Beginning Visual C++ 4

Ivor Horton

Wrox Press Ltd.®

Beginning Visual C++ 4

Published by Wrox Press Ltd. Site 16, 20 James Road, Birmingham, B11 2BA, UK
Printed in Canada
1 2 3 4 5 TRI 99 98 97 96

Library of Congress Catalog no. 95-61104
ISBN 1-874416-59-1

Trademark Acknowledgements

Wrox has endeavored to provide trademark information about all the companies and products mentioned in this book by the appropriate use of capitals. However, Wrox cannot guarantee the accuracy of this information.

Credits

Author
Ivor Horton

Editors
Julian Dobson
Alex Stockton

Managing Editor
John Franklin

Technical Reviewers
Julian Templeman
Abe Klagsbrun
Bill Ibbetson
Justin Rudd
Lynn Mettler
Curt Krone
Hugh Gibson

Production Manager
Greg Powell

Design/Layout
Neil Gallagher
Graham Butler
Damon Creed
Andrew Guillaume

Proof Readers
Melanie Orgee
Pam Brand

Index
Simon Gilks

Cover Design
Third Wave

For more information on Third Wave, contact Ross Alderson on 44-121 236 6616
Cover photo: Greg Powell

Beginning
Visual C++
4

Summary of Contents

Beginning
Visual C++
4

Table of Contents

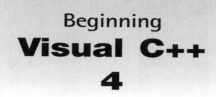

Beginning
Visual C++
4

Introduction

Who's This Book For?

This book is for everyone. Well, that's not strictly true. If you've been using Visual C++ since version 1.0, this book will be of little use to you. If, on the other hand, you're just starting out into the world of C++ and Windows programming, this is the book for you.

We have assumed no prior knowledge of programming in any language, although if you do have some experience, that's bound to help.

What's Covered in This Book

The book is split into two halves; the first half covers C++, while the second half covers Windows programming with MFC.

We begin with a full tutorial to the C++ language. It starts with an introduction to Developer Studio, the integrated development environment provided with Visual C++, briefly covering the main components of the interface. The next ten chapters cover all you need to know about the C++ language. Starting with the basics of the language, such as data types and program flow, and ending with a gentle tour through the essence of object oriented programming, the first section provides a solid foundation for the section to follow. There is a brief interlude in Chapter 7 where you will write your first Windows program.

The second half is where you will get to grips with MFC and Windows programming for real. We'll tell you about AppWizard and ClassWizard, two tools to speed up your application development. We'll cover building applications with menus, dialogs and scrollbars. Saving and reading data to and from the disk will be discussed, along with how to print documents, connect to databases and write dynamic link libraries. We'll finish off by showing you how to write programs to utilize OLE, including developing your own controls, known as OCXs. Throughout this section, we'll be designing and building a drawing package called Sketcher.

What You Need to Use This Book

To use this book, you need Visual C++ 4.0. This is the latest version of Microsoft's best selling C++ compiler. This version is 32-bit only, so you will need to install it on Windows 95 or Windows NT 3.51, which means a 486 or better CPU and a minimum 16MB of memory.

For Visual C++, you'll need quite a lot of hard disk space - a typical installation is 100 Mbytes. You can do a minimal installation which takes up only 15 Mbytes, but this will mean longer compile times as the CD-ROM will be utilized more.

Source Code is Freely Available

As you may have noticed, there is no disk with this book. However, the source code is available for free download from our web site. The full URL is:

http://www.wrox.com/wrox/download/591.zip

The Wrox Press website also contains source code and information on many of our other books.

If you don't have access to the internet, we can provide a disk for a nominal fee to cover postage and packing. You'll find details of this service at the back of the book.

Academic Pack

For those of you who may be looking at this book in light of using it as part of a Visual C++ course, there is an academic pack available. This contains a set of questions and model answers for each chapter.

Please contact Martin Anderson on **1-800-USE-WROX**, or e-mail him at **martina@wrox.com**

Conventions Used

We use a number of different styles of text and layout in the book to help differentiate between the different kinds of information. Here are examples of the styles we use and an explanation of what they mean:

FYI Extra details, for your information, come in boxes like this.

 Important Words are in a bold type font.

 Words that appear on the screen, such as menu options, are a similar font to the one used on screen, for example, the File menu.

 Keys that you press on the keyboard, like *Ctrl* and *Enter*, are in italics.

 All filenames are in this style: **Wineshop.mdb**.

➤ Function names look like this: **sizeof**

➤ Code which is new, important or discussed will be shown in the following format:

```
void main()
{
    cout << "Beginning Visual C++";
}
```

Code which has previously been discussed, or is unimportant to the current discussion will be shown as:

```
void main()
{
    cout << "Beginning Visual C++";
}
```

Tell Us What You Think

We have tried to make this book as accurate and enjoyable for you as possible, but what really matters is what the book actually does for you. Please let us know your views, whether positive or negative, either by returning the reply card in the back of the book or by contacting us at Wrox Press by any of the following methods:

feedback@wrox.com
http://www.wrox.com/
Compuserve: 100063,2152

We have made every effort to make sure there are no errors in the text or the code. However, to err is human and, as such, we recognize the need to keep you, the reader, informed of these mistakes as they are spotted and amended. Please visit our web site for the latest errata sheet, or call us on **1-800-USE-WROX** and we'll gladly send it to you by post.

If you spot a mistake for which there is no reference on the errata sheet, please get in touch and let us know. We'll endeavor to solve the problem and get back to you with the solution as soon as humanly possible. This not only helps you, but others who may come across the same problem.

Finally, thank you for buying this book, or if you are merely browsing in the store, please buy and enjoy!

Programming with Visual C++

Windows programming isn't difficult. In fact, Microsoft Visual C++ Version 4.0 makes it remarkably easy, as you will see throughout the course of this book. There's just one obstacle in our path: before we get to the specifics of Windows programming, we have to be thoroughly familiar with the capabilities of the C++ programming language, particularly the object oriented aspects of the language. Object oriented techniques are central to the effectiveness of all the tools provided by Visual C++ for Windows programming, so it is essential that you gain a good understanding of these. That is exactly what this book will provide.

In this chapter, as a base for tackling the C++ language, we are going to take a rapid tour of the Developer Studio - the integrated development environment that comes with Visual C++. Becoming reasonably fluent with the Developer Studio will make the whole process of developing your applications much easier and, since Microsoft are promoting the Developer Studio as the IDE for all their future programming language products, learning about it now will put you one step ahead of everyone else.

The Developer Studio is very straightforward, and generally intuitive in its operation, so you will be able to pick up most of it as you go along. The best approach to getting familiar with it is to work through creating, compiling and executing a simple program. You'll get some insight into the philosophy and mechanics of the Developer Studio as you use it. We'll take you through this process and beyond so that, by the end of this chapter, you will have learned about:

- The principal components of Visual C++
- Projects and how you create them
- How to create and edit a program
- How to compile, link and execute your first C++ program
- How to create a basic Windows program

So power up your PC, start Windows, load the mighty Visual C++ and we can begin our journey.

Learning C++ and Windows Programming

With this book, you will learn how to write programs using C++ and how to write Windows programs. We will approach both topics in that order, insulating C++ from Windows considerations until you are comfortable with the language. You should find that it is a natural progression from understanding C++ to applying it to the development of Windows applications.

To give you a feel for where we are ultimately headed, we can take look at the characteristics of a typical Windows program. We can also introduce the development context that we will use while you are grappling with C++.

Introducing Windows Programming

Our approach to Windows programming will be to use all the tools that Visual C++ provides. AppWizard which, as you will see, can generate a basic Windows program automatically, will be the starting point for all the Windows examples later in the book, and we will be using ClassWizard in the process of developing what AppWizard produces into something more useful. To get the flavor of how AppWizard works, later in this chapter we will look at the mechanics of starting a Windows program.

A Windows program has quite a different structure to that of the typical DOS program, and it is rather more complicated. There are two reasons for this. Firstly, in a DOS program you can get input from the keyboard or write to the display directly, whereas a Windows program can only access the input and output facilities of the computer by way of Windows functions. No direct access to these hardware resources is permitted. Since several programs can be active at one time under Windows, Windows has to determine which application a given input is destined for and signal the program concerned accordingly. Windows has primary control of all communications with the user.

Secondly, the nature of the interface between a user and a Windows application is such that a range of different inputs are possible at any given time. A user may key some data, select any of a number of menu options, or click the mouse somewhere in the application window. A well designed Windows application has to be prepared to deal with any type of input at any time, because there is no way of knowing in advance which type of input is going to occur.

These user actions are all regarded by Windows as events and will typically result in a particular piece of your program code being executed. How program execution proceeds is therefore determined by the sequence of user actions, or **events**. Programs that operate in this way are referred to as **event-driven programs**.

Therefore, a Windows program consists primarily of pieces of code that respond to events caused by the action of the user, or by Windows itself. This sort of program structure can be represented as illustrated:

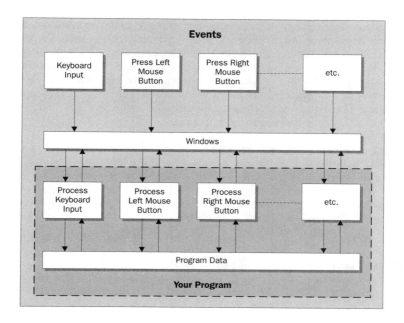

Each block in the illustration represents a piece of code written specifically to deal with a particular event. Although the program may appear to be somewhat fragmented, the primary factor welding the program into a whole is Windows itself. You can think of your Windows program as customizing Windows to provide a particular set of capabilities. Of course, the modules servicing various external events, such as selecting a menu or clicking the mouse, will all typically have access to a common set of application specific data in a particular program. This application data will contain information that relates to what the program is about, blocks of text in an editor for example, or player scoring records in a program aimed at tracking how your baseball team is doing, as well as information about some of the events that have occurred during execution of the program. This shared collection of data allows various parts of the program which look independent to communicate and operate in a coordinated and integrated fashion. We will, of course, go into this in much more detail later in the book.

Even an elementary Windows program involves quite a few lines of code and, with AppWizard based Windows programs, 'quite a few' turns out to be quite a lot. To make the process of understanding how C++ works easy, you really need a context which is as simple as possible. Fortunately, Visual C++ comes with an environment that is ready made for the purpose.

Console Applications

As well as developing Windows applications, Visual C++ also allows you to write, compile, and test C++ programs that have none of the baggage required for Windows programs - that is, applications that are essentially character-based DOS programs. These programs are called **console applications** in Visual C++ because you communicate with them through the keyboard and the screen in character mode.

Writing console applications might seem as though you are being sidetracked from the main objective here, but when it comes to learning C++ - which you do need to do before embarking on Windows-specific programming - it's the best way to learn. As we said earlier, there is a lot of code in even a simple Windows program, and it's very important not to be distracted by the complexities of Windows when learning the ins and outs of C++. Therefore, in the early chapters of the book where we are concerned with how C++ works, we'll spend time walking with a few lightweight console applications before we get to run with the heavyweight sacks of code in the world of Windows.

While you are learning C++, you will be able to concentrate on the language features without worrying about the environment in which we are operating. With the console applications that we'll write, we only have a text interface, but this will be quite sufficient for understanding all of C++. There is no graphical capability within the definition of the language. Naturally, we will provide extensive coverage of graphical user interface programming when we come to write programs specifically for Windows using MFC.

What is the Developer Studio?

The Developer Studio is a completely self-contained environment for creating, compiling, linking and testing Windows programs. It is the Integrated Development Environment (IDE) that comes with Visual C++ version 4.0 and it also happens to be a great environment in which to learn C++ (particularly when combined with a great book).

The Developer Studio incorporates a range of fully integrated tools designed to make the whole process of writing Windows programs easy. We will see something of these in this chapter, but rather than grind through a boring litany of features and options in the abstract, we will first take a look at the basics to get a view of how the Developer Studio works and then pick up the rest in context as we go along.

Components of the System

The fundamental parts of Visual C++, provided as part of the Developer Studio, are the editor, the compiler, the linker and the libraries. These are the basic tools that are essential to writing and executing a C++ program. The functions of these are as follows:

The Editor

The editor provides an interactive environment for creating and editing C++ source code. As well as the usual facilities, such as cut and paste, which you are certainly already familiar with, the editor also provides color cues to differentiate between various language elements. The editor automatically recognizes fundamental words in the C++ language and assigns a color to them according to what they are. This not only helps to make your code more readable, but also provides a clear indicator of when you make errors in keying such words.

The Compiler

The compiler converts your source code into machine language, and detects and reports errors in the compilation process. The compiler can detect a wide range of errors that are due to invalid or unrecognized program code, as well as structural errors, where, for example, part of a program can never be executed. The output from the compiler is known as **object code** and is stored in files called **object files**, which usually have the extension **.obj**.

The Linker

The linker combines the various modules generated by the compiler from source code files, adds required code modules from program libraries supplied as part of C++, and welds everything into an executable whole. The linker can also detect and report errors, for example if part of your program is missing or a non-existent library component is referenced.

The Libraries

A library supports and extends the C++ language by providing routines to carry out operations which are not part of the language. For example, libraries can contain routines such as calculating a square root, comparing two character strings or obtaining date and time information. There are two kinds of libraries provided by Visual C++.

The first kind contains routines that aren't platform-specific. There is a basic set of routines common to all C++ compilers which make up the **Standard Library**. There are also extensions to the standard set which will be supported in many other C++ compilers, but their universality isn't guaranteed. You will get to know quite a number of these as you develop your knowledge of C++.

The other kind of library is called the **Microsoft Foundation Class Library**, or **MFC** for short, which is the cornerstone of Windows programming with Visual C++. MFC provides the basis for all the Windows programs that you will write. MFC is also referred to as an **application framework** because it provides a set of structured components that provide a ready-made basis for almost any Windows program. We will see a lot more of MFC when we get to the details of Windows programming.

Other Tools

The Developer Studio also includes two important tools which work in a wholly integrated way to help you write Windows programs. These are the **AppWizard** and the **ClassWizard**. They are not essential to the process of writing Windows programs but provide such immense advantages in simplifying the development process, reducing the incidence of errors and shortening the time to completing a program that we will use them for all of our major examples. Read on for an idea of the services that these tools provide.

AppWizard

The AppWizard automatically generates a basic framework for your Windows program. In fact, the framework is a complete, executable Windows program, as we shall see later in this chapter. Of course, you need to add the specific functionality necessary to make the program do what you want which is an essential part of developing a Windows program.

ClassWizard

Classes are the most important language feature of C++ and are fundamental to Windows programming with Visual C++. The ClassWizard provides an easy means of extending the classes generated by AppWizard as part of your basic Windows program and also helps you to add new classes based on classes in MFC to support the functionality you want to include in your program. Note that ClassWizard neither recognizes nor deals with classes that are not based on MFC classes.

Using the Visual C++ Development Environment

All our program development and execution will be performed from within the Developer Studio. When you start Visual C++, assuming no project was active when you shut it down last (we will see what a project is exactly in a moment), you will see the window shown below:

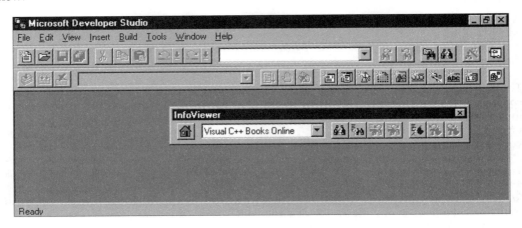

The toolbars below the main menu that you see above provide icons which act as an instant route to some of the functions available from the main menus. Just clicking on a toolbar icon will directly perform the function that it corresponds to. The Developer Studio offers a whole range of dockable and customizable toolbars that you can use.

Dockable Toolbars

A **dockable** toolbar is one that you can drag around with the mouse to position it at a convenient place in the window. When it is placed at any of the four borders of the application, it is said to be docked and will look like the toolbars that you see at the top of the application window. If you drag a dockable toolbar away from its docked position, it will look like the InfoViewer toolbar that you see above, enclosed in a little window but, of course, with a different caption. In this state, it is called a floating toolbar. All the toolbars that you see above are dockable and can be floating, so you can experiment with dragging any of them around.

Toolbars Options

The toolbars that you see below the menu bar are the Standard and Project toolbars. Right-clicking on any toolbar will bring up a list of the other toolbars that are available. You can add any of them to the Developer Studio just by clicking on its entry in the pop-up. Similarly, if you click on an entry in the pop-up that corresponds to a toolbar that is already selected, it will be removed.

You needn't clutter up the application window with all the toolbars you think you might need at some time. The other toolbars will appear automatically when required, so you will probably find the default toolbar selections are perfectly adequate.

Just like many other Windows applications, the toolbars that make up the Developer Studio come complete with tooltips. Just let the mouse pointer linger over a button for a second or two and a little yellow label will provide you with the function and shortcut key combination of that button.

You'll be familiar with many of the toolbars' icons from using other Windows applications, but you may not appreciate exactly what these icons do in terms of Visual C++, so we'll describe them as we use them.

Since we will use a new project for every program we develop, looking at what exactly a project is and understanding how the mechanism for defining a project works, a good place to start is to find out how we use the Developer Studio.

Defining a Project Workspace

A project workspace defines and keeps track of all the bits that go to make up your program, as well as the Developer Studio options that you are using. It is contained in a single file folder which will hold the project definition files and all your source code. This project folder will also contain other folders to store the output from compiling and linking your project for example. A project definition includes:

▶ A project name.

▶ A list of all the source files.

▶ A definition of what sort of program is to be built from the source files, for example, a Windows **.exe** program, or a console application.

▶ The default options set for the editor, the compiler, the linker and other components of Visual C++ that might be involved.

▶ The windows to be displayed in Developer Studio when the project is opened.

The basic definition of a project is actually stored on disk in a file called a makefile with the extension **.mak**. This contains information about how your program is to be created from the files in the project workspace and is produced when you create a project workspace. Your project workspace will also contain a file with the extension **.mdp** which contains all the settings for the Developer Studio, such as which windows you use and where they are positioned. This file isn't created until you close your project workspace, since it needs to contain the Developer Studio settings for your project. It is used to configure Developer Studio when you open the project and will be updated each time you close the project.

Both of these files are created and maintained automatically by Visual C++ and the Developer Studio, so you shouldn't attempt to edit or amend them directly yourself. Any changes you want to make - for example, to the options in effect for a program - you should introduce using the menus for that purpose in Developer Studio.

Debug and Release Versions of Your Program

When you create a new project workspace, Developer Studio will automatically create configurations for producing two versions of your application. One includes information which will help you to debug the program and is called the **Debug Version**. The other, called the **Release Version**, has no debug information included and has the code optimization options for the compiler turned on to provide you with the most efficient executable module.

You can choose which version of your program to work with by selecting the configuration you want from the drop-down list that appears on the project toolbar.

TRY IT OUT - Creating a New Project

Let's take a look at creating a project for a console application. First select <u>N</u>ew... from the <u>F</u>ile menu to bring up the list of items shown here:

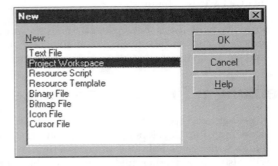

Select Project Workspace from the list and click OK to bring up the New Project Workspace dialog.

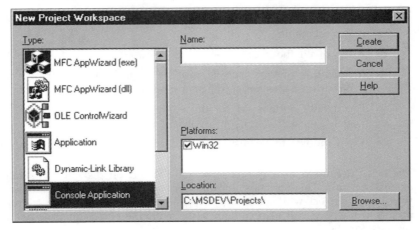

This dialog allows you to enter the type, name and location for your project as well as the platforms upon which you'd like it to run, where applicable. (We won't need to change this setting at all for the examples in this book.) If you simply enter a name for your project in the Name: text box, the Location will automatically be set to a folder with that name. The folder will be created for you if it doesn't already exist. Alternatively, you can use the Browse... button to select another folder for your project's files.

The selection that you make from the Type: list determines what kind of program you are creating. For many of these options, a basic set of program source modules will be created automatically. For the project we are creating here, you should select Console Application as the project's type. This won't generate any code, but will set the options for this kind of application. You can now enter a suitable name for your project - you could call this one TrialRun, for instance - or any other name that takes your fancy. Visual C++ supports long file names, so you have a lot of flexibility.

When you click on the Create button, a new project workspace folder will be created in the folder that you have specified as the Location: entry. The folder will have the name that you supplied as the project name and will store all the files making up the project definition. If you used the location shown above, you'll find the project in the **C:\MSDEV\Projects\TrialRun** folder on your hard drive. If you use Explorer to look in this folder, you will see there are just two files initially: the makefile, **TrialRun.mak**, and a file, **TrialRun.ncb**, which you can safely ignore since this is used internally by the Developer Studio. The file, **TrialRun.mdp**, containing the Developer Studio settings for the project, will be created when you close the project workspace.

The new workspace will automatically be opened in Developer Studio. You will see that two tabs have been added to the Project Workspace window, showing a ClassView and a FileView for your project. You can switch between these windows by clicking the tab for the window you want to see. All three tabs are shown below:

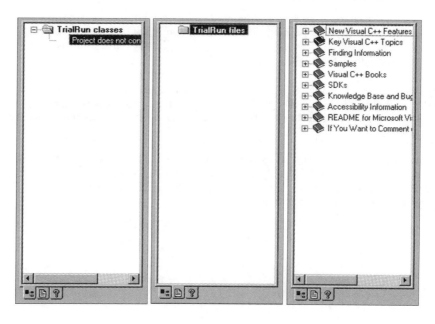

Although these views are looking rather empty at the moment, you'll see later that they provide a quick and convenient way of viewing and accessing various aspects of your project.

The **ClassView** displays the classes defined in your project and will also show the contents of each class. We don't have any classes in this application, so the view is empty. When we get into discussing classes, you will see that you can use ClassView to move around the code relating to the definition and implementation of all your application classes very quickly and easily.

The **FileView** shows the files that make up your project. You can display the contents of any of your project files by double clicking on a file name in FileView. This will open a window for the file and automatically invoke an editor to enable you to modify the file contents.

The **InfoView** is a standard view that is the same for every project. It shows the contents for the Books Online reference material supplied with ClassWizard, or a subset of those contents if you've defined one. You can access this material by clicking on pages displayed on the InfoView tab, or by using the <u>H</u>elp menu option to search the material.

Projects for Windows applications will also have a tab to display a **ResourceView** which will display the dialogs, icons, menus and toolbars that are used by the program.

Like most elements of the Developer Studio, the Project Workspace window provides context-sensitive pop-up menus when you right-click in the window. If you find that the Project Workspace window gets in your way when writing code, you can hide and show it most easily by using the Project Workspace button provided on the Standard toolbar.

Entering Your First Program

Since a project workspace isn't really a great deal of use without a program file, it's time we entered our first program. Select <u>F</u>ile then <u>N</u>ew... from the main menu. Select Text File from the list provided, or simply click the leftmost button on the Standard toolbar to create a new text file.

This will open a new window to display the file which will have the default name `Text1`. You'll see that the file name is displayed in the Developer Studio title bar at the top. The asterisk following the name indicates that the contents of the file displayed in the window have been modified.

Because you chose to open the file as a text file, the editor is already active, so go right ahead and type in the program code exactly as shown in the window below. Don't worry about what it does. This is a very simple program which outputs some lines of text and is just meant to exercise the Developer Studio facilities.

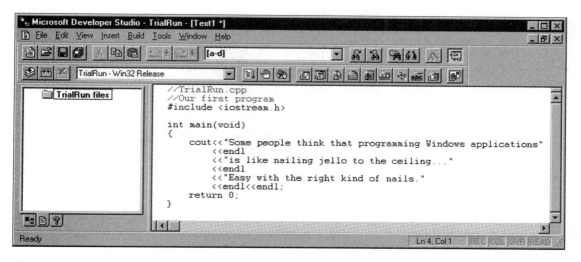

```
//TrialRun.cpp
//Our first program
#include <iostream.h>

int main(void)
{
    cout<<"Some people think that programming Windows applications"
        <<endl
        <<"is like nailing jello to the ceiling..."
        <<endl
        <<"Easy with the right kind of nails."
        <<endl<<endl;
    return 0;
}
```

Note the automatic indenting that occurs as you type in the code. C++ uses indenting to make programs more readable and the editor automatically indents each line of code that you enter, based on what was in the previous line. You can also see the syntax color highlighting in action as you type. Some elements of the program are shown in different colors as the editor automatically assigns colors to language elements depending on what they are.

All the executable code is contained between the curly braces. The block of code here is called a function and has the name **main**. Every C++ console program has this function and execution of the program starts at the beginning of **main**. Windows programs, on the other hand, are very different in structure. We will come back to the structure of console programs in the next chapter and will look at the structure of a Windows program in Chapter 7.

Having entered the program, you need to save it with a suitable file name. C++ source programs are usually assigned a name with the extension **.cpp**, so, using the Save As... option from the File menu, call this file **TrialRun.cpp**. Files with the extensions **.cpp** or **.cxx** are recognized as C++ source files, whereas files with the extension **.c** are assumed to be C source files. If you don't use one of these extensions, Developer Studio won't recognize the file as a source file. It's best to stick to the **.cpp** extension for C++ as this is most commonly used in the PC environment. You can save a file in any folder that you feel like, but, since we intend this file to be part of the TrialRun project that we just created, it's a good idea to store it in the same directory as the project files.

Adding a Source File to a Project

Now that we have a program source file, we need to add it to our project (saving it in the project directory doesn't do that, it just stores it on disk). The easiest way to do this is to right-click in the text file window and select the Insert File into Project item from the pop-up. Alternatively, you could have chosen this item from the Insert menu on the main menu bar and browsed for the file that you wished to add.

```
//TrialRun.cpp
//Our first program
#include <iostream.h>

int main(void)
{
    cout<<"Some people thi                    indows applications"
        <<endl
        <<"is like nailing                    .."
        <<endl
        <<"Easy with the r
        <<endl<<endl;
    return 0;
}
```

| Cut |
| Copy |
| Paste |
| Insert/Remove Breakpoint |
| Enable Breakpoint |
| Insert File into Project ▶ | TrialRun |
| Open |
| Go To Definition |
| Go To Reference |
| ClassWizard... |
| Toolbar |
| Properties |

If you had chosen the Insert File into Project item from the pop-up before the file had been saved, you would have been prompted to save the file first. The same menu item from the Insert menu won't do this for you because it assumes that you want to add a file from disk rather than the file that you are currently working on. If you haven't saved it, it won't appear in the file list.

Building a Project

The combined process of compiling the source files in a project to produce object code modules and then linking these to produce an executable file is referred to as **building** a project. The makefile, with the extension **.mak**, is used by Visual C++ in the build process to set the options for the compiler and linker to create the executable file. You can build a project in a number of ways:

▶ Click the Build button on the Project toolbar.

▶ Choose the Build item from the menu that appears when you right-click the TrialRun files folder in the FileView.

▶ Choose the Build TrialRun.exe item from the Build menu on the main menu bar.

> *Note that open source files are automatically saved when a build is performed.*

When you build the executable, the Output window which provides you with status and error information about the process will appear.

```
--------------------Configuration: TrialRun - Win32 Release--------------------
TrialRun.exe - 0 error(s), 0 warning(s)
```
Build / Debug / Find in Files / Profile /

Dealing with Errors

Of course, if you didn't type in the program correctly, you will get errors reported. To show how this works we could deliberately introduce an error into the program. If you already have errors of your own, you can use those to exercise this bit. Go back to the Text Editor window and delete the semicolon at the end of the second to last line and then rebuild the source file. The Output window should appear like this:

```
--------------------Configuration: TrialRun - Win32 Release--------------------
Compiling...
TrialRun.cpp
C:\Msdev\Projects\TrialRun\TrialRun.cpp(14) : error C2143: syntax error : missing ';' before '}'
Error executing cl.exe.
TrialRun.exe - 1 error(s), 0 warning(s)
```
Build ╲ Debug ╲ Find in Files ╲ Profile /

The error message here is very clear. It specifically states that a semicolon is missing and, if you double click on the error message you will be taken directly to the line in error. You can then correct the error and rebuild the executable.

Using Help with the Output Window

Sometimes, the cause of an error may not be quite so obvious, in which case some additional information can be very helpful. You can get more information about any error reported by placing the cursor in the output window, anywhere in the line containing the error code (in this case, C2143). You can position the cursor just by clicking with the mouse anywhere in the line. If you now press the function key *F1*, you will automatically bring up a help page with more information on the particular error in question, often containing examples of the sort of incorrect code that can cause the problem.

The build operation works very efficiently because the project definition keeps track of the status of the files making up the project. During a normal build, Visual C++ only recompiles the files that have changed since the programs were last compiled or built. This means that if your project had several source files and you edited only one of the files since the project was last built, only that file is recompiled before linking to create a new **.exe** file.

You also have the option of rebuilding all files from the start if you want, regardless of when they were last compiled. You just need to use the Rebuild All menu option instead of Build TrialRun.exe (or whatever the name of the executable is).

Files Created by Building a Console Application

Once the example has been built without error, if you take a look in the project folder, you will see a new subfolder called **Debug**. This folder contains the output of the build that you just performed on the project. You will see that this folder contains seven new files.

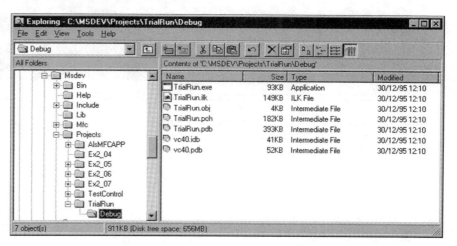

Other than the **.exe** file, which is your program in executable form, you don't need to know much about what is in these files. However, in case you're curious, let's do a quick run-through of what the more interesting ones are for:

.exe   This is the executable file for the program. You only get this file if both the compile and link steps are successful.

.obj   The compiler produces these object files containing machine code from your program source files. These are used by the linker, along with files from the libraries, to produce your **.exe** file.

.ilk   This file is used by the linker when you rebuild your project. It enables the linker to incrementally link the object files produced from the modified source code into the existing **.exe** file. This avoids the need to re-link everything each time you change your program.

.pch   This is a **pre-compiled header** file. With pre-compiled headers, large tracts of code which are not subject to modification - particularly code supplied by Visual C++ - can be processed once and stored in the **.pch** file. Using the **.pch** file substantially reduces the time needed to build your program.

.pdb   This file contains debugging information that is used when you execute the program in debug mode. In this mode, you can dynamically inspect information that is generated during program execution.

If you have a **.exe** file for the TrialRun project, you can take it for a trial run, so let's see how to do that.

Executing Your First Program

We can, of course, execute the program in the normal way by double clicking the **.exe** file from Explorer, but we can also execute it without leaving the Visual C++ development environment. You can do this by selecting Execute TrialRun.exe from the Build menu. Our example will produce the output shown below:

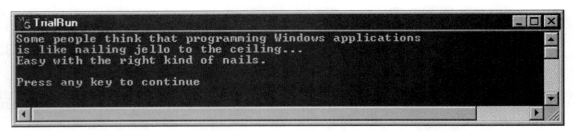

If we had changed any of the source files since the last build of the executable, or if we hadn't built the executable at all, we would be prompted to rebuild the project when we clicked the Execute TrialRun.exe menu item.

Creating and Executing a Windows Program

Just to show how easy it is going to be, we'll now create a working Windows program. We'll defer discussion of the program that we generate until we've covered the necessary ground for you to understand it in detail. You will see, though, that the process really is very easy.

To start with, if an existing project is active - this will be indicated by the project makefile name appearing in the title bar of the Developer Studio main window - you can select Close Workspace from the File menu. Alternatively, you can just go ahead and create a new project and Developer Studio will close the current project for you. To create the Windows program, we are going to use AppWizard, so select New... from the File menu then Project Workspace from the list. Leave the project type as MFC AppWizard (exe) and enter TrialWin as the project's name.

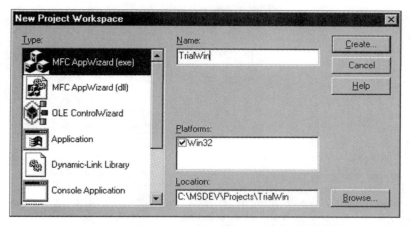

This will result in the MFC AppWizard window being displayed. The AppWizard consists of a number of dialog pages with options that let you choose which feature you'd like to have included in your application, for example, whether you'd like database support or various levels of OLE support, toolbars, and so on.

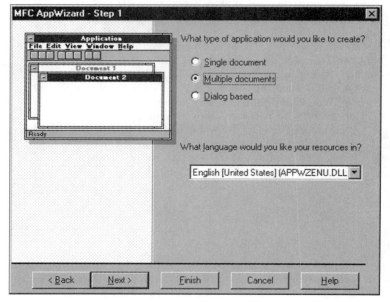

We'll ignore all these options and just accept the default settings, so click the Finish button. Another window will be displayed as shown here:

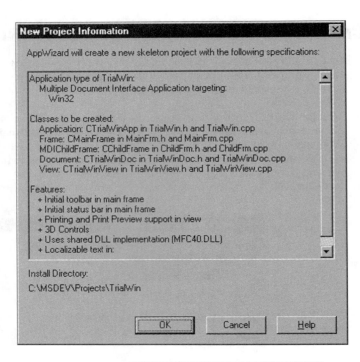

This is to advise you of what AppWizard is about to do and provides you with an opportunity to abort the whole thing if it doesn't seem to be what you want. It defines a list of the classes that it is going to create, and what the basic features of the program are going to be. We won't worry about what all these signify - we'll get to them eventually. It also indicates the folder that it will use to store the project and program files. Just click on the OK button and let AppWizard out of its cage. AppWizard will spend a few moments generating the necessary files and then eventually return to the main window. If you now expand the FileView in the Project Workspace window, you'll see the file list shown here:

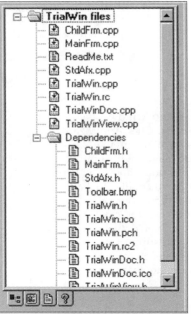

The list shows a large number of files that have been created. You need plenty of space on your hard drive when writing Windows programs. The files with the extension **.cpp** contain executable C++ source code, and the **.h** files contain C++ code consisting of definitions which are used by the executable code. The **.ico** files contain icons.

If you now take a look at the **TrialWin** folder using Explorer, or whatever else you may have handy for looking at the files on your hard disk, you will see that we have generated a total of 22 files. The files that contain the resources used by the program, such as the menus and icons, are kept in a subfolder called **res**. We get all this as a result of just entering the name we want to assign to the project. You can see why, with so many files and file names being created automatically, a separate directory for each project becomes more than just a good idea.

One of the files in the **TrialWin** subdirectory, **ReadMe.txt** file, provides an explanation of the purpose of each of the files that AppWizard has generated. You can take a look at it if you wish, using Notepad, WordPad or even the Visual C++ editor.

Executing a Windows Program

Before we can execute our program, we have to compile and link the program modules. You do this in exactly the same way that you did with the console application example. To save time, just select the Execute TrialWin.exe item from the Build menu. Since you haven't built the executable yet, you will be asked whether you want to do so. Click Yes.

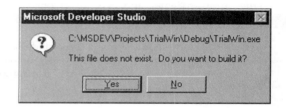

Compiling and linking the project will take a little time, even if you have a fast machine, since we already have quite a complex program. Once the project has been built, the Output window will indicate that there were no errors and the executable will start running. The window for the program that we have generated is shown here:

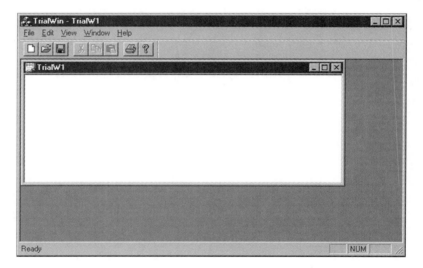

As you see, it's complete with menus and a toolbar. Although there is no specific functionality in the program - that's what we need to add to make it *our* program - all the menus work. You can try them out. You can even create further windows by selecting the New item from the File menu.

I think you'll agree that creating a Windows program with AppWizard has not really stressed too many brain cells. We'll need to get a few more ticking away when we come to developing the basic program we have here into a program that does something more interesting, but it won't be that hard. Certainly, for many people, writing a serious Windows program the old-fashioned way, without the aid of Visual C++, required at least a couple of months on a fish diet before making the attempt. That's why so many programmers used to eat sushi. That's all gone now with Visual C++. However, you never know what's around the corner in programming technology. If you like sushi, it's best to continue with it to be on the safe side.

Summary

In this chapter, we have run through the basic mechanics of using Developer Studio. We used the Studio to enter and execute a console application program and, with the help of AppWizard, we created a complete Windows program.

Every program should have a project defined for it. The project will store information as to the kind of program it is, what files need to be combined to construct the program and the options in effect for the program. All programs in this book will have a project defined.

Starting with the next chapter, we'll be using console applications extensively throughout the book. All the examples illustrating how C++ language elements are used will be executed using console applications. We will return to AppWizard as soon as we have finished delving into the secrets of C++.

Data, Variables and Calculations

In this chapter, we will get down to the essentials of programming in C++. By the end of the chapter you will be able to write a simple C++ program of the traditional form: input - process - output.

As we will explore aspects of the language using working examples, you will have an opportunity to get some additional practice with the Developer Studio. You should create a project for each of the examples before you build and execute them. Remember that when you are defining a project, they are all console applications.

In this chapter you will learn about:

▶ C++ program structure

▶ Variables in C++

▶ Defining variables and constants

▶ Basic input from the keyboard and output to the screen

▶ Performing arithmetic calculations

▶ Variable scope

The Structure of a C++ Program

Programs that will run as console applications under Visual C++ are text based MS-DOS programs. All the examples that we will write to understand how C++ works will be MS-DOS programs, so let's look at how such programs are structured.

A program in C++ consists of one or more **functions**. In Chapter 1, we saw an example consisting simply of the function **main()**, where **main** is the name of the function. This was an MS-DOS program. Every C++ program in the DOS environment contains the function **main()** and all C++ programs of any size consist of several functions. A function is simply a self-contained block of code with a unique name which is invoked by using the name of the function.

A typical DOS program might be structured as shown in the figure:

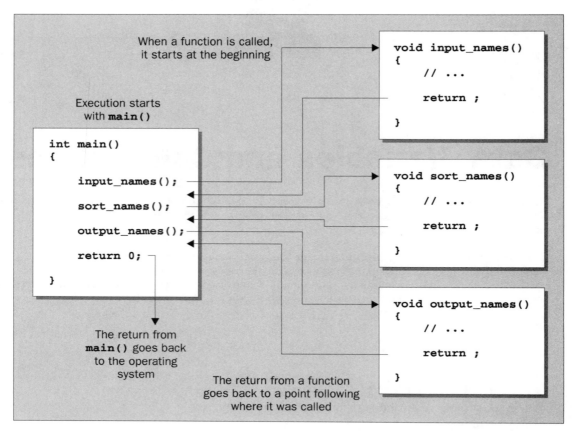

The figure above illustrates that execution of the program shown starts at the beginning of the function **main()**. From **main()**, execution transfers to a function **input_names()** which returns execution to the position immediately following the point where it was called in **main()**. The function **sort_names()** is then called from **main()** and, once control returns to **main()**, the final function **output_names()** is called. Eventually, once output has been completed, execution returns once again to **main()** and the program ends.

Of course, different programs under DOS may have radically different functional structures, but they all start execution at the beginning of **main()**. The principle advantage of having a program broken up into functions is that you can write and test each piece separately. There is a further advantage in that functions written to perform a particular task can be re-used in other programs. The libraries that come with C++ provide a lot of standard functions that you can use in your programs. They can save you a great deal of work.

> *We will see more on creating and using functions in Chapter 5.*

TRY IT OUT - A Simple Program

Let's look at a simple example to understand the elements of a program a little better. Start by creating a new project by selecting Project Workspace from the range of alternatives offered when you click the New... item in the File menu. When the New Project Workspace dialog appears, select Console Application and name the project Ex2_01.

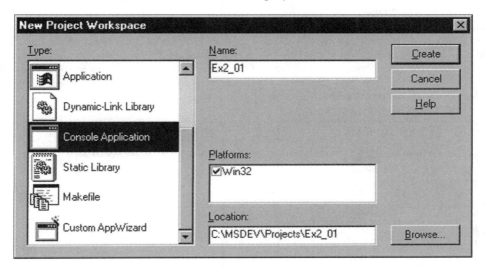

We will start by entering the following program as a new source file, so click the leftmost icon on the standard toolbar to create a new text file into which you can type the code.

```cpp
// EX2_01.CPP
// A Simple Example of a Program
#include <iostream.h>
int main()
{
   int apples, oranges;        // Declare two integer variables
   int fruit;                  // ..then another one

   apples = 5; oranges = 6;    // Set initial values
   fruit = apples + oranges;   // Get the total fruit

   cout << endl;               // Start output on a new line
   cout << "Oranges are not the only fruit... " << endl
        << "- and we have " << fruit << " fruits in all.";
   cout << endl;               // Start output on a new line

   return 0;                   // Exit the program
}
```

Note that the above example is intended to illustrate some of the ways in which you can write C++ statements, rather than to be a model of good programming style.

Once you have keyed it in, save it as **Ex2_01.cpp** using the File menu Save As... option. The Save As... dialog will offer to save it in the project directory that you just created and, since this file is part of that project, that's the best place for it.

If you look at the FileView tab for your new project, you'll notice that the source file doesn't appear as part of the project's files. We need to add the file to the project using the Files into Project... item from the Insert menu, or by right-clicking in the window containing the source, just as we did for the project in Chapter 1. Once this is done, you'll see the newly created source file in the FileView and the **main()** function will appear under the Globals section of the ClassView. We'll consider the meaning of this later.

If you now build this program by using the Build button on the Project toolbar, and execute it using the Execute Ex2_01.exe item in the Build menu, you should get the following output:

```
Ex2_01                                                                    _ ☐ ✕

Oranges are not the only fruit...
- and we have 11 fruits in all.
Press any key to continue
```

Program Comments

The first two lines in the program are comments. Comments are an important part of any program, but they are not executable code - they are there simply to help the human reader. All comments are ignored by the compiler. Two successive slashes on a line that are not contained within a text string (we shall see what text strings are later) indicate that the rest of the line is a comment.

You can see that several lines of the program contain comments as well as program statements. You can also use an alternative form of comment bounded by */* and **/*. For example, the first line of the program could have been written:

```
/* EX2_01.CPP   */
```

The comment using *//* only covers the portion of the line following the two successive slashes, whereas the */*....*/* form defines whatever is enclosed as a comment and can span several lines. For example, we could write:

```
/*
    EX2_01.CPP
    A Simple Program Example
*/
```

All four lines are comments. If you want to highlight some particular comment lines, you can always embellish them with a frame of some description:

```
/*****************************
 *  EX2-01.CPP              *
 *  A Simple Program Example *
 *****************************/
```

As a rule, you should always comment your programs comprehensively. The comments should be sufficient for another programmer, or you at a later date, to understand the purpose of any particular piece of code, and to understand how it works.

The #include Directive - Header Files

Following the comments, we have the **#include** directive,

```
#include <iostream.h>
```

which makes the compiler insert the contents of the file **iostream.h** into the program before compilation. This file is called a **header file** because it is usually brought in at the beginning of a program file. This particular header file contains definitions that are necessary for you to be able to use input and output statements in C++. If we didn't include **iostream.h** in our program, it wouldn't compile because we use input and output statements which depend on some of the definitions in this file. There are many different header files provided by Visual C++ that cover a wide range of capabilities. We shall be seeing more of them as we progress through the language facilities.

An **#include** statement is one of several **preprocessor directives**. The Visual C++ editor recognizes these and highlights them in blue in an edit window. Preprocessor directives are commands executed by the compiler that generally act on your source code in some way before it is compiled. They all start with the **#** character. We will be introducing other preprocessor directives as we need them.

The Function main()

The function **main()** in our example consists of the function header defining it as **main()** plus everything from the first opening curly brace to the corresponding closing curly brace. The curly braces enclose the executable statements in the function which are referred to collectively as the **body** of the function.

As we shall see, all functions consist of a header which defines, amongst other things, the function name, followed by the function body which consists of a number of program statements enclosed between a pair of curly braces. The body of a function may contain no statements at all, in which case it doesn't do anything.

A function that doesn't do anything may seem somewhat superfluous, but when you are writing a large program, you may map out the complete program structure in functions but, initially, leave the code for many of them with empty bodies. Doing this means that you can compile and execute the whole program with all its functions but add detailed coding for them incrementally.

Program Statements

The program statements making up the function body of **main()** are each terminated with a semicolon. The program statement is the basic unit in defining what a program does. This is a bit like a sentence in a paragraph of text where each sentence stands by itself in expressing an action or an idea, but relates to and combines with the other sentences in the paragraph in expressing a more general idea. A statement is a self-contained definition of an action that the computer is to carry out but which can be combined with other statements to define a more complex action or calculation.

The action of a function is always expressed by a number of statements, each ending with a semicolon. Let's take a quick look at each of the statements in the example that we have just written, just to get a general feel for how it works. We will discuss each type of statement more fully later in this chapter.

The first statement in the program,

```
int apples, oranges;        // Declare two integer variables
```

declares two variables, **apples** and **oranges**. A variable is a named bit of computer memory that you can use to store data. A statement introducing the names of variables is called a **variable declaration**. The keyword, **int**, indicates that the variables are to store values that are whole numbers or integers. The next statement declares another integer variable, **fruit**. While you can declare several variables in the same statement, as we did for **apples** and **oranges**, it is generally a good idea to declare them separately. This enables you to comment them individually.

In the example, the line,

```
apples = 5; oranges = 6;    // Set initial values
```

contains two statements, each terminated by a semicolon. While it isn't obligatory, it's good programming practice to write only one statement on a line. The two statements store the values **5** and **6** in the variables **apples** and **oranges** respectively. These statements are called **assignment statements** because they assign a new value to a variable.

The next statement,

```
fruit = apples + oranges;   // Get the total fruit
```

is also an assignment statement which adds the values stored in the variables **apples** and **oranges** and stores the result in the variable **fruit**.

The next three statements are:

```
cout << endl;                 // Start output on a new line
cout << "Oranges are not the only fruit... " << endl
     << "- and we have " << fruit << " fruits in all.";
cout << endl;                 // Start output on a new line
```

These are all output statements. The first sends a newline character, denoted by the word **endl**, to the screen. In C++, a source of input or a destination for output is referred to as a stream. The word **cout** specifies the standard output stream, and the operator **<<** indicates that what appears to the right of the operator is to be sent to the output stream, **cout**. The operator, **<<**, 'points' in the direction that the data flows - from the variable or string on the right to the output destination on the left.

The meaning of the word **cout** and the operator << are defined by the contents of **iostream.h** which we added to our program code in the **#include** directive at the beginning of the program. Because **cout** has been defined to represent the standard output stream to your display screen, you shouldn't use the word **cout** for other purposes; for example, as a variable in your program.

31

The second statement sends a text string defined between quotes to the screen, followed by another newline character - **endl**, then another text string, followed by the value stored in the variable **fruit**, then finally another text string. There is no problem stringing together a sequence of things that you want to output in this way. The statement executes from left to right, with each item being sent to **cout** in turn. Note that each item is preceded by its own **<<** operator.

The third statement sends another newline character to the screen. These statements produce the output from the program that you see. Note that the second statement runs over two lines. The successive lines are combined into a single statement until the compiler finds the semicolon that defines the end of the statement. This means that if you forget a semicolon for a statement, the compiler will assume the next line is part of the same statement and join them together. This usually results in something the compiler cannot understand, so you will get an error.

The last statement in our program,

```
    return 0;                    // Exit the program
```

stops execution of the program and returns control to the operating system. We will be discussing all of these statements in more detail later on.

The statements in a program are executed in the sequence in which they are written, unless a statement specifically causes the natural sequence to be altered. In Chapter 3, we will look at statements which alter the sequence of execution.

Whitespace

Whitespace is the term used in C++ to describe blanks, tabs, newline characters and comments. Whitespace separates one part of a statement from another and enables the compiler to identify where one element in a statement, such as **int**, ends and the next element begins. Therefore, in the statement,

```
    int fruit;                   // ..then another one
```

there must be at least one whitespace character - usually a space between **int** and **fruit** - for the compiler to be able to distinguish them. On the other hand, in the statement,

```
    fruit = apples + oranges;    // Get the total fruit
```

no whitespace characters are necessary between **fruit** and **=**, or between **=** and **apples**, although you are free to include some if you wish. This is because the **=** is not alphabetic or numeric so the compiler can separate it from its surroundings. Similarly, no whitespace characters are necessary either side of the **+** sign.

Apart from its use as a separator between elements in a statement that might otherwise be confused, whitespace is ignored by the compiler (except, of course, in a string of characters between quotes). You can, therefore, include as much whitespace as you like to make your program more readable, as we did when we spread our output statement in the last example over several lines. In some programming languages, the end of a statement is at the end of the line, but in C++ the end of a statement is wherever the semicolon occurs.

Since variable names must be made up of single words, you must not put whitespace characters in the middle. If you do, the single variable name will not be seen by the compiler as such and will not be interpreted correctly.

Statement Blocks

We can enclose several statements between a pair of curly braces, in which case they become a **block**, or a **compound statement**. The body of a function is an example of a block. Such a compound statement can be thought of as a single statement (as we shall see when we look at the decision making possibilities in C++ in Chapter 3). In fact, wherever you can put a single statement in C++, you could equally well put a block of statements between braces. As a consequence, blocks can be placed inside other blocks. In fact, blocks can be nested, one within another, to any depth.

 A statement block also has important effects on variables, but we will defer discussion of this until later in this chapter when we discuss something called variable scope.

Defining Variables

Now that we are beyond our first program, we are going to want to manipulate some meaningful information and get some answers. An essential element in this process is having a piece of memory that we can call our own, that we can refer to using a meaningful name and where we can store an item of data. Each individual piece of memory so specified is called a **variable**.

Each variable will store a particular kind of data which is fixed when we define the variable in our program. One variable might store whole numbers (that is, integers) in which case it couldn't be used to store numbers with fractional values. The value that each variable contains at any point is determined by the instructions in our program and, of course, its value will usually change many times as the program calculation progresses.

Let's look first at the rules for naming a variable when we introduce it into a program.

Naming Variables

The name we give to a variable is called an **identifier**, or more conveniently a **variable name**. Variable names can include the letters A-z (upper or lower case), the digits 0-9 and the underscore character. All other characters are illegal. Variable names must also begin with either a letter or an underscore. Names are usually chosen to indicate the kind of information to be stored.

In Visual C++, up to 247 characters are permitted for variable names which gives you a reasonable amount of flexibility. In fact, apart from variables, there are quite a few things that have names in C++. We shall see they can all have names of up to 247 characters with the same definition rules as a variable name. Using names of the maximum length can make your programs a little difficult to read and, unless you have amazing keyboard skills, they are the very devil to type in. A more serious consideration is that not all compilers support such long names. If you anticipate compiling your code in other environments, names with up to 31 characters are usually adequate and will not cause problems in most instances.

Although you can use variable names that begin with an underscore, for example **_this** and **_that**, this is best avoided because of potential clashes with standard system variables which have the same form. You should also avoid using names starting with a double underscore for the same reason.

Examples of good variable names are:

- **Price**
- **discount**
- **pShape**
- **Value_**
- **COUNT**

8_Ball, **7Up**, and **6_pack** are not legal. Neither is **Hash!** or **Mary-Ann**. This last example is a common mistake although **Mary_Ann** would be quite acceptable. Of course, **Mary Ann** would not be, because blanks are not allowed in variable names. Note that the variable names **republican** and **Republican** are quite different, as upper and lower case letters are differentiated.

Keywords in C

There are reserved words in C++, also called **keywords**, which have special significance within the language. They will be highlighted with a particular color by the Visual C++ editor as you enter your program. If keywords you type do not appear highlighted, the keyword has been entered incorrectly.

 Remember that keywords, like the rest of the C++ language, are case-sensitive.

For example, the program that you entered earlier in the chapter contained the keywords **int** and **return**. You will see many more as you progress through the book. You must ensure that the names you choose for entities in your program, such as variables, are not the same as any of the keywords in C++. A complete list of keywords used in Visual C++ appears in Appendix A.

Declaring Variables

A variable **declaration** is a program statement which specifies the name of a variable and the sort of data that it can store. For example, the statement,

```
int value;
```

declares a variable with the name **value** that can store integers. The type of data that can be stored in the variable **value** is specified by the keyword **int**. Because **int** is a keyword, you can't use **int** as a name for one of your variables.

 Note that a declaration always ends with a semicolon.

A single declaration can specify the names of several variables but, as we have said, it is generally better to declare variables in individual statements, one per line. We will deviate from this from time to time in this book, but only in the interests of not spreading code over too many pages.

You must declare a variable at any point between the beginning of your program and when the variable is used for the first time. In C++, it is good practice to declare variables close to their first point of use.

Initial Values for Variables

When you declare a variable, you can also assign an initial value to it. A variable declaration that assigns an initial value to a variable is called a **definition**. To initialize a variable when you declare it, you just need to write an equals sign followed by the initializing value after the variable name. We can write the following statements to give each of the variables an initial value:

```
int value = 0;
int count = 10;
int number = 5;
```

In this case, **value** will have the value **0**, **count** will have the value **10** and **number** will have the value **5**.

There is another way of writing the initial value for a variable in C++ called **functional notation**. Instead of an equals sign and the value, you can simply write the value in parentheses following the variable name. So we could rewrite the previous declarations as:

```
int value(0);
int count(10);
int number(5);
```

If you don't supply an initial value for a variable, it will usually contain whatever garbage was left in the memory location that it occupies by the previous program you ran (there is an exception to this as we shall see later). Wherever possible, you should always initialize your variables when you declare them. If your variables start out with known values, it makes it easier to work out what is happening when things go wrong. And one thing you can be sure of, things will go wrong.

Data Types in C++

The sort of information that a variable can hold is determined by its **data type**. All data and variables in your program must be of some defined type. C++ provides you with a range of standard data types, specified by particular keywords. We have already seen the keyword **int** for defining integer variables. As part of the object oriented aspects of the language, you can also create your own data types, as we shall see later. For the moment, let's take a look at elementary numerical data types.

Integer Variables

As we have said, integer variables are variables that can only have values that are whole numbers. The number of players in a football team is an integer, at least at the beginning of the game. We already know that you can declare integer variables using the keyword **int**. These are variables which occupy 4 bytes in memory and can take both positive and negative values.

The upper and lower limits for the values of a variable of type **int** correspond to the maximum and minimum signed binary numbers which can be represented by 32 bits. The upper limit for a variable of type **int** is 2^{31}, and the lower limit is -2^{31}.

In Visual C++, the keyword **short** also defines an integer variable, this time occupying two bytes. The keyword **short** is equivalent to **short int**.

C++ also provides another integer type, **long**, which can also be written as **long int**. In this case, we can write the statement,

```
long BigNumber = 1000000L, LargeValue = 0L;
```

where we declare the variables **BigNumber** and **LargeValue** with initial values **1000000** and **0** respectively. The letter **L** appended to the end of the constant values specifies that they are **long** constants. You can also use the small letter **l** for the same purpose, but it has the disadvantage that it is easily confused with the numeral 1.

Note that we don't include commas when writing large numeric values in a program.

Integer variables declared as **long** occupy 4 bytes and can have values from -2,147,483,648 to 2,147,483,647. This is the same as variables declared as **int** using Visual C++ 4.0.

Note that with other C++ compilers **long** and **long int** may not be the same as **int**, so if you expect your programs to be compiled in other environments, do not assume that **long** and **int** are equivalent. For truly portable code, you should not even assume that an **int** is 4 bytes (for example, under older 16-bit versions of Visual C++ an **int** was 2 bytes).

The char Data Type

The **char** data type serves a dual purpose. It specifies a one byte variable that you can use to store integers, or to store a single **ASCII** character, which is the **A**merican **S**tandard **C**ode for **I**nformation **I**nterchange. The ASCII character set appears in Appendix B. We can declare a **char** variable with this statement:

```
char letter = 'A';
```

This declares the variable **letter** and initializes it with the value **'A'**. Note that we specify a constant which is a single character between single quotes, not double quotes which we used previously for defining a string of characters to be displayed. A string of characters is a series of values, of type **char**, that are grouped together into a single entity called an array. We will discuss arrays and how strings are handled in C++ in Chapter 4.

Because the character **'A'** is represented as the decimal value 65 (have a look at Appendix B if you don't believe me), we could have written this,

```
char letter = 65;      // Equivalent to A
```

to produce the same result as the previous statement. The range of integers that can be stored in a variable of type **char** is from -128 to 127.

We can also use hexadecimal constants to initialize **char** variables (and other integer types). A hexadecimal constant is written using the standard representation for hexadecimal digits, 0 to 9, and A to F (or a to f) for digits with values from 10 to 15. It is also preceded by 0x (or 0X) to distinguish it from a decimal value. Thus, to get exactly the same result ,we could rewrite the last statement as follows:

```
char letter = 0x41;      // Equivalent to A
```

 Do not write decimal integer values with a leading zero. The compiler will interpret such values as octal (base 8), so a value written as 065 will be equivalent to 53 in normal decimal notation.

Integer Type Modifiers

Variables of the integral types **char**, **int**, **short** or **long** which we have just discussed, contain signed values by default. That is, they can store both positive and negative values. This is because the type modifier **signed** is assumed for these types by default. So wherever we wrote **char**, **int**, or **long**, we could have written **signed char**, **signed int**, or **signed long** respectively. If you are sure that you don't need to store negative values in a variable, if you were recording the number of miles you drive in a week for instance, you can specify a variable as **unsigned**:

```
unsigned long mileage = 0UL;
```

In this case, the minimum value that can be stored is zero and the maximum increases to 4,294,967,295 (2^{32}). The maximum value of an unsigned variable is larger than that of a signed variable because the bit used to determine the sign of the integer counts as part of the numeric value instead. Note how a **U** (or **u**) is appended to **unsigned** constant values. In the above example we also have **L** appended to indicate that the value is **long**. You can use either upper or lower case for **U** and **L** and the sequence is unimportant, but it is a good idea to adopt a consistent way of specifying such constants.

> *Of course, both* **signed** *and* **unsigned** *are keywords, so you can't use them as variable names.*

Floating Point Variables

Values which are not integral are stored as **floating point** numbers. A floating point number can be expressed as a decimal value such as 112.5, or with an exponent such as 1.125E2 where the decimal part is multiplied by the power of 10 specified after the E (for Exponent). Our example is, therefore, 1.125×10^2, which is 112.5.

 FYI Note that a floating point constant must contain a decimal point or an exponent or both. If you write neither, you have an integer.

You can specify a floating point variable using the keyword **double**, as in this statement:

```
double in_to_mm = 25.4;
```

A **double** variable occupies 8 bytes of memory and stores values accurate to 15 decimal digits. The range of values stored is much wider than that indicated by the 15 digits accuracy, being from 1.7×10^{-308} to 1.7×10^{308}, positive and negative.

If you don't need 15 digits precision, and you don't need the massive range of values provided by **double** variables, you can opt to use the keyword **float** to declare floating point variables occupying 4 bytes. For example, the statement,

```
float Pi = 3.14159f;
```

defines a variable **Pi** with the initial value 3.14159. The **f** at the end of the constant specifies it to be a **float** type. Without the **f**, the constant would have been of type **double**. Variables declared as **float** are of 7 decimal digits precision and can have values from 3.4×10^{-38} to 3.4×10^{38}, positive and negative.

FYI You can find a complete summary of the various data types in the online documentation provided with Visual C++.

Variables with Specific Sets of Values

You will sometimes be faced with the need for variables that have a limited set of possible values which can be usefully referred to by labels - the days of the week, for example, or months of the year. There is a specific facility in C++ to handle this situation, called an **enumeration**. Let's take one of the examples we have just mentioned - a variable that can assume values corresponding to days of the week. We can define this as follows:

```
enum Week {Mon, Tues, Wed, Thurs, Fri, Sat, Sun} This_week;
```

This declares an enumeration type called **Week**, and the variable **This_week** that is an instance of the enumeration type **Week** that can only assume the values specified between the braces. If you try to assign to **This_week** anything other than the set of values specified, it will cause an error. The symbolic names listed between the braces are known as **enumerators**. In fact, each of the names of the days will be automatically defined as representing a fixed integer value. The first name in the list, **Mon**, will have the value 0, **Tues** will be 1, and so on.

By default, each successive enumerator is one larger than the value of the previous one but, if you would prefer the implicit numbering to start at a different value, you can just write,

```
enum Week {Mon = 1, Tues, Wed, Thurs, Fri, Sat, Sun} This_week;
```

and they will be equivalent to 1 through 7. The enumerators don't need to have unique values. You could define **Mon** and **Tues** as both having the value 1 for example, with the statement:

```
enum Week {Mon = 1, Tues = 1, Wed, Thurs, Fri, Sat, Sun} This_week;
```

As it's the same as an **int**, the variable **This_week** will occupy four bytes, as will all variables which are of an enumeration type.

Having defined the form of an enumeration, you can define another variable thus:

```
enum Week Next_week;
```

This defines a variable **Next_week** as an enumeration that can assume the values previously specified. You can also omit the keyword **enum** in declaring a variable so, instead of the previous statement, you could write:

```
Week Next_week;
```

If you wish, you can assign specific values to all the enumerators. For example, we could define this enumeration:

```
enum Punctuation {Comma=',', Exclamation='!', Question='?'}things;
```

Here we have defined the possible values for the variable **things** as the numerical equivalents of the appropriate symbols. If you look in the ASCII table in Appendix B, you will see that the symbols are 44, 33 and 63 respectively in decimal . As you can see, the values assigned don't have to be in ascending order. If you don't specify all the values explicitly, values continue to be assigned incrementing by 1 from the last specified value, as in our second **Week** example. You could also use this to define the idea of logical variables as:

```
enum Boolean {False, True} B1, B2, B3;
```

This defines three variables having the possible values **False** or **True**. Note that here the sequence of values results in **True** and **False** being assigned the values of 1 and 0 respectively, consistent with the usual interpretation of **True** and **False**.

If you don't intend to define any other enumeration variables of the same type, you can omit the type, in which case you have an anonymous enumeration. For example, we could write,

```
enum {False, True} B1, B2, B3;
```

which would define variables **B1**, **B2**, and **B3** that can each be given the values **True** or **False**.

Defining Your Own Data Types

The **typedef** keyword enables you to define your own data type specifier. Using **typedef**, you could define the type name **BigOnes** as equivalent to the standard **long int** type with the declaration:

```
typedef long int BigOnes;        // Defining BigOnes as a type name
```

This defines **BigOnes** as an alternative type specifier for **long int**, so you could declare a variable **mynum** as **long int** with the declaration:

```
BigOnes mynum = 0;               // Define a long int variable
```

There is no difference between this declaration and the one using the built in type name. You could equally well use,

```
long int mynum = 0;              // Define a long int variable
```

for exactly the same result. In fact, if you define your own type name such as **BigOnes**, you can use both type specifiers within the same program for declaring different variables that will end up as having the same type.

Since **typedef** only defines a synonym for an existing type, it may appear to be a bit superficial. We will see later that it can fulfill a very useful role in enabling us to simplify more complex declarations than we have met so far. We will also see later that classes provide us with a means of defining completely new data types.

Basic Input/Output Operations

Here, we will only look at enough of C++ input and output to get us through learning about C++. It's not that it's difficult - quite the opposite in fact - but for Windows programming we won't need it at all.

C++ input/output revolves around the notion of a data stream where we can insert data into an output stream or extract data from an input stream. We have already seen that the standard output stream to the screen is referred to as **cout**. The input stream from the keyboard is referred to as **cin**.

Input from the Keyboard

We obtain input from the keyboard through the stream **cin**, using the extractor operator for a stream **>>**. To read two integer values from the keyboard into integer variables **num1** and **num2**, you can write this:

```
cin >> num1 >> num2;
```

The operator 'points' in the direction that data flows - in this case, from **cin** to each of the two variables in turn. Any leading whitespace is skipped and the first integer value you key in is read into **num1**. This is because the input statement executes from left to right. Whitespace following **num1** is ignored and the second integer value that you enter is read into **num2**. There has to be some whitespace between successive values though, so that they can be differentiated. The stream input operation ends when you press the *Enter* key and execution then continues with the next statement. Of course, errors can arise if you key in the wrong data, but we will assume that you always get it right!

Floating point values are read from the keyboard in exactly the same way as integers and, of course, we can mix the two. The stream input and operations automatically deal with variables and data of any of the basic types. For example, in the statements,

```
int num1 = 0, num2 = 0;
double factor = 0.0;
cin >> num1 >> factor >> num2;
```

the last line will read an integer into **num1**, then a floating point value into **factor** and, finally, an integer into **num2**.

TRY IT OUT - Output to the Display

Writing information to the display operates in a complementary fashion to input. The stream is called **cout** and we use the insertion operator **<<**. This also 'points' in the direction of data movement. We have already used this operator to output a text string between quotes. We can demonstrate the process of outputting the value of a variable with a simple program. We'll assume that you've got the hang of creating a new project and a new source file, adding the source file to the project and building it into an executable. Here's the code:

```
// EX2_02.CPP
// Exercising output
#include <iostream.h>
int main()
{
   int num1 = 1234, num2 = 5678;
   cout << endl;                        //Start on a new line
   cout << num1 << num2;                //Output two values
   cout << endl;                        //End on a new line
   return 0;                            //Exit program
}
```

How It Works

The first statement in the body of **main()** declares and initializes two integer variables, **num1** and **num2**. This is followed by two output statements, the first of which moves the screen cursor position to a new line. Because output statements execute from left to right, the second output statement displays the value of **num1** followed by the value of **num2**.

When you compile and execute this, you will get the output:

This is correct, but not exactly helpful. We really need the two output values separated by at least one space. The default for stream output is to just output the digits in the output value, which doesn't provide for spacing different values out nicely so they can be differentiated. As it is, we have no way to tell where the first number begins and the second one ends.

TRY IT OUT - Manipulators

We can fix this quite easily, though, just by outputting a space between the two values. We can do this by replacing the 8th line in our original program with the statement:

```
cout << num1 << ' ' << num2;                    //Output two values
```

Of course, if we had several rows of output that we wanted to align in columns, we would need some extra capability as we do not know how many digits there will be in each value. We can take care of this situation by using what is called a **manipulator**. A manipulator modifies the way in which data output to (or input from) a stream is handled.

Manipulators are defined in the header file **iomanip.h**, so we need to add an **#include** statement for it. The manipulator that we will use is **setw(n)** which will output the following value left justified in a field **n** spaces wide, so **setw(6)** puts the output in a field with a width of six spaces. To get something more like the output we want, we can change our program to the following:

```
// EX2_03.CPP
// Exercising output
#include <iostream.h>
#include <iomanip.h>
int main()
{
    int num1 = 1234, num2 = 5678;
    cout << endl;                               //Start on a new line
    cout << setw(6) << num1 << setw(6) << num2; //Output two values
    cout << endl;                               //Start on a new line
    return 0;                                   //Exit program
}
```

How It Works

The only changes from the last example are the addition of the **#include** statement for **iomanip.h**, and the insertion of the **setw()** manipulator in the output stream preceding each value, to output the values in a field six characters wide. Now we get nice neat output where we can actually separate the two values:

Note that the **setw()** manipulator only works for the single output value immediately following it. We have to insert it into the stream immediately preceding each value that we want to output within a given field width. If we put only one **setw()**, it would apply to the first value to be output after it was inserted. Any following value would be output in the default manner. You could try this out by deleting the second **setw(6)** and its insertion operator in our example.

Escape Sequences

When we write a character string between quotes, we can include special characters called **escape sequences**. They are called escape sequences because they allow characters to be included in a string that otherwise could not be represented. An escape sequence starts with a backslash character, ****. For example, a tab character is written as **\t**, so these two output statements,

```
cout << endl << "This is output.";
cout << endl << "\tThis is output after a tab.";
```

will produce these lines:

This is output.
        This is output after a tab.

In fact, instead of using **endl** ,we could include the escape sequence for the newline character, **\n**, in each string, so we could rewrite the statements above as follows:

```
cout << "\nThis is output.";
cout << "\n\tThis is output after a tab.";
```

Here are some escape sequences which may be particularly useful:

Escape sequence	What it does
\a	Sounds a beep
\n	Newline
\'	Single quote
\\	Backslash
\b	Backspace
\t	Tab
\"	Double quote

Obviously, if you want to be able to include a backslash or a double quote as a character to be output in a string between quotes, you must use the escape sequences to represent them. Otherwise, the backslash would be interpreted as another escape sequence and a double quote would indicate the end of the character string.

You can also use characters specified by escape sequences in the initialization of **char** variables. For example:

```
char Tab = '\t';        // Initialize with tab character
```

That gives us enough of a toehold in input/output. We will collect a few more bits as and when we need them.

Calculating in C++

This is where we actually start doing something with the data that we enter. We are beginning the 'processing' part of a C++ program. Almost all of the computational aspects of C++ are fairly intuitive, so we should slide through this like a hot knife through butter.

The Assignment Statement

We have already seen examples of the assignment statement. A typical assignment statement would look like this:

```
whole = part1 + part2 + part3;
```

The assignment statement enables you to calculate the value of an expression which appears on the right hand side of the equals sign, in this case the sum of **part1**, **part2** and **part3**, and store the result in the variable specified on the left hand side, in this case **whole**. In this statement, the **whole** is only the sum of its parts, and no more.

FYI   Note that the statement, as always, ends with a semicolon.

You can also write repeated assignments such as,

```
A = B = 1;
```

where this is equivalent to assigning the value 1 to **B**, then assigning the value of **B** to **A**.

Understanding Lvalues

An **lvalue** is something that refers to an address in memory, and is so-called because it can appear on the left of an equals sign in an assignment. Most variables are lvalues since they specify a place in memory. However, as we shall see, there are variables which are not lvalues and so cannot appear on the left of an assignment because their values have been defined as constant. The variables **A** and **B** appearing in the preceding paragraph are lvalues, whereas the expression **A+B** would not be, since its result does not determine an address in memory where a value might be stored.

> *Lvalues will pop up at various times throughout the book, sometimes where you least expect it, so keep the idea in mind.*

Arithmetic Operations

The basic arithmetic operators we have at our disposal are addition, subtraction, multiplication and division, represented by the symbols **+**, **-**, ***** and **/** respectively. These operate generally as you would expect, with the exception of division which has a slight aberration when working with integer variables or constants as we'll see. You can write statements such as the following:

```
NetPay = Hours*Rate - Deductions;
```

Here, the product of **Hours** and **Rate** will be calculated, then **Deductions** subtracted from the value produced. The multiply and divide operators are executed before addition and subtraction. We will discuss the order of execution more fully later in this chapter. The overall result of the expression will be stored in the variable **NetPay**.

The minus sign used in the last statement applies to two operands - it subtracts one from another. This is called a binary operation because two values are involved. The minus sign can also be used with one operand to change the sign of its value, in which case it is called a unary minus. You could write this:

```
int A = 0; B = -5;
A = -B;                      // Changes the sign of the operand
```

Here, **A** will be assigned the value +5 because the unary minus changes the sign of the value of the operand **B**.

Note that an assignment is not the equivalent of the equations you saw in high school algebra. It specifies an action to be carried out rather than a statement of fact. The statement,

```
A = A + 1;
```

means add 1 to the current value stored in **A** and then store the result back in **A**. As a normal algebraic statement it wouldn't make sense.

TRY IT OUT - Exercising Basic Arithmetic

We can exercise basic arithmetic in C++ by calculating how many standard rolls of wallpaper are needed to paper a room. This is done with the following example:

```cpp
// EX2_04.CPP
// Calculating how many rolls of wallpaper are required for a room
#include <iostream.h>
int main()
{
   double height = 0.0, width = 0.0, length = 0.0; // Room dimensions
   double perimeter = 0.0;                         // Room perimeter

   const double ROLLWIDTH =21.0;          // Standard roll width
   const double ROLLLENGTH = 12.*33.;     // Standard roll length(33ft.)

   int Strips_per_Roll = 0;               // Number of strips in a roll
   int Strips_Reqd = 0;                   // Number of strips needed
   int Nrolls = 0;                        // Total number of rolls
```

```
    cout << endl                          // Start a new line
        << "Enter the height of the room in inches: ";
    cin >> height;

    cout  << endl                         // Start a new line
        << "Now enter the length and width in inches: ";
    cin >> length >> width;

    Strips_per_Roll = ROLLLENGTH/height;   // Get number of strips in a roll
    perimeter = 2.0*(length + width);      // Calculate room perimeter
    Strips_Reqd = perimeter/ROLLWIDTH;     // Get total strips required
    Nrolls = Strips_Reqd/Strips_per_Roll;  // Calculate number of rolls

    cout << endl
        << "For your room you need " << Nrolls << " rolls of wallpaper."
        << endl;

    return 0;
}
```

Note that compiling this program will produce a couple of warnings but, as you'll see, this is nothing to worry about. The program will run just fine.

How It Works

One thing needs to be clear at the outset. No responsibility is assumed for you running out of wallpaper as a result of using this program! As we shall see, all errors in the estimate of the number of rolls required are due to the way C++ works and to the wastage that inevitably occurs when you hang your own wallpaper - usually 50%+!

We can work through the statements in this example in sequence, picking out the interesting, novel, or even exciting features. The statements down to the start of the body of **main()** are familiar territory by now, so we will take those for granted.

A couple of general points worth noting are about the layout of the program. Firstly, the statements in the body of **main()** are indented to make the extent of the body visually clearer and, secondly, various groups of statements are separated by a blank line to indicate that they are functional groups. Indenting statements is a fundamental technique in laying out program code in C++. You will see that this is applied universally to provide visual cues for various logical blocks in a program.

The const Modifier

We have a block of declarations for the variables used in the program right at the beginning of the body of **main()**. These statements are also fairly familiar but there are two which contain some new features:

```
    const double ROLLWIDTH =21.0;       // Standard roll width
    const double ROLLLENGTH = 12.*33.;  // Standard roll length(33ft.)
```

They both start out with a new keyword **const**. This is a type modifier which indicates that the variables are not just of type **double**, but are also constants. Because we effectively tell the compiler that these are constants, the compiler will check for any statements which attempt to change the values of these variables and, if it finds any, it will generate an error message. This is relatively easy since a variable declared as **const** is not an lvalue and, therefore, can't legally be placed on the left of an assignment operation.

You could check this out by adding, anywhere after the declaration of **ROLLWIDTH**, a statement such as:

```
ROLLWIDTH = 0;
```

You will find the program no longer compiles.

Note that the variable names declared as **const** are written here with capital letters. It is a common convention in C++ to write identifiers that represent constants in capitals to distinguish them from other variables which are, well, more variable. It can be very useful defining constants by means of **const** variable types, particularly when you use the same constant several times in a program. For one thing, if you need to change it, you will only need to change its definition at the beginning to ensure that the change automatically appears throughout. We will see this technique used quite often.

Constant Expressions

The **const** variable **ROLLLENGTH** is also initialized with an arithmetic expression **(12.*33.)**. Being able to use constant expressions to initialize variables saves having to work out the value yourself, and can also be more meaningful, as 33 feet times 12 inches is much clearer than simply writing 396. The compiler will generally evaluate constant expressions accurately, whereas if you do it yourself, depending on the complexity of the expression and your ability to number crunch, there is a finite probability that it may be wrong.

You can use any expression that can be calculated as a constant at compile time, including **const** objects that you have already defined. So for instance, if it was useful in the program to do so, we could declare the area of a standard roll of wallpaper as:

```
const double ROLLAREA = ROLLWIDTH*ROLLLENGTH;
```

This statement obviously would need to be placed after the declarations for the two **const** variables used in the initialization of **ROLLAREA**.

Program Input

The next four statements in the program handle input:

```
cout << endl                           // Start a new line
     << "Enter the height of the room in inches: ";
cin >> height;

cout  << endl                          // Start a new line
     << "Now enter the length and width in inches: ";
cin >> length >> width;
```

Here we have used **cout** to prompt for the input required and then read the input from the keyboard using **cin**. We first obtain the room **height** and then read the **length** and **width** successively. In a practical program, we would need to check for errors and possibly make sure that the values that are read are sensible, but we don't have enough knowledge to do that yet!

Calculating the Result

We have four statements involved in calculating the number of standard rolls of wallpaper required for the size of room given:

```
Strips_per_Roll = ROLLLENGTH/height;      // Get number of strips in a roll
perimeter = 2.0*(length + width);         // Calculate room perimeter
Strips_Reqd = perimeter/ROLLWIDTH;        // Get total strips required
Nrolls = Strips_Reqd/Strips_per_Roll;     // Calculate number of rolls
```

The first statement calculates the number of strips of paper with a length corresponding to the height of the room that we can get from a standard roll, by dividing one into the other. So, if the room is 8 feet high, we divide 96 into 396, which would produce the floating point result 4.125. There is a subtlety here, however. The variable where we store the result, **Strips_per_Roll**, was declared as **int**, so it can only store integer values. Consequently, any floating point value to be stored as an integer is rounded down to the nearest integer, 4 in our case, and this value is stored. This is actually the result that you want here since, although it may fit under a window or over a door, fractions of a strip are best ignored when estimating. Note that the compiler will issue a warning here. It recognizes that the result is being truncated and lets you know in case that was not what you intended . We could avoid the error message by **casting** the value on the right of the assignment to **int**, so the statement would become:

```
Strips_per_Roll = int(ROLLLENGTH/height); //Get number of strips in a roll
```

The addition of **int** with the parentheses around the expression on the right tells the compiler explicitly to convert the value of the expression to **int**. Although this means that we still lose the fractional part of the value, the compiler assumes that we know what we are doing and does not issue a warning. We will see more about casting later.

Note how we calculate the perimeter of the room in the next statement. In order to multiply the sum of the **length** and the **width** by two, we enclose the expression summing the two variables between parentheses. This ensures that the addition is performed first and the result is multiplied by 2.0 to give us the correct value for the perimeter. We can use parentheses to make sure that a calculation is carried out in the order we require since expressions in parentheses are always evaluated first. Where there are nested parentheses, the expressions within the parentheses are evaluated in sequence, from the innermost to the outermost.

The third statement, calculating how many strips of paper are required to cover the room, uses the same effect that we observed in the first statement: the result is rounded down to the nearest integer because it is to be stored in the integer variable, **Strips_Reqd**. This is not what we need in practice. It would be best to round up for estimating, but we don't have enough knowledge of C++ to do this yet. Once you have read the next chapter you can come back and fix it!

The last arithmetic statement calculates the number of rolls required by dividing the number of strips required (integer) by the number of strips in a roll (also integer). Because we are dividing one integer by another, the result has to be integer and any remainder is ignored. This would still be the case if the variable **Nrolls** were floating point. The resulting integer value would be converted to floating point form before it was stored in **Nrolls**. The result that we obtain is essentially the same as if we had produced a floating point result and rounded down to the nearest integer. Again, this is not what we want, so if you want to use this, you will need to fix it.

Displaying the Result

The result of the calculation is displayed by the following statement:

```
cout << endl
    << "For your room you need " << Nrolls << " rolls of wallpaper."
    << endl;
```

This is a single output statement spread over three lines. It first outputs a newline character, then the text string **"For your room you need "**. This is followed by the value of the variable **Nrolls**, and finally the text string **"rolls of wallpaper."**. As you can see, output statements are very easy in C++.

Finally, the program ends when this statement is executed:

```
return 0;
```

The value zero here is a return value which, in this case, will be returned to the operating system. We will see more about return values in Chapter 6.

Calculating a Remainder

We have seen in the last example that dividing one integer value by another produces an integer result which ignores any remainder, so that 11 divided by 4 gives the result 2. Since the remainder after division can be of great interest, particularly when you are dividing cookies amongst children, for example, C++ provides a special operator **%** for this. So we can write the statements,

```
int Residue = 0, Cookies = 19, Children = 5;
Residue = Cookies%Children;
```

and the variable **Residue** will end up with the value 4, the number left after dividing 19 by 5. To calculate how many each of them received, you just need to use division, as in the statement:

```
Each = Cookies/Children;
```

Modifying a Variable

It's often necessary to modify the existing value of a variable, such as incrementing it or doubling it. We could increment a variable **count** using the statement:

```
count = count + 5;
```

This simply adds 5 to the current value stored in **count**, and stores the result back in **count**, so if **count** started out at 10, it would end up as 15. You have an alternative shorthand way of writing the same thing in C++:

```
count += 5;
```

This says, 'Take the value in **count**, add 5 to it and store the result back in **count**.'

We can also use other operators with this notation. For example,

```
count *=5;
```

has the effect of multiplying the current value of **count** by 5 and storing the result back in **count**. In general, we can write statements of the form,

```
rhs op= lhs;
```

where **op** is any of the following operators:

```
+      -      *      /      %
<<     >>     &      ^      |
```

The first five of these we have already met, and the remainder, which are shift and logical operators, we will see later in this chapter. **rhs** stands for any legal expression for the right-hand side of the statement, and is usually (but not necessarily) a variable name. **lhs** stands for any legal expression on the left-hand side of the statement.

The general form of the statement is equivalent to this:

```
rhs = rhs op (lhs);
```

This means that we can write statements such as

```
A /= B + C;
```

which will be identical in effect to

```
A = A/(B + C);
```

The Increment and Decrement Operators

We will now take a brief look at some unusual arithmetic operators called the increment and decrement operators, as we will find them to be quite an asset once we get further into applying C++ in earnest. These are unary operators used to increment or decrement a variable. For example, assuming the variables are of type **int**, the following three statements all have exactly the same effect:

```
count = count + 1;      count += 1;        ++count;
```

They each increment the variable **count** by 1. The last form using the increment operator is clearly the most concise. The action of this operator in an expression is to increment the value of the variable, then use the incremented value in the expression. For example, if **count** has the value 5, the statement,

```
total = ++count + 6;
```

results in the variable **total** being assigned the value 12.

So far, we have written the operator in front of the variable to which it applies. This is called the **prefix** form. It can also be written after the variable to which it applies, the **postfix** form, where the effect is slightly different. The incrementing of the variable to which it applies occurs after its value is used in context. For example, if we rewrite the previous example as,

```
total = count++ + 6;
```

with the same initial value for **count**, **total** is assigned the value 11, since the initial value of **count** is used to evaluate the expression, then the increment by 1 is applied. The statement above is equivalent to the two statements:

```
total = count + 6;
++count;
```

Generally, it isn't a good idea to use the increment operator in the way that we have here. It would be clearer to write:

```
total = 6 + count++;
```

Where we have an expression such as **a++ + b**, or **a+++b**, it becomes less obvious what is meant or what the compiler will do. They are actually the same, but in the second case you might really have meant **a + ++b** which is different. It evaluates to one more than the other two expressions.

Exactly the same rules that we have discussed in relation to the increment operator apply to the decrement operator, **--**. For example, if **count** has the initial value 5, the statement,

```
total = --count + 6;
```

results in **total** having the value 10 assigned, whereas,

```
total = 6 + count-- ;
```

sets the value of **total** to 11. Both operators are usually applied to integers, particularly in the context of loops, as we shall see in Chapter 3. We shall also see in later chapters that they can also be applied to other data types in C++.

TRY IT OUT - The Comma Operator

The comma operator allows you to specify several expressions where normally only one might occur. This is best understood by looking at an example of how it is used:

```cpp
// EX2_05.CPP
// Exercising the comma operator
#include <iostream.h>
int main()
{
   long num1 = 0, num2 = 0, num3 = 0, num4 = 0;

   num4 = (num1 = 10, num2 = 20, num3 = 30);
   cout << endl
          << "The value of a series of expressions "
          << "is the value of the right most: "
          << num4;
   cout << endl;

   return 0;
}
```

How It Works

If you compile and run this program you will get this output,

which is fairly self explanatory. The variable **num4** receives the value of the last of the series of three assignments, the value of an assignment being the value assigned to the left-hand side. The parentheses in the assignment for **num4** are essential. You could try executing this without them to see the effect. Without the parentheses, the first expression separated by commas in the series will become:

```
num4 = num1 = 10
```

So, **num4** will have the value 10.

Of course, the expressions separated by the comma operator do not have to be assignments. We could equally well write the following:

```
long num1 = 1, num2 = 10, num3 = 100, num4 = 0;
num4 = (++num1, ++num2, ++num3);
```

The effect of this assignment would be to increment the variables **num1**, **num2** and **num3** by 1, and to set **num4** to the value of the last expression which will be 101. This example is aimed at illustrating the effect of the comma operator, and is not an example of how to write good code.

The Sequence of Calculation

So far, we haven't talked about how we arrive at the sequence of calculations involved in evaluating an expression. It generally corresponds to what you will have learnt at school when dealing with basic arithmetic operators, but there are many other operators in C++. To understand what happens with these we need to look at the mechanism used in C++ to determine this sequence. It is referred to as **operator precedence**.

Operator Precedence

Operator precedence orders the operators in a priority sequence. In any expression, operators with the highest precedence are always executed first, followed by operators with the next lowest precedence, and so on, down to those with the lowest precedence of all. The precedence of the operators in C++ is shown in the following table:

Operators	Associativity
`()  []  ->  ::  .`	Left to right
`!  ~  +`(unary) `-`(unary) `++  &`(unary) `*`(unary) `(typecast) sizeof new delete`	Right to left
`.*`(unary) `->*`	Left to right
`*  /  %`	Left to right
`+  -`	Left to right
`<<  >>`	Left to right
`<  <=  >  >=`	Left to right
`==  !=`	Left to right
`&`	Left to right
`^`	Left to right
`|`	Left to right
`&&`	Left to right
`||`	Left to right
`?:`(conditional operator)	Right to left
`=  *=  /=  %=  +=  &=  ^=  |=  <<=  >>=`	Right to left
`,`	Left to right

There are a lot of operators that you haven't seen yet, but you will know them all by the end of the book. Rather than being spread around, they all appear in the precedence table here so that you can always refer back to it if you are uncertain about the precedence of one operator relative to another.

Operators with the highest precedence appear at the top of the table. Operators in the same row are all of equal precedence. If there are no parentheses in an expression, operators of equal precedence are executed in a sequence determined by their **associativity**. Thus, if the associativity is 'left to right', the left-most operator in an expression is executed first, progressing through the expression to the right-most.

Note that where an operator has a unary (working with one operand) and a binary (working with two operands) form, the unary form is always of a higher precedence and is, therefore, executed first.

FYI

You can always override the precedence of operators by using parentheses. Since there are so many operators in C++, it is sometimes hard to be sure what takes precedence over what. It is a good idea to insert parentheses to make sure. A further plus is that parentheses often make the code much easier to read.

Variable Types and Casting

Calculations in C++ can only be carried out between values of the same type. When you write an expression involving variables or constants of different types, for each operation to be performed the compiler has to convert the type of one of the operands to match that of the other. This conversion process is called **casting**. For example, if you want to add a double value to an integer, the integer value is first converted to **double**, after which the addition is carried out. Of course, the variable which contains the value to be cast is itself not changed. The compiler will store the converted value in a temporary memory location which will be discarded when the calculation is finished.

There are rules which govern the selection of the operand to be converted in any operation. Any expression to be calculated breaks down into a series of operations between two operands. For example, the expression **2*3-4+5** amounts to the series **2*3** resulting in **6**, **6-4** resulting in **2**, and finally **2+5** resulting in **7**. Thus, the rules for casting operands where necessary only need to be defined in terms of decisions about pairs of operands. So, for any pair of operands of different types, the following rules are checked in the order that they are written. When one applies, that rule is used.

Rules for Casting Operands

1 If either operand is **long double**, the value of the other is cast to **long double**.

2 If either operand is **double**, the value of the other is cast to **double**.

3 If either operand is **float**, the value of the other is cast to **float**.

4 If either operand is **long**, the value of the other is cast to **long**.

5 If either operand is **int**, the value of the other is cast to **int**.

We could try these rules on a hypothetical expression to see how they work. Let's suppose that we have a sequence of variable declarations as follows:

```
double value = 31.0;
int count = 16;
float many = 2.0f;
char num = 4;
```

Let's also suppose that we have the following rather arbitrary arithmetic statement:

```
value = (value - count)*(count - num)/many + num/many;
```

We can now work out what casts the compiler will apply. The first operation is to calculate **(value - count)**. Rule 1 doesn't apply but Rule 2 does, so the value of **count** is converted to **double** and the **double** result 15.0 is calculated. Next **(count - num)** must be evaluated, and here the first rule in sequence which applies is Rule 5, so **num** is converted from **char** to **int** and the result 12 is produced as a value of type **int**. The next calculation is the product of the first two results, a **double** 15.0 and an **int** 12. Rule 2 applies here and the 12 is converted to 12.0 as **double**, and the **double** result 180.0 is produced. This result now has to be divided by **many**, so Rule 2 applies again and the value of **many** is converted to **double** before generating the **double** result 90.0. The expression **num/many** is calculated next, and here Rule 3 applies to produce the **float** value 2.0f after converting the value of **num** from

char to **float**. Lastly, the **double** value 90.0 is added to the **float** value 2.0f for which Rule 2 applies, so after converting the 2.0f to 2.0 as **double**, the final result of 92.0 is stored in **value**.

In spite of the last paragraph reading a bit like *The Auctioneer's Song*, I hope you get the general idea.

Casts in Assignment Statements

As we saw in example **Ex2_04.cpp** earlier in this chapter, you can cause an implicit cast by writing an expression of the right-hand side of an assignment that is of a different type to the variable on the left-hand side. This can cause values to be changed and information to be lost. For instance, if you assign a **float** or **double** value to an **int** or a **long** variable, at least the fractional part of the **float** or **double** will be lost and just the integer part will be stored, assuming that does not exceed the range of values available for the integer type concerned.

For example, after executing the following code fragment,

```
int number = 0;
float decimal = 2.5f;
number = decimal;
```

the value of **number** will be 2. Note the **f** at the end of the constant 2.5. This indicates to the compiler that this constant is single precision floating point. Without the **f**, the default would have been **double**. Any constant containing a decimal point is floating point. If you don't want it to be double precision, you need to append the **f**. A capital **F** would do the job just as well.

Explicit Casts

Sometimes the default cast rules can be inconvenient. Suppose you have an expression,

```
result = x+i/j;
```

where **x** is double and **i** and **j** are integers. Because of the way integer division works, you won't get an exact result here unless **i** is a multiple of **j**. You can use an explicit type cast to convert a value from one type to another. We can rewrite the last statement as:

```
result = x + (double)i/j;
```

It may be obvious to you that the value of **i** and **j** are converted to type **double** before the division occurs, (the **(double)** operator only acts on the variable immediately following it, but the automatic type conversion rules ensure that **j** is also cast as **double**) so we now get an exact result produced.

The way the cast is written above is called **cast notation**. You can also use functional notation which would look like this:

```
result = x + double(i)/j;
```

This works exactly the same as the previous version. As **i** is cast to double, **j** is cast to double according to the rules for mixed expressions that we saw earlier.

You can write an explicit cast for any standard type, but you should be conscious of the possibility of losing information. If you cast a **float** or **double** value to **long**, for example, you will lose the fractional part of the value converted, so if the value started out as less than 1.0, the result will be 0. If you cast **double** to **float**, you will lose accuracy because a **float** variable has only 7 digits precision, whereas **double** variables maintain 19. Even casting between integer types provides the potential for losing data, depending on the values involved. For example, the value of an integer of type **long** can exceed the maximum that you can store in a variable of type **short**, so casting from a **long** value to a **short** may lose information.

In general, you should avoid casting as far as possible. If you find that you need a lot of casts in your program, the overall design of your program may well be at fault. You need to look at the structure of the program and the ways in which you have chosen data types to see whether you can eliminate, or at least reduce, the number of casts in your program.

The Bitwise Operators

The bitwise operators treat their operands as a series of individual bits rather than a numerical value. They only work with integer variables or constants as operands, so only data types **short**, **int**, **long** and **char** can be used. They are useful in programming hardware devices where the status of a device is often represented as a series of individual flags (that is, each bit of a byte may signify the status of a different aspect of the device), or for any situation where you might want to pack a set of on-off flags into a single variable. You will see them in action when we look at input/output in detail, where single bits are used to control various options in the way data is handled.

There are six bitwise operators:

- **&** bitwise AND
- **|** bitwise OR
- **^** bitwise exclusive OR
- **~** bitwise NOT
- **>>** shift right
- **<<** shift left

Let's take a look at how each of them works.

The Bitwise AND

The bitwise AND, **&**, is a binary operator that combines corresponding bits in its operands. If both corresponding bits are 1, the result is a 1 bit, and if either or both operand bits are 0, the result is a 0 bit. We can represent this in a table:

Bitwise AND	0	1
0	0	0
1	0	1

For each row and column combination, the result of **&** combining the two is the entry at the intersection of the row and column.

Let's see how this works on an example:

```
char Letter1 = 'A', Letter2 = 'Z', Result = 0;
Result = Letter1 & Letter2;
```

We need to look at the bit patterns to see what happens. The letters **'A'** and **'Z'** correspond to hexadecimal values 41h and 5Ah respectively (see Appendix B) for ASCII codes. The way in which the bitwise AND operates on these two values is shown below:

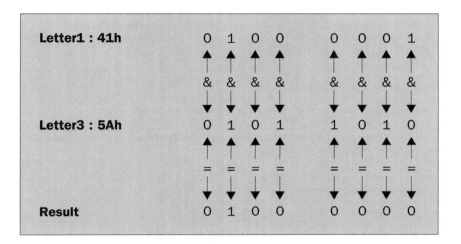

You can confirm this by looking at how corresponding bits combine with **&** in the truth table. After the assignment, **Result** will have the value 40h which corresponds to the character **'@'**.

Because the **&** produces zero, if either bit is zero, we can use this operator to make sure that unwanted bits are zero in a variable. We achieve this by creating what is called a 'mask' which is combined with the original variable using **&**. We create the mask by putting 1 where we want to keep a bit, and 0 where we want to set a bit to zero. The result will be 0s where the mask bit is 0, and the same value as the original bit in the variable where the mask is 1. Suppose we have a **char** variable **Letter** where, for the purposes of illustration, we want to eliminate the high order 4 bits, but keep the low order 4 bits. This is easily done by setting up a mask as **0Fh** and combining it with the letter using **&** like this,

```
Letter = Letter & 0x0F;
```

or, more concisely:

```
Letter &= 0x0F;
```

If **Letter** started out as 41h, it would end up as 01h as a result of either of these statements. This operation is shown in the illustration next:

57

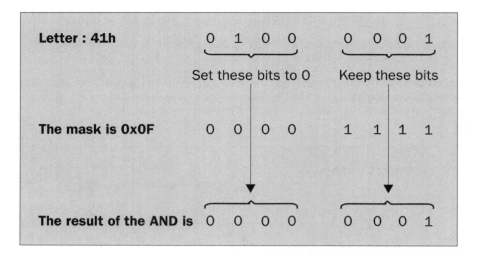

The 0 bits in the mask cause corresponding bits in **Letter** to be set to 0, and the 1 bits in the mask cause corresponding bits to be kept.

Similarly, you can use a mask of **0xF0** to keep the 4 high order bits, and zero the 4 low order bits. Therefore, this statement,

```
Letter &= 0xF0;
```

will result in the value of **Letter** being changed from 41h to 40h.

The Bitwise OR

The bitwise OR, |, sometimes called the inclusive OR, combines corresponding bits such that the result is a 1 bit if either operand bit is a 1, and 0 if both operand bits are 0. The truth table for the bitwise OR is:

Bitwise OR	0	1
0	0	1
1	1	1

We can exercise this with an example of how we could set individual flags packed into a variable of type **int**. Let's suppose that we have a variable **style** of type **short** which contains 16 individual 1 bit flags. Let's suppose further that we are interested in setting individual flags in the variable style. One way of doing this is by defining values that we can combine with the OR operator to set particular bits on. To use in setting the rightmost bit, we can define:

```
short VREDRAW=0x0001;
```

For use in setting the second to rightmost bit, we could define the variable **HREDRAW** as:

```
short HREDRAW=0x0002;
```

So we could set the rightmost two bits in the variable style to 1 with the statement:

```
style = HREDRAW|VREDRAW;
```

The effect of this statement is illustrated in the diagram below:

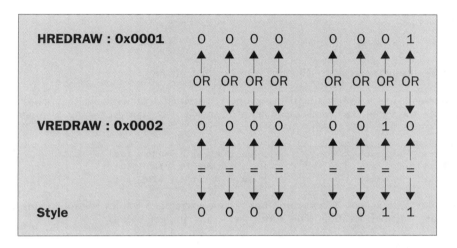

Because the OR operation results in 1 if either of two bits is a 1, ORing the two variables together produces a result with both bits set on.

A very common requirement is to be able to set flags in a variable without altering any of the others which may have been set elsewhere. We can do this quite easily with a statement such as:

```
style |= HREDRAW|VREDRAW;
```

This statement will set the two rightmost bits of the variable **style** to 1, leaving the others at whatever they were before the execution of this statement.

The Bitwise Exclusive OR

The exclusive OR, ^, is so called because it operates similarly to the inclusive OR but produces 0 when both operand bits are 1. Therefore, its truth table is as follows:

Bitwise EOR	0	1
0	0	1
1	1	0

59

Using the same variable values that we used with the OR, we can look at the result of the following statement:

```
Result = Letter1 ^ Letter2;
```

This operation can be represented as:

Letter1	0100 0001
Letter2	0101 1010

EORed produce:

Result	0001 1011

The variable **Result** is set to 1Bh or 27 in decimal notation.

The ^ operator has a rather surprising property. Suppose that we have two **char** variables, **First** with the value **'A'**, and **Last** with the value **'Z'**, corresponding to binary values 0100 0001 and 0101 1010. If we write the statements,

```
First ^= Last;        // Result First is 0001 1011
Last ^= First;        // Result Last is 0100 0001
First ^= Last;        // Result First is 0101 1010
```

the result of these is that **First** and **Last** have exchanged values without using any intermediate memory location. This works with any integer values.

The Bitwise NOT

The bitwise NOT, ~, takes a single operand for which it inverts the bits: 1 becomes 0, and 0 becomes 1. Thus, if we execute the statement,

```
Result = ~Letter1;
```

if **Letter1** is 0100 0001, the variable **Result** will have the value 1011 1110, which is BEh or 190 as a decimal value.

The Bitwise Shift Operators

These operators shift the value of an integer variable a specified number of bits to the left or right. The operator >> is for shifts to the right and << is the operator for shifts to the left. Bits that go off either end of the variable are lost. The following illustration shows the effect of shifting the 2 byte variable left and right, with the initial value shown.

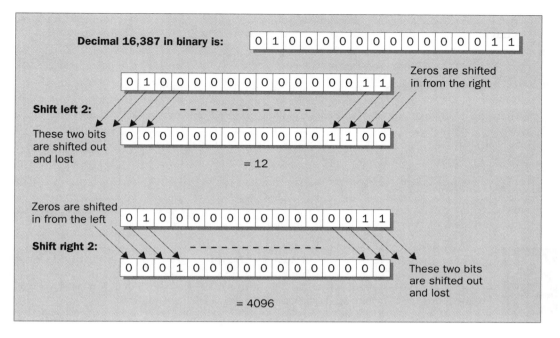

The operand on the right of the shift operator determines how many positions the bits in the variable on the right are to be shifted. Let's take a **char** variable **Number** with the decimal value 14. The statement,

```
    Number <<= 2;
```

results in the value of **Number** which to start with is 0000 1110 in binary, being shifted two positions left. This results in **Number** ending up as the value 0011 1000. This is equivalent to decimal 56, which is four times the original value. As long as bits are not lost, shifting left *n* bits is equivalent to multiplying the value by 2, *n* times. In other words, it is equivalent to multiplying by 2^n. Similarly, shifting right *n* bits is equivalent to dividing by 2^n. But beware - if we initialize **Number** with the value 16385 and execute the statement,

```
    Number <<= 2;
```

the variable **Number** will have the value 4, which might not be what you anticipated. This is because the high order bits have fallen off the end and are lost.

You might imagine that confusion could arise with the operators that we have been using for input and output. As far as the compiler is concerned, the meaning will always be clear from the context. If it isn't, the compiler will generate a message, but you need to be careful. For example, if you want to output the result of shifting a variable **Number** left by two bits, you could write;

```
    cout << (Number << 2);
```

Here, the parentheses are essential. Without them, the shift operator will be interpreted by the compiler as a stream operator, so you will not get the result that you intended.

In the main, the right shift operation is similar to the left shift. For example, if the variable **Number** has the value 24, and we execute the statement,

```
Number >>= 2;
```

it will result in **Number** having the value 6, effectively dividing by 4.

The right shift operates in a special way with **signed** integer types that are negative (that is, the sign bit, which is the leftmost bit, is 1). In this case, the sign bit is propagated to the right. So if **Number** of type **char** has the value -104 in decimal, which is 1001 1000 in binary, and we shift it right 2 bits with the operation,

```
Number >>= 2;          // Result 1110 0110
```

the decimal value of the result is -26 as the sign bit is repeated. With operations on **unsigned** integer types, of course, the sign bit is not repeated and zeros appear.

FYI These shift operations can be faster than the regular multiply or divide on some computers - on a 486, for example, a multiply is slower than a shift left by a least a factor of 3. However, you should only use them in this way if you are sure you are not going to lose bits that you can ill-afford to be without.

Understanding Scope

Everything that you give a name to in a program (a variable or a function, or anything else) only exists for a finite period of time, the maximum being the entire duration of program execution. It is only accessible in a prescribed part of the program code, at most from where it is declared to the end of the program code. The area of the program over which you can use a name is called its **scope**. All ordinary functions have **file scope**, which is also called **global scope**. This means that they are accessible anywhere within the file in which they are defined.

All variables have a finite lifetime. They come into existence from the point you declare them and then, at some point, at the latest when your program terminates, they disappear. The scope of a variable is determined by wherever you declare it in your program. Variables that are declared within the braces delimiting the body of a function are called **automatic variables**, so let's take a closer look at them.

Automatic Variables

All of the variables that we have declared so far have been declared within a block, that is, within the extent of a pair of curly braces. These are called **automatic** variables and are said to have **local scope** or **block scope**. They are born when they are declared and automatically cease to exist at the end of the block containing the declaration. There are also other kinds of variables which we shall see later in this chapter when we come to discuss **static** and **dynamic** variables.

TRY IT OUT - Automatic Variables

We can demonstrate the effect of scope on automatic variables with the following example:

```cpp
// EX2_06.CPP
// Demonstrating variable scope.
#include <iostream.h>
int main()
{                                          // Function scope starts here
   int count1 = 10;
   int count3 = 50;
   cout << endl
       << "Value of outer count1 = " << count1;

   {                                       // New scope starts here...
      int count1 = 20;          //This hides the outer count1
      int count2 = 30;
      cout << endl
          << "Value of inner count1 = " << count1;
      count1 += 3;             // This affects the inner count1
      count3 += count2;
   }                                       // ...and ends here.

   cout << endl
       << "Value of outer count1 = " << count1
       << endl
       << "Value of outer count3 = " << count3;

   // cout << endl << count2;  // uncomment to get an error
   cout << endl;
   return 0;
}                                          // Function scope ends here
```

How It Works

The output from this example will be:

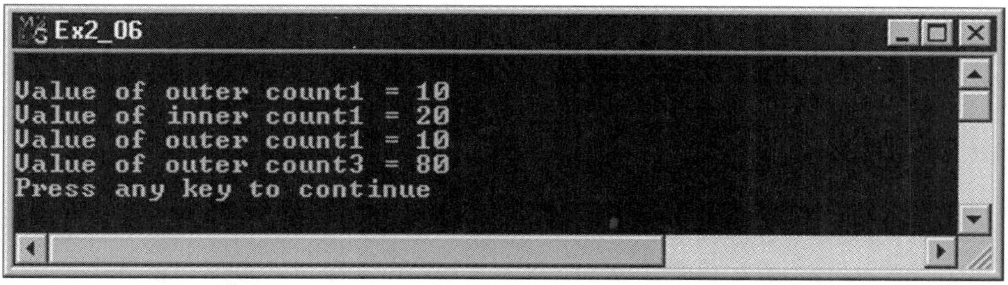

```
Ex2_06
Value of outer count1 = 10
Value of inner count1 = 20
Value of outer count1 = 10
Value of outer count3 = 80
Press any key to continue
```

The first two statements declare and define two integer variables **count1** and **count3** with initial values of **10** and **50** respectively. Both these variables exist from this point to the closing brace at the end of the program. Following the variable definitions, the value of **count1** is output to produce the first of the lines shown above.

There is then a second curly brace which starts a new scope. Two variables **count1** and **count2** are defined with values **20** and **30** respectively. This **count1** is different from the first **count1**, but the first is masked by the second because they have the same name.

Note this is not a good approach to programming in general. It is confusing and it is very easy to accidentally hide variables defined in an outer scope. The output statement shows by the value in the second line that we are using the **count1** in the inner scope - that is, inside the innermost braces. If it were the outer **count1**, it would have the value 10. The variable **count1** is incremented and the increment applies to the variable in the inner scope since the outer one is still hidden. However, **count3**, which was defined in the outer scope, is incremented without any problem showing that the variables that were defined at the beginning of the outer scope are accessible in the inner scope. Note that they could be defined after the second of the inner pair of braces and still be within the outer scope, but in that case they would not exist at the point that we used them.

After the brace ending the inner scope, **count2** and the inner **count1** cease to exist. The variables **count1** and **count3** are still there in the outer scope and the values displayed show that **count3** was indeed incremented in the inner scope. If you uncomment the line,

```
// cout << endl << count2;  // uncomment to get an error
```

the program will no longer compile correctly because it attempts to output a non-existent variable. You will get the error message,

C:\Msdev\Projects\Ex2_06\Ex2_06.cpp(25) : error C2065: 'count2' : undeclared identifier

since **count2** is out of scope at this point.

Positioning Variable Declarations

You have great flexibility in where you place the declarations for your variables. The most important aspect to consider is what scope the variables need to have. Beyond that, you should generally place a declaration close to where the variable is to be first used in a program. You should write your programs with a view to making them as easy as possible for another programmer to understand, and declaring a variable at its first point of use can be helpful in achieving that. It is also possible to place declarations for variables outside of all of the functions that make up a program. Let's look what effect that has on the variables concerned.

Global Variables

Variables declared outside of all blocks and classes (you might not know what classes are yet but we will come to them later) are called **globals** and have **global scope** or **file scope**. This means that they are accessible throughout all the functions in the file, following the point at which they are declared. If you declare them at the very beginning, they will be accessible anywhre in the file. The following illustration shows the contents of a source file, **Example.cpp**, and the scope of each of the variables is indicated by the arrows.

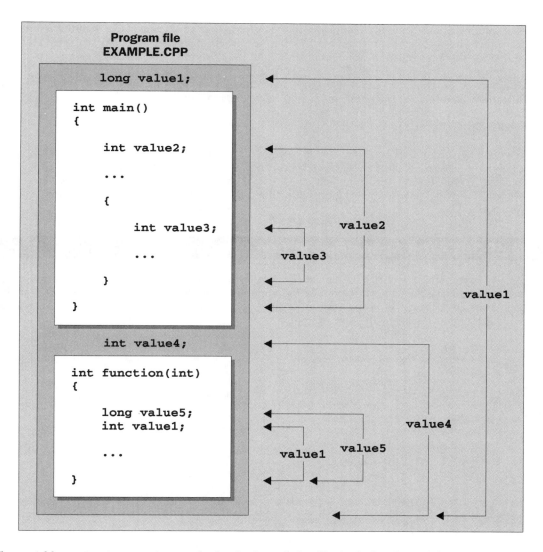

The variable **value1** appearing at the beginning of the file is declared at global scope, as is the variable **value4** which appears after the function **main()**. The scope of each variable is shown by the arrows. The global variables have a scope which extends from the point at which they are defined to the end of the file. Note that a local variable called **value1** in **function()** hides the global variable of the same name.

Since global variables are declared outside of all the blocks in a program, they continue to exist as long as the program is running. This might raise the question in your mind 'why not make all variables global and avoid all this messing about with local variables that disappear?' This sounds very attractive at first, but as with the Sirens of mythology, there are serious disadvantages which completely outweigh any advantages that you might gain.

Real programs are generally composed of a large number of statements, a significant number of functions and a great many variables. Declaring all variables at the global scope greatly magnifies the possibility of accidental erroneous modification of a variable, as well as making the job of naming them sensibly quite intractable. They will also occupy memory for the duration of program execution. By keeping variables local to a function or a block, you can be sure they have almost complete protection from external effects, they will only exist and occupy memory from the point at which they are defined to the end of the enclosing block, and the whole development process becomes much easier to manage.

If you take a look at ClassView for any of the examples that you have created so far, and extend the classes tree for the project by clicking on the +, you will see an entry called Globals. If you extend this, you will see a list of everything in your program that has global scope. This will include all the global functions, as well as any global variables that you have declared.

TRY IT OUT - The Scope Resolution Operator

As we have seen, a global variable can be hidden by a local variable with the same name if we use just the variable name to reference the variable. However, it is still possible to get at the global variable using the **scope resolution operator**, **::**. We can demonstrate how this works with a revised version of the last example:

```cpp
// EX2_07.CPP
// Demonstrating variable scope.
#include <iostream.h>

int count1 = 100;                    // Global version of count1

int main()
{                                        // Function scope starts here
    int count1 = 10;
    int count3 = 50;
    cout << endl
        << "Value of outer count1 = " << count1;

    cout << endl
        << "Value of global count1 = "<< ::count1;

    {                                // New scope starts here...
        int count1 = 20;          //This hides the outer count1
        int count2 = 30;
        cout << endl
            << "Value of inner count1 = " << count1;

        cout << endl
            << "Value of global count1 = " << ::count1;

        count1 += 3;              // This affects the inner count1
        count3 += count2;
    }                                  // ...and ends here.

    cout << endl
        << "Value of outer count1 = " << count1
        << endl
        << "Value of outer count3 = " << count3;
```

```
        //cout << endl << count2;  // uncomment to get an error
        cout << endl;
        return 0;
    }                                    // Function scope ends here
```

How It Works

If you compile and run this example, you will get the following output:

```
Value of outer count1 = 10
Value of global count1 = 100
Value of inner count1 = 20
Value of global count1 = 100
Value of outer count1 = 10
Value of outer count3 = 80
Press any key to continue
```

From the listing, you can see the changes that we have made to the previous example. We will simply discuss the effects of those. The declaration of **count1** prior to the definition of the function **main()** is global, so it is available in principle anywhere through the function **main()**. This global variable is initialized with the value of 100. However, we have two other variables called **count1** which are also defined in **main()** so throughout the program the global **count1** is hidden by the local **count1** variables. In fact, in the inner block it is hidden behind two variables called **count1**, the inner **count1** and the outer **count1**. The first additional output statement,

```
cout << endl
    << "Value of global count1 = " << ::count1;
```

uses the scope resolution operator to make it clear to the compiler that we want to reference the global variable **count1**. You can see that this works from the value displayed by this statement. The global scope resolution operator also does its stuff within the inner block as you can see from the output generated by the statement we have added there. A global is always reached by the long arm of the scope resolution operator.

We shall see a lot more of this operator when we get to object oriented programming where it is used extensively in referencing data members of a class.

Static Variables

It is conceivable that you might want to have a variable that is defined and accessible locally, but which also continues to exist after exiting the block in which it is declared. The need for this will become more apparent when we come to deal with functions. The **static** specifier provides you with the means of doing this. In fact, a **static** variable will continue to exist for the life of a program even though it is declared within a block and only available from within that block (or its sub-blocks). To declare the **static** variable called **count** you would write:

```
static int count;
```

Static variables are always initialized for you if you don't provide an initial value yourself. The variable **count** declared here will be initialized with 0. If you don't specify an initial value when you declare a static variable, it will be initialized with 0, converted to the type applicable to the variable.

Summary

In this chapter, we have covered the basics of computation in C++. We have learnt about all of the elementary types of data provided for in the language, and all the operators that manipulate these types directly. The essentials of what we have discussed up to now are as follows:

▶ A DOS program in C++ consists of at least one function called **main()**.

▶ The executable part of a function is made up of statements contained between curly braces.

▶ A statement in C++ is terminated by a semicolon.

▶ Named objects in C++, such as variables or functions, can have names that consist of a sequence of letters and digits, the first of which is a letter, and where an underscore is considered to be a letter. Upper and lower case letters are distinguished.

▶ All the objects, such as variables, that you name in your program must not have a name that coincides with any of reserved words in C++. The full set of reserved words in Visual C++ appears in Appendix A.

▶ All constants and variables in C++ are of a given type. The basic types are **char**, **int**, **long**, **float** and **double**.

▶ The name and type of a variable is defined in a declaration statement ending with a semicolon. Variables may also be given initial values in a declaration.

▶ You can protect the value of a variable of a basic type by using the modifier **const**. This will prevent direct modification of the variable within the program and give you compiler errors everywhere that a constant's value is altered.

▶ By default, a variable is automatic, which means that it only exists from the point at which it is declared to the end of the scope in which it is defined, indicated by the corresponding closing brace after its declaration.

▶ A variable may be declared as **static**, in which case it continues to exist for the life of the program. It can only be accessed within the scope in which it was defined.

▶ Variables can be declared outside of all blocks within a program, in which case they have global scope. Variables with global scope are accessible throughout a program, except where a local variable exists with the same name as the global variable. Of course, they can still be reached by using the scope resolution operator.

▶ An lvalue is an object that can appear on the left-hand side of an assignment. Non-**const** variables are examples of lvalues.

▶ You can mix different types of variables and constants in an expression, but they will be automatically converted to a common type where necessary. Conversion of the type of the right hand side of an assignment to that of the left-hand side will also be made where necessary. This can cause loss of information when the left-hand side type can't contain the same information as the right-hand side: **double** converted to **int**, or **long** converted to **short**, for example.

▶ The keyword **typedef** allows you to define synonyms for other types.

Although we have discussed all the basic types, don't be misled into thinking that's all there is. There are more complex types based on the basic set as we shall see, and eventually you will be creating original types of your own.

Decisions and Loops

In this chapter, we will look at how to add decision-making capabilities to your C++ programs. You will also learn how to make your programs repeat a set of actions until a specific condition is met. This will enable you to handle variable amounts of input, as well as make validity checks on the data that you read in. You will also be able to write programs that can adapt their actions depending on the input data, and to deal with problems where logic is fundamental to the solution. By the end of this chapter you will have learnt:

> How to compare data values

> How to alter the sequence of program execution based on the result

> What logical operators and expressions are and how you can apply them

> How to deal with multiple choice situations

> How to write and use loops in your programs

We will start with one of the most powerful programming tools: the ability to compare variables and expressions with other variables and expressions and, based on the outcome, execute one set of statements or another.

Comparing Values

Unless we want to make decisions on a whim for the rest of our lives, we need a mechanism for comparing things. This involves some new operators called **relational operators**. Because all information in your computer is ultimately represented by numerical values (we saw in the last chapter how character information is represented by numeric codes), comparing numerical values is the essence of practically all decision making. We have six fundamental operators for comparing two values:

<	less than	<=	less than or equal to
>	greater than	>=	greater than or equal to
==	equal to	!=	not equal to

FYI The 'equal to' comparison operator has two successive equal signs. This is *not* the same as the assignment operator which only consists of a single equal sign. It's pretty common to mistakenly use one equals sign in situations where you should be using two, so watch out for this potential cause of confusion.

Each of these operators compares two values and gives either a value of **1**, representing **TRUE**, if the comparison is true, or **0**, representing **FALSE** if it is not. We can see how this works by having a look at a few simple examples of comparisons. Suppose we have integer variables **i** and **j** with the values 10 and -5 respectively. Then the expressions,

```
i > j          i != j          j > -8          i <= j+15
```

are all true.

Let's further assume that we have the following variables defined:

```
char First = 'A', Last = 'Z';
```

We can now write some examples of comparisons using character variables. Take a look at these:

```
First==65       First<Last       'E'<=First       First!=Last
```

All four of these involve comparing ASCII code values. The first expression is true since **First** was initialized with 'A' which is the equivalent of decimal 65. The second expression checks whether the value of **First**, which is 'A', is less than the value of **Last**, which is 'Z'. If you check the ASCII codes for these characters in Appendix B, you will see that the capital letters are represented by an ascending sequence of numerical values from 65 to 90, 65 representing 'A' and 90 representing 'Z', so this comparison will result in 1 since it is true. The third expression is false and so returns 0, since 'E' is greater than the value of **First**. The last expression is true since 'A' is definitely not equal to 'Z'.

Let's consider some slightly more complicated numerical comparisons. With variables defined by the statements,

```
int i = -10, j = 20;
double x = 1.5, y = -0.25E-10;
```

take a look at the following:

```
-1<y          j <(10 - i)          2.0*x >=(3 + y)
```

As you can see, we can use expressions resulting in a numerical value as operands in comparisons. If you check with the precedence table that we saw in Chapter 2, you will see that none of the parentheses are strictly necessary, but they do help to make the expressions clearer. The first comparison is true and so produces 1. The variable **y** has a very small negative value, -0.000000000025, and so is greater than -1. The second comparison results in 0 since it is false. The expression **10-i** has the value 20 which is the same as **j**. The third expression is true since the expression **3+y** is slightly less than 3.

We can use relational operators to compare values of any of the basic types, so all we need now is a practical way of using the results of a comparison to modify the behavior of a program. Let's look into that immediately.

The if Statement

The basic **if** statement allows your program to execute a single statement, or a block of statements enclosed within curly braces, if a given condition is **TRUE**. This is illustrated in the figure:

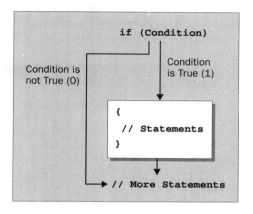

A simple example of an **if** statement is as follows:

```
if(Letter == 'A')
    cout << "The first capital, alphabetically speaking.";
```

The condition to be tested appears in parentheses immediately following the keyword, **if**. Note the position of the semicolon here. It goes after the statement following the **if**. There shouldn't be a semicolon after the condition in parentheses. You can also see how the statement following the **if** is indented to indicate it that is only executed as a result of the **if** condition being **TRUE**. The indentation is not necessary for the program to execute, but it helps you to recognize the relationship between the **if** condition and the statement that depends on it.

The relational operators return 1 as representing **TRUE**, but actually any non-zero value will be interpreted as **TRUE** in an **if** statement.

The output statement will only be executed if the variable **Letter** has the value **'A'**. We could extend this example to change the value of **Letter** if it contains the value **'A'**:

```
if(Letter == 'A')
{
    cout << "The first capital, alphabetically speaking.";
    Letter = 'a';
}
```

Here we execute the statements in the block only if the condition is **TRUE**. Without the braces, only the first statement would be the subject of the **if**, and the statement assigning the value **'a'** to **Letter** would always be executed. Note that there is a semicolon after each of the statements in the block, and not after the closing brace at the end of the block. There can be as many statements as you like within the block. Now, as a result of **Letter** having the value **'A'**, we change its value to **'a'** after outputting the same message as before. Neither of these will be executed if the condition is **FALSE**.

Nested if Statements

The statement that is to be executed when the condition in an **if** statement is **TRUE** can also be an **if**. This arrangement is called a **nested if**. The inner **if** is only executed if the condition for the outer **if** is **TRUE**. An **if** that is nested inside another can also contain a nested **if**. You can generally continue nesting **if**s one inside the other like this for as long as you know what you are doing.

TRY IT OUT - Using Nested ifs

We can demonstrate the nested **if** with a working example:

```
// EX3_01.CPP
// A nested if demonstration
#include <iostream.h>
int main()
{
   char Letter = 0;                       // Store input in here

   cout << endl
        << "Enter a letter: ";            // Prompt for the input
   cin >> Letter;                         // then read a character

   if(Letter >= 'A')                      // Test for 'A' or larger
      if(Letter <= 'Z')                   // Test for 'Z' or smaller
      {
         cout << endl
              << "You entered a capital letter."
              << endl;
         return 0;
      }

   if(Letter >= 'a')                      // Test for 'a' or larger
      if(Letter <= 'z')                   // Test for 'z' or smaller
      {
         cout << endl
              << "You entered a small letter."
              << endl ;
         return 0;
      }

   cout << endl << "You did not enter a letter." << endl;
   return 0;
}
```

How It Works

This program starts with the usual comment lines and the **#include** statement for the header file supporting input/output. The first action in the body of **main()** is to prompt for a letter to be entered. This is stored in the **char** variable **Letter**.

The **if** statement that follows the input checks whether the character entered is **'A'** or larger. Since the ASCII codes for lower case letters (97 to 122) are greater than those for upper case letters(65 to 90), entering a lower case letter causes the program to execute the first **if** block, as **(Letter >= 'A')** will be **TRUE** for all letters. In this case, the nested **if**, which checks for the input being **'Z'** or less, is executed. If it is **'Z'** or less, we know that we have a capital letter, the message is displayed and we are done, so we execute a **return** statement to end the program. Both statements are enclosed between braces, so they are both executed when the nested **if** condition is **TRUE**.

The next **if** checks whether the character entered is lower case using essentially the same mechanism as the first **if**, displays a message and returns.

If the character entered was not a letter, the output statement following the last **if** block will be executed. This displays a message to the effect that the character entered was not a letter. The return is then executed.

You can see that the relationship between the nested **if**s and the output statement is much easier to follow because of the indentation applied to each.

A typical output from this example is:

You could easily arrange to change upper case to lower case by adding just one extra statement to the **if**, checking for upper case:

```
if(Letter >= 'A')                    // Test for 'A' or larger
    if(Letter <= 'Z')                // Test for 'Z' or smaller
    {
        cout << endl
            << "You entered a capital letter.";
        Letter += 'a' - 'A';           // Convert to lower case
        return 0;
    }
```

This involves adding one additional statement. This statement for converting from upper to lower case increments the **Letter** variable by the value **'a' - 'A'**. It works because the ASCII codes for **'A'** to **'Z'** and **'a'** to **'z'** are two groups of consecutive numerical codes, so that the expression **'a'-'A'** represents the value to be added to an upper case letter to get the equivalent lower case letter.

You could equally well use the equivalent ASCII values for the letters here, but using the letters means that this would work on computers where the characters were not ASCII, as long as the set of upper case letters and the lower case set are both represented by a contiguous sequence of numeric values.

There is a library function provided with Visual C++ to convert letters to upper case so you don't normally need to program for this yourself. It has the name **toupper()** *and appears in the library* **ctype.h***. You will see more about standard library facilities when we get to look specifically at how functions are written.*

The Extended if Statement

The **if** statement that we have been using so far executes a statement if the condition specified is **TRUE**. Program execution then continues with the next statement in sequence. We also have a version of the **if** which allows one statement to be executed if the condition is **TRUE**, and another to be executed if the condition is **FALSE**. Execution then continues with the next statement in sequence. As we saw in Chapter 2, a block of statements can always replace a single statement, so this also applies to these **if**s.

TRY IT OUT - Extending the if

An example of using an extended **if** would be as follows:

```
// EX3_02.CPP
// Using the extended if
#include <iostream.h>
int main()
{
   long number = 0;                    // Store input here
   cout << endl
        << "Enter an integer number less than 2 billion: ";
   cin >> number;

   if(number%2L)                       // Test remainder after division by 2
      cout << endl                     // Here if remainder 1
           << "Your number is odd." << endl;
   else
      cout << endl                     // Here if remainder 0
           << "Your number is even." << endl;
   return 0;
}
```

A typical example of output from this program is:

```
Ex3_02
Enter an integer number less than 2 billion: 12345

Your number is odd.
Press any key to continue
```

How It Works

After reading the input value into **number**, the value is tested by taking the remainder after division by two (using the remainder operator **%** that we saw in the last chapter) and using that as the condition for the **if**. If the remainder is a positive integer (**TRUE**), the statement immediately following the **if** is executed. If the remainder is anything else (**FALSE**), the statement following the **else** keyword is executed. Since the remainder of a division of an integer by two can only be one or zero, we have commented the code to indicate this fact. After either outcome, the **return** statement is executed to end the program.

FYI Note that the `else` keyword is written without a semicolon, similar to the `if` part of the statement. Again, indentation is used as a visible indicator of the relationship between various statements. You can clearly see which statement is executed for a **TRUE** result, and which for a **FALSE** result. You should always indent the statements in your programs to show their logical structure.

The **if-else** combination provides a choice between two options. The general logic of the **if-else** is shown in the illustration here:

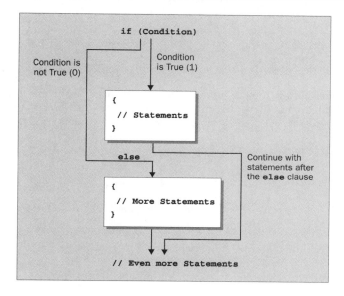

The arrows in the diagram indicate the sequence in which statements are executed, depending on whether the **if** condition is **TRUE** or **FALSE**.

Nested if-else Statements

As we have seen, you can nest **if** statements within **if** statements. You can also nest **if-else** statements within **if**s, **if**s within **if-else** statements, and **if-else** statements within **if-else** statements. This provides us with considerable room for confusion, so let's look at a few examples. Taking the first case first, an example of an **if-else** nested within an **if** might be:

```
if(coffee == 'y')
    if(donuts == 'y')
        cout << "We have coffee and donuts.";
    else
        cout << "We have coffee, but not donuts";
```

The test for **donuts** is executed if the result of the test for **coffee** is **TRUE**, so the messages reflect the correct situation in each case. However, it is easy to get this confused. If we write much the same thing with incorrect indentation, we can be trapped into the wrong conclusion:

```
if(coffee == 'y')
    if(donuts == 'y')
        cout << "We have coffee and donuts.";
else                                         // This else is indented incorrectly
    cout << "We have no coffee...";   // Wrong!
```

This mistake is easy to see here, but with more complicated **if** structures we need to keep in mind the rule about which **if** owns which **else**.

 An **else** always belongs to the nearest preceding **if** that is not already spoken for by another **else**.

Whenever things look a bit complicated you can apply this rule to sort things out. When you are writing your own programs you can always use braces to make the situation clearer. It isn't really necessary in such a simple case, but we could write the last example as follows:

```
if(coffee == 'y')
{
    if(donuts == 'y')
        cout << "We have coffee and donuts.";
    else
        cout << "We have coffee, but not donuts";
}
```

Now it should be absolutely clear.

Now that we know the rules, understanding the case of an **if** nested within an **if-else** becomes easy:

```
if(coffee == 'y')
{
    if(donuts == 'y')
        cout << "We have coffee and donuts.";
}
else
    if(tea == 'y')
        cout << "We have tea, but not coffee";
```

Here the braces are essential. If we leave them out, the **else** would belong to the **if** which is looking out for **donuts**. In this kind of situation, it is easy to forget to include them and create an error which may be hard to find. A program with this kind of error will compile fine, and even produce the right results some of the time.

If we removed the braces in this example, we'd get the right results only as long as **coffee** and **donuts** are both equal to **'y'** so that the **if(tea == 'y')** check wouldn't be executed.

Here we'll look at **if-else** statements nested in **if-else** statements. This can get very messy, even with just one level of nesting. Let's beat the coffee and donuts analysis to death by using it again:

```
if(coffee == 'y')
   if(donuts == 'y')
      cout << "We have coffee and donuts.";
   else
      cout << "We have coffee, but not donuts";
else
   if(tea == 'y')
      cout << "We have tea, but not coffee";
   else
      cout << "No tea or coffee, but maybe donuts...";
```

This starts to look a bit muddled. No braces are necessary as the rule you saw earlier will verify that this is correct, but it would look a bit clearer if they were there:

```
if(coffee == 'y')
{
   if(donuts == 'y')
      cout << "We have coffee and donuts.";
   else
      cout << "We have coffee, but not donuts";
}
else
{
   if(tea == 'y')
      cout << "We have tea, but not coffee";
   else
      cout << "No tea or coffee, but maybe donuts...";
}
```

There are much better ways of dealing with this kind of logic in a program. If you put enough nested **if**s together, you can almost guarantee a mistake somewhere. The following section will help to simplify things.

Logical Operators and Expressions

As we have just seen, using **if**s where we have two or more related conditions can be a bit cumbersome. We have tried our iffy talents on looking for coffee and donuts, but in practice you may want to check much more complex conditions. You could be searching a personnel file for someone who is over 21 but under 35, female with a college degree, unmarried and speaks Hindi or Urdu. Defining a test for this could involve the mother of all **if**s.

Logical operators provide a neat and simple solution. Using logical operators, we can combine a series of comparisons into a single expression, so we end up needing just one **if**, virtually regardless of the complexity of the set of conditions.

We have just three logical operators:

&&	logical AND
||	logical OR
!	logical negation(NOT)

We'll first consider what each of these are used for in general terms, then we'll look at an example.

Logical AND

You would use the AND operator, **&&**, where you have two conditions that must both be **TRUE** for a true result. You want to be rich *and* healthy. For example, you could use the **&&** operator when you are testing a character to determine whether it's an upper case letter. The value being tested must be both greater than or equal to **'A'** AND less than or equal to **'Z'**. Both conditions must be **TRUE** for the value to be a capital letter.

Taking the example of a value stored in a **char** variable **Letter**, we could replace the test using two **if**s for one that uses only a single **if** and the **&&** operator:

```
if((Letter >='A') && (Letter<='Z'))
    cout << "This is a capital letter.";
```

The parentheses inside the **if** expression ensure that there is no doubt that the comparison operations are executed first, and makes the statement clearer. Here, the output statement will be executed only if both of the conditions combined by the operator **&&** are **TRUE**.

The effect of a particular logical operator is often shown using what is called a **truth table**. This shows, for various possible combinations of operands, what the result is. The truth table for **&&** is as follows:

&&	0	1
0	0	0
1	0	1

The row headings of the left and the column headings at the top represent the value of the logical expressions to be combined by the operator **&&**. Thus, to determine the result of combining a **TRUE** condition (1) with a **FALSE** condition (0), select the row with 1 at the left and the column with 0 at the top and look at the intersection of the row and column for the result (0).

Logical OR

The OR operator, **||**, applies when you have two conditions and you want a **TRUE** result if either or both of them are true. For example, you might be considered creditworthy for a loan from the bank if your income was at least $100,000 a year, or you had $1,000,000 in cash. This could be tested using the following **if**:

```
if((Income >= 100000.00) || (Capital >= 1000000.00))
    cout << "How much would you like to borrow, Sir, (grovel, grovel)?";
```

The ingratiating response emerges when either or both of the conditions are **TRUE**. (A better response might be '*Why* do you want to borrow?' It's strange how banks will only lend you money if you don't need it.)

We can also construct a truth table for the || operator:

||	0	1
0	0	1
1	1	1

As you can see, you only get a **FALSE** result if both conditions are **FALSE**.

Logical NOT

The third logical operator, **!**, takes one operand with a logical value, **TRUE** or **FALSE**, and inverts its value. So if the value of **Test** is **TRUE** then **!Test** becomes **FALSE**, and if it is **FALSE** then **!Test** becomes **TRUE**. To take the example of a simple expression, if **x** has the value 10, the expression,

    !(x>5)

is **FALSE**, since **x >5** is **TRUE**.

We could also apply the ! operator in an expression that was a favorite of Charles Dickens:

    !(Income>Expenditure)

If this expression is **TRUE**, the result is misery, at least as soon as the bank starts bouncing your checks.

TRY IT OUT - Combining Logical Operators

You can combine conditional expressions and logical operators to any degree that you feel comfortable with. For example, we could construct a test for whether a variable contained a letter just using a single **if**. Let's write it as a working example:

```cpp
// EX3_03.CPP
// Testing for a letter using logical operators
#include <iostream.h>
int main()
{
 char Letter = 0;                                // Store input in here

   cout << endl
        << "Enter a character: ";
   cin >> Letter;

   if(((Letter>='A')&&(Letter<='Z')) ||
      ((Letter>='a')&&(Letter<='z')))            // Test for alphabetic
      cout << endl
           << "You entered a letter." << endl;
   else
      cout << endl
           << "You didn't enter a letter." << endl;
   return 0;
}
```

How It Works

This example starts out in the same way as **Ex3_01.cpp** by reading a character after a prompt for input. The interesting part of the program is in the **if** statement condition. This consists of two logical expressions combined with the **||** (OR) operator, so that, if either is true, the condition returns **TRUE** and the message You entered a letter is displayed. If both logical expressions are **FALSE**, the **else** statement is executed which displays the message You didn't enter a letter.

Each of the logical expressions combines a pair of comparisons with the operator **&&** (AND), so both comparisons must be **TRUE** if the logical expression is to be true. The first logical expression is **TRUE** if the input is a capital letter, and the second is **TRUE** if the input is a small letter.

The Conditional Operator

The conditional operator is sometimes called the ternary operator because it involves three operands. It is best understood by looking at an example. Suppose we have two variables, **a** and **b**, and we want to assign the maximum of **a** and **b** to a third variable **c**. We can do this with the statement:

```
c = a>b?a : b;            // Set c to the maximum of a and b
```

The conditional operator has a logical expression as its first argument, in this case **a>b**. If this expression is **TRUE**, the second operand - in this case **a** - is selected as the value resulting from the operation. If the first argument is **FALSE** the third operand - in this case **b** - is selected as the value. Thus, the result of the conditional expression is **a** if **a** is greater than **b**, and **b** otherwise. This value is stored in **c**. This use of the conditional operator in this assignment statement is equivalent to the **if** statement:

```
if(a>b)
   c = a;
else
   c = b;
```

The conditional operator can be written generally as:

```
condition ?expression1 : expression2
```

If the condition evaluates as **TRUE**, the result is the value of **expression1**, and if it evaluates to **FALSE**, the result is the value of **expression2**.

TRY IT OUT - Using the Conditional Operator with Output

A common use of the conditional operator is to control output, depending on the result of an expression or the value of a variable. You can vary a message by selecting one text string or another depending on the condition specified.

```
// EX3_04.CPP
// The conditional operator selecting output.
#include <iostream.h>
```

```
    int main()
    {
       int nCakes = 1;              // Count of number of cakes

       cout << endl
            << "We have " << nCakes << " cake" << ((nCakes>1)?"s.":".")
            << endl;

       ++nCakes;

       cout << endl
            << "We have " << nCakes << " cake" << ((nCakes>1)?"s.":".")
            << endl;
       return 0;

    }
```

The output from
this program will
be:

```
Ex3_04                                                          _ □ ×
We have 1 cake.

We have 2 cakes.
Press any key to continue
```

How It Works

First we initialize the **nCakes** variable with the value 1, then perform an output statement that shows us the number of cakes. The part that uses the conditional operator simply tests the variable to determine whether we have a singular cake or plural cakes:

```
((nCakes>1)?"s.":".")
```

This expression evaluates to **"s."** if **nCakes** is greater than 1, or **"."** otherwise. This allows us to use the same output statement for any number of cakes. We show this in the example by incrementing the **nCakes** variable and repeating the output statement.

There are many other situations where you can apply this sort of mechanism, selecting between **"is"** and **"are"**, for example.

The switch Statement

The **switch** statement enables you to select from multiple choices based on a set of fixed values for a given expression. It operates like a physical rotary switch in that you can select one of a fixed number of choices - some makes of washing machine provide a means of choosing an operation for processing your laundry in this way. There are a given number of possible positions for the switch such as cotton, wool, synthetic fiber, and so on, and you can select any one of them by turning the knob to point to the option that you want.

In the **switch** statement, the selection is determined by the value of an expression that you specify. You define the possible switch positions by one or more **case values**, a particular one being selected if the value of the switch expression is the same ·as the particular case value. There is one case value for each possible choice in the switch. You can also specify a default

83

case which is selected when the value of the expression for the switch does not correspond with any of the case values that you've defined.

TRY IT OUT - The switch Statement

We can examine how the **switch** statement works with the following example:

```
// EX3_05.CPP
// Using the switch statement
#include <iostream.h>
int main()
{
   int choice = 0;                      // Store selection value here

   cout << endl
        << "Your electronic recipe book is at your service." << endl
        << "You can choose from the following delicious dishes: "
        << endl
        << endl << "1 Boiled eggs"
        << endl << "2 Fried eggs"
        << endl << "3 Scrambled eggs"
        << endl << "4 Coddled eggs"
        << endl << endl << "Enter your selection number: ";
   cin >> choice;

   switch(choice)
   {
      case 1: cout << endl << "Boil some eggs." << endl;
              break;
      case 2: cout << endl << "Fry some eggs." << endl;
              break;
      case 3: cout << endl << "Scramble some eggs." << endl;
              break;
      case 4: cout << endl << "Coddle some eggs." << endl;
              break;
      default: cout << endl <<"You entered a wrong number, try raw eggs."
                       << endl;
   }
   return 0;
}
```

How It Works

After defining your options in the stream output statement, and reading a selection number into the variable **choice**, the **switch** statement is executed with the condition specified as simply **choice** in parentheses, immediately following the keyword **switch**. The possible choices in the **switch** are enclosed between braces and are each identified by a **case label**. A case label is the keyword **case** followed by the value of **choice** that corresponds to this option and terminated by a colon.

As you can see, the statements to be executed for a particular case are written following the colon at the end of the case label, and are terminated by a **break** statement. The **break** transfers execution to the statement after the **switch**. The **break** isn't mandatory, but if you don't include it, all the statements for the cases following the one selected will be executed, which isn't usually what you want. You can demonstrate this by removing the **break** statements from this example and seeing what happens.

If the value of **choice** doesn't correspond with any of the case values specified, the statements preceded by the **default** label are executed. A **default** case isn't essential. In its absence, if the value of the test expression does not correspond to any of the cases, the **switch** is exited and the program continues with the next statement after the **switch**.

TRY IT OUT - Sharing a Case

Each of the case constant expressions must be constant and must be unique. The reason that no two case constants can be the same is that the compiler would have no way of knowing which case statement should be executed for that particular value. However, different cases don't need to have a unique action. Several cases can share the same action, as shown in the following example:

```
// EX3_06.CPP
// Multiple case actions
#include <iostream.h>
int main()
{
   char Letter = 0;
   cout << endl
        << "Enter a small letter: ";
   cin >> Letter;

   switch(Letter*(Letter>='a' && Letter <='z'))
   {
      case 'a':
      case 'e':
      case 'i':
      case 'o':
      case 'u': cout << endl << "You entered a vowel.";
                break;

      case 0: cout << endl << "It is not a small letter.";
              break;

      default: cout << endl << "You entered a consonant.";
   }
   cout << endl;
   return 0;
}
```

How It Works

In this example, we have a more complex expression in the **switch**. If the character entered is not a small letter, the expression,

```
(Letter>='a' && Letter <='z')
```

will result in the value 0. **Letter** is multiplied by this expression, so the **switch** expression would be set to 0 if a small letter was not entered. This will then cause the statements following the case label **case 0** to be executed.

85

If a small letter was entered, the expression above will result in the value 1. Multiplying **Letter** by one results in the **switch** expression having the same value as **Letter**. For all values corresponding to vowels, the same output statement is executed since we haven't used **break** statements to separate these case labels. You can see that we can make a single action be taken for a number of different cases by writing each of the case labels one after the other before the statements to be executed. If a small letter that is a consonant is entered as program input, the **default** case label statement is executed.

Unconditional Branching

The **if** statement provides you with the flexibility to choose to execute one set of statements or another, depending on a specified condition, so the statement execution sequence is varied, depending on the values of the data in the program. The **goto** statement, in contrast, is a blunt instrument. It enables you to branch to a specified program statement unconditionally. The statement to be branched to must be identified by a statement label which is an identifier defined according to the same rules as a variable name. This is followed by a colon and placed before the statement requiring labeling. Here is an example of a labeled statement:

```
MyLabel: x = 1;
```

This statement has the label **MyLabel**, and an unconditional branch to this statement would be written as follows:

```
goto MyLabel;
```

Whenever possible, you should avoid using **goto**s in your program. They tend to encourage very convoluted code that can be extremely difficult to follow.

As the **goto** is theoretically unnecessary - there is always an alternative approach to using **goto** - a significant cadre of programmers say you should never use the **goto**. I don't subscribe to such an extreme view. It is a legal statement after all, and there are occasions when it can be convenient. However, I do recommend that you only use it where you can see an obvious advantage over other options that are available.

Repeating a Block of Statements

The ability to repeat a group of statements is fundamental to most applications. Without this ability, an organization would need to modify the payroll program every time an extra employee was hired. Without it, you would need to reload Tetris every time you wanted to play another game. So let's first understand how a loop works.

What is a Loop?

A loop executes a sequence of statements until a particular condition is true (or false). We can actually write a loop with the C++ statements that we have met so far. We just need an **if** and the dreaded **goto**. Look at this example:

```cpp
// EX3_07.CPP
// Creating a loop with an if and a goto
#include <iostream.h>
int main()
{
   int i = 0, sum = 0;
   const int MAX = 10;

   i = 1;
loop:
   sum += i;                   // Add current value of i to sum
   if(++i <= MAX)
      goto loop;               // Go back to loop until i = 11

   cout << endl
        << "sum = " << sum
        << endl
        << "i = " << i
        << endl;
   return 0;
}
```

This example accumulates the sum of integers from 1 to 10. The first time through the sequence of statements, **i** is 1 and is added to **sum** which starts out as zero. In the **if**, **i** is incremented to 2 and, as long as it is less than or equal to **MAX,** the unconditional branch to **loop** occurs and the value of **i**, now 2, is added to **sum**. This continues with **i** being incremented and added to **sum** each time, until finally, when **i** is incremented to 11 in the **if**, the branch back will not be executed. If you run this example, you will get this output:

This shows quite clearly how the loop works. However, it uses a **goto** and introduces a label into our program, both of which are things we should avoid if possible. We can achieve the same thing, and more, with the next statement which is specifically for writing a loop.

TRY IT OUT - Using the for Loop

We can rewrite the last code fragment as a working example using what is known as a **for** loop:

```cpp
// EX3_08.CPP
// Summing integers with a for loop
#include <iostream.h>
int main()
{
   int i = 0, sum = 0;
   const int MAX = 10;
```

```
    for(i = 1 ; i <= MAX ; i++ )      // Loop specification
       sum += i;                       // Loop statement
```

```
    cout << endl
            << "sum = " << sum
            << endl
            << "i = " << i
            << endl;
    return 0;
}
```

How It Works

If you compile and run this, you will get exactly the same output as the previous example, but the code is much simpler here. The conditions determining the operation of the loop appear in parentheses after the keyword **for**. There are three expressions that appear within the parentheses:

> The first sets **i** to 1.

> The second determines that the loop statement on the following line is executed as long as **i** is less than or equal to **MAX**.

> The third increments **i** each iteration.

Actually, this loop is not exactly the same as the version in **Ex3_07.cpp**. You can demonstrate this if you set the value of **MAX** to 0 in both programs and run them again. You will find that the value of **sum** is 1 in **Ex3_07.cpp** and 0 in the **for** loop version, and the value of **i** differs too. The reason for this is that the **if** version of the program always executes the loop at least once, since we don't check the condition until the end. The **for** loop does not do this because the condition is actually checked at the beginning.

The general form of the **for** loop is as follows:

for(*initializing_expression* **;** *test_expression* **;** *increment expression* **)**
    *loop_statement***;**

Of course, *loop_statement* can be a block between braces. The sequence of events in executing the **for** loop is shown in the figure here:

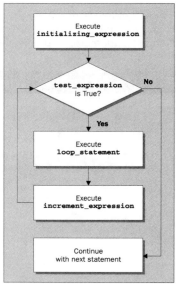

As we have said, the loop statement shown in the diagram can also be a block of statements. The expressions controlling the **for** loop are very flexible. You can even put multiple expressions for each, separated by the comma operator. This gives you a lot of scope in applying the **for** loop.

Variations on the for Loop

Most of the time, the expressions in a **for** loop are used in a fairly standard way, the first for initializing one or more loop counters, the second to test if the loop should continue and the third to increment or decrement one or more loop counters. However, you are not obliged to use these expressions in this way and quite a few variations are possible.

The initialization expression in a **for** loop can also include a declaration for a loop variable. Using our previous example, we could have written the loop to include the declaration for the loop counter **i**:

```
for(int i = 1 ; i <= MAX ; i++)        // Loop specification
    sum += i;                          // Loop statement
```

Naturally, the original declaration for **i** would need to be omitted in the program. If you make this change to the last example, you will find that it runs exactly as before, but there is something odd about this. A loop has a scope which extends from the **for** expression to the end of the body of the loop, which of course can be a block of code between braces, as well as just a single statement. The counter **i** is now declared within the loop scope, but we are still able to refer to it in the output statement which is outside the scope of **i**. This is because a special extension has been allowed for loop counters to extend their scope to the scope enclosing the loop.

> *I recommend that you don't write programs which rely on the value of a counter that is declared within the loop scope being available outside the loop scope. This is because recent changes to the draft standard for C++ suggest that this may not be supported by future C++ compilers. If you need to use the value in the counter after the loop has executed, declare it outside the scope of the loop.*

You can also omit the initialization expression altogether. If we initialize **i** appropriately in the declaration, we can write the loop as follows:

```
int i = 1;
for(; i <= MAX ; i++)                  // Loop specification
    sum += i;                          // Loop statement
```

You still need to put the semicolon that separates the initialization expression from the test condition for the loop. In fact, both semicolons must always appear. If you omitted the semicolon, the compiler would be unable to decide which expression you had omitted.

The increment expression is also flexible as to what it can contain. For example, we could actually put the loop statement in the last example into the increment expression, so the loop would become:

```
for(i = 1 ; i <= MAX ; sum += i++);    // The whole loop
```

We still need the semicolon after the closing parentheses to indicate that the loop statement is now empty. If it is omitted, the next statement will be interpreted as the loop statement.

TRY IT OUT - Using Multiple Counters

You can use the comma operator to include multiple counters in a **for** loop. We can show this in operation in the following program:

```
// EX3_09.CPP
// Using multiple counters to show powers of 2
#include <iostream.h>
#include <iomanip.h>
int main()
{

    long i = 0, power = 0;
    const int MAX = 10;

    for(i = 0, power = 1 ; i <= MAX ; i++, power += power)
       cout << endl
            << setw(10) << i << setw(10) << power;      // Loop statement

    cout << endl;
    return 0;
}
```

How It Works

We initialize two variables in the initialization part of the **for**, separated by the comma operator, and increment each of them in the increment part. Clearly, you can put as many expressions as you like in each position. You can even specify multiple conditions, separated by commas, in the test part of the **for**, but only the right-most one will affect when the loop ends. Note that the assignments defining the initial values for **i** and **power** are expressions, not statements. A statement always ends with a semicolon.

For each increment of **i**, the value of the variable **power** is doubled by adding it to itself. This produces the powers of two that we are looking for and so the program will produce the following output:

```
 Ex3_09                                                    _ □ ✕

          0           1
          1           2
          2           4
          3           8
          4          16
          5          32
          6          64
          7         128
          8         256
          9         512
         10        1024
Press any key to continue
```

The **setw()** manipulator that we saw in the previous chapter is used to align the output nicely. We have included **iomanip.h** so that we can use **setw()**.

TRY IT OUT - The Infinite for Loop

If you omit the test condition, the value is assumed to be **TRUE** so the loop will continue indefinitely unless you provide some other means of exiting from it. In fact, if you like, you can omit all the expressions in the parentheses after **for**. This may not seem to be very useful, but in fact, quite the reverse is true. You will often come across situations where you want to execute a loop a number of times, but you do not know in advance how many iterations you will need. Have a look at the following example:

```cpp
// EX3_10.CPP
// Using an infinite for loop to compute an average
#include <iostream.h>
int main()
{
   double value = 0.0;             // Value entered stored here
   double sum = 0.0;               // Total of values accumulated here
   int i = 0;                      // Count of number of values
   char indicator = 'n';           // Continue or not?

   for(;;)                         // Infinite loop
   {
      cout << endl
           << "Enter a value: ";
      cin >> value;                // Read a value
      ++i;                         // Increment count
      sum += value;                // Add current input to total

      cout << endl
           << "Do you want to enter another value ( enter n to end )?";
      cin >> indicator;            // Read indicator
      if ((indicator == 'n') || (indicator == 'N'))
         break;                    // Exit from loop
   }

   cout << endl
        << "The average of  the " << i
        << " values you entered is " << sum/i << "."
        << endl;
   return 0;
}
```

How It Works

This program will compute the average of an arbitrary number of values. After each value is entered you need to indicate whether you want to enter another value by entering a single character y or n. Typical output from executing this example is as follows:

```
Ex3_10                                                    _ □ X
Enter a value: 10
Do you want to enter another value ( enter n to end )?y
Enter a value: 20
Do you want to enter another value ( enter n to end )?y
Enter a value: 30
Do you want to enter another value ( enter n to end )?n
The average of  the 3 values you entered is 20.
Press any key to continue
```

After declaring and initializing the variables that we are going to use, we start a **for** loop with no expressions specified, so there is no provision for ending it here. The block immediately following is the subject of the loop which is to be repeated.

The loop block performs two basic actions:

> It reads a value.

> It checks whether you want to continue to enter values.

The first action within the block is to prompt you for input and then read a value into the variable **value**. The value that you enter is added to **sum** and the count of the number of values, **i**, is incremented. After accumulating the value in **sum**, you are prompted to enter **'n'** if you have finished. The character that you enter is stored in the variable **indicator** for testing against **'n'** or **'N'** in the **if**. If neither is found, the loop continues, otherwise a **break** is executed. The effect of **break** in a loop is similar to its effect in the context of the **switch** statement. In this instance, it exits the loop immediately by transferring to the statement following the closing brace of the loop block.

Finally, we output the count of the number of values entered and the average, calculated by dividing **sum** by **i**. Of course, **i** will be promoted to **double** before the calculation, as you will remember from the casting discussion in Chapter 2.

The continue Statement

There is another statement besides **break** that is used to affect the operation of a loop: the **continue** statement. This is written simply as:

```
continue;
```

Executing **continue** within a loop starts the next loop iteration immediately, skipping over any statements remaining in the current iteration. We can demonstrate how this works with the following code fragment:

```
#include <iostream.h>
int main()
{
    int i = 0, value = 0, product = 1;
```

```
    for(i = 1 ; i <= 10 ; i++)
    {
       cin >> value;

       if(value == 0)                        // If value is zero
          continue;                          // skip to next iteration

       product *= value;
    }
    cout << "Product (ignoring zeros): " << product
         << endl;

    return 0;                                // Exit from loop
}
```

This loop reads 10 values with the intention of producing the product of the values entered. The **if** checks whether the value entered was zero, and if it was, the **continue** statement skips to the next iteration. This is so that we don't end up with the product as zero if one of the values is zero. Obviously, if a zero value occurred on the last iteration, the loop would end. There are clearly other ways of achieving the same result, but **continue** provides a very useful capability, particularly with complex loops where you may need to skip to the end of the current iteration from various points in the loop.

The effect of the **break** and **continue** statements on the logic of a **for** loop is illustrated in the figure shown here:

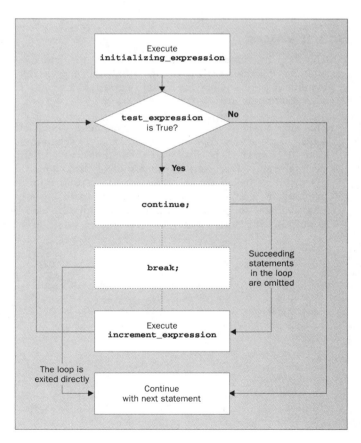

Obviously, in a real situation, the **break** and **continue** statements are used with some condition testing logic to determine when the loop should be exited, or when an iteration of the loop should be skipped. The **break** and **continue** statements can also be used with the other kinds of loop which we will discuss later on in this chapter, where they work in exactly the same way.

TRY IT OUT - Using Other Types in Loops

So far, we have only used integers to count loop iterations. You are in no way restricted as to what type of variable you use to count iterations. Look at the following example:

```cpp
// EX3_11.CPP
// Display ASCII codes for alphabetic characters
#include <iostream.h>
#include <iomanip.h>
int main()
{
  for(char capital='A',small='a'; capital<='Z'; capital++,small++)
    cout << endl
         << "\t" << capital                  // Output capital as character
         << hex << setw(10) << int (capital) // Output capital as hex
         << dec << setw(10) << int (capital) // Output capital as decimal
         << "    " << small                  // Output small as character
         << hex << setw(10) << int (small)   // Output small as hex
         << dec << setw(10) << int (small);  // Output small as decimal

  cout << endl;
  return 0;
}
```

How It Works

The loop in this example is controlled by the **char** variable **capital** which we declare along with the variable **small** in the initializing expression. We also increment both variables in the increment part, so that the value of **capital** varies from **'A'** to **'Z'**, and the value of **small** correspondingly varies from **'a'** to **'z'**.

The loop contains just one output statement spread over seven lines. The first line, **cout << endl**, starts a new line on the screen. On each iteration after outputting a tab character, the value of **capital** is displayed three times, as a character, as a hexadecimal value and as a decimal value. We insert the manipulator **hex** which causes succeeding data values to be displayed as hexadecimal values for the second output of **capital**, and we then insert the manipulator **dec** to cause succeeding values to be output as decimal once more. We get the **char** variable **capital** to output as a numeric value by casting it to **int**. The value of **small** is output in a similar way. As a result, the program will generate the following output:

A	41	65	a	61	97
B	42	66	b	62	98
C	43	67	c	63	99
D	44	68	d	64	100
E	45	69	e	65	101
F	46	70	f	66	102
G	47	71	g	67	103
H	48	72	h	68	104
I	49	73	i	69	105
J	4a	74	j	6a	106
K	4b	75	k	6b	107
L	4c	76	l	6c	108
M	4d	77	m	6d	109
N	4e	78	n	6e	110
O	4f	79	o	6f	111

P	50	80	p	70	112
Q	51	81	q	71	113
R	52	82	r	72	114
S	53	83	s	73	115
T	54	84	t	74	116
U	55	85	u	75	117
V	56	86	v	76	118
W	57	87	w	77	119
X	58	88	x	78	120
Y	59	89	y	79	121
Z	5a	90	z	7a	122

You can also use a floating point value as a loop counter. An example of a **for** loop with this kind of counter is as follows:

```
double a = 0.3, b = 2.5;
for(double x = 0.0 ; x <= 2.0 ; x += .25)
   cout << "\n\tx = " << x
        << "\ta*x +b = " << a*x + b;
```

This calculates the value of **a*x+b** for values of **x** from 0.0 to 2.0 in steps of 0.25. You need to take care with using a floating point counter in a loop, though. Many decimal values are not represented exactly in binary floating point, so discrepancies can build up when values are accumulated.

The while Loop

A second kind of loop in C++ is the **while** loop. Where the **for** loop is primarily used to repeat a statement or a block for a prescribed number of iterations, the **while** loop will continue as long as a specified condition is true. The general form of the **while** loop is as follows,

while(*condition***)**
    *loop_statement***;**

where ***loop_statement*** will be executed repeatedly as long as the ***condition*** expression has the value **TRUE**. Once the condition becomes **FALSE**, the program continues with the statement following the loop. Of course, a block of statements between braces could replace the single ***loop_statement***. The logic of the **while** loop is represented in the figure shown here:

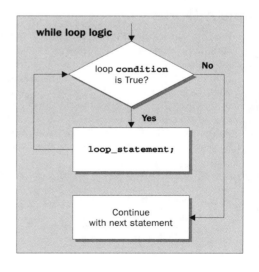

TRY IT OUT - Using the while Loop

We could rewrite our program (**Ex3_10.cpp**) to compute averages to use the **while** form of loop:

```
// EX3_12.CPP
// Using a while loop to compute an average
#include <iostream.h>
int main()
{
    double value = 0.0;              // Value entered stored here
    double sum = 0.0;                // Total of values accumulated here
    int i = 0;                       // Count of number of values
    char indicator = 'y';            // Continue or not?

    while(indicator == 'y')          // Loop as long as y is entered
    {
        cout << endl
            << "Enter a value: ";
        cin >> value;                // Read a value
        ++i;                         // Increment count
        sum += value;                // Add current input to total

        cout << endl
            << "Do you want to enter another value ( enter n to end )?";
        cin >> indicator;            // Read indicator
    }

    cout << endl
        << "The average of  the " << i
        << " values you entered is " << sum/i << "."
        << endl;
    return 0;
}
```

How It Works

For the same input, this version of the program will produce the same output as before. The statement that has changed and the one that has been added are highlighted above. The **for** loop statement was replaced by the **while** statement and the test for **indicator** in the **if** was deleted, as this function is performed by the **while** condition. You need to initialize **indicator** with **'y'** in place of **'n'** which appeared previously, otherwise the **while** loop will terminate immediately. As long as the condition in the **while** is **TRUE**, the loop continues. You can put any expression resulting in **TRUE** or **FALSE** as the loop condition. The example would be a better program if the loop condition were extended to allow **'Y'** to be entered to continue the loop as well as **'y'**. Modifying the **while** to this,

```
    while((indicator=='y') || (indicator=='Y'))
```

would do the trick.

You can also create an infinite **while** loop by using a condition that is always **TRUE**. This can be written as follows:

```
while(1)
{
    ...
}
```

Naturally, the same requirement applies here as in the case of the infinite **for** loop, namely that there must be some way of exiting the loop within the loop block. We will see some other ways to use the **while** loop in Chapter 4.

The do-while Loop

The **do-while** loop is similar to the **while** loop in that the loop continues as long as the specified loop condition remains **TRUE**. The main difference is that the condition is checked at the end of the **do-while** loop, not at the beginning, as in the case of the **while** loop (and the **for** loop). Thus the loop statement is always executed at least once. The general form of the **do-while** loop is as follows:

```
do
{
    loop_statements;
}while(condition);
```

The logic of this form of loop is shown in the illustration here:

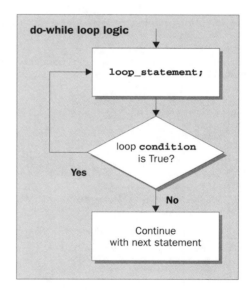

We could replace the **while** loop in the last version of the program to calculate an average with a **do-while** loop:

```
do
{
    cout << endl
         << "Enter a value: ";
    cin >> value;                    // Read a value
    ++i;                             // Increment count
    sum += value;                    // Add current input to total
```

```
                   cout << "Do you want to enter another value ( enter n to end )?";
                   cin >> indicator;                // Read indicator
        }while((indicator=='y') || (indicator=='Y'));
```

There is little to choose between them, except that this version doesn't depend on the initial value set in **indicator** for correct operation. As long as you want to enter at least one value, which is not unreasonable for the calculation in question, this version of the loop is preferable.

Nested Loops

You can nest one loop inside another. The usual application of this will become more apparent in Chapter 4, as it is typically applied to repeating actions at different levels of classification. An example might be calculating the total marks for each student in a class, then repeating the whole thing for each class in a school.

TRY IT OUT - Nested Loops

We can illustrate the effects of nesting one loop inside another by calculating a simple formula. A factorial of an integer is the product of all the integers from 1 to the integer in question, so the factorial of 3 for example, is 1 times 2 times 3, which is 6. The following program will compute the factorial of integers that you enter (until you have had enough):

```cpp
// EX3_13.CPP
// Demonstrating nested loops to compute factorials
#include <iostream.h>
int main()
{
    char indicator = 'n';
    long value = 0,
         factorial = 0;

    do
    {
        cout << endl
             << "Enter an integer value: ";
        cin >> value;

        factorial = 1;
        for(int i = 2 ; i<=value ; i++)
            factorial *= i;

        cout << "Factorial " << value << " is " << factorial;
        cout << endl
             << "Do you want to enter another value( y or n )? ";
        cin >> indicator;
    }while((indicator=='y') || (indicator=='Y'));

    return 0;
}
```

How It Works

If you compile and execute this example, the typical output produced will be as follows:

```
Ex3_13                                              _ □ ×

Enter an integer value: 5
Factorial 5 is 120
Do you want to enter another value( y or n )? y

Enter an integer value: 10
Factorial 10 is 3628800
Do you want to enter another value( y or n )? y

Enter an integer value: 23
Factorial 23 is 862453760
Do you want to enter another value( y or n )? n
Press any key to continue
```

Factorial values grow very fast. In fact, 23 is the last value for which this example will produce a correct value. If you run it with larger values, leading digits will be lost in the result stored in the variable **factorial**, and you may well get negative values for the factorial.

 FYI

Note that this situation doesn't cause any error messages, so it is of paramount importance that you are sure that the values you are dealing with in a program can be contained in the permitted range of the type of variable you are using. You also need to consider the effects of incorrect input values. Errors of this kind, which occur silently, can be very hard to find.

The outer of the two nested loops is the **do-while** loop which controls when the program ends. As long as you keep entering y or Y at the prompt, the program will continue to calculate factorial values. The factorial for the integer entered is calculated in the inner **for** loop. This is executed **value** times to multiply the variable **factorial** (with an initial value of 1) with successive integers from 2 to **value**.

TRY IT OUT - Another Nested Loop

If you haven't dealt much with nested loops they can be a little confusing, so let's try another example. This program will generate a multiplication table of a given size:

```cpp
// EX3_14.CPP
// Using nested loops to generate a multiplcation table
#include <iostream.h>
#include <iomanip.h>
int main()
{
   const int SIZE = 12;                 // Size of table
   int i = 0, j = 0;                    // Loop counters

   cout << endl                         // Output table title
        << SIZE << " by " << SIZE
        << " Multiplication Table" << endl << endl;
```

```
    cout << endl << "    |";
    for(i=1 ; i<=SIZE ; i++)              // Loop to output
       cout << setw(3) << i << "  ";       // column headings

    cout << endl;                         // Newline for underlines
    for(i=0 ; i<=SIZE ; i++)
       cout << "_____";                   // Underline each heading

    for(i=1 ; i<=SIZE ; i++)                        // Outer loop for rows
    {
       cout << endl
            << setw(3) << i << "  |";       // Output row label

       for(j=1 ; j<=SIZE ; j++)            // Inner loop to output the
          cout << setw(3) << i*j << "  ";   // rest of the row

    }                                      // End of outer loop
    cout << endl;
    return 0;
 }
```

How It Works

If you build this example and execute it, you will see the output shown in the figure below. This shows the output window when execution is complete:

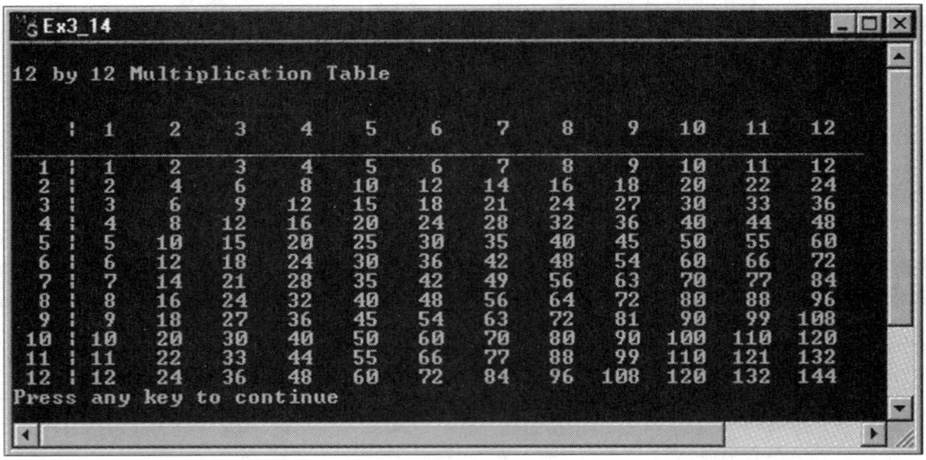

The table title is produced by the first output statement in the program. The next output statement, combined with the loop following it, generates the column headings. Each column will be five characters wide, so the heading value is displayed in a field width of three specified by the **setw(3)** manipulator, followed by two blanks. The output statement preceding the loop outputs four spaces and a vertical bar above the first column which will contain the row headings. A series of underline characters are then displayed beneath the column headings.

The nested loop generates the main table contents. The outer loop repeats once for each row, so **i** is the row number. The output statement,

```
    cout << endl
        << setw(3) << i << " |";        // Output row label
```

goes to a new line for the start of a row and then outputs the row heading given by the value of **i** in a field width of three, followed by a space and a vertical bar.

A row of values is generated by the inner loop:

```
    for(j=1 ; j<=SIZE ; j++)             // Inner loop to output the
        cout << setw(3) << i*j << "  ";   // rest of the row
```

This loop outputs values **i*j** corresponding to the product of the current row value **i**, and each of the column values in turn by varying **j** from 1 to **SIZE**. So for each iteration of the outer loop, the inner loop executes **SIZE** iterations. The values are positioned in the same way as the column headings.

When the outer loop is completed, the **return** is executed to end the program.

Summary

In this chapter, we have assembled all of the essential mechanisms for making decisions in C++ programs. We have also gone through all the facilities for repeating a group of statements. The essentials of what we have discussed are as follows:

- The basic decision-making capability is based on the set of relational operators, which allow expressions to be tested and compared yielding a value **TRUE** or **FALSE**.

- **TRUE** is represented by 1 and **FALSE** is represented by 0, although any non-zero value will be interpreted as **TRUE** when a condition is tested.

- The primary decision making capability in C++ is provided by the **if** statement. Further flexibility is provided by the **switch** statement and the conditional operator.

- There are three basic methods provided for repeating a group of statements: the **for** loop, the **while** loop and the **do-while** loop. The **for** loop allows the loop to repeat a given number of times, the **while** loop allows a loop to continue as long as a specified condition is **TRUE** and **do-while** executes the loop at least once and allows continuation of the loop as long as a specified condition is **TRUE**.

- Any kind of loop may be nested within any other kind of loop.

- The keyword **continue** allows you to skip the remainder of the current iteration in a loop and go straight to the next iteration.

- The keyword **break** provides an immediate exit from a loop. It also provides an exit from a switch at the end of a group of **case** statements.

Arrays, Pointers and References

So far, we have covered all the basic data types of consequence and have accumulated a basic knowledge of how to perform calculations and make decisions in a program. This chapter is about broadening the application of the basic programming techniques that we have covered so far, from using single data elements to working with whole collections of data items. In this chapter, you will learn:

 What an array is and how you can use it

 How to declare and initialize arrays of different types

 How to declare and use multi-dimensional arrays

 What a pointer is and how you can use it

 How to declare and initialize pointers of different types

 The relationship between arrays and pointers

 What a reference is, how it is declared and some initial ideas on its uses

 How to create and allocate memory for variables dynamically

You will also learn how to execute a program one statement at a time for debugging purposes and how to monitor the values of variables you are interested in.

Handling Multiple Data Values of the Same Type

We already know how to declare and initialize variables of various types which each hold a single item of information and which we will refer to as a **data element**. We know how to create a single character in a **char** variable, a single integer in a variable of type **int** or of type **long**, or a single floating point number in a variable of type **float**. The most obvious extension to these ideas is to be able to reference several data elements of a particular type with a single variable name. This would enable you to handle applications of a much broader scope.

Let's think about an example of where you might need this. Suppose that you needed to write a payroll program. Using a separately named variable for each individual's pay, tax liability, and so on, would be an uphill task to say the least. A much more convenient way to handle such a problem would be to reference an employee by some kind of generic name - **EmployeeName** to take an imaginative example - and to have other generic names for the kinds of data related to each employee, such as **Pay**, **Tax**, and so on. Of course, you would also need some means of picking out a particular employee from the whole bunch, together with the data from the generic variables associated with him or her. This kind of requirement arises with any collection of like entities that you want to handle in your program, whether they are baseball players or battleships. Naturally, C++ provides you with a way to deal with this.

Arrays

The basis for the solution to all of these problems is provided by the **array** in C++. An array is simply a number of memory locations, each of which can store an item of data of the same data type and which are all referenced through the same variable name. The employee names in a payroll program could be stored in one array, the pay for each employee in another, and the tax due for each employee could be stored in a third array.

Individual items in an array are specified by an index value which is simply an integer representing the sequence number of the elements in the array, the first having the sequence number 0, the second 1, and so on. You can also envisage the index value of an array element as an offset from the first element in an array. The first element has an offset of 0 and, therefore, an index of **0**, and an index value of **3** will refer to the fourth element of an array. For our payroll, we could arrange that, for an employee corresponding to a given index value in an array called **EmployeeName**, the arrays **Pay** and **Tax** would store the associated data on pay and tax in the array positions referenced by the same index value.

The basic structure of an array is illustrated in the figure below:

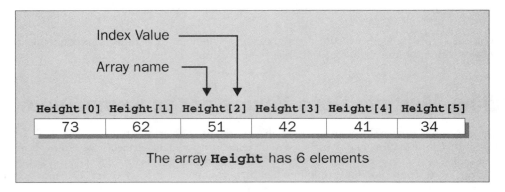

The array **Height** has 6 elements

This shows an array, **Height**, with six elements, each storing a different value. These might be the heights of the members of a family, for instance, recorded to the nearest inch. As there are six elements, the index values run from **0** through to **5**. To refer to a particular element, you write the array name, followed by the index value of the particular element between square brackets, the third element being referred to as **Height[2]**, for example. Some people like to think of the index as the offset from the first element, so for example, the fourth element is offset by 3 from the first element.

The amount of memory required to store each element will be determined by its type, and all the elements of an array will be stored in a contiguous block of memory.

Declaring Arrays

You declare an array in essentially the same way as you declared the variables that we have seen up to now, the only difference being that the number of elements in the array is specified between square brackets immediately following the array name. For example, we could declare the integer array **Height**, shown in the previous figure, with the following declaration statement:

```
long Height[6];
```

Since each **long** value occupies 4 bytes in memory, the whole array requires 24 bytes. Arrays can be of any size, subject to the constraints imposed by the amount of memory in the personal computer that your program will be running on.

You can declare arrays to be of any type. For example, to declare arrays intended to store the capacity and power output of a series of engines, you could write the following:

```
double cubic_inches[10];
double horsepower[10];
```

If auto mechanics are your thing, this would enable you to store the cubic capacity and power output of up to 10 engines, referenced by index values from **0** to **9**. As we have seen before with other variables, you can declare multiple arrays of a given type in a single statement but, in practice, it is better to declare variables in separate statements.

TRY IT OUT - Using Arrays

As a basis for an exercise in using arrays, let's imagine that we have kept a record of the amount of gas we have bought for the car and have recorded the odometer reading on each occasion. We can write a program to analyze this data to see how the gas consumption looks on each occasion that we bought gas:

```
// EX4_01.CPP
// Calculating gas mileage
#include <iostream.h>
#include <iomanip.h>

int main()
{
   const int MAX = 20;                      // Maximum number of values
   double gas[ MAX ];                       // Gas quantity in gallons
   long miles[ MAX ];                       // Odometer readings
   int count = 0;                           // Loop counter
   char indicator = 'n';                    // Input indicator

   for(count=0 ; count < MAX ; count++)
   {
      cout << endl
           << "Enter gas quantity: ";
      cin >> gas[count];                     // Read gas quantity
```

```
                cout << "Enter odometer reading: ";
                cin >> miles[count];                    // Read odometer value

                cout << "Do you want to enter another( y or n )? ";
                cin >> indicator;
                if(indicator =='n' || indicator == 'N')
                    break;                              // Exit loop if N or n entered
        }

        if(count < 1)                                   // First was index 0 so index
        {                                               // on exit should be at least 1
            cout << endl
                 << "Sorry - at least two readings are necessary.";
            return 0;
        }

    // Output results from 2nd entry to last entry
        for(int i=1 ; i <= count ; i++)
        cout << endl
             << setw(2) << i << "."                     // Output sequence number
             << "Gas purchased = " << gas[ i] << " gallons" // Output gas
             << " resulted in "                         // Output miles per gallon
             << (miles[i] - miles[i-1])/gas[i] << " miles per gallon.";

        cout << endl;
        return 0;
    }
```

How It Works

Since we need to take the difference between two odometer readings to calculate the miles covered for the gas used, we only use the odometer reading from the first pair of input values - we ignore the gas bought in the first instance. The typical output produced by this example is shown in the figure below:

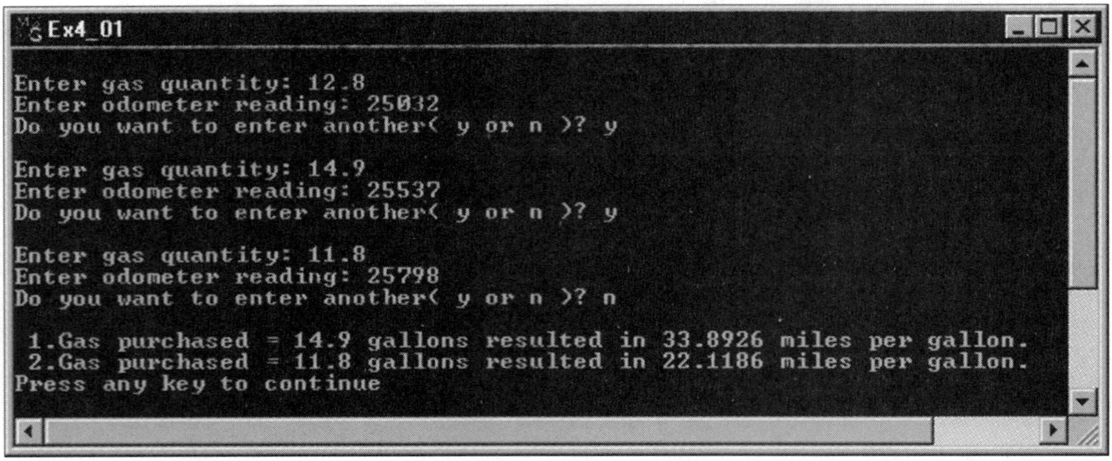

During the second period shown in the output, traffic must have been really bad - or maybe the parking brake was always on.

The dimensions of the two arrays **gas** and **miles**, used to store the input data, is determined by the value of the constant variable **MAX**. By changing the value of **MAX**, you can change the program to accommodate a different maximum numbers of input values. This technique is commonly used to make a program flexible in the amount of information that it can handle. Of course, all the program code must be written to take account of the array dimensions, or of any other parameters being specified by **const** variables. However, this presents little difficulty in practice, so there is no reason why you should not adopt this approach. We'll also see later how to allocate memory for storing data as the program executes so that we don't need to fix the amount of memory allocated for data storage in advance.

Inputting the Data

The data values are read in the first **for** loop. Since the loop variable **count** can run from **0** to **MAX-1**, we haven't allowed the user of our program to enter more values than the array can handle. There is a prompt for each input value required and the value is read into the appropriate array element. The element used to store a particular value is determined by the loop control variable **count**. The array element is specified in the **cin** statement by using **count** as an index. Since **count** varies from **0** to **MAX-1** in integer steps, successive values of each array are used according to the current value of **count**.

After you enter each value, the program prompts you for confirmation that another value is to be entered. The character entered is read into the variable **indicator** and then tested in the **if** statement. If you enter n or N, the program terminates the loop by executing the **break** statement. In any event, the loop will end once **MAX** pairs of input values have been read.

Once the input loop ends (by whatever means), the value of **count** contains the index value of the last element entered in each array. This is checked to verify that at least two pairs of values were entered. If this wasn't the case, since two odometer values are necessary to calculate a mileage value, the program ends with a suitable message.

Producing the Results

The output is generated in the second **for** loop. The control variable **i** runs from **1** to **count**, allowing mileage to be calculated as the difference between the current element, **miles[i]** and the previous element, **miles[i-1]**. Note that an index value can be any expression that evaluates to an integer that represents a legal index for the array in question.

If the value of an index expression lies outside of the range corresponding to legitimate array elements, you will be referencing a spurious data location that may contain other data, garbage, or even program code. If the reference to such an element appears in an expression, you will be using some arbitrary data value in the calculation which will certainly produce a result that you did not intend. If you are storing a result in an array element using an illegal index value, you will overwrite whatever happens to be in that location. When this is part of your program code, the results will be catastrophic. If you use illegal index values, there are no warnings produced either by the compiler or at run-time. The only way to guard against this is to code your program to prevent it happening.

The output is generated by a single **cout** statement for all values entered, except for the first. A line number is also generated for each line of output using the loop control variable **i**. The miles per gallon is calculated directly in the output statement. You can use array elements in exactly the same way as any other variables in an expression.

Initializing Arrays

To initialize an array, the initializing values are enclosed within braces in the declaration and placed following an equals sign after the array name. An example of a declaration and initialization of an array would be this:

```
int cubic_inches[5] = { 200, 250, 300, 350, 400 };
```

The values in the initializing list correspond to successive index values of the array so, in this case, **cubic_inches[0]** will have the value **200**, **cubic_inches[1]** the value **250**, **cubic_inches[2]** the value **300**, and so on.

You mustn't specify more initializing values than there are elements in the list, but you can include fewer. If there *are* fewer, the values are assigned to successive elements, starting with the first element which has the index **0**. The array elements for which you didn't provide an initial value will be initialized with zero. This is not the same as supplying no initializing list. Without an initializing list, the array elements will contain junk values. Also, if you include an initializing list, there must be at least one initializing value in it, otherwise the compiler will generate an error message. We can illustrate this with the following, rather limited, example.

TRY IT OUT - Initializing an Array

```cpp
// EX4_02.CPP
// Demonstrating array initialization
#include <iostream.h>
#include <iomanip.h>

int main()
{
   int value[5] = { 1, 2, 3 };
   int Junk [5];

   cout << endl;
   for(int i=0 ; i<5 ; i++)
      cout << setw(12) << value[i];

   cout << endl;
   for(i=0 ; i<5 ; i++)
      cout << setw(12) << Junk[i];

   cout << endl;
   return 0;
}
```

In this example we declare two arrays, the first of which, **value**, is initialized in part, and the second, **Junk**, is not initialized at all. The program generates two lines of output which on my computer look like this:

```
Ex4_02                                                          _ □ ×
              1           2           3           0           0
  -2125014104     5505024     6618628     4211914     4276756
Press any key to continue
```

The second line (corresponding to values of `Junk[0]` to `Junk[4]`) may well be different on your computer.

How It Works

The first three values of the array **value** are the initializing values and the last two have the default value of **0**. In the case of **Junk**, all the values are spurious since we did not provide any initial values at all. The array elements will contain whatever values were left there by the program which last used these memory locations.

A convenient way to initialize a whole array to zero is simply to specify a single initializing value as **0**. For example, the statement,

```
long data[100] = {0};    // Initialize all elements to zero
```

declares the array **data**, with all elements initialized with **0**.

Providing you supply initializing values, you can also omit the dimension of an array of numeric type. The number of elements in the array will be determined by the number of initializing values. For example, the array declaration,

```
int value[] = { 2, 3, 4 };
```

defines an array with three elements which will have the initial values **2**, **3**, and **4**.

Character Arrays and String Handling

An array of type **char** is called a character array and is generally used to store a character string. A character string is a sequence of characters with a special character appended to indicate the end of the string. The string terminating character is defined by the escape sequence **'\0'**, and is sometimes referred to as a null character, being a byte with all bits as zero. The representation of a string in memory is shown in the figure below:

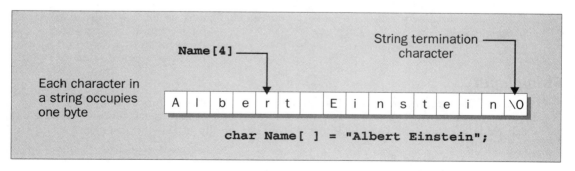

This illustrates how a string looks in memory and shows a form of declaration for a string that we will get to in a moment.

 Each character in the string occupies one byte, so together with the null character, a string requires a number of bytes that is one greater than the number of characters contained in the string.

We can declare a character array and initialize it with a string constant between quotation marks. For example:

```
char movie_star[15] = "Marilyn Monroe";
```

Note that the terminating `'\0'` will be supplied automatically by the compiler. If you include one explicitly in the string constant, you will end up with two of them. You must, however, include space for the terminating null in the number of elements that you allot to the array.

You can let the compiler work out the length of an initialized array for you, as we saw in the previous illustration. Have a look at the following declaration:

```
char President[] = "Ulysses Grant";
```

Because the dimension is unspecified, the compiler will allocate space for enough elements to hold the initializing string, plus the terminating null, in this case, 14 elements for the array **President**. Of course, if you want to use this array later for storing a different string, its length (including the terminating null) must not exceed 14 bytes. In general, it is your responsibility to ensure that the array is large enough for any string that you might subsequently want to store.

> *You may well have heard of Unicode, or seen references to it in the Visual C++ documentation so we'll just outline it here so that you know what it refers to. For supporting international character sets, a character type* **wchar_t** *is supported which uses 2 bytes for each character. This allows 65,536 different characters to be represented, which makes it possible for all the national characters sets to be given unique 16 bit codes, so they can coexist within a single 2 byte character set. This makes creating applications intended for multinational markets much easier.*
>
> *The definition of the 2 byte character set which incorporates all national character sets, as well as all other standard technical and publishing symbols, is called Unicode. MFC provides facilities for using the Unicode character set in your Windows programs. We will not be going into any further detail on Unicode in this book, not because it's difficult - it isn't - but simply because we have to stop somewhere.*

String Input

The header file **iostream.h** contains definitions of a number of functions for reading characters from the keyboard. The one that we shall look at here is the function **getline()** which reads a string into a character array. This is typically used with statements such as this:

```
const int MAX = 80;
char name[MAX];
...
cin.getline(name, MAX, '\n');
```

These statements first declare a **char** array name with **MAX** elements and then read characters from **cin** using the function **getline()**. The source of the data, **cin**, is written as shown, with a period separating it from the function name. The significance of various parts of the input statement is shown here:

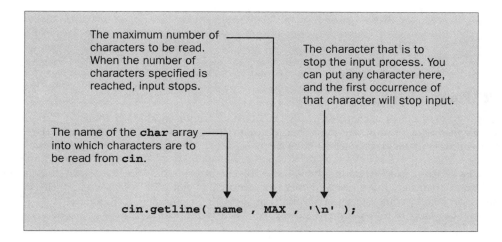

The maximum number of characters to be read. When the number of characters specified is reached, input stops.

The character that is to stop the input process. You can put any character here, and the first occurrence of that character will stop input.

The name of the **char** array into which characters are to be read from **cin**.

```
cin.getline( name , MAX , '\n' );
```

Characters are read from **cin** until the **'\n'** (newline or endline character) character is read, or when **MAX-1** characters have been read (plus the terminating **'\0'** is appended), whichever occurs first. The **'\n'** character is generated when you press the *Return* key on your keyboard, and thus is usually the most convenient character to end input. You can, though, specify something else if you wish by changing the last argument. The **'\n'** isn't stored in the input array **name**, but a **'\0'** is added at the end of input string in the array.

We will learn more about this form of syntax when we discuss classes later on. Meanwhile, we can take it for granted and use it in an example.

TRY IT OUT - Programming with Strings

We now have enough knowledge to write a simple program to read a string and then count how many characters it contains.

```cpp
// EX4_03.CPP
// Counting string characters
#include <iostream.h>

int main()
{
   const int MAX = 80;                // Maximum array dimension
   char buffer[MAX];                  // Input buffer
   int count = 0;                     // Character count

   cout << "Enter a string of less than 80 characters:\n";
   cin.getline(buffer, MAX, '\n');    // Read a string until \n

   while(buffer[count] != '\0')       // Increment count as long as
      count++;                        // the current character is not null

   cout << endl
        << "The string \"" << buffer
```

111

```
                << "\" has " << count << " characters.";

        cout << endl;
        return 0;
    }
```

How It Works

This program declares a character array **buffer** and reads a character string from the keyboard after displaying a prompt for the input. Reading from the keyboard ends when the user presses *Return*, or when **MAX-1** characters have been read.

A **while** loop is used to count the number of characters read. The loop continues as long as the current character referenced to **buffer[count]** is not **'\0'**. This sort of checking on the current character (while stepping through an array) is a common technique in C++. The only action in the loop is to increment **count** for each non-null character.

 There is also a library function, **strlen()**, that can save you the trouble of coding it yourself. If you use it, you need to include the **string.h** header file in your program.

Finally in our example, the string and the character count is displayed with a single output statement. Note how we need to use the escape character **'\"'** to output a quote. The typical output from this program is illustrated below:

```
Ex4_03                                                    _ □ ×
Enter a string of less than 80 characters:
Radiation fades your genes

The string "Radiation fades your genes" has 26 characters.
Press any key to continue
```

Multi-Dimensional Arrays

The arrays that we have defined so far with one index are referred to as **one-dimensional** arrays. An array can also have more than one index value - in which case it is a **multi-dimensional** array. Suppose we have a field in which we are growing bean plants in rows of 10, and the field contains 12 such rows (so 120 plants in all). We could perhaps declare an array to record the weight of beans produced by each plant, using the following statement:

```
    double beans[12][10];
```

This declares the two-dimensional array **beans**, the first index being the row number and the second index the number within the row. To refer to any particular element requires two indices. For example, we could set the value of the element reflecting the fifth plant in the third row with the following statement:

```
    beans[2][4] = 10.7;
```

Remembering that the index values start from zero, the row index value is **2** and the index for the fifth plant within the row is **4**.

Being successful bean farmers, we might have several identical fields planted with beans in the same pattern. Assuming that we have eight fields, we could use a three-dimensional array declared thus:

```
double beans[8][12][10];
```

This will record production for all of the plants in each of the fields, the leftmost index referencing a particular field. If we ever get to bean farming on an international scale, we will be able to use a four-dimensional array, with the extra dimension designating the country. Assuming that you are as good a salesman as farmer, growing this quantity of beans to keep up with the demand may start to affect the ozone layer.

Arrays are stored in memory such that the rightmost index value varies most rapidly. You can visualize the array **data[3][4]** as three one-dimensional arrays of four elements each. The arrangement of this array is illustrated below:

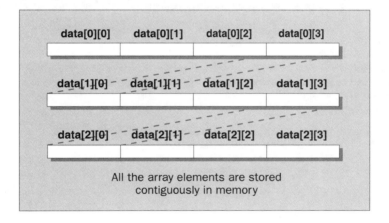

All the array elements are stored
contiguously in memory

Initializing Multi-Dimensional Arrays

To initialize a multi-dimensional array, you use an extension of the method used for a one-dimensional array. For example, you can initialize a two-dimensional array, **data**, with the following declaration:

```
long data[2][4] = {
                    { 1,   2 ,  3 ,  5 },
                    { 7,  11 , 13 , 17 }
                  };
```

Thus, the initializing values for each row of the array are contained within their own pair of braces. Since there are four elements in each row, there are four initializing values in each group and, since there are two rows, there are two groups between braces, each group of initializing values being separated from the next by a comma.

113

You can omit initializing values in any row, in which case the remaining array elements in the row will be zero. For example, with the declaration,

```
long data[2][4] = {
                    { 1,   2 , 3        },
                    { 7, 11             }
                  };
```

the initializing values have been spaced out here to show where values have been omitted. The elements **data[0][3]**, **data[1][2]** and **data[1][3]** have no initializing values and will, therefore, be zero.

If you wanted to initialize the whole array with zeros you could simply write:

```
long data[2][4] = {0};
```

If you are initializing arrays with even more dimensions, remember that you need as many nested braces for groups of initializing values as there are dimensions in the array.

TRY IT OUT - Storing Multiple Strings

We can use a single two-dimensional array to store several strings. We can see how this works with an example:

```
// EX4_04.CPP
// Storing strings in an array.
#include <iostream.h>
int main()
{
    char stars[6][80] = { "Robert Redford",
                          "Hopalong Cassidy",
                          "Lassie",
                          "Slim Pickens",
                          "Boris Karloff",
                          "Oliver Hardy"
                        };
    int dice = 0;

    cout << endl
         << " Pick a lucky star!"
         << " Enter a number between 1 and 6: ";
    cin >> dice;

    if(dice >= 1 && dice <= 6)               // Check input validity
       cout << endl                          // Output star name
            << "Your lucky star is " << stars[dice-1];
    else
       cout << endl                          // Invalid input
            << "Sorry, you haven't got a lucky star.";

    cout << endl;
    return 0;
}
```

How It Works

Apart from its incredible inherent entertainment value, the main point of interest in this example is the declaration of the array stars. It is a two-dimensional **char** array, which can hold up to 6 strings, each of which can be up to 80 characters including the terminating null character. The terminating null for each string is automatically added by the compiler. The initializing strings for the array are enclosed between braces and separated by commas.

 One disadvantage of using arrays in this way is the memory that is almost invariably left unused. All of our strings are less than 80 characters and the surplus elements in each row of the array are wasted.

You can also let the compiler work out how many strings you have by omitting the first array dimension and declaring it as follows:

```
char stars[][80] = { "Robert Redford",
                     "Hopalong Cassidy",
                     "Lassie",
                     "Slim Pickens",
                     "Boris Karloff",
                     "Oliver Hardy"
                   };
```

This will cause the compiler to define the first dimension to accommodate the number of initializing strings that you have specified. Since we have six, the result is exactly the same, but it avoids the possibility of an error. Here you cannot omit both array dimensions. The rightmost dimension must always be defined.

 Note the semicolon at the end of the declaration. It is easy to forget it when there are initializing values for an array.

Where we need to reference a string for output in the statement,

```
cout << endl                              // Output star name
     << "Your lucky star is " << stars[dice-1];
```

we only need to specify the first index value. A single index value selects a particular 80 element subarray, and the output operation will display the contents up to the terminating null character. The index is specified as **dice-1**, as the **dice** values are from **1** to **6**, whereas the index values clearly need to be from **0** to **5**.

Indirect Data Access

The variables that we have dealt with so far provide you with the ability to name a memory location in which you can store data of a particular type. The contents of a variable are either entered from an external source, such as the keyboard, or calculated from other values that are entered. There is another kind of variable in C++ which does not store data that you normally enter or calculate, but greatly extends the power and flexibility of your programs. This kind of variable is called a **pointer**.

What is a Pointer?

Each memory location that you use to store a data value has an address. The address provides the means for your PC hardware to reference a particular data item. A pointer is a variable that stores an address of another variable of a particular type. A pointer has a variable name just like any other variable and also has a type which designates what kind of variables its contents refer to. Note that the type of a pointer variable includes the fact that it is a pointer. A variable that is a pointer which can contain addresses of locations in memory containing values of type **int**, is of type 'pointer to **int**'.

Declaring Pointers

The declaration for a pointer is similar to that of an ordinary variable, except that the pointer name has an asterisk in front of it to indicate that it is a variable which is a pointer. For example, to declare a pointer **pnumber** of type **long**, you could use the following statement:

```
long* pnumber;
```

This declaration has been written with the asterisk close to the type name. You can also write it as,

```
long *pnumber;
```

if you wish - the compiler won't mind at all. However, the type of the variable **pnumber** is 'pointer to **long**' which is often indicated by placing the asterisk close to the type name.

You can mix declarations of ordinary variables and pointers in the same statement. For example:

```
long* pnumber, number = 99;
```

This declares the pointer **pnumber** of type **long** as before, and also declares the variable **number**, also of type **long**. On balance, it's probably better to declare pointers separately from other variables, otherwise the statement can appear misleading as to the type of the variables declared, particularly if you prefer to place the ***** adjacent to the type name. The following statements certainly look clearer. Putting declarations on separate lines enables you to add comments for them individually - making for a program that is easier to read.

```
long number = 99; // Declaration and initialization of long variable
long* pnumber;    // Declaration of variable of type pointer to long
```

It is a common convention in C++ to use variable names beginning with **p** to denote pointers. This makes it easier to see which variables in a program are pointers, which in turn can make a program easier to follow.

Let's take an example to see how this works, without worrying about what it is for. We will come on to how this is used very shortly. Suppose we have the **long** integer variable **number**, as we declared it above, containing the value **99**. We also have the pointer **pnumber** of type **long**, which we could use to store the address of our variable **number**. But how can we obtain the address of a variable?

The Address-Of Operator

What we need is the address-of operator, **&**. This is a unary operator which obtains the address of a variable. It is also called the reference operator for reasons we will discuss later in this chapter. To set up the pointer that we have just discussed, we could write this assignment statement:

```
pnumber = &number;          // Store address of number in pnumber
```

The result of this operation is illustrated below:

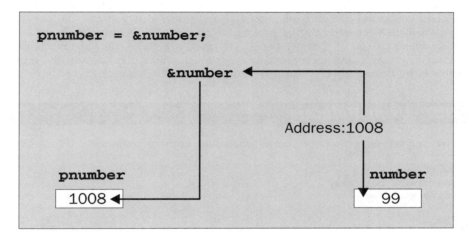

You can use the operator **&** to obtain the address of any variable, but you need a pointer of the same type to store it. If you want to store the address of a **double** variable for example, the pointer must have been declared as **double***, which is type 'pointer to **double**'.

Using Pointers

Taking the address of a variable and storing it in a pointer is all very well, but the really interesting aspect is how you can use it. Fundamental to using a pointer is accessing the data value in the variable to which a pointer points. This is done using the indirection operator, *****.

The Indirection Operator

The indirection operator, *****, is used with a pointer to access the contents of the variable pointed to. The name **indirection operator** stems from the fact that the data is accessed indirectly. It is also called the **de-reference operator**, and the process of accessing the data in the variable pointed to by a pointer is termed **de-referencing** the pointer.

One aspect of this operator that can seem confusing is the fact that we now have several different uses for the same symbol, *****. It is the multiply operator, the indirection operator, and it is used in the declaration of a pointer. Each time you use *****, the compiler is able to distinguish its meaning by the context. When you multiply two variables, **A*B** for instance, there is no meaningful interpretation of this expression for anything other than a multiply operation.

Why Use Pointers?

A question that usually springs to mind at this point is, 'Why use pointers at all?' After all, taking the address of a variable you already know and sticking it in a pointer so that you can de-reference it seems like overhead you can do without. There a several reasons why pointers are important.

First of all, as you will see shortly, you can use pointer notation to operate on data stored in an array, which often executes faster than if you use array notation. Secondly, when we get to define our own functions later in the book, you'll see that pointers are used extensively for enabling access to large blocks of data, such as arrays within a function, that are defined outside. Thirdly, and most importantly, you'll also see later that you can allocate space for variables dynamically - that is during program execution. This sort of capability allows your program to adjust its use of memory depending on the input to the program. Since you don't know in advance how many variables you are going to create dynamically, the only way you can do this is by using pointers - so make sure you get the hang of this bit.

TRY IT OUT - Using Pointers

We can try out various aspects of pointer operations with an example:

```
//EX4_05.CPP
// Exercising pointers
#include <iostream.h>

int main()
{
   long* pnumber;                     // Pointer declaration
   long number1 = 55, number2 = 99;

   pnumber = &number1;                // Store address in pointer
   *pnumber += 11;                    // Increment number1 by 11
   cout << endl
        << "number1 = " << number1
        << "   &number1 = " << hex << pnumber;

   pnumber = &number2;                // Change pointer to address of number2
   number1 = *pnumber*10;             // 10 times number2

   cout << endl
        << "number1 = " << dec << number1
        << "   pnumber = " << hex << pnumber
        << "   *pnumber = " << dec << *pnumber;

   cout << endl;
   return 0;
}
```

How It Works

There is no input to this example. All operations are carried out with the initializing values for the variables. After storing the address of **number1** in the pointer **pnumber**, the value of **number1** is incremented indirectly through the pointer in this statement:

```
   *pnumber += 11;                        // Increment number1 by 11
```

The indirection operator determines that we are adding 11 to the contents of the variable pointed to, **number1**. If we forget the *****, we would be attempting to add 11 to the address stored in the pointer.

The values of **number1**, and the address of **number1** stored in **pnumber**, are displayed. We use the **hex** manipulator to generate the address output in hexadecimal notation.

You can obtain the value of ordinary integer variables as hexadecimal output by using the manipulator **hex**. You send it to the output stream in the same way that we have applied **endl**, with the result that all following output will be in hexadecimal notation. If you want the following output to be decimal, you need to use the manipulator **dec** in the next output statement to switch the output back to decimal mode again.

After the first line of output, the contents of **pnumber** are set to the address of **number2**. The variable **number1** is then changed to the value of 10 times **number2**:

```
number1 = *pnumber*10;                    // 10 times number2
```

This is calculated by accessing the contents of **number2** indirectly through the pointer. The second line of output shows the results of these calculations. On my computer, the example generates the following output:

```
Ex4_05
number1 = 66    &number1 = 0x0064FDF0
number1 = 990   pnumber = 0x0064FDEC    *pnumber = 99
Press any key to continue
```

The address values on your computer may well be different, since they reflect where the program is loaded in memory, which depends on how your operating system is configured. The **0x** prefixing the address values indicate that they are hexadecimal numbers. Note that the addresses for **number1** and **pnumber** when it contains **&number2**, differ by four bytes. This shows that **number1** and **number2** occupy adjacent memory locations, as a **long** variable requires four bytes. The output demonstrates that everything is working as we expect.

Debugging

The last example is a good vehicle for an initial exploration of the basic debug capabilities of the Developer Studio. When you have written a program that doesn't work as it should, the debug facilities enable you to work through a program one step at a time to find out where and how it is going wrong. We'll arrange to execute our program one statement at a time and to monitor the contents of the variables that we're interested in. In this case, we want to look at **pnumber**, the contents of the location pointed to by **pnumber** (which is ***pnumber**), **number1** and **number2**.

First, we need to be sure that the Build configuration for the example is set to Win32 Debug rather than Win32 Release (it will be unless you've changed it). The configuration is shown in the drop-down list on the Project toolbar. You can change it by extending the drop-down list and choosing the alternative. The toolbar is shown on the next page.

119

The tooltips will tell you what each of the toolbar buttons are for. Just let the cursor linger over a toolbar button and the tooltip for that button will appear.

The Debug configuration in the project causes additional information to be included in your executable program so that the debugging facilities can be used. In this example, we won't use all the debugging facilities available to us, but we'll consider some of the more important features, starting with the buttons available on the Project toolbar. This will get you started on using debugging, so you should be able to experiment with using debugging on other examples as we go through the book.

Setting Breakpoints

Setting breakpoints enables you to define where in a program you want execution to pause so that you can look at variables within the program and change them if they don't have the values they should. We're going to execute our program one statement at a time but, with a large program, this would be impractical. Usually, you'll only want to look at a particular area of the program where you think there might be an error. Consequently, you would usually set breakpoints where you think the error is and run the program so that it halts at the first breakpoint.

To set a breakpoint, you simply place the cursor in the statement where you want execution to stop and click the Insert/Remove Breakpoint button or press *F9*.

You would normally set several breakpoints, each chosen to show when the variables that you think are causing a problem are changing. Execution will stop *before* the statement indicated by the breakpoint is executed.

A breakpoint is indicated by a large circle at the start of a line of code, as you can see from this screenshot:

```
//EX4_05.CPP
// Exercising pointers
#include <iostream.h>

int main()
{
    long* pnumber;                    // Pointer declaration
    long number1 = 55, number2 = 99;

●   pnumber = &number1;               // Store address in pointer
    *pnumber += 11;                   // Increment number1 by 11
    cout << endl
```

Although you can set breakpoints for each line of text, the compiler can only break before a complete statement and not halfway through it, so you may see this message when you try and run your code:

120

To avoid this message, make sure that you position your breakpoints on the last line of a multi-line statement. In other words, position your breakpoints on the same line as the semicolon that ends the statement.

Removing Breakpoints

You can remove breakpoints by positioning the cursor on the same line as an existing breakpoint and clicking the Insert/Remove Breakpoint button or pressing *F9*.

Alternatively, you can remove all the breakpoints in the active project by clicking the Remove All Breakpoints button or by pressing *Ctrl+Shift+F9*.

Note that this will remove breakpoints from all files in the project, even if they're not currently open in Developer Studio.

Starting Debugging

There are three ways of starting your application in debug mode, which you can see if you look at the options under Debug in the Build menu.

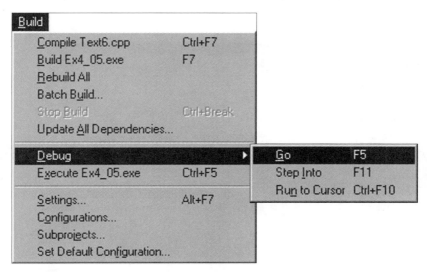

The <u>G</u>o option (also available from the button on the Project toolbar) simply executes a program to the first breakpoint, where execution will halt. After you've examined all you need to at a breakpoint, selecting <u>G</u>o again will continue execution up to the next breakpoint. In this way, you can move through a program from breakpoint to breakpoint, and at each halt in execution have a look at critical variables, changing their values if you need to.

Of course, just because you started debugging using <u>G</u>o doesn't mean that you have to continue using it; at each halt in execution you can choose any of the possible ways of moving through your code.

<u>Ru</u>n to Cursor does exactly what it says - it executes the program up to the statement where you left the cursor in the Text Editor window. In this way, you can set the position where you want the program to stop as you go along.

Step <u>I</u>nto executes your program one statement at a time. This would be something of a nuisance for us if we used it throughout the debugging process, since it would also execute all the code for stream output which we're not really interested in since we didn't write it. To avoid having to step through all that code, we'll use the Step Over facility provided by the debugger. This will simply execute the statements in our function **main()** and jump over all the code used by the stream operations without stopping. First, though, we'll start the program using Step <u>I</u>nto, so click the menu item or press *F11* to begin.

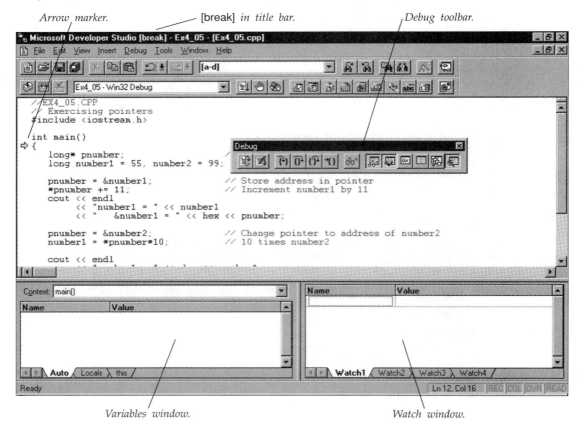

Arrow marker.   [break] *in title bar.*   *Debug toolbar.*

Variables window.   *Watch window.*

After a short pause (assuming that you've already built the project), the Developer Studio will switch to debugging mode. The Project Workspace and Output windows will disappear, to be replaced by the Variables window and the Watch window at the bottom of the screen. The <u>B</u>uild menu will be replaced by the <u>D</u>ebug menu and the Debug toolbar will appear. If you look at the <u>D</u>ebug menu or the Debug toolbar, you'll see that it contains an option for Step O<u>v</u>er , as well as a number of other features, some of which we'll discuss shortly.

In the Text Editor window, you'll see that the opening brace of our **main()** function is highlighted by an arrow to indicate that this is the current point in execution. At this point in the program, we can't choose any variables to look at because none exist at present. Until a declaration for a variable has been executed, you can't look at its value or change it.

Inspecting Variable Values

Defining a variable that you want to inspect is referred to as **setting a watch** for the variable. Before we set any watches, we need to invoke Step O<u>v</u>er twice to get the declarations for our variables executed. Use the Step O<u>v</u>er menu item, the toolbar icon or press *F10* twice so that the arrow now appears at the start of the line:

```
    pnumber = &number1;              // Store address in pointer
```

If you look at the Variables window now, you should see the following (although the values for **&number1** and **pnumber** may be different on your system as they represent memory locations). Note that the values for **&number1** and **pnumber** are not equal to each other, since the line that the arrow is pointing at hasn't yet been executed.

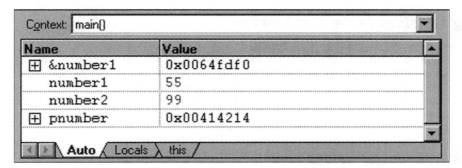

The Variables window has three tabs, each representing a different view of some of the variables in use in your program:

> The Auto tab shows the variables in use in the current and previous statements (in other words, the statement pointed to by the arrow and the one before it).

> The Locals tab shows the values of the variables local to the current function. In general, new variables will come into scope as you trace through a program and then go out of scope as you exit a function. In our case, this window will always show values for **number1**, **number2** and **pnumber** as we only have the function **main()**.

> The this tab will become more useful to you as we progress into object oriented programming as **this** has a special meaning that only applies in that context.

You'll have noticed that **&number1** and **pnumber** both have plus signs next to their names in the Variables window. Plus signs will appear for any variable, such as an array or a pointer, for which there is additional information that can be displayed. In our case, we do have some pointer variables, so you can expand the view for each of these by clicking the plus signs. This will display the value stored at the address contained in the pointer.

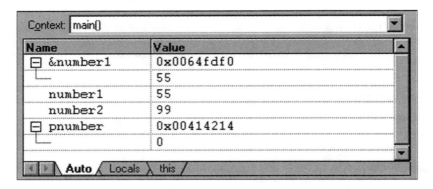

As you can see, the Variables window automatically provides us with all the information we need, providing both the memory address and the data value stored at that address for pointers. You can also view the variables that are local to the current function by selecting the Locals tab. There are also other ways that we can inspect variables using the debugging facilities of the Developer Studio.

Viewing Variables in the Edit Window

If we need to look at the value of a single variable, and that variable is visible in the Text Editor window, the easiest way to look at its value is to position the cursor over the variable for a second. A tooltip will pop up showing the current value of the variable. You can also look at more complicated expressions by highlighting them and resting the cursor over the highlighted area. Again a tooltip will pop up to display the value. Unfortunately, this method won't show the extended information that appears in the Variables window, such as the data stored at the address contained in a pointer, but there is another way to get at this information.

Watching Variables' Values

You can monitor a variable and its extended information where it has any by setting a **watch**. You can also monitor the value of an expression in this way. To set a watch for the pointer **pnumber**, first position the cursor in the Text Editor window in the middle of the pointer name, **pnumber**, then select QuickWatch... from the Debug menu. You could also click on the Debug toolbar icon showing the spectacles to do this.

You should see the next window:

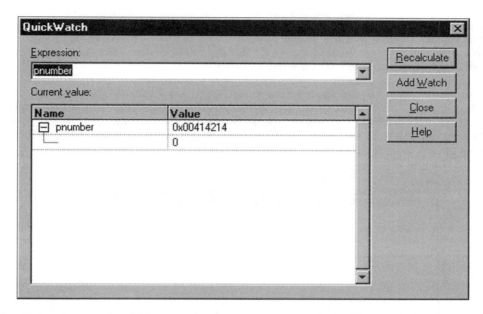

It should be clear to the debugger what you want to watch in this case but, in general, if you have any problems setting a watch, highlight the whole name of the variable or expression in which you are interested.

In the QuickWatch window, as in the Variables window, the variable **pnumber** is automatically displayed in hexadecimal notation, because this is usually the most convenient form for an address. The QuickWatch facility shows us both the memory address and the value stored there, which is just what we want, but it only allows us to watch one expression at a time and, since the dialog is modal, we can't continue executing our code.

We can get around this by setting a permanent watch (or a SlowWatch if we extend Microsoft's terminology, which is what mine always seems to be!). Do this now by clicking the Add Watch button. This will add the watched expression into the Watch window. As execution proceeds, the Watch window will show all the variables we are watching, with their values and extended values.

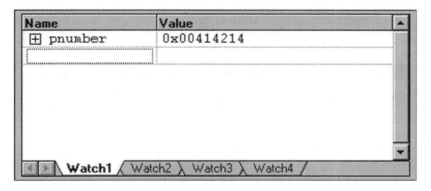

You can also add variables or expressions to the Watch window in two other ways: either type the name of the variable into the Name field of a line in the Watch window or highlight and drag a variable or expression from the Text Editor window or the Variables window. We'll add some more expressions to the Watch window now.

First, expand the view on **pnumber** in the Watch window by clicking the plus sign, then type ***pnumber** into the Name field of the last blank line. Since ***pnumber** is the value stored at the address given by **pnumber**, the last two lines should always have the same value throughout the execution of the program. With the help of the Watch window, you'll be able to confirm this for yourself.

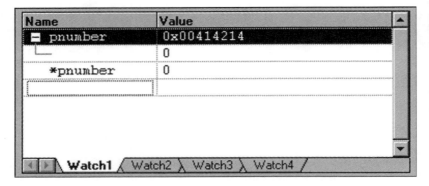

You could have achieved exactly the same result by highlighting the line under **pnumber** in the Variables window (the line that is shown when you click the plus sign) and dragging it into the Watch window. Now add the rest of the variables shown by dragging them from the Auto tab of the Variables window into the Watch window. Remember to start your drag by clicking in the Name field of the Variables window, otherwise you'll just drag the value. You can remove items from the Watch window by highlighting the line that they're on and pressing the *Delete* key.

Name	Value
⊟ pnumber	0x00414214
└	0
*pnumber	0
⊞ &number1	0x0064fdf0
number1	55
number2	99

Watch1 / Watch2 / Watch3 / Watch4 /

Now you're in a position to step through each line of code in the program, using Step Over, so that you don't have to step through all the stream output code. If you do accidentally step into some code that you don't recognize, you can always step out of it again by using the Step Out item from the Debug menu or the button on the Debug toolbar.

At each stage, you can see that everything operates as described just by looking at the values of the variables in the Watch window. The program will end as soon as the last line of code has been executed but, if you wish, you can end debugging before that by choosing the Stop Debugging item from the Debug menu, clicking the Stop Debugging button on the Debug toolbar or pressing *Shift+F5*. Make sure that you don't leave your programs hanging in the middle of the code.

There are various options you can experiment with for watching variables. For example, you can specify various formats for the value to be displayed. You can use any of the ways of stepping through a program in any combination and, in debugging a program for real, this is exactly what you would do. Don't forget to try the Help menu if you get stuck.

You'll probably find it useful to run a few more of the examples in debug mode as we progress through this chapter. It will enable you to get a good feel for how the programs work, as well as getting you familiar with the way that debugging operates under various conditions.

Initializing Pointers

Just as with arrays, using pointers that aren't initialized is extremely hazardous. If you do this, you can overwrite random areas of memory. The resulting damage just depends on how unlucky you are, so it's more than just a good idea to initialize your pointers. It's very easy to initialize a pointer to the address of a variable that has already been defined. Here, you can see that we have initialized the pointer **pnumber** with the address of the variable **number**, just using the operator **&** with the variable name:

```
int number = 0;              // Initialized integer variable
int* pnumber = &number;      // Initialized pointer
```

When initializing a pointer with another variable, remember that the variable must already have been declared prior to the pointer declaration.

Of course, you may not want to initialize a pointer with the address of a specific variable when you declare it. In this case, you can initialize it with the pointer equivalent of zero. For this, Visual C++ provides the symbol **NULL** that is already defined as **0**, so you can declare and initialize a pointer using the following statement:

```
int* pnumber = NULL;         // Pointer not pointing to anything
```

This ensures that the pointer doesn't contain an address that will be accepted as valid, and provides the pointer with a value that you can check in an **if** statement, such as:

```
if(pnumber == NULL)
    cout << endl << "pnumber is null.";
```

Of course, you can also initialize a pointer explicitly with **0**, which will also ensure that it is assigned a value that doesn't point to anything. In spite of it being arguably somewhat less legible, if you expect to run your code with other compilers, it is preferable to use **0** as an initializing value for a pointer that you want to be null.

To use **0** as the initializing value for a pointer, you'd simply write:

```
int* pnumber = 0;               // Pointer not pointing to anything
```

To check whether a pointer contains a valid address you could use the statement,

```
if(pnumber == NULL)            // or pnumber == 0
   cout << endl << "pnumber is null.";
```

or you could equally well use the statement,

```
if(!pnumber)
   cout << endl << "pnumber is null.";
```

which does exactly the same as the previous example.

Of course, you can also use the form:

```
if(pnumber != 0)
   // Pointer is valid, so do something useful
```

A pointer of type **char** has the interesting property that it can be initialized with a string constant. For example, we can declare and initialize such a pointer with the statement:

```
char* proverb = "A miss is as good as a mile.";
```

This looks very similar to initializing a char array, but it is slightly different. This will create the string constant (actually a constant array of type **char**) with the character string appearing between the quotes, and terminated with **\0**, and store the address of the constant in the pointer **proverb**. This is shown in the figure:

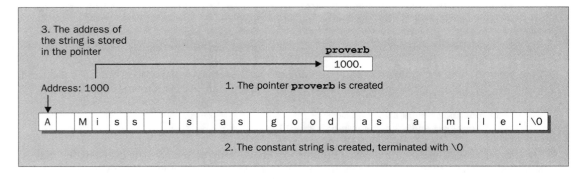

TRY IT OUT - Lucky Stars with Pointers

We could rewrite our lucky stars example, using pointers instead of an array, to see how that would work:

```
// EX4_06.CPP
// Initializing pointers with strings
#include <iostream.h>
int main()
{
   char* pstr1 = "Robert Redford";
   char* pstr2 = "Hopalong Cassidy";
   char* pstr3 = "Lassie";
   char* pstr4 = "Slim Pickens";
   char* pstr5 = "Boris Karloff";
   char* pstr6 = "Oliver Hardy";
   char* pstr  = "Your lucky star is ";

   int dice = 0;

   cout << endl
        << " Pick a lucky star!"
        << " Enter a number between 1 and 6: ";
   cin >> dice;

   cout << endl;
   switch(dice)
   {
      case 1: cout << pstr << pstr1;
              break;

      case 2: cout << pstr << pstr2;
              break;

      case 3: cout << pstr << pstr3;
              break;

      case 4: cout << pstr << pstr4;
              break;

      case 5: cout << pstr << pstr5;
              break;

      case 6: cout << pstr << pstr6;
              break;

      default: cout << "Sorry, you haven't got a lucky star.";
   }

   cout << endl;
   return 0;
}
```

How It Works

The array in **EX4_04.CPP** has been replaced by the six pointers, **pstr1** to **pstr6**, each initialized with a name. We've also declared an additional pointer, **pstr**, initialized with the phrase that we want to use at the start of a normal output line. Because we have discrete pointers, it's easier to use a **switch** statement to select the appropriate output message than to use an **if** as we had in the original version. Any incorrect values that are entered are all taken care of by the **default** option of the **switch**.

Outputting the string pointed to by a pointer couldn't be easier. As you can see, you simply write the pointer name. It may cross your mind at this point that in **EX4_05.CPP** we wrote a pointer name in the output statement and the address that it contained was displayed. Why is it different here? The answer lies in the way the output operation views a pointer of type 'pointer to **char**'. It treats a pointer of this type as a string (which is an array of **char**) and so outputs the string itself, rather than its address.

Using pointers has eliminated the waste of memory that occurred with the array version of this program, but the program seems a little long winded now - there must be a better way. Indeed there is - using an array of pointers.

TRY IT OUT - Arrays of Pointers

With an array of pointers of type **char**, each element can point to an independent string, and the length of each string can be different. We can declare an array of pointers in the same way that we declare a normal array. Let's go straight to rewriting the previous example, using a pointer array:

```cpp
// EX4_07.CPP
// Initializing pointers with strings
#include <iostream.h>
int main()
{
   char* pstr[] =  { "Robert Redford",   // Initializing a pointer array
                     "Hopalong Cassidy",
                     "Lassie",
                     "Slim Pickens",
                     "Boris Karloff",
                     "Oliver Hardy"
                  };
   char* pstrt = "Your lucky star is ";

   int dice = 0;

   cout << endl
        << " Pick a lucky star!"
        << " Enter a number between 1 and 6: ";
   cin >> dice;

   cout << endl;
   if(dice >= 1 && dice <= 6)                     // Check input validity
      cout << pstrt << pstr[dice-1];              // Output star name

   else
      cout << "Sorry, you haven't got a lucky star.";  // Invalid input
```

```
        cout << endl;
        return 0;
}
```

How It Works

In this case, we're nearly getting the best of all possible worlds. We have a one-dimensional array of **char** pointers declared such that the compiler works out what the dimension should be from the number of initializing strings. The memory usage that results from this is illustrated below:

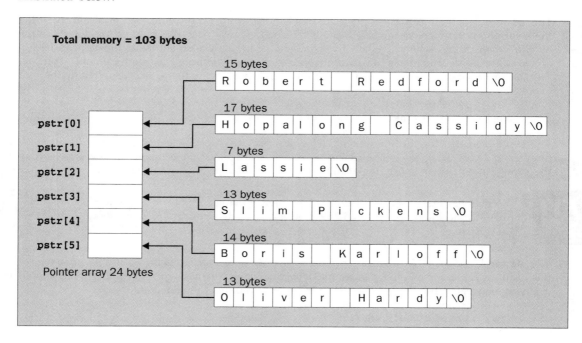

Of course, compared to using an array, the pointer array is less overhead in terms of space. With an array, we would need to make each row the length of the longest string, so we would need 6x17 bytes which is 104 bytes so, by using a pointer array, we save a whole byte here. However, you would save more with longer and more variable length strings.

Since we are using **pstr** as the array name, the variable holding the start of the output message needs to be different, so we have called it **pstrt**. We select the string that we want to output by means of a very simple **if** statement, similar to that of the original version of the example. We either display a star selection or a suitable message if the user enters an invalid value.

One weakness of the way we have written the program is that the code assumes there are six options, even though the compiler is allocating the space for the pointer array from the number of initializing strings that we supply. So, if we add a string to the list, we have to alter other parts of the program to take account of this. It would be nice to be able to add strings and have the program automatically adapt to however many strings there are.

The sizeof Operator

A new operator will help us here. The **sizeof** operator produces an integer constant that gives the number of bytes occupied by its operand. For example, with the variable **dice** from the previous example, this expression,

```
cout << sizeof dice;
```

will output the value **4** since **dice** was declared as **int** and, therefore, occupies 4 bytes.

The **sizeof** operator can be applied to an element in an array or to the whole array. When the operator is applied to an array name by itself, it produces the number of bytes occupied by the whole array, whereas when it is applied to a single element with the appropriate index value or values, it results in the number of bytes occupied by that element. Thus, in the last example, we could output the number of elements in the **pstr** array with the expression:

```
cout << (sizeof pstr)/(sizeof pstr[0]);
```

The expression divides the number of bytes occupied by the whole pointer array by the number of bytes occupied by one element of the array. Since all elements of the array occupy the same amount of memory, the result is the number of elements in the array.

 Remember that **pstr** is an array of pointers - using the **sizeof** operator on the array or on individual elements will not tell us anything about the memory occupied by the text strings.

The **sizeof** operator can also be applied to a type name rather than a variable, in which case the result is the number of bytes occupied by a variable of that type. The type name should be enclosed between parentheses. For example, after executing the statement,

```
long_size = sizeof(long);
```

the variable **long_size** will have the value **4**.

The result returned by **sizeof** is obviously an integer and you can always treat it as such. Its precise type is actually **size_t** which is used for values measured in bytes. The type **size_t**, which will pop up in various contexts from time to time, is defined in various standard libraries in Visual C++ and is equivalent to **unsigned int**.

TRY IT OUT - Using the sizeof Operator

We can use this to amend the last example so that it automatically adapts to an arbitrary number of string values from which to select:

```
// EX4_08.CPP
// Flexible array management using sizeof
#include <iostream.h>
int main()
{
    char* pstr[] =                          // Initializing a pointer array
```

```
                    { "Robert Redford",
                      "Hopalong Cassidy",
                      "Lassie",
                      "Slim Pickens",
                      "Boris Karloff",
                      "Oliver Hardy"
                    };
   char* pstrt = "Your lucky star is ";
   int count = (sizeof pstr)/(sizeof pstr[0]); // Number of array elements

   int dice = 0;

   cout << endl
       << " Pick a lucky star!"
       << " Enter a number between 1 and " << count << ": ";
   cin >> dice;

   cout << endl;
   if(dice >= 1 && dice <= count)                 // Check input validity
       cout << pstrt << pstr[dice-1];             // Output star name

   else
       cout << "Sorry, you haven't got a lucky star."; // Invalid input

   cout << endl;
   return 0;
}
```

How It Works

As you can see, the changes required in the example are very simple. We just calculate the number of elements in the pointer array **pstr** and store the result in **count**. Then, wherever the total number of elements in the array is referenced as **6**, we just use the variable **count**. You could now just add a few more names to the list of lucky stars and everything affected in the program will be adjusted automatically.

Constant Pointers and Pointers to Constants

The array **pstr** in the last example is clearly not intended to be modified in the program - nor are the strings being pointed to, or the variable **count**. It would be a good idea to ensure that these didn't get modified in error in the program. We could very easily protect the variable **count** from accidental modification by writing this:

```
   const int count = (sizeof pstr)/(sizeof pstr[0]);
```

However, the array of pointers deserves closer examination. As the program stands, a statement such as this,

```
   *pstr[0] = 'X';
```

is perfectly legal and results in Mr. Redford being re-christened Xobert. If we rewrite the declaration of the array as follows,

```
   const char* pstr[] = { "Robert Redford",     // Array of pointers
                          "Hopalong Cassidy",   // to constants
```

133

```
                    "Lassie",
                    "Slim Pickens",
                    "Boris Karloff",
                    "Oliver Hardy"
                };
```

we are declaring the objects pointed to by elements of the pointer array as constant. Therefore, the compiler will inhibit any direct attempt to change these, so the last assignment statement would be flagged as an error. However, we could still legally write this statement,

```
    pstr[0] = pstr[1];
```

so those lucky individuals due to be awarded Mr. Redford would get Mr. Cassidy instead, since both pointers now point to the same name. Note that this isn't changing the values of the objects pointed to by the pointer array element - it is changing the value of the pointer stored in **pstr[0]**. We should, therefore, inhibit this kind of change as well, since some people may reckon that good old Hoppy may not have the same sex appeal as Robert. We can do this with the following statement:

```
// Array of constant pointers to constants
const char* const pstr[] = { "Robert Redford",
                             "Hopalong Cassidy",
                             "Lassie",
                             "Slim Pickens",
                             "Boris Karloff",
                             "Oliver Hardy"
                };
```

To summarize, we can distinguish three situations relating to **const**, pointers and the objects to which they point:

A pointer to a constant object,

```
const char* pstring = "Some text";
```

Here, the object pointed to cannot be modified but we can set the pointer to point to something else.

A constant pointer to an object,

```
char* const pstring =  "Some text";
```

Here, the address stored in the pointer can't be changed, but the object pointed to can be.

A constant pointer to a constant object,

```
const char* const pstring = "Some text";
```

Here, both the pointer and the object pointed to have been defined as constant and, therefore, neither can be changed.

Of course, all this applies to pointers of any type. Type `char` is used here purely for illustration purposes.

Pointers and Arrays

Array names can behave like pointers under some circumstances. In most situations, if you use the name of a one-dimensional array by itself, it's automatically converted to a pointer to the first element of the array. Note that this is not the case when the array name is used as the operand of the **sizeof** operator.

If we have these declarations,

```
double* pdata;
double data[5];
```

we can write this assignment:

```
pdata = data;          // Initialize pointer with the array address
```

This is assigning the address of the array **data** to the pointer **pdata**. Using the array name by itself refers to the address of the array. If we use the array name **data** with an index value, it defines the contents of the element corresponding to that index value. So, if we want to store the address of that element in the pointer, we have to use the address-of operator,

```
pdata = &data[1];
```

and the pointer **pdata** will contain the address of the second element of the array.

Pointer Arithmetic

You can perform arithmetic operations with pointers. You are limited to addition and subtraction in terms of arithmetic, but you can also perform comparisons using pointers to produce a logical result. Arithmetic with a pointer implicitly assumes that the pointer points to an array, and that the arithmetic operation is on the address contained in the pointer. For the pointer **pdata** for example, we could assign the address of the third element of the array **data** to a pointer with this statement:

```
pdata = &data[2];
```

In this case, the expression **pdata+1** would refer to the address of **data[3]**, the fourth element of the **data** array, so we could make the pointer point to this element by writing this statement:

```
pdata += 1;            // Increment pdata to the next element
```

This statement has incremented the address contained in **pdata** by the number of bytes occupied by one element of the array **data**. In general, the expression **pdata+n**, where **n** can be any expression resulting in an integer, will add **n*sizeof(double)** to the address contained in the pointer **pdata**, since it was declared to be of type pointer to **double**. This is illustrated on the following page:

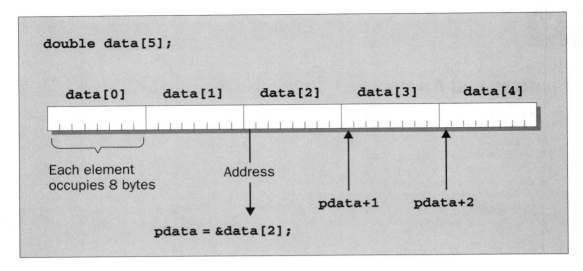

In other words, incrementing or decrementing a pointer works in terms of the type of the object pointed to. Increasing a pointer to **long** by one changes its contents to the next **long** address, and so increments the address by four. Similarly, incrementing a pointer to **short** by one will increment the address by two. The more common notation for incrementing a pointer is using the increment operator. For example, this,

```
pdata++;                 // Increment pdata to the next element
```

is equivalent to (and more usual than) the **+=** form. However, the **+=** form was used above to make it clear that, while the increment value is actually specified as one, the effect is usually an increment greater than one, except in the case of a pointer to **char**.

The address resulting from an arithmetic operation on a pointer can be a value from the address of the first element of the array to which it points, to the address which is one beyond the last element. Outside of these limits, the behavior of the pointer is undefined.

You can, of course, de-reference a pointer on which you have performed arithmetic, (there wouldn't be much point to it otherwise). For example, assuming that **pdata** is still pointing to **data[2]**, this statement,

```
*(pdata+1) = *(pdata+2);
```

is equivalent to this:

```
data[3] = data[4];
```

When you want to de-reference a pointer after incrementing the address it contains, the parentheses are necessary as the precedence of the indirection operator is higher than that of the arithmetic operators, **+** or **-**. If you write the expression ***pdata+1**, instead of

*(pdata+1), this would add one to the value stored at the address contained in **pdata**, which is equivalent to executing **data[2] +1**. Since this is not an lvalue, its use in the assignment statement above would cause the compiler to generate an error message.

We can use an array name as though it were a pointer for addressing elements of an array. If we have the same one-dimensional array as before, declared as,

```
long data[5];
```

using pointer notation, we can refer to the element **data[3]** for example as ***(data+3)**. This kind of notation can be applied generally so that, corresponding to the elements **data[0]**, **data[1]**, **data[2]**, **...**, we can write ***data**, ***(data+1)**, ***(data+2)**, and so on.

TRY IT OUT - Array Names as Pointers

We could exercise this aspect of array addressing with a program to calculate prime numbers (a prime number is a number divisible only by itself and one).

```cpp
// EX4_09.CPP
// Calculating primes
#include <iostream.h>
#include <iomanip.h>
int main()
{
    const int MAX = 100;            // Number of primes required
    long primes[MAX] = { 2,3,5 };   // First three primes defined
    long trial = 5;                 // Candidate prime
    int count = 3;                  // Count of primes found
    int found = 0;                  // Indicates when a prime is found

    do
    {
        trial += 2;                         // Next value for checking
        found = 0;                          // Set found indicator
        for(int i = 0; i < count; i++)      // Try division by existing primes
        {
            found = (trial % *(primes+i)) == 0;  // True for exact division
            if(found)                            // If division is exact
                break;                           // it's not a prime
        }
        if (found == 0)                     // We got one...
            *(primes+count++) = trial;      // ...so save it in primes array
    }while(count < MAX);

    // Output primes 5 to a line
    for( int i = 0 ; i < MAX ; i++)
    {
        if(i%5 == 0)                        // New line on 1st, and every 5th line
            cout << endl;
        cout << setw(10) << *(primes+i);
    }
    cout << endl;
    return 0;
}
```

How It Works

We have the usual **#include** statements for **iostream.h** for input and output, and for **iomanip.h**, since we will be using a stream manipulator to set the field width for output.

We use the constant **MAX** to define the number of primes that we want the program to produce. The **primes** array which stores the results has the first three primes already defined to start the process off. All the work is done in two loops, the outer **do-while** loop which picks the next value to be checked and adds the value to the **primes** array if it is prime and the inner **for** loop that actually checks the value to see whether it is prime or not.

The algorithm in the **for** loop is very simple and is based on the fact that if a number is not a prime, it must be divisible by one of the primes found so far, all of which are less than the number in question, since all numbers are either prime or a product of primes. In fact, only division by primes less than the square root of the number in question needs to be checked, so this example isn't as efficient as it might be.

This statement,

```
found = (trial % *(primes+i)) == 0; // True for exact division
```

sets the variable **found** to be **1** if there is no remainder from dividing the value in **trial** by the current prime ***(primes+i)** (remember that this is equivalent to **primes[i]**) and **0** otherwise. The **if** statement causes the **for** loop to be terminated if **found** has the value **1**, since the candidate in **trial** can't be a prime in that case.

After the **for** loop ends (for whatever reason), it's necessary to decide whether or not the value in **trial** was prime. This is indicated by the value in the indicator variable **found**. If **trial** *does* contain a prime, this statement,

```
*(primes+count++) = trial;      // ...so save it in primes array
```

stores the value in **primes[count]** and then increments **count** through the postfix increment operator.

Once **MAX** number of primes have been found, they are output with a field width of 10 characters, 5 to a line, as a result of this statement,

```
if(i%5 == 0)                // New line on 1st, and every 5th line
      cout << endl;
```

which starts a new line when **i** has the values **0**, **5**, **10**, and so on.

If you compile and execute this example, you should get the output shown here:

```
 Ex4_09
        2          3          5          7         11
       13         17         19         23         29
       31         37         41         43         47
       53         59         61         67         71
       73         79         83         89         97
      101        103        107        109        113
      127        131        137        139        149
      151        157        163        167        173
      179        181        191        193        197
      199        211        223        227        229
      233        239        241        251        257
      263        269        271        277        281
      283        293        307        311        313
      317        331        337        347        349
      353        359        367        373        379
      383        389        397        401        409
      419        421        431        433        439
      443        449        457        461        463
      467        479        487        491        499
      503        509        521        523        541
Press any key to continue
```

TRY IT OUT - Counting Characters Revisited

To see how handling strings works in pointer notation, we could produce a version of the program we looked at earlier for counting the characters in a string:

```cpp
// EX4_10.CPP
// Counting string characters using a pointer
#include <iostream.h>

int main()
{
   const int MAX = 80;                  // Maximum array dimension
   char buffer[MAX];                    // Input buffer
   char* pbuffer=buffer;                // Pointer to array buffer

   cout << endl                         // Prompt for input
        << "Enter a string of less than "
        << MAX << " characters:"
        << endl;

   cin.getline(buffer, MAX, '\n');      // Read a string until \n

   while(*pbuffer)                      // Continue until \0
      pbuffer++;

   cout << endl
```

```
            << "The string \"" << buffer
            << "\" has " << pbuffer-buffer << " characters.";
    cout << endl;
    return 0;
}
```

How It Works

Here, the program operates using the pointer **pbuffer** rather than the array name **buffer**. We don't need the **count** variable, since the pointer is incremented in the **while** loop until **\0** is found. When the **\0** is found, **pbuffer** will contain the address of that position in the string. The count of the number of characters in the string entered is, therefore, the difference between the address stored in the pointer **pbuffer** and the address of the beginning of the array denoted by **buffer**.

We could also have incremented the pointer in the loop by writing the loop like this:

```
while(*pbuffer++);                              // Continue until \0
```

Now the loop contains no statements, only the test condition. This would work adequately, except for the fact that the pointer would be incremented after **\0** was encountered, so the address would be one more than the last position in the string. We would, therefore, need to express the count of the number of characters in the string as **pbuffer-buffer-1**.

Note that, here, we can't use the array name in the same way that we have used the pointer. The expression **buffer++** is strictly illegal since you can't modify an array name - it is not a pointer.

Using Pointers with Multi-Dimensional Arrays

Using a pointer to store the address of a one-dimensional array is relatively straightforward, but with multi-dimensional arrays, things can get a little complicated. If you don't intend to do this, you can skip this section as it's a little obscure, but if your previous experience is with C, this section is worth a glance.

If you have to use a pointer with multi-dimensional arrays, you need to keep clear in your mind what is happening. By way of illustration, we can use an array **beans**, declared as follows:

```
double beans[3][4];
```

We can declare and assign a value to the pointer **pbeans** as follows:

```
double* pbeans;
pbeans = &beans[0][0];
```

Here, we are setting the pointer to the address of the first element of the array which is of type **double**. We could also set the pointer to the address of the first row in the array with the statement:

```
pbeans = beans[0];
```

This is equivalent to using the name of a one-dimensional array which is replaced by its address. We used this in the earlier discussion. However, because **beans** is a two-dimensional array, we cannot set an address in the pointer with the following statement:

```
pbeans=beans;              // Will cause an error!!
```

The problem is one of type. The type of the pointer you have defined is **double***, but the array is of type **double[3][4]**. A pointer to store the address of this array must be of type **double*[4]**. C++ associates the dimensions of the array with its type and the statement above is only legal if the pointer has been declared with the dimension required. This is done with a slightly more complicated notation than we have seen so far:

```
double (*pbeans)[4];
```

The parentheses here are essential, otherwise you would be declaring an array of pointers. Now the previous statement is legal, but this pointer can only be used to store addresses of an array with the dimensions shown.

Pointer Notation with Multi-Dimensional Arrays

You can use pointer notation with an array name to reference elements of the array. You can reference each element of the array **beans** that we declared earlier which had three rows of four elements, in two ways:

> Using the array name with two index values.

> Using the array name in pointer notation.

Therefore, the following are equivalent:

```
beans[i][j]
```

```
*(*(beans+i)+j)
```

Let's look at how these work.

The first line uses normal array indexing to refer to the element with offset **j** in row **i** of the array.

We can determine the meaning of the second line by working from the inside, outwards. **beans** refers to the address of the first row of the array, so **beans+i** refers to row **i** of the array. The expression ***(beans+i)** is the address of the first element of row **i**, so ***(beans+i)+j** is the address of the element in row **i** with offset **j**. The whole expression, therefore, refers to the value of that element.

If you really want to be obscure, and it's not recommended that you do so, the following are also legal references to the same element of the array,

```
*(beans[i]+j)
```

```
(*(beans+i))[j]
```

where we have mixed array and pointer notation.

There is yet another aspect to the use of pointers which is really the most important of all - the ability to create variables dynamically. We'll look into that next.

Dynamic Memory Allocation

Working with a fixed set of variables in a program can be very restrictive. The need often arises within an application to decide the amount of space to be allocated for storing different types of variables at execution time, depending on the input data for the program. With one set of data it may be appropriate to use a large integer array in a program, whereas with a different set of input data, a large floating point array may be required. Obviously, since any dynamically allocated variables can't have been defined at compile time, they can't be named in your source program. When they're created, they're identified by their address in memory which is contained within a pointer. With the power of pointers and the dynamic memory management tools in Visual C++, writing your programs to have this kind of flexibility is quick and easy.

The Free Store, Alias the Heap

In most instances, when your program is executed, there is unused memory in your computer. This unused memory is called the **heap** in C++, or sometimes the **free store**. You can allocate space within the free store for a new variable of a given type, using a special operator in C++ which returns the address of the space allocated. This is the operator **new**, which is complemented by the operator **delete** which de-allocates memory previously allocated by **new**.

You can allocate space in the free store for some variables in one part of a program, and then release the allocated space and return it to the free store once you have finished with the variables concerned. This makes it available for reuse by other dynamically allocated variables, later in the same program. This enables you to use memory very efficiently, and in many cases it results in programs that can handle much larger problems, involving considerably more data than otherwise might be possible.

The Operators new and delete

Suppose that we need space for a **double** variable. We can define a pointer to type **double** and then request that the memory be allocated at execution time. We can do this using the operator **new** with the following statements:

```
double* pvalue=0;        // Pointer initialized with null
pvalue = new double;     // Request memory for a double variable
```

This is a good moment to recall that *all pointers should be initialized*. Using memory dynamically typically involves a number of pointers floating around, so it's important that they should not contain spurious values. You should try to arrange that if a pointer doesn't contain a legal address value, it is set to **NULL**.

The **new** operator in the second line of code above should return the address of the memory in the free store allocated to a **double** variable, and this address will be stored in the pointer **pvalue**. We can then use this pointer to reference the variable using the indirection operator as we have seen. For example:

```
*pvalue = 9999.0;
```

However, using a dynamic variable as shown here is very risky. The memory may not have been allocated, because the free store has been used up. Alternatively, it could be that the free store is fragmented by previous usage, meaning that there is not a sufficient number of contiguous bytes to accommodate the variable for which you want to obtain space. In this case, the operator **new** will return a **NULL** pointer value so, before using it, we should always test for a valid address being returned and stored in our pointer. We could have done this by writing the following:

```
if(!(pvalue = new double))
{
    cout << endl
        << "Out of memory.";
    exit(1);
}
```

Here we have called for the space to be allocated and the address to be stored in the pointer, **pvalue**, all within the **if** statement. If a **NULL** pointer value was returned, the **if** expression will be **TRUE**, so the message will be displayed and the **exit()** function called to end the program. The **exit()** function is used when you want to terminate a program abnormally. The value between the parentheses is an integer (**int**) value that can be used to indicate the circumstances under which the program was terminated. If you use the **exit()** function, you need to include the header file **STDLIB.H** into your program.

You can also initialize a variable created by **new**. Taking our example of the **double** variable which was allocated by **new** and the address stored in **pvalue**, we could have set the value to **999.0** as it was created with this statement:

```
pvalue = new double(999.0);    // Allocate a double and initialize it
```

When you no longer need a variable that has been dynamically allocated, you can free up the memory that it occupies in the free store with the **delete** operator:

```
delete pvalue;                 // Release memory pointed to by pvalue
```

This ensures that the memory can be used subsequently by another variable. If you don't use **delete**, and subsequently store a different address value in the pointer **pvalue**, it will be impossible to free up the memory or to use the variable that it contains since access to the address will have been lost.

Allocating Memory Dynamically for Arrays

Allocating memory for an array dynamically is very straightforward. If we wanted to allocate an array of type **char**, assuming **pstr** is a pointer to **char**, we could write this:

```
pstr = new char[20];       // Allocate a string of twenty characters
```

This allocates space for a **char** array of 20 characters and stores its address in **pstr**.

To remove the array that we have just created in the free store, we must use the **delete** operator. The statement would look like this:

```
delete [] pstr;               // Delete array pointed to by pstr
```

Note the use of square brackets to indicate that what we are deleting is an array. When removing arrays from the free store, you should always include the square brackets or the results will be unpredictable. Note also that you do not specify any dimensions here, simply [].

TRY IT OUT - Using Free Store

We can see how this works in practice by rewriting our program to calculate an arbitrary number of primes, but use memory in the free store to store them.

```cpp
// EX4_11.CPP
// Calculating primes using dynamic memory allocation
#include <iostream.h>
#include <iomanip.h>
#include <stdlib.h>                    // For the exit function

int main()
{
    long* pprime=0;                    // Pointer to prime array
    long trial = 5;                    // Candidate prime
    int count = 3;                     // Count of primes found
    int found = 0;                     // Indicates when a prime is found
    int max = 0;                       // Number of primes required

    cout << endl
        << "Enter the number of primes you would like: ";
    cin >> max;                        // Number of primes required

    if(!(pprime=new long[max]))
    {
        cout << endl
            << "Memory allocation failed.";
        exit(1);                       // Terminate program
    }

    *pprime = 2;                       // Insert three
    *(pprime+1) = 3;                   // seed primes
    *(pprime+2) = 5;

    do
    {
        trial += 2;                               // Next value for checking
        found = 0;                                // Set found indicator
        for(int i = 0 ; i < count ; i++)          // Division by existing primes
        {
            found =(trial % *(pprime+i)) == 0;    // True for exact division
            if(found)                             // If division is exact
                break;                            // it's not a prime
        }
        if (found == 0)                           // We got one...
            *(pprime+count++) = trial;            // ...so save it in primes array
    }while(count < max);
```

```
      // Output primes 5 to a line
      for(int i = 0 ; i < max ; i++)
      {
         if(i%5 == 0)                    // New line on 1st, and every 5th line
            cout << endl;
         cout << setw(10) << *(pprime+i);
      }
      delete [] pprime;                  // Free up memory
      cout << endl;
      return 0;
   }
```

How It Works

Apart for the prompt for the number of primes required, the output from this example is the same as the previous version (assuming that the same number of primes is being generated) so we won't reproduce it again here.

In fact, the program is very similar to the previous version. We have an extra **#include** statement for **stdlib.h** because we are using the function **exit()** if we run out of memory. After receiving the number of primes required in the **int** variable **max**, we allocate an array of that size in the free store using the operator **new**. We specify the size of the array required by putting the variable **max** between the square brackets following the array type specification. The pointer value returned by **new** and stored in the pointer **pprime** is validated in the **if**. If it turns out to be **NULL**, a message is displayed and the program is exited.

```
   if(!(pprime=new long[max]))
   {
      cout << endl
           << "Memory allocation failed.";
      exit(1);                           // Terminate program
   }
```

Assuming that the memory allocation is successful, the first three array elements are set to the values of the first three primes.

 Note that we can't specify initial values for elements of an array allocated dynamically. We have to use explicit assignment statements if we want to set initial values for elements of the array.

The calculation of the prime numbers is exactly as before. The only change is that the name of the pointer we have here, **pprime**, is substituted for the array name **primes**, used in the previous version. Equally, the output process is the same. Acquiring space dynamically is really not a problem at all. Once it has been allocated, it in no way affects how the computation is written.

Once we have finished with the array, we remove it from the free store using the **delete** operator, not forgetting to include the square brackets to indicate that it is an array we are deleting.

```
   delete [] pprime;                     // Free up memory
```

Dynamic Allocation of Multi-Dimensional Arrays

Allocating memory in the free store for a multi-dimensional array involves using the operator **new** in only a slightly more complicated form than that for a one-dimensional array. Assuming that we have already declared the pointer **pbeans** appropriately, to obtain the space for our array **beans[3][4]** that we used earlier in this chapter, we could write this:

```
pbeans = new double [3][4];          // Allocate memory for a 3x4 array
```

Allocating space for a three-dimensional array simply requires the extra dimension specified with **new**, as in this example:

```
pBigArray = new double [5][10][10]; // Allocate memory for a 5x10x10 array
```

However many dimensions there are in the array that has been created, to destroy it and release the memory back to the free store you write the following:

```
delete [] pBigArray;                // Release memory for array
```

You use just one pair of square brackets regardless of the dimensionality of the array with which you are dealing.

We've already seen that we can use a variable as the specification of the dimension of a one-dimensional array to be allocated by **new**. This extends to two or more dimensions only in that the leftmost dimension may be specified by a variable. All the other dimensions must be constants or constant expressions. So we could write this,

```
pBigArray = new double[max][10][10];
```

where **max** is a variable. However, specifying a variable for any other dimension will cause an error message to be generated by the compiler.

Using References

A **reference** appears to be similar to a pointer in many respects, which is why we've introduced it here, but it isn't the same. Its real significance will only become apparent when we get to discuss its use with functions, particularly in the context of object oriented programming. So don't be misled by its simplicity and what might seem to be a trivial concept. As you'll see later, references provide some extraordinarily powerful facilities and, in some contexts, it will enable you to achieve results that would be impossible without using them.

What is a Reference?

A reference is an alias for another variable. It has a name that can be used in place of the original variable name. Since it is an alias, and not a pointer, the variable for which it is an alias has to be specified when the reference is declared, and unlike a pointer, a reference can't be altered to represent another variable.

Declaring and Initializing References

If we have a variable declared as follows,

```
long number = 0;
```

we can declare a reference for this variable using the following declaration statement:

```
long& rnumber=number;     // Declare a reference to variable number
```

The ampersand following the type **long**, and preceding the name **rnumber**, indicates that a reference is being declared, and the variable name it represents, **number**, is specified as the initializing value following the equals sign. Therefore, **rnumber** is of type 'reference to **long**'. The reference can now be used in place of the original variable name. For example, this statement,

```
rnumber += 10;
```

has the effect of incrementing the variable **number** by 10.

Let's contrast the reference **rnumber** with the pointer **pnumber**, declared in this statement:

```
long* pnumber = &number;        // Increment number through a pointer
```

This declares the pointer **pnumber**, and initializes it with the address of the variable **number.** This then allows the variable number to be incremented with a statement such as:

```
*pnumber += 10;                 // Increment number through a pointer
```

You should see a significant distinction between using a pointer and using a reference. The pointer needs to be de-referenced and whatever address it contains is used to access the variable to participate in the expression. With a reference, there is no need for de-referencing. In some ways, a reference is like a pointer that has already been de-referenced, although it can't be changed to reference another variable. The reference is the complete equivalent of the variable for which it is a reference. A reference may seem like just an alternative notation for a given variable, and here it certainly appears to behave like that. However, we shall see when we come to discuss functions in C++ that this is not quite true and that it can provide some very impressive extra capabilities.

Summary

You are now familiar with all of the basic types of values in C++: how to create and use arrays of those types and how to create and use pointers. You have also been introduced to the idea of a reference. However, we have not exhausted all of these topics. We will come back to arrays, pointers and references again later in the book. The important points that we have discussed in this chapter are:

▶ An array allows you to manage a number of variables of the same type using a single name. Each dimension of an array is defined between square brackets following the array name in the declaration of the array.

▶ Each dimension of an array is indexed starting from zero. Thus the fifth element of a one-dimensional array will have the index value 4.

▶ Arrays can be initialized by placing the initializing values between braces in the declaration.

▶ A pointer is a variable that contains the address of another variable. A pointer is declared as a 'pointer to *type*', and may only be assigned addresses of variables of the given type.

▶ A pointer can point to a constant object. Such a pointer can be reassigned to another object. A pointer may also be defined as **const**, in which case it can't be reassigned.

▶ A reference is an alias for another variable, and can be used in the same places as the variable it references. A reference must be initialized in its declaration.

▶ A reference can't be reassigned to another variable.

▶ The operator **sizeof** returns the number of bytes occupied by the object specified as its argument. Its argument may be a variable or a type name between parentheses.

▶ The operator **new** allocates memory dynamically in the free store. When memory has

Introducing Structure to Your Programs

Up to now, we have not really been able to structure our program code in a modular fashion, since we have only been able to construct a program as a single function, **main()**, but we *have* been using library functions of various kinds. Whenever you write a C++ program, you should have a modular structure in mind from the outset and, as we shall see, a good understanding of how to implement functions is essential to object oriented programming in C++. In this chapter, you will learn:

- How to declare and write your own C++ functions
- What are function arguments and how they are defined and used
- How arrays can be passed to and from a function
- What pass-by-value means.
- How to pass pointers to functions
- How to use references as function arguments and what pass-by-reference means
- How the **const** modifier affects function arguments.
- How to return values from a function
- What recursion is and how it can be used

There is quite a lot to structuring your C++ program so, to avoid indigestion, we won't try to swallow the whole thing in one gulp. Once we have chewed over and gotten the full flavor of the morsels listed above, we'll move on to the next chapter where we'll get further into the meat of the topic.

Understanding Functions

Let's first look at the broad principles of how a function works. A function is a self-contained block of code with a specific purpose. A function has a name that both identifies it and is used to call it for execution in a program. The name of a function is global, but is not necessarily unique in C++, as we shall see in the next chapter. However, functions which perform different actions should generally have different names.

The name of a function is governed by the same rules as those for a variable. A function name is, therefore, a sequence of letters and digits, the first of which is a letter and where an underscore counts as a letter. The name of a function should generally reflect what it does so, for example, you might call a function that counts beans, **CountBeans()**.

You pass information to a function by means of arguments specified when you invoke it. The arguments that you specify need to correspond with parameters appearing in the definition of the function. The arguments that you specify replace the parameters used in its definition when the function is executed. The code in the function then executes as though it was written using your argument values. The relationship between arguments in the function call and its parameters is illustrated below:

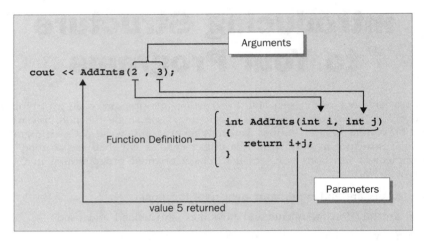

In this example, the function returns the sum of the two arguments passed to it. In general, a function returns either a single value to the point in the program where it was called, or nothing at all, depending on how the function is defined. You might think that returning a single value from a function is a constraint, but the single value returned can be a pointer which might contain the address of an array, for example. We'll see more about how data is returned from a function a little later in this chapter.

Why Do You Need Functions?

One major advantage that a function offers is that it can be executed as many times as necessary from different points in a program. Without the ability to package a block of code into a function, programs would end up being much larger, since you would typically need to replicate the same code at various points in it. But the real reason that you need functions is to break up a program into easily manageable chunks.

Imagine a really big program, a million lines of code let's say. A program of this size would be virtually impossible to write without functions. Functions allow a program to be segmented so that it can be written piecemeal, and each piece tested independently before bringing it together with the other pieces. It also allows the work to be divided among members of a programming team, with each team member taking responsibility for a tightly specified piece of the program, with a well defined functional interface to the rest of the code.

Structure of a Function

As we have seen when writing the function **main()**, a function consists of a function header which identifies the function, followed by the body of the function between curly braces containing the executable code for the function. Let's look at an example. We could write a function to raise a value to a given power, that is - compute x^n:

```
double power(double x, int n)        // Function header
{                                    // Function body starts here...
   double result = 1.0;              // Result stored here
   for(int i = 1 ; i<=n ; i++)
      result *= x;
   return result;
}                                    // ...and ends here
```

The Function Header

Let's first examine the function header in this example. This is the first line of the function:

```
double power(double x, int n)        // Function header
```

It consists of three parts: the type of the **return value** which is **double** in this case, the name of the function, **power**, and then the parameters of the function enclosed between parentheses.

The return value is returned to the calling function when the function is executed, so when the function is called, it will have a value of type **double** in the expression in which it appears.

Our function has two parameters which are **x**, the value to be raised to a given power, which is of type **double**, and the value of the power, **n**, which is of type **int**. The computation that the function performs is written using these parameter variables together with another variable, **result**, declared in the body of the function.

 Note that no semicolon is required at the end of the function header.

The General Form of a Function Header

The general form of a function header can be written as follows:

return_type   FunctionName(parameter_list)

The **return_type** can be any legal type. If the function does not return a value, the return type is specified by the keyword **void**. The keyword **void** is also used to indicate the absence of parameters, so a function that has no parameters and does not return a value would have this header:

```
void MyFunction(void)
```

An empty parameter list also indicates that a function takes no arguments, so you could omit the keyword **void** between the parentheses as follows:

```
void MyFunction()
```

A function with a return type specified as **void** should not be used in an expression in the calling program. Because it doesn't return a value, it can't sensibly be part of an expression, so using it in this way will cause the compiler to generate an error message.

The Function Body

The desired computation in a function is performed by the statements in the function body following the function header. The first of these in our example declares a variable **result** which is initialized with the value **1.0**. The variable **result** is local to the function, as are all automatic variables declared within a function body. This means that the variable **result** ceases to exist after the function has completed execution.

The calculation is performed in the **for** loop. A loop control variable **i** is declared in the **for** loop which will assume successive values from **1** to **n**. The variable **result** is multiplied by **x** once for each loop iteration, so this occurs **n** times to generate the required value. If **n** is **0**, the statement in the loop will not be executed at all because the loop continuation condition will immediately fail, and **result** will be left as **1.0**.

As we have said, all the variables declared within the body of a function, as well as the parameters, are local to the function. There is nothing to prevent you from using the same names for variables in other functions for quite different purposes. Indeed, it is just as well this is so because it would be extremely difficult to ensure variables names were always unique within a program containing a large number of functions, particularly if the functions were not all written by the same person.

The scope of variables declared within a function is determined in the same way that we have already discussed. A variable is created at the point at which it is defined and ceases to exist at the end of the block containing it. There is one type of variable that is an exception to this - variables declared as static. We shall discuss static variables a little later in this chapter.

 Be careful about masking global variables with local variables of the same name. We discussed this situation back in Chapter 2 and saw how we could use the scope resolution operator :: to avoid any problems.

The return Statement

The **return** statement returns the value of **result** to the point where the function was called. What might immediately strike you is that we have just said **result** ceases to exist on completing execution of the function - so how is it returned? The answer is that a copy is automatically made of the value being returned and this copy is available to the return point in the program.

The general form of the return statement is as follows,

```
return expression;
```

where ***expression*** must evaluate to a value of the type specified in the function header for the return value. The expression can be any expression as long as you end up with a value of the required type. It can include function calls - even a call of the same function in which it appears, as we shall see later in this chapter.

If the type of return value has been specified as **void**, there must be no expression appearing in the **return** statement. It must be written simply as:

```
return;
```

Using a Function

Before you can use a function in a program, you must declare the function using a statement called a **function prototype**.

Function Prototypes

A prototype for a function provides the basic information that the compiler needs to check that a function is used correctly. It specifies the parameters to be passed to the function, the function name and the type of the return value, so it contains essentially the same information as appears in the function header, with the addition of a semicolon. Clearly, the number of parameters and their types must be the same in the function prototype and the function header in the definition of the function.

The prototypes for the functions used in a program must appear before the statements calling them and are usually placed at the beginning of a program. The header files (that is, the files with the extension **.h** which appear between **<** and **>** in an **include** statement) that we have been including for standard library functions include the prototypes of the functions provided by the library.

For our **power()** example, we could write the prototype as follows:

```
double power(double value, int index);
```

 Don't forget that a semicolon is required at the end of a function prototype. Without it, you will get error messages from the compiler.

Note that we have specified different names for the parameters in the function prototype to those we used in the function header when we defined the function. This is just to indicate that it is possible. Most often, the same names are used in the prototype and in the function header in the definition of the function, but this doesn't *have* to be so. The parameter names in the function prototype can be selected to aid understanding of the significance of the parameters.

If you like, you can also omit the names altogether in the prototype and just write the following:

```
double power(double, int);
```

155

This is enough for the compiler to do its job. However, it's better practice to use some meaningful name in a prototype as it aids readability, and in some cases it can make all the difference between opacity and lucidity. If you have a function with two parameters of the same type (suppose our index was also of type **double** in the function **power()** for example), the use of suitable names can indicate which parameter appears first and which second.

TRY IT OUT - Using a Function

We can see how all this goes together in an example exercising our **power()** function:

```cpp
// EX5_01.CPP
// Declaring, defining, and using a function
#include <iostream.h>

double power(double x, int n);    // Function prototype

int main(void)
{
   int index = 3;               // Raise to this power
   double x = 3.0;              // Different x from that in function power
   double y = 0.0;

   y = power(5.0, 3);          // Passing constants as arguments
   cout << endl
        << "5.0 cubed = " << y;

   cout << endl
        << "3.0 cubed = "
        << power(3.0, index);   // Outputting return value

   x = power(x, power(2.0, 2.0)); // Using a function as an argument
   cout << endl                   // with auto conversion of 2nd parameter
        << "x = " << x;

   cout << endl;
   return 0;
}

// Function to compute integral powers of a double value
// First argument is value, second argument is power index
double power(double x, int n)
   {                                    // Function body starts here...
      double result = 1.0;                    // Result stored here
      for(int i = 1 ; i<=n ; i++)
         result *= x;
      return result;
   }                                    // ...and ends here
```

FYI Note that this example produces some compiler warnings because of type conversion, but it runs just fine. We will explain the reasons for the warnings in the following discussion.

This shows some of the ways in which we can use the function **power()**, specifying the arguments in a variety or ways. If you run this example, you'll get the following output:

```
Ex5_01                                              _ □ X
5.0 cubed = 125
3.0 cubed = 27
x = 81
Press any key to continue
```

How It Works

After the usual **#include** statement for input/output, we have the prototype for the function **power()**. If you tried deleting this and recompiling the program, the compiler wouldn't be able to process the calls to the function in **main()**.

In a change to previous examples, we have used the new keyword **void** in the function **main()** where the parameter list would usually appear to indicate that no parameters are to be supplied. Previously, we left the parentheses enclosing the parameter list empty, which is also interpreted in C++ as indicating that there are no parameters, but it is better to specify the fact by using the keyword **void**. As we saw, the keyword **void** can also be used as the return type for a function to indicate that no value is returned. If you specify the return type of a function as **void**, you must not place a value in any **return** statement within the function, otherwise you will get an error message from the compiler.

You will have gathered from some of our previous examples that using a function is very simple. To use the function **power()** to calculate 5.0^3 and store the result in a variable **y** in our example, we have written this:

```
y = power(5.0, 3);
```

The values **5.0** and **3** here are called **arguments**. They happen to be constants, but any expression can be used as an argument, as long as a value of the correct type is ultimately produced. The arguments substitute for the parameters **x** and **n** which were used in the definition of the function. The computation is performed using these values and a copy of the result, **125**, will be returned to the calling function, **main()**, and will be stored in **y**. You can think of the function as having this value in the statement or expression in which it appears. We then output the value of **y** to the screen:

```
cout << endl
     << "5.0 cubed = " << y;
```

The next call of the function is used within the output statement,

```
cout << endl
     << "3.0 cubed = "
     << power(3.0, index); // Outputting return value
```

so the value returned is transferred directly to the output stream. Since we have not stored the returned value anywhere, it is otherwise unavailable to us. The first argument in the call of the function here is a constant and the second is a variable.

157

The function **power()** is next used in this statement:

```
x = power(x, power(2.0, 2.0));   // Using a function as an argument
```

Here the function will be called twice. The first call of the function will be the rightmost in the expression, appearing as an argument to the leftmost call. Although the arguments are both specified as **2.0**, the function will actually be called with the first argument as **2.0** and the second argument as **2**. The compiler will convert the **double** value specified for the second argument to **int** because it knows from the function prototype (shown again here) that the type of the second parameter has been specified as **int**.

```
double power(double x, int n);        // Function prototype
```

This will produce the first compiler warning since there is a possible loss of data in converting from a **double** to an **int** and the compiler has instituted this conversion. This results from the checking that the compiler performs to ensure that variable and data types are consistent.

The **double** result **4.0** will be returned and, after converting this to **int** (producing the second compiler warning for possible data loss), the compiler will insert this value as the second argument in the next call of the function, with **x** as the first argument. Since **x** has the value **3.0**, the value of 3.0^4 will be computed and the result, **81.0**, stored in **x**. This sequence of events is illustrated here:

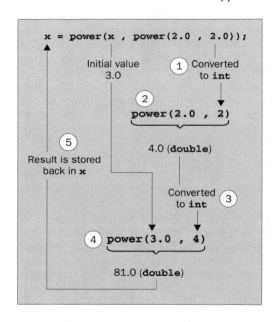

You can eliminate the warnings from the compiler by explicitly casting the values to the required type, as follows:

```
x = power(x, (int)power(2.0, (int)2.0));
```

Although there are no warning messages now, you have not removed the possibility of losing data in the conversion from one type to another but. since it was you that specified that it should be done, the compiler assumes that you know what you are doing.

Passing Arguments to a Function

It is very important to understand how arguments are passed to a function as it will affect how you write functions and how they will ultimately operate. There are also a number of pitfalls to be avoided, so we will look at the mechanism for this quite closely.

The arguments specified when a function is called should usually correspond in type and sequence to the parameters appearing in the definition of the function. As we have seen in the last example, if the type of an argument specified in a function call doesn't correspond with the type of parameter in the function definition, where possible, it will be converted to the required type. If this turns out not to be possible, you will get an error message from the compiler. You will also get a warning message if any conversion needs to be introduced which could cause loss of data, as in conversion from a floating point to an integer, or from type **long** to type **short**, for example. We saw this in the last example that we looked at.

One mechanism used generally in C++ to pass parameters to functions applies when the parameters are specified in the function definition or prototype as ordinary variables (*not* references). This is called the **pass-by-value** method of transferring data to a function.

The Pass-by-value Mechanism

With this mechanism, the variables or constants that you specify as arguments are not passed to a function at all. Instead, copies of the arguments are created and these copies are used as the values to be transferred. We can show this in a diagram using the example of our function **power()**:

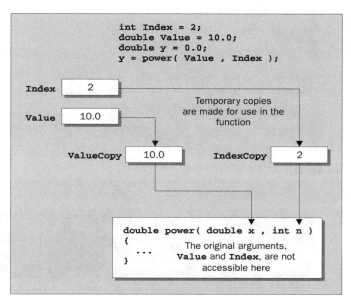

Each time you call the function **power()**, the compiler arranges for copies of the arguments that you specify to be stored in a temporary location in memory. During execution of the functions, all references to the function parameters will be mapped to these temporary copies of the arguments.

> *Purely to help your understanding of the diagram, we have used pseudo-names for the copies generated in the illustration. In reality, they do not exist in this form.*

TRY IT OUT - Passing-by-value

One consequence of the pass-by-value mechanism is that a function can't directly modify the arguments passed. We can demonstrate this by deliberately trying to do so in an example:

```
// EX5_02.CPP
// A futile attempt to modify caller arguments
#include <iostream.h>

int incr10(int num);                    // Function prototype

int main(void)
{
   int num = 3;

   cout << endl
        << "incr10(num) = " << incr10(num)
        << endl
        << "num = " << num;

   cout << endl;
   return 0;
}

// Function to increment a variable by 10
int incr10(int num)           // Using the same name might help...
{
   num += 10;                 // Increment the caller argument - hopefully
   return num;                // Return the incremented value
}
```

How It Works

Of course, this program is doomed to failure. If you run it, you will get this output,

confirming that the original value of **num** remains untouched. The incrementing occurred on the copy of **num** that was generated and was eventually discarded on exiting from the function.

Clearly, the pass-by-value mechanism provides you with a high degree of protection from having your caller arguments mauled by a rogue function, but it is conceivable that we might actually want to arrange to modify caller arguments. Of course, there is a way to do this. Didn't you just know that pointers would turn out to be incredibly useful?

Pointers as Arguments to a Function

When you use a pointer as an argument, the pass-by-value mechanism still operates as before. However, a pointer is an address of another variable and, if you take a copy of this address, the copy still points to the same variable. This is how specifying a pointer as a parameter enables your function to get at a caller argument.

TRY IT OUT - Pass-by-pointer

We can change the last example to use a pointer to demonstrate the effect:

```cpp
// EX5_03.CPP
// A successful attempt to modify caller arguments
#include <iostream.h>

int incr10(int* num);                    // Function prototype

int main(void)
{
   int num = 3;
   int* pnum = &num;                     // Pointer to num

   cout << endl
        << "Address passed = " << pnum;

   cout << endl
        << "incr10(pnum) = " << incr10(pnum);

   cout << endl
           << "num = " << num;

   cout << endl;
   return 0;
}

// Function to increment a variable by 10
int incr10(int* num)            // Function with pointer argument
{
   cout << endl
        << "Address received = " << num;

   *num += 10;                  // Increment the caller argument - confidently
   return *num;                 // Return the incremented value
}
```

How It Works

In this example, the principal alterations from the previous version relate to passing a pointer **pnum** in place of the original variable **num**. The prototype for the function now has the parameter type specified as a pointer to **int** and the **main()** function has the pointer **pnum** declared and initialized with the address of **num**. The function **main()** and the function **incr10** output the address sent and the address received respectively, to verify that the same address is indeed being used in both places.

If you run this
program, you
will get output
similar to this:

```
Ex5_03
Address passed = 0x0064FDF0
Address received = 0x0064FDF0
incr10( pnum ) = 13
num = 13
Press any key to continue
```

 FYI   The address values produced by your computer may be different from those shown above, but the two values should be identical to each other.

The output shows that, this time, the variable **num** has been incremented and has a value that is now identical to that returned by the function.

In the rewritten version of the function **incr10()**, both the statement incrementing the value passed to the function and the **return** statement now need to de-reference the pointer in order to use the value stored.

Passing Arrays to a Function

You can also pass an array to a function but, in this case, the array is not copied, even though a pass-by-value method of passing arguments still applies. The array name is converted to a pointer and a copy of the pointer to the beginning of the array is passed to the function. This is quite advantageous, as copying large arrays could be very time consuming.

TRY IT OUT - Passing Arrays

We can illustrate the ins and outs of this by writing a function to compute the average of a number of values that are passed to a function in an array:

```cpp
// EX5_04.CPP
// Passing an array to a function
#include <iostream.h>
double average(double array[], int count);        //Function prototype

int main(void)
{
   double values[] =
             { 1.0, 2.0, 3.0, 4.0, 5.0, 6.0, 7.0, 8.0, 9.0, 10.0 };

   cout << endl
        << "Average = "
        << average(values, (sizeof values)/(sizeof values[0]));

   cout << endl;
   return 0;
}

// Function to compute an average
double average(double array[], int count)
```

```
{
    double sum = 0.0;                    // Accumulate total in here
    for(int i = 0 ; i<count ; i++)
        sum += array[i];                 // Sum array elements

    return sum/count;                    // Return average
}
```

How It Works

The function **average()** is designed to work with an array of any length. As you can see from the prototype, it accepts two arguments: the array and a count of the number of elements. Since we want it to work with arrays of arbitrary length, the array parameter appears without a dimension specified.

The function is called in **main()** in this statement,

```
cout << endl
     << "Average = "
     << average(values, (sizeof values)/(sizeof values[0]));
```

with the first argument as the array name, **values**, and the second argument as an expression which evaluates to the number of elements in the array.

> *You will recall this expression using the operator **sizeof** from when we looked at arrays in Chapter 4.*

Within the body of the function, the computation is expressed in the way you would expect. There is no significant difference between this and the way we would write the same computation if we implemented it directly in **main()**.

If you run the example, it will produce the following output:

This confirms that everything works as we anticipated.

TRY IT OUT - Using Pointer Notation when Passing Arrays

However, we haven't exhausted all the possibilities here. As we determined at the outset, the array name is passed as a pointer, in fact, as a copy of a pointer so, within the function, we need not necessarily deal with the data as an array at all. We could modify the function in the example to work with pointer notation throughout, in spite of the fact that we are using an array.

```
// EX5_05.CPP
// Handling an array in a function as a pointer
#include <iostream.h>
```

```
    double average(double* array, int count);        //Function prototype

int main(void)
{
    double values[] =
                { 1.0, 2.0, 3.0, 4.0, 5.0, 6.0, 7.0, 8.0, 9.0, 10.0 };

    cout << endl
            << "Average = "
            << average(values, (sizeof values)/(sizeof values[0]));

    cout << endl;
    return 0;
}

// Function to compute an average
double average(double* array, int count)
{
    double sum = 0.0;                          // Accumulate total in here
    for(int i = 0 ; i<count ; i++)
        sum += *array++;                       // Sum array elements

    return sum/count;                          // Return average
}
```

How It Works

As you can see, the program needed very few changes to make it work with the array as a pointer. The prototype and the function header have been changed, although neither change is absolutely necessary. If you change both back to the original version with the first parameter specified as a **double** array, and leave the function body written in terms of a pointer, it will work just as well. The most interesting aspect of this version is the **for** loop statement:

```
    sum += *array++;                    // Sum array elements
```

Here, we apparently break the rule about not being able to modify an address specified as an array name because we are incrementing the address stored in **array**. In fact, we are not breaking the rule at all. Remember that the pass-by-value mechanism makes a copy of the original array address and passes that so, here, we are modifying the copy and the original array address will be quite unaffected. As a result, whenever we pass a one-dimensional array to a function, we are free to treat the value passed as a pointer in every sense and change the address in any way we wish.

Naturally, this version produces exactly the same output as the original.

Passing Multi-Dimensional Arrays to a Function

Passing a multi-dimensional array to a function is quite straightforward. To pass a two-dimensional array, for instance, the array declared as follows,

```
    double beans[2][4];
```

you could write the prototype of a hypothetical function **yield()** like this:

```
    double yield(double beans[2][4]);
```

164

FYI You may be wondering how the compiler can know that this is defining an array of the dimensions shown as an argument and not a single array element. The answer is simple. You can't write a single array element as a parameter in a function definition or prototype, although you can pass one as an argument when you call a function. For a parameter accepting a single element of an array as an argument, the parameter would have just a variable name. The array context doesn't apply.

When you are defining a multi-dimensional array as a parameter, you can also omit the first dimension value. Of course, the function will need some way of knowing the extent of the first dimension. For example you could write this,

```
double yield(double beans[][4], int index);
```

where the second parameter would provide the necessary information about the first dimension. Here, the function can operate with a two-dimensional array with any value for the first dimension, but with the second dimension fixed at **4**.

TRY IT OUT - *Passing Multi-Dimensional Arrays*

We could define such a function in an example:

```cpp
// EX5_06.CPP
// Passing a two-dimensional array to a function
#include <iostream.h>

double yield(double array[][4], int n);


int main(void)
{
   double beans[3][4] =
               {   { 1.0,   2.0,   3.0,   4.0 },
                   { 5.0,   6.0,   7.0,   8.0 },
                   { 9.0, 10.0, 11.0, 12.0 }  };

   cout << endl
        << "Yield = " << yield(beans, sizeof beans/sizeof beans[0]);

   cout << endl;
   return 0;
}

// Function to compute total yield
double yield(double beans[][4], int count)
{
   double sum = 0.0;
   for(int i=0 ; i<count ; i++)          // Loop through number of rows
      for(int j=0 ; j<4 ; j++)           // Loop through elements in a row
         sum += beans[i][j];
   return sum;
}
```

How It Works

Here, we have used different names for the parameters in the function header from those in the prototype just to remind you that this is possible but, in this case, it doesn't really improve the program at all. The first parameter is defined as an array of an arbitrary number of rows, each row having four elements. We actually call the function using the array **beans** with three rows. The second argument is specified by dividing the total length of the array in bytes by the length of the first row. This will evaluate to the number of rows in the array.

The computation in the function is simply a nested **for** loop with the inner loop summing elements of a single row and the outer loop repeating this for each row. For what it's worth, the program will display this result:

Using a pointer in a function as an alternative to a multi-dimensional array as an argument doesn't really apply particularly well. When the array is passed, it passes an address value which points to an array of four elements (a row). This doesn't lend itself to an easy pointer operation within the function. We would need to modify the statement in the nested **for** loop to the following,

```
sum += *(*(beans+i)+j);
```

so the computation is probably clearer in array notation.

References as Arguments to a Function

Specifying a parameter to a function as a reference changes the method of passing data for that parameter. The method used is not pass-by-value where an argument is copied before being passed, but **pass-by-reference** where the parameter acts as an alias for the argument passed. This eliminates any copying and allows the function to access the caller argument directly. It also means that the de-referencing, which is required when passing and using a pointer to a value, is also unnecessary.

TRY IT OUT - Pass-by-reference

Let's go back to a revised version of a very simple example, **Ex5_03.cpp**, to see how it would work using reference parameters:

```
// EX5_07.CPP
// Using a reference to modify caller arguments
#include <iostream.h>

int incr10(int& num);                 // Function prototype

int main(void)
{
```

```
        int num = 3;
        int value = 6;

        cout << endl
             << "incr10(num) = " << incr10(num);

        cout << endl
             << "num = " << num;

        cout << endl
             << "incr10(value) = " << incr10(value);

        cout << endl
             << "value = " << value;

     cout << endl;
     return 0;
}

// Function to increment a variable by 10
int incr10(int& num)          // Function with reference argument
{
   cout << endl
        << "Value received = " << num;

   num += 10;                 // Increment the caller argument - confidently
   return num;                // Return the incremented value
}
```

How It Works

You should find the way this works quite remarkable. This is essentially the same as **Ex5_03.cpp**, except that the function uses a reference as a parameter. The prototype has been changed to reflect this. When the function is called, the argument is specified just as though it was a pass-by-value operation, so it is used in the same way as the earlier version. The argument value isn't passed to the function. Here, the function parameter is **initialized** with the address of the argument so, whenever the parameter **num** is used in the function, it accesses the caller argument directly.

Just to reassure you that there is nothing fishy about the use of the identifier **num** in **main()** as well as in the function, the function is called a second time with the variable **value** as the argument. At first sight this may give you the impression that it contradicts what we said was a basic property of a reference - that once declared and initialized, it couldn't be reassigned to another variable. The reason that it isn't contradictory is that a reference as a function parameter is created and initialized when the function is called and destroyed when the function ends, so we get a completely new reference each time we use the function.

Within the function, the value received from the calling program is displayed on the screen. Although the statement is essentially the same as the one used to output the address stored in a pointer, because **num** is now a reference, we obtain the data value rather than the address.

This clearly demonstrates the difference between a reference and a pointer. A reference is an alias for another variable and, therefore, can be used as an alternative way of referring to it. It is equivalent to using the original variable name.

The output from this example is as follows:

```
Ex5_07                                                    _ □ ×
Value received = 3
incr10( num ) = 13
num = 13
Value received = 6
incr10( value ) = 16
value = 16
Press any key to continue
```

This shows that the function **incr10()** is directly modifying the variable passed as a caller argument.

You will find that if you try to use a numeric value, such as 20, as an argument to **incr10()**, the compiler will output an error message. This is because the compiler recognizes that a reference parameter can be modified within a function and the last thing you want is to have your constants changing value now and again. It would introduce the kind of excitement in your programs that you can do without.

This security is all very well but, if the function did not modify the value, we would not want the compiler to create all these error messages every time we pass a reference argument that was a constant. Surely there ought to be some way to accommodate this? As Ollie would have said, "There most certainly is Stanley!"

Use of the const Modifier

We can use the **const** modifier with a parameter to a function to tell the compiler that we don't intend to modify it in any way. This will cause the compiler to check that your code indeed does not modify the argument and there will be no error messages when you use a constant argument.

TRY IT OUT - Passing a const

We can modify the previous program to show how the **const** modifier changes the situation.

```cpp
// EX5_08.CPP
// Using a reference to modify caller arguments
#include <iostream.h>

int incr10(const int& num);                    // Function prototype

int main(void)
{
    const int num = 3;   // Declared const to test for temporary creation
    int value = 6;

    cout << endl
         << "incr10(num) = " << incr10(num);

    cout << endl
         << "num = " << num;

    cout << endl
```

```
                       << "incr10(value) = " << incr10(value);

          cout << endl
                 << "value = " << value;

          cout << endl;
          return 0;
      }

      // Function to increment a variable by 10
      int incr10(const int& num)        // Function with const reference argument
      {
          cout << endl
                 << "Value received = " << num;

      //    num += 10;                   // this statement would now be illegal
          return num+10;                 // Return the incremented value
      }
```

How It Works

We declare the variable **num** in **main()** as **const** to show that when the parameter to the function **incr10()** is declared as **const**, we no longer get a compiler message when passing a **const** object.

It has also been necessary to comment out the statement which increments **num** in the function **incr10()**. If you uncomment this line, you will find that the program will no longer compile as the compiler won't allow **num** to appear on the left-hand side of an assignment. When you specified **num** as **const** in the function header and prototype, you promised not to modify it, so the compiler checks that you kept your word.

Everything works as before, except that the variables in **main()** are no longer changed in the function, so the program produces the following output:

```
Ex5_08
Value received = 3
incr10( num ) = 13
num = 3
Value received = 6
incr10( value ) = 16
value = 6
Press any key to continue
```

Now, by using reference arguments we have the best of both worlds. On the one hand, we can write a function that can access caller arguments directly and avoid the copying that is implicit in the pass-by-value mechanism. On the other hand, where we do not intend to modify an argument, we can get all the protection against accidental modification we need by using a **const** modifier with a reference.

Returning Values from a Function

All the example functions that we have created have returned a single value. Is it possible to return anything other than a single value? Well, not directly but, as we said earlier, the single value returned need not be a numeric value; it could also be an address, which provides the key to returning any amount of data. You simply use a pointer. Unfortunately, here is where the pitfalls start, so you need to keep your wits about you for the adventure ahead.

Returning a Pointer

Returning a pointer value is very easy. A pointer value is just an address, so if you want to return the address of some variable **value**, you can just write the following:

```
    return &value;              // Returning an address
```

As long as the function header and function prototype indicate the return type appropriately, we have no problem - at least no apparent problem. Assuming that the variable **value** is of type **double**, the prototype of a function called **treble** which might contain the above **return** statement might be as follows:

```
    double* treble(double data);
```

The parameter list has been defined arbitrarily here.

So let's look at a function that will return a pointer. It's only fair that I warn you in advance - this function doesn't work. Let's assume that we need a function which will return a pointer to three times its argument value. Our first attempt might look like this:

```
// Function to treble a value - mark 1
double* treble(double data)
{
    double result = 0;

    result = 3.0*data;
    return &result;
}
```

TRY IT OUT - Returning a Bad Pointer

We could create a little test program to see what happens (remember that the **treble** function won't work as expected) :

```
//EX5_09.CPP
#include <iostream.h>

double* treble(double);                     // Function prototype

int main(void)
{
    double num = 5.0;                       // Test value
    double* ptr=0;                          // Pointer to returned value

    ptr = treble(num);

    cout << endl
        << "Three times num = " << 3.0*num;
```

```
      cout << endl
           << "Result = " << *ptr;              // Display 3*num

      cout << endl;
      return 0;
  }


  // Function to treble a value - mark 1
  double* treble(double data)
  {
      double result = 0;

      result = 3.0*data;
      return &result;
  }
```

How It Works (or Why It Doesn't)

The function **main()** calls the function **treble()** and stores the address returned, which should point to a value which is three times the argument **num**, in the pointer **ptr**. We then display the result of computing three times **num** followed by the value at the address returned from the function.

On my computer, I get this output:

Clearly, the second line doesn't reflect the correct value of 15, but where's the error? The error arises because we are returning the address of a variable which is local to the function. The variable **result** in the function **treble()** is created when the function begins execution, and is destroyed on exiting from the function, so the memory that the pointer is pointing to no longer contains the original variable value. The memory previously allocated to **result** becomes available for other purposes, and here it has evidently been used for something else.

A Cast Iron Rule for Returning Addresses

There is an absolutely cast iron rule for returning addresses:

Never return the address of a local automatic variable from a function.

Now we have a function that doesn't work, we need to think about what we do to rectify that. We could use a reference and modify the original variable, but that's not what we set out to do. We are trying to return a pointer to some useful data so that, ultimately, we can return more than one item of data. One answer lies in dynamic memory allocation (we saw this in action in the last chapter). With the operator **new**, we can create a new variable in the free store which will continue to exist until it is eventually destroyed by **delete** or until the program ends. The function would then look like this:

171

```
// Function to treble a value - mark 2
double* treble(double data)
{
   double* result = new double(0.0);
   if(!result)
   {
      cout << "Memory allocation failed.";
      exit(1);
   }

   *result = 3.0*data;
   return result;
}
```

Rather than declaring **result** as of type **double**, we now declare it as **double*** and store in it the address returned by the operator **new**. We then have the necessary check that we received a valid address, and exit the program if anything is wrong.

Since the result is a pointer, the rest of the function is changed to reflect this and the address contained in the result is finally returned to the calling program. You could exercise this by replacing the function in the last working example with this version.

You need to remember that with dynamic memory allocation within a function like this, more memory is allocated each time the function is called. The onus is on the calling program to delete the memory when it is no longer required. It is easy to forget to do this in practice, with the result that the free store is gradually eaten up until at some point it is exhausted and the program will fail. This sort of problem is often referred to as a 'memory leak'.

Here you can see how the function would be used. The only changes that we needed to make to the original code once the function was replaced were including the standard library header file and using **delete** to free the memory as soon as we finished with the returned pointer.

```
#include <iostream.h>
#include <stdlib.h>

double* treble(double);                      // Function prototype

int main(void)
{
   double num = 5.0;                         // Test value
   double* ptr=0;                            // Pointer to returned value

   ptr = treble(num);

   cout << endl
        << "Three times num = " << 3.0*num;

   cout << endl
        << "Result = " << *ptr;              // Display 3*num
   delete ptr;                               // Don't forget to free the memory

   cout << endl;
   return 0;
}
```

```
// Function to treble a value - mark 2
double* treble(double data)
{
   double* result = new double(0.0);
   if(!result)
   {
      cout << "Memory allocation failed.";
      exit(1);
   }

   *result = 3.0*data;
   return result;
}
```

Returning a Reference

You can also return a reference from a function. This is just as fraught with potential error as returning a pointer, so you need to take care with this too. Because a reference has no existence in its own right (as it is always an alias for something else), you must ensure that the object referred to still exists after the function completes execution. It's very easy to forget this when you use references in a function because they appear to be just like ordinary variables.

References as return types are of primary significance in the context of object oriented programming. As you will see later in the book, they will enable you to do things which would be impossible without them (for the advanced reader this particularly applies to 'operator overloading'). The principal characteristic that a reference type return value has is that it is an lvalue. This means that you can use the result of a function on the left side of an assignment statement.

TRY IT OUT - Returning a Reference

Let's look at one example which illustrates the use of reference return types and also demonstrates how a function can be used on the left of an assignment operation when it returns an lvalue. We will assume that we have an array containing a mixed set of values. Whenever we want to insert a new value into the array, we want to replace the lowest value.

```
// EX5_10.CPP
// Returning a reference
#include <iostream.h>
#include <iomanip.h>

double& lowest(double A[], int len);   // Prototype of function
                                       //   returning a reference

int main(void)
{
   double array[] =
               { 3.0, 10.0, 1.5, 15.0, 2.7, 23.0,
                 4.5, 12.0, 6.8, 13.5, 2.1, 14.0 };
   int len = sizeof array/sizeof array[0]; // Initialize to number
                                           // of elements
```

173

```
      cout << endl;
      for(int i = 0 ; i<len ; i++)
         cout << setw(6) << array[i];

      lowest(array, len) = 6.9;              // Change lowest to 6.9
      lowest(array, len) = 7.9;              // Change lowest to 7.9

      cout << endl;
      for(i = 0 ; i<len ; i++)
         cout << setw(6) << array[i];

      cout << endl;
      return 0;
   }

double& lowest(double A[], int len)
{
   int j=0;                          // Index of lowest element
   for(int i=1 ; i<len ; i++)
      if(A[j]>A[i])                  // Test for a lower value...
         j = i;                      // ...if so update j
   return A[j];                      // Return reference to lowest element
}
```

How It Works

Let's first take a look at how the function is implemented. The prototype uses **double&** as the specification of the return type for the function **lowest()**, which is, therefore, of type 'reference to **double**'. You write a reference type return value in exactly the same way as we've already seen for variable declarations, appending the **&** to the data type. The function has two parameters specified: a one-dimensional array of type **double**, and an **int** parameter **len** which should specify the length of the array.

The body of the function has a straightforward **for** loop to determine which element of the array passed contains the lowest value. The index, **j**, of the array element with the lowest value is arbitrarily set to **0** at the outset, and then modified within the loop if the current element, **A[i]**, is less than **A[j]**. Thus, on exit from the loop, **j** will contain the index value corresponding to the array element with the lowest value. The **return** statement is as follows:

```
   return A[j];                      // Return reference to lowest element
```

In spite of the fact that this looks identical to the statement which would return a value, because the return type was declared as a reference, this returns a reference to **A[j]** rather than the value that the element contains. The address of **A[j]** is used to initialize the reference to be returned. This reference is created by the compiler because the return type was declared as a reference.

Don't confuse returning **&A[j]** with returning a reference. If you write **&A[j]** as the return value, you are specifying the address of **A[j]** which is a *pointer*. If you do this after having specified the return type as a *reference*, you will get an error message from the compiler.

The function **main()**, which exercises our function **lowest()**, is very simple. An array of type **double** is declared and initialized with 12 arbitrary values, and an **int** variable **len** is initialized to the length of the array. The initial values in the array are output for comparison purposes.

Again, we've used the stream manipulator `setw()` to space the values uniformly, requiring the `#include` statement for `iomanip.h`.

The function **main()** then calls the function **lowest()** on the left side of an assignment to change the lowest value in the array. This is done twice to show that it does actually work and is not an accident. The contents of the array are then output to the display again, with the same field width as before, so corresponding values line up. If you run this example, you should see the following output:

As you can see, with the first call to **lowest()**, the third element of the array, **array[2]**, contained the lowest value, so the function returned a reference to it and its value was changed to **6.9**. Similarly, on the second call, **array[10]** was changed to **7.9**.

This demonstrates quite clearly that returning a reference allows the use of the function on the left side of an assignment statement. The effect is as if the variable specified in the **return** statement appeared on the left of the assignment.

Of course, if you want to, you can also use it on the right side of an assignment, or in any other suitable expression. If we had two arrays **X** and **Y**, with **lenX** and **lenY** elements respectively, we could set the lowest element in the array **X** to twice the lowest element in the array **Y** with this statement:

```
lowest(X, lenX) = 2.0*lowest(Y, lenY);
```

This statement would call our function **lowest()** twice, once with arguments **Y** and **lenY** in the expression on the right side of the assignment, and once with arguments **X** and **lenX** to obtain the address where the result of the right-hand expression is to be stored.

A Teflon-Coated Rule: Returning References

A similar rule to that applicable to returning a pointer from a function also applies to returning references:

 Never return a reference to a local variable in a function.

We will leave the topic of returning a reference from a function for now, but we haven't finished with it yet. We will come back to it again in the context of user-defined types and object oriented programming, when we shall unearth a few more magical things that we can do with references.

Static Variables in a Function

There are some things you can't do with automatic variables within a function. You can't count how many times a function is called, for example, because you can't accumulate a value from one call to the next. There is more than one way to get around this if you need to. For instance, you could use a reference parameter to update a count in the calling program, but this wouldn't help if the function was called from lots of different places within a program. You could use a global variable which you increment from within the function, but globals are risky things to use as they can be accessed from anywhere in a program, which makes it very easy to change them accidentally.

For a general solution, you can declare a variable within a function as **static**. You use exactly the same form of declaration for a **static** variable that we saw in Chapter 2. For example, to declare a variable **count** as **static** you could use this statement:

```
static int count = 0;
```

This also initializes the variable to zero.

 Initialization of a static variable within a function only occurs the first time that the function is called. In fact, on the first call of a function, the **static** variable is created and initialized. It then continues to exist for the duration of program execution, and whatever value it contains when the function is exited is available when the function is next called.

TRY IT OUT - Using Static Variables in Functions

We can demonstrate how a **static** variable behaves in a function with the following simple example:

```
// EX5_11.CPP
// Using a static variable within a function
#include <iostream.h>
void record(void);    // Function prototype, no arguments or return value

int main(void)
{
   record();

   for(int i = 0 ; i<= 3 ; i++)
      record();

   cout << endl;
   return 0;
}

// A function that records how often it is called
void record(void)
{
   static int count = 0;
   cout << endl
```

```
                 << "This is the " << ++count;
     if((count>3) && (count<21))                     // All this....
         cout <<"th";
     else
         switch(count%10)                            // is just to get...
         {
            case 1: cout << "st";
                    break;
            case 2: cout << "nd";
                    break;
            case 3: cout << "rd";
                    break;
            default: cout << "th";                   // the right ending for...
         }                                           // 1st, 2nd, 3rd, 4th, etc.
     cout << " time I have been called";
     return;
}
```

How It Works

Our function here serves only to record the fact that it was called. If you build and execute it, you will get this output:

```
Ex5_11                                                    _ □ ×
This is the 1st time I have been called
This is the 2nd time I have been called
This is the 3rd time I have been called
This is the 4th time I have been called
This is the 5th time I have been called
Press any key to continue
```

The **static** variable **count** is initialized with **0**, and is incremented in the first output statement in the function. Because the increment operation is prefix, the incremented value is displayed by the output statement. It will be **1** on the first call, **2** on the second, and so on. Because the variable **count** is **static**, it continues to exist and retain its value from one call of the function to the next.

The remainder of the function is concerned with working out when **"st"**, **"nd"**, **"rd"**, or **"th"** should be appended to the value of **count** that is displayed. It's surprisingly irregular. (I guess 101 should be 101st rather than 101th, shouldn't it?)

FYI Note the **return** statement. Because the return type of the function is **void**, to include a value would cause a compiler error. You don't actually need to put a **return** statement in this particular case as running off the closing brace for the body of the function is equivalent to the **return** statement without a value. The program would compile and run without error even if you didn't include the **return**.

Recursive Function Calls

When a function contains a call to itself it is referred to as a **recursive function**. A recursive function call can also be indirect, where a function **fun1** calls a function **fun2**, which in turn calls **fun1**.

Recursion may seem to be a recipe for an infinite loop and, if you're not careful, it certainly can be. An infinite loop will lock up your machine and require *Ctrl-Alt -Del*, which is always a nuisance. A prerequisite for avoiding an infinite loop is that the function contains some means of stopping the process.

Unless you have come across the technique before, the sort of things to which recursion may be applied may not be obvious. In physics and mathematics, there are many things which can be thought of as involving recursion. A simple example is the factorial of an integer which for a given integer N, is the product 1x2x3...xN. This is very often the example given to show recursion in operation. However, we shall look at something even simpler.

TRY IT OUT - A Recursive Function

At the start of the chapter (see **Ex5_01.cpp**), we produced a function to compute the integral power of a value, that is to compute x^n . This is equivalent to x multiplied by itself n times. We'll implement this as a recursive function as an elementary illustration of recursion in action.

```cpp
// EX5_12.CPP (based on EX5_01.CPP)
// A recursive version of x to the power n
#include <iostream.h>
#include <stdlib.h>                     // This is for the exit() function

double power(double x, int n);          // Function prototype

int main(void)
{
    int index = 3;                  // Raise to this power
    double x = 3.0;                 // Different x from that in function power
    double y = 0.0;

    y = power(5.0, 3);             // Passing constants as arguments
    cout << endl
        << "5.0 cubed = " << y;

    cout << endl
        << "3.0 cubed = "
        << power(3.0, index);      // Outputting return value

    x = power(x, power(2.0, 2.0)); // Using a function as an argument
    cout << endl                   // with auto conversion of 2nd parameter
        << "x = " << x;

    cout << endl;
    return 0;
}
// Recursive function to compute integral powers of a double value
// First argument is value, second argument is power index
double power(double x, int n)
{
    if(n<0)
    {
```

```
        cout << endl
             << "Negative index, program terminated.";
        exit(1);
    }
    if(n)
        return x*power(x, n-1);
    else
        return 1.0;
}
```

The function **main()** is exactly the same as the previous version so the output is also the same:

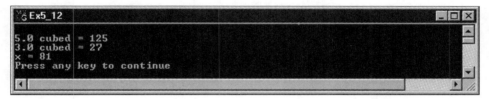

> *Remember that the compiler will produce two type conversion warnings, just as we discussed with* **Ex5_01.cpp**. *These can be safely ignored in this case. You could put explicit conversions in to eliminate them, as we discussed earlier.*

We have added the **#include** statement for **stdlib.h** because we use the **exit()** function in our revised function **power()**. Let's now look at how the function works.

How It Works

We only intend to support positive powers of **x**, so the first action is to check that the value for the power that **x** is to be raised to **n**, is not negative. With a recursive implementation this is essential, otherwise we could get an infinite loop with a negative value for **n** because of the way the rest of the function is written. The **if** statement provides for the value 1.0 being returned if **n** is zero, and in all other cases it returns the result of the expression, **x*power(x, n-1)**. This causes a further call of the function **power()** with the index value reduced by 1.

Clearly, within the function **power()**, if the value of **n** is greater than zero, a further call of the function **power()** will occur. In fact, for a given value of **n** greater than 0, the function will call itself **n** times. The mechanism is illustrated in the figure below, assuming the value 3 for the index argument.

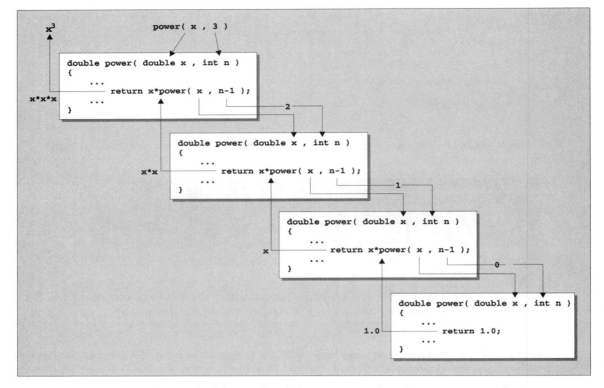

As you see, we need a total of four calls of the **power()** function to generate x^3.

Using Recursion

Unless you have a problem which particularly lends itself to using recursive functions, or if you have no obvious alternative, it's generally better to use a different approach such as a loop. This will be much more efficient than using recursive function calls. Think about what happens with our last example to evaluate a simple product, **x*x*...x n** times. On each call, the compiler will generate copies of the two arguments to the function, and it also has to keep track of the location to return to when each **return** is executed. It will also be necessary to arrange to save the contents of various registers in your computer so that they can be used within the function **power()**, and of course these will need to be restored to their original state at each return from the function. With a quite modest depth of recursive call, the overhead can be considerably greater than if you use a loop.

This is not to say you should never use recursion. Where the problem suggests the use of recursive function calls as a solution, it can be an immensely powerful technique, greatly simplifying the code. We'll see an example where this is the case in the next chapter.

Summary

In this chapter, you have learned about the basics of program structure. You should have a good grasp of how functions are defined, how data can be passed to a function, and how results are returned to a calling program. Functions are fundamental to programming in C++, so everything we do from here on will involve using multiple functions in a program. The key points that you should keep in mind about writing your own functions are these:

▶ Functions should be compact units of code with a well-defined purpose. A typical program will consist of a large number of small functions, rather than a small number of large functions.

▶ Always provide a function prototype for each function defined in your program positioned before you call that function.

▶ Passing values to a function using a reference can avoid the copying implicit in the call-by-value transfer of arguments. Parameters which are not modified in a function should be specified as **const**.

▶ When returning a reference or a pointer from a function, ensure that the object being returned has the correct scope. Never return a pointer or a reference to an object which is local to a function.

The use of references as arguments is a very important concept, so make sure you are confident about using them. We'll see a lot more about references as arguments to functions when we look into object oriented programming.

More about Program Structure

In the previous chapter, you learned about the basics of defining functions and the various ways in which data can be passed to a function. You also saw how results are returned to a calling program.

In this chapter, we will cover the further aspects of how functions can be put to good use, including:

> What is a pointer to a function

> How to define and use pointers to functions

> How to write a function to manage dynamic memory allocation errors

> How to define and use arrays of pointers to functions

> How to write multiple functions with a single name to handle different kinds of data automatically

> How to write a substantial program example using several functions

Pointers to Functions

A pointer stores an address value which, up to now, has been the address of another variable with the same basic type as the pointer. This has provided considerable flexibility in allowing us to use different variables at different times through a single pointer. A pointer can also point to the address of a function. This enables you to call a function through a pointer, that function being the function at the address that was last assigned to the pointer.

As with pointers to variables, pointers to functions must contain the memory address of the function being pointed to. To work properly, however, the pointer must also maintain information about the parameter list for the function it points to, as well as the return type. Therefore, when we declare a pointer to a function, we have to specify the parameter types and the return type of the functions that it can point to, in addition to the name of the pointer.

Declaring Pointers to Functions

Let's declare a pointer **pfun** that can point to functions which take two arguments of type **char*** and **int**, and will return a value of type **double**. The declaration would be as follows:

```
double (*pfun)(char*, int);        // Pointer to function declaration
```

This may look a little weird at first because of all the parentheses. This declares a pointer, **pfun**, which can point to functions which accept two arguments of type pointer to **char** and of type **int**, and which return a value of type **double**. The parentheses around the pointer name, **pfun** and the asterisk are necessary, since without them, it would be a function declaration rather than a pointer declaration. In this case, it would look like this:

```
double *pfun(char*, int); // Prototype for a function
                          // returning type double*
```

This is a prototype for a function **pfun()** with two parameters and returning a pointer to a **double** value. Since we were looking to declare a pointer, this is clearly not what we want at the moment.

The general form of a declaration of a pointer to a function is given here:

return_type (*pointer_name)(list_of_parameter_types);

> *The pointer can only point to functions with the same* **return_type** *and* **list_of_parameter_types** *specified in the declaration.*

This shows that the declaration breaks down into three components:

▶ The return type of the functions that can be pointed to.

▶ The pointer name preceded by an asterisk to indicate it is a pointer.

▶ The parameter types of the functions that can be pointed to.

> *If you attempt to assign a function to a pointer that does not conform to the types in the pointer declaration, you will get an error message from the compiler.*

You can initialize a pointer to a function with the name of a function within the declaration of the pointer. This is what it might look like:

```
long sum(long num1, long num2);    // Function prototype
long (*pfun)(long, long) = sum;    // Pointer to function points to sum()
```

Here, the pointer can be set to point to any function that accepts two arguments of type **long** and also returns a value of type **long**.

Of course, you can also initialize a pointer to a function by using an assignment statement. Assuming that the pointer **pfun** has been declared as above, we could set the value of the pointer to a different function with these statements:

```
long product(long, long);        // Function prototype
    . . .
pfun = product;                  // Set pointer to function product()
```

As with pointers to variables, you must ensure that a pointer to a function is initialized before you use it to call a function. Without initialization, catastrophic failure of your program is guaranteed.

TRY IT OUT - *Pointers to Functions*

To get a proper feel for these newfangled pointers and how they perform in action, let's try one out in a program:

```
// EX6_01.CPP
// Exercising pointers to functions
#include <iostream.h>

long sum(long a, long b);              // Function prototype
long product(long a, long b);          // Function prototype

int main(void)
{
   long (*pdo_it)(long, long);         // Pointer to function declaration

   pdo_it = product;
   cout << endl
        << "3*5 = " << pdo_it(3, 5);   // Call product thru a pointer

   pdo_it = sum;                       // Reassign pointer to sum()
   cout << endl
        << "3*(4+5) + 6 = "
        << pdo_it(product(3, pdo_it(4, 5)), 6); // Call thru a pointer
                                                // twice

   cout << endl;
   return 0;
}

// Function to multiply two values
long product(long a, long b)
{
   return a*b;
}

// Function to add two values
long sum(long a, long b)
{
   return a+b;
}
```

How It Works

This is hardly a useful program, but it does show very simply how a pointer to a function is declared, assigned a value and subsequently used to call a function.

After the usual preamble, we declare a pointer to a function, **pdo_it**, which can point to either of the other two functions that we have defined, **sum()** or **product()**. The pointer is given the address of the function **product()** in this assignment statement:

```
   pdo_it = product;
```

When initializing an ordinary pointer, the name of the function is used in a similar way to that of an array name in that no parentheses or other adornments are required. The function name is automatically converted to an address which is stored in the pointer.

The function **product()** is then called indirectly through the pointer **pdo_it** in the output statement.

```
cout << endl
     << "3*5 = " << pdo_it(3, 5);      // Call product thru a pointer
```

The name of the pointer is used just as if it were a function name and is followed by the arguments between parentheses, exactly as they would appear if the original function name were being used directly.

Just to show that we can do it, we change the pointer to point to the function **sum()**. We then use it again in a ludicrously convoluted expression to do some simple arithmetic. This shows that a pointer to a function can be used in exactly the same way as the function that it points to. The sequence of actions in the expression is shown here:

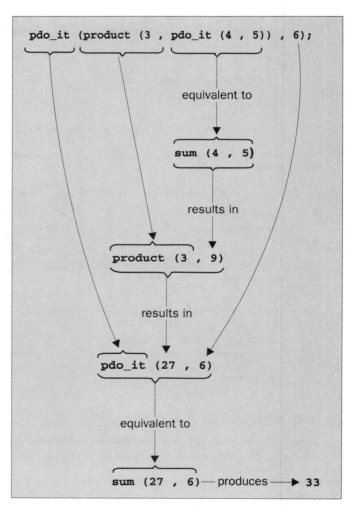

A Pointer to a Function as an Argument

Since 'pointer to a function' is a perfectly reasonable type, a function can also have a parameter that is a pointer to a function. The function can then call the function pointed to by the argument. Since the pointer can be made to point at different functions in different circumstances, this allows the particular function that is to be called from inside a function to be determined in the calling program. In this case, you can pass a function explicitly as an argument.

TRY IT OUT - Passing a Function Pointer

We can look at this with an example. Suppose we need a function that will process an array of numbers by producing the sum of the squares of each of the numbers on some occasions, and the sum of the cubes on other occasions. One way of achieving this is by using a pointer to a function as an argument.

```cpp
//EX6_02.CPP
// A pointer to a function as an argument
#include <iostream.h>

// Function prototypes
double squared(double);
double cubed(double);
double sumarray(double array[], int len, double (*pfun)(double));

int main(void)
{
    double array[] = { 1.5, 2.5, 3.5, 4.5, 5.5, 6.5, 7.5 };
    int len = sizeof array/sizeof array[0];

    cout << endl
         << "Sum of squares = "
         << sumarray(array,len,squared);

    cout << endl
         << "Sum of cubes = "
         << sumarray(array,len,cubed);

    cout << endl;
    return 0;
}

// Function for a square of a value
double squared(double x)
{
    return x*x;
}

// Function for a cube of a value
double cubed(double x)
{
    return x*x*x;
}
```

```
// Function to sum functions of array elements
double sumarray(double array[], int len, double (*pfun)(double))
{
    double total = 0.0;        // Accumulate total in here

    for(int i=0 ; i<len ; i++)
        total +=pfun(array[i]);

    return total;
}
```

How It Works

The first statement of interest is the prototype for the function **sumarray()**. Its third parameter is a pointer to a function which has a parameter of type **double** and returns a value of type **double**.

```
double sumarray(double array[], int len, double (*pfun)(double));
```

The function **sumarray()** processes each element of the array passed as its first argument with whatever function is pointed to by its third argument. The function then returns the sum of the processed array elements.

We call the function **sumarray()** twice in **main()**, the first time with **squared** as the third argument, and the second time using **cubed**. In each case, the address corresponding to the function name used as an argument will be substituted for the function pointer in the body of the function **sumarray()**, so the appropriate function will be called within the **for** loop.

There are obviously easier ways of achieving what this example does, but using a pointer to a function provides you with a lot of generality. You could pass any function to **sumarray()** that you care to define as long as it takes one **double** argument and returns a value of type **double**.

The example will generate this output:

Writing a Function to Handle Memory Allocation Errors

When we used the operator **new** to allocate memory for our variables (as we saw in Chapters 4 and 5), we had to test the value of the pointer returned for null, since **new** returns null if the memory was not allocated. If the memory wasn't allocated, we used the **exit()** function to quit the execution of our program. This is quite adequate in most situations as having no memory left is usually a terminal condition for a program. However, there can be circumstances where you might be able to do something about it if you had the chance. For instance, you might be allocating several blocks of memory for different purposes and, if the program ran out, you could conceivably delete one of the blocks to allow the program to stagger on for a bit. Under these circumstances, there is something you can do which depends on the ability to define a pointer to a function.

Visual C++ supplies a function called **_set_new_handler()** which accepts a pointer to a function as an argument. The function name begins with an underscore which is used to distinguish system functions in Visual C++. This enables you to avoid naming functions that clash with system functions. All you need to do is to avoid using names for your own functions that begin with an underscore. The pointer argument to **_set_new_handler()** should point to a function that you supply which will handle the problem of the operator **new** not being able to allocate memory. This is how the function gets its name. The function that you write will then be called whenever **new** fails to allocate the memory requested. Once you have called the function **_set_new_handler()** with a pointer to your function as an argument, the problem of dealing with the failure of **new** to work properly is fixed for the entire program, assuming that the action in your function is effective. To use the function **_set_new_handler()**, you must include the header file **new.h** into your program.

The function that you supply to handle out-of-memory conditions must have a prototype of the form:

```
int mem_error(size_t space);     // Function to handle memory depletion
```

You can give the function any name you like, but the parameter list and return type must correspond to that shown above. The argument passed to your function will be a count of the number of bytes required. Its type, **size_t** is defined in **new.h** and, as we saw in Chapter 4, is the same as that of values returned by the operator **sizeof**. It is generally used for values which are a count of a number of bytes. With this value available, you may have a chance to scrape up enough memory to carry on. The statement to set the function **mem_error()** to be called when memory is exhausted might be:

```
_set_new_handler(mem_error);
```

The function **_set_new_handler()** actually returns a pointer to the previous handler (which would be the default function if you haven't called **_set_new_handler()** previously). Most of the time, you'll find that it's a good idea to store the pointer returned by the function in a variable so that you can restore the old handler when you no longer need your handler to be active. You can do this by calling **_set_new_handler()** once more, using the pointer to the old handler as the argument.

The header file, **new.h**, also defines a type **_PNH** (for **P**ointer to **N**ew **H**andler) which you can use to declare a pointer to store the address of the previous handler. So, the statement,

```
_PNH pOldHandler=_set_new_handler(mem_error);
```

declares the pointer **pOldHandler**, sets **mem_error()** as the function to handle out of memory conditions and stores the address of the old handler in the pointer **pOldHandler**. If you want to restore the old handler, you just call **_set_new_handler()** once more:

```
_set_new_handler(pOldHandler);
```

Having done whatever you feel is necessary to free up memory in your **mem_error** function, you may want to try again to allocate the memory which previously caused a failure. To do this, you should return a positive value from your function, in which case the **new** operator will automatically retry the failed memory allocation. Of course, if it fails again, it will call your function again. To avoid this, you should make sure that your function doesn't keep returning positive values if it hasn't freed up enough memory. Otherwise, you risk being trapped in an infinite loop. If you return zero from your function, the operator **new** will terminate.

To implement a function to handle the out-of-memory situations with some positive effect, clearly you must have some means of returning memory to the free store. This implies that some dynamically allocated memory must be accessible at the global scope in order that you can make sure that the function is able to release it using **delete**. In most practical cases, this involves some serious work on the program to manage memory, unless you are just setting some memory aside for a rainy day.

Arrays of Pointers to Functions

In the same way as with regular pointers, you can declare an array of pointers to functions. You can also initialize them in the declaration. An example of declaring an array of pointers would be:

```
double sum(double, double);          // Function prototype
double product(double, double);      // Function prototype
double difference(double, double);   // Function prototype
double (*pfun[3])(double,double) =
            { sum, product, difference }; // Array of function pointers
```

Each of the elements in the array are initialized by the corresponding function address appearing in the initializing list between braces. To call the function **product()** using the second element of the pointer array, you would write:

```
pfun[1](2.5, 3.5);
```

The square brackets which selects the function pointer array element appear immediately after the array name and before the arguments to the function being called. Of course, you place a function call through an element of a function pointer array in any appropriate expression that the original function might legitimately appear in, and the index value selecting the pointer can be any expression producing a valid index value.

Initializing Function Parameters

You can initialize the parameters to a function in its prototype. For example, let's suppose that we write a function to display a message, where the message to be displayed is to be passed as an argument. Here is the definition of such a function:

```
void showit(char* message)
{
   cout << endl
        << message;
   return;
}
```

We can initialize the parameter to this function by specifying the initializing string value in the function prototype, as follows:

```
void showit(char* message = "Something is wrong.");
```

Here, the parameter **message** is initialized with the string shown. If you initialize a parameter to a function in the prototype, you can leave out that argument when you call the function and the initializing string is used in the call.

TRY IT OUT - Omitting Function Arguments

Leaving out the function argument when you call the function will execute it with the default value. If you supply the argument, it will replace the default value. We can use the previous function to output a variety of messages.

```
//EX6_03.CPP
// Omitting function arguments
#include <iostream.h>

void showit(char* = "Something is wrong.");

int main(void)
{
   char* mymess = "The end of the world is nigh.";

   showit();                                  // Display the basic message
   showit("Something is terribly wrong!");    // Display an alternative
   showit();                                  // Display the default again
   showit(mymess);                            // Display a predefined message

   cout << endl;
   return 0;
}

void showit(char* message)
{
   cout << endl
        << message;
   return;
}
```

How It Works

If you execute this example, it will produce the following apocalyptic output:

```
Ex6_03
Something is wrong.
Something is terribly wrong!
Something is wrong.
The end of the world is nigh.
Press any key to continue
```

As you can see, we get the default message specified in the function prototype whenever the argument is left out. Otherwise, the function behaves normally.

If you have a function with several arguments, you can provide initial values for as many of them as you like. If you want to omit more than one argument to take advantage of a default value, all arguments to the right of the leftmost argument that you omit must also be left out. For example, if you have this function,

```
int do_it(long arg1=10, long arg2=20, long arg3=30, long arg4=40);
```

and you want to omit one argument in a call to it, you can omit only the last one, **arg4** or if you want to omit **arg3**, you must also omit **arg4**. If you omit **arg2**, **arg3** and **arg4** must also be omitted, and if you want to use the default value for **arg1**, you have to omit all of the arguments in the function call.

You can conclude from this that you need to put the arguments which have default values in the function prototype together in sequence at the end of the parameter list, with the argument most likely to be omitted appearing last.

Exceptions

An exception can be loosely described as an event that you did not expect to occur. Error conditions that arise in your program are exceptions, but any unusual condition that arises, such as erroneous input, could be considered as an exception. So far, we have typically handled error conditions by using an **if** statement to test some expression and then executing some specific code to deal with the error. C++ also provides another, more general mechanism for handling exceptions which allows you to separate the code that deals with these conditions from the code that executes when such conditions do not arise. This mechanism uses three new keywords:

try	identifies a code block in which an exception can occur.
throw	causes an exception condition to be originated.
catch	identifies a block of code which handles an exception generated by a **throw** expression.

Throwing and Catching Exceptions

We can see how exception handling works by working through an example. Let's use a very simple context for this. Suppose we write a program to read the height of a person in inches and then display the height in meters. Let's also suppose that we want to validate the height entered so that we won't accept any values greater than 100 inches, or less than 9 inches.

We could code this, using exception handling, as follows:

```
// EX6_04.CPP  Using exception handling
#include <iostream.h>

int main(void)
{
    int Height = 0;
    double InchesToMeters = 0.0254;
```

```
      char ch = 'y';

      while(ch == 'y'||ch =='Y')
      {
         cout << "Enter a height in inches: ";
         cin >> Height;          // Read the height to be converted

         try                     // Defines try block in which
         {                       // exceptions may be thrown
            if(Height > 100)
               throw "Height exceeds maximum";    // Exception thrown
            if(Height < 9)
               throw "Height below minimum";       // Exception thrown

               cout << (double)Height*InchesToMeters << " meters" << endl;

               cout << "Do you want to continue (y or n)?";
               cin >> ch;
         }

         catch(char* aMessage)         // start of catch block which
         {                             // catches exceptions of type char*
            cout << aMessage << endl;
         }
      }
      return 0;
}
```

If you run this example, typical output will be as shown below:

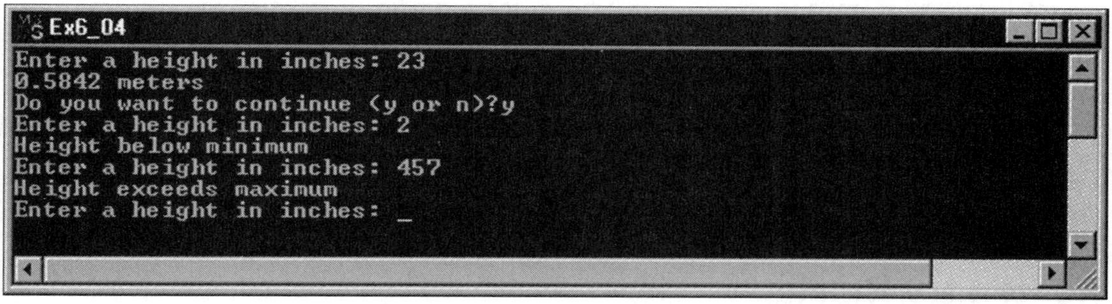

```
M₅ Ex6_04                                                        _ □ ✕
Enter a height in inches: 23
0.5842 meters
Do you want to continue (y or n)?y
Enter a height in inches: 2
Height below minimum
Enter a height in inches: 457
Height exceeds maximum
Enter a height in inches: _
```

The code in the **try** block is executed in the normal sequence. The **try** block serves to define where an exception can be raised. You can see from the output that when an exception is thrown, the **catch** block is executed and execution continues with the statement following the **catch** block. When no exception is thrown, the **catch** block is not executed. Because the **try** block encloses the statement to output the converted value of **Height** and read a value for **ch** and, because these follow the **throw** statements, they are not executed when an exception is thrown. When a throw statement is executed, control passes immediately to the first statement in the **catch** block.

Throwing Exceptions

Exceptions can be thrown anywhere within a **try** block. In our example, we throw two exceptions in the **throw** statements that you see. The operand of the **throw** statements determines a type for the exception - both the exceptions thrown here are of type **char***. The operand following the **throw** keyword can be any expression and the type of the result of the expression determines the type of exception thrown.

Exceptions can also be thrown in functions called from within a **try** block and caught by a **catch** block following the **try** block. You could add a function to the previous example to demonstrate this, with the definition:

```
void TestThrow(void)
{
    throw "An exception from within a function!";
}
```

If you place a call to this function after the statement reading the value for **ch**, this exception will be thrown and caught by the **catch** block on every iteration when no other exception is thrown. Don't forget the function prototype if you add the definition of **TestThrow()** to the end of the source code.

Catching Exceptions

The **catch** block following the **try** block in our example catches any exception of type **char***. This is determined by the exception declaration that appears in parentheses following the keyword **catch**. You must supply at least one **catch** block for a **try** block, and the **catch** blocks must immediately follow the **try** block. A **catch** block will catch all exceptions (of the correct type) that occur anywhere in the code in the immediately preceding **try** block, including those thrown in any functions that are called directly or indirectly within the **try** block.

If you want to specify that a **catch** block is to handle any exception that is thrown in a **try** block, you must put an ellipsis, **...**, between the parentheses enclosing the exception declaration:

```
catch (...)
{
    // code to handle any exception
}
```

This **catch** block must appear last if you have other **catch** blocks defined for the **try** block.

Nested try Blocks

You can nest **try** blocks one within another. With this situation, if an exception is thrown from within an inner **try** block which is not followed by a **catch** block corresponding to the type of exception thrown, the catch handlers for the outer **try** block will be searched. You can demonstrate this by modifying the previous example as follows:

```
// EX6_04A.cpp
// Nested try blocks
#include <iostream.h>

int main(void)
{
    int Height = 0;
    double InchesToMeters = 0.0254;
    char ch = 'y';
```

```
   try                          // Outer try block
   {
      while(ch == 'y'||ch =='Y')
      {
         cout << "Enter a height in inches: ";
         cin >> Height;          // Read the height to be converted

         try                     // Defines try block in which
         {                       // exceptions may be thrown
            if(Height > 100)
               throw "Height exceeds maximum";    // Exception thrown
            if(Height < 9)
               throw Height;                       // Exception thrown

               cout << (double)Height*InchesToMeters
                    << " meters" << endl;

               cout << "Do you want to continue( y or n)?";
               cin >> ch;
         }

         catch(char* aMessage)      // start of catch block which
         {                          // catches exceptions of type char*
            cout << aMessage << endl;
         }
      }
   }
   catch(int BadHeight)
   {
      cout << BadHeight << " inches is below minimum" << endl;
   }
   return 0;
}
```

Here, there is an extra **try** block enclosing the **while** loop and the second exception thrown in the inner **try** block has been changed to throw the value of **Height** when this value is below the minimum. If you run this version of the program, the exception of type **char*** is caught by the **catch** block for the inner **try** block. The exception of type **int** has no catch handler for exceptions of this type, so the catch handler for the outer try block is executed. In this case, the program ends immediately because the statement following the **catch** block is a **return**.

Function Overloading

Suppose we have a function which generates the maximum value of an array of values of type **double**:

```
// Function to generate the maximum value in an array of type double
double maxdouble(double array[], int len)
{
   double max = array[0];

   for(int i=1 ; i<len ; i++)
      if(max<array[i])
         max = array[i];
```

```
        return max;
    }
```

We now want to create a function which produces the maximum value from an array of type **long**, so we write another function very similar to the first, with this prototype:

```
    long maxlong(long array[], int len);
```

We now have to be careful to choose the appropriate function name to match the particular task in hand. We may also need the same function for other types of argument. It seems a pity that we have to keep inventing new names. Ideally, we would want to use the function **max()** for whatever type and have the appropriate version executed.

The mechanism which enables you to do this is called **function overloading**.

What is Function Overloading?

Function overloading allows you to use the same name in different functions and, in each instance, to have the compiler choose the correct version for the job. There has to be a clear method for the compiler to decide which function is to be called in any particular instance. The key to this is the parameter list. A series of functions with the same name, but which are differentiated by their parameter lists, is a set of overloaded functions. So, following on from our **max()** function example, we could have overloaded functions with the following prototypes:

```
    int max(int array[], int len);           // Prototypes for
    long max(long array[], int len);         // a set of overloaded
    double max(double array[], int len);     // functions
```

Each of the functions must have a different parameter list. Note that a different return type does not distinguish a function adequately. You can't add the function,

```
    double max(long array[], int len);
```

to the above set as it would clash with this prototype,

```
    long max(long array[], int len);
```

causing the compiler to complain and the program not to compile. This may seem slightly unreasonable, until you remember that you can write statements such as this:

```
    long numbers[] = {1,2,3,3,6,7,11,50,40};
    int len = sizeof numbers/sizeof number[0];
    ...
    max(numbers, len);
```

If the return type were permitted as a distinguishing feature, the version of **max()** taking a **long** array as an argument and returning a **double** value would be allowed, along with the original three. In the instance of the code above, the compiler would be unable to decide whether to choose the version with a **long** return type or a **double** return type. You could however *replace* the **long** function with the **double** function in the set as the parameter lists would remain unique.

Each function in a set of overloaded functions is sometimes said to have a unique **signature**, determined by the parameter list.

TRY IT OUT - *Using Overloaded Functions*

We can exercise the overloading capability with the function **max()** that we have already defined. We can include the three versions for **int**, **long** and **double** arrays.

```
// EX6_05.CPP
// Using overloaded functions
#include <iostream.h>

int max(int array[], int len);              // Prototypes for
long max(long array[], int len);            // a set of overloaded
double max(double array[], int len);        // functions

int main(void)
{
   int small[] = { 1,24,34,22};
   long medium[] = { 23,245,123,1,234,2345};
   double large[] = { 23.0,1.4,2.456,345.5,12.0, 21.0};
   int lensmall = sizeof small/sizeof small[0];
   int lenmedium = sizeof medium/sizeof medium[0];
   int lenlarge = sizeof large/sizeof large[0];

   cout << endl << max(small, lensmall);
   cout << endl << max(medium, lenmedium);
   cout << endl << max(large, lenlarge);

   cout << endl;
   return 0;
}

// Maximum of ints
int max(int x[], int len)
{
   int max = x[0];
   for(int i=1 ; i<len ; i++)
      if(max<x[i])
         max = x[i];
   return max;
}

// Maximum of longs
long max(long x[], int len)
{
   long max = x[0];
   for(int i=1 ; i<len ; i++)
      if(max<x[i])
         max = x[i];
   return max;
}

// Maximum of doubles
double max(double x[], int len)
{
```

```
    double max = x[0];
    for(int i=1 ; i<len ; i++)
        if(max<x[i])
            max = x[i];
    return max;
}
```

How It Works

We have three prototypes for the three overloaded versions of the function **max()**. In each of the three output statements, the appropriate version of the function **max()** is selected by the compiler based on the argument list types. The example works as expected and produces this output:

```
Ex6_05
34
2345
345.5
Press any key to continue
```

When to Overload Functions

Function overloading provides you with the means of ensuring that a function name describes the function being performed and is not confused by extraneous information such as the type of data being processed. This is akin to what happens with basic operations in C++. To add two numbers, you use the same operator, regardless of the type of the operands. Our overloaded function **max()** has the same name, regardless of the type of data being processed. This helps to make the code more readable and makes these functions easier to use.

> *The intent of function overloading is clear: to enable the same operation to be performed with different operands using a single function name. So, whenever you have a series of functions that do essentially the same thing, but with different types of arguments, you should overload them and use a common function name.*

Function Templates

The last example was somewhat tedious in that we had to repeat essentially the same code for each function, but with different variable and parameter types. We also have the possibility of having a recipe for automatically generating functions of various types. The code to do this for a particular group of functions is called a **function template**.

The functions generated by a function template all have the same basic code, but have one or more types defined as parameters to the template. As you use a particular form of a template function, a version is automatically generated to support the type of arguments that you use. We can demonstrate this by defining a function template for the function **max()** in the previous example.

Using a Function Template

We can define a template for the function **max()** as follows:

```
template<class T> T max( T x[], int len )
{
    T max = x[0];
    for(int i=1 ; i<len ; i++)
        if(max<x[i])
            max = x[i];
    return max;
}
```

The **template** keyword identifies this as a template definition. The angled brackets following the **template** keyword enclose the type parameters that are used to create a particular instance of the function. The keyword **class** before the **T** indicates that the **T** is the type parameter for this template, class being a generic term for type. We shall see later in the book that defining a class is essentially defining your own data type. Consequently, you have basic types in C++, such as **int** and **char**, and you also have the types that you define yourself.

Wherever **T** appears in the definition of the template, it is to be replaced by a specific type, such as **long** for example, when an instance of the template is created. If you try this out manually, you will see that this will generate a perfectly satisfactory function for calculating the maximum value from an array of type **long**. The creation of a particular function instance is referred to as **instantiation**. In our case, we have just one type parameter **T**, but in general there can be more.

Each time you use the function **max()** in your program, the compiler will check to see if a function corresponding to the type of arguments that you have used in the function call already exists. If the function required does not exist, the compiler will create one by substituting the argument type that you have used in place of the parameter **T** throughout the source code in the template definition. You could exercise this template with the same function **main()** that we used in the previous example:

```
// EX6_05A.CPP
// Using function templates
#include <iostream.h>

// Template for function to compute the maximum element of an array
template<class T> T max( T x[], int len )
{
    T max = x[0];
    for(int i=1 ; i<len ; i++)
        if(max<x[i])
            max = x[i];
    return max;
}

int main(void)
{
    int small[] = { 1,24,34,22};
    long medium[] = { 23,245,123,1,234,2345};
    double large[] = { 23.0,1.4,2.456,345.5,12.0, 21.0};
    int lensmall = sizeof small/sizeof small[0];
    int lenmedium = sizeof medium/sizeof medium[0];
    int lenlarge = sizeof large/sizeof large[0];
```

```
    cout << endl << max(small, lensmall);
    cout << endl << max(medium, lenmedium);
    cout << endl << max(large, lenlarge);

    cout << endl;
    return 0;
}
```

If you run this program, it will produce exactly the same output as the previous example. For each of the statements outputting the maximum value in an array, a new version of **max()** is instantiated using the template. Of course, if you add another statement calling the function **max()** with one of the types used previously, no new version of the code is generated.

Note that using a template does not reduce the size of your compiled program in any way. A version of the source code is generated for each function that you require. In fact, using templates can generally increase the size your program as functions can be created automatically, even though an existing version might satisfactorily be used by casting the argument accordingly. You can force the creation of particular instances of a template by explicitly including a declaration for it. For example, if you wanted to ensure that an instance of the template for the function **max()** was created corresponding to the type **float**, you could place the following declaration after the definition of the template:

```
    float max(float, int);
```

This will force the creation of this version of the function template. It does not have much value in the case of our program example, but it can be useful when you know that several versions of a template function might be generated, but you want to force the generation of a subset that you plan to use with arguments cast to the appropriate type where necessary.

An Example Using Functions

We have covered a lot of ground in C++ up to now, and a lot on functions in this chapter. After wading through a varied menu of language capabilities, it's not always easy to see how they relate to one another. Now would be a good point to see how some of this goes together to produce something with more meat than a simple demonstration program.

Let's work through a more realistic example to see how a problem can be broken down into functions. The process will involve defining the problem to be solved, analyzing the problem to see how it can be implemented in C++, and finally writing the code. The approach here is aimed at illustrating how various functions go together to make up the final result, rather than a tutorial on how to develop a program.

Implementing a Calculator

Suppose we need a program that will act as a calculator, not one of these fancy devices with lots of buttons and gizmos designed for those who are easily pleased, but one for people who know where they are going, arithmetically speaking. We can really go for it and enter a calculation from the keyboard as a single arithmetic expression, and have the answer displayed immediately. An example of the sort of thing that we might enter is:

2*3.14159*12.6*12.6/2 + 25.2*25.2

To avoid unnecessary complications, for the moment we won't allow parentheses in the expression and the whole computation must be entered in a single line. However, to allow the user to make the input look attractive, we *will* allow blanks to be placed anywhere. The expression entered may contain the operators multiply, divide, add, and subtract represented by *, /, +, and - respectively, and should be evaluated with normal arithmetic rules, so that multiplication and division take precedence over addition and subtraction.

The program should allow as many successive calculations to be performed as required and should terminate if an empty line is entered. It should also have helpful and friendly error messages.

Analyzing the Problem

A good place to start is with the input. The program will read in an arithmetic expression of any length on a single line, which can be any construction within the terms given. Since nothing is fixed about the elements making up the expression, we will have to read it as a string of characters and then work out within the program how it's made up. We can decide arbitrarily that we will handle a string of up to 80 characters, so we could store it in an array declared within these statements:

```
const int MAX = 80;      // Maximum expression length including '\0'
char buffer[MAX];        // Input area for expression to be evaluated
```

To change the maximum length of the string processed by the program, we will only need to alter the initial value of **MAX**.

We need to determine the basic structure of the information in the input string, so let's break it down step-by-step.

The first thing to do is to make sure that it is as uncluttered as possible so, before we start analyzing, we will get rid of all the blanks in the input string. The function that we will use to do this we can call **eatspaces()**. This can work by moving through the input buffer - which will be the array **buffer[]** where we store the input - using two indexes to it, **i** and **j**, and shuffling elements up to overwrite any blank characters. The indexes **i** and **j** start out at the beginning of the buffer, and we store element **j** at position **i**. As we progress through the elements, each time we find a blank we don't increment **i**, so it will get overwritten by the next element. We can illustrate the logic of this in the following figure:

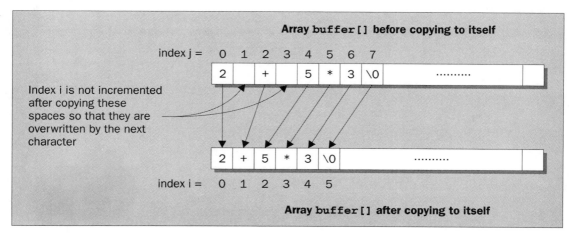

Array buffer[] before copying to itself

index j = 0 1 2 3 4 5 6 7

| 2 | | + | | 5 | * | 3 | \0 | .... | |

Index i is not incremented after copying these spaces so that they are overwritten by the next character

| 2 | + | 5 | * | 3 | \0 | .... | |

index i = 0 1 2 3 4 5

Array buffer[] after copying to itself

This process is one of copying the contents of the array buffer[] to itself, but not copying any blanks. The diagram shows the array buffer before the copying process and after it has been completed.

The next thing we need to do is to evaluate the expression. We will define the function **expr()**, which will return the value of the whole expression in the input buffer. To decide what goes on inside the function, we need to look into the structure of the input in more detail. The add and subtract operators have the lowest precedence and so are evaluated last. We can envisage the string as one or more terms, we can refer to as a **term**, connected by 'add' operators which can be either the operator + or the operator -. We can refer to any of these using the mnemonic **addop**. With this terminology, we can represent the general expression as follows:

    expression: term addop term ... addop term

The expression will contain at least one **term** and can have an arbitrary number of following **addop term** combinations. In fact, assuming that we have removed all the blanks, there are only three legal possibilities for the character following each **term**:

> The next character is `'\0'`, so we are at the end of the string.

> The next character is `'-'`, in which case we should subtract the next **term** from the value accrued for the expression up to this point.

> The next character is `'+'`, in which case we should add the value of the next **term** to the value of the expression accumulated so far.

If anything else follows a **term**, the string is not what we expect, so we will display a message and exit from the program. The structure of an expression is illustrated below:

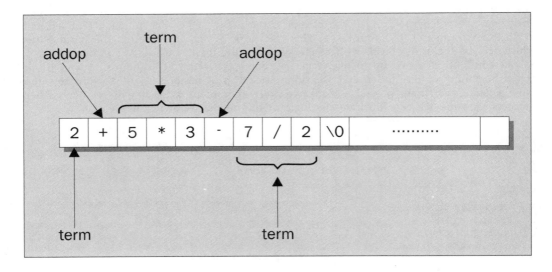

The next thing that we need to know about an input expression is a more detailed and precise definition of a **term**. A **term** is simply a series of numbers that are connected by either the operator ***** or the operator **/**. Therefore, a **term** (in general) will look like this:

```
term: number multop number ... multop number
```

By **multop**, we mean either multiply or divide. What we need is a function **term()** to return the value of a **term**. This will need to progress through the string first by finding a number and then looking for a **multop** followed by another number. If a character is found that is not a **multop**, we will assume that it is an **addop** and return the value that we have found up to that point.

The last thing that we need to understand before writing the program is what a number is. To avoid unnecessary complications, we will only allow a number to be unsigned. Therefore, a number consists of a series of digits that may be followed by a decimal point and some more digits. To determine the value of a number, we move through the buffer finding digits. If we find anything that isn't a digit, we check whether it is a decimal point. If it's not a decimal point, it has nothing to do with a number so we return what we have got. If it is a decimal point, we look for more digits. As soon as we find anything that's not a digit, we have the complete number and we return that. Imaginatively, we'll call the function to sort this out **number()**.

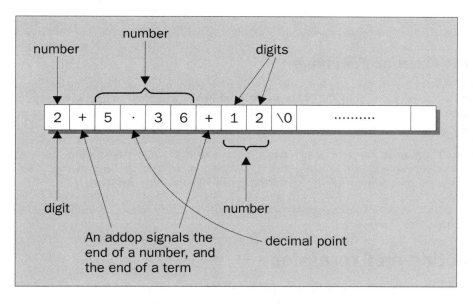

We now have enough understanding of the problem to write some code. We can work through the functions we need, then write a **main()** function to tie them all together. The first, and perhaps easiest, function to write is **eatspaces()** which is going to eliminate the blanks from the input string.

Eliminating Blanks from a String

We can write the prototype for **eatspaces()** as follows:

```
void eatspaces(char* str); // Function to eliminate blanks
```

It doesn't need to return any value since the blanks can be eliminated from the string *in situ*, modifying the original string directly through the pointer provided as an argument. The process for eliminating blanks is a very simple one. We need to copy the string to itself, but overwriting any blanks as we saw earlier in this chapter.

We can define the function to do this as follows:

```
// Function to eliminate blanks from a string
void eatspaces(char* str)
{
   int i=0;             // 'Copy to' index to string
   int j=0;             // 'Copy from' index to string

   while((*(str+i) = *(str+j++)) != '\0')    // Loop while character
                                              // copied is not \0
      if(*(str+i) != ' ')                     // Increment i as long as
         i++;                                 // character is not a blank
   return;
}
```

How the Function Functions

All the action is in the **while** loop. The loop condition copies the string by moving the character at position **j** to the character at position **i**, and then increments **j** to the next character. If the character copied was **'\0'**, we have reached the end of the string, and we are done.

The only action in the loop statement is to increment **i** to the next character if the last character copied was not a blank. If it *is* a blank, **i** will not be incremented and the blank will therefore be overwritten by the character copied on the next iteration.

That wasn't hard, was it? Next, we can try writing the function providing the result of evaluating the expression.

Evaluating an Expression

The function **expr()** needs to return the value of the expression specified in the string that is supplied as an argument, so we can write its prototype as follows:

```
double expr(char* str); // Function evaluating an expression
```

The function declared here accepts a string as an argument and returns the result as type **double**.

Based on the structure for an expression that we worked out earlier, we can draw a logic diagram for the process of evaluating an expression as shown here:

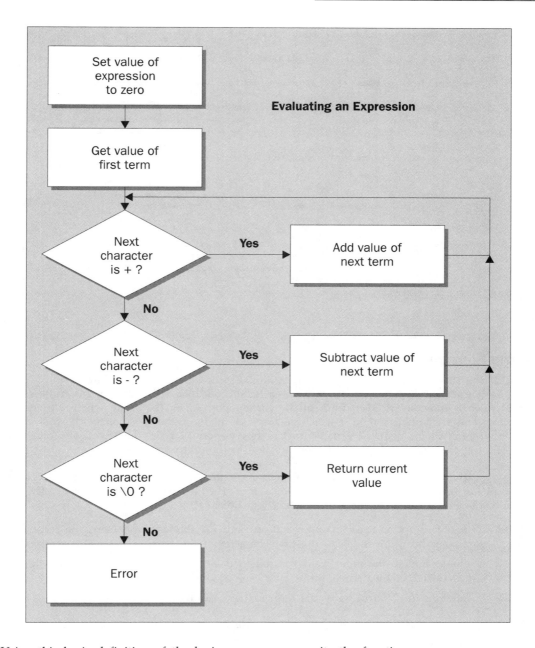

Evaluating an Expression

Using this basic definition of the logic, we can now write the function:

```cpp
// Function to evaluate an arithmetic expression
double expr(char* str)
{
   double value = 0;        // Store result here
   int index = 0;           // Keeps track of current character position
```

```
    value = term(str, index);// Get first term

    for(;;)                    // Infinite loop, all exits inside
    {
        switch(*(str+index++)) // Choose action based on current character
        {
            case '\0':                    // We're at the end of the string
                return value;             // so return what we have got

            case '+':                     // + found so add in the
                value += term(str, index);  // next term
                break;

            case '-':                     // - found so subtract
                value -= term(str, index);  // the next term
                break;

            default:                      // If we reach here the string
                cout << endl              // is junk
                    << "Arrrgh!*#!! There's an error"
                    << endl;
                exit(1);
        }
    }
}
```

How the Function Functions

Considering this function is analyzing any arithmetic expression that you care to throw at it (as long as it uses our operator subset), it's not a lot of code. We define a variable **index** of type **int**, which is intended to keep track of the current position in the string where we are working, and we initialize it to 0 which corresponds to the index position of the first character in the string. We also define a variable **value** of type **double** in which we will accumulate the value of the expression passed to the function in the **char** array **str**.

Since an expression must have at least one term, the first action in the function is to get the value of the first term by calling the function **term()** which we have yet to write. This actually places three requirements on the function **term()**:

▶ It should accept a **char*** pointer and an **int** variable as parameters, the second parameter being an index to the first character of the term in the string supplied.

▶ It should update the index value passed to position it at the character following the last character of the term found.

▶ It should return the value of the term as type **double**.

The rest of the program is an infinite **for** loop. Within the loop, the action is determined by a **switch** statement which is controlled by the current character in the string. If it is a **'+'**, we call the function **term()** to get the value of the next term in the expression and add it to the variable **value**. If it is a **'-'**, we subtract the value returned by **term()** from the variable value. If it is a **'\0'**, we are at the end of the string, so we return the current contents of the variable **value** to the calling program. If it is any other character, it shouldn't be there so, after remonstrating with the user, we end the program!

If either a `'+'` or a `'-'` was found, the loop continues. Each call to `term()` will have moved the value of the variable `index` to the next character after the last term, which should be either another `'+'` or `'-'`, or the end of string character `'\0'`. Thus, the function either terminates normally when `'\0'` is reached, or abnormally by calling `exit()`. We need to remember the `#include` for `stdlib.h` to provide the prototype for the function `exit()` when we come to put the whole program together.

It would also be possible to analyze an arithmetic expression using a recursive function. If we think about the definition of an expression slightly differently, we could specify it as being either a term, or a term followed by an expression. The definition here is recursive and this approach is very common in defining language structures. This definition provides just as much flexibility as the first, but using this as the base concept, we could arrive at a recursive version of `expr()` instead of using a loop as we did in the implementation above. You might wish to try this alternative approach as an exercise, once we have completed the first version.

Getting the Value of a Term

The function `term()` needs to return a **double** value and receive two arguments: the string being analyzed and an index to the current position in the string. There are other ways of doing this, but this arrangement is quite straightforward. We can, therefore, write the prototype of the function `term()` as follows:

```
double term(char* str, int& index);        // Function analyzing a term
```

We have specified the second parameter as a reference. This is because we want the function to modify the value of the variable `index` in the calling program to position it at the character following the last character of the term found in the input string. We could return `index` as a value but then we would need to return the value of the term in some other way, so the arrangement we have chosen seems quite natural.

The logic for analyzing a term is going to be similar in structure to that for an expression. It is a number, potentially followed by one or more combinations of a multiply or a divide operator and another number. We can write the definition of the function `term()` as follows:

```
// Function to get the value of a term
double term(char* str, int& index)
{
   double value = 0;                // Somewhere to accumulate the result

   value = number(str, index);     // Get the first number in the term

   // Loop as long as we have a good operator
   while((*(str+index)=='*')||(*(str+index)=='/'))
   {

      if(*(str+index)=='*')                // If it's multiply,
         value *= number(str, ++index);    // multiply by next number

      if(*(str+index)=='/')                // If it's divide,
         value /= number(str, ++index);    // divide by next number
   }
   return value;               // We've finished so return what we've got
}
```

How the Function Functions

We first declare a local **double** variable value in which we will accumulate the value of the current term. Since a term must contain at least one number, the first action in the function is to obtain the value of the first number by calling the function **number()** and storing the result in the variable **value**. We implicitly assume that the function **number()** will accept the string and an index to the string as arguments and will return the value of the number found. Since the function **number()** must also update the index to the string to the position after the number that was found, we will again specify the second parameter as a reference when we come to define that function.

The rest of the function is a **while** loop which continues as long as the next character is **'*'** or **'/'**. Within the loop, if the character found at the current position is **'*'**, we increment the variable **index** to position it at the beginning of the next number, call the function **number()** to get the value of the next number, and then multiply the contents of the variable **value** by the value returned. In a similar manner, if the current character is **'/'**, we increment the variable **index** and divide the contents of **value** by the value returned from **number()**. Since the function **number()** automatically alters the value of the variable index to the character following the number found, **index** is already set to select the next available character in the string on the next iteration.

The loop terminates when a character other than a multiply or divide operator is found, whereupon the current value of the term accumulated in the variable **value** is returned to the calling program.

The last analytical function that we require is **number()** which needs to determine the numerical value of any number appearing in the string.

Analyzing a Number

Based on the way we have used the function **number()** within the function **term()**, we need to declare it with this prototype:

```
double number(char* str, int& index);   // Function to recognize a number
```

The specification of the second parameter as a reference will allow the function to update the argument in the calling program directly, which is what we require.

We can make use of a function provided in a standard C++ library here. The header file **ctype.h** provides declarations for a range of functions for testing single characters. They include these functions:

Declaration	Function
`int isalpha(int c)`	Returns **True** if the argument is alphabetic, **False** otherwise.
`int isupper(int c)`	Returns **True** if the argument is an upper case letter, **False** otherwise.
`int islower(int c)`	Returns **True** if the argument is a lower case letter, **False** otherwise.
`int isdigit(int c)`	Returns **True** if the argument is a digit, **False** otherwise.

> *There are also a number of other functions provided by* **ctype.h**, *but we won't grind through all the detail. If you're interested, you can look them up in Visual C++* **Help**. *Simply do a search on 'is routines' or look at* **Visual C++ Books\C/ C++\Run-Time Library Reference\Run-Time Routines by Category\Character Classification** *for a fuller listing.*

We only need the last of the functions shown above in our program. Remember that **isdigit()** is testing a character, such as the character '9' (ASCII character 57 in decimal notation) for instance, not a numeric 9, because the input is a string.

We can define the function **number()** as follows:

```
// Function to recognize a number in a string
double number(char* str, int& index)
{
   double value = 0.0;                 // Store the resulting value

   while(isdigit(*(str+index)))        // Loop accumulating leading digits
      value=10*value + (*(str+index++) - 48);

                                       // Not a digit when we get to here
   if(*(str+index)!='.')               // so check for decimal point
      return value;                    // and if not, return value

   double factor = 1.0;                // Factor for decimal places
   while(isdigit(*(str+(++index))))    // Loop as long as we have digits
   {
      factor *= 0.1;                   // Decrease factor by factor of 10
      value=value + (*(str+index)-48)*factor;   // Add decimal place
   }

   return value;                       // On loop exit we are done
}
```

How the Function Functions

We declare the local variable **value** as **double** which will hold the value of the number. We initialize it with **0.0** because we will add in the digit values as we go along.

As the number in the string is a series of digits as ASCII characters, the function will walk through the string accumulating the value of the number digit by digit, as we saw earlier in the logic diagram for this function. This will occur in two steps, accumulating digits before the decimal point, and then if we find a decimal point, accumulating the digits after it.

The first step is in the **while** loop that continues as long as the current character selected by the variable **index** is a digit. The value of the digit is extracted and added to the variable **value** in the loop statement:

```
   value = 10*value + (*(str+index++) - 48);
```

The way this is constructed might bear a little closer examination. A digit character will have an ASCII value between 48, corresponding to the digit 0, and 57 corresponding to the digit 9. Thus, if we subtract 48 from the ASCII code for a digit, we will convert it to its equivalent numeric value, which is the actual digit. We have put parentheses around the subexpression `*(str+index++) - 48` to make it a little clearer what's going on. The contents of the variable `value` are multiplied by 10 in order to shift the value left one decimal place before adding in the digit, since we will find digits from left to right - that is, the most significant digit first. This process is illustrated here:

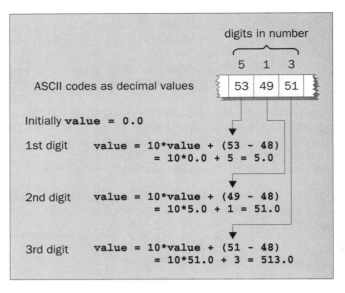

As soon as we come across something other than a digit, it is either a decimal point, or something else. If it's not a decimal point, we have finished, so we return the current contents of the variable `value` to the calling program. If it is a decimal point, we accumulate the digits corresponding to the fractional part of the number in the second loop. In this loop, we use the variable `factor`, which has the initial value 1.0, to set the decimal place for the current digit, and consequently it is multiplied by 0.1 for each digit found. Thus, the first digit after the decimal point will be multiplied by 0.1, the second by 0.01, the third by 0.001, and so on. This process is illustrated here:

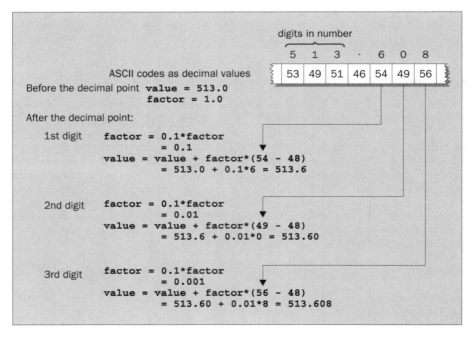

As soon as we find a non-digit character, we are done so, after the second loop, we return the value of the variable **value**.

We now have almost the whole thing. We just need a **main()** function to read the input and drive the process.

Putting the Program Together

The first thing we need to do is to collect the **#include** statements together and assemble the function prototypes at the beginning of the program for all the functions used in this program:

```
// EX6_06.CPP
// A program to implement a calculator

#include <iostream.h>                   // For stream input/output
#include <stdlib.h>                     // For the exit() function
#include <ctype.h>                      // For the isdigit() function

void eatspaces(char* str);             // Function to eliminate blanks
double expr(char* str);                // Function evaluating an expression
double term(char* str, int& index);   // Function analyzing a term
double number(char* str, int& index); // Function to recognize a number

const int MAX = 80;            // Maximum expression length including '\0'
```

We have also defined a global variable **MAX**, which is the maximum number of characters in the expression processed by the program (including the terminating null).

Now all we need to define is the function **main()** and our program is complete. It needs to read a string and exit if it is empty, otherwise call the function **expr()** to evaluate the input and display the result. This process should repeat indefinitely. That doesn't sound too difficult, so let's give it a try.

```
int main(void)
{
    char buffer[MAX] = {0};     // Input area for expression to be evaluated

    cout << endl
         << "Welcome to your friendly calculator."
         << endl
         << "Enter an expression, or an empty line to quit."
         << endl;

    for(;;)
    {
        cin.getline(buffer, sizeof buffer);   // Read an input line
        eatspaces(buffer);                     // Remove blanks from input

        if(!buffer[0])                         // Empty line ends calculator
            return 0;

        cout << "\t= " << expr(buffer)         // Output value of expression
             << endl << endl;
    }
}
```

211

How the Function Functions

In **main()**, we set up the **char** array **buffer** to accept an expression up to 80 characters long (including the terminating null). The expression is read within the infinite **for** loop using the input function **getline()**, and after obtaining the input, blanks are eliminated from the string by calling the function **eatspaces()**.

The only other things that the function **main()** provides for are within the loop. They are to check for an empty string which will consist of just the null character, **'\0'**, in which case the program ends, and to output the value of the string produced by the function **expr()**.

Once you've typed in all the functions, you should get output similar to that shown:

```
Ex6_06                                                    _ □ ✕

Welcome to your friendly calculator.
Enter an expression, or an empty line to quit.
22/7
        = 3.14286

2*3 +4 - 0.35*6
        = 7.9

2.5*3.5/1.4 + 7.8*.76/7
        = 7.09686

1/2 + 1/3 + 1/4 + 1/5 + 1/6 + 1/7
        = 1.59286

1/3 + 1/5 + 1/7 + 1/9
        = 0.787302

Press any key to continue
```

You can enter as many calculations as you like and when you are fed up with it, you just press *Enter* to end the program.

Extending the Program

Now that we've got a working calculator, we can start to think about extending it. Wouldn't it be nice to be able to handle parentheses in an expression? It can't be that difficult, can it? Let's give it a try. We need to think about the relationship between something in parentheses which might appear in an expression, and the kind of expression analysis that we have made so far. Let's look at an example of the kind of expression we want to handle:

2*(3+4)/6-(5+6)/(7+8)

The first thing to notice is that the expressions in parentheses always form part of a term in our original parlance. Whatever sort of computation you come up with, this is always true. In fact, if we could substitute the value of the expressions within parentheses back in the original string, we would have something that we can already deal with. This indicates a possible approach to handling parentheses. Why don't we treat an expression in parentheses as just another number, and modify the function **number()** to sort out the value of whatever appears between the parentheses?

That sounds like a good idea, but 'sorting out' the expression in parentheses requires a bit of thought - but not much as it happens. The clue to success is in our terminology. An **expression** appears within parentheses, a minute replica of a full-blown expression, and we already have a function **expr()** which will return the value of an expression. All we need to do is to get the function **number()** to work out what the contents of the parentheses are and extract those from the string to be passed to the function **expr()**, so recursion really simplifies the problem. What's more, we don't need to worry about nested parentheses. Since any set of parentheses will contain what we have defined as an expression, they will be taken care of automatically. Recursion wins again.

Let's have a stab at rewriting the function **number()** to recognize an expression between parentheses:

```cpp
// Function to recognize an expression in parentheses
// or a number in a string
double number(char* str, int& index)
{
    double value = 0.0;                    // Store the resulting value

    if(*(str+index) == '(')               // Start of parentheses
    {
        char* psubstr = 0;                 // Pointer for substring
        psubstr = extract(str, ++index);   // Extract substring in brackets
        value = expr(psubstr);             // Get the value of the substring
        delete[]psubstr;                   // Clean up the free store
        return value;                      // Return substring value
    }

    while(isdigit(*(str+index)))          // Loop accumulating leading digits
        value=10*value + (*(str+index++) - 48);
                                          // Not a digit when we get to here
    if(*(str+index)!='.')                 // so check for decimal point
        return value;                      // and if not, return value

    double factor = 1.0;                   // Factor for decimal places
    while(isdigit(*(str+(++index))))       // Loop as long as we have digits
    {
        factor *= 0.1;                     // Decrease factor by factor of 10
        value=value + (*(str+index)-48)*factor; // Add decimal place
    }

    return value;                          // On loop exit we are done
}
```

How the Function Functions

Look how little has changed to support parentheses. I suppose it's a bit of a cheat, since we use a function (**extract()**) that we haven't written yet, but for one extra function you get as many levels of nested parentheses as you want. This really is icing on the cake. All down to the magic of recursion!

The first thing that the function **number()** now does is to test for a left parenthesis. If it finds one, it calls another function, **extract()** to extract the substring between the parentheses from the original string. The address of this new substring is stored in the pointer **psubstr** so we then apply the function **expr()** to the substring by passing this pointer as an argument. The result is stored in **value**, and after releasing the memory allocated on the free store in the function **extract()** (as we will eventually implement it), we return the value obtained for the substring as though it were a regular number. Of course, if there is no left parenthesis to start with, the function **number()** continues exactly as before.

We now need to write the function **extract()**. It's not difficult, but it's also not trivial. The main complication comes from the fact that the expression within parentheses may also contain other sets of parentheses, so we can't just go looking for the first right parenthesis we can find. We need to watch out for more left parentheses as well, and for every one we find, ignore the corresponding right parenthesis. We can do this by maintaining a count of left parentheses as we go along, adding one to the count for each left parenthesis we find, and if the count is not zero, subtracting one for each right parenthesis. Of course, if the count is zero, and we find a right parenthesis, we are at the end of the substring. The mechanism is illustrated in the following figure:

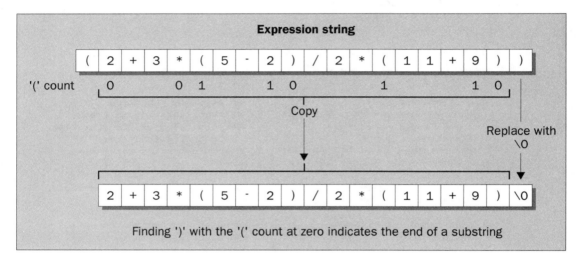

Finding ')' with the '(' count at zero indicates the end of a substring

Since the string extracted here contains subexpressions enclosed within parentheses, eventually **extract()** will be called again to deal with those.

The function **extract()** will also need to allocate memory for the substring and return a pointer to it. Of course, the index to the current position in the original string will need to end up selecting the character following the substring, so the parameter for that will need to be specified as a reference. The prototype of **extract()** will, therefore, be as follows:

```
char* extract(char* str, int& index);    //Function to extract a substring
```

We can now have a shot at the definition of the function.

```
// Function to extract a substring between parentheses
// (requires string.h)
char* extract(char* str, int& index)
{
    char buffer[MAX];        // Temporary space for substring
    char* pstr=0;            // Pointer to new string for return
    int numL = 0;            // Count of left parentheses found
    int bufindex = index;    // Save starting value for index
```

```
        do
        {
            buffer[index-bufindex] = *(str+index);
            switch(buffer[index-bufindex])
            {
                case ')':
                    if(numL==0)
                    {
                        buffer[index-bufindex] = '\0';  // Replace ')' with '\0'
                        ++index;
                        pstr = new char[index-bufindex];
                        if(!pstr)
                        {
                            cout << "Memory allocation failed,"
                                 << " program terminated.";
                            exit(1);
                        }
                        strcpy(pstr,buffer);  // Copy substring to new memory
                        return pstr;          // Return substring in new memory
                    }
                    else
                        numL--;               // Reduce count of '(' to be matched
                    break;

                case '(':
                    numL++;                   // Increase count of '(' to be matched
                    break;
            }
        }while(*(str+index++) != '\0');// Loop - don't overrun end of string

        cout << "Ran off the end of the expression, must be bad input."
             << endl;
        exit(1);
        return pstr;
}
```

How the Function Functions

We declare a **char** array to hold the substring temporarily. We don't know how long the substring will be, but it can't be more than **MAX** characters. We can't return the address of **buffer** to the calling function because it is local and will be destroyed on exit from the function. Therefore, we will need to allocate some memory on the free store when we know how long the string is. We do this by declaring a variable, **psubstr**, of type 'pointer to **char**' which we will return by value when we have the substring safe and sound in the free store memory.

We also declare a counter **numL**, to keep track of left parentheses in the substring (as we discussed earlier). The initial value of **index** (when the function begins execution) is stored in the variable **bufindex**. This will be used in combination with incremented values of **index** to index the array **buffer**.

The executable part of the function is basically one big **do-while** loop. Within the loop, the substring is copied from **str** to **buffer** one character at each iteration, with a check for left or right parentheses each cycle. If a left parenthesis is found, **numL** is incremented, and if a right parenthesis is found and **numL** is non-zero, it is decremented. When we find a right parenthesis and **numL** is zero, we have found the end of the substring. The **')'** in the

215

substring in **buffer** is then replaced by **'\0'**, and sufficient memory is obtained on the free store to hold the substring. The substring in **buffer** is then copied to the memory obtained through the operator **new** by using the function **strcpy()**, which is defined in the header file **string.h**. This function copies the string specified by the second argument, **buffer**, to the address specified by the first argument, **pstr**.

If we fall through the bottom of the loop, it means that we hit the **null** at the end of the expression in **str** without finding the complementary right bracket, so we display a message and terminate the program.

Running the Modified Program

After replacing the function **number()** in the old version of the program, adding the **#include** statement for **string.h**, and incorporating the prototype and the definition for the new function, **extract()**, we have just written, you are ready to roll with an all-singing, all-dancing calculator. If you have assembled all that without error, you will get output something like that shown below:

```
Ex6_06A                                                    _ □ ✕

Welcome to your friendly calculator.
Enter an expression, or an empty line to quit.
1/(1+1/(1+1/(1+1)))
        = 0.6

(1/2 - 1/3)*(1/3 - 1/4)*(1/4 - 1/5)
        = 0.000694444

2.5*(1.5 - 3/(1.3-2*1.5))-1
        = 7.16176

2,5 - 28

Arrrgh!*#!! There's an error
Press any key to continue
```

The friendly and informative error message in the last output line is due to the use of the comma instead of the decimal point in the expression above it, in what should be 2.5. As you can see, we get nested parentheses to any depth with a relatively simple extension of the program, all due to the amazing power of recursion.

Summary

You now have a reasonably comprehensive knowledge of writing and using functions. You have used a pointer to a function in a practical context for handling out-of-memory conditions in the free store, and you have used overloading to implement a set of functions providing the same operation with different types of parameters. We will also see more of overloading functions in the following chapters.

You also worked through the calculator example which we implemented using several functions. But remember that all the uses of functions up to now have been in the context of a traditional procedural approach to programming. When we come to look at object oriented programming, we will still use functions extensively, but with a very different approach to program structure and the design of a solution to a problem.

A Taste of Old-Fashioned Windows

In this chapter, we're going to take a break from delving into C++ language features. Instead, we're going to take a look at the nuts and bolts of a Windows program to see how you can put one together without the assistance of the AppWizard and MFC.

In later chapters, you will be using MFC for your Windows application development so that you can take advantage of its object-oriented approach and have the application framework set up for you by the AppWizard. Here though, you'll see how Windows operates behinds the scenes, knowledge that will be useful to you even when you are developing applications using MFC.

You can almost write a Windows program with the knowledge that you have of C++ so far. However, before we can go any further in our quest for Windows enlightenment, there is one other feature of the language that you need to understand - the **struct**. So, after first taking a look at how to define and use a **struct**, we will write a simple Windows program to display text in a window.

By the end of this chapter you will have learnt:

> What a **struct** is in C++ and how it is used in Windows programming

> What the basic structure of a window is

> What the Windows API is and how it is used

> What Windows messages are and how you deal with them

> What notation is commonly used in Windows programs

> What the basic structure of a Windows program is

The struct in C++

Before we start programming in Windows, there is one language feature that we need to understand because it is used so extensively in the programming interface to Windows. It is called a structure and is defined using the keyword **struct**. The **struct** is something of a hangover from the C language that preceded C++, and is functionally replaceable by a class. (We'll meet classes in the next chapter.) However, because Windows was written in C before C++ became widely used, the **struct** appears pervasively in Windows programming, so we have to take a look at it here.

What is a struct?

All the variables and data types that we have seen up to now have consisted of a single type of entity - a number of some kind, a character, or a string. Life, the universe and everything are usually a bit more complicated than that, unless you are among those who believe the answer is 42, in which case all you'll ever need is an **int**.

Describing virtually anything requires you to define several values, in order that the description is of practical use in a program. If you think about the information that might be needed to describe something as simple as a book for instance, you might consider title, author, publisher, date of publication, number of pages, price, topic or classification and ISBN number just for starters, and you can probably come up with a few more without too much difficulty. You could specify separate variables to contain each of the parameters that you need to describe a book, but ideally you would want to have a single data type, **BOOK** say, which embodied all of these parameters. I'm sure you won't be surprised to hear that this is exactly what a **struct** can do for you.

Defining a struct

Let's stick with the notion of a book, and suppose that we just want to include the title, author, publisher and year of publication within our definition of a book. We could declare a structure to accommodate this as follows:

```
struct BOOK
{
    char Title[80];
    char Author[80];
    char Publisher[80];
    int Year;
};
```

This doesn't define any variables, but it actually creates a new variable type, called **BOOK**. The keyword **struct** defines **BOOK** as such, and the elements making up a **struct** of this type are defined within the curly braces. Note that each line defining an element in the **struct** is terminated by a semicolon, and that a semicolon also appears after the closing brace. The elements of a **struct** can be of any type, except the same type as the **struct** being defined. We couldn't have an element of type **BOOK** included in the structure definition for **BOOK**, for example. You may think this to be a limitation, but note that we could include a pointer to a variable of type **BOOK**, as we shall see a little later on.

The elements **Title**, **Author**, **Publisher** and **Year** enclosed between the braces in the definition above may also be referred to as members or fields of the structure **BOOK**. Each variable of type **BOOK** will contain the members **Title**, **Author**, **Publisher** and **Year**. We can now create variables of type **BOOK** in exactly the same way that we create variables of any other type:

```
BOOK Novel;                 // Declare variable Novel of type BOOK
```

This declares a variable **Novel** which we can now use to store information about a book. All we need now is to understand how we get data into the various members that make up a variable of type **BOOK**.

Initializing a struct

The first way to get data into the members of a **struct** is to define initial values in the declaration. Suppose we wanted to initialize the variable **Novel** to contain the data for one of my favorite books, *Paneless Programming*, published in 1981 by the Gutter Press. This is a story of a guy performing heroic code development while living in an igloo, and as you probably know, inspired the famous Hollywood box office success, *Gone with the Window*. It was written by I.C. Fingers, who is also the author of that seminal three volume work, *The Connoisseur's Guide to the Paper Clip*, so with this wealth of information we can write the declaration for the variable **Novel** as:

```
BOOK Novel =
{
    "Paneless Programming",      // Initial value for Title
    "I.C. Fingers",              // Initial value for Author
    "Gutter Press",              // Initial value for Publisher
    1981                         // Initial value for Year
};
```

The initializing values appear between braces, separated by commas, in much the same way that we defined initial values for members of an array. As with arrays, the sequence of initial values obviously needs to be the same as the sequence of the members of the **struct** in its definition. Each member of the structure **Novel** will have the corresponding value assigned to it, as indicated in the comments.

Accessing the Members of a struct

To access individual members of a **struct**, you can use the **member selection operator**, which is a period. To refer to a particular member, you write the **struct** variable name, followed by a period, followed by the name of the member that you want to access. To change the member **Year** of our structure, **Novel**, we could write,

```
Novel.Year = 1988;
```

which would set the value of this particular member to 1988. You can use a member of a structure in exactly the same way as any other variable of the same type as the member. To increment the member **Year** by two, for example, we can write:

```
Novel.Year += 2;
```

This increments the value of the member **Year** just like any other variable.

TRY IT OUT - Using structs

Let's use another console application example to exercise a little further how referencing the members of a **struct** works. Suppose we want to write a program to deal with some of the things you might find in a yard, such as those that are illustrated in the professionally landscaped yard on the next page:

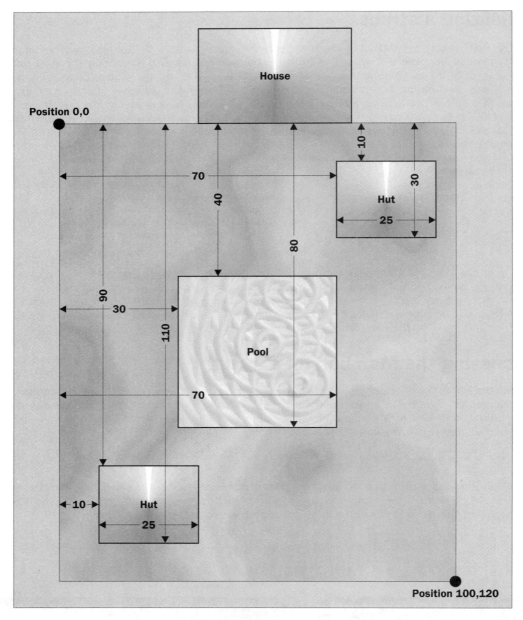

The Yard Layout

We have arbitrarily assigned the coordinates 0,0 to the top left corner of the yard. The bottom right corner has the coordinates 100,120. Thus, the first coordinate value is a measure of the horizontal position relative to the top left corner, with values increasing from left to right, and the second coordinate is a measure of the vertical position from the same reference point, with values increasing from top to bottom. The illustration also shows the position of the pool and that of the two huts relative to the top left-hand corner of the yard. Since the yard, the huts and the pool are all rectangular, we could define a **struct** which will be convenient for us to use in their representation:

```
struct RECTANGLE
{
    int Left;                   // Top left point
    int Top;                    // coordinate pair

    int Right;                  // Bottom right point
    int Bottom;                 // coordinate pair
};
```

The first two members of the **RECTANGLE** structure type correspond to the coordinates of the top left point of a rectangle, and the next two to the coordinates of the bottom right point. We can use this in an elementary example dealing with the objects in the yard as follows:

```
// EX7_01.CPP
// Exercising structures in the yard
#include <iostream.h>

// Definition of a struct to represent rectangles
struct RECTANGLE
{
    int Left;                   // Top left point
    int Top;                    // coordinate pair

    int Right;                  // Bottom right point
    int Bottom;                 // coordinate pair
};

// Prototype of function to calculate the area of a rectangle
long Area(RECTANGLE& aRect);

// Prototype of a function to move a rectangle
void MoveRect(RECTANGLE& aRect, int x, int y);

int main(void)
{
    RECTANGLE Yard = { 0, 0, 100, 120 };
    RECTANGLE Pool = { 30, 40, 70, 80 };
    RECTANGLE Hut1, Hut2;

    Hut1.Left = 70;
    Hut1.Top = 10;
    Hut1.Right = Hut1.Left + 25;
    Hut1.Bottom = 30;

    Hut2 = Hut1;                        // Define Hut2 the same as Hut1
    MoveRect(Hut2, 30, 90);            // Now move it to the right position

    cout << endl
        << "Coordinates of Hut2 are "
        << Hut2.Left << "," << Hut2.Top << " and "
        << Hut2.Right << "," << Hut2.Bottom;

    cout << endl
        << "The area of the yard is "
```

```
                    << Area(Yard);

        cout << endl
             << "The area of the pool is "
             << Area(Pool)
             << endl;

        return 0;
}

// Function to calculate the area of a rectangle
long Area(RECTANGLE& aRect)
{
        return (aRect.Right - aRect.Left)*(aRect.Bottom - aRect.Top);
}

// Function to Move a Rectangle
void MoveRect(RECTANGLE& aRect, int x, int y)
{
        int length = aRect.Right - aRect.Left;    // Get length of rectangle
        int width = aRect.Bottom - aRect.Top;     // Get width of rectangle

        aRect.Left = x;                           // Set top left point
        aRect.Top = y;                            // to new position
        aRect.Right = x + length;                 // Get bottom right point as
        aRect.Bottom = y + width;                 // increment from new position

        return;
}
```

How It Works

Note that the **struct** definition appears at global scope in this example. You'll be able to see it in the ClassView of the Project Workspace Window. This allows us to declare a variable of type **RECTANGLE** anywhere in our **.cpp** file of source code. With a program with a more significant amount of code, such definitions are normally stored in a **.h** file and then added to each **.cpp** file where necessary by using an **#include** directive.

We have defined two functions to process **RECTANGLE** objects. The function **area()** calculates the area of a **RECTANGLE** passed as a reference argument as the product of the length and the width, where the length is the difference between the horizontal positions of the defining points, and the width is the difference between the vertical positions of the defining points. The function **MoveRect()** modifies the defining points of a **RECTANGLE** object to position it at the coordinates **x,y** which are passed as arguments. The position of a **RECTANGLE** object is assumed to be the position of the **Left,Top** point. Since the **RECTANGLE** variable is passed as a reference, the function is able to modify the members of the **RECTANGLE** object directly. After calculating the length and width of the **RECTANGLE** object passed, the **Left** and **Top** members are set to **x** and **y** respectively, and the new **Right** and **Bottom** members are calculated by incrementing **x** and **y** by the length and width of the original **RECTANGLE** object.

In the function **main()**, we initialize the **Yard** and **Pool RECTANGLE** variables with their coordinate positions as shown in the illustration. The variable **Hut1**, represents the hut at the top right in the illustration and its members are set to the appropriate values using assignment statements. The variable **Hut2**, corresponding to the hut at the bottom left of the yard, is first set to be the same as **Hut1** in the assignment statement

```
    Hut2 = Hut1;                        // Define Hut2 the same as Hut1
```

This statement results in copying the values of the members of **Hut1** to the members of **Hut2**. You can only assign a **struct** of a given type to another of the same type. For example, you can't increment a **struct** directly, or use a **struct** in an arithmetic expression.

To alter the position of **Hut2** to its place at the bottom left of the yard, we call the **MoveRect()** function with the coordinates of the required position as arguments. This roundabout way of getting the coordinates of **Hut2** is totally unnecessary and serves only to show how we can use a **struct** as an argument to a function.

After displaying the coordinates of the final version of **Hut2**, we display the area of the **RECTANGLE** objects **Yard** and **Pool** using the function **area()**. If you build and execute this example, you should see the output shown below:

```
Ex7_01                                                        _ □ ×

Coordinates of Hut2 are 30,90 and 55,110
The area of the yard is 12000
The area of the pool is 1600
Press any key to continue
```

The values displayed are what you would expect from the positions and dimensions shown in the illustration of the yard.

The struct RECT

Rectangles are used a great deal in Windows programs. For this reason, there is a **RECT** structure predefined in the header file **windows.h**. Its definition is essentially the same as the structure that we defined in the last example:

```
struct RECT
{
    int left;                      // Top left point
    int top;                       // coordinate pair

    int right;                     // Bottom right point
    int bottom;                    // coordinate pair
};
```

As we shall see, this **struct** is usually used to define rectangular areas on your display for a variety of purposes. Since **RECT** is used so extensively, **windows.h** also contains prototypes for a number of functions to manipulate and modify rectangles. For example, **windows.h** provides the function **InflateRect()** to increase the size of a rectangle and the function **EqualRect()** to compare two rectangles. MFC also defines a class **CRect** which is the equivalent of a **RECT** structure. Once we have understood classes, we will be using this in preference to the **RECT** structure. The **CRect** class provides a very extensive range of functions for manipulating rectangles, and you will be using a number of these when we are writing Windows programs using MFC. You can find the complete list of functions for manipulating **RECT** structures by looking up SDKs\Win32 SDK\Win32\Overviews\Window Management\Rectangles in InfoView.

Using Pointers with a struct

As you might expect, you can create a pointer to a variable of a structure type. In fact, many of the functions declared in **windows.h** that work with **RECT** objects require pointers to a **RECT** as arguments because this avoids the copying of the whole structure when a **RECT** argument is passed to a function. To define a pointer to a **RECT** object for example, the declaration is what you might expect:

```
RECT* pRect = NULL;              // Define a pointer to RECT
```

Assuming that we have defined a **RECT** object, **aRect**, we can set our pointer to the address of this variable in the normal way, using the address-of operator:

```
pRect = &aRect;                 // Set pointer to the address of aRect
```

As we saw when we introduced the idea of a **struct**, a **struct** can't contain a member of the same type as the **struct** being defined, but it can contain a pointer to a **struct**, including a pointer to a **struct** of the same type. For example, we could define the structure:

```
struct ListElement
{
    RECT aRect;                        // RECT member of structure
    ListElement* pNextListElement;     // Pointer to a list element
};
```

The first element of the **ListElement** structure is of type **RECT**, and the second element is a pointer to a structure of type **ListElement** - the same type as that being defined. (Remember that this element isn't of type **ListElement**, it's of type 'pointer to **ListElement**'.) This allows elements to be daisy-chained together, where each element of type **ListElement** can contain the address of the next **ListElement** object in a chain, the last in the chain having the pointer as zero. This is illustrated in the diagram:

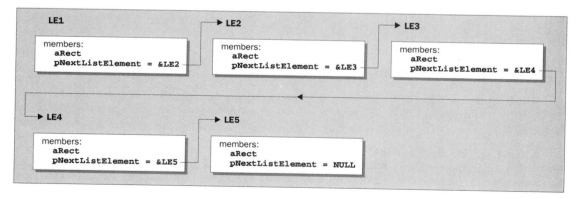

Each box in the diagram represents an object of type **ListElement**. This kind of arrangement is usually referred to as a **linked list**. It has the advantage that as long as you know the first element in the list, you can find all the others. This is particularly important when variables are created dynamically since a linked list can be used to keep track of them all. Every time a new one is created, it's simply added to the end of the list. We will see this sort of thing in operation in a Windows programming example later on.

Accessing Elements through a Pointer

Consider the following statements:

```
RECT aRect = { 0, 0, 100, 100 };
RECT* pRect = &aRect;
```

The first declares and defines the **RECT** object, **aRect**, with the first pair of members initialized to 0,0 and the second pair to 100,100. The second statement declares the pointer to **RECT**, **pRect**, and initializes it with the address of **aRect**. We can now access the members of **aRect** through the pointer with a statement such as:

```
(*pRect).Top += 10;                // Increment the Top member by 10
```

The parentheses to de-reference the pointer here are essential since the member selection operator takes precedence over the de-referencing operator. Without the parentheses, we would be attempting to treat the pointer as a **struct** and to de-reference the member, so the statement would not compile. After executing this statement the **Top** member will have the value **10** and, of course, the remaining members will be unchanged.

The Indirect Member Selection Operator

The method that we used to access the member of a **struct** through a pointer looks rather clumsy. Since this kind of operation crops up very frequently in C++, the language includes a special operator to enable you to express the same thing in a much more readable and intuitive form. It's specifically for accessing members of a **struct** through a pointer and is called the **indirect member selection operator**. We could use it to rewrite the statement to access the **Top** member of **aRect** through the pointer **pRect**, as follows:

```
pRect->Top += 10;                  // Increment the Top member by 10
```

The operator looks like a little arrow and is formed from a minus sign followed by the symbol for 'greater than'. It's much more expressive of what's going on, isn't it? This operator is also used with classes and we will be seeing a lot more of it throughout the rest of the book.

Windows Programming Basics

Now that we've seen how **structs** can be used in C++, let's move on to Windows programming. You have already created a Windows program in Chapter 1 with the aid of the AppWizard and without writing a single line of code. The user interface that was created was actually very sophisticated - we're going to create a much more elementary window for our example in this chapter - but we'll use the window generated by our example in Chapter 1 to illustrate what the various elements that go to make up a window are.

Elements of a Window

You will inevitably be familiar with most, if not all, of the principal elements of the user interface to a Windows program. However, we will go through them anyway since we will be concerned with programming them as elements rather than just using them. The best way for us to understand what the elements of a window can be is to look at one. An annotated version of the window displayed by the example that we saw in Chapter 1 is shown on the following page:

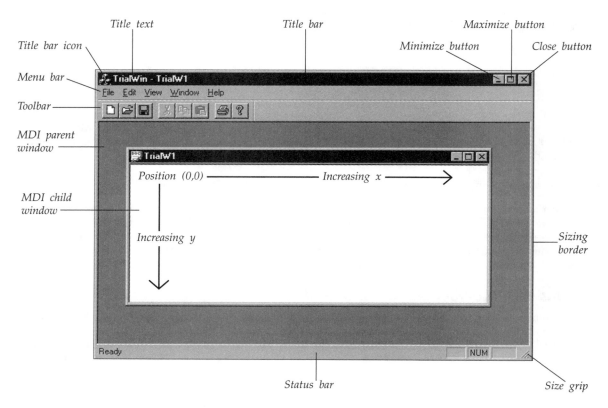

Title text   Title bar   Maximize button

Title bar icon   Minimize button   Close button

Menu bar

Toolbar

MDI parent window

MDI child window

Position (0,0) —————— Increasing x —————→

Increasing y

Sizing border

Status bar   Size grip

The example actually generated two windows. The larger window with the menu and the tool bars is the main, or **parent window**, and the smaller window is a **child window** of the parent. If you ran the example you will have seen that, while the child window can be closed by double-clicking the title bar icon without closing the parent window, closing the parent window automatically closes the child window as well. This is because the child window is owned by, and dependent upon, the parent window. In general, a parent window may have a number of child windows, as we shall see.

The most fundamental parts of a typical window are its **border**, the **title bar icon**, the **title bar** showing the name that you give to the window, and the **client area** (the area in the center of the window not used by the title bar or borders). We can get all of these for free in a Windows program. As you will see, all we have to do is provide some text for the title bar.

The border defines the boundary of a window and may be fixed or sizable. If the border is sizable, you can drag it to alter the size of the window. The window may also possess a size grid which you can use to alter the size of a window while maintaining its aspect ratio - that is the ratio of the width to the height. When we define a window, if we need to, we can modify how the border behaves and appears. Most windows will also have the maximize, minimize and close buttons in the top-right corner of the window. These allow the window to be increased to full screen size, reduced to an icon or closed.

When you click on the title bar icon with the left mouse button, it provides a standard menu for altering or closing the window called the system menu or control menu. The system menu also appears when you right-click on the title bar of a window. While it's optional, it's a good idea to always include the title bar icon in any main windows that your program generates. It can be a very convenient way of closing the program when things don't work as you anticipated.

The client area is the part of the window where you will usually want your program to write text or graphics. You address the client area for this purpose in exactly the same way as the yard that we saw in the example earlier in this chapter. The top-left corner of the client area has the coordinates 0,0, with x increasing from left to right, and y increasing from top to bottom.

The menu bar is optional, but is probably the most common way to control an application. The contents of a menu and the physical appearance of many objects that are displayed in a window, such as the icons on the toolbar that appear above, the cursor and many others, are defined by a **resource file**. We will see a lot more of resource files when we get to write some more sophisticated Windows programs.

The toolbar provides a set of icons that usually act as alternatives to menu options that you use most often. Because they have a pictorial cue to the function provided, they can often make a program easier and faster to use.

Comparing DOS and Windows Programs

When you write a program for DOS, the operating system is essentially subservient. When you want some service to be provided, you call an operating system function. You can even bypass the operating system and provide your own function to communicate with your PC hardware if you want. You can address any of the hardware in your machine directly, and for some application areas where the ultimate performance is required - games programs, for example - this is how programs are regularly implemented.

With Windows, it's all quite different. Here your program is subservient and Windows is in control. You must not deal directly with the hardware and all communications with the outside must pass through Windows. When you use a Windows program you are interacting primarily with Windows. Windows is then communicating with the application program on your behalf. Your Windows program is the tail, Windows is the dog, and your program wags only when Windows tells it to.

There are a number of reasons why this is so. First and foremost, since you are potentially always sharing the computer with other programs that may be executing at the same time, Windows has to have primary control in order to manage the sharing of machine resources. If one application was allowed to have primary control in a Windows environment, as well as inevitably making programming more complicated because of the need to provide for the possibility of others, information intended for other applications could be lost. A second reason for Windows being in control is that Windows embodies a standard user interface and needs to be in charge to enforce that standard. You can only display information on the screen using the tools that Windows provides, and then only when authorized.

Event-driven Programs

We already saw in Chapter 1 that a Windows program is event-driven. A significant part of the code required for a Windows application is dedicated to processing events caused by external actions of the user. Activities that aren't directly associated with your application can nonetheless require that bits of your program code are executed. For example, if the user drags the window of another application that is active alongside yours, and this action uncovers part of the client area of the window devoted to your application, your application will need to redraw that part of the window.

Windows Messages

Events are occurrences such as the user clicking the mouse, pressing a key, or a timer reaching zero. For every event, Windows records the event as a message and places the message in a message queue for the program for which the message is intended. If your program is properly organized, by sending a message Windows can tell it that something needs to be done, that some information has become available, or that an event such as a mouse click has occurred. There are many different kinds of messages and they can occur very frequently - many times per second when the mouse is being dragged, for example.

A Windows program must contain a function specifically for handling these messages. The function is often called **WndProc()** or **WindowProc()**, although it doesn't have to be, since Windows accesses the function through a pointer to a function that you supply. So the sending of a message to your program boils down to Windows calling a function that you provide, typically called **WindowProc()**, and passing any necessary data to your program by means of arguments to this function. Within your function **WindowProc()**, it's up to you to sort out what the message is from the data supplied and what to do about it.

Fortunately, you don't need to write code to process every message. You can filter out those that are of interest in your program, deal with those in whatever way you want, and pass the rest back to Windows. Passing a message back to Windows is done by calling a standard function provided by Windows called **DefWindowProc()**, which provides default message processing.

The Windows API

All of the communications between a Windows application and Windows itself use the Windows application programming interface, otherwise known as the **Windows API**. This consists of literally hundreds of functions that are provided as standard with Windows to be used by your application. Structures are often used for passing some kinds of data between Windows and your program which is why we needed to look at them first.

The Windows API covers all aspects of the dialog necessary between Windows and your application. Because there's such a large number of functions, using them in the raw can be very difficult. Just understanding what they all are is a task in itself. This is where Visual C++ comes in. Visual C++ packages the Windows API in a manner which structures the functions in an object oriented manner, and provides an easier way to use the interface with more default functionality. This takes the form of MFC.

Visual C++ also provides an application framework in the form of code generated by the

AppWizard which includes all of the boiler-plate code necessary for a Windows application, leaving you to just customize this for your particular purposes. The example in Chapter 1 illustrated how much functionality Visual C++ is capable of providing without any coding effort on our part. We will discuss this in much more detail when we get to write some examples using AppWizard.

Notation in Windows Programs

In many Windows programs, variable names have a prefix which indicates what kind of value the variable holds and how it's used. There are quite a few prefixes and they are often used in combination. For example, the prefix **lpfn** signifies a long pointer to a function. A sample of what you might come across by way of prefixes is:

Prefix	Meaning
b	A logical variable of type **BOOL**, which is equivalent to **int**
by	Type **unsigned char** - a byte
c	Type **char**
dw	Type **DWORD** which is **unsigned long**
fn	A function
h	A handle, which is used to identify something (usually an **int** value)
i	Type **int**
l	Type **long**
lp	**Long** pointer
n	Type **int**
p	A pointer
s	A string
sz	A zero terminated string
w	Type **WORD** which is **unsigned short**

This use of these prefixes is called Hungarian notation. It was introduced to minimize the possibility of misusing a variable by interpreting it differently from how it was defined or intended to be used. This was easily done in the C language, a precursor of C++. With C++ and its stronger type checking, to avoid such problems you don't need to make such a special effort with your notation. The compiler will always flag an error for type inconsistencies in your program, and many of the kind of bugs that plagued earlier C programs can't occur with C++.

On the other hand, it can still help to make programs easier to understand, particularly when you are dealing with a lot of variables of different types that are arguments to Windows API functions. Since a lot of Windows programs are still written in C, and of course since parameters for Windows API functions are still defined using Hungarian notation, it's still widely used.

You can make up your own mind as to the extent to which you want to use Hungarian notation. It is by no means obligatory. You may choose not to use it at all, but in any event, if you have an idea of how it works, you will find it easier to understand what the arguments to the Windows API functions are. There's a small caveat, however. As Windows has developed, the types of some of the API function arguments have changed slightly, but the variable names that are used remain the same. As a consequence, the prefix may not be quite correct in specifying the variable type.

The Structure of a Windows Program

For a minimum Windows program written using just the Windows API, we will write two functions. These will be a **WinMain()** function where execution of the program begins and basic program initialization is carried out, and a **WindowProc()** function which will be called by Windows to process messages for the application. Usually, the **WindowProc()** part of a Windows program is the larger portion because this is where most of the application specific code will be - responding to messages caused by user input of one kind or another.

While these two functions make up a complete program, they are not directly connected. **WinMain()** doesn't call **WindowProc()**, Windows does. In fact, Windows also calls **WinMain()**. This is illustrated in the diagram:

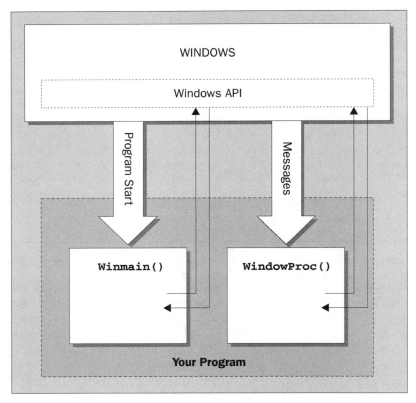

Links between Your Program and Windows

The function **WinMain()** communicates with Windows by calling some of the Windows API functions. The same applies to the function **WindowProc()**. The integrating factor in your Windows program is Windows itself, and Windows links to both **WinMain()** and **WindowProc()**. We will take a look at what the pieces are that make up the functions **WinMain()** and **WindowProc()**, and then assemble the parts into a working example of a simple Windows program.

The WinMain() Function

The **WinMain()** function is the equivalent of the **main()** function in a DOS program. This is where execution starts and where the basic initialization for the rest of the program is carried out. To allow Windows to pass data to it, **WinMain()** has four parameters and a return value of type **int**. Its prototype is:

```
int WINAPI WinMain(
                HINSTANCE hInstance,
                HINSTANCE hPrevInstance,
                LPSTR lpCmdLine,
                int nCmdShow
                );
```

Following the return type specifier, **int**, we have a specification for the function, **WINAPI**, which is new to us. This is a Windows-defined macro which causes the function name and the arguments to be handled in a special way, which happens to correspond to the way that a function is handled in the Pascal language (and the Fortran language). This is different from the way functions are normally handled in C++, in that parameters are passed on to the stack with first or leftmost parameter at the top, and the calling program is responsible for cleaning up the stack after the function has executed. The precise details are unimportant - this is simply the way Windows requires things to be - so we need to put the **WINAPI** specifier in front of the names of functions called by Windows.

You may wonder why there are so many types, such as **HINSTANCE** and others, defined by Windows. This is to provide for implementations of Windows in different machine environments. By defining its own specific Windows types, Windows can control how these types are interpreted and they can be adjusted to suit the needs of different computers. All the types used by Windows, as well as the prototypes of the Windows API functions, are contained in the header file **windows.h**, so we will need to include this header file when we put our basic Windows program together.

The four arguments passed by Windows to your **WinMain()** function contain important data. The first argument, **hInstance**, is of type **HINSTANCE** which is a handle to an instance, an instance here being a running program. A handle is a 32-bit integer value which identifies an object of some kind - in this case, the instance of the application. This allows for the possibility of multiple copies of a Windows program being active simultaneously. As we will see shortly, handles are also used to identify other things.

With DOS, only one program can be executed at one time, whereas with Windows there can be several. This raises the possibility of several copies of the same application being active at once, and this needs to be recognized. Hence the need for the **hInstance** handle to identify a particular copy. If you start more than one copy of the program, each one will have its own unique **hInstance** value.

The next argument, **hPrevInstance**, is a legacy from 16-bit days. Under Windows 3.*x* this parameter gave you the handle to the previous instance of the program, if there was one. If **hPrevInstance** was **NULL**, you knew that there was no previous instance of the program so this must be the only copy of the program executing (at the moment anyway). This information was necessary in many cases because programs running under Windows 3.*x* share the same address space and multiple copies of a program executing simultaneously could cause complications. For this reason, programmers often limit their application to only one running instance at a time, and having the **hPrevInstance** argument passed to **WinMain()** allowed them to provide for this very easily by testing it in an **if** statement.

Under 32-bit systems (Windows 95 and Windows NT) the **hPrevInstance** parameter is completely irrelevant since each application runs in its own address space, and one application has no direct knowledge of the existence of another that is executing concurrently. This parameter is always **NULL**, even if another instance of an application is running.

The next argument, **lpCmdLine**, is a pointer to a string containing the command line that started the program. For instance, if you have started it using the Run... command from the Start button menu of Windows 95, the string will contain everything that appears in the Open box. Having this pointer allows you to pick up any parameter values that may appear in the command line. The type **LPSTR** is another Windows type, specifying a 32-bit pointer to a string.

The last argument, **nCmdShow**, indicates how the window is to look when it's created. It could be displayed normally or it might to be minimized; for example, if the shortcut for the program specifies that the program should be minimized when it starts. This argument can take one of a fixed set of values that are defined by symbolic constants such as **SW_SHOWNORMAL** and **SW_SHOWMINNOACTIVE**. There are a number of other constants like these which define the way a window is to be displayed and they all begin **SW_**. Other examples are **SW_HIDE** or **SW_SHOWMAXIMIZED**. You don't usually need to examine the value of **nCmdShow**. You typically pass it directly to the Windows API function responsible for displaying your application window.

If you want to know what all the other constants are that specify how a window will be displayed, you can find a complete list of possible values if you search on WinMain in the Visual C++ help facility and look at the WinMain topic.

The function **WinMain()** in our Windows program needs to do three things:

▶ Tell Windows what kind of window the program requires.

▶ Create and initialize the program window.

▶ Retrieve Windows messages intended for the program.

Let's take a look at each of these in turn and then create a complete **WinMain()** function.

Specifying a Program Window

The first step in creating a window is to define just what sort of window it is that we want to create. Windows defines a special **struct** called **WNDCLASS** to contain the data specifying a window. We need to create a variable from this **struct** and give values to each of its members (just like filling in a form). Once we've filled in the variable, we can pass it to Windows (via a function that we'll see later) in order to register the class. Once done, whenever we want to create a window of that class we can tell Windows to look up the class that we've already registered.

The definition of the **WNDCLASS struct** is as follows:

```
struct WNDCLASS
{
    UINT style;              // Window style
    WNDPROC lpfnWndProc;     // Pointer to message processing function
    int cbClsExtra;          // Extra byte after the window class
    int cbWndExtra;          // Extra bytes after the window instance
    HINSTANCE hInstance;     // The application instance handle
    HICON hIcon;             // The application icon
    HCURSOR hCursor;         // The window cursor
    HBRUSH hbrBackground;    // The brush defining the background color
    LPCSTR lpszMenuName;     // A pointer to the name of the menu resource
    LPCSTR lpszClassName;    // A pointer to the class name
};
```

The **style** member of the **struct** determines various aspects of the window's behavior, in particular, the conditions under which the window should be redrawn. You can select from a number of options for this member's value, each defined by a symbolic constant beginning **CS_**.

You'll find the possible constant values for **style** if you look at the section for **WNDCLASS** under **SDKs\Win32 SDK\Win32\Reference\Structures** in InfoView.

Where two or more options are required, to produce a composite value these are combined using the bitwise OR operator, |. For example, assuming that we have declared the variable **WindowClass**, we could write:

```
WindowClass.style = CS_HREDRAW | CS_VREDRAW;
```

The option **CS_HREDRAW** indicates to Windows that the window is to be redrawn if its horizontal width is altered, and **CS_VREDRAW** indicates that it is to be redrawn if the vertical height of the window is changed. In the statement above we have elected to have our window redrawn in either case. As a result, Windows will send a message to our program indicating that we should redraw the window whenever the width or height of the window is altered by the user. Each of the possible options for the window style is defined by a unique bit being 1 in a 32-bit word. That's why the bitwise OR is used to combine them. The complete set of options can be found under Visual C++ help.

The member **lpfnWndProc** stores a pointer to the function in your program which will handle messages for the window that we will create. The prefix to the name signifies that this is a **long** pointer to a function. If you followed the herd and called the function to handle messages for the application **WindowProc()**, you would initialize this member with the statement:

```
WindowClass.lpfnWndProc = WindowProc;
```

The next two members, **cbClsExtra** and **cbWndExtra**, allow you to ask for some extra space internal to Windows for your own use. An example of this could be when you want to associate additional data with each instance of a window to assist in message handling for each window instance. If you don't need extra space allocated for you, you must set the **cbClsExtra** and **cbWndExtra** members to zero. The **hInstance** member holds the handle for the current application instance, so you should set this to the **hInstance** value passed to **WinMain()** by Windows.

235

The members **hIcon**, **hCursor** and **hbrBackground** are handles which in turn define the icon which will represent the application when minimized, the cursor the window is to use and the background color of the client area of the window. These are set using Windows API functions. For example:

```
WindowClass.hIcon = LoadIcon(0, IDI_APPLICATION);
WindowClass.hCursor = LoadCursor(0, IDC_ARROW);
WindowClass.hbrBackground = GetStockObject(GRAY_BRUSH);
```

All three members are set to standard Windows values by these function calls. The icon is a default provided by Windows and the cursor is the standard arrow cursor used by the majority of Windows applications. A brush is a Windows object which is used to fill an area, in this case the client area of the window. The background color is therefore set as gray so that a handle to the standard gray brush will be returned by the function **GetStockObject()**. This function can also be used to obtain other standard objects for a window, such as fonts for example.

The **lpszMenuName** member is set to the name of a resource defining the window menu and to **0** if there is no menu for the window. We will be looking into creating and using menu resources when we use AppWizard.

The last member of the **struct** is **lpszClassName**. This member stores the name that you supply to identify this particular class of window. You would usually use the name of the application for this. You need to keep track of this name because you will need it again when a window is created. This member would therefore be typically set with the statements:

```
static char szAppName[] = "OFWin";      // Define window class name
WindowClass.lpszClassName = szAppName;  // Set class name
```

Creating and Initializing a Program Window

After all the members of your **WNDCLASS** structure have been set to the values required, the next step is to tell Windows about it. You do this using the Windows API function **RegisterClass()**. Assuming that our structure is **WindowClass**, the statement to do this would be:

```
RegisterClass(&WindowClass);
```

Easy, wasn't it? The address of the **struct** is passed to the function, and Windows will extract and squirrel away all the values that you have set in the structure members. This process is called **registering** the window class. The term *class* here is used in the sense of classification. This is not identical to the idea of a **class** in C++, so don't confuse the two. Each instance of the application must make sure that it registers the window classes that it needs.

Once Windows knows the characteristics of the window that we want, and the function that is going to handle messages for it, we can go ahead and create it. You use the function **CreateWindow()** for this. The window class that we've already created determines the broad characteristics of a window, and further arguments to the function **CreateWindow()** add additional characteristics. Since in general, an application may have several windows, the function **CreateWindow()** returns a handle to the window created which you can store to enable you to refer to the particular window later. There are a lot of API calls that will require you to specify the window handle as a parameter if you want to use them. We will just look at a typical use of the **CreateWindow()** function at this point. This might be:

```
HWND hWnd;                                   // Window handle
//...
hWnd = CreateWindow(
        szAppName,                           // the window class name
        "A Basic Window the Hard Way",       // The window title
        WS_OVERLAPPEDWINDOW,                 // Window style as overlapped
        CW_USEDEFAULT,         // Default  screen position of upper left
        CW_USEDEFAULT,         // corner of our window as x,y...
        CW_USEDEFAULT,         // Default window size
        CW_USEDEFAULT,         // ....
        0,                     // No parent window
        0,                     // No menu
        hInstance,             // Program Instance handle
        0                      // No window creation data
        );
```

The variable **hWnd** of type **HWND**, is a 32-bit integer handle to a window. We will use this variable to record the value that identifies the window that is returned from the function **CreateWindow()**. The first argument that we pass to the function is the class name. This is used by Windows to identify the **WNDCLASS struct** that we passed to it previously, in the **RegisterClass()** function call, so that the information from this **struct** can be used in the window creation process.

The second argument to **CreateWindow()** defines the text that is to appear on the title bar. The third argument specifies the style that the window will have once it is created. The option specified here, **WS_OVERLAPPEDWINDOW**, actually combines several options. It defines the window as having the **WS_OVERLAPPED**, **WS_CAPTION**, **WS_SYSMENU**, **WS_THICKFRAME**, **WS_MINIMIZEBOX** and **WS_MAXIMIZEBOX** styles. This results in an overlapped window with a title bar and a thick frame which has a title bar icon, system menu and maximize and minimize buttons. A window specified as having a thick frame has borders that can be resized.

The following four arguments determine the position and size of the window on the screen. The first pair are the screen coordinates of the top-left corner of the window, and the second pair define the width and height of the window. The value **CW_USEDEFAULT** indicates that we want Windows to assign the default position and size for the window. This tells Windows to arrange successive windows in cascading positions down the screen. This only applies to windows specified as **WS_OVERLAPPED**.

The next argument value is zero, indicating that the window being created is not a child window. It we wanted it to be a child window, we would set this argument to the handle of the parent window. The next argument is also zero, indicating that no menu is required. We then specify the handle of the current instance of the program and the last argument is zero.

The window now exists but is not yet displayed on the screen. We need to call another Windows API function to get it displayed:

```
ShowWindow(hWnd, nCmdShow);    // Display the window
```

Only two arguments are required here. The first identifies the window and is the handle returned by the function **CreateWindow()**. The second is the value **nCmdShow** which was passed to **WinMain()**, and which indicates how the window is to appear on screen.

Initializing the Client Area of the Window

After calling the function **ShowWindow()**, the window will appear on screen but will still have no application content so let's get our program to draw in the client area of the window. We could just put together some code to do this directly in the **WinMain()** function, but this would be most unsatisfactory: the contents of the client area can't be considered to be permanent - we can't afford to output what we want and forget about it. Any action on the part of the user which modifies the window in some way, such as dragging a border or dragging the whole window, will typically require that the window and its client area are redrawn.

When the client area needs to be redrawn for any reason, Windows will send a particular message to our program and our **WindowProc()** function will need to respond by reconstructing the client area of the window. Therefore, the best way to get the client area drawn in the first instance is to get Windows to send the message requesting this to our program. Indeed, whenever we know in our program that the window should be redrawn, when we change something for example, we just need to tell Windows to send a message back to this effect.

We can do this by calling another Windows API function, **UpdateWindow()**. The statement to accomplish this is:

```
UpdateWindow(hWnd);          // Cause window client area to be drawn
```

This function only requires one argument: the window handle **hWnd**, which identifies our particular program window. (In general, there can be several windows in an application.) The result of the call is that Windows will send a message to our program requesting that the client area be redrawn.

Dealing with Windows Messages

The last task that **WinMain()** needs to address is dealing with the messages that Windows may have queued for our application. This may seem a bit odd since we said that we needed the function **WindowProc()** to deal with messages.

Queued and Non-Queued Messages

There are, in fact, two kinds of Windows messages. Firstly, there are **queued messages** which Windows places in a queue and which the **WinMain()** function needs to extract from the queue for processing. The code in **WinMain()** that does this is called the **message loop**. Queued messages include those arising from user input from the keyboard, moving the mouse and clicking the mouse buttons. Messages from a timer and the Windows message to request that a window be repainted are also queued.

Secondly, there are **non-queued messages** which result in the **WindowProc()** function being called directly by Windows. A lot of the non-queued messages arise as a consequence of processing queued messages. What we are doing in the message loop in **WinMain()** is retrieving a message that Windows has queued for our application and then asking Windows to invoke our function **WindowProc()** to process it. Why can't Windows just call **WindowProc()** whenever necessary? Well, it could, but it just doesn't work this way. The reasons are to do with how Windows manages multiple applications executing simultaneously.

The Message Loop

Retrieving messages from the message queue is a standard mechanism in Windows programming called the message loop. The code for this would be:

```
MSG msg;                            // Windows message structure
while(GetMessage(&msg, 0, 0, 0) == TRUE)  // Get any messages
{
    TranslateMessage(&msg);            // Translate the message
    DispatchMessage(&msg);             // Dispatch the message
}
```

This involves three steps in dealing with each message:

GetMessage()	retrieves a message from the queue.
TranslateMessage()	performs any conversion necessary on the message retrieved.
DispatchMessage()	causes Windows to call the **WindowProc()** function in our application, to deal with the message.

The operation of **GetMessage()** is important since it has a significant contribution to the way Windows works with multiple applications. Let's look into it in a little more detail.

The **GetMessage()** function will retrieve a message queued for our application window and will store information about the message in the variable **msg**, pointed to by the first argument. The variable **msg** which is a **struct** of type **MSG** contains a number of different members which we will not be accessing here. Still, for completeness, the definition of the structure is:

```
struct MSG
{
    HWND    hwnd;       // Handle for the relevant window
    UINT    message;    // The message ID
    WPARAM  wParam;     // Message parameter (32-bits)
    LPARAM  lParam;     // Message parameter (32-bits)
    DWORD   time;       // The time when the message was queued
    POINT   pt;         // The mouse position
};
```

The **wParam** member is an example of a slightly misleading Hungarian notation prefix that we mentioned was now possible. You might assume that it was of type **WORD** which is **int**, which used to be true in earlier Windows versions, but now it's of type **WPARAM** which is a 32-bit integer value.

The exact contents of the members **wParam** and **lParam** are dependent on what kind of message it is. The message ID in the member **message** is an integer value that can be one of a set of values that are predefined in the header file **windows.h** as symbolic constants. They all start with **WM_** and typical examples are **WM_PAINT** to redraw the screen or **WM_QUIT** to end the program. The function **GetMessage()** will always return **TRUE** unless the message is **WM_QUIT** to end the program in which case the value returned is **FALSE**, or until an error occurs in which case the return value is **-1**. Thus, the **while** loop here will continue until a quit message is generated to close the application or until an error condition arises. In either case, we would then need to end the program by passing the **wParam** value back to Windows in a **return** statement.

239

The second argument in the call to **GetMessage()** is the handle of the window for which we want to get messages. This parameter can be used to retrieve messages for one window separately from another. If this argument is **0** as it is here, **GetMessage()** will retrieve all messages for an application, so this is an easy way of retrieving all messages for an application regardless of how many windows it has. It's also the safest way since you are sure of getting all the messages for your application. When the user of your Windows program closes the application window for example, the window is closed before the **WM_QUIT** message is generated. Consequently, if you only retrieve messages by specifying a window handle to the **GetMessage()** function, you will not retrieve the **WM_QUIT** message and your program will not be able to terminate properly.

The last two arguments to **GetMessage()** are integers that are minimum and maximum values for the message IDs you want to retrieve from the queue. This allows messages to be retrieved selectively. A range is usually specified by symbolic constants. Using **WM_MOUSEFIRST** and **WM_MOUSELAST**, as these two arguments would select just mouse messages for example. If both arguments are zero, as we have them here, all messages are retrieved.

Multi-Tasking

If there are no messages queued, the **GetMessage()** function will not come back to our program. Windows will allow execution to pass to another application and we will only get a value returned from calling **GetMessage()** when a message appears in the queue. This mechanism is fundamental in enabling multiple applications to run under Windows 3.x, and is referred to as **cooperative multitasking** because it depends on concurrent applications giving up their control of the processor from time to time. Once your program calls **GetMessage()**, unless there is a message for your program, another application will be executed and your program will only get another opportunity to do something if the other application calls **GetMessage()**.

With Windows 3.x, a program that doesn't call **GetMessage()** or includes code for a heavy computation that doesn't make provision for returning control to Windows from time to time, can retain use of the processor indefinitely. With Windows 95 the operating system can interrupt an application after a period of time and transfer control to another application. This is called **pre-emptive multitasking**. However, you still need to program the message loop in **WinMain()** using **GetMessage()** as before, and make provision for relinquishing control of the processor to Windows from time to time in a long running calculation (this is usually done using the **PeekMessage()** API function). If you don't do this, your application may be unable to respond to messages to repaint the application window when these arise. This can be for reasons that are quite independent of your application - when an overlapping window for another application is closed for example.

The conceptual operation of the **GetMessage()** function is illustrated on the following page:

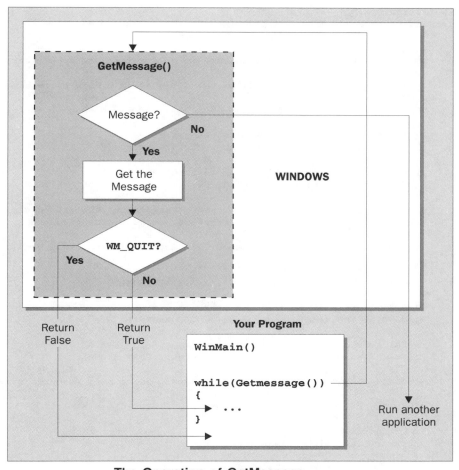

The Operation of GetMessage

Within the **while** loop, the first function call to **TranslateMessage()** requests Windows to do some conversion work for keyboard-related messages. Then the call to the function **DispatchMessage()** causes Windows to dispatch the message, or in other words, to call the **WindowProc()** function in our program to process the message. The return from **DispatchMessage()** will not occur until **WindowProc()** has finished processing the message.

A Complete WinMain() Function

We have looked at all the bits that need to go into the function **WinMain()**. So now let's assemble them into a complete function.

```cpp
// Listing OFWIN_1
int WINAPI WinMain(HINSTANCE hInstance, HINSTANCE hPrevInstance,
                   LPSTR lpCmdLine, int nCmdShow)
{
    WNDCLASS WindowClass;  // Structure to hold our window's attributes

    static char szAppName[] = "OFWin";      // Define window class name
    HWND hWnd;                              // Window handle
    MSG msg;                               // Windows message structure

    // Redraw the window if the size changes
    WindowClass.style   = CS_HREDRAW | CS_VREDRAW;

    // Define our procedure for message handling
    WindowClass.lpfnWndProc = WindowProc;

    WindowClass.cbClsExtra = 0;// No extra bytes after the window class
    WindowClass.cbWndExtra = 0;// structure or the window instance

    WindowClass.hInstance = hInstance;   // Application instance handle

    // Set default application icon
    WindowClass.hIcon = LoadIcon(0, IDI_APPLICATION);

    // Set window cursor to be the standard arrow
    WindowClass.hCursor = LoadCursor(0, IDC_ARROW);

    // Set gray brush for background color
    WindowClass.hbrBackground = GetStockObject(GRAY_BRUSH);

    WindowClass.lpszMenuName = 0;   // No menu, so no menu resource name

    WindowClass.lpszClassName = szAppName;  // Set class name

    // Now register our window class
    RegisterClass(&WindowClass);

    //  Now we can create the window
    hWnd = CreateWindow(
        szAppName,                       // the window class name
        "A Basic Window the Hard Way",   // The window title
        WS_OVERLAPPEDWINDOW,             // Window style as overlapped
        CW_USEDEFAULT,             // Default  screen position of upper left
        CW_USEDEFAULT,             // corner of our window as x,y...
        CW_USEDEFAULT,             // Default window size
        CW_USEDEFAULT,             // ....
        0,                         // No parent window
        0,                         // No menu
        hInstance,                 // Program Instance handle
        0                          // No window creation data
        );

    ShowWindow(hWnd, nCmdShow); // Display the window
    UpdateWindow(hWnd);          // Cause window client area to be drawn

    // The message loop
    while(GetMessage(&msg, 0, 0, 0) == TRUE)    // Get any messages
```

```
    {
        TranslateMessage(&msg);         // Translate the message
        DispatchMessage(&msg);          // Dispatch the message
    }

    return msg.wParam;                  // End so return to Windows
}
```

How It Works

After declaring the variables we need in the function, all the members of the **WindowClass** structure are initialized and the window is registered.

The next step is to call the **CreateWindow()** function to create the data for the physical appearance of the window based on the arguments passed and the data established in the **WindowClass** structure that was previously passed to Windows using the **RegisterClass()** function. The call to **ShowWindow()** causes the window to be displayed according to the mode specified by **nCmdShow**, and the **UpDateWindow()** function signals that a message to draw the window client area should be generated.

Finally, the message loop will continue to retrieve messages for the application until a **WM_QUIT** message is obtained, whereupon the **GetMessage()** function will return **False** and the loop will end. The value of the **wParam** member of the **msg** structure is passed back to Windows in the **return** statement.

Message Processing Functions

The function **WinMain()** contained nothing that was application specific beyond the general appearance of the application window. All of the code that will make the application behave in the way that we want is going to be included in the message processing part of the program. This is the function **WindowProc()** that we identified to Windows in the **WindowClass** structure. Windows will call this function each time a message for our main application window is dispatched.

Our example is going to be very simple, so we will be putting all the code to process messages in the one function, **WindowProc()**. More generally though, the **WindowProc()** function would be responsible for analyzing what a given message was and which window it was destined for, and then calling one of a whole range of functions, each of which would be geared to handling a particular message in the context of the particular window concerned. However, the overall sequence of operations, and the way in which the function **WindowProc()** analyzes an incoming message, will be much the same in most application contexts.

The WindowProc() Function

The prototype of our **WindowProc()** function is:

```
long WINAPI WindowProc(HWND hWnd, UINT message,
                       WPARAM wParam, LPARAM lParam);
```

Since the function will be called by Windows, we need to qualify the function as **WINAPI**. The four arguments that are passed provide information about the particular message causing the function to be called. The meaning of each of these arguments is:

243

`HWND   hWnd:`	a handle to the window in which the event causing the message occurred.
`UINT   message:`	the message ID which is a 32-bit value indicating the type of message.
`WPARAM   wParam:`	a 32-bit value containing additional information depending on what sort of message it is.
`LPARAM   lParam:`	a 32-bit value containing additional information depending on what sort of message it is.

The window that the incoming message relates to is identified by the first argument, **hWnd**, that is passed to the function. In our case, we only have one window, so we can ignore it.

Messages are identified by the value, **message**, that is passed to **WindowProc()**. You can test this value against predefined symbolic constants, each of which relate to a particular message. They all begin with **WM_** and typical examples are **WM_PAINT** which corresponds to a request to redraw part of the client area of a window, or **WM_LBUTTONDOWN** which indicates the left mouse button was pressed. You can find the whole set of these by searching for WM_ in the Visual C++ Help menu.

Decoding a Windows Message

The process of decoding the message that Windows is sending is usually done using a **switch** statement in the **WindowProc()** function, based on the value of **message**. Selecting the message types that you want to process is then just a question of putting a **case** statement for each case in the **switch**. The typical structure of such a **switch** statement, with arbitrary cases included, is as follows:

```
switch(message)
{
    case WM_PAINT:
        // Code to deal with drawing the client area
        break;

    case WM_LBUTTONDOWN:
        // Code to deal with the left mouse button being pressed
        break;

    case WM_LBUTTONUP:
        // Code to deal with the left mouse button being released
        break;

    case WM_DESTROY:
        // Code to deal with a window being destroyed
        break;

    default:
        // Code to handle any other messages
}
```

Every Windows program will have something like this somewhere, although it will be hidden from sight in the Windows programs that will write later using MFC. Each case corresponds to a particular value for the message ID and provides suitable processing for that message. Any messages that a program doesn't want to deal with individually are handled by the default statement which should hand the messages back to Windows by calling **DefWindowProc()**. This is the Windows API function providing default message handling.

In a complex program, dealing specifically with a wide range of possible Windows messages, this **switch** statement can become very large and rather cumbersome. When we get to use AppWizard we won't have to worry about this because it's all taken care of for us and we will never see the **WindowProc()** function. All we will need to do is to supply the code to process the particular messages that we are interested in.

Drawing the Window Client Area

To signal that the client area of an application should be redrawn, Windows sends a **WM_PAINT** message to the program. So in our example, we will need to draw the text in the window in response to the **WM_PAINT** message. We can't go drawing in the window willy nilly. Before we can write to our window, we need to tell Windows that we want to do so and get Windows' authority to go ahead. We do this by calling the Windows API function **BeginPaint()**. This function should only be called in response to a **WM_PAINT** message. It's used as follows:

```
HDC hDC;                         // A display context handle
PAINTSTRUCT PaintSt;       // Structure defining area to be redrawn

hDC = BeginPaint(hWnd, &PaintSt); // Prepare to draw in the window
```

The type **HDC** defines what's called a **display context**, or more generally a **device context**. A device context provides the link between the device independent Windows API functions for outputting information to the screen or a printer and the device drivers which support writing to the specific devices attached to your PC. You can also regard a device context as a token of authority which is handed to you on request by Windows and grants you permission to output some information. Without a device context you just can't generate any output.

The **BeginPaint()** function provides us with a display context as a return value and requires two arguments to be supplied. The window to which we want to write is identified by the window handle, **hWnd**, which we pass as the first argument. The second argument is the address of a **PAINTSTRUCT** variable **PaintSt**, in which Windows will place information about the area to be redrawn in response to the **WM_PAINT** message. We will ignore the details of this since we aren't going to use it. We will just redraw the whole of the client area. We can obtain the coordinates of the client area in a **RECT** structure with the statements:

```
RECT aRect;                              // A working rectangle
GetClientRect(hWnd, &aRect);
```

The **GetClientRect()** function supplies the coordinates of the upper-left and lower-right corners of the client area for the window specified by the first argument. These coordinates will be stored in the **RECT** structure **aRect**, which is passed through the second argument as a pointer. We can then use this definition of the client area for our window when we write the text to the window using the **DrawText()** function. Because our window has a gray background, we should alter the background of the text to be transparent, to allow the gray to show through, otherwise the text will appear against a white background. We can do this with the API function call:

```
SetBkMode(hDC, TRANSPARENT);            // Set text background mode
```

245

The first argument identifies the device context and the second sets the background mode. The default option is **OPAQUE**.

We can now write the text with the statement:

```
DrawText(
        hDC,                      // Device context handle
        "But, soft! what light through yonder window breaks?",
        -1,                       // Indicate null terminated string
        &aRect,                   // Rectangle in which text is to be drawn
        DT_SINGLELINE|            // Text format - single line
        DT_CENTER|                //                - centered in the line
        DT_VCENTER                //                - line centered in aRect
        );
```

The first argument is our certificate of authority, the display context **hDC**. The next argument is the text string that we want to output. We could equally well have defined this in a variable and passed the pointer to the text. The argument with the value **-1** signifies our string is terminated with a null character. If it wasn't, we would put the count of the number of characters in the string here. The fourth argument is a pointer to a **RECT** structure defining a rectangle in which we want to write the text. In our case it's the whole client area defined in **aRect**. The last argument defines the format for the text in the rectangle. Here we have combined three specifications with a bitwise OR. Our string will be a single line, with the text centered on the line and the line centered vertically within the rectangle. This will place it nicely in the center of the window. There are also a number of other options which include the possibility to place text at the top or the bottom of the rectangle, and to left or right justify it.

Once we have output all the text we want, we must tell Windows that we have finished drawing the client area. For every **BeginPaint()** function call, there must be a corresponding **EndPaint()** function call. Thus, to end processing the **WM_PAINT** message, we need the statement:

```
        EndPaint(hWnd, &PaintSt);   // Terminate window redraw operation
```

The **hWnd** argument identifies our program window and the second argument is the address of the **PAINTSTRUCT** structure that was filled in by the **BeginPaint()** function.

Ending the Program

You may assume that closing the window will close the application, but to get this behavior we have to add some code. The reason that our application won't close when the window is closed is that we may need to do some clearing up. It's also possible that the application may have more than one window. When the user closes the window by double-clicking the title bar icon or clicking the close button, this causes a **WM_DESTROY** message to be generated. Therefore, in order to close the application we need to process the **WM_DESTROY** message in our **WindowProc()** function. We do this by generating a **WM_QUIT** message with the following statement:

```
        PostQuitMessage(0);
```

The argument here is an exit code. This Windows API function does exactly what its name suggests - it posts a **WM_QUIT** message in the message queue for our application. This will result in the **GetMessage()** function in **WinMain()** returning **False** and ending the message loop, so ending the program.

A Complete WindowProc() Function

We have covered all the elements necessary to make up the complete **WindowProc()** function for our example. The code for the function is as follows:

```
// Listing OFWIN_2
long PASCAL WindowProc(HWND hWnd, UINT message,
                       WPARAM wParam, LPARAM lParam)
{
   HDC hDC;                          // Display context handle
   PAINTSTRUCT PaintSt;             // Structure defining area to be drawn
   RECT aRect;                       // A working rectangle

   switch(message)                   // Process selected messages
   {
   case WM_PAINT:                    // Message is to redraw the window
     hDC = BeginPaint(hWnd, &PaintSt); // Prepare to draw the window

     // Get upper left and lower right of client area
     GetClientRect(hWnd, &aRect);

     SetBkMode(hDC, TRANSPARENT);         // Set text background mode

     // Now draw the text in the window client area
     DrawText(
         hDC,                     // Device context handle
         "But, soft! what light through yonder window breaks?",
         -1,                      // Indicate null terminated string
         &aRect,                  // Rectangle in which text is to be drawn
         DT_SINGLELINE|           // Text format - single line
         DT_CENTER|               //               - centered in the line
         DT_VCENTER);             //               - line centered in aRect

     EndPaint(hWnd, &PaintSt); // Terminate window redraw operation
     return 0;

   case WM_DESTROY:                  // Window is being destroyed
     PostQuitMessage(0);
     return 0;

   default:                  // Any other message - we don't want to know,
                             // so call default message processing
     return DefWindowProc(hWnd, message, wParam, lParam);
   }
}
```

How It Works

The function consists wholly of a **switch** statement. A particular **case** will be selected, based on the message ID passed to our function in the parameter **message**. Because our example is very simple, we only need to process two different messages, **WM_PAINT** and **WM_DESTROY**. We hand all other messages back to Windows by calling the **DefWindowProc()** function in the **default** case for the **switch**. The arguments to **DefWindowProc()** are those that were passed to our function, so we are just passing them back as they are. Note the **return** statement at the end of processing each message type. For the messages we handle, a zero value is returned.

A Simple Windows Program

Since we have written **WinMain()** and **WindowProc()** to handles messages, we have enough to create a complete source file for our Windows program. The complete source file will simply consist of an **#include** statement for the Windows header file, a prototype for the **WindowProc** function and the **WinMain** and **WindowProc** functions that we've already seen:

```
// OFWIN.CPP    Native windows program to display text in a window
#include <windows.h>

long   WINAPI   WindowProc(HWND hWnd, UINT message,
                           WPARAM wParam, LPARAM lParam);

    // Insert code for WinMain() here (Listing OFWIN_1)

    // Insert code for WindowProc() here (Listing OFWIN_2)
```

Of course you'll need to create a project for this program, but instead of choosing Console Application as you've done up to now, you should create this project as an Application.

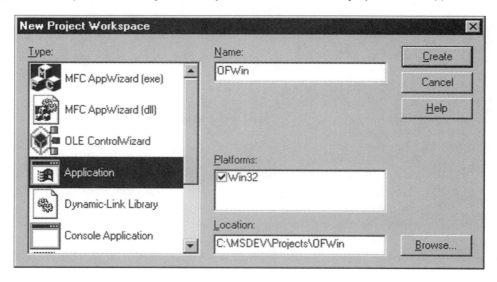

TRY IT OUT - Old-Fashioned Windows

If you build and execute the example, it will produce the window shown below:

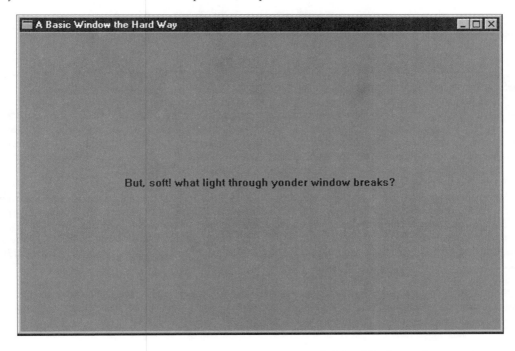

Note that the window has a number of properties provided by Windows that require no programming effort on our part to manage. The boundaries of the window can be dragged to resize it, and the whole window can be moved about on the screen. The maximize and minimize buttons also work. Of course, all of these actions do affect the program. Every time you modify the position or size of the window, a **WM_PAINT** message will be queued and our program will have to redraw the client area but all the work of drawing and modifying the window itself is done by Windows.

The system menu and close button is also a standard feature of our window because of the options that we specified in the **WindowClass** structure. Again, Windows takes care of the management. The only additional effect on our program arising from this is the passing of a **WM_DESTROY** message if you close the window, as we have previously discussed.

Summary

In this chapter, we have described the idea of a **struct** because Windows uses structures for passing data, but all the capabilities of a **struct** are provided by a **class** in C++, which we'll discuss in the next chapter. Since we can always use a **class** instead of a **struct**, and since a **class** provides much more extensive capabilities, we will not be elaborating on the **struct** any further. For the remainder of the book, we will just use classes.

The example that we developed in this chapter was designed to introduce you to the basic mechanics of operating a program under Windows. As we said at the beginning of this chapter, we don't actually need to know about this when using the full capabilities of Visual C++ because all the details of creating and displaying a window, the message loop, and analyzing messages passed to an application are all submerged in the code that Visual C++ can provide automatically. However, you should find that the operation of programs generated by the AppWizard is much easier to understand if you have plowed through the material in this chapter, and this should make the AppWizard even easier to apply.

You may also be like me - never quite comfortable with taking things on trust, and not happy about using things without understanding how they really work. This has its downside of course. It can take a while to get comfortable with using something as mundane as a microwave oven, or even taking a plane. With the latter, understanding the theory still doesn't make sitting in a metal tube seven miles above the earth feel like a secure and natural thing to be doing.

In the next chapter we are back to C++, this time looking into the basis for object oriented programming: the **class**.

Structuring Your Data Using Classes

This chapter is about creating your own data types to suit your particular problem. This will go far beyond the notion of a **struct** which we saw in the last chapter. It is also about creating objects, the building-blocks of object oriented programming. An object can seem a bit mysterious to the uninitiated but, as we shall see in this chapter, an object is just an instance of one of your own data types.

In this chapter you will learn about:

- Classes and how they are used
- The basic components of a class and how a class is declared
- Creating and using objects of a class
- Controlling access to members of a class
- Constructors and how to create them
- The default constructor
- References in the context of classes
- The copy constructor and how it is implemented

Data Types, Objects, Classes and Instances

Before we get into the language, syntax and programming techniques of classes, we'll start by considering how our existing knowledge relates to the concept of classes.

So far, we have learnt that C++ lets you create variables which can be any of a range of basic data types: **int**, **long**, **double** and so on. In the previous chapter, you saw how you could use the **struct** keyword to define a structure which, in turn, defined a variable representing a composite of several other variable types.

The variables of the basic types don't allow you to model real world objects (or even imaginary objects) adequately. It's hard to model a box in terms of an **int**, for example. However, as we saw in the previous chapter, you could use a **struct** and its members to define extended attributes of your object. You could define variables, **length**, **breadth** and **height** to represent the dimensions of the box and bind them together as members of a **Box** structure as follows:

```
struct Box
{
    double length;
    double breadth;
    double height;
};
```

With this definition of a new data type called **Box**, you could go ahead and define variables of this type just as you did with variables of the basic types. You could then create, manipulate and destroy as many **Box** objects as you need to in your program. This means that you can model objects using **struct**s and write your programs around them. So - that's object oriented programming all wrapped up then?

Well, not quite. You see, object oriented programming (OOP) is based on a number of foundations (famously encapsulation, polymorphism and inheritance) and the **struct** doesn't quite fit the bill. Don't worry about what these terms mean for the moment - we'll be exploring that in the rest of this chapter and throughout the book. Suffice to say, though, that where the **struct** falls flat, the class comes through with flying colors.

As we said in the previous chapter, a **class** can do everything that a **struct** can, and more, so let's look at how we'd define a class for boxes:

```
class CBox
{
    public:
        double m_Length;
        double m_Breadth;
        double m_Height;
};
```

Just like when we defined the **Box** structure, when we define **CBox** as a class we are essentially defining a new data type. The only differences here are the use of the keyword **class** instead of **struct**, and the use of the keyword **public** followed by a colon that precedes the definition of the members of the class.

We have also called the class **CBox** instead of **Box**. We could have called the class **Box**, but MFC adopts the convention of using the prefix **C** for all class names, so we might as well get into the habit now. MFC also prefixes data members of classes with **m_** to distinguish them from other variables, so we'll use this convention too.

The **public** keyword is the first clue as to the difference between a structure and a class. It just defines the members of the class as being generally accessible in the same way as the members of the structures that we used in the last chapter were. As you'll see a little later in the chapter, though, it's also possible to place restrictions on the accessibility of the class members - something that isn't possible with structures.

We can declare a variable, **BigBox** say, that is an instance of the **CBox** class like this:

```
CBox BigBox;
```

This is exactly the same as declaring a variable for a **struct** or for any other variable type. Once we have defined the class **CBox**, the declaration of variables of this type is quite standard. The variable **BigBox** here is also referred to as an **object** or an **instance** of the class **Box**.

First Class

The notion of class was invented by an Englishman to keep the general population happy. It derives from the theory that people who knew their place and function in society would be much more secure and comfortable in life than those who did not. The famous Dane, Bjarne Stroustrup, who invented C++, undoubtedly acquired a deep knowledge of class concepts while at Cambridge University in England and appropriated the idea very successfully for use in his new language.

Class in C++ is similar to the English concept in that each class usually has a very precise role and a permitted set of actions. However, it differs from the English idea because class in C++ has largely socialist overtones, concentrating on the importance of working classes. Indeed, in some ways it is the reverse of the English ideal because, as we shall see, working classes in C++ often live on the backs of classes that do nothing at all.

Operations on Classes

In C++ you can create new data types as classes to represent whatever kinds of objects you like. As you'll come to see, classes aren't limited to just holding data like **struct**s are; you can also define member functions or even operations that act between objects of your classes using the standard C++ operators. You can define the class **CBox**, for example, so that the following statements work and have the meaning you want them to have:

```
CBox Box1;
CBox Box2;

if(Box1 > Box2)          // Fill the larger box
  Box1.Fill();
else
  Box2.Fill();
```

You could also implement operations as part of the **CBox** class for adding subtracting or even multiplying boxes - in fact, almost any operation to which you can ascribe a sensible meaning in the context of boxes.

We are talking about incredibly powerful medicine here and it constitutes a major change in the approach that we can take to programming. Instead of breaking down a problem in terms of what are essentially computer-related data types (integer numbers, floating point numbers and so on) and then writing a program, we are going to be programming in terms of problem-related data types, in other words classes. These classes might be named **CEmployee**, or **CCowboy**, or **CCheese**, or **CChutney**, each defined specifically for the kind of problem that you want to solve, complete with the functions and operators that are necessary to manipulate instances of your new types.

Program design now starts with deciding what new application-specific data types you need to solve the problem in hand and writing the program in terms of operations on the specifics that the problem is concerned with, be it **CCoffins** or **CCowpokes**.

Terminology

Let's summarize some of the terminology that we will be using when discussing classes in C++:

▶ A **class** is a user defined data type.

▶ **Object oriented programming** is the programming style based on the idea of defining your own data types as classes.

▶ Declaring an object of a class is sometimes referred to as **instantiation** because you are creating an **instance** of a class.

▶ Instances of a class are referred to as **objects**.

▶ The idea of an object containing the data implicit in its definition, together with the functions that operate on that data, is referred to as **encapsulation**.

When we get into the detail of object oriented programming, it may seem a little complicated in places, but getting back to the basics of what you are doing can often help to make things clearer, so always keep in mind what objects are really about. They are about writing programs in terms of the objects that are specific to the domain of your problem. All the facilities around classes in C++ are there to make this as comprehensive and flexible as possible. Let's get down to the business of understanding classes.

Understanding Classes

A class is a data type that you define. It can contain data elements which can be variables of the basic types in C++, or of other user-defined types. The data elements of a class may be single data elements, arrays, pointers, arrays of pointers of almost any kind or objects of other classes, so you have a lot of flexibility in what you can include in your data type. A class can also contain functions which operate on objects of the class by accessing the data elements that they include. So, a class combines both the definition of the elementary data that makes up an object and the means of manipulating the data belonging to individual objects of the class.

The data and functions within a class are called **members** of the class. Funnily enough, the members of a class that are data items are called **data members** and the members that are functions are called **function members** or **member functions**. The member functions of a class are also sometimes referred to as **methods** but we will not use this term in this book.

When you define a class, you define a blueprint for a data type. This doesn't actually define any data but it defines what the class name means, that is, what an object of the class will consist of and what operations can be performed on such an object. It's much the same as if you wrote a description of the basic type **double**. This wouldn't be a variable of type **double** but a definition of how it's made up and how it operates. To create a variable, you need to use a declaration statement. It's exactly the same with classes, as you will see.

Defining a Class

Let's look again at the class we started talking about at the start of the chapter - a class of boxes. We defined the **CBox** data type using the keyword **class** as follows:

```
class CBox
{
    public:
        double m_Length;            // Length of a box in inches
        double m_Breadth;           // Breadth of a box in inches
        double m_Height;            // Height of a box in inches
};
```

The name that we have given to our class appears following the keyword and the three data members are defined between the curly braces. The data members are defined for the class using the declaration statements that we already know and love and the whole class definition is terminated with a semicolon. The names of all the members of a class are local to a class. You can therefore use the same names elsewhere in a program without causing any problems.

Access Control in a Class

The keyword **public** looks a bit like a label, but in fact it is more than that. It determines the access attributes of the members of the class that follow it. Specifying the data members as **public** means that these members of an object of the class can be accessed anywhere within the scope of the class object. You can also specify the members of a class as **private** or **protected**. In fact, if you omit the access specification altogether, the members have the default attribute, **private**. We shall look into the effect of these keywords in a class definition a bit later.

Remember that all we have defined so far is a class, which is a data type. We have not declared any objects of the class. When we talk about accessing a class member, say **m_Height**, we are talking about accessing the data member of a particular object and that object needs to be declared somewhere.

Declaring Objects of a Class

We declare objects of a class with exactly the same sort of declaration that we use to declare objects of basic types. We saw this at the beginning of this chapter. We could declare objects of our class **CBox** with these statements:

```
        CBox Box1;          // Declare Box1 of type Box
        CBox Box2;          // Declare Box2 of type Box
```

Both of the objects **Box1** and **Box2** will, of course, have their own data members. This is illustrated in the following figure:

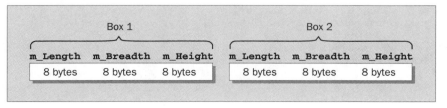

The object name **Box1** embodies the whole object, including its three data members. Of course, they are not initialized to anything. The data members of each object will simply contain junk values. So we need to look at how we can access them for the purpose of setting them to some specific values.

Accessing the Data Members of a Class

The data members of objects of a class can be referred to using the **direct member selection operator** that we used to access members of a **struct**. So, to set the value of the data member **m_Height** of the object **Box2** to 18.0 say, we could write this assignment statement:

```
Box2.m_Height = 18.0;          // Setting the value of a data member
```

We can only access the data member in this way, in a function outside the class, because the member **m_Height** was specified as having **public** access. If it was not defined as **public**, this statement would not compile. We will see more about this shortly.

TRY IT OUT - Your First Use of Classes

Let's first verify that we can use our class in the same way as the structure. We'll try it out in the following console application:

```cpp
// EX8_01.CPP
// Creating and using boxes
#include <iostream.h>

class CBox                          // Class definition at global scope
{
   public:
      double m_Length;             // Length of a box in inches
      double m_Breadth;            // Breadth of a box in inches
      double m_Height;             // Height of a box in inches
};

int main(void)
{
   CBox Box1;                      // Declare Box1 of type CBox
   CBox Box2;                      // Declare Box2 of type CBox

   double volume = 0.0;            // Store the volume of a box here

   Box1.m_Height = 18.0;           // Define the values
   Box1.m_Length = 78.0;           // of the members of
   Box1.m_Breadth = 24.0;          // the object Box1

   Box2.m_Height = Box1.m_Height - 10;     // Define Box2
   Box2.m_Length = Box1.m_Length/2.0;      // members in
   Box2.m_Breadth = 0.25*Box1.m_Length;    // terms of Box1

// Calculate volume of Box1
   volume = Box1.m_Height*Box1.m_Length*Box1.m_Breadth;

   cout << endl
```

```
                 << "Volume of Box1 = " << volume;

        cout << endl
             << "Box2 has sides which total "
             << Box2.m_Height+ Box2.m_Length+ Box2.m_Breadth
             << " inches.";

        cout << endl                    // Display the size of a box in memory
             << "A Box object occupies "
             << sizeof Box1 << " bytes.";

        cout <<endl;
        return 0;
    }
```

How It Works

We are back to console application examples again for the moment, so the project should be defined accordingly. Everything here works as we would have expected from our experience with structures. The definition of the class appears outside of the function **main()** and, therefore, has global scope. This enables objects to be declared in any function in the program and causes the class to show up in the ClassView..

We have declared two objects of type **CBox** within the function **main()**, **Box1** and **Box2**. Of course, as with variables of the basic types, the objects **Box1** and **Box2** are local to **main()**. Objects of a class obey the same rules with respect to scope as variables declared as one of the basic types (such as the variable **volume** used in this example).

The first three assignment statements set the values of the data members of **Box1**. We define the values of the data members of **Box2** in terms of the data members of **Box1** in the next three assignment statements.

We then have a statement which calculates the volume of **Box1** as the product of its three data members. This value is then output to the screen. Next, we output the sum of the data members of **Box2** by writing the expression for the sum of the data members directly in the output statement. The final action in the program is to output the number of bytes occupied by **Box1**, which is produced by the operator **sizeof**.

If you run this program, you should get this output:

The last line shows that the object **Box1** occupies 24 bytes of memory, which is a result of having 3 data members of 8 bytes. The statement which produced the last line of output could equally well have been written as you see on the next page.

```
            cout << endl                  // Display the size of a box in memory
                 << "A Box object occupies "
                 << sizeof (CBox) << " bytes.";
```

Here, we have used the type name between parentheses, rather than a specific object name. You'll remember that this is standard syntax for the **sizeof** operator, as you saw in Chapter 4.

This example has demonstrated the mechanism for accessing the **public** data members of a class. It also shows that they can be used in exactly the same way as ordinary variables. We are now ready to break new ground by taking a look at member functions of a class.

Member Functions of a Class

A member function of a class is a function that has its definition or its prototype within the class definition. It operates on any object of the class of which it is a member, and has access to all the members of a class for that object.

TRY IT OUT - Adding a Member Function to CBox

To see how accessing the members of the class works, let's create an example extending the **CBox** class to include a member function.

```
// EX8_02.CPP
// Calculating the volume of a box with a member function
#include <iostream.h>

class CBox                              // Class definition at global scope
{
   public:
      double m_Length;                  // Length of a box in inches
      double m_Breadth;                 // Breadth of a box in inches
      double m_Height;                  // Height of a box in inches

// Function to calculate the volume of a box
      double Volume(void)
      {
         return m_Length*m_Breadth*m_Height;
      }
};

int main(void)
{
   CBox Box1;                           // Declare Box1 of type CBox
   CBox Box2;                           // Declare Box2 of type CBox

   double volume = 0.0;                 // Store the volume of a box here

   Box1.m_Height = 18.0;                   // Define the values
   Box1.m_Length = 78.0;                   // of the members of
   Box1.m_Breadth = 24.0;                  // the object Box1

   Box2.m_Height = Box1.m_Height - 10;     // Define Box2
   Box2.m_Length = Box1.m_Length/2.0;      // members in
```

```
        Box2.m_Breadth = 0.25*Box1.m_Length;      // terms of Box1

    volume = Box1.Volume();                       // Calculate volume of Box1
    cout << endl
         << "Volume of Box1 = " << volume;

    cout << endl
         << "Volume of Box2 = "
         << Box2.Volume();

    cout << endl
         << "A Box object occupies "
         << sizeof Box1 << " bytes.";

    cout << endl;
    return 0;
  }
```

How It Works

The new code that we have added to the class definition is shaded. It's just the definition of the function **Volume()**, which is a member function of the class. It also has the access attribute **public** which the data members have. It returns the volume of a **CBox** object as a value of type **double**. The expression in the **return** statement is just the product of the three data members of the class.

Note that there is no need to qualify the names of the members in any way when accessing them in member functions. The unqualified member names automatically refer to the members of the object that is current when the member function is executed.

The member function **Volume()** is used in the highlighted statements in **main()**, after initializing the data members (as in the first example). Using the same name for a variable in **main()** causes no conflict or problem. You can call a member function of a particular object by writing the name of the object to be processed, followed by a period, followed by the member function name. As we noted above, the function will automatically access the data members of the object for which it was called, so the first use of **Volume()** calculates the volume of **Box1**. Using only the name of a member will always refer to the member of the object for which the member function has been called.

The member function is used a second time directly in the output statement to produce the volume of **Box2**. If you execute this example, it will produce this output:

```
Ex8_02                                              _ □ ✕

Volume of Box1 = 33696
Volume of Box2 = 6084
A Box object occupies 24 bytes.
Press any key to continue
```

Note that the **Box** object is still the same number of bytes. Adding a function member to a class doesn't affect the size of the objects. Obviously, a member function has to be stored in memory somewhere, but there is only one copy, regardless of how many class objects have been declared and it is not counted when the operator **sizeof** produces the number of bytes that an object occupies.

The names of the class data members in the member function automatically refer to the data members of the specific object used to call the function, and the function can only be called for a particular object of the class. In this case, this is done by using the direct member selection operator with the name of an object.

 FYI If you try to call a member function without specifying an object name, your program will not compile.

Positioning a Member Function Definition

A member function need not be placed inside the class definition. If you want to put it outside the class definition, you need to put the prototype for the function inside the class. If we rewrite the previous class with the function definition outside, the class definition would look like this:

```
class CBox                      // Class definition at global scope
{
    public:
        double m_Length;        // Length of a box in inches
        double m_Breadth;       // Breadth of a box in inches
        double m_Height;        // Height of a box in inches
        double Volume(void);    // Member function prototype
};
```

Now we need to write the function definition, but there has to be some way of telling the compiler that the function belongs to the class **Box**. This is done by prefixing the function name with the name of the class and separating the two with the **scope resolution operator**, **::** which is formed from two successive colons. The function definition would now look like this:

```
// Function to calculate the volume of a box
double CBox::Volume(void)
{
    return m_Length*m_Breadth*m_Height;
}
```

It will produce the same output at the last example. However, it isn't exactly the same program. In the second case, all calls to the function are treated in the way that we are already familiar with. However, when we defined the function within the definition of the class in **Ex8_02.cpp**, the compiler implicitly treated the function as an **inline** function.

Inline Functions

With an **inline** function, the compiler tries to expand the code in the body of the function in place of a call of the function. This avoids much of the overhead of calling the function and, therefore, speeds up your code. This is illustrated in the following figure:

The compiler replaces
inline function calls
with body code

```
Main()
{
    ...
    InlineFunction()
    { body }

    ...

    InlineFunction()
    { body }
    ...

}
```

InlineFuction()
{ body }

FYI

Of course, the compiler takes care of ensuring that expanding a function **inline** doesn't cause any problems with variable names or scope.

The compiler may not always be able to insert the code for a function inline (such as with recursive functions or functions for which you have obtained an address) but, generally, it will work. It's best used for very short simple functions such as our function **Volume()** because they will execute faster and will not significantly increase the size of the executable module.

With the function definition outside of the class definition, the compiler treats the function as a normal function and a call of the function will work in the usual way. However, it is also possible to tell the compiler that, if possible, we would like the function to be considered as inline. This is done by simply placing the keyword **inline** at the beginning of the function header. So, for our function, the definition would be as follows:

```
// Function to calculate the volume of a box
inline double CBox::Volume(void)
{
    return m_Length*m_Breadth*m_Height;
}
```

With this definition for the function, the program would be exactly the same as the original. This allows you to put the member function definitions outside of the class definition, if you so choose, and still retain the speed benefits of inlining.

You can apply the keyword **inline** to ordinary functions in your program that have nothing to do with classes and get the same effect. However, remember that it's best used (and only likely to work) for short, simple functions. The compiler can decide not to treat a function as **inline** simply because it is too large.

We now need to understand a little more about what happens when we declare an object of a class.

Class Constructors

In the program above, we declared our **CBox** objects, **Box1** and **Box2**, and then laboriously worked through each of the data members for each object in order to assign an initial value to it. This is unsatisfactory from several points of view. First of all, it would be easy to overlook initializing a data member, particularly with a class which had many more data members than our **Box** class. Initializing the data members of several objects of a complex class could involve pages of assignment statements. The final constraint on this approach arises when we get to defining data members of a class that do not have the attribute **public** - we won't be able to access them from outside the class anyway. There has to be a better way. Of course there is - it is known as the class **constructor**.

What is a Constructor?

A class constructor is a special function in a class which is called when a new object of the class is declared. It therefore provides the opportunity to initialize objects as they are created and to ensure that data members only contain valid values.

You have no leeway in naming a class constructor. It always has the same name as the class in which it is defined. The function **CBox()**, for example, is a constructor for our class **CBox**. It also has no return type. It is wrong to specify a return type for a constructor - you must not even write it as **void**. The primary function of a class constructor is to assign initial values to the data elements of the class and no return type is necessary, or permitted.

TRY IT OUT - Adding a Constructor to the CBox Class

Let's extend our **CBox** class to incorporate a constructor.

```
// EX8_03.CPP
// Using a constructor
#include <iostream.h>

class CBox                          // Class definition at global scope
{
   public:
      double m_Length;              // Length of a box in inches
      double m_Breadth;             // Breadth of a box in inches
      double m_Height;              // Height of a box in inches

      CBox(double lv, double bv, double hv)    // Constructor definition
      {
         cout << endl << "Constructor called.";
         m_Length = lv;                        // Set values of
         m_Breadth = bv;                       // data members
         m_Height = hv;
      }

// Function to calculate the volume of a box
      double Volume()
      {
         return m_Length* m_Breadth* m_Height;
      }
```

```
};

int main(void)
{
    CBox Box1(78.0,24.0,18.0);      // Declare and initialize Box1
    CBox CigarBox(8.0,5.0,1.0);     // Declare and initialize CigarBox

    double volume = 0.0;            // Store the volume of a box here

    volume = Box1.Volume();         // Calculate volume of Box1
    cout << endl
         << "Volume of Box1 = " << volume;

    cout << endl
         << "Volume of CigarBox = "
         << CigarBox.Volume();

    cout << endl;
    return 0;
}
```

How It Works

The constructor **CBox()** has been written with three parameters of type **double** corresponding to the initial values for the **m_Length**, **m_Breadth** and **m_Height** members of an object. The first statement in the constructor outputs a message so that we can tell when it's called. You wouldn't do this in production programs but, since it's very helpful in showing when a constructor is called, it is often used when testing a program. We will use it regularly for the purposes of illustration. The code in the body of the constructor is very simple. It just assigns the arguments passed to the corresponding data members. If necessary, we could also include checks that valid, non-negative arguments are supplied and in a real context you probably would want to do this but, here, our primary interest is in seeing how the mechanism works.

Within **main()**, we declare the object **Box1** with initializing values for the data members **m_Length**, **m_Breadth**, and **m_Height**, in sequence. These are in parentheses following the object name. This uses the functional notation for initialization which, as we saw in Chapter 2, can also be applied to initializing ordinary variables of basic types. We also declare a second object of type **CBox**, called **CigarBox** which also has initializing values.

The volume of **Box1** is calculated using the member function **Volume()** as in the previous example and is then displayed on the screen. We also display the value of the volume of **CigarBox**. The output from the example is as follows:

```
Ex8_03                                                    _ □ X

Constructor called.
Constructor called.
Volume of Box1 = 33696
Volume of CigarBox = 40
Press any key to continue
```

The first two lines are output from the two calls of the constructor **CBox()**, once for each variable declared. The constructor that we have supplied in the class definition is automatically called when a **CBox** object is declared, so both **CBox** objects are initialized with the initializing values appearing in the declaration. These are passed to the constructor as arguments, in the sequence that they are written in the declaration. As you can see, the volume of **Box1** is the same as before and **CigarBox** has a volume looking suspiciously like the product of its dimensions, which is quite a relief.

The Default Constructor

Try modifying the last example by adding the declaration for **Box2** that we had previously:

```
CBox Box2;          // Declare Box2 of type CBox
```

Here, we have left **Box2** without initializing values. When you rebuild this version of the program, you will get the error message:

error C2512: 'CBox' : no appropriate default constructor available

This means that the compiler is looking for a default constructor for **Box2**, either one that needs no arguments because none are specified in the constructor definition, or one whose arguments are all optional because we haven't supplied any initializing values for the data members. Well, this statement was perfectly satisfactory in **Ex8_02.cpp**, so why doesn't it work now?

The answer is that the previous example used a default constructor that was supplied by the compiler because we didn't supply one. Since in this example we did supply a constructor, the compiler assumed that we were taking care of everything and didn't supply the default. So if you still want to use declarations for **CBox** objects which are not initialized, you have to include the default constructor yourself. What exactly does the default constructor look like? In the simplest case, it's just a constructor that accepts no arguments, it doesn't even need to do anything:

```
CBox()      // Default constructor
{}          // Totally devoid of statements
```

TRY IT OUT - Supplying a Default Constructor

Let's add our version of the default constructor to the last example, along with the declaration for **Box2**, plus the original assignments for the data members of **Box2**. We must enlarge the default constructor just enough to show that it is called. Here is the next version of the program:

```
// EX8_04.CPP
// Supplying and using a default constructor
#include <iostream.h>

class CBox                         // Class definition at global scope
{
   public:
      double m_Length;            // Length of a box in inches
      double m_Breadth;           // Breadth of a box in inches
      double m_Height;            // Height of a box in inches

      CBox(double lv, double bv, double hv)      // Constructor definition
      {
```

```
                cout << endl << "Constructor called.";
                m_Length = lv;                          // Set values of
                m_Breadth = bv;                         // data members
                m_Height = hv;
        }

    // Default constructor definition
        CBox()
        { cout << endl << "Default constructor called."; }

    // Function to calculate the volume of a box
        double Volume()
        {
            return m_Length*m_Breadth*m_Height;
        }
};

int main(void)
{
    CBox Box1(78.,24.0,18.0);    // Declare and initialize Box1 of type CBox
    CBox Box2;                   // Declare Box2 - no initial values
    CBox CigarBox(8.0,5.0,1.0);  // Declare and initialize CigarBox

    double volume = 0.0;             // Store the volume of a box here

    volume = Box1.Volume();          // Calculate volume of Box1
    cout << endl
        << "Volume of Box1 = " << volume;

    Box2.m_Height = Box1.m_Height - 10;      // Define Box2
    Box2.m_Length = Box1.m_Length/2.0;       // members in
    Box2.m_Breadth = 0.25*Box1.m_Length;     // terms of Box1

    cout << endl
        << "Volume of Box2 = "
        << Box2.Volume();

    cout << endl
        << "Volume of CigarBox = "
        << CigarBox.Volume();

    cout << endl;
    return 0;
}
```

How It Works

Now that we have included our own version of the default constructor, there are no error messages from the compiler and everything works. The program produces this output:

```
Ex8_04
Constructor called.
Default constructor called.
Constructor called.
Volume of Box1 = 33696
Volume of Box2 = 6084
Volume of CigarBox = 40
Press any key to continue
```

All that our default constructor does is to display a message. Evidently, it was called when we declared the object **Box2**. We also get the correct value for the volumes of all three **CBox** objects, so the rest of the program is working as it should.

One aspect of this example that you may have noticed is that we now know we can overload constructors just as we overloaded functions in Chapter 6. We have just run an example with two constructors that differ only in their parameter list. One has three parameters of type **double** and the other has no parameters at all.

Assigning Default Values in a Constructor

When we discussed functions in C++, we saw how we could specify default values for the parameters to a function in the function prototype. We can also do this for class member functions, including constructors. If we put the definition of the member function inside the class definition, we can put the default values for the parameters in the function header. If we only include the prototype of a function in the class definition, the default parameter value should go in the prototype.

If we decided that the default size for a **CBox** object was a unit box with all sides of length 1, we could alter the class definition in the last example to this:

```cpp
class CBox                          // Class definition at global scope
{
   public:
      double m_Length;              // Length of a box in inches
      double m_Breadth;             // Breadth of a box in inches
      double m_Height;              // Height of a box in inches

// Constructor definition
      CBox(double lv = 1.0, double bv = 1.0, double hv = 1.0)
      {
         cout << endl << "Constructor called.";
         m_Length = lv;                        // Set values of
         m_Breadth = bv;
         m_Height = hv;                         // data members
      }

// Default constructor definition
      CBox()
      { cout << endl << "Default constructor called."; }

// Function to calculate the volume of a box
      double Volume()
      {
         return m_Length*m_Breadth*m_Height;
      }
};
```

If we make this change to the last example, what happens? We get another error message from the compiler, of course. We get these useful comments:

```
warning C4520: 'CBox' : multiple default constructors specified
error C2668: 'CBox::CBox' : ambiguous call to overloaded function
```

This means that the compiler can't work out which of the two constructors to call - the one for which we have set default values for the parameters or the constructor that doesn't accept any parameters. This is because the declaration of **Box2** requires a constructor without parameters and either constructor can now be called without parameters. The immediately obvious solution to this is to get rid of the constructor that accepts no parameters. This is actually beneficial. Without this constructor, any **Box** object that is declared without being explicitly initialized will automatically have its members initialized to **1**.

TRY IT OUT - Supplying Default Values for Constructor Arguments

We can demonstrate this with the following simplified example:

```
// EX8_05.CPP
// Supplying default values for constructor arguments
#include <iostream.h>

class CBox                          // Class definition at global scope
{
   public:
      double m_Length;             // Length of a box in inches
      double m_Breadth;            // Breadth of a box in inches
      double m_Height;             // Height of a box in inches

// Constructor definition
      CBox(double lv=1.0, double bv=1.0, double hv=1.0)
      {
         cout << endl << "Constructor called.";
         m_Length = lv;                        // Set values of
         m_Breadth = bv;                       // data members
         m_Height = hv;
      }

// Function to calculate the volume of a box
      double Volume()
      {
         return m_Length*m_Breadth*m_Height;
      }
};

int main(void)
{
   CBox Box2;                       // Declare Box2 - no initial values

   cout << endl
        << "Volume of Box2 = "
        << Box2.Volume();

   cout << endl;
   return 0;
}
```

How It Works

We only declare a single uninitialized **CBox** variable, **Box2**, because that's all we need for demonstration purposes. This version of the program produces the output shown on the next page.

```
Ex8_05                                                      _ □ ✕
Constructor called.
Volume of Box2 = 1
Press any key to continue
```

This shows that the constructor with default parameter values is doing its job of setting the values of objects that have no initializing values specified.

You shouldn't assume from this that this is the only, or even the recommended, way of implementing the default constructor. There will be many occasions where you won't want to assign default values in this way, in which case you will need to write a separate default constructor. There will even be times when you don't want to have a default constructor operating at all, even though you have defined another constructor. This would ensure that all declared objects of a class must have initializing values explicitly specified in their declaration.

Using an Initialization List in a Constructor

Previously, we initialized the members of an object in the class constructor using explicit assignment. We could also have used a different technique, using what is called an **initialization list**. We can demonstrate this with an alternative version of the constructor for the class **Box**:

```
// Constructor definition using an initialization list
   CBox(double lv=1.0, double bv=1.0, double hv=1.0): m_Length(lv),
                                                      m_Breadth(bv),
                                                      m_Height(hv)
   {
      cout << endl << "Constructor called.";
   }
```

Now the values of the data members are not set in assignment statements in the body of the constructor. As in a declaration, they are specified as initializing values using functional notation and appear in the initializing list as part of the function header. The member **m_Length** is initialized by the value of **lv**, for example. This can be rather more efficient than using assignments as we did in the previous version. If you substitute this version of the constructor in the previous example, you will see that it works just as well.

Note that the initializing list for the constructor is separated from the parameter list by a colon and each of the initializers is separated by a comma. This technique for initializing parameters in a constructor is important because, as we shall see, it is the only way of setting values for certain types of data members for an object.

Private Members of a Class

Having a constructor that sets the values of the data members of a class object but still admits the possibility of any part of a program being able to mess with what are really the guts of an object is almost a contradiction in terms. To draw an analogy, once you have arranged for a brilliant surgeon such as Dr. Kildare to do things to your insides, whose skills were honed over years of training, letting the local plumber, bricklayer or the folks from Hill Street Blues have a go hardly seems appropriate somehow. We need some protection for our class data members.

We can get it by using the keyword **private** when we define the class members. Class members which are **private** can, in general, only be accessed by member functions of a class. There is one exception, but we will worry about that later. A normal function has no direct means of accessing the **private** members of a class. This is shown in the diagram below:

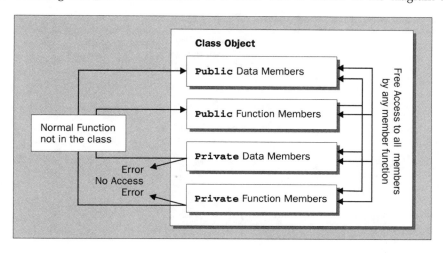

Having the possibility of specifying class members as **private** also enables you to separate the interface to the class from its internal implementation. The interface to a class is composed of the **public** members and the **public** member functions in particular, since they can provide indirect access to all the members of a class, including the **private** members. By keeping the internals of a class **private**, you can later modify the internals, for example, to improve performance, without necessitating modifications to code that uses the class through its public interface. To keep them safe from unnecessary meddling, it's good practice to declare data and function members of a class that do not need to be exposed as **private**. Only make **public** what is essential to the use of your class.

TRY IT OUT - private Data Members

We can rewrite the **CBox** class to make its data members **private**.

```
// EX8_06.CPP
// A class with private members
#include <iostream.h>

class CBox                          // Class definition at global scope
{
   public:
// Constructor definition
      CBox(double lv=1.0, double bv=1.0, double hv=1.0)
      {
         cout << endl << "Constructor called.";
         m_Length = lv;                       // Set values of
         m_Breadth = bv;                      // data members
         m_Height = hv;
      }
```

```
    // Function to calculate the volume of a box
        double Volume()
        {
            return m_Length*m_Breadth*m_Height;
        }

    private:
        double m_Length;            // Length of a box in inches
        double m_Breadth;           // Breadth of a box in inches
        double m_Height;            // Height of a box in inches

};
int main(void)
{
    CBox Match(2.2, 1.1, 0.5);      // Declare Match box
    CBox Box2;                      // Declare Box2 - no initial values

    cout << endl
        << "Volume of Match = "
        << Match.Volume();

// Uncomment the following line to get an error
// Box2.m_Length = 4.0;

    cout << endl
        << "Volume of Box2 = "
        << Box2.Volume();

    cout << endl;
    return 0;
}
```

How It Works

The definition of the class **CBox** now has two sections. The first is the **public** section containing the constructor and the member function **Volume()**. The second section is specified as **private** and contains the data members. Now the data members can only be accessed by the member functions of the class. We don't have to modify any of the member functions - they can access all the data members of the class anyway. However, if you uncomment the statement in the function **main()**, assigning a value to the member **length** of the object **Box2**, you will get a compiler error message confirming that the data member is inaccessible.

> *A point to remember is that using a constructor or a member function is now the only way to get a value into a **private** data member of an object. You have to make sure that all the ways in which you might want to set or modify **private** data members of a class are provided for through member functions.*

We could also put functions into the **private** section of a class. In this case, they can only be called by other member functions. If you put the function **Volume()** in the **private** section, you will get a compiler error from the statements that attempt to use it in the function **main()**. If you put the constructor in the **private** section, you won't be able to declare any members of the class.

The example generates this output:

```
Ex8_06                                                    _ □ X
Constructor called.
Constructor called.
Volume of Match = 1.21
Volume of Box2 = 1
Press any key to continue
```

This demonstrates that the class is still working satisfactorily, with its data members defined as having the access attribute **private**. The major difference is that they are now completely protected from unauthorized access and modification.

If you don't specify otherwise, the default access attribute which applies to members of a class is **private**. You could, therefore, put all your **private** members at the beginning of the class definition and let them default to **private** by omitting the keyword. However, it is better to take the trouble to explicitly state the access attribute in every case, so there can be no doubt about what you intend.

Of course, you don't have to make all your data members **private**. If the application for your class requires it, you can have some data members defined as **private** and some as **public**. It all depends on what you are trying to do. If there is no reason to make members of a class **public**, it is better to make them **private** as it makes the class more secure. Ordinary functions won't be able to access any of the **private** members of your class.

Accessing private Class Members

On reflection, declaring the data members of a class as **private** is rather extreme. It's all very well protecting them from unauthorized modification but that's no reason to keep their values a secret. What we need is a Freedom of Information Act for **private** members.

You don't need to start writing to your state senator to get it. It's already available to you. All you need to do is to write a member function to return the value of a data member. Look at this member function for the class **CBox**:

```
inline double CBox::GetLength(void)
{
    return m_Length;
}
```

Just to show how it looks, this has been written as a member function definition which is external to the class. We've specified it as **inline** since we'll benefit from the speed increase without increasing the size of our code too much. Assuming that you have the declaration of the function in the **public** section of the class, you can use it by writing this statement:

```
len = Box2.GetLength();    // Obtain data member length
```

All you need to do is to write a similar function for each data member that you want to make available to the outside world, and their values can be accessed without prejudicing the security of the class. Of course, if you put the definitions for these functions within the class definition, they will be **inline** by default.

273

The friend Functions of a Class

There may be circumstances when, for one reason or another, you want certain selected functions which are not members of a class to, nonetheless, be able to access all the members of a class - a sort of elite group with special privileges. Such functions are called **friend functions** of a class and are defined using the keyword **friend**. You can either include the prototype of a friend function in the class definition, or you can include the function definition. Functions which are friends of a class and are defined within the class definition are also by default **inline**.

Let's suppose that we wanted to implement a friend function in the **CBox** class to compute the surface area of a **CBox** object.

TRY IT OUT - Using a friend to Calculate the Surface Area

We can see how this works in the following example:

```cpp
// EX8_07.CPP
// Creating a friend function of a class
#include <iostream.h>

class CBox                        // Class definition at global scope
{
   public:
// Constructor definition
      CBox(double lv=1.0, double bv=1.0, double hv=1.0)
      {
         cout << endl << "Constructor called.";
         m_Length = lv;                      // Set values of
         m_Breadth = bv;                     // data members
         m_Height = hv;
      }

// Function to calculate the volume of a box
      double Volume()
      {
         return m_Length*m_Breadth*m_Height;
      }


   private:
      double m_Length;           // Length of a box in inches
      double m_Breadth;          // Breadth of a box in inches
      double m_Height;           // Height of a box in inches

   //Friend function
   friend double BoxSurface(CBox aBox);

};


// friend function to calculate the surface area of a Box object
double BoxSurface(CBox aBox)
{
   return 2.0*(aBox.m_Length*aBox.m_Breadth +
```

```
                        aBox.m_Length*aBox.m_Height +
                        aBox.m_Height*aBox.m_Breadth);
    }


    int main(void)
    {
       CBox Match(2.2, 1.1, 0.5);      // Declare Match box
       CBox Box2;                      // Declare Box2 - no initial values

       cout << endl
            << "Volume of Match = "
            << Match.Volume();

       cout << endl
            << "Surface area of Match = "
            << BoxSurface(Match);

       cout << endl
            << "Volume of Box2 = "
            << Box2.Volume();

       cout << endl
            << "Surface area of Box2 = "
            << BoxSurface(Box2);

       cout << endl;
       return 0;
    }
```

How It Works

We declare the function **BoxSurface()** as a friend of the **CBox** class by writing the function prototype with the keyword **friend** at the front. Since the **BoxSurface()** function itself is a global function, it makes no difference where we put the **friend** declaration within the definition of the class, but it's a good idea to be consistent when you position this sort of declaration. You can see that we have chosen to position ours after all the **public** and **private** members of the class. Remember that a **friend** function is not a member of the class.

The definition of the function follows that of the class. Note that we specify access to the data members of the object within the definition of **BoxSurface()**, using the **CBox** object passed to the function as a parameter. Because a **friend** function is not a class member, the data members can't be referenced just by their names. They each have to be qualified by the object name in exactly the same way as they might in an ordinary function, except, of course, that an ordinary function can't access the **private** members of a class. A **friend** function is the same as an ordinary function except that it can access all the members of a class without restriction.

The example produces the output:

```
Ex8_07                                                    _ □ ×
Constructor called.
Constructor called.
Volume of Match = 1.21
Surface area of Match = 8.14
Volume of Box2 = 1
Surface area of Box2 = 6
Press any key to continue
```

275

This is exactly what you would expect. The **friend** function is computing the surface area of the **CBox** objects from the values of the **private** members.

Placing friend Function Definitions inside the Class

We could have combined the definition of the function with its declaration as a friend of the **CBox** class within the class definition and the code would run as before. This has a number of disadvantages relating to the readability of the code. Although the function would still have global scope, this wouldn't be obvious to readers of the code, since the function would be hidden in the body of the class definition and particularly since the function would no longer show up in the ClassView.

The Default Copy Constructor

Suppose we declare and initialize a **CBox** object **Box1** with this statement:

```
CBox Box1(78.0, 24.0, 18.0);
```

We now want to create another **CBox** object, identical to the first. We would like to initialize the second **CBox** object with **Box1**.

TRY IT OUT - Copying Information between Instances

We can try this out with the **main()** function which follows:

```
// EX8_08.CPP
// Initializing an object with an object of the same class
#include <iostream.h>

class CBox                       // Class definition at global scope
{
   public:
// Constructor definition
      CBox(double lv=1.0, double bv=1.0, double hv=1.0)
      {
         cout << endl << "Constructor called.";
         m_Length = lv;                   // Set values of
         m_Breadth = bv;                  // data members
         m_Height = hv;
      }

// Function to calculate the volume of a box
      double Volume()
      {
         return m_Length*m_Breadth*m_Height;
      }


   private:
      double m_Length;           // Length of a box in inches
      double m_Breadth;          // Breadth of a box in inches
      double m_Height;           // Height of a box in inches
```

```
    };

    int main(void)
    {
        CBox Box1(78.0, 24.0, 18.0);
        CBox Box2 = Box1;              // Initialize Box2 with Box1

        cout << endl
             << "Box1 volume = " << Box1.Volume()
             << endl
             << "Box2 volume = " << Box2.Volume();

        cout << endl;
        return 0;
    }
```

How It Works

This example will produce this output:

```
Ex8_08
Constructor called.
Box1 volume = 33696
Box2 volume = 33696
Press any key to continue
```

Clearly, the program is working as we would want, with both boxes having the same volume. However, as you can see from the output, our constructor was called only once for the creation of **Box1**. The question is, how was **Box2** created? The mechanism is similar to the one that we experienced when we had no constructor defined and the compiler supplied a default constructor to allow an object to be created. In this case, the compiler generates a default version of what is referred to as a **copy constructor**.

A copy constructor does exactly what we are doing here - it creates an object of a class by initializing it with an existing object of the same class. The default version of the copy constructor creates the new object by copying the existing object, member by member.

This is fine for simple classes such as **Cbox**, but for many classes, classes that have pointers or arrays as members for example, it won't work properly. Indeed, with such classes it can create serious errors in your program. In this case, you need to create your own class copy constructor. This requires a special approach, so we will look into this more fully towards the end of this chapter and again in the next chapter.

The Pointer this

In our class **CBox**, we wrote the function **Volume()** in terms of the class member names in the definition of the class. Of course, every object of type **CBox** that we create contains these members, so there has to be a mechanism for the function to refer to the members for the particular object for which the function is called.

277

When any member function executes, it automatically contains a hidden pointer with the name **this**, which points to the object used with the function call. Therefore, when the member **m_Length** is accessed in the function **Volume()** during execution, it is actually referring to **this.m_Length**, which is the fully specified reference to the object member that is being used. The compiler takes care of adding the necessary pointer name **this** to the member names in the function.

If you need to, you can use the pointer **this** explicitly within a member function, for example, when you want to return a pointer to the current object.

TRY IT OUT - Explicit Use of this

We could add a public function to our class **CBox** to compare the volume of two **CBox** objects.

```cpp
// EX8_09.CPP
// Using the pointer this
#include <iostream.h>

class CBox                          // Class definition at global scope
{
    public:
// Constructor definition
        CBox(double lv=1.0, double bv=1.0, double hv=1.0)
        {
            cout << endl << "Constructor called.";
            m_Length = lv;                          // Set values of
            m_Breadth = bv;                         // data members
            m_Height = hv;
        }

// Function to calculate the volume of a box
        double Volume()
        {
            return m_Length*m_Breadth*m_Height;
        }

// Function to compare two boxes which returns TRUE (1)
// if the first is greater that the second, and FALSE (0) otherwise
        int compare(CBox xBox)
        {
            return this->Volume() > xBox.Volume();
        }

    private:
        double m_Length;            // Length of a box in inches
        double m_Breadth;           // Breadth of a box in inches
        double m_Height;            // Height of a box in inches

};

int main(void)
{
    CBox Match(2.2, 1.1, 0.5);      // Declare Match box
    CBox Cigar(8.0, 5.0 ,1.0);      // Declare Cigar box
```

```
        if(Cigar.compare(Match))
            cout << endl
                 << "Match is smaller than Cigar";
        else
            cout << endl
                 << "Match is equal to or larger than Cigar";

    cout << endl;
    return 0;
}
```

How It Works

The member function **compare()** returns **1** if the prefixed **CBox** object in the function call has a greater volume than the **CBox** object specified as an argument, and **0** if it doesn't. In the **return** statements, the prefixed object is referred to through the pointer **this**, used with the indirect member selection operator, **->**, that we saw in the previous chapter.

 FYI Remember that you use the direct member selection operator "**.**" when dealing with objects and the indirect member selection operator "**->**" when dealing with pointers to objects. **this** is a pointer.

It works the same for pointers to class objects as it did when we were dealing with a **struct**. Here, using the pointer **this** demonstrates that it exists and *does* work, but it's quite unnecessary to use it explicitly in this case. If you change the **return** statement in the **compare()** function to be,

```
    return Volume() > xBox.Volume();
```

you will find that it works just as well. Any references to unadorned member names are automatically assumed to be the members of the object pointed to by **this**.

The **compare()** function is used in **main()** to check the relationship between the volumes of the objects **Match** and **Cigar**. The output from the program is as follows:

```
Ex8_09
Constructor called.
Constructor called.
Match is smaller than Cigar
Press any key to continue
```

This confirms that the **Cigar Box** object is larger than the **Match Box** object.

It also wasn't essential to write the **compare()** function as a class member. We could just as well have written it as an ordinary function with the objects as arguments. Note that this is not true of the function **Volume()**, since it needs to access the **private** data members of the class. Of course if the function **compare()** was implemented as an ordinary function, it wouldn't have the pointer **this**, but it would still be very simple.

```
// Comparing two CBox objects - ordinary function version
int compare(CBox B1, CBox B2)
{
    return B1.Volume() > B2.Volume();
}
```

This has both objects as arguments and returns **TRUE** if the volume of the first is greater than the last. You would use this function to perform the same function as in the last example with this statement:

```
if(compare(Cigar, Match))
    cout << endl
        << "Match is smaller than Cigar";
else
    cout << endl
        << "Match is equal to or larger than Cigar";
```

If anything, this looks slightly better and easier to read than the original version. However, there is a much better way to do this, which we shall see before the end of this chapter.

Arrays of Objects of a Class

We can declare an array of objects of a class in exactly the same way that we have declared an ordinary array where the elements are one of the built-in types. Each element of an array of class objects causes the default constructor to be called.

TRY IT OUT - Arrays of Class Objects

We can use the class definition of **Box** from the last example, but modified to include a specific default constructor:

```
// EX8_10.CPP
// Using an array of class objects
#include <iostream.h>

class CBox                          // Class definition at global scope
{
    public:
// Constructor definition
        CBox(double lv, double bv=1.0, double hv=1.0)
        {
            cout << endl << "Constructor called.";
            m_Length = lv;                      // Set values of
            m_Breadth = bv;                     // data members
            m_Height = hv;
        }

        CBox()                              // Default constructor
        {
            cout << endl
                << "Default constructor called.";
            m_Length = m_Breadth = m_Height = 1.0;
        }
```

```
    // Function to calculate the volume of a box
        double Volume()
        {
            return m_Length*m_Breadth*m_Height;
        }

    private:
        double m_Length;                // Length of a box in inches
        double m_Breadth;               // Breadth of a box in inches
        double m_Height;                // Height of a box in inches

};
int main(void)
{
    CBox Boxes[5];                      // Array of CBox objects declared
    CBox Cigar(8.0, 5.0 ,1.0);          // Declare Cigar box

    cout << endl
        << "Volume of Boxes[3] = " << Boxes[3].Volume()
        << endl
        << "Volume of Cigar = " << Cigar.Volume();

    cout << endl;
    return 0;
}
```

How It Works

We have modified the constructor accepting arguments so that only two default values are supplied, and we have added a default constructor which initializes the data members to **1** after displaying a message that it was called. We will now be able to see *which* constructor was called *when*. The constructors now have quite distinct parameter lists, so there is no possibility of the compiler confusing them. The program produces this output:

```
Ex8_10                                                          _ □ X
Default constructor called.
Default constructor called.
Default constructor called.
Default constructor called.
Default constructor called.
Constructor called.
Volume of Boxes[3] = 1
Volume of Cigar = 40
Press any key to continue
```

We can see that the default constructor was called five times, once for each element of the array **Boxes**. The other constructor was called to create the object **Cigar**. It's clear from the output that the default constructor initialization is working satisfactorily, as the volume of the array element is **1**.

Static Members of a Class

Both data members and function members of a class can be declared as **static**. Because the context is a class definition, there is a little more to it than the effect of the keyword **static** outside of a class, so let's look at static data members.

Static Data Members of a Class

When we declare data members of a class as **static**, the effect is that the **static** data members are defined only once and are shared between all objects of the class. Each object gets its own copies of each of the ordinary data members of a class, but only one instance of each static data member exists, regardless of how many class objects have been defined.

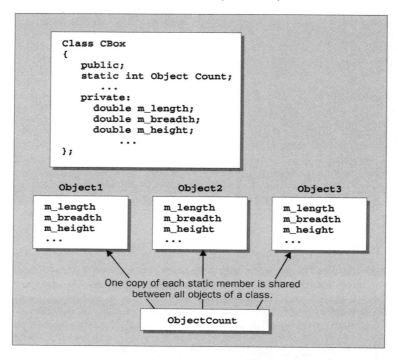

```
Class CBox
{
    public;
    static int Object Count;
        ...
    private:
        double m_length;
        double m_breadth;
        double m_height;
            ...
};
```

Object1	Object2	Object3
m_length m_breadth m_height ...	m_length m_breadth m_height ...	m_length m_breadth m_height ...

One copy of each static member is shared between all objects of a class.

ObjectCount

One use for a **static** data member is to count how many objects actually exist. We could add a **static** data member to the public section of the **CBox** class by adding the following statement to the previous class definition:

```
static int ObjectCount;      // Count of objects in existence
```

We now have a problem. How do we initialize the static data member? We can't put it in the class definition - that is simply a blueprint for an object - and initializing values are not allowed. We don't want to initialize it in a constructor, because we want to increment it every time the constructor is called. We can't initialize it in another member function since a member function is associated with an object, and we want it initialized before any object is created. The answer is to write the initialization outside of the class definition with this statement:

```
int CBox::ObjectCount = 0; // Initialize static member of class CBox
```

FYI Note that the keyword **static** is not included here. However, we do need to qualify the member name by using the class name and the scope resolution operator so that the compiler understands we are referring to a static member of the class. Otherwise, we would simply create a global variable that was nothing to do with the class.

TRY IT OUT - Counting Instances

Let's add the **static** data member and the object counting capability to the last example.

```cpp
// EX8_11.CPP
// Using a static data member in a class
#include <iostream.h>

class CBox                         // Class definition at global scope
{
   public:
      static int ObjectCount;      // Count of objects in existence

// Constructor definition
      CBox(double lv, double bv=1.0, double hv=1.0)
      {
         cout << endl << "Constructor called.";
         m_Length = lv;                         // Set values of
         m_Breadth = bv;
         m_Height = hv;                         // data members
         ObjectCount++;
      }

      CBox()                                    // Default constructor
      {
         cout << endl
              << "Default constructor called.";
         m_Length = m_Breadth = m_Height = 1.0;
         ObjectCount++;

      }

// Function to calculate the volume of a box
      double Volume()
      {
         return m_Length*m_Breadth*m_Height;
      }

   private:
      double m_Length;             // Length of a box in inches
      double m_Breadth;            // Breadth of a box in inches
      double m_Height;             // Height of a box in inches

};

int CBox::ObjectCount = 0;    // Initialize static member of class CBox

int main(void)
{
   CBox Boxes[5];                        // Array of CBox objects declared
   CBox Cigar(8.0, 5.0 ,1.0);            // Declare Cigar box

   cout << endl << endl
        << "Number of objects (through class) = "
        << CBox::ObjectCount;

   cout << endl
```

```
                   << "Number of objects (through object) = "
                   << Boxes[2].ObjectCount;

     cout << endl;
     return 0;
}
```

How It Works

This example will produce the output:

```
Ex8_11                                                    _ □ ✕
Default constructor called.
Default constructor called.
Default constructor called.
Default constructor called.
Default constructor called.
Constructor called.

Number of objects (through class) = 6
Number of objects (through object) = 6
Press any key to continue
```

This code shows that it doesn't matter how we refer to the static member **ObjectCount** (whether through the class itself or any of the objects of that class). The value is the same and is equal to the number of objects of that class that have been created. The six objects are obviously the five elements of the **Boxes** array, plus the object **Cigar**. It's interesting to note that **static** members of a class exist even though there may be no members of the class in existence. This is evidently the case, since we initialized the **static** member **ObjectCount** before any class objects were declared.

FYI — Note that you must initialize a static data member, otherwise the compiler will complain. The declaration in the class definition doesn't define a static variable so, until you define its initial value, it doesn't exist.

Static Function Members of a Class

By declaring a function member as **static**, you make it independent of any particular object of the class. Referencing members of the class must be done using qualified names (as you would do with an ordinary member function). The **static** member function has the advantage that it exists and can be called, even if no objects of the class exist. In this case, only **static** data members can be used, since they are the only ones that exist. You can thus call a **static** function member of a class to examine **static** data members, even when you do not know for certain that any objects of the class exists. You could, therefore, use a **static** member function to determine whether some objects of the class have been created or, indeed, how many have been created.

Of course, once the objects have been defined, a **static** member function can access **private** as well as **public** members of class objects. A **static** function might have this prototype:

```
      static void afunction(int n);
```

A **static** function can be called in relation to a particular object by a statement such as the following,

```
    aBox.afunction(10);
```

where **aBox** is an object of the class. The same function could also be called without reference to an object. In this case, the statement would be in the following form,

```
    CBox::afunction(10);
```

where **CBox** is the class name. Using the class name and the scope resolution operator serves to tell the compiler to which class the function **afunction()** belongs.

Pointers and References to Class Objects

Using pointers, and particularly references to class objects, is very important to object oriented programming. Class objects can involve considerable amounts of data, so using a pass-by-value mechanism by specifying objects as parameters can be very time consuming and inefficient. There are also some techniques involving the use of references which are essential to some operations with classes. As we shall see, you can't write a copy constructor without using a reference parameter.

Pointers to Class Objects

You declare a pointer to a class object in the same way that you declare other pointers. For example, a pointer to objects of the class **Box** is declared in this statement:

```
    CBox* pBox = 0;            // Declare a pointer to CBox
```

You can now use this to store the address of a **CBox** object in an assignment in the usual way, using the address operator:

```
    pBox = &Cigar;           // Store address of CBox object Cigar in pBox
```

As we saw when we used the pointer **this** in the definition of the member function **compare()**, you can call a function using a pointer to an object. We can call the function **Volume()** for the pointer **pBox** in this statement:

```
    cout << pBox->Volume(); // Display volume of object pointed to by pBox
```

Again, this uses the indirect member selection operator. This is the typical notation used by most programmers for this kind of operation, so from now on we will use it universally.

TRY IT OUT - Pointers to Classes

Let's try exercising the indirect member selection operator a little more. We will use the example **Ex8_09.cpp** as a base, but change it a little.

```
// EX8_12.CPP
// Exercising the indirect member selection operator
#include <iostream.h>

class CBox                          // Class definition at global scope
{
   public:
// Constructor definition
      CBox(double lv=1.0, double bv=1.0, double hv=1.0)
      {
         cout << endl << "Constructor called.";
         m_Length = lv;                         // Set values of
         m_Breadth = bv;                        // data members
         m_Height = hv;
      }

// Function to calculate the volume of a box
      double Volume()
      {
         return m_Length*m_Breadth*m_Height;
      }

// Function to compare two boxes which returns TRUE (1)
// if the first is greater that the second, and FALSE (0) otherwise
      int compare(CBox* pBox)
      {
         return this->Volume() > pBox->Volume();
      }

   private:
      double m_Length;             // Length of a box in inches
      double m_Breadth;            // Breadth of a box in inches
      double m_Height;             // Height of a box in inches

};

int main(void)
{
   CBox Boxes[5];                  // Array of CBox objects declared
   CBox Match(2.2, 1.1, 0.5);   // Declare Match box
   CBox Cigar(8.0, 5.0 ,1.0);   // Declare Cigar Box
   CBox* pB1 = &Cigar;     // Initialize pointer to Cigar object address
   CBox* pB2 = 0;          // Pointer to CBox initialized to null

   cout << endl
      << "Address of Cigar is " << pB1          // Display address
      << endl
      << "Volume of Cigar is " << pB1->Volume(); // Volume of object
                                                 // pointed to

   pB2 = &Match;
   if(pB2->compare(pB1))                         // Compare via pointers
      cout << endl
         << "Match is greater than Cigar";
   else
      cout << endl
         << "Match is less than or equal to Cigar";
```

```
    pB1 = Boxes;                        // Set to address of array
    Boxes[2] = Match;                   // Set 3rd element to Match
    cout << endl                        // Now access thru pointer
        << "Volume of Boxes[2] is " << (pB1 + 2)->Volume();

  cout << endl;
  return 0;
}
```

How It Works

The only change to the class definition is not one of great substance. We have only modified the **compare()** function to accept a pointer to a **CBox** object as an argument. The function **main()** merely exercises pointers to **CBox** type objects in various, rather arbitrary, ways.

Within the function **main()**, after declaring an array **Boxes**, and the **CBox** objects **Cigar** and **Match**, we declare two pointers to **CBox** objects. The first, **pB1**, is initialized with the address of the object **Cigar**, and the second, **pB2**, is initialized to **NULL**. All of this uses the pointer in exactly the same way as when you are applying a pointer to a basic type. The fact that we are using a pointer to a type that we have defined makes no difference.

We use **pB1** with the indirect member selection operator to generate the volume of the object pointed to, and the result is displayed. We then assign the address of **Match** to **pB2** and use both pointers in calling the compare function. Because the argument of the function **compare()** is a pointer to a **CBox** object passed by value, the function uses the indirect member selection operator in calling the **Volume()** function for the object.

To demonstrate that we can use address arithmetic on the pointer **pB1** when using it to select the member function, we set **pB1** to the address of the first element of the array of type **CBox**, **Boxes**. In this case, we select the third element of the array and calculate its volume. This is the same as the volume of **Match**.

If you run the example, the output window will look something like that shown below:

```
Ex8_12                                                    _ □ ✕

Constructor called.
Constructor called.
Constructor called.
Constructor called.
Constructor called.
Constructor called.
Constructor called.
Address of Cigar is 0x0064FDE0
Volume of Cigar is 40
Match is less than or equal to Cigar
Volume of Boxes[2] is 1.21
Press any key to continue
```

> *Of course, the value of the address for the object* **Cigar** *may well be different on your PC.*

You can see that there were seven calls of the constructor for **CBox** objects, five due to the array **Boxes**, plus one each for the objects **Cigar** and **Match**.

Overall, there is virtually no difference between using a pointer to a class object and using a pointer to a basic type, such as **double**.

References to Class Objects

References really come into their own when they are used with classes. As with pointers, there is virtually no difference between the way you declare and use references to class objects and the way in which we have already declared and used references to variables of basic types. To declare a reference to the object **Cigar**, for instance, we would write this:

```
CBox& rCigar = Cigar;          // Define reference to object Cigar
```

To use a reference to calculate the volume of the object **Cigar**, you would just use the reference name where the object name would otherwise appear:

```
cout << rCigar.Volume();   // Output volume of Cigar thru a reference
```

As you may remember, a reference acts as an alias for the object it refers to, so the usage is exactly the same as using the original object name.

Implementing a Copy Constructor

The importance of references is really in the context of arguments and return values in functions, particularly class member functions. Let's return to the question of the copy constructor as a first toe in the water. For the moment, we will sidestep the question of *when* you need to write your own copy constructor and concentrate on the problem of *how* you can write one. We will use the class **CBox** just to make the discussion more concrete.

The copy constructor is a constructor which creates an object by initializing it with an object of the same class which has been created previously. It therefore needs to accept an object of the class as an argument. We might consider writing the prototype like this:

```
CBox(CBox initB);
```

Let's now consider what happens when this constructor is called. If we write this declaration,

```
CBox myBox = Cigar;
```

this will generate a call of the copy constructor as follows:

```
CBox::CBox(Cigar);
```

This seems to be no problem, until you realize that the argument is passed by value. So, before the object **Cigar** can be passed, the compiler needs to arrange to make a copy of it. Therefore, it calls the copy constructor to make a copy of the argument for the call of the copy constructor. Unfortunately, since it is passed by value, this call also needs a copy of its argument to be made, so the copy constructor is called ..., and so on, and so on. We end up with an infinity of calls to the copy constructor.

The solution, as I'm sure you have guessed, is to use a **const** reference parameter. If the prototype of the copy constructor is this,

```
CBox(const Box& initB);
```

the argument to the copy constructor does not now need to be copied. It will be used to initialize the reference parameter, so no copying takes place. We could implement the copy constructor as follows:

```
CBox::CBox(const CBox& initB)
{
   m_Length = initB.m_Length;
   m_Breadth = initB.m_Breadth;
   m_Height = initB.m_Height;
}
```

This definition of the copy constructor assumes that it appears outside of the class definition. The name is, therefore, qualified with the class name using the scope resolution operator. Each data member of the object being created is initialized with the corresponding member of the object passed as an argument. Of course, we could equally well use the initialization list to set the values of the object.

This case is not an example of when we need to write a copy constructor. . As we have seen, the default copy constructor works perfectly well with **CBox** objects. We will get to *why* and *when* we need to write our own copy constructor in the next chapter.

Summary

You now understand the basic ideas behind classes in C++. We are going to see more and more about using classes throughout the rest of the book.

The key points to keep in mind from this chapter are:

▶ A **class** provides a means of defining your own data types. These can reflect whatever types of **objects** your particular problem requires.

▶ A class can contain **data members** and **function members**. The function members of a class always have free access to the data members of the same class.

▶ Objects of a class are created and initialized using functions called **constructors**. These are automatically called when an object declaration is encountered. Constructors may be overloaded to provide different ways of initializing an object.

▶ Members of a class can be specified as **public**, in which case they are freely accessible by any function in a program. Alternatively, they may be specified as **private**, in which case they may only be accessed by member functions or **friend** functions of the class.

▶ Members of a class can be defined as **static**. Only one instance of each static member of a class exists, which is shared amongst all instances of the class, no matter how many objects of the class are created.

▶ Every non-**static** member of a class contains the pointer **this**, which points to the current object for which the function was called.

▶ Using references to class objects as arguments to function calls can avoid substantial overhead in passing complex objects to a function.

▶ A copy constructor, which is a constructor for an object that is initialized with an existing object of the same class, must have its parameter specified as a **const** reference.

More on Classes

In this chapter, you will extend your knowledge of classes by understanding how to make your class objects work more like the basic types in C++. You will learn:

- What a class destructor is and when and why it is necessary
- How to implement a class destructor
- How to allocate data members of a class in the free store
- How to delete data members of a class when they are no longer required
- When you must write a copy constructor for a class
- What a union is and how it can be used
- How to make objects of your class work with C++ operators such as + or *
- How to use classes in a practical example

Class Destructors

Although this section heading refers to destructors, it is also about dynamic memory allocation. Allocating memory in the free store for class members can only be managed with the aid of a destructor, in addition to a constructor of course, and, as you'll see, using dynamically allocated class members will require you to write your own copy constructor.

What is a Destructor?

A **destructor** is a function that destroys an object when it is no longer required or when it goes out of scope. It's called automatically when an object goes out of scope. Destroying an object involves freeing the memory occupied by the data members of the object (except for **static** members which continue to exist even when there are no class objects in existence). The destructor for a class is a member function with the same name as the class preceded by a tilde ~. The class destructor doesn't return a value and doesn't have parameters defined. For the class **CBox**, the prototype of the class destructor is as follows:

```
    ~CBox();                    // Class destructor prototype
```

FYI   It's an error to specify either a return value or parameters for a destructor.

The Default Destructor

All the objects that we have been using up to now have been destroyed automatically by the default destructor for the class. This is generated by the compiler in the absence of any explicit destructor being provided with a class. The default destructor doesn't delete objects or object members that have been allocated in the free store by the operator **new**. You must explicitly use the **delete** operator to destroy objects that have been created using the operator **new**, just as you would with ordinary variables. If you decide to allocate memory for members of an object dynamically, you must use the operator **delete** to supply a class destructor which frees any memory that was allocated by the operator **new** .

TRY IT OUT - A Simple Destructor

We need some practice in writing our own destructor. First, to show when the destructor is called, we can include a destructor in the class **CBox** . This class definition in this example is based on the last example in the previous chapter, **Ex8_12.cpp**.

```cpp
// EX9_01.CPP
// Class with an explicit destructor
#include <iostream.h>

class CBox                      // Class definition at global scope
{
   public:
// Destructor definition
      ~CBox()
      { cout << "Destructor called." << endl; }

// Constructor definition
      CBox(double lv=1.0, double bv=1.0, double hv=1.0)
      {
         cout << endl << "Constructor called.";
         m_Length = lv;                      // Set values of
         m_Breadth = bv;                     // data members
         m_Height = hv;
      }

// Function to calculate the volume of a box
      double Volume()
      {
         return m_Length*m_Breadth*m_Height;
      }

// Function to compare two boxes which returns TRUE (1)
// if the first is greater that the second, and FALSE (0) otherwise
      int compare(CBox* pBox)
      {
```

```
            return this->Volume() > pBox->Volume();
        }

    private:
        double m_Length;            // Length of a box in inches
        double m_Breadth;           // Breadth of a box in inches
        double m_Height;            // Height of a box in inches

};
```

```
int main(void)
{
    CBox Boxes[5];                  // Array of CBox objects declared
    CBox Cigar(8.0, 5.0 ,1.0);      // Declare Cigar box
    CBox Match(2.2, 1.1, 0.5);      // Declare Match box
    CBox* pB1 = &Cigar;        // Initialize pointer to Cigar object address
    CBox* pB2 = 0;                  // Pointer to CBox initialized to null

    cout << endl
        << "Volume of Cigar is "
        << pB1->Volume();           // Volume of obj. pointed to

    pB2 = Boxes;                    // Set to address of array
    Boxes[2] = Match;               // Set 3rd element to Match
    cout << endl                    // Now access thru pointer
        << "Volume of Boxes[2] is " << (pB2 + 2)->Volume();

    cout << endl;
    return 0;
}
```

How It Works

The only thing that our destructor does is to display a message showing that it was called. The output is as follows:

```
Ex9_01
Constructor called.
Constructor called.
Constructor called.
Constructor called.
Constructor called.
Constructor called.
Constructor called.
Volume of Cigar is 40
Volume of Boxes[2] is 1.21
Destructor called.
Destructor called.
Destructor called.
Destructor called.
Destructor called.
Destructor called.
Destructor called.
Press any key to continue
```

We get one call of the destructor at the end of the program for each of the objects which exist. For each constructor call that occurred, there is a matching destructor call. We don't need to call the destructor explicitly here. The compiler arranges for a destructor call for each object. When an object of a class goes out of scope, the compiler will also arrange that the destructor for the class is called automatically. In our example, the destructors are called after **main()** has finished executing, so if there's an error in a destructor, it's quite possible for a program to crash after **main()** has safely terminated.

Destructors and Dynamic Memory Allocation

You'll find that you often want to allocate memory for class data members dynamically. We can use the operator **new** in a constructor to allocate space for an object member. In such a case, we must assume responsibility for deleting the space by providing a suitable destructor. Let's first define a simple class where we can do this.

Suppose we want a class where each object is a message of some description, for example, a text string. We want the class to be as memory efficient as possible so, rather than defining a data member as a **char** array big enough to hold the maximum length string that we might require, we will allocate memory on the free store for a message when an object is created. Here's the class definition:

```
//Listing 02_01
class CMessage
{
   private:
      char* pmessage;                  // Pointer to object text string

   public:

// Function to display a message
      void ShowIt(void)
      {
          cout << endl << pmessage;
      }

// Constructor definition
      CMessage(const char* text = "Default message")
      {

          pmessage = new char[strlen(text)+1];// Allocate space for text
          strcpy(pmessage, text);              // Copy text to new memory
      }

      ~CMessage();                             // Destructor prototype
};
```

This class has only one data member defined, **pmessage**, which is a pointer to a text string. This is defined in the **private** section of the class so that it can't be accessed from outside the class.

In the **public** section, we have a function **ShowIt()** which will output a **CMessage** object to the screen. We also have the definition of a constructor and we have the prototype for the class destructor **~CMessage()** which we will come to in a moment.

The constructor for the class requires a string as an argument, but if none is passed, it uses the default value specified. The constructor obtains the length of the string supplied as an argument, excluding the terminating null, using the function **strlen()**. For the constructor to use this library function, there must be an **#include** statement for the header file **string.h**. By adding 1 to the value that the function **strlen()** returns, the constructor defines the number of bytes of memory necessary to store the string in the free store.

> *We are assuming that we have our own function to handle out-of-memory conditions, so we don't bother to test the pointer returned for **NULL**. (See Chapter 4 for information on handling out-of-memory conditions.)*

Having obtained the memory for the string, using the operator **new**, we use the **strcpy()** function, which is also declared in the header file **string.h**, to copy the string supplied as an argument into the memory allocated for it. This function copies the string specified by the second pointer argument to the address contained in the first pointer argument.

We now need to write a class destructor that will free up the memory allocated for a message. If we don't provide this, there's no way to delete the memory allocated for an object. If we use this class in a program where a large number of **CMessage** objects are created, the free store will be gradually eaten away until the program fails. It's easy for this to happen almost invisibly. For example, if you create a temporary **CMessage** object in a function which is called many times in a program, you might assume that the objects are being destroyed at the return from the function. Of course, they will be, but the free store memory will not be released.

The code for the destructor is as follows:

```
// Listing 02_02
// Destructor to free memory allocated by new
CMessage::~CMessage()
{
    cout << "Destructor called."        // Just to track what happens
         << endl;
    delete[] pmessage;                   // Free memory assign to pointer
}
```

Because we are defining it outside of the class definition, we need to qualify the name of the destructor with the class name, **CMessage**, and the scope resolution operator. All the destructor does is displays a message so that we can see what's going on and uses the operator **delete** to free the memory pointed to by the member **pmessage**. Note that we must include the square brackets with **delete** because we are deleting an array (of type **char**).

TRY IT OUT - Using the Message Class

We can exercise this class with a little example:

```
// EX9_02.CPP
// Using a destructor to free memory
#include <iostream.h>           // For stream I/O
#include <string.h>             // For strlen() and strcpy()

// Put the CMessage class definition here (Listing 02_01)
```

```
// Put the destructor definition here (Listing 02_02)
```

```
int main(void)
{
// Declare object
   CMessage Motto("A miss is as good as a mile.");
// Dynamic object
   CMessage* pM = new CMessage("A cat can look at a queen.");

   Motto.ShowIt();              // Display 1st message
   pM->ShowIt();                // Display 2nd message
   cout << endl;

   //delete pM;                 //Manually delete object created with new
   return 0;
}
```

How It Works

At the beginning of **main()**, we declare and define an initialized **CMessage** object, **Motto**, in the usual manner. In the second declaration we define a pointer to a **CMessage** object, **pM**, and allocate memory for the **CMessage** object pointed to by using the operator **new**. The call to **new** invokes the **CMessage** class constructor, which has the effect of calling **new** again to allocate space for the message text pointed to by the data member **pmessage**. If you build and execute this example, it will produce the output:

```
Ex9_02
A miss is as good as a mile.
A cat can look at a queen.
Destructor called.
Press any key to continue
```

We have only one destructor call, even though we created two message objects. We said earlier that the compiler doesn't take responsibility for objects created in the free store. The compiler arranged to call our destructor for the object **Motto** because this is a normal automatic object, even though the memory for the data member was allocated in the free store by the constructor. The object pointed to by **pM** is different. We allocated memory for the **object** in the free store, so we have to use **delete** to remove it. You need to uncomment this statement,

```
//delete pM;                 //Manually delete object created with new
```

which appears just before the **return** statement in **main()**. If you run the code now, it will produce this output:

```
Ex9_02
A miss is as good as a mile.
A cat can look at a queen.
Destructor called.
Destructor called.
Press any key to continue
```

298

Now we get an extra call of our destructor. This is surprising in a way. Clearly, **delete** is only dealing with the memory allocated by the call to **new** in the function **main()**. It only freed the memory pointed to by **pM**. Since our pointer to **pM** is a pointer to a **CMessage** object for which a destructor has been defined, **delete** also calls our destructor to allow us to clean up the details of the members of the object. So when you use **delete** for an object created dynamically with **new**, **delete** will always call the destructor for the object allocated on the free store.

Implementing a Copy Constructor

When you allocate space for class members dynamically, there are denizens lurking in the free store. For our class **CMessage**, the default copy constructor is woefully inadequate. If we have these statements,

```
CMessage Motto1("Radiation fades your genes.");
CMessage Motto2(Motto1);
```

the effect of the default copy constructor will be to copy the address in the pointer member from **Motto1** to **Motto2**. Consequently, there will be only one text string shared between the two objects, as illustrated in the diagram below:

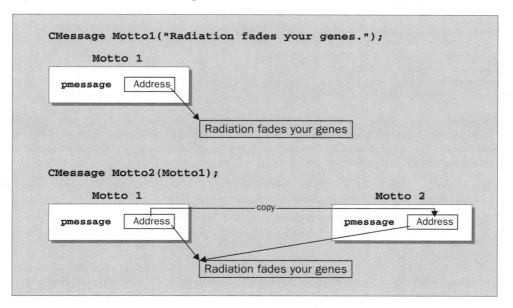

If the string is changed from either of the objects, it will be changed for the other. If **Motto1** is destroyed, the pointer in **Motto2** will be pointing at a memory area which may now be used for something else, and chaos will surely follow. Of course, the same problem arises if **Motto2** is deleted. **Motto1** would then contain a member pointing to a non-existent string.

The solution is to supply a class copy constructor to replace the default version. This could be implemented in the **public** section of the class as follows on the next page.

```
CMessage(const CMessage& initM)        // Copy Constructor definition
{
   // Allocate space for text
   pmessage = new char[ strlen(initM.pmessage) +1 ];
   // Copy text to new memory
   strcpy(pmessage, initM.pmessage);
}
```

You will remember from the previous chapter that, to avoid an infinite spiral of calls to the copy constructor, the parameter must be specified as a **const** reference. This copy constructor first allocates enough memory to hold the string in the object **initM**, storing the address in the data member of the new object, and copies the text string from the initializing object. Now, our new object will be identical to, but quite independent of, the old one.

Just because you don't initialize one **CMessage** class object with another, don't think that you are safe and need not bother with the copy constructor. Another monster lurks in the free store. Consider the following statements,

```
CMessage Thought("Eye awl weighs yews my spell checker.");
DisplayMessage(Thought);        // Call a function to output a message
```

where the function **DisplayMessage()** is defined as:

```
void DisplayMessage(CMessage LocalMsg)
{
   cout << endl << "The message is: "
        << LocalMsg.ShowIt();
   return;
}
```

Looks simple enough, doesn't it? What could be wrong with that? A catastrophic error, that's what! What the function **DisplayMessage()** does is actually irrelevant. The problem lies with the argument. The argument is a **CMessage** object which is passed by value. With the default copy constructor, the sequence of events is as follows:

- The object **Thought** is created with the space for the message **"Eye awl weighs yews my spell checker"** allocated in the free store.

- The function **DisplayMessage()** is called and, because the argument is passed by value, a copy, **LocalMsg** is made using the default copy constructor. Now the pointer in the copy of the object points to the same string in the free store as the original object.

- At the end of the function, the local object goes out of scope, so the destructor for the **Message** class is called. This deletes the local object by deleting the memory pointed to by the pointer **pmessage.**

- On return from the function **DisplayMessage()**, the pointer in the original object, **Thought**, still points to the memory area that has just been deleted. Next time you try to use the original object, or even if you don't since it will need to be deleted sooner or later, your program will behave in weird and mysterious ways.

Any call to a function that passes by value an object of a class that has a member defined dynamically will cause problems. So, out of this, we have an absolutely 100 percent, 24 carat golden rule:

If you allocate space for a class member dynamically, always implement a copy constructor.

Sharing Memory between Variables

As a relic of the days when 64K was quite a lot of memory, we have a facility in C++ which allows more than one variable to share the same memory (but obviously not at the same time). This is called a **union**.

There are two basic ways in which you can use a union:

First, you can use it so that a variable **A** occupies a block of memory at one point in a program, which is then occupied by another variable **B** of a different type, because **A** is no longer required. I recommend that you don't do this. It's not worth the risk of error that is implicit in such an arrangement. You can achieve the same effect by allocating memory dynamically.

Alternatively, you could have a situation in a program where a large array of data is required but you don't know in advance of execution what the data type is. This will be determined by the input data. I also recommend that you don't use unions for this, since you can achieve the same result using a couple of pointers of different types and again allocating the memory dynamically.

A third possible use for a union is the one that you may need now and again - when you want to interpret the same data in two or more different ways. This could happen when you have a variable that is of type **long**, and you want to treat it as two values of type **int**. Windows will sometimes package two **int** values in a single parameter of type **long** passed to a function. Another instance arises when you want to treat a block of memory containing numeric data as a string of bytes, just to move it around.

Defining Unions

A union is defined using the keyword **union**. It's best understood by taking an example of a definition:

```
union shareLD          // Sharing memory between long and double
{
    double dval;
    long lval;
};
```

This defines a union type **shareLD** which provides for the variables of type **long** and **double** to occupy the same memory. The union type name is usually referred to as a **tag name**. This statement is rather like a class definition in that we haven't defined a union instance yet, so we don't have any variables at this point. Once it has been defined, we can declare instances of a union in a declaration. For example:

```
shareLD MyUnion;
```

This declares an instance of the union, **shareLD**, that we defined previously. We could also have declared **MyUnion** by including it in the union definition statement:

```
union shareLD            // Sharing memory between long and double
{
    double dval;
    long lval;
}MyUnion;
```

If we want to refer to a member of the union, we use the direct member selection operator (the period) with the union instance name, just as we have done when accessing members of a class. So, we could set the long variable **lval** to 100 in the union instance **MyUnion** with this statement:

```
MyUnion.lval = 100;       // Using a member of a union
```

The basic problem with using a union to store different types of values in the same memory is that, because of the way a union works, you also need some means of determining which of the member values is current. This is usually achieved by maintaining another variable which acts as an indicator of the type of value stored.

A union isn't limited to sharing between two variables. If you wish, you can share the same memory between several variables. The memory occupied by the union will be that which is required by its largest member. For example, if we define this union,

```
union shareDLF
{
    double dval;
    long lval;
    float fval;
} uinst = {1.5};
```

it will occupy 8 bytes, as illustrated in the figure below:

In the example, we defined an instance of the union, **uinst**, as well as the tag name for the union. We also initialized it with the value 1.5.

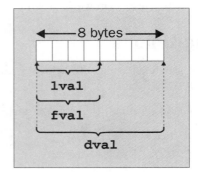

You can only initialize the first member of the union when you declare an instance.

Anonymous Unions

You can define a union without a union type name, in which case an instance of the union is automatically declared. For example, if we define a union like this,

```
union
{
    char* pval;
    double dval;
    long lval;
};
```

it defines both a union with no name and an instance of the union with no name. Consequently, the variables that it contains may be referred to just by their names, as they appear in the union definition. This can be more convenient than a normal union with a type name, but you need to be careful that you don't confuse the members with ordinary variables. The members of the union will still share the same memory. As an illustration of how the anonymous union above works, to use the **double** member, you could write this statement:

```
dval = 99.5;      // Using a member of an anonymous union
```

As you can see, there's nothing to distinguish the variable **dval** as being used as a union member. It you need to use anonymous unions, you could use a naming convention to make the members more obvious.

Unions in Classes

You can include an instance of a union in a class. If you intend storing different types of value at different times, this usually necessitates maintaining a class data member to indicate what kind of value is stored in the union. There isn't usually a great deal to be gained by using unions as class members.

Operator Overloading

Operator overloading enables you to make standard operators such as **+**, **-**, ***** and so on, work with objects of your own data types. It allows you to write a function which redefines a particular operator so that it performs a particular action when it's used with objects of a class. For example, you could redefine the operator **>**, so that, when it was used with objects of the class **CBox** (which we saw earlier), it would return **TRUE** if the first **CBox** argument had a greater volume than the second.

Operator overloading doesn't allow you to invent new operators, nor can you change the precedence of an operator, so your overloaded version of an operator will have the same priority in the sequence of evaluating an expression as the original base operator.

Although you can't overload all the operators, the restrictions aren't particularly oppressive. These are the operators that you can't overload:

The scope resolution operator	`::`
The conditional operator	`?:`
The direct member selection operator	`.`
The size of operator	**sizeof**
The dereference pointer to class member operator	`.*`

Anything else is fair game, which gives you quite a bit of scope. Obviously, it's a good idea to ensure that your version of the standard operators are reasonably consistent with their normal usage, or at least reasonably intuitive in their operation. It wouldn't be a very sensible approach to produce an overloaded **+** operator for a class that performed the equivalent of a multiply on class objects. The best way to understand how operator overloading works is to work through an example, so let's implement what we just referred to, the greater than operator, **>**, for the **CBox** class .

Implementing an Overloaded Operator

If we want to implement an overloaded operator for a class, we have to write a special function. Assuming that it's a member of the class **CBox**, the prototype for the function to overload the **>** operator will be as follows:

```
int operator>(CBox& aBox);      // Overloaded 'greater than'
```

The word **operator** here is a keyword. Combined with an operator, in this case **>**, it defines an operator function. The function name in this case is **operator>**. You can write an operator function with or without a space between the keyword **operator** and the operator itself, as long as there's no ambiguity. The ambiguity arises with operators using normal letters such as **new** or **delete**. If they are written without a space, **operatornew** and **operatordelete**, they are legal names for ordinary functions. So, for operator functions with these operators, you must leave a space between the keyword and the operator.

With our operator function **operator>()**, the right operand of the operator is that which is defined between parentheses. The left operand will be defined implicitly by the pointer **this**. So, if we have the following **if** statement,

```
if(Box1 > Box2)
    cout << endl << "Box1 is greater than Box2";
```

the expression between parentheses in the **if** will call our operator function. It's equivalent to this function call:

```
Box1.operator>(Box2);
```

The correspondence between the **CBox** objects in the expression and the operator function parameters are illustrated as follows:

```
if(Box1 > Box2)
                        Function
                        Parameter

                        int CBox::operator>(CBox& aBox)
                        {
   The object pointed
   to by this
                        return (this->volume())> (aBox,volume());

                        }
```

Let's look at how the code for the **operator>()** function works:

```
// Operator function for 'greater than' which
// compares volumes of CBox objects.
int CBox::operator>(CBox& aBox)
{
   return (this->Volume()) > (aBox.Volume())
}
```

We use a reference parameter to the function to avoid unnecessary copying when the function is
called. The **return** expression uses the member function **Volume()** to calculate the volume of
the **CBox** object pointed to by **this**, and compares the result, using the basic operator **>** , with
the volume of the object **aBox**. Thus, **1** is returned if the **CBox** object pointed to by the pointer
this has a larger volume than the object **aBox** passed as a reference argument, and **0**
otherwise.

TRY IT OUT - Operator Overloading

We can exercise this function with an example:

```
//EX9_03.CPP
// Exercising the overloaded 'greater than' operator
#include <iostream.h>                    // For stream I/O

class CBox                               // Class definition at global scope
{
   public:
// Constructor definition
      CBox(double lv=1.0, double bv=1.0, double hv=1.0)
      {
         cout << endl << "Constructor called.";
         m_Length = lv;                  // Set values of
         m_Breadth = bv;                 // data members
         m_Height = hv;
      }
```

```
    // Function to calculate the volume of a box
        double Volume()
        {
            return m_Length*m_Breadth*m_Height;
        }

        int operator>(CBox& aBox);          // Overloaded 'greater than'

    // Destructor definition
        ~CBox()
        { cout << "Destructor called." << endl; }

    private:
        double m_Length;            // Length of a box in inches
        double m_Breadth;           // Breadth of a box in inches
        double m_Height;            // Height of a box in inches

    };
```

```
// Operator function for 'greater than' which
// compares volumes of CBox objects.
int CBox::operator>(CBox& aBox)
{
    return (this->Volume()) > (aBox.Volume());
}

int main(void)
{
    CBox SmallBox(4.0,2.0, 1.0);
    CBox MediumBox(10.0, 4.0, 2.0);
    CBox BigBox(30.0, 20.0, 40.0);

    if(MediumBox > SmallBox)
        cout << endl
            << "MediumBox is Bigger than SmallBox";

    if(MediumBox > BigBox)
        cout << endl
            << "MediumBox is Bigger than BigBox";
    else
        cout << endl
            << "MediumBox is not Bigger than BigBox";

    cout << endl;
    return 0;
}
```

How It Works

The prototype of the operator function **operator>()** appears in the **public** section of the class. As the function definition is outside the class definition, it won't default to **inline**. This is quite arbitrary. We could just as well have put the definition in place of the prototype in the class definition. In this case, we wouldn't need to qualify the function name with **CBox::** in front of it. As you will remember, this is needed in order to tell the compiler that this function is a member of the class **CBox**.

The function **main()** has two **if** statements using the operator **>** with class members. These automatically invoke our overloaded operator. If you wanted to get confirmation of this, you could add an output statement to the operator function. The output from the example as written will be as follows:

```
Ex9_03                                                         _ □ ×
Constructor called.
Constructor called.
Constructor called.
MediumBox is Bigger than SmallBox
MediumBox is not Bigger than BigBox
Destructor called.
Destructor called.
Destructor called.
Press any key to continue
```

The output demonstrates that the **if** statements work fine with our operator function, so being able to express the solution to **CBox** problems directly in terms of **CBox** objects is beginning to be a realistic proposition.

Implementing Full Support for an Operator

With our operator function **operator>()**, there's still a lot of things that you can't do. Specifying a problem solution in terms of **CBox** objects might well involve statements such as the following:

```
if(aBox > 20.0)
```

Our function won't deal with that. If you try to use an expression comparing a **CBox** object with a numerical value, you will get an error message. In order to support this, we would need to write another version of the function **operator>()** as an overloaded function.

We can quite easily support the type of expression that we have seen. The prototype of the function would be:

```
// Compare a CBox object with a constant
int operator>(const double& value);
```

This would appear in the definition of the class. The **CBox** object will be passed as the implicit pointer **this**.

The implementation is also easy. It's just one statement in the body of the function:

```
// Function to compare a CBox object with a constant
int CBox::operator>(const double& value)
{
    return (this->Volume()) > value;
}
```

This couldn't be much simpler, could it? But we still have a problem with the operator **>** with **CBox** objects. We may well want to write statements such as you see over the page.

```
if(20.0 > aBox)
    .....                         // do something
```

You might argue that this could be done by implementing the operator function **operator<()** and rewriting the statement above to use it, which is quite true. Indeed, the **<** operator is likely to be a requirement for comparing **CBox** objects anyway, but an implementation of support for an object type shouldn't artificially restrict the ways in which you use the objects in an expression.

The use of the objects should be as natural as possible. The problem is how to do it. A member operator function always provides the left argument as the pointer **this**. Since, in this case, the left argument is of type **double**, we can't implement it as a member function. That leaves us with two choices: an ordinary function or a **friend** function. Since we don't need to access the **private** members of the class, we can implement it as an ordinary function. The prototype would need to be,

```
int operator>(const double& value, CBox& aBox);
```

placed outside the class definition. The implementation would be this:

```
// Function comparing a constant with a CBox object
int operator>(const double& value, CBox& aBox)
{
    return value > aBox.Volume();
}
```

As we have seen already, an ordinary function (and a **friend** function for that matter) accesses the data members of an object by using the direct member selection operator and the object name. The member function **Volume()** is **public**, so there's no problem using it here.

If the class didn't have the **public** function **Volume()**, we could either use a **friend** function that could access the **private** data members directly, or we could provide a set of member functions to return the values of the **private** data members and use those in an ordinary function to implement the comparison.

TRY IT OUT - Complete Overloading of the > Operator

We can put all this together in an example to show how it works:

```
//EX9_04.CPP
// Implementing a complete overloaded 'greater than' operator
#include <iostream.h>                    // For stream I/O

class CBox                               // Class definition at global scope
{
   public:
// Constructor definition
      CBox(double lv=1.0, double bv=1.0, double hv=1.0):
             m_Length(lv), m_Breadth(bv), m_Height(hv)
      {
         cout << endl << "Constructor called.";
      }
```

```
// Function to calculate the volume of a box
    double Volume()
    {
        return m_Length*m_Breadth*m_Height;
    }

// Operator function for 'greater than' which
// compares volumes of CBox objects.
    int operator>(CBox& aBox)
    {
        return (this->Volume()) > (aBox.Volume());
    }

// Function to compare a CBox object with a constant
    int operator>(const double& value)
    {
        return (this->Volume()) > value;
    }

// Destructor definition
    ~CBox()
    { cout << "Destructor called." << endl;}

  private:
    double m_Length;              // Length of a box in inches
    double m_Breadth;             // Breadth of a box in inches
    double m_Height;              // Height of a box in inches

};

int operator>(const double& value, CBox& aBox); // Function prototype

int main(void)
{
   CBox SmallBox(4.0,2.0, 1.0);
   CBox MediumBox(10.0, 4.0, 2.0);

   if(MediumBox > SmallBox)
      cout << endl
           << "MediumBox is Bigger than SmallBox";

   if(MediumBox > 50.0)
      cout << endl
           << "MediumBox capacity is more than 50";
   else
      cout << endl
           << "MediumBox capacity is not more than 50";

   if(10.0 > SmallBox)
      cout << endl
           << "SmallBox capacity is less than 10";
   else
      cout << endl
           << "SmallBox capacity is not less than 10";

   cout << endl;
   return 0;
}
```

```
// Function comparing a constant with a CBox object
int operator>(const double& value, CBox& aBox)
{
   return value > aBox.Volume();
}
```

How It Works

The constructor for the class **CBox** has been updated to initialize the data members rather than use assignments, since it's a bit more efficient. Note the position of the prototype for the ordinary function version of **operator>()**. It needs to follow the class definition because it refers to a **CBox** object in the parameter list. If you place it before the class definition, the example will not compile.

There's a way to place it at the beginning of the program file following the **#include** statement - use an **incomplete class declaration**. This would precede the prototype and would look like this:

```
class CBox;                             // Incomplete class declaration
int operator>(const double& value, CBox& aBox);   // Function prototype
```

The incomplete class declaration identifies **CBox** to the compiler as a class and is sufficient to allow the compiler to properly process the prototype for the function, since it now knows that **aBox** is a variable of a user-defined type to be specified later.

This mechanism is also essential in circumstances such as those where you have two classes, each of which has an object of the other class as a member. They each will then require the other to be declared first. It's possible to resolve this impasse through the use of an incomplete class declaration.

The output from the example is as follows:

After the constructor messages due to the declarations of the objects **SmallBox** and **MediumBox**, we have the output lines from the three **if** statements, each of which is working as we expected. The first of these is calling the operator function that is a class member and works with two **CBox** objects. The second is calling the member function that has a parameter of type **double**. The expression in the third **if** statement calls the operator function that we implemented as an ordinary function.

As it happens, we could have made both the operator functions which are class members ordinary functions, since they only need access to the member function **Volume()**, which is **public**.

> *Any comparison operator can be implemented in much the same way as we have implemented these. They would only differ in the minor details and the general approach to implementing them would be exactly the same.*

Overloading the Assignment Operator

If you don't provide an overloaded assignment operator function for your class, the compiler will provide a default. The default version will simply provide a member-by-member copying process, similar to that of the default copy constructor. However, don't confuse the default copy constructor with the default assignment operator. The default copy constructor is called by a declaration of a class object that is initialized with an existing object of the same class, or by passing an object to a function by value whereas the default assignment operator is called when an assignment statement has a class object on both sides of the assignment operator.

For our **CBox** class, the default assignment operator works with no problem but, for any class which has space for members allocated dynamically, you need to look carefully at the requirements of the class in question. There may be considerable potential for chaos in your program if you leave it out under these circumstances.

For a moment, let's return to our message class that we used when talking about copy constructors. You'll remember that it had a member, **pmessage**, that was a pointer to a string. Now consider the effect that the default assignment operator can have. Suppose we had two instances of the class **Motto1** and **Motto2**. We could set the members of **Motto2** equal to the members of **Motto1**, using the default assignment operator as follows:

```
Motto2 = Motto1;                    // Use default assignment operator
```

The effect of using the default assignment operator for this class is essentially the same as using the default copy constructor - disaster will result! Since each object will have a pointer to the same string, if the string is changed for one object, it's changed for both. There's also the problem that when one of the instances of the class is destroyed, its destructor will deallocate the memory used for the string and the other object will be left with a pointer to memory that may now be used for something else.

What we need the assignment operator to do is to copy the text to a memory area owned by the destination object.

Fixing the Problem

We can fix this with our own assignment operator which we will assume is defined within the class definition:

```
// Overloaded assignment operator for CMessage objects
CMessage& operator=(const CMessage& aMess)
{
    // Release memory for 1st operand
    delete[] pmessage;
    pmessage = new char[ strlen(aMess.pmessage) +1];

    // Copy 2nd operand string to 1st
    strcpy(this->pmessage, aMess.pmessage);

    // Return a reference to 1st operand
```

```
        return *this;
    }
```

You need to take note of a couple of subtleties here. The first is that we return a reference from the operator function because, as you may recall from our discussion of references in the last chapter, this allows the result to appear on the left of an equals sign. This is because we could have a statement such as,

```
    Motto1 = Motto2 = Motto3;
```

which will translate into,

```
    (Motto1.operator=(Motto2)) = Motto3;
```

with the result of the first operator function call on the left. This, in turn, will finally become this:

```
    (Motto1.operator=(Motto2)).operator=(Motto3);
```

The second subtlety you need to remember is that each object already has memory for a string allocated, so the first thing that the operator function has to do is to delete the memory allocated to the first object and reallocate sufficient memory to accommodate the string belonging to the second object. Once this is done, the string from the second object can be copied to the new memory now owned by the first.

There is still a defect in this operator function. What if we were to write the following statement?

```
    Motto1 = Motto1;
```

Obviously, you wouldn't do anything as stupid as this directly, but it could easily be hidden behind a pointer, for instance, as in the following statement,

```
    Motto1 = *pMess;
```

where the pointer **pMess** points to **Motto1**. In this case, the operator function as it stands would delete the memory for **Motto1**, allocate some more memory based on the length of the string that has already been deleted and try to copy the old memory which, by then, could well have been corrupted. We can fix this with a check at the beginning of the function, so now it would become this:

```
    // Overloaded assignment operator for CMessage objects
    CMessage& operator=(const CMessage& aMess)
    {
        if(this == &aMess)              // Check addresses, if equal
            return *this;               // return the 1st operand
        // Release memory for 1st operand
        delete[] pmessage;
        pmessage = new char[ strlen(aMess.pmessage) +1];

        // Copy 2nd operand string to 1st
        strcpy(this->pmessage, aMess.pmessage);

        // Return a reference to 1st operand
        return *this;
    }
```

TRY IT OUT - Overloading the Assignment Operator

Let's put this together in a working example. We'll add a function, called **Reset()**, to the class at the same time. This just resets the message to a string of asterisks.

```cpp
// EX9_05.CPP
// Overloaded copy operator perfection
#include <iostream.h>
#include <string.h>

class CMessage
{
   private:
      char* pmessage;                  // Pointer to object text string

   public:
// Function to display a message
      void ShowIt(void)
      {
         cout << endl << pmessage;
      }

//Function to reset a message to *
      void Reset(void)
      {
         char* temp=pmessage;
         while(*temp)
            *(temp++)='*';
      }

// Overloaded assignment operator for CMessage objects
      CMessage& operator=(const CMessage& aMess)
      {
         if(this == &aMess)                     // Check addresses, if equal
            return *this;                       // return the 1st operand

         // Release memory for 1st operand
         delete[] pmessage;
         pmessage = new char[ strlen(aMess.pmessage) +1];

         // Copy 2nd operand string to 1st
         strcpy(this->pmessage, aMess.pmessage);

         // Return a reference to 1st operand
         return *this;
      }

// Constructor definition
      CMessage(const char* text = "Default message")
      {
         pmessage = new char[ strlen(text)+1 ]; // Allocate space for text
         strcpy(pmessage, text);                // Copy text to new memory
      }
// Destructor to free memory allocated by new
      ~CMessage()
      {
         cout << "Destructor called."   // Just to track what happens
```

```
                        << endl;
            delete[] pmessage;                    // Free memory assigned to pointer
      }
};
```

```
int main(void)
{

    CMessage Motto1("The devil takes care of his own");
    CMessage Motto2;

    cout << "Motto2 contains - ";
    Motto2.ShowIt();
    cout << endl;

    Motto2 = Motto1;                    // Use new assignment operator

    cout << "Motto2 contains - ";
    Motto2.ShowIt();
    cout << endl;

    Motto1.Reset();                     // Setting Motto1 to * doesn't
                                        // affect Motto2

    cout << "Motto1 now contains - ";
    Motto1.ShowIt();
    cout << endl;

    cout << "Motto2 still contains - ";
    Motto2.ShowIt();
    cout << endl;

    return 0;
}
```

You can see from the output of this program that everything works exactly as required, with no linking between the messages of the two objects, except where we explicitly set them equal.

So let's have another golden rule out of all of this:

Always implement an assignment operator if you allocate space dynamically for a member of an object.

Having implemented the assignment operator, what happens with operations such as **+=**? Well, they don't work unless you implement them. For each form of **op=** that you want to use with your class objects, you need to write another operator function.

Overloading the Addition Operator

Let's look at overloading the addition operator for our **CBox** class. This is interesting because it involves creating and returning a new object. The new object will be the sum (whatever we define that to mean) of the two **CBox** objects that are its operands.

So what do we want the sum to mean? Let's define the sum of two **CBox** objects as a **CBox** object which is large enough to contain the other two boxes stacked on top of each other. We can do this by making the new object have a **m_Length** member which is the larger of the **m_Length** members of the objects being added, and a **m_Breadth** member derived in a similar way. The **m_Height** member will be the sum of the **m_Height** members of the two operand objects, so that the resultant **CBox** object can contain the other two **CBox** objects. This isn't necessarily an optimal solution, but it will be sufficient for our purposes. By altering the constructor, we'll also arrange that the **m_Length** member of a **CBox** object is always greater than or equal to the **m_Breadth** member.

The addition operation is easier to explain graphically, so it's illustrated below:

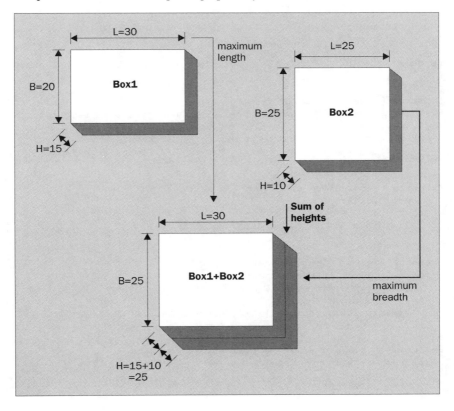

Since we need to get at the members of an object directly, we'll make the **operator+()** a member function. The prototype of the function will be this:

```
CBox operator+(const CBox& aBox);// Function adding two CBox objects
```

We define the parameter as a **const** reference to avoid unnecessary copying of the right argument when the function is called. The operation function definition would now be as follows:

```
// Function to add two CBox objects
CBox CBox::operator+(const CBox& aBox)
{
// New object has larger length and breadth, and sum of heights
   return CBox(m_Length>aBox.m_Length? M_Length:aBox.m_Length,
               m_Breadth>aBox.m_Breadth? M_Breadth:aBox.m_Breadth,
               m_Height+aBox.m_Height);
}
```

TRY IT OUT - Exercising Our Addition

We can see how this works in an example:

```
// EX9_06.CPP
// Adding CBox objects
#include <iostream.h>                   // For stream I/O

class CBox                              // Class definition at global scope
{
   public:
// Constructor definition
      CBox(double lv=1.0, double bv=1.0, double hv=1.0):m_Height(hv)
      {
         m_Length = lv > bv ? lv : bv;       // Ensure that
         m_Breadth = bv < lv ? bv : lv;      // length >= breadth
      }

// Function to calculate the volume of a box
      double Volume()
      {
         return m_Length*m_Breadth*m_Height;
      }

// Operator function for 'greater than' which
// compares volumes of CBox objects.
      int CBox::operator>(CBox& aBox)
      {
         return (this->Volume()) > (aBox.Volume());
      }

// Function to compare a CBox object with a constant
      int operator>(const double& value)
      {
         return Volume() > value;
      }

// Function to add two CBox objects
```

```
            CBox operator+(const CBox& aBox)
            {
                // New object has larger length & breadth, and sum of heights
                return CBox(
                        m_Length>aBox.m_Length ? m_Length : aBox.m_Length,
                        m_Breadth>aBox.m_Breadth ? m_Breadth : aBox.m_Breadth,
                        m_Height + aBox.m_Height);
            }

    // Function to show the dimensions of a box
        void ShowBox(void)
        {
            cout << m_Length << " " << m_Breadth << " " << m_Height
                << endl;
        }

    private:
        double m_Length;            // Length of a box in inches
        double m_Breadth;           // Breadth of a box in inches
        double m_Height;            // Height of a box in inches

};

int operator>(const double& value, CBox& aBox); // Function prototype

int main(void)
{
    CBox SmallBox(4.0,2.0, 1.0);
    CBox MediumBox(10.0, 4.0, 2.0);
    CBox aBox;
    CBox bBox;

    aBox = SmallBox+MediumBox;
    cout << "aBox dimensions are ";
    aBox.ShowBox();

    bBox = aBox+SmallBox+MediumBox;
    cout << "bBox dimensions are ";
    bBox.ShowBox();

    return 0;
}

// Function comparing a constant with a CBox object
int operator>(const double& value, CBox& aBox)
{
    return value > aBox.Volume();
}
```

How It Works

In this example, we have changed the **CBox** class members a little. The destructor has been deleted as it isn't necessary for this class, and the constructor has been modified to ensure that the **m_Length** member is not less than the **m_Breadth** member. Knowing that the length of a box is always greater than the breadth makes the add operation a bit easier. We have also added the function **ShowBox()** to output the dimensions of a **CBox** object. This will enable us to verify that our overloaded add operation is working as we expect.

The output from this program is as follows:

```
Ex9_06                                                    _ □ ×
aBox dimensions are 10 4 3
bBox dimensions are 10 4 6
Press any key to continue_
```

This seems to be consistent with the notion of adding **CBox** objects that we have defined and, as you can see, the function also works with multiple add operations in an expression. For the computation of **bBox**, the overloaded addition operator will be called twice.

We could equally well have implemented the **add** operation for the class as a **friend** function. Its prototype would then be this:

```
friend CBox operator+(const CBox& aBox, const CBox& bBox);
```

The method to produce the result would be much the same, except that the direct member selection operator would need to be used to obtain the members of the arguments to the function. It would work just as well as the first version of the operator function.

Using Classes

We have touched on most of the basic aspects of defining a class, so maybe we should look at how a class might be used to solve a problem. We will still need to keep the problem simple in order to keep this book down to a reasonable number of pages! So we'll consider problems in which we can use an extended version of the **CBox** class.

The Idea of a Class Interface

The implementation of an extended **CBox** class should incorporate the notion of a **class interface**. What we are going to provide is a tool kit for anyone wanting to work with **CBox** objects, so we need to assemble a set of functions that represent the interface to the world of boxes. Since the interface will represent the only way to deal with **CBox** objects, it needs to be defined to adequately cover the likely things one would want to do with a **CBox** object, and be implemented, as far as possible, in a manner that protects against misuse or accidental errors.

The first question that we need to consider is the nature of the problem we intend to solve and, from that, derive the kind of functionality we need to provide in the class interface.

Defining the Problem

The principal function of a box is to contain objects of one kind or another so, in a word, our problem is *packaging*. We will attempt to provide a class that eases packaging problems in general and then see how it might be used. We will assume that we will always be working on packing **CBox** objects into other **CBox** objects since, if you want to pack candy in a box, you could always represent each of the pieces of candy as an idealized **CBox** object. The basic operations that we might want to provide for our **CBox** class include:

➧ Calculate the volume of a **CBox**. This is a fundamental characteristic of a **CBox** object and we have an implementation of this already.

➧ Compare the volumes of two **CBox** objects to determine which is the larger. We probably should support a complete set of comparison operators for **CBox** objects. We already have a version of the operator **>**.

➧ Compare the volume of a **CBox** object with a specified value and vice versa. We also have an implementation of this for the operator **>**, but we will also need the other comparison operators.

➧ Add two **CBox** objects to produce a **CBox** object which will contain both the original objects. Thus, the result will be at least the sum of the volumes, but may be larger. We have a version of this already by overloading the **+** operator.

➧ Multiply a **CBox** object by an integer (and vice versa) to provide a **CBox** object which will contain the specified number of the original object. This is effectively designing a carton.

➧ Determine how many **CBox** objects of a given size can be packed in another **CBox** object of a given size. This is effectively division, so we could overload the operator **/**.

➧ Determine the volume of space remaining in a **CBox** object after packing it with the maximum number of **CBox** objects of a given size.

We had better stop right there! There are undoubtedly other functions that would be very useful but, in the interest of saving trees, we'll consider the set complete, apart from ancillaries such as accessing dimensions, for example.

Implementing the CBox Class

We really need to consider the degree of error protection that we want to build into the **CBox** class. The basic class that we defined to illustrate various aspects of a class is a starting point, but we should also consider some aspects a little more deeply. The constructor is a little weak in that it doesn't ensure that we have valid dimensions for a **CBox**, so perhaps the first thing we should do is to ensure we always have valid objects. We could redefine the basic class as follows:

```cpp
class CBox                          // Class definition at global scope
{
   public:
      // Constructor definition
      CBox(double lv=1.0, double bv=1.0, double hv=1.0)
      {
         lv = lv<=0 ? 1.0 : lv;              // Ensure positive
         bv = bv<=0 ? 1.0 : bv;             // dimensions for
         hv = hv<=0 ? 1.0 : hv;             // the object

         m_Length = lv>bv ? lv : bv;         // Ensure that
         m_Breadth = bv < lv ? bv : lv;      // length >= breadth
         m_Height = hv;
      }

// Function to calculate the volume of a box
      double Volume()
      {
```

```
            return m_Length*m_Breadth*m_Height;
      }

// Function providing the length of a box
     double GetLength() { return m_Length; }

// Function providing the breadth of a box
     double GetBreadth() { return m_Breadth; }

// Function providing the height of a box
     double GetHeight() { return m_Height; }

   private:
      double m_Length;           // Length of a box in inches
      double m_Breadth;          // Breadth of a box in inches
      double m_Height;           // Height of a box in inches

};
```

Our constructor is now secure, since any dimension that the user of the class tries to set to a negative number or zero will be set to 1 in the constructor. You could also consider displaying a message for a negative or zero dimension, since there is obviously an error when this occurs and arbitrarily and silently setting a dimension to 1 might not be the best solution.

The default copy constructor is satisfactory for our class, since we have no dynamic memory allocation for data members and the default assignment operator will also work well with the class. Perhaps now we should consider comparisons for objects of our class.

Comparing CBox Objects

We should support the operators **>**, **>=**, **==**, **<**, **<=** for two **CBox** objects as well as for a **CBox** object and a value of type **double**. We should implement these as ordinary global functions, since they don't need to be member functions. We can also write the functions to compare two **CBox** objects in terms of the functions to compare a **CBox** object with a **double** value, so let's start with the latter. We can repeat the **operator>()** function that we had before:

```
// Function for testing if a constant is > a CBox object
   int operator>(const double& value, CBox& aBox)
   {
      return value > aBox.Volume();
   }
```

We can now write the **operator<()** function in a similar way:

```
// Function for testing if a constant is < CBox object
   int operator<(const double& value, CBox& aBox)
   {
      return value < aBox.Volume();
   }
```

The implementation of the same operators, but with the arguments reversed, can now be specified using these two functions:

```
// Function for testing if CBox object is > a constant
   int operator>(CBox& aBox, const double& value)
```

```
      { return value<aBox; }

// Function for testing if CBox object is < a constant
   int operator<(CBox& aBox, const double& value)
   { return value>aBox; }
```

We just use the appropriate overloaded operator function that we wrote before, with the arguments from the call to this function switched.

We now need `>=` and `<=` , which will be the same as the first two functions but with the `<=` operator replacing each use of `<` and `>=` instead of `>`. The `operator==()` functions are also very similar:

```
// Function for testing if constant is == a CBox object
   int operator==(const double& value, CBox& aBox)
   {
       return value == aBox.Volume() ;
   }

// Function for testing if CBox object is == a constant
   int operator==(CBox& aBox, const double& value)
   {
       return value==aBox;
   }
```

We now have a complete set of comparison operators for **CBox** objects. Also keep in mind that these will also work with expressions as long as the expressions result in objects of the required type, so we will be able to combine these with the use of other overloaded operators.

Combining CBox Objects

Now we come to the question of overloading the operators `+`, `*`, `/`, and `%`. We will take them in order. The add operation that we already have from **Ex9_06.cpp** has this prototype:

```
   CBox operator+(const CBox& aBox);    // Function adding two CBox objects
```

Although our original implementation of this is not an ideal solution, we'll use it to avoid overcomplicating our class. A better version would need to see if the operands had any faces with the same dimension and join along those faces, but coding this can get a bit messy. Of course, if this were a practical application, a better **add** operation could be developed later and substituted for the existing version and any programs written using the original would still run without change. The separation of the interface to a class from its implementation is crucial to good C++ programming.

The multiply operation is very easy. It represents the process of creating a box to contain **n** boxes, where **n** is the multiplier. The simplest solution would be to take the **m_Length** and **m_Breadth** of the object to be packed and multiply the height by **n** to get the new **CBox** object. We will make it a little more clever by checking whether or not the multiplier is even and, if it is, stacking the boxes side by side by doubling the **m_Length** value and only multiplying the **m_Height** value by half of **n**. This is illustrated in the following figure:

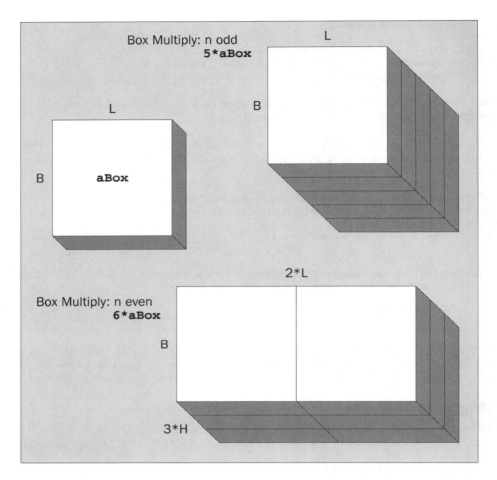

Of course, we will need to check which is the larger of the length and breadth for the new object, and make that the length. This is not shown in the diagram. We'll write the version of the operator function, **operator*()** as a member function, with the left operand as a **CBox** object:

```
// CBox multiply operator this*n
CBox operator*(int n)
{
    if(n%2)
        return CBox(m_Length, m_Breadth, n*m_Height);        // n odd
    else
        return CBox(m_Length>2.0*m_Breadth? m_Length:2.0*m_Breadth,
                    m_Length<2.0*m_Breadth? m_Length:2.0*m_Breadth,
                    (n/2)*m_Height); // n even
}
```

Here, we use the conditional operator to produce the length and breadth arguments for creating the new **CBox** object when **n** is even. The length of the new object corresponds to the maximum of the length and twice the breadth of the original box. The breadth is the minimum of these values.

We can now use the function we have just written in the implementation of the version with the left operand as an integer. We can write this as a non-member function:

```
// CBox multiply operator n*aBox
   CBox operator*(int n, CBox aBox)
   {
       return aBox*n;
   }
```

This version of the multiply operation simply reverses the order of the operands so as to use the previous version of the function directly. That completes the set of combinatorial operators for **CBox** objects that we defined. We can finally look at the two analytical operator functions **operator/()** and **operator%()**.

Analyzing CBox Objects

As we have said, the division operation will be determining how many of a **CBox** object given by the right operand can be contained in the **CBox** object specified by the left operand. To keep it relatively simple, we'll assume that all the **CBox** objects are packed the right way up, that is, with the height dimensions vertical. We will also assume that they are all packed the same way round, so that their length dimensions are aligned. Without these assumptions, it can get rather complicated.

The problem will then amount to determining how many of the right operand objects can be placed in a single layer and then deciding how many layers we can get inside the right operand **CBox**.

We will code this as a member function as follows:

```
int operator/(const CBox& aBox)
{
    int tc1 = 0;     // Temporary for number in horizontal plane this way
    int tc2 = 0;     // Temporary for number in a plane that way

    tc1 = int(m_Length/aBox.m_Length)*
                  (int)(m_Breadth/aBox.m_Breadth);   // to fit this way..
    tc2 = int(m_Length/aBox.m_Breadth)*
                  (int)(m_Breadth/aBox.m_Length);     // ...and that way

//Return best fit
    return int(m_Height/aBox.m_Height)*( tc1>tc2?tc1:tc2);
}
```

This function first determines how many of the second operand **CBox** objects can fit in a layer with the length aligned with the length dimension of the first operand **CBox**. This is stored in **tc1**. We then calculate how many fit in a layer with the length of the second operand **CBox** lying in the breadth direction of the first operand **CBox**. We then multiply the larger of **tc1** and **tc2** by the number of layers we can pack in, and return that value. This process is illustrated on the following page:

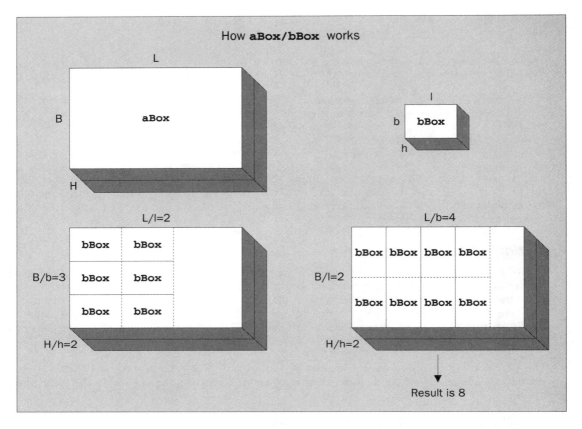

We look at two possibilities - fitting **bBox** into **aBox** with the length aligned with that of **aBox**, and with the length of **bBox** aligned with the breadth of **aBox**. You can see from the illustration that the best packing results from rotating **bBox** so that the breadth divides into the width of **aBox**.

The other analytical operator function, **operator%()**, for obtaining the free volume in a packed **aBox** is easier, since we can use the operator we have just written. We can write it as an ordinary global function, since we don't need access to the **private** members of the class.

```
// Operator to return the free volume in a packed box
double operator%(CBox& aBox, CBox& bBox)
{
    return aBox.Volume() - (aBox/bBox) * bBox.Volume();
}
```

This computation falls out very easily using existing class functions. The result is the volume of the big box, **aBox**, minus the volume of the **bBox** boxes in it. The number of **bBox** objects packed is given by the expression **aBox/bBox** which uses the previous overloaded operator. We multiply this by the volume of **bBox** objects to get the volume to be subtracted from the volume of the large box, **aBox**.

That completes our class interface. There are, clearly, many more functions that might be required for a production problem solver but, as an interesting working model demonstrating how we can produce a class for solving a particular kind of problem, it will suffice. Now we should try it out on a problem.

TRY IT OUT - A Multifile Project Using the CBox Class

Before we can actually start writing the code to *use* our **CBox** class and its overloaded operators, the first thing we need to do is to assemble the definition for the class into a coherent whole. We're going to take a slightly different approach from what you've seen previously, in that we are going to write multiple files for our project.

Start by creating a new Project Workspace for a console application called **Ex9_07**. Start a new source file and save it as **Ex9_07.h** (make sure that it's saved in the project directory, but don't add the file to the project). We'll use this header file to store the definition of the **CBox** class and the prototypes for the functions that aren't members of the class. Type in the code that you see below, then save the file.

```cpp
// EX9_07.H
// Header file containing the definition of the CBox class
#ifndef EX9_07_H
#define EX9_07_H

#include <iostream.h>

class CBox;

// Function prototypes

// Operators for comparing a double value with a CBox object
int operator>(const double& value, CBox& aBox);
int operator<(const double& value, CBox& aBox);
int operator>=(const double& value, CBox& aBox);
int operator<=(const double& value, CBox& aBox);
int operator==(const double& value, CBox& aBox);

// Operators for comparing a CBox object with a double value
int operator>(CBox& aBox, const double& value);
int operator<(CBox& aBox, const double& value);
int operator==(CBox& aBox, const double& value);

CBox operator*(int n, CBox aBox);           // CBox capacity n x aBox
double operator%(CBox& aBox, CBox& bBox);   // for remainder

class CBox                       // Class definition at global scope
{
   public:
      // Constructor definition
      CBox(double lv=1.0, double bv=1.0, double hv=1.0)
      {
         lv = lv<=0.0 ? 1.0:lv;             // Ensure positive
         bv = bv<=0.0 ? 1.0:bv;             // dimensions for
         hv = hv<=0.0 ? 1.0:hv;             // the object

         m_Length = lv>bv ? lv:bv;          // Ensure that
         m_Breadth = bv<lv ? bv:lv;         // length >= breadth
         m_Height = hv;
      }
```

325

```
        // Function to calculate the volume of a box
        double Volume() { return m_Length*m_Breadth*m_Height; }

        // Function providing the length of a box
        double GetLength() { return m_Length; }

        // Function providing the breadth of a box
        double GetBreadth() { return m_Breadth; }

        // Function providing the height of a box
        double GetHeight() { return m_Height; }

        // Function to add two CBox objects - this+aBox
        CBox operator+(const CBox& aBox)
        {
            // New object has larger length and breadth of the two,
            // and sum of the two heights
            return CBox(m_Length>aBox.m_Length? m_Length:aBox.m_Length,
                        m_Breadth>aBox.m_Breadth? m_Breadth:aBox.m_Breadth,
                        m_Height+aBox.m_Height);
        }

        // CBox multiply operator this*n
        CBox operator*(int n)
        {
            if(n%2)
                return CBox(m_Length, m_Breadth, n*m_Height);    // n odd
            else
                return CBox(m_Length>2.0*m_Breadth?m_Length:2.0*m_Breadth,
                            m_Length<2.0*m_Breadth?m_Length:2.0*m_Breadth,
                            (n/2)*m_Height);                       // n even
        }

        // CBox divide operator this/aBox
        int operator/(const CBox& aBox)
        {
            // Temporary for number in horizontal plane this way
            int tc1 = 0;
            // Temporary for number in a plane that way
            int tc2 = 0;

            tc1 = int(m_Length/aBox.m_Length)*
                    (int)(m_Breadth/aBox.m_Breadth); // to fit this way..
            tc2 = (int)(m_Length/aBox.m_Breadth)*
                    (int)(m_Breadth/aBox.m_Length);  // ...and that way

            //Return best fit
            return (int)(m_Height/aBox.m_Height)*(tc1>tc2?tc1:tc2);
    }

    private:
        double m_Length;                // Length of a box in inches
        double m_Breadth;               // Breadth of a box in inches
        double m_Height;                // Height of a box in inches

};
#endif                          // EX9_07_H
```

We've already discussed the code contained here, which is just the definition for the class **CBox** in its latest guise, but you've probably noticed the new preprocessor commands beginning with **#**. The **#ifndef** works rather like an **if**, in that it tests whether the name specified (in this case **EX9_07_H**) has not already been defined and, if it hasn't, the following statements down to **#endif** are included. If the name exists, all the statements and commands down to **#endif** are ignored. The command **#define** defines the name.

If this file were included in a program more than once, the first **#include** directive that was executed would include the file contents and define the name **EX9_07_H** with the **#define** command. For any subsequent inclusions of the file, the symbol **EX9_07_H** would already exist, so the **#ifndef** test would fail and the contents would be ignored. This is a common technique to avoid duplicate definitions in your code.

Now create a new source file with the name **Ex9_07f.cpp** and add the file to the project. We'll use this file to hold the definitions for all the functions that aren't members of the class. In other words, this file will hold all the overloaded operator functions that don't need access to the **private** members of the **CBox** class.

```
// EX9_07F.CPP
// CBox object operations that don't rely on private members
#include "EX9_07.H"

// Function for testing if a constant is > a CBox object
int operator>(const double& value, CBox& aBox)
{ return value > aBox.Volume(); }

// Function for testing if a constant is < CBox object
int operator<(const double& value, CBox& aBox)
{ return value < aBox.Volume(); }

// Function for testing if CBox object is > a constant
int operator>(CBox& aBox, const double& value)
{ return value < aBox; }

// Function for testing if CBox object is < a constant
int operator<(CBox& aBox, const double& value)
{ return value > aBox; }

// Function for testing if a constant is >= a CBox object
int operator>=(const double& value, CBox& aBox)
{ return value >= aBox.Volume(); }

// Function for testing if a constant is <= CBox object
int operator<=(const double& value, CBox& aBox)
{ return value <= aBox.Volume(); }

// Function for testing if CBox object is >= a constant
int operator>=(CBox& aBox, const double& value)
{ return value <= aBox; }

// Function for testing if CBox object is <= a constant
int operator<=(CBox& aBox, const double& value)
{ return value <= aBox; }

// Function for testing if a constant is == CBox object
int operator==(const double& value, CBox& aBox)
```

```
    { return value == aBox.Volume(); }

    // Function for testing if CBox object is == a constant
    int operator==(CBox& aBox, const double& value)
    { return value == aBox; }

    // CBox multiply operator n*aBox
    CBox operator*(int n, CBox aBox)
    { return aBox * n; }

    // Operator to return the free volume in a packed CBox
    double operator%(CBox& aBox, CBox& bBox)
    { return aBox.Volume() - (aBox/bBox) * bBox.Volume(); }
```

Again, you've seen this code before, but we've presented it all in one place for your convenience. As you can see, the code contains an **#include** statement for the file **Ex9_07.h**, which we have just created and which contains the definition of the **CBox** class. This is necessary because the functions in **EX9_07f.cpp** refer to this class. The **#include** statement for including user defined files has the file name between double quotes so that Visual C++ will first look for the file in the same folder as the base **.cpp** file was found, then in the standard include folders if it is not found. Now that we've prepared the ground for the use of the **CBox** class, let's consider a problem that we can solve with its help.

Using Our CBox Class

Let's suppose that we need to package candies. They are on the big side, real jaw breakers, occupying an envelope 1.5 inches long by 1 inch wide by 1 inch high. We have access to a standard candy box that is 4.5 inches by 7 inches by 2 inches and we want to know how many candies fit in the box so that we can set the price. We also have a standard carton that is 2 feet 6 inches long, by 18 inches wide and 18 inches deep, and we want to know how many boxes of candy it can hold and how much space we are wasting.

In case the standard candy box is not a good solution, we would also like to know what custom candy box would be suitable. We know that we can get a good price on boxes with a length from 3 inches to 7 inches, a breadth from 3 inches to 5 inches and a height from 1 inch to 2.5 inches, where each dimension can vary in steps of half an inch. We also know that we need to have at least 30 candies in a box, because this is the minimum quantity consumed by our largest customers at a sitting. Also, the candy box should not have empty space because the complaints from customers who think they are being cheated goes up. Further, ideally we want to pack the standard carton completely so they don't rattle around.

With our **CBox** class, the problem becomes almost trivial. The solution is represented by the following **main()** function. So, create a new source file called **Ex9_07.cpp**, type in the code shown here and add the file to the project.

```
// EX9_07.CPP
// A sample packaging problem
#include <iostream.h>
#include "EX9_07.H"

int main(void)
{
    CBox Candy(1.5,1.0,1.0);                    // Candy definition
    CBox CandyBox(7.0, 4.5, 2.0);               // Candy box definition
```

```
        CBox Carton(30.0, 18.0, 18.0);                    // Carton definition

// Calculate candies per candy box
    int NumCandies = CandyBox/Candy;

// Calculate candy boxes per carton
    int NumCboxes = Carton/CandyBox;

// Calculate wasted carton space
    double space = Carton%CandyBox;

    cout << endl
        << "There are " << NumCandies
        << " candies per candy box"
        << endl
        << "For the standard boxes there are " << NumCboxes
        << " candy boxes per carton " << endl << "with "
        << space << " cubic inches wasted.";

    cout << endl << endl << "CUSTOM CANDY BOX ANALYSIS (No Waste)";

// Try the whole range of custom candy boxes
    for(double length = 3.0 ; length <= 7.5 ; length += 0.5)
        for(double breadth = 3.0 ; breadth <= 5.0 ; breadth += 0.5)
            for(double height = 1.0 ; height <= 2.5 ; height += 0.5)
            {
                // Create new box each cycle
                CBox TryBox(length, breadth, height);

                if(Carton%TryBox < TryBox.Volume() &&
                            TryBox%Candy == 0.0 && TryBox/Candy >= 30)
                    cout << endl << endl
                        << "TryBox L = " << TryBox.GetLength()
                        << " B = " << TryBox.GetBreadth()
                        << " H = " << TryBox.GetHeight()
                        << endl
                        << "TryBox contains " << TryBox/Candy << " candies"
                        << " and a carton contains " << Carton/TryBox
                        << " candy boxes.";
            }
    cout << endl;
    return 0;
}
```

We should first look at how our program is structured. We have divided it into a number of files, which is common when writing in C++. You should be able to see them if you look at the FileView.

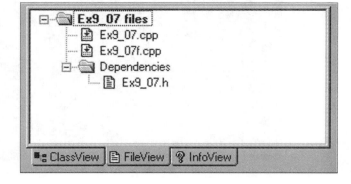

The file **Ex9_07.cpp** contains our function **main()**. It contains an **include** statement for the file **Ex9_07.h** , which contains the prototypes for the functions in **Ex9_07f.cpp,** which are not class members, and the definition of the class **CBox**. So, a C++ program is usually divided into a number of files that each fall into one of three basic categories:

> **.h** files containing library **#include** commands, global constants and variables, class definitions and function prototypes - in other words everything except executable code. Where a program has several class definitions, they are often each placed in a separate **.h** file.

> **.cpp** files containing the executable code for the program, plus **#include** commands for all the definitions required by the executable code.

> Another **.cpp** file containing the function **main()**.

All the **.cpp** files are added explicitly to the project for the program. Visual C++ automatically incorporates all the files that are dependencies (the **.h** files), deducing these from the **#include** directives in the **.cpp** files.

The code in our function **main()** really doesn't need a lot of explanation. It's almost a direct expression of the definition of the problem in words, because the operators in the class interface perform problem oriented actions on **CBox** objects.

The solution to the question of the use of standard boxes is in the declaration statements, which also compute the answers we require as initializing values. We then output these values with some explanatory comment.

The second part of the problem is solved using the three nested **for** loops iterating over the possible ranges of **m_Length**, **m_Breadth** and **m_Height** so we evaluate all possible combinations. We could output them all but, since this would involve 200 combinations of which we might only be interested in a few, we have an **if** which defines the options that we are actually interested in. The **if** expression is only **TRUE** if there is no space wasted in the carton *and* the current trial candy box has no wasted space *and* it also contains at least 30 candies.

The output from this program is shown below:

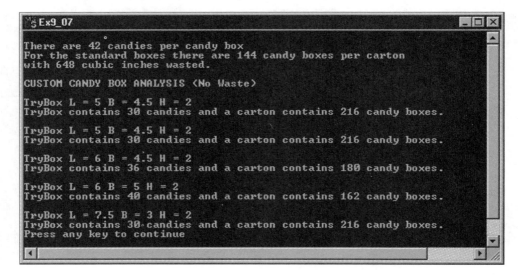

We have a duplicate solution due to the fact that, in the nested loop, we will evaluate boxes that have a length of 5 and a breadth of 4.5, as well as boxes that have a length of 4.5 and a breadth of 5. Because our class constructor ensures that the length is not less than the breadth, these two are identical. We could include some additional logic to avoid presenting duplicates, but it hardly seems worth the effort. You could treat it as a small exercise if you like.

Organizing Your Program Code

In this last example, we distributed the code among several files for the first time. This is not only common practice with Windows programming, it is essential. The sheer volume of code involved in even the simplest program necessitates dividing it into workable chunks.

As we discussed in the previous section, there are basically two kinds of source code in a C++ program. This is illustrated in the diagram below:

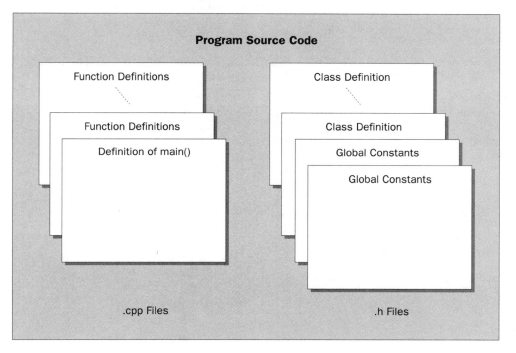

First of all, there is the executable code which corresponds to the definitions of the functions that make up the program. Secondly, there are definitions of various kinds that are necessary for the executable code to compile correctly - global constants and variables, data types - which are classes, structures, and unions, and function prototypes. The executable source code is stored in files with the extension **.cpp**, and the definitions are stored in files with the extension **.h**.

You should add all the **.cpp** files that make up your program to the project definition. As you know, you can do this using the Insert/Files into Project... menu option. The definition code stored in **.h** files that are required for each **.cpp** file are added using **#include** directives at the beginning of each **.cpp** file. These will consist of header files for standard library functions and other standard definitions, as well as your own header files. Developer Studio automatically keeps track of all these files, and enables you to view them in FileView. You can also view the class definitions and globals in ClassView.

In a Windows program, there are other kinds of definitions for the specification of such things as menus and toolbar buttons. These are stored in files with various extensions such as **.rc** and **.ico**. Just like **.h** files, these do not need to be explicitly added to a project as they are tracked automatically by Developer Studio.

Naming Program Files

For classes of any complexity, it is usual to store the class definition in a **.h** file with a filename based on the class name, and the implementation of the function members of the class that are defined outside of the class definition in a **.cpp** file with the same name. On this basis, the definition of our **CBox** class should appear in a file with the name **CBox.h**. Similarly, the class implementation would be stored in the file **CBox.cpp**. We did not follow this convention in this chapter because it's easier to reference the examples with names derived from the chapter number and the sequence number of the example within a chapter.

This is a very convenient approach for the most part, as it's easy to find the definition or implementation of any class. As long as you know the class name, you can go directly to the file you want. This is not a rigid rule, however. It's sometimes useful to group the definitions of a set of closely related classes together in a single file and assemble their implementations similarly. The ClassView will still display all the individual classes, as well as all the members of each class, as you can see here:

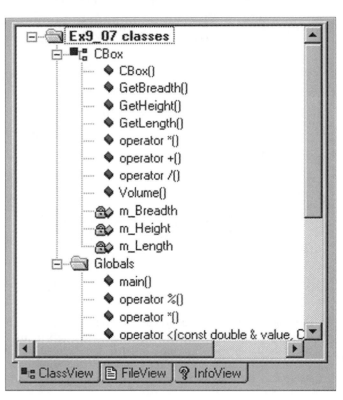

Here, you can see the details of the classes and globals for the last example. Double-clicking on any of the entries in the tree will take you directly to the relevant source code.

Summary

In this chapter, we have laid the foundations for object oriented programming and the basis for understanding how the Microsoft Foundation Classes (MFC) that are provided as part of Visual C++ work, since MFC is based on a set of classes specially designed to make programming Windows easy. In the same way as we defined a **CBox** class interface for working with **CBox** objects, MFC implements a set of classes providing an easy-to-use set of tools for programming Windows. You will also be applying classes to the application specific parts of your Windows programs. Classes become extremely useful for managing application data that subsequently needs to be displayed in response to a **WM_PAINT** message. The next chapter will complete the knowledge of classes that you will need to understand how to apply classes to your own applications, and how to use MFC.

The key points to keep in mind from this chapter are:

▶ Objects are destroyed using functions called **destructors**. It is essential to define a destructor to destroy objects which contain members that are allocated by **new**, as the default constructor will not do this.

▶ The compiler will supply a default copy constructor for your class if you do not define one. The default copy constructor will not deal correctly with objects of classes that have data members allocated on the free store.

▶ When you define your own copy constructor, you must use a reference parameter.

▶ If you do not define an assignment operator for your class, the compiler will supply a default version. As with the copy constructor, the default assignment operator will not work correctly with classes that have data members allocated on the free store.

▶ It is essential that you provide a destructor, a copy constructor and an assignment operator for classes that have members allocated by **new**.

▶ A class may be designated as a **friend** of another class. In this case, all the function members of the **friend** class may access all the members of the other class. If class **A** is a **friend** of **B**, class **B** is not a **friend** of **A** unless it has been declared as such.

▶ Most basic operators can be overloaded to provide actions specific to objects of a class. You should only implement operator functions for your classes that are consistent with the normal interpretation of the basic operators.

Class Inheritance

In this chapter, we are going to look into what lies at the heart of object oriented programming and what will enable you to use the facilities of MFC and AppWizard to program Windows applications - inheritance. Inheritance is simply the means by which you can define a new class in terms of one you already have. You will use this in programming for Windows by redefining the classes provided by MFC to suit your own particular needs, so it is important that you understand how inheritance works.

In this chapter you will learn about:

▶ How inheritance fits into the idea of object oriented programming

▶ Defining a new class in terms of an existing one

▶ The use of the keyword **protected** to define a new access specification for class members

▶ Virtual functions and how you can use them

▶ Pure virtual functions

▶ Abstract classes

▶ Virtual destructors and when to use them

▶ Multiple inheritance

Basic Ideas of OOP

As we saw in the last chapter, a class is a data type that you define to suit your own application requirements. Classes in object oriented programming also define the objects to which your program relates. You program the solution to a problem in terms of the objects that are specific to the problem, using operations that work directly with those objects. You can define a class to represent something abstract, such as a complex number which is a mathematical concept, or a truck which is decidedly physical (especially if you run into one on the highway). So, as well as being a data type, a class can also be a definition of a real world object, at least to the degree necessary to solve a given problem.

You can think of a class as defining the characteristics of a particular group of things that are specified by a common set of parameters and share a common set of operations that may be performed on them. The operations that are possible are defined by the class interface contained in the **public** section of the class definition. The class **CBox** that we used in the last chapter is a good example of this. This defined a box in the most elementary terms.

Of course, in the real world there are many different kinds of boxes: there are cartons, coffins, candy boxes or cereal boxes and you will certainly be able to come up with a few others. You can differentiate various kinds of box by the kind of things they hold, the materials they are made of and in a multitude of other ways, but even though there are many different kinds of box, they share common characteristics, so you can still visualize them as actually being related to one another. You could define a particular kind of box as having the characteristics of a generic box - perhaps just a length, a breadth and a height - plus some additional parameters which serve to differentiate your kind of box from the rest. You may also find that there may be new things you can do with your particular kind of box.

Equally, some objects may be the result of combining a particular kind of box with some other kind of object, a box of candy, or a crate of beer, for example. You can, of course, define one kind of box as a generic box plus some additional characteristics and then specify another sort of box as a further specialization of that. An example of the kinds of relationships you might define between different sorts of boxes is illustrated below:

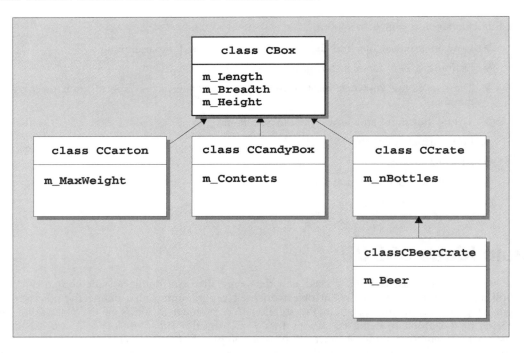

Here, we have three different kinds of box defined based on the generic type. We also have beer crates defined as a further refinement of crates designed to hold bottles.

You could deduce from this that a good way to approximate the real world relatively well, using classes in C++, would be through the ability to define classes that are interrelated. A candy box can be considered to be a box, with all the characteristics of a basic box, plus a few characteristics of its own. This precisely illustrates the relationship between classes in C++, when one class is defined, based on another, and is shown in the diagram above. Let's look at how this works in practice.

Inheritance in Classes

When one class is defined based on another class, or more generally, based on several others, the class is referred to as a **derived class**. It automatically contains all the data members of the class or classes which are used to define it and, with some restrictions, the function members as well. In this case, the class is said to **inherit** the data members and function members of the classes on which it is based.

The only members of a base class which are not inherited by a derived class are the destructor, the constructors and any member functions overloading the assignment operator. All other function members, together with all the data members of a base class, will be inherited by a derived class.

What is a Base Class?

A base class is any class that is used in the definition of another class. This can be a direct base class when, for example, a class **B** is defined directly in terms of a class **A**. **A** is said to be a **direct base class** of **B**. In the previous diagram, the class **CCrate** was a direct base class of **CBeerCrate**. When a class such as **CBeerCrate** is defined in terms of another class **CCrate**, **CBeerCrate** is said to be derived from **CCrate**. Because the class **CCrate** is also defined in terms of the class **CBox**, **CBox** is said to be an **indirect base class** of **CBeerCrate.** We shall see how this is expressed in the class definition in a moment. The relationship between a derived class and a base class is illustrated in the following figure:

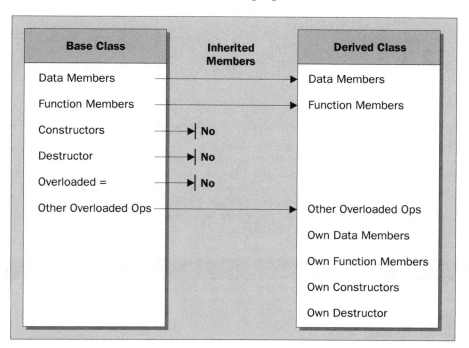

Deriving Classes from a Base Class

Let's go back to the original **CBox** class with **public** data members that we had at the beginning of the last chapter:

```
// Listing 10_01-01
class CBox
{
    public:
        double m_Length;
        double m_Breadth;
        double m_Height;

        CBox(double lv=1.0, double bv=1.0, double hv=1.0)
        {
            m_Length = lv;
            m_Breadth = bv;
            m_Height = hv;
        }
};
```

We have included a constructor in the class so that we can initialize objects when we declare them. Suppose we now need another class **CCandyBox**, which is the same as a **CBox** object, but also has another data member - a pointer to a text string. We can define **CCandyBox** as a derived class with the class **CBox** as the base class, as follows:

```
// Listing 10_01-02
class CCandyBox : CBox
{
    public:
        char* m_Contents;

        CCandyBox(char* str= "Candy")                   // Constructor
        {
            m_Contents = new char[ strlen(str) + 1 ];
            strcpy(m_Contents, str);
        }

        ~CCandyBox()                                    // Destructor
        { delete[] m_Contents; };
};
```

The base class, **CBox**, appears after the class name for the derived class **CCandyBox** and is separated from it by a colon. In all other respects, it looks like a normal class definition. We have added the new member, **m_Contents**, and, since it is a pointer to a string, we need a constructor to initialize it and a destructor to release the memory for the string. We have also put a default value for the string describing the contents of a **CCandyBox** object in the constructor. Objects of the class **CCandyBox** contain all the members of the base class, **CBox**, plus the additional data member, **m_Contents**.

TRY IT OUT - Using a Derived Class

We can see how our derived class works in an example:

```
// EX10_01.CPP
// Using a derived class
#include <iostream.h>                      // For stream I/O
#include <string.h>                        // For strlen() and strcpy()


// Insert CBox definition (Listing 10_01-01)

// Insert CCandyBox definition (Listing 10_01-02)

int main(void)
{
   CBox myBox(4.0,3.0,2.0);                // Create CBox object
   CCandyBox myCandyBox;
   CCandyBox myMintBox("Wafer Thin Mints");  // Create CCandyBox object

   cout << endl
       << "myBox occupies " << sizeof  myBox    // Show how much memory
       << " bytes" << endl                       // the objects require
       << "myCandyBox occupies " << sizeof myCandyBox
       << " bytes" << endl
       << "myMintBox occupies " << sizeof myMintBox
       << " bytes";

   cout << endl
       << "myBox length is " << myBox.m_Length;

   myBox.m_Length = 10.0;

// myCandyBox.m_Length = 10.0;              // uncomment this for an error

   cout << endl;
   return 0;
}
```

How It Works

After declaring a **CBox** object and two **CCandyBox** objects, we output the number of bytes occupied by each object. Let's look at the output:

```
Ex10_01
myBox occupies 24 bytes
myCandyBox occupies 32 bytes
myMintBox occupies 32 bytes
myBox length is 4
Press any key to continue
```

The first line is what we would expect from our discussion in the last chapter. A **CBox** object has three data members of type **double**, each of which will be 8 bytes, making 24 bytes in all. Both our **CCandyBox** objects are the same size - 32 bytes. The length of the string doesn't affect the size of an object, as the memory for it is allocated in the free store. The 32 bytes are made up of 24 bytes for the three **double** members inherited from the base class, **CBox**, plus 4 bytes for the pointer member, **m_Contents** - so where did the other 4 bytes come from? This is due to the compiler aligning members at addresses that are a multiple of 8 bytes. You should be able to demonstrate this by adding an extra member of type **int**, say, to the class **CCandyBox**. You'll find that the size of a class object is still 32 bytes.

We also output the value of the **m_Length** member of the **CBox** object **myBox**. Even though we have no difficulty accessing this member of the **CBox** object, if you uncomment the following statement in the function **main()**,

```
// myCandyBox.m_Length = 10.0;              // uncomment this for an error
```

the program will no longer compile. The compiler will generate a message,

error C2248: 'm_Length' : cannot access public member declared in class 'CBox'

which says that the **m_Length** member from the base class is not accessible. In the derived class, the member **m_Length** has become **private**.

The reason for this is that there is a default access specifier of **private** for a base class. There always has to be an access specification for a base class which will determine the status of the inherited members in the derived class. Omitting an access specification when specifying a base class causes the compiler to assume that it's **private**. If we change the definition of the class **CCandyBox** to the following,

```
class CCandyBox : public CBox
{
    // Contents the same as in Listing 10_01-02
};
```

the member **m_Length** in the derived class will be inherited as **public** and will be accessible in the function **main()**. With the access specifier **public** for the base class, all the inherited members originally specified as **public** in the base class will have the same access level in the derived class.

Access Control Under Inheritance

The whole question of the access of inherited members in a derived class needs to be looked at more closely. Firstly, we should consider the **private** members of a base class in a derived class.

There was a good reason for choosing the version of the class **CBox** with **public** data members, rather than the later, more secure version with **private** data members that we looked at. The reason was that, although **private** data members of a base class are also members of a derived class, they remain **private** to the base class member functions. They are only accessible in the derived class through function members of the base class that are not in the **private** section of the base class. You can demonstrate this very easily by changing all the **CBox** class data members to **private** and putting a function **Volume()** in the derived class **CCandyBox**, so that the class definitions become as follows:

```
// Version of the classes that will not compile
class CBox
{
    public:

        CBox(double lv=1.0, double bv=1.0, double hv=1.0)
        {
            m_Length = lv;
```

```
                  m_Breadth = bv;
                  m_Height = hv;
             }

      private:
          double m_Length;
          double m_Breadth;
          double m_Height;
};

class CCandyBox : public CBox
{
      public:
          char* m_Contents;

// Function to calculate the volume of a CCandyBox object
          double Volume(void)                // Error - members not accessible
          { return m_Length*m_Breadth*m_Height; }

          CCandyBox(char* str= "Candy")      // Constructor
          {
             m_Contents = new char[ strlen(str) + 1 ];
             strcpy(m_Contents, str);
          }

          ~CCandyBox()                       // Destructor
          { delete[] m_Contents; }
};
```

A program using these classes will not compile. The function **Volume()** in the class **CCandyBox** attempts to access the **private** members of the base class, which is not legal.

TRY IT OUT - Accessing private Members of the Base Class

It is, however, legal to use the **Volume()** function in the base class, so if you move the definition of the function **Volume()** to the base class, **CBox**, not only will the program compile but you can use the function to obtain the volume of a **CCandyBox** object:

```
// EX10_02.CPP
// Using a function inherited from a base class
#include <iostream.h>           // For stream I/O
#include <string.h>             // For strlen() and strcpy()

class CBox
{
      public:

//Function to calculate the volume of a CBox object
          double Volume(void)
          { return m_Length*m_Breadth*m_Height; }


          CBox(double lv=1.0, double bv=1.0, double hv=1.0)
          {
             m_Length = lv;
             m_Breadth = bv;
```

```
            m_Height = hv;
        }
    private:
        double m_Length;
        double m_Breadth;
        double m_Height;

};

class CCandyBox : public CBox
{
    // Contents the same as in Listing 10_01-02
};

int main(void)
{
    CBox myBox(4.0,3.0,2.0);                    // Create CBox object
    CCandyBox myCandyBox;
    CCandyBox myMintBox("Wafer Thin Mints");   // Create CCandyBox object

    cout << endl
        << "myBox occupies " << sizeof  myBox       // Show how much memory
        << " bytes" << endl                          // the objects require
        << "myCandyBox occupies " << sizeof myCandyBox
        << " bytes" << endl
        << "myMintBox occupies " << sizeof myMintBox
        << " bytes";
    cout << endl                           // Get volume of a CCandyBox object
        << "myMintBox volume is " << myMintBox.Volume();
    cout << endl;
    return 0;
}
```

How It Works

This example will produce the following output:

```
Ex10_02

myBox occupies 24 bytes
myCandyBox occupies 32 bytes
myMintBox occupies 32 bytes
myMintBox volume is 1
Press any key to continue_
```

The interesting additional output is the last line. This shows the value produced by the function **Volume()** which is now in the **public** section of the base class. Within the derived class, it operates on the members of the derived class that are inherited from the base. It is a full member of the derived class, so it can be used freely with objects of the derived class.

The value for the volume of the derived class object is **1** because, in creating the **CCandyBox** object, the default constructor **CBox()** was called first to create the base class part of the object, and this sets default **CBox** dimensions to **1**.

Constructor Operation in a Derived Class

The constructor for the base part of the derived class was called automatically in the last example. This doesn't have to be the case. We can arrange to call a particular constructor for a base class from the derived class constructor. This will enable us to initialize the base class data members with a constructor other than the default, or indeed to choose one or other base class constructor, depending on the data supplied to the derived class constructor.

TRY IT OUT - Calling Constructors

We can demonstrate this in action using a modified version of the last example. We really need to provide a constructor for the derived class which allows you to specify the dimensions of the object to make the class usable. We can produce an additional constructor in the derived class to do this, and call the base class constructor explicitly to set the values of the data members inherited from the base class.

```cpp
// EX10_03.CPP
// Calling a base consructor from a derived class constructor
#include <iostream.h>          // For stream I/O
#include <string.h>            // For strlen() and strcpy()

class CBox
{
   public:

//Function to calculate the volume of a CBox object
      double Volume(void)
        { return m_Length*m_Breadth*m_Height; }

// Base class constructor
      CBox(double lv=1.0, double bv=1.0, double hv=1.0)
        {
          cout << endl << "CBox constructor called";
          m_Length = lv;
          m_Breadth = bv;
          m_Height = hv;
        }

   private:
      double m_Length;
      double m_Breadth;
      double m_Height;

};

class CCandyBox : public CBox
{
   public:
      char* m_Contents;

// Constructor to set dimensions and contents
// with explicit call of CBox constructor
      CCandyBox(double lv, double bv, double hv, char* str= "Candy")
             :CBox(lv,bv,hv)
```

```
        {
            cout << endl <<"CCandyBox constructor2 called";
            m_Contents = new char[ strlen(str) + 1 ];
            strcpy(m_Contents, str);
        }

// Constructor to set contents
// calls default CBox constructor automatically
        CCandyBox(char* str= "Candy")
        {
            cout << endl << "CCandyBox constructor1 called";
            m_Contents = new char[ strlen(str) + 1 ];
            strcpy(m_Contents, str);
        }
```

```
    ~CCandyBox()                                          // Destructor
    { delete[] m_Contents; }
};

int main(void)
{
    CBox myBox(4.0,3.0,2.0);
    CCandyBox myCandyBox;
    CCandyBox myMintBox(1.0,2.0,3.0,"Wafer Thin Mints");

    cout << endl
        << "myBox occupies " << sizeof  myBox  // Show how much memory
        << " bytes" << endl                    // the objects require
        << "myCandyBox occupies " << sizeof myCandyBox
        << " bytes" << endl
        << "myMintBox occupies " << sizeof myMintBox
        << " bytes";
    cout << endl
        << "myMintBox volume is "              // Get volume of a
        << myMintBox.Volume();                 // CCandyBox object
    cout << endl;
    return 0;
}
```

How It Works

As well as adding the additional constructor in the derived class, we have put an output statement in each constructor so we will know when either gets called. The explicit call of the constructor for the **CBox** class appears after a colon in the function header of the derived class constructor. You will have perhaps noticed that the notation is exactly the same as that used for initializing members in a constructor, which we saw in the last chapter.

```
// Initializing members
    CBox(double lv=1.0, double bv=1.0, double hv=1.0)
        :m_Length(lv), m_Breadth(bv), m_Height(hv)
    {
    ...
    }

// Calling the base class constructor
    CCandyBox(double lv, double bv, double hv, char* str= "Candy")
            :CBox(lv,bv,hv)
    {
```

```
        ...
    }
```

This is quite consistent with what we are doing here, since we are essentially initializing a **CBox** sub-object of the derived class object. In the first case, we are explicitly calling the default constructors for the **double** types **m_Length**, **m_Breadth** and **m_Height** in the initialization list. In the second instance, we are calling the constructor for **CBox**.

If you build and run this example, it will produce the output shown below:

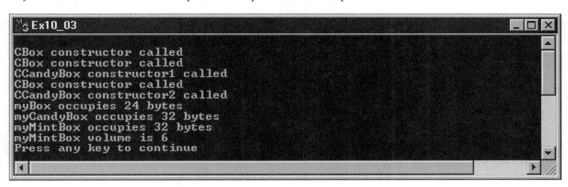

The calls to the constructors are explained in the table below:

Screen Output	Object being constructed
CBox constructor called	Constructing **myBox**
CBox constructor called	Constructing **myCandyBox**
CCandyBox constructor1 called	Constructing **myCandyBox**
CBox constructor called	Constructing **myMintBox**
CCandyBox constructor2 called	Constructing **myMintBox**

The first line of output is due to the **CBox** class constructor call, originating from the declaration of the **CBox** object, **myBox**. The second line of output arises from the automatic call of the base class constructor caused by the declaration of the **CCandyBox** object **myCandyBox**.

 Note how the base class constructor is always called before the derived class constructor.

The following line is due to our version of the default derived class constructor being called for the object **myCandyBox**. This constructor is invoked because the object is not initialized. The fourth line of output arises from the explicit call of the **CBox** class constructor from our new constructor for **CCandyBox** objects. This call passes the argument values specified for the dimensions of the object to the base class constructor. Next, comes the output from the new derived class constructor itself, so constructors are again called for the base class first, followed by the derived class.

The last line shows that the initialization of the base part of the object **myMintBox** is working as it should, with the **private** members having been initialized by the **CBox** class constructor.

Having the **private** members of a base class only accessible to function members of the base isn't always convenient. There will be many instances where we want to have **private** members of a base class that can be accessed within the derived class. As you will surely have anticipated by now, C++ provides a way to do this.

Declaring protected Members of a Class

In addition to the **public** and **private** access specifiers for members of a class, you can also declare members of a class as **protected**. Within the class, the keyword **protected** has the same effect as the keyword **private**: members of a class that are **protected** can only be accessed by member functions of the class, by **friend** functions of the class and member functions of a class that is declared as a **friend** of the class. Using the keyword **protected**, we could redefine our class **CBox** as follows:

```
// Listing 10_04-01
class CBox
{
    public:
        CBox(double lv=1.0, double bv=1.0, double hv=1.0)
        {
          cout << endl << "CBox constructor called";
          m_Length = lv;
          m_Breadth = bv;
          m_Height = hv;
        }

// CBox destructor - just to track calls
    ~CBox()
    { cout << "CBox destructor called" << endl; }

    protected:
        double m_Length;
        double m_Breadth;
        double m_Height;

};
```

Now, the data members are still effectively **private**, in that they can't be accessed by ordinary global functions but they will still be accessible to member functions of a derived class.

TRY IT OUT - Using protected Members

We can demonstrate this by using this version of the class **CBox** to derive a new version of the class **CCandyBox**, which accesses the members of the base class through its own member function **Volume()**.

```
// EX10_04.CPP
// Using the protected access specifier
#include <iostream.h>              // For stream I/O
#include <string.h>               // For strlen() and strcpy()

// Insert CBox class definition here (Listing 10_04-01)

class CCandyBox : public CBox
```

```
    {
    public:
        char* m_Contents;

// Derived class function to calculate volume
        double Volume()
        { return m_Length*m_Breadth*m_Height; }

// Constructor to set dimensions and contents
// with explicit call of CBox constructor
        CCandyBox(double lv, double bv, double hv, char* str= "Candy")
            :CBox(lv,bv,hv)                  // Constructor
        {
            cout << endl <<"CCandyBox constructor2 called";
            m_Contents = new char[ strlen(str) + 1 ];
            strcpy(m_Contents, str);
        }

 // Constructor to set contents
 // calls default CBox constructor automatically
        CCandyBox(char* str= "Candy")                 // Constructor
        {
            cout << endl << "CCandyBox constructor1 called";
            m_Contents = new char[ strlen(str) + 1 ];
            strcpy(m_Contents, str);
        }

        ~CCandyBox()                                  // Destructor
        {
            cout << "CCandyBox destructor called" << endl;
            delete[] m_Contents;
        }
};

int main(void)
{
   CCandyBox myCandyBox;
   CCandyBox myToffeeBox(2,3,4,"Stickjaw Toffee");

   cout << endl
        << "myCandyBox volume is " << myCandyBox.Volume()
        << endl
        << "myToffeeBox volume is " << myToffeeBox.Volume();

// cout << endl << myToffeeBox.m_Length; // Uncomment this for an error

   cout << endl;
   return 0;
}
```

How It Works

In this example, the volumes of the two **CCandyBox** objects are calculated by invoking the function **Volume()**, which is a member of the derived class. This function accesses the inherited members **m_Length**, **m_Breadth** and **m_Height** to produce the result. The members were declared as **protected** in the base class and remain **protected** in the derived class. The program produces the output shown on the following page.

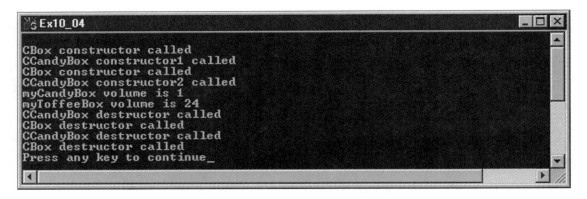

This shows that the volume is being calculated properly for both **CCandyBox** objects. The first object has the default dimensions produced by calling the default **CBox** constructor, so the volume is **1**, and the second object has the dimension defined as initial values in its declaration.

The output also shows the sequence of constructor and destructor calls.

 FYI Note that destructors for a derived class object are called in the reverse sequence to constructors for the object. This is a general rule that always applies. Constructors are invoked starting with the base class constructor and then the derived class constructor, whereas the destructor for the derived class is called first when an object is destroyed, followed by the base class destructor.

You can demonstrate that the **protected** members of the base class remain **protected** in the derived class by uncommenting the statement preceding the **return** statement in the function **main()**. If you do this, you will get the following error message from the compiler,

error C2248: 'm_Length' : cannot access protected member declared in class 'CBox'

which indicates quite clearly that the member **m_Length** is inaccessible.

The Access Level of Inherited Class Members

We know that if we have no access specifier for the base class in the definition of a derived class, the default specification is **private**. This has the effect of causing the inherited **public** and **protected** members of the base class to become **private** in the derived class. The **private** members of the base class remain **private** to the base and, therefore, inaccessible to member functions of the derived class. In fact, they remain **private** to the base class, regardless of how the base class is specified in the derived class definition.

We have also used **public** as the specifier for a base class. This leaves the members of the base class with the same access level in the derived class as they had in the base, so **public** members remain **public** and **protected** members remain **protected**.

The last possibility is to declare a base class as **protected**. This has the effect of making the inherited **public** members of the base **protected** in the derived class. The **protected** (and **private**) inherited members retain their original access level in the derived class.

This is summarized in the following illustration:

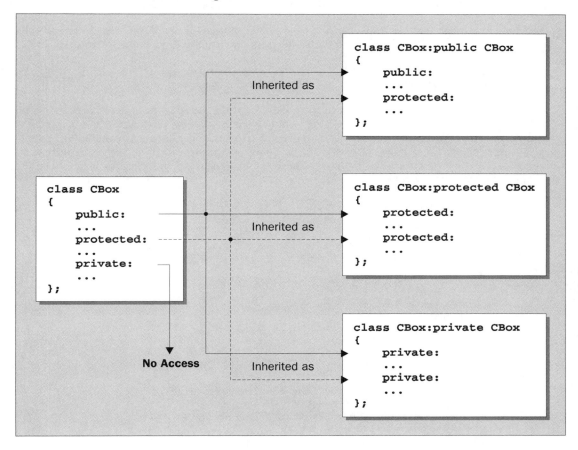

This may look a little complicated, but you can reduce it to the following three points about the inherited members of a derived class:

- **private** members of a base class are never accessible in a derived class.

- Defining a base class as **public** doesn't change the access level of its members in the derived class.

- Defining a base class as **protected** changes its **public** members to **protected** in the derived class.

Being able to change the access level of inherited members in a derived class gives you a degree of flexibility, but remember that you can only make the access level more stringent. In no way can you relax the level specified in the base class. This suggests that your base classes need to have **public** members if you want to be able to vary the access level in derived classes. This may seem to run contrary to the idea of encapsulating data in a class in order to protect it from unauthorized access but, as we shall see, it will often be the case that we construct base classes in such a manner that their only purpose is to act as a base for other classes and they are not intended to be used for instantiating objects in their own right.

The Copy Constructor in a Derived Class

You will remember that the copy constructor is called automatically when you declare an object which is initialized with an object of the same class. For example, in these statements,

```
CBox myBox(2.0, 3.0, 4.0);      // Calls constructor
CBox CopyBox(myBox);            // Calls copy constructor
```

the first statement will call the constructor accepting three **double** arguments and the second will call the copy constructor. If you don't supply your own copy constructor, the compiler will supply one that copies the initializing object member by member to the corresponding members of the new object. So that we can see what is going on during execution, let's add our own version of a copy constructor to the class **CBox**. We can then use this class as a base for defining the class **CCandyBox**.

```
// Listing 10_05-01
class CBox                  // Base class definition
{
   public:
       CBox(double lv=1.0, double bv=1.0, double hv=1.0)
       {
         cout << endl << "CBox constructor called";
         m_Length = lv;
         m_Breadth = bv;
         m_Height = hv;
       }

   // Copy constructor
       CBox(const CBox& initB)
       {
          cout << endl << "CBox copy constructor called";
          m_Length = initB.m_Length;
          m_Breadth = initB.m_Breadth;
          m_Height = initB.m_Height;
       }

// CBox destructor - just to track calls
       ~CBox()
       { cout << "CBox destructor called" << endl; }

   protected:
      double m_Length;
      double m_Breadth;
      double m_Height;

};
```

You'll also recall that the copy constructor needs to have its parameter specified as a reference in order to avoid an infinity of calls of itself, caused by the need to copy an argument that is transferred by value. When the copy constructor in our example is invoked, it will output a message to the screen, so we will be able to see from the output when this is happening.

We'll use the **CCandyBox** class from **Ex10_04.cpp**:

```
// Listing 10_05-02
class CCandyBox : public CBox
```

```
    {
        public:
            char* m_Contents;

// Derived class function to calculate volume
            double Volume()
            { return m_Length*m_Breadth*m_Height; }

// Constructor to set dimensions and contents
// with explicit call of CBox constructor
            CCandyBox(double lv, double bv, double hv, char* str= "Candy")
                :CBox(lv,bv,hv)                    // Constructor
            {
                cout << endl <<"CCandyBox constructor2 called";
                m_Contents = new char[ strlen(str) + 1 ];
                strcpy(m_Contents, str);
            }

// Constructor to set contents
// calls default CBox constructor automatically
            CCandyBox(char* str= "Candy")                    // Constructor
            {
                cout << endl << "CCandyBox constructor1 called";
                m_Contents = new char[ strlen(str) + 1 ];
                strcpy(m_Contents, str);
            }

            ~CCandyBox()                                      // Destructor
            {
                cout << "CCandyBox destructor called" << endl;
                delete[] m_Contents;
            }
    };
```

This doesn't have a copy constructor added yet, so we'll rely on the compiler-generated version.

TRY IT OUT - The Copy Constructor in Derived Classes

We can exercise the copy constructor that we have just defined with the following example:

```
// EX10_05.CPP
// Using a derived class copy constructor
#include <iostream.h>          // For stream I/O
#include <string.h>            // For strlen() and strcpy()

// Insert CBox class definition here (Listing 10_05-01)

// Insert CCandyBox class definition here (Listing 10_05-02)

int main(void)
{
    CCandyBox ChocBox(2.0, 3.0, 4.0, "Chockies"); // Declare and initialize
    CCandyBox ChocolateBox(ChocBox);              // Use copy constructor

    cout << endl
        << "Volume of ChocBox is " << ChocBox.Volume()
```

```
              << endl
              << "Volume of ChocolateBox is " << ChocolateBox.Volume()
              << endl;

       return 0;
}
```

How It Works (or Why It Doesn't)

When you run this example, in addition to the expected output, you'll see the following message:

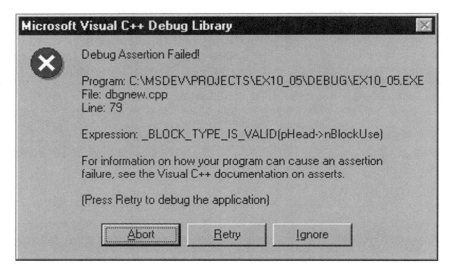

Press **Abort** to clear the dialog and you'll see the output in the console window that you might expect. The output shows that the compiler-generated copy constructor for the derived class automatically called the copy constructor for the base class.

However, as you've probably realized, all is not as it should be. In this particular case, the compiler-generated copy constructor causes problems because the memory pointed to by the member **m_Contents** of the derived class in the second object declared will point to the same memory as the first object. When one object is destroyed, it releases the memory occupied by the text. When the second object is destroyed, the destructor attempts to release some memory that has already been freed by the destructor call for the previous object.

The way we can fix this is to supply a copy constructor for the derived class that will allocate some additional memory for the new object.

TRY IT OUT - Fixing the Copy Constructor Problem

We can do this by adding the following code for the copy constructor to the **public** section of the derived class:

```
// Derived class copy constructor
   CCandyBox(const CCandyBox& initCB)
```

```
{
    cout << endl << "CCandyBox copy constructor called";
    // Get new memory
    m_Contents = new char[ strlen(initCB.m_Contents) + 1 ];
    // Copy string
    strcpy(m_Contents, initCB.m_Contents);
}
```

We can now run this new version of the last example with the same function **main()** to see how our copy constructor works.

How It Works

Now when we run the example, it behaves rather better and produces the output shown in the screen below:

However, there is still something wrong. The third line of output shows that the default constructor for the **CBox** part of the object **ChocolateBox** is called, rather than the copy constructor. As a consequence, the object has the default dimensions rather than the dimensions of the initializing object, so the volume is incorrect. The reason for this is that when you write a constructor for an object of a derived class, you are responsible for ensuring that the members of the derived class object are properly initialized. This includes the inherited members.

The fix for this is to call the copy constructor for the base part of the class in the initialization list for the copy constructor for the **CCandyBox** class. The copy constructor would then become:

```
// Derived class copy constructor
CCandyBox(const CCandyBox& initCB): CBox(initCB)
{
    cout << endl << "CCandyBox copy constructor called";
    // Get new memory
    m_Contents = new char[ strlen(initCB.m_Contents) + 1 ];
    // Copy string
    strcpy(m_Contents, initCB.m_Contents);
}
```

Now, the **CBox** class copy constructor is called with the **initBC** object. Only the base part of the object will be passed to it, so everything will work out. If you modify the last example by adding the base copy constructor call, the output will now be as shown:

353

```
Ex10_05
CBox constructor called
CCandyBox constructor2 called
CBox copy constructor called
CCandyBox copy constructor called
Volume of ChocBox is 24
Volume of ChocolateBox is 24
CCandyBox destructor called
CBox destructor called
CCandyBox destructor called
CBox destructor called
Press any key to continue_
```

The output shows that all the constructors and destructors are called in the correct sequence and the copy constructor for the **CBox** part of **ChocolateBox** is called before the **CCandyBox** copy constructor. The volume of the object **ChocolateBox** of the derived class is now the same as that of its initializing object, which is as it should be.

We, therefore, have another golden rule to remember:

 If you write any kind of constructor for a derived class, you are responsible for the initialization of all members of the derived class object, including all its inherited members.

Virtual Functions

We need to look more closely at the behavior of inherited member functions and their relationship to derived class member functions. Let's add a function to the class **CBox** to output the volume of a **CBox** object. The simplified class would then become as follows:

```cpp
// Listing 10_06-01
class CBox          // Base class
{
   public:

// Function to show the volume of an object
      void ShowVolume(void)
      {
         cout << endl
            << "CBox usable volume is " << Volume();
      }

// Function to calculate the volume of a CBox object
      double Volume(void)
      { return m_Length*m_Breadth*m_Height; }

// Constructor
      CBox(double lv=1.0, double bv=1.0, double hv=1.0)
         :m_Length(lv), m_Breadth(bv), m_Height(hv) {}

   protected:
```

```
        double m_Length;
        double m_Breadth;
        double m_Height;

};
```

Now, we can produce the output of the usable volume of a **CBox** object just by calling this function for any object for which we require the output. The constructor sets the data member values in the initialization list, so no statements are necessary in the body of the function. The data members are as before and are specified as **protected**, so they will be accessible to the member functions of any derived class.

Let's suppose we want to derive a class for a different kind of box called a **CGlassBox**, to hold glassware for instance. Because the contents are fragile, the capacity of the box is less than the capacity of a basic **CBox** object because packing material is added to protect the contents. We therefore need a different **Volume()** function to account for this, so we add it to the derived class:

```
// Listing 10_06-02
class CGlassBox: public CBox       // Derived class
{
   public:

// Function to calculate volume of a CGlassBox
// allowing 15% for packing
       double Volume(void)
         { return 0.85*m_Length*m_Breadth*m_Height; }

// Constructor
       CGlassBox(double lv, double bv, double hv): CBox(lv,bv,hv){}

};
```

There could conceivably be other additional members of the derived class, but we'll keep it simple and concentrate on how the inherited functions work for the moment. The constructor for the derived class objects just calls the base class constructor in its initialization list to set the data member values. No statements are necessary in its body. We have included a new version of the function **Volume()** to replace the version from the base class, the idea being that we can get the inherited function **ShowVolume()** to call the derived class version of the member function **Volume()** when we call it for an object of the class **CGlassBox**.

TRY IT OUT - Using an Inherited Function

Now, we should see how our derived class works in practice. We can try this out very simply by creating an object of the base class and an object of the derived class with the same dimensions and then verifying that the correct volumes are being calculated. The **main()** function to do this would be as follows:

```
// EX10_06.CPP
// Behavior of inherited functions in a derived class
#include <iostream.h>

// Insert CBox class definition (Listing 10_06-01)
```

```
// Insert CGlassBox class definition (Listing 10_06-02)

int main(void)
{
    CBox myBox(2.0, 3.0, 4.0);          // Declare a base box
    CGlassBox myGlassBox(2.0,3.0,4.0);  // Declare derived box - same size

    myBox.ShowVolume();                 // Display volume of base box
    myGlassBox.ShowVolume();            // Display volume of derived box

    cout << endl;
    return 0;
}
```

How It Works

If you run this example, it will produce this output:

This isn't only dull and repetitive, it's also disastrous. It isn't working the way we want at all, and the only interesting thing about it is why. Evidently, the fact that the second call is for an object of the derived class **CGlassBox** is not being taken into account. We can see this from the incorrect result in the output. The volume of a **CGlassBox** object should definitely be less than that of a basic **CBox** with the same dimensions.

The reason for the incorrect output is that the call of the function **Volume()** in the function **ShowVolume()** is being set once and for all by the compiler as the version defined in the base class. This is called **static** resolution of the function call, or **static linkage**. The function call is fixed before the program is executed. This is also sometimes called **early binding** because the particular function **Volume()** chosen is bound to the call from the function **ShowVolume()** during the compilation of the program.

> Note that the function **Volume()** here in the derived class actually hides the base class version from the view of derived class functions. If you wanted to call the base version of **Volume()** from a derived class function, you would need to use the scope resolution operator to refer to the function as **CBox::Volume()**.

What we were hoping for in this example was that the question of which **Volume()** function call to use in any given instance would be resolved when the program was executed. This sort of operation is referred to as **dynamic linkage**, or **late binding**. We want the actual version of the function **Volume()** called by **ShowVolume()** to be determined by the kind of object being processed, and not arbitrarily fixed by the compiler before the program is executed.

No doubt you won't be astonished that C++ does, in fact, provide us with a way to do this, since this whole discussion would have been futile otherwise! We need to use what is called a **virtual function**.

What's a Virtual Function?

A virtual function is a function in a base class that is declared using the keyword **virtual**. Defining a function as **virtual** in a base class that has another version in a derived class signals to the compiler that we don't want static linkage for this function. What we *do* want is the selection of the function to be called at any given point in the program to be based on the kind of object for which it is called.

TRY IT OUT - Fixing the CGlassBox

To make our example work as we originally hoped, we just need to add the keyword **virtual** to the definition of the function **Volume()** in the base class:

```
// EX10_07.CPP (based on Ex10_06.cpp)
// Using a virtual function
#include <iostream.h>

class CBox              // Base class
{
   public:
...
// Function to calculate the volume of a CBox object
      virtual double Volume(void)
         { return m_Length*m_Breadth*m_Height; }
...
};

class CGlassBox : public CBox
{
   public:
...
// Function to calculate volume of a CGlassBox
// allowing 15% for packing
      virtual double Volume(void)
         { return 0.85*m_Length*m_Breadth*m_Height; }
...
};

int main(void)
{
...
}
```

How It Works

If you run this version of the program with just the little word **virtual** added to the definition of **Volume()** in the base class, it will produce this output:

```
Ex10_07
CBox usable volume is 24
CBox usable volume is 20.4
Press any key to continue_
```

This is now clearly doing what we wanted in the first place. The first call to the function **ShowVolume()** with the **CBox** object, **myBox**, calls the inherited base version of **Volume()**. The second call with the **CGlassBox** object, **myGlassBox**, calls the version defined in the derived class.

Note that, although we have put the keyword **virtual** in the derived class definition of the function **Volume()**, it's not essential to do so. The definition of the base version of the function as **virtual** is sufficient. However, I recommend that you *do* specify the keyword in derived classes for the virtual functions since it makes it clear to anyone reading the derived class definition that they are virtual functions and that they will be selected dynamically.

In order for a function to behave as **virtual**, it must have the same name, parameter list, and return type in any derived class as the function has in the base class. If you use different parameters or return types, the virtual function mechanism won't work. The function will operate with static linkage established and fixed at compile time.

The operation of virtual functions is an extraordinarily powerful mechanism. You may have heard the term **polymorphism** in relation to object oriented programming. This refers to the virtual function capability. Something that is polymorphic can appear in different guises, such as a werewolf, or Dr. Jekyll, for example. Calling a virtual function will produce different effects, depending on the kind of object for which it is being called.

Using Pointers to Class Objects

Using pointers with objects of a base class and of a derived class is a very important technique. A pointer to a base class object can be assigned the address of a derived class object as well as that of the base. We can thus use a pointer of the type 'pointer to base', to obtain different behavior with virtual functions, depending on what kind of object the pointer is pointing to. We can see how this works more clearly by looking at an example.

TRY IT OUT - Pointers to Base and Derived Classes

Let's use the same classes as in the previous example, but make a small modification to the function **main()** so that it uses a pointer to a base class object.

```
// EX10_08.CPP
// Using a base class pointer to call a virtual function
#include <iostream.h>

class CBox           // Base class
{
   public:

// Function to show the volume of an object
      void ShowVolume(void)
      {
         cout << endl
              << "CBox usable volume is " << Volume();
      }

// Function to calculate the volume of a CBox object
      virtual double Volume(void)
      { return m_Length*m_Breadth*m_Height; }
```

```
        // Constructor
            CBox(double lv=1.0, double bv=1.0, double hv=1.0)
                :m_Length(lv), m_Breadth(bv), m_Height(hv) {}

        protected:
            double m_Length;
            double m_Breadth;
            double m_Height;

    };
    class CGlassBox: public CBox          // Derived class
    {
        public:

    // Function to calculate volume of a CGlassBox
    // allowing 15% for packing
            virtual double Volume(void)
                { return 0.85*m_Length*m_Breadth*m_Height; }

    // Constructor
            CGlassBox(double lv, double bv, double hv): CBox(lv,bv,hv){}

    };
```

```
    int main(void)
    {
        CBox myBox(2.0, 3.0, 4.0);            // Declare a base box
        CGlassBox myGlassBox(2.0,3.0,4.0); // Declare derived box of same size
        CBox* pBox = 0;                      // Declare a pointer to base class objects

        pBox = &myBox;                       // Set pointer to address of base object
        pBox->ShowVolume();                  // Display volume of base box
        pBox = &myGlassBox;                  // Set pointer to derived class object
        pBox->ShowVolume();                  // Display volume of derived box

        cout << endl;
        return 0;
    }
```

How It Works

The classes are the same as in example **Ex10_07.cpp**, but the function **main()** has been altered to use a pointer to call the function **ShowVolume()**. Because we are using a pointer, we use the indirect member selection operator, **->**, to call the function. The function **ShowVolume()** is called twice and both calls use the same pointer to base class objects, **pBox**. On the first occasion, the pointer contains the address of the base object, **myBox**, and, on the occasion of the second call, it contains the address of the derived class object **myGlassBox**.

The output produced is as follows,

```
Ex10_08                                                          _ □ ×
CBox usable volume is 24
CBox usable volume is 20.4
Press any key to continue
```

which is exactly the same as that from the previous example where we used explicit objects in the function call.

We can, therefore, conclude from this example that the virtual function mechanism works just as well through a pointer to a base class, with the specific function being selected based on the type of object being pointed to. This is illustrated in the following figure:

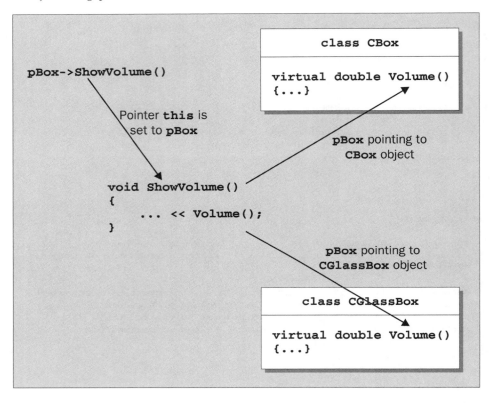

This means that, even when we don't know the precise type of the object pointed to by a base class pointer in a program (when a pointer is passed to a function as an argument for example), the virtual function mechanism will ensure that the correct function is called.

Using References with Virtual Functions

A reference to a base class used as a function parameter can be passed an argument of a derived object type and can also select the appropriate virtual function to call. We could show this happening by modifying the function **main()** in the last example to call a function that has a reference as a parameter.

TRY IT OUT - Using References with Virtual Functions

Let's move the call to the function which outputs the volume of an object to a separate function, and call that from **main()**:

```
// EX10_09.CPP
// Using a reference to call a virtual function
#include <iostream.h>

class CBox;                          // Required for prototype following

void Output(CBox& aBox);            // Prototype of function
```

```
// Insert class definitions for CBox and CGlassBox (as in Ex10_08.cpp)
```

```
int main(void)
{
    CBox myBox(2.0, 3.0, 4.0);             // Declare a base box
    CGlassBox myGlassBox(2.0,3.0,4.0);     // Declare derived box of same size

    Output(myBox);                         // Output volume of base class object
    Output(myGlassBox);                    // Output volume of derived class object

    cout << endl;
    return 0;
}

// Function to output a volume via a virtual function call
// using a reference
void Output(CBox& aBox)
{
    aBox.ShowVolume();
}
```

How It Works

At the beginning of the program, we have an incomplete definition of the class **CBox**. This is included so that the compiler will know of the existence of **CBox** as a class when it gets to the prototype of the function **Output()**. Without this, the prototype would cause an error message to be generated.

The function **main()** now basically consists of two calls of the function **Output()**, the first with an object of the base class as an argument and the second with an object of the derived class. Because the parameter is a reference to the base class, the function accepts objects of either class as an argument and the appropriate version of the virtual function **ShowVolume()** is called, depending on the object that is initializing the reference.

The program produces exactly the same output as the previous example, demonstrating that the virtual function mechanism does indeed work through a reference parameter.

Pure Virtual Functions

It's possible that you may want to include a virtual function in a base class so that it may be suitably redefined in a derived class to suit the objects of that class. There is, however, no meaningful definition you can give for the function in the base class.

For example, we could conceivably have a class **CContainer**, which could be used as a base for defining our **CBox** class or a **CBottle** class, or even a **CTeapot** class. The container class wouldn't have data members, but you might want to provide a virtual member function **Volume()** for any derived classes. Since the **CContainer** class has no data members and, therefore, no dimensions, there is no sensible **Volume()** definition that we can write, but we can still define the class, including the member function **Volume()**, as follows:

```
// Listing 10_10-01
class CContainer              // Generic base class for specific containers
{
   public:

// Function for calculating a volume - no content
// This is defined as a 'pure' virtual function, signified by '=0'
      virtual double Volume(void) = 0;

// Function to display a volume
      virtual void ShowVolume()
      {
         cout << endl
              << "Volume is " << Volume();
      }
};
```

The statement for the virtual function **Volume()** defines it as having no content by placing the equals sign and zero in the function header. This is called a **pure virtual function**. Any class derived from this class must either define the **Volume()** function or redefine it as a pure virtual function.

The class also contains the function **ShowVolume()**, which will display the volume of objects of derived classes. Since this is declared as **virtual**, it can be replaced in a derived class, but if it isn't, the base class version that you see here will be called.

Abstract Classes

A class containing a pure virtual function is called an **abstract class**. It's called **abstract** because you can't define objects of a class containing a pure virtual function. It exists only for the purpose of defining classes which are derived from it. If a class derived from an abstract class still defines a pure virtual function of the base as pure, it too is an abstract class.

Note that you should not conclude from the example of the **CContainer** class above that an abstract class can't have data members. An abstract class can have both data members and function members. The presence of a pure virtual function is the only condition that determines that a given class is abstract. Of course, an abstract class can also have more than one pure virtual function. In this case, a derived class must have definitions for every pure virtual function in its base, if it is not also to be an abstract class.

TRY IT OUT - An Abstract Class

We could implement a **CCan** class, representing beer or cola cans perhaps, together with our original **CBox** class, with both being derived from the **CContainer** class. The definitions of these two classes would be as follows:

```
// Listing 10_10-02
class CBox : public CContainer          // Derived class
{
   public:
```

```
// Function to show the volume of an object
      virtual void ShowVolume(void)
      {
         cout << endl
               << "CBox usable volume is " << Volume();
      }

// Function to calculate the volume of a CBox object
      virtual double Volume(void)
         { return m_Length*m_Breadth*m_Height; }

// Constructor
      CBox(double lv=1.0, double bv=1.0, double hv=1.0)
            :m_Length(lv), m_Breadth(bv), m_Height(hv){}

   protected:
      double m_Length;
      double m_Breadth;
      double m_Height;

};
```

```
// Listing 10_10-03
class CCan : public CContainer
{
   public:
// Function to calculate the volume of a can
      virtual double Volume()
         { return 0.25*PI*m_Diameter*m_Diameter*m_Height;    }

// Constructor
      CCan(double hv=4.0, double dv=2.0) : m_Height(hv),
                                                m_Diameter(dv){}

   protected:
      double m_Height;
      double m_Diameter;
};
```

The **CBox** class is essentially as we had it in the previous example, except this time we have specified that it is derived from the **CContainer** class. The **Volume()** function is fully defined within this class (as it must be if this class is to be used to define objects). The only other option would be to specify it as a pure virtual function, since it is pure in the base class, but then we couldn't create **CBox** objects.

The **CCan** class also defines a **Volume()** function based on the formula $h\pi r^2$, where h is the height and r is the radius of the cross-section of a can. This is essentially the height multiplied by the area of the base, to produce the volume. The expression in the function definition assumes a global constant **PI** is defined, so we'll need to remember that.

We can exercise these classes with the following function **main()**:

```
// EX10_10.CPP
// Using an abstract class
#include <iostream.h>          // For stream I/O

const double PI= 3.14159265;   // Global definition for PI
```

```
// Insert definition of CContainer class (Listing 10_10-01)
// Insert definition of CBox class      (Listing 10_10-02)
// Insert definition of CCan class      (Listing 10_10-03)

int main(void)
{
// Pointer to abstract base class
// initialized with address of CBox object
   CContainer* pC1 = new CBox(2.0 ,3.0 ,4.0);

// Pointer to abstract base class
// initialized with address of CCan object
   CContainer* pC2 = new CCan(6.5, 3.0);

   pC1->ShowVolume();              // Output the volumes of the two
   pC2->ShowVolume();              // objects pointed to
   cout << endl;

   delete pC1;                     // Now clean up the free store
   delete pC2;                     // ....

   return 0;
}
```

How It Works

In this program, we declare two pointers to the base class, **CContainer**. Although we can't define **CContainer** objects because **CContainer** is an abstract class, we can still define a pointer to a **CContainer**, which we can then use to store the address of a derived class object. The pointer **pC1** is assigned the address of a **CBox** object created in the free store by the operator **new**. The second pointer is assigned the address of a **CCan** object in a similar manner.

The output produced by this example is as follows:

```
Ex10_10

CBox usable volume is 24
Volume is 45.9458
Press any key to continue
```

Because **ShowVolume()** is a virtual function, the derived class version is called for the **CBox** object, but the base class version is invoked for the **CCan** object. Since **Volume()** is also a virtual function that is implemented in both the derived classes (necessarily - because it is a pure virtual function in the base class), the call to it is resolved when the program is executed by selecting the version belonging to the class of the object being pointed to. Thus, for the pointer **pC1**, the version from the class **CBox** is called and, for the pointer **pC2**, the version in the class **CCan** is called, so in each case we obtain the correct result.

We could equally well have used just one pointer **pC1** and assigned the address of the **CCan** object to it (after calling the **Volume()** function for the **CBox** object). A base class pointer can contain the address of any derived class object, even when several different classes are derived from the same base class, and so we can have automatic selection of the appropriate virtual function across a whole range of derived classes. Impressive stuff, isn't it?

Of course, because the derived class objects were created dynamically, we need to use the operator `delete` to clean up the free store when we have finished with them.

Indirect Base Classes

At the beginning of this chapter, we said that a base class of one class could in turn be derived from another, more base class. A small extension of the last example will provide us with an illustration of this, as well as demonstrating the use of a virtual function across a second level of inheritance.

TRY IT OUT - More than One Level of Inheritance

All we need to do is add the class **CGlassBox** to the classes we have in the last example. The relationship between the classes we now have is illustrated below:

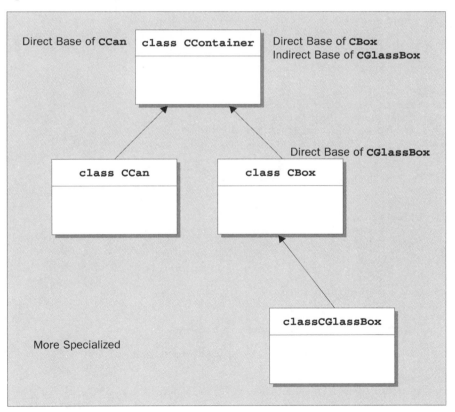

The class **CGlassBox** is derived from the **CBox** class exactly as before, but we will omit the derived class version of **ShowVolume()** to show that the base class version still propagates through the derived classes. With the class hierarchy shown above, the class **CContainer** is an indirect base of the class **CGlassBox** and a direct base of the classes **CBox** and **CCan**.

Our new example, with an updated function **main()** to use the additional class in the hierarchy, will be as follows:

```cpp
// EX10_11.CPP
// Using an abstract class with multiple levels of inheritance
#include <iostream.h>                      // For stream I/O

const double PI= 3.14159265;               // Global definition for PI

class CContainer            // Generic base class for specific containers
{
   public:

// Function for calculating a volume - no content
// This is defined as a 'pure' virtual function, signified by '=0'
      virtual double Volume(void) = 0;

// Function to display a volume
      virtual void ShowVolume()
      {
         cout << endl
            << "Volume is " << Volume();
      }
};
class CBox : public CContainer           // Derived class
{
   public:
// Function to calculate the volume of a CBox object
      virtual double Volume(void)
      { return m_Length*m_Breadth*m_Height; }

// Constructor
      CBox(double lv=1.0, double bv=1.0, double hv=1.0)
           :m_Length(lv), m_Breadth(bv), m_Height(hv){}

   protected:
      double m_Length;
      double m_Breadth;
      double m_Height;

};

class CCan : public CContainer
{
   public:
// Function to calculate the volume of a can
      virtual double Volume()
      { return 0.25*PI*m_Diameter*m_Diameter*m_Height;    }

// Constructor
      CCan(double hv=4.0, double dv=2.0) : m_Height(hv),
                                                m_Diameter(dv){}

   protected:
      double m_Height;
      double m_Diameter;
};
```

```
class CGlassBox: public CBox        // Derived class
{
   public:

// Function to calculate volume of a CGlassBox
// allowing 15% for packing
      virtual double Volume(void)
      { return 0.85*m_Length*m_Breadth*m_Height; }

// Constructor
      CGlassBox(double lv, double bv, double hv): CBox(lv,bv,hv){}

};

int main(void)
{
// Pointer to abstract base class initialized with address of CBox object
   CContainer* pC1 = new CBox(2.0 ,3.0 ,4.0);

   CCan myCan(6.5, 3.0);                      // Define CCan object
   CGlassBox myGlassBox(2.0, 3.0, 4.0);       // Define CGlassBox object

// initialized with address of CCan object

   pC1->ShowVolume();                // Output the volume of CBox
   delete pC1;                       // Now clean up the free store

   pC1 = &myCan;                     // Put myCan address in pointer
   pC1->ShowVolume();                // Output the volume of CCan

   pC1 = &myGlassBox;                // Put myGlassBox address in pointer
   pC1->ShowVolume();                // Output the volume of CGlassBox

   cout << endl;
   return 0;
}
```

How It Works

We have the three-level class hierarchy shown in the previous illustration, with **CContainer** as an abstract base class, because it contains the pure virtual function, **Volume()**. The function **main()** now calls the function **ShowVolume()** three times, using the same pointer to the base class, but with the pointer containing the address of an object of a different class each time. Since **ShowVolume()** is not defined in any of the derived classes we have here, the base class version is called in each instance. A separate branch from the base **CContainer** defines the derived class **CCan**.

The example produces this output,

```
Ex10_11                                              _ □ ×
Volume is 24
Volume is 45.9458
Volume is 20.4
Press any key to continue
```

showing that we execute the three different version of the function **Volume()** according to the type of object involved.

FYI
Note that we need to delete the **CBox** object from the free store before we assign another address value to it. If we don't do this, we wouldn't be able to clean up the free store because we would have no record of the original address. This is an easy mistake to make when reassigning pointers and using the free store.

Virtual Destructors

One problem that arises with using objects of derived classes using a pointer to the base class is that the correct destructor may not be called. We can show this effect by modifying the last example.

TRY IT OUT - Calling the Wrong Destructor

We just need to add destructors to each of the classes so that we can track which destructor is called when the objects are destroyed. Therefore, the program would be as follows:

```
// EX10_12.CPP
// Destructor calls with derived classes
// using objects via a base class pointer
#include <iostream.h>                    // For stream I/O

const double PI= 3.14159265;             // Global definition for PI

class CContainer                         // Generic base class for containers
{
    public:
// Destructor
        ~CContainer()
            { cout << "CContainer destructor called" << endl; }

// Insert other members of CContainer as in EX10_11.CPP
};

class CBox : public CContainer           // Derived class
{
    public:
// Destructor
        ~CBox()
            { cout << "CBox destructor called" << endl; }

// Insert other members of CBox as in EX10_11.CPP
};

class CCan : public CContainer
{
    public:
```

```
// Destructor
    ~CCan()
    { cout << "CCan destructor called" << endl; }

// Insert other members of CCan as in EX10_11.CPP
};

class CGlassBox: public CBox        // Derived class
{
    public:
// Destructor
    ~CGlassBox()
    { cout << "CGlassBox destructor called" << endl; }

// Insert other members of CGlassBox as in EX10_11.CPP
};

int main(void)
{
// Pointer to abstract base class initialized with address of CBox object
    CContainer* pC1 = new CBox(2.0 ,3.0 ,4.0);

    CCan myCan(6.5, 3.0);                    // Define CCan object
    CGlassBox myGlassBox(2.0, 3.0, 4.0);     // Define CGlassBox object

    pC1->ShowVolume();                       // Output the volume of CBox
    cout << endl << "Delete CBox" << endl;
    delete pC1;                              // Now clean up the free store

    pC1 = new CGlassBox(4.0, 5.0, 6.0);  // Create CGlassBox dynamically
    pC1->ShowVolume();                   // ...output its volume...
    cout << endl << "Delete CGlassBox" << endl;
    delete pC1;                          // ...and delete it

    pC1 = &myCan;                            // Get myCan address in pointer
    pC1->ShowVolume();                       // Output the volume of CCan

    pC1 = &myGlassBox;                       // Get myGlassBox address in pointer
    pC1->ShowVolume();                       // Output the volume of CGlassBox

    cout << endl;
    return 0;
}
```

How It Works

Apart from adding a destructor to each class, which outputs a message to the effect that it was called, the only other change is a couple of additions to the function **main()**. There are additional statements to create a **CGlassBox** object dynamically, output its volume and then delete it. There is also a message displayed to indicate when the dynamically created **CBox** object is deleted. The output generated by this example is shown on the following page.

```
Ex10_12                                                    _ □ ✕

Volume is 24
Delete CBox
CContainer destructor called

Volume is 102
Delete CGlassBox
CContainer destructor called

Volume is 45.9458
Volume is 20.4
CGlassBox destructor called
CBox destructor called
CContainer destructor called
CCan destructor called
CContainer destructor called
Press any key to continue_
```

You can see from this that, when we delete the **CBox** object pointed to by **PC1**, the destructor for the base class **CContainer** is called. Similarly, when the **CGlassBox** object that we added is deleted, again the destructor for the base class **CContainer** is called. For the other objects, the correct destructor calls occur with the derived class constructor being called first, followed by the base class constructor. For the first **CGlassBox** object created in a declaration, three destructors are called: first, the destructor for the derived class, followed by the direct base destructor and, finally, the indirect base destructor.

All the problems are with objects created in the free store. In both cases, the wrong destructor is called. The reason for this is that the linkage to the destructors is resolved statically, at compile time. For the automatic objects there is no problem. The compiler knows what they are and arranges for the correct destructor to be called.

With objects created dynamically and accessed through a pointer, things are different. The only information that the compiler has when the **delete** operation is executed is that the pointer type is a pointer to the base class. The type of object the pointer is pointing to is unknown. The compiler then simply ensures that the **delete** operation is set up to call the base class destructor. In a real application, this can cause a lot of problems, with bits of objects left strewn around the free store and possibly more serious problems, depending on the nature of the objects involved.

The solution is simple. We need the calls to be resolved dynamically as the program is executed. We can organize this by using virtual destructors in our classes. As we said when we first discussed virtual functions, it's sufficient to declare the base class function as virtual, for all functions in any derived classes with the same name, parameter list and return type, to be virtual as well. This applies to destructors in addition to ordinary member functions. We just need to add the keyword **virtual** to the definition of the destructor in the class **CContainer**, so that it becomes as follows:

```
class CContainer                    // Generic base class for containers
{
  public:
// Destructor
    virtual ~CContainer()
      { cout<< endl << "CContainer destructor called"; }
```

```
    // Insert other members of CContainer as in Listing 10_10-01
    };
```

Now, the destructors in all the derived classes are automatically **virtual**, even though you don't explicitly specify them as such. Of course, you can specify them as **virtual** if you want the code to be absolutely clear.

If you re-run the example with this modification, it will produce the following output:

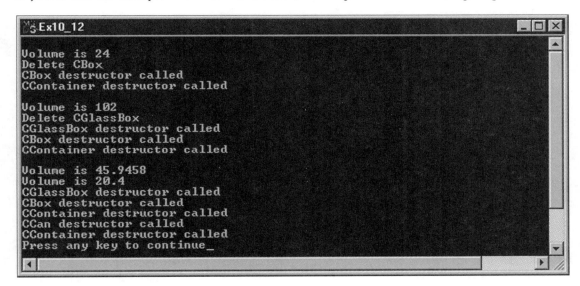

As you can see, all the objects are now destroyed with a proper sequence of destructor calls. Destroying the dynamic objects produces the same sequence of destructor calls as the automatic objects of the same type in the program.

 It's a good idea to always declare your base class destructor as **virtual** as a matter of course when using inheritance. There is a small overhead in the execution of the class destructors, but you won't notice it in the majority of circumstances. Using virtual destructors ensures that your objects will be properly destroyed and avoids potential program crashes that might otherwise occur.

Multiple Inheritance

This is the last major topic before we get to writing some Windows programs, so we're nearly finished with C++ language specifics. Note that this discussion is included because you are certain to become aware of multiple inheritance but, in fact, we don't need it to write Windows programs using Visual C++ and we will not be using it in any of the examples in the book. Multiple inheritance can get you into quite deep water, so we'll just outline the basic considerations here.

All our derived classes so far have had a single direct base class. We're not limited to this, however. A derived class can have several base classes. This is referred to as **multiple inheritance**. Of course, this means that multiple indirect bases are also possible.

371

Multiple Base Classes

It's quite difficult to come up with an example of a class with multiple base classes that is based on relationships in the real world. Defining a class, such as **CBox**, in terms of the class **CContainer** reflects the real world relationship between a box and a container. A box is a form of container, so we are defining a more specific object from a more general one. With most real world objects, this unidirectional specialization pattern applies. Multiple base classes are often used in practice for the convenience of implementation rather than to reflect any particular relationships between objects.

However, we could consider the example of a **CPackage**, which might be a combination of a **CContainer**, or some specialized form of container such as a **CBox**, together with the contents of the container defined by a class **CContents**. We could define the class **CPackage** as derived from both the class **CBox** and the class **CContents**. This could be represented like this:

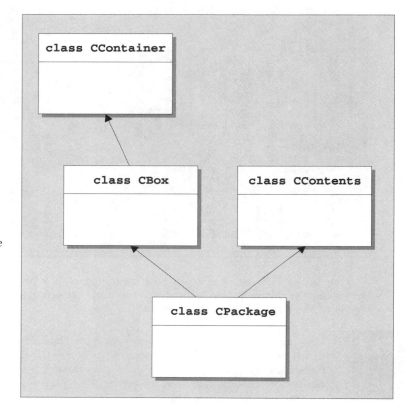

The definition of the class would look like this:

```
class CPackage : public CBox, public CContents
{
    . . .
};
```

The class **CPackage** will now inherit all the members of both classes, with the same access specifiers as appear in the definitions of the base classes, since they are defined as **public** base classes. The access limitations for inherited class members, as we discussed earlier in this chapter, apply equally well to classes with multiple bases.

Things can get a little more complicated now. For example, it's conceivable that both base classes could have a **public** member function, **Show()**, to display the contents of an object. If so, a statement such as,

```
        myPackage.Show();
```

where **myPackage** is an object of the class **CPackage**, will be ambiguous, since the class **CPackage** contains two members with the same name, **Show()**, one inherited from each of the base classes. The compiler has no way of knowing which one should be called, so this will result in an error message from the compiler. If you need to call one or the other, you have to use the scope resolution operator to specify which of the two functions you want to invoke. For example, you could write this,

```
        myPackage.CContents::Show();
```

which makes it quite clear that you want to call the function that is inherited from the class **CContents**.

Virtual Base Classes

A further complication can arise with multiple inheritance if the direct base classes are themselves derived from another class or classes. The possibility arises that both base classes could be derived from a common class. For instance, the classes **CContents** and **CBox**, which we used in the definition of the class package, could be derived from another base called **CRockBottom**. Their definitions could then be something like this:

```
class CContents: public CRockBottom
{
...
};

class CBox: public CRockBottom
{
...
};
```

Now, the class **CPackage** will contain two copies of the members of the class **CRockBottom**, as illustrated here:

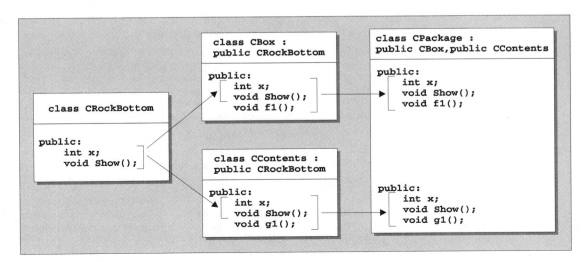

In the class **CPackage**, we end up with two data members called **x**, and two function members **Show()**. The duplication of the members of the indirect base can at best be confusing, and at worst, it can cause a lot of problems. However, it's easy to avoid by simply modifying the definitions of the base classes **CBox** and **CContents** such that the class **CRockBottom** is specified as a **virtual base class**. Their definitions in outline would then be as follows:

```
class CContents: public virtual CRockBottom
{
    ...
};

class CBox: public virtual CRockBottom
{
    ...
};
```

Now, there will be only one instance of the members of the base class **CRockBottom** in any class derived from these two classes, and any problems with the original definition of the class **CPackage** disappear.

Summary

In this chapter, we've covered all of the principle ideas involved in using inheritance. The fundamentals that you should keep in mind are these:

> A derived class inherits all the members of a base class except for constructors, the destructor and the overloaded assignment operator.

> Members of a base class which are declared as **private** in the base class are not accessible in any derived class. To obtain the effect of the keyword **private** but allow access in a derived class, you should use the keyword **protected** in place of **private**.

> A base class can be specified for a derived class with the keyword **public**, **private**, or **protected**. If none is specified, the default is **private**. Depending on the keyword specified for a base, the access level of the inherited members may be modified.

> If you write a derived class constructor, you must arrange for data members of the base class to be initialized properly, as well as those of the derived class.

> A function in a base class may be declared as **virtual**. This allows other definitions of the function appearing in derived classes to be selected at execution time, depending on the type of object for which the function call is made.

> You should declare the destructor in a base class containing a virtual function as **virtual**. This will ensure correct selection of a destructor for dynamically-created derived class objects.

> A virtual function in a base class can be specified as pure, by placing **=0** in the function declaration. The class will then be an abstract class for which no objects can be created. In any derived class, all the pure virtual functions must be defined; if not, it too becomes an abstract class.

> A class may be derived from multiple base classes, in which case in inherits members from all of its bases, with the exception of destructors, constructors and overloaded assignment operator functions.

▶ An indirect base class may be specified as **virtual** for derived classes in order to avoid possible multiple occurrences of its members in a class with multiple bases, two or more of which are derived from the indirect base.

You have now gone through all of the important language features of C++ and it's important that you feel comfortable with the mechanism for defining and deriving classes and the process of inheritance. With the exception of multiple inheritance, Windows programming with Visual C++ will involve extensive use of all these concepts. If you have any doubts, go back over the last three chapters and try playing around with the source code of the examples related to the areas that you are unsure about. Just to make sure, the next chapter is devoted to a sizable complete example using class inheritance. After that, we'll be focusing solely on programming for Windows.

An Example Using Classes

In this chapter, we're going to develop an application using a class-based approach to programming. This will provide you with some insight into how to approach a problem from an object oriented point of view. The example we will use is that of a calculator like the one we developed in Chapter 6 but, this time, we're going to build it from an object oriented perspective.

Although this isn't a perfect candidate for an object oriented program, having two versions of the calculator will give you a feel for the differences in approach to program design. You'll also see how an object oriented program looks in comparison to the same problem developed in a traditional way. Our implementation here isn't necessarily ideal, since the objective is to exercise the techniques that we've learnt in the previous chapters in a practical context. It is, however, reasonably efficient and you can get some additional practice by trying out your own ideas on how it should work or by adding functionality to it.

Using Classes

Before we can begin creating our calculator program, we need to decide what objects our problem is concerned with and how they need to behave. Based on that, we'll decide what classes to define to implement the calculator and what operations they'll need to support. Before we get to that stage, however, and well before we get into coding at all, we need to make sure that we have a clear understanding of the problem.

Defining the Problem

We'll aim to create a calculator with the same capabilities as the previous version. It should handle any arithmetic expression involving the operators *, /, + and -, and also allow parentheses to any depth. The only limitation on the complexity of an expression will be that it must be entered on a single input line. Numerical values can be entered with or without a decimal point. A typical expression which the calculator should handle might be:

3.5*(2.45*7.1 - 4.7/1.25)*(3+1.5*(8.2-7*125/88.9)/5.7)

Blanks can appear anywhere in an expression and an expression is terminated by pressing the *Enter* key.

We'll assume that the calculator will act like a real calculator in that, once a result has been computed, it's retained in the display. When one value has been calculated and displayed, we can then just enter,

*3

for example, to multiply it by 3.

Solely for the sake of brevity, we'll also assume that the expressions entered are well formed, so we won't do any error checking. It's not that it is difficult, but it does tend to inflate the numbers of lines of source code, and we'll have quite a few anyway.

 FYI Note that leaving out error checking is the last thing you would do in a real application. Dealing with error conditions is as important as the rest of the program code.

Analyzing the Problem

Deciding which objects and classes suit a particular problem isn't a clear cut process, with no hard and fast rules. Indeed, for many problems, there may be a number of alternative object sets possible, each with their own advantages and disadvantages. However, we can set down some general points about the process which might help:

- You are not only looking for objects and classes, but also relationships between them. Representing class and object relationships in a diagram can be very helpful.

- Approach the problem top-down. Decide what candidates there are for the objects the problem is concerned with and then break these down into their constituents.

- You can define the outline of classes as you go along, but you need to be prepared to go back and modify existing classes from time to time, as getting to a final set of classes will often be an iterative process.

- Remember that classes will not all be representative of physical objects. You may find quite abstract ideas can be conveniently expressed as a class.

- Sometimes, the most difficult thing to do is to start. Don't worry about making mistakes. Get some initial ideas down, even if you know they are not quite right. It will give you something to modify and improve.

- You may find it helpful, as a first pass, to describe the problem and its solution by writing down sentences. You often find that the nouns can give you a guide to the classes needed, while the verbs help define the functionality required from the classes.

When you use this approach, you may need to alter your thinking slightly. For example, our particular problem is not so much to perform calculations, but more to model a calculating machine that will perform calculations for us.

Let's begin by modeling our classes on a real calculator. Using a top-down approach, we might start by breaking a calculator into its constituent parts. The most obvious of these are a keyboard for input, a logic unit for processing the input and a display for outputting the results of the calculation. It's quite likely that we may wish to further subdivide the logic unit but, at this stage, we'll keep it fairly simple and see what develops. As mentioned above, developing an application is often an iterative process.

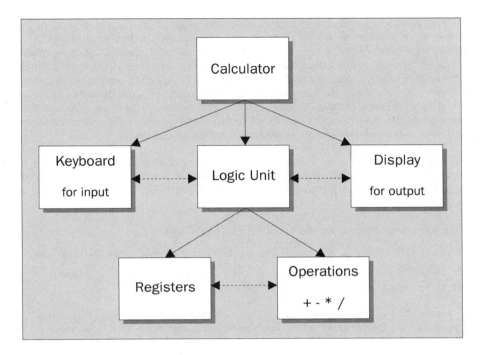

Here, you can see a diagram representing our initial thoughts. The blocks represent the main elements of a calculator. Most of them will certainly translate into classes. We can envisage a **CCalculator** class for the whole thing, a **CKeyboard** class, a **CDisplay** class and a **CLogicUnit** class. **Operations** doesn't seem a likely candidate for a class at the moment, as these are actions rather than things, but we can't really be certain at this point so let's wait and see. **Registers** does look like a good prospect for a **CRegister** class, though.

The solid arrows in the diagram indicate an ownership relationship modeled on the real world. A calculator has a keyboard, a logic unit and a display, so we'll give our **CCalculator** class a member of type **CKeyboard**, one of type **CLogicUnit** and one of type **CDisplay**. The dashed arrows indicate a communications requirement, so objects of type **CKeyboard** will need to pass information to objects of type **CLogicUnit** who, in turn, will need to communicate with **CDisplay** objects. We'll see how we might take account of this when we get into the detail of the classes.

Deciding between Class Membership and Class Inheritance

Getting your classes defined with the proper relationships, and deciding when to define classes in an inheritance hierarchy rather than using class members to create an ownership hierarchy, is of fundamental importance to good object oriented programs. Unfortunately, this isn't always easy and there are no hard and fast rules which will guarantee the desired result. However, we can identify some general guidelines that will help in many cases.

Generally, you should try to reflect the intent of the relationship between a base class and a derived class. A derived class usually represents an object that is a form of the object described by the base class so that, in deriving one class from another, you are going from the general to the particular. In our example, a calculator is not a type of logic unit, a type of keyboard, or even a type of display, but rather has these things as components, so class derivation is not appropriate.

379

Usually, if you can say one object is a version of another, as a chicken is a type of bird, for example, you have a situation where deriving one class from another is appropriate. You could derive a class **CChicken** from a base class **CBird**. An object of class **CChicken**, **Chukkie**, for example, would then be a particular instance of a chicken. You might want to differentiate between birds that can fly, such as owls and eagles, and ones that cannot, such as ostriches or emus. In this case, you could derive two classes, **CFlyingBird** and **CNonFlyingBird**, from the more general class **Bird**, and then derive classes for types of birds from either of these, depending on whether they can fly or not. Objects of each derived class then represent a set of objects that is a subset of the objects represented by its base class.

Where an object has an object as a component, as with a chicken having wings, for example, you have a situation where defining objects as members of another class is appropriate. So, a **CChicken** class might contain the member variables **m_LeftWing** and **m_RightWing** of class **CWing**, for example.

This can be summarized by using the 'is a' versus 'has a' test:

> A chicken *is a* bird so it's reasonable to derive **CChicken** from the base class **CBird**

> A chicken *has a* wing so it makes sense for **CChicken** to have a member of type **CWing** (it makes even more sense for it to have two).

The 'is a' versus 'has a' test is quite a good way of deciding which way you should go in defining your classes, particularly when you are starting out with C++. However, it's not a universal or cast iron method. Sometimes, you may need to derive a class from more than one base class, particularly when you are dealing with abstract and complex objects that don't have the simple physical reality of birds. Experience is probably the single most important factor in enhancing your ability to design effective classes in such circumstances.

Let the Coding Commence

At this stage, it's time to get ourselves into a position where we can actually enter some code, so start a new project workspace for a console application called **Ex11_01** and we can begin.

Defining the CCalculator Class

One kind of object that we definitely need is a calculator object, so **CCalculator** will be the first class that we will define. Begin the process by creating a new source file (click the leftmost icon on the Standard toolbar) and save the file in the project directory as **CCalculator.h**. Don't add the file to the project explicitly because this file will be a header file, so will be added to the project's code using **#include** statements.

Type in the code shown below:

```
// CCALCULATOR.H - Interface of CCalculator class
#ifndef CCALCULATOR_H
#define CCALCULATOR_H

class CCalculator
{
};

#endif
```

This will be the standard format for the header files for the classes in this example. You can see that we have included a comment describing the function of the file and an empty definition for the **CCalculator** class. The preprocessor commands surrounding the code (the lines beginning with **#**) will ensure that we don't include duplicate definitions of this class. We saw these directives in action back in Chapter 9.

Now create another new source file and insert it into the project as **CCalculator.cpp**. We'll use this to hold the code for the definitions of the member functions for the class **CCalculator** (once we've decided what they should be). Type in the code shown below and save the file.

```
// CCALCULATOR.CPP - Implementation of CCalculator class
#include "CCalculator.h"
```

Again, this will be standard for the **.cpp** files for the classes in this project. All of them will include a comment describing the function of the file and an **#include** statement for the header file of the class. In this way, we can make a clear separation between the interface of the class and its implementation.

The ClassView should now show the **CCalculator** class and the FileView should show **CCalculator.cpp**, with **CCalculator.h** as a dependency.

Now we need to give a little more thought to the structure of the **CCalculator** class and how we might use objects created from it. As shown in our diagram, a real calculator can be thought of as containing a logic unit to perform individual calculations and control what goes on, a keyboard for input and a display to show results. We'll consider our model from this perspective. This gives us three member variables to add to the class: **m_Display** of class **CDisplay**, **m_LogicUnit** of class **CLogicUnit** and **m_Keyboard** of class **CKeyboard**.

We'll add these using the context menu for **CCalculator** provided by the ClassView, so right-click on the class icon for **CCalculator** in the ClassView:

This will bring up a menu with many useful options relating to classes. You can ignore most of these for now, just select Add Variable... from the menu.

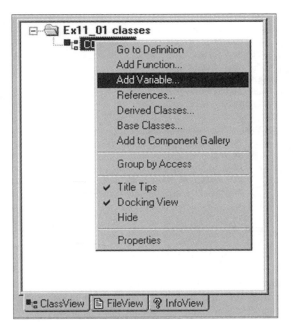

381

This will bring up the Add Member Variable dialog that allows you to easily add variables to your classes. Start by adding the variable **m_Display** by setting the dialog options as you see in the screen shot.

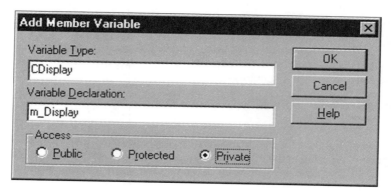

Note that you should set the Access for this variable to Private, since it won't need to be accessible from outside the **CCalculator** class. Now repeat the process to add the variables **m_LogicUnit** and **m_Keyboard**, both of which should also be specified as **private**. You'll be able to see the fruits of your labor if you expand the view of the **CCalculator** class in ClassView. Double-clicking on any of the icons for the member variables will take you to their declaration in **CCalculator.h**.

Since we have added member variables of other classes, we need to ensure that those classes are defined before the **CCalculator** class. We do this by adding **#include** statements for the header files for those classes to **CCalculator.h**. At this stage, the header file for **CCalculator** should look something like this:

```
// Preliminary class definition
// CCALCULATOR.H
#ifndef CCALCULATOR_H
#define CCALCULATOR_H
#include "CLogicUnit.h"
#include "CKeyboard.h"
#include "CDisplay.h"

class CCalculator
{
private:
    CLogicUnit m_LogicUnit;
    CDisplay m_Display;
    CKeyboard m_Keyboard;
};

#endif
```

Note that the header file names are contained in quotes in the **#include** statements since this tells the compiler to look for them in the same directory as the file containing the **#include** statements. In this case, that's the project directory. Don't worry that we haven't actually created the files referred to in the **#include** statements, we'll be doing that a little later in the chapter.

Connecting the Logic Unit to the Display

Thinking back to the communication relationships we saw earlier, we decided that the logic unit would need to know about the display. We'll use the constructor of the **CCalculator** class to forge a link between the **m_LogicUnit** and **m_Display** members of a calculator by passing a pointer to **m_Display** to a member function of the **m_LogicUnit** object. We'll give the **CLogicUnit** class a function called **ConnectDisplay()** which will accept a pointer of type **CDisplay** for this purpose.

We'll delay actually creating the **CLogicUnit** class and the **DisplayConnect()** function for a while; for now, we'll just concentrate on creating the constructor for **CCalculator** using the context menu for **CCalculator** provided by the ClassView. This time, select Add Function... from the pop-up menu and just type **CCalculator** as the Function Declaration.

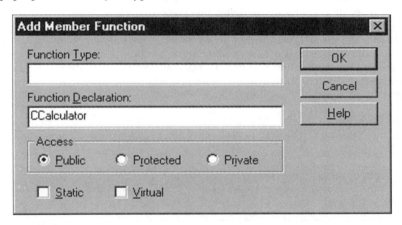

When you click OK, the source code window will change to display **CCalculator.cpp** and you'll see that an empty function definition has been created for the constructor ready for you to enter your code. If you switch to the header file for the class, you'll see that a prototype for the function has also been added to the class definition.

Switch back to the **.cpp** file by double-clicking the ClassView icon for the **CCalculator()** function ◆ and type in the code shown:

```
// Constructor - connects the display to the logic unit
CCalculator::CCalculator()
{
    m_LogicUnit.DisplayConnect(&m_Display);
}
```

Note that we can refer to members of the **CCalculator** object in the constructor, since they will exist at this point. The memory for the members has already been allocated by the time the constructor begins execution.

Don't forget to add comments to your code to help you understand it at a later date, particularly when you use ClassView's context menus to add members, as it's easy to forget them using this mechanism.

Starting a Calculator

We're going to give the **CCalculator** class one more member function and then it will be complete. We'd like the process of using a calculator to be as simple as creating a **myCalculator** object and then running it using a function in the interface of the **CCalculator** class. We could use some creativity here and call it **Run()**.

This seems straightforward enough, but we're going to complicate matters slightly by using an approach similar to the way we used recursive functions back in Chapter 6. Instead of creating only a single calculator object, we plan to create a number of calculators, each of which will process different levels of parentheses. For each level of parentheses in an expression, there will be a new **CCalculator** created. Thus, if you have an expression with three levels of parentheses, for example, there will be three **CCalculator** objects in existence concurrently, while the lowest level of parentheses is being processed.

New **CCalculator** objects will be created when there is an opening parenthesis, will process the expression in parentheses and will terminate upon finding a closing parenthesis matching the opening parenthesis that started the process. The actual creation and destruction of these **CCalculator** objects will be handled in the **CLogicUnit** and **CKeyboard** classes, but we'll use the **Run()** function to return the value of the expression.

Add a new function, **Run()** to the **CCalculator** class using the context menu in the ClassView and make it of type **double**. The function doesn't need to accept any parameters, so we specify the parameter list as **void**.

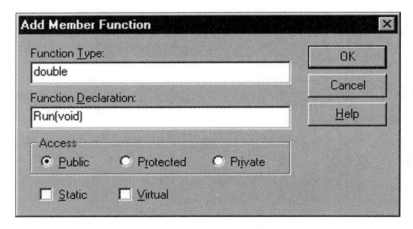

Once again, an empty function definition will be added to **CCalculator.cpp**. Add the code you see below:

```
double CCalculator::Run(void)
{
    m_Keyboard.GetKey(m_LogicUnit);      // Start keyboard manager
    return m_LogicUnit.GetDisplay();     // CCalculator terminated so
                                         // return display value
}
```

This code simply starts the keyboard manager represented by the **GetKey()** member function of **m_Keyboard**, then returns a result. We won't really be able to see exactly what's going on until we define the other classes and functions, so don't worry too much at the moment. We'll get on with defining these classes shortly. First, though, we'll present the complete **CCalculator** class for your convenience:

```cpp
// CCALCULATOR.H - Interface of CCalculator class
#ifndef CCALCULATOR_H
#define CCALCULATOR_H
#include "CLogicUnit.h"
#include "CKeyboard.h"
#include "CDisplay.h"

class CCalculator
{
public:
    double Run(void);      // Prototype of function to run calculator
    CCalculator();         // A constructor

private:
    CLogicUnit m_LogicUnit;
    CDisplay m_Display;
    CKeyboard m_Keyboard;
};

#endif

// CCALCULATOR.CPP - Implementation of CCalculator class
#include "CCalculator.h"

// Constructor - connects the display to the logic unit
CCalculator::CCalculator()
{
    m_LogicUnit.DisplayConnect(&m_Display);
}

double CCalculator::Run(void)
{
    m_Keyboard.GetKey(m_LogicUnit);       // Start keyboard manager
    return m_LogicUnit.GetDisplay();      // CCalculator terminated so
                                          // return display value
}
```

The CDisplay Class

Now we're going to look at the **CDisplay** class. This class will be relatively simple since we'll just give it responsibility for displaying the result of a calculation. We can implement this in the form of a member function called **ShowRegister()**. The function will accept one parameter of type **double**, which will be the numerical result of the calculation. The function will then display the result on whatever device the programmer feels is appropriate. In our case, we'll just use the standard output device for a console application, the screen.

This does raise a slight problem, though. Since we'll be creating multiple **CCalculator** objects, and each of them has a **m_Display** member, there will be multiple **CDisplay** objects. If we allowed all of them to output their results to the screen, we'd be outputting many intermediate results which is not what we want. We can prevent this by keeping a count of the number of **CDisplay** objects in a static data member and using this to control the output mechanism.

We could define the class as follows:

```
// CDISPLAY.H - Interface of CDisplay class
#ifndef CDISPLAY_H
#define CDISPLAY_H

class CDisplay
{
public:
    CDisplay();
    void ShowRegister(double RegisterValue);
    ~CDisplay();

private:
    static int m_DisplayCount;
};

#endif

// CDISPLAY.CPP - Implementation of CDisplay class
#include "CDisplay.h"
#include <iostream.h>
#include <iomanip.h>

// Class constructor - increments the count of CDisplay objects
CDisplay::CDisplay()
{
    ++m_DisplayCount;
}

// Function to display calculated value
void CDisplay::ShowRegister (double RegisterValue)
{
    if(m_DisplayCount>1)            // Only the first display should work
        return;                     // so do nothing if we are secondary
                                    // Otherwise display the value
    cout << endl << setw(12) << RegisterValue << endl;
    return;
}

// Class destructor - decrements the count of CDisplay objects
CDisplay::~CDisplay()
{
    --m_DisplayCount;
}
```

The class contains one function in addition to the constructor and the destructor: **ShowRegister()**. The static member **m_DisplayCount** in the **private** section of the class is incremented by the class constructor and decremented by the class destructor. We can check this value in the function **ShowRegister()**, and inhibit output if it is greater than 1, since this will indicate that a second or subsequent calculator display is operating. We must remember to initialize the value of **m_DisplayCount** to zero at global scope. We can do this when we write the function **main()** for our program.

The **CDisplay** class only supports output of values of type **double**, since that's all we'll be using in our calculator program. If we needed to support output for other types, it would be a simple matter of overloading the **ShowRegister()** member function to accept different types of arguments.

Note that we have had to include the header files for output, **iostream.h** and **iomanip.h**.

The CKeyboard Class

Now that we've got an idea about how the **CCalculator** and **CDisplay** classes operate, we can turn our attention to the **CKeyboard** class. We'll design this class so that it has responsibility for handling keyboard input and for performing some preliminary processing before passing messages to the **m_LogicUnit** object to indicate which particular key was pressed. It won't need any data members, so we can specify the class interface as:

```
// CKEYBOARD.H - Interface of CKeyboard class
#ifndef CKEYBOARD_H
#define CKEYBOARD_H
#include "CLogicUnit.h"

class CKeyboard
{
public:
    void GetKey(CLogicUnit& aLogicUnit);
};

#endif
```

The **GetKey()** member function, which will receive keyboard input, will need to communicate with the **m_LogicUnit** member of the calculator, so we have arranged that this will be passed as a reference argument to the function when the function is called. (You'll remember that it gets called from the **Run()** member function of the **CCalculator** class.) The **GetKey()** function will determine which character has been entered from the keyboard and then it will call a different **CLogicUnit** interface function, depending on what kind of input character has been identified.

Note that we have added the preprocessor directive,

```
#include "CLogicUnit.h"
```

because the class definition requires the **CLogicUnit** class to be defined before **CKeyboard**.

On the following page, you can see the relationship between the classes.

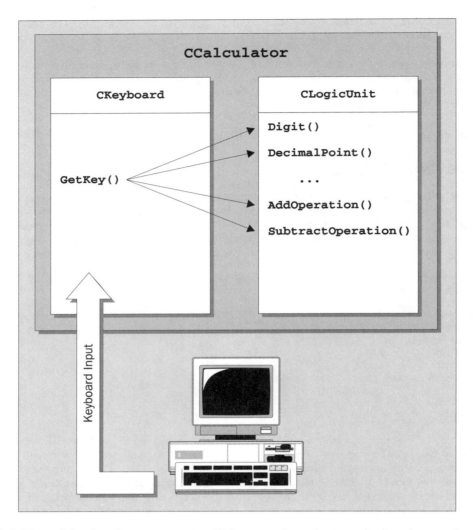

The definition of the function **GetKey()** will be very dependent on the interface to the **CLogicUnit** class, since its main task will be carried out using that interface. As we define the **GetKey()** function, we'll also be defining the interface for **CLogicUnit**.

Analyzing Keystrokes

We can write the **GetKey()** function as a huge **switch** statement inside a loop. The function will keep reading characters from the keyboard until the loop is exited.

```
// CKEYBOARD.CPP - Implementation of CKeyboard class
#include "CKeyboard.h"
#include "CCalculator.h"
#include <iostream.h>

// Keyboard manager function to get key presses and act on
```

```cpp
// valid key presses
void CKeyboard::GetKey(CLogicUnit& rLogicUnit)
{
    char achar = 0;                 // Key press stored here
    int ExitKey = 0;                // Flag to end calculator operation
    CCalculator* pCalc=0;           // Pointer to a CCalculator

    while(!ExitKey)                 // Get key presses until there is
    {                               // a reason not to...
        achar = cin.get();          // Get a key depression

        switch (achar)              // Test key press
        {
        case ' ':                   // For blank
            break;                  // do nothing

        case '0': case '1': case '2': case '3': case '4':
        case '5': case '6': case '7': case '8': case '9':
        // For any digit send numeric value of digit to rLogicUnit
            rLogicUnit.Digit(achar - '0');
            break;

        case '.':
            // Send decimal point to rLogicUnit
            rLogicUnit.DecimalPoint();
            break;

        case '(':                           // Open parenthesis,
            pCalc = new CCalculator;        // so create a new calculator
            rLogicUnit.SetDisplay(pCalc->Run()); // and run it
            delete pCalc;                   // Finally destroy it
            break;

        case ')' :
            // We must be a secondary calculator
            // and this is the signal to end
            rLogicUnit.EnterOperation();
            ExitKey = 1;
            break;

        case '*':
            rLogicUnit.MultiplyOperation(); // Send a multiply message
            break;

        case '/':
            rLogicUnit.DivideOperation();   // Send a divide message
            break;

        case '+':
            rLogicUnit.AddOperation();      // Send an add message
            break;

        case '-':
            rLogicUnit.SubtractOperation(); // Send a subtract message
            break;

        case 'Q': case 'q' :                // Quit key pressed
            ExitKey = 1;                    // So set flag to exit
```

389

```
            break;

        case 'c': case 'C':              // Clear key pressed
            rLogicUnit.Reset();          // so reset the logic unit
            break;

        case '\n':
            rLogicUnit.EnterOperation(); // Send Enter message
            break;

        default:                         // Wrong key pressed
            ExitKey = 1;                 // so set flag to exit
        }
    }
    return;
}
```

It looks like a lot of code, but it's simply testing for each of the possible kinds of key depression. All the testing is done in a single **switch** statement. Most of the cases simply call the relevant function of the **CLogicUnit** class which will then do the real processing. If the character read is a blank, it is ignored and another character is read. For any digit key that is pressed, the numeric value (not the ASCII value) is passed to the **Digit()** function of the **CLogicUnit** object. A decimal point causes the **DecimalPoint()** function of **rLogicUnit** to be invoked.

If an arithmetic operation key is pressed, the **CLogicUnit** is signaled by calling the appropriate function in the **rLogicUnit** object. The function called will then process the operation.

The most important code to look at is the code that processes an opening parenthesis:

```
        case '(':                             // Open parenthesis,
            pCalc = new CCalculator;          // so create a new calculator
            rLogicUnit.SetDisplay(pCalc->Run());   // and run it
            delete pCalc;                     // Finally destroy it
            break;
```

When such a parenthesis is entered, a new **CCalculator** object is created and its address is stored in **pCalc**. The new **CCalculator** object starts execution through the **Run()** function in the statement:

```
            rLogicUnit.SetDisplay(pCalc->Run());   // and run it
```

As we discussed earlier, the new **CCalculator** object will process the expression in parentheses and will terminate when it finds a right parenthesis matching the left parenthesis that started the process. You can also see this in the code above.

```
        case ')' :                          // We must be a secondary calculator
            rLogicUnit.EnterOperation();  // and this is the signal to end
            ExitKey = 1;
            break;
```

This will result in the value of the expression that it found being returned by the function **Run()**, and thus passed as an argument to the function **SetDisplay()** for the **rLogicUnit** object in the current calculator. Finally, the new **CCalculator** object is deleted.

Note that the creation of the **CCalculator** object in the body of the function requires us to include the header file **CCalculator.h**.

Pressing **'Q'** or **'q'** causes the **ExitKey** flag to be set, which will end the **while** loop and, therefore, end the calculator. The characters **'C'** or **'c'** are interpreted as a clear key, so either will result in the **CLogicUnit** object being reset. Any other key value is handled by the **default** case and will cause the loop to be exited, thus ending operations with the calculator.

The CLogicUnit Class

We can see already, from the number of functions that we will need to give it to process each of the key presses, that the **CLogicUnit** class will be fairly complicated. In our definition of **GetKey()** for the **CKeyboard** class, we've already anticipated the creation of nine **public** functions: **Digit()**, **DecimalPoint()**, **SetDisplay()**, **EnterOperation()**, **MultiplyOperation()**, **DivideOperation()**, **AddOperation()**, **SubtractOperation()** and **Reset()**.

You probably also remember that we need to add a **DisplayConnect()** function, as used in the constructor for the **CCalculator** class, so that the logic unit can communicate directly with the display. We'll store the pointer to the display that is passed to the **DisplayConnect()** function in a member variable called **m_pDisplay**.

In addition to all of this, we're going to need somewhere to store values as they are passed to the logic unit, so that means more member variables for the class. We won't implement these member variables as simple data types, though; we'll give them their own functionality by creating them as objects of a new class **CRegister**. (Note that there can't be a class called **register**, because **register** is a reserved word in C++.)

What registers are we likely to need? We need a display register to hold the value of any result that will appear on the display. We'll also need at least two others. When we discussed arithmetic expressions in the context of the previous calculator implementation in Chapter 6, we determined that an expression breaks down into a series of terms connected by addition or subtraction operators. The terms are a series of numbers or parenthesized expressions connected by multiply or divide operators. This suggests that we will need a multiply register to hold the value of a term, and an add register to hold any intermediate result that is a combination of one or more terms. We could call the three registers we need **m_DisplayRegister**, **m_MultiplyRegister** and **m_AddRegister**.

A register is an electronic storage for data which is a component of a logic unit. Since a logic unit has registers, we should define **CRegister** objects as members of the **CLogicUnit** class, rather than relating them by inheritance. This suggests that the **CLogicUnit** class interface will be at least:

```
// Preliminary interface for CLogicUnit
class CLogicUnit
{
public:
    double GetDisplay(void);
    void Reset(void);
    void EnterOperation(void);
    void AddOperation(void);
```

```
        void SubtractOperation(void);
        void DivideOperation(void);
        void MultiplyOperation(void);
        void DecimalPoint(void);
        void Digit(const int& digit);
        void DisplayConnect(CDisplay* pDisplay);

    private:
        CRegister m_DisplayRegister;
        CRegister m_AddRegister;
        CRegister m_MultiplyRegister;
        CDisplay* m_pDisplay;
    };
```

Connecting the Display

We can define the **DisplayConnect()** function as follows:

```
void CLogicUnit::DisplayConnect(CDisplay* pDisplay)
{
    m_pDisplay = pDisplay;
    return;
}
```

Storing a pointer to the display will allow the **CLogicUnit** object to send a message to the **CDisplay** object when a result needs to be presented.

Handling Digits

The **Digit()** function will need to send the digit to the display register, as that is normally how a calculator operates. It would be reasonable to assume that the **CRegister** class will contain a function to accept a digit from somewhere, so we could write this function as:

```
// Send a digit to display register
void CLogicUnit::Digit(const int& digit)
{
    m_DisplayRegister.Digit(digit);
}
```

This function receives the digit as a reference and passes it on to the **CRegister** class function **Digit()** operating on the **m_DisplayRegister** object. The **CRegister** object will have responsibility for assembling the input value from a succession of digits (and possibly a decimal point) that are passed to it. There's no problem with having a function called **Digit()** in both the **CRegister** class and the **CLogicUnit** class. They can only be called in the context of a particular object, so there's no risk of confusion. It's also reasonable to give them the same name, since they do much the same sort of thing in context.

Handling a Decimal Point

To handle a decimal point in the **CLogicUnit** class, we could add a function **DecimalPoint()** which will simply pass the message on to the appropriate **CRegister** object. We can call the **CRegister** class function by the same name here as well:

```
// Send a point to display register
void CLogicUnit::DecimalPoint(void)
{
    m_DisplayRegister.DecimalPoint();
}
```

This perhaps is a good point for us to digress into the **CRegister** class. We'll come back and fill in the rest of the detail of the **CLogicUnit** class later.

The CRegister Class

We've already identified two functions that we need a **CRegister** object to have, so, if we add the fact that a **CRegister** object will need to store a value, we can put a stake in the ground with a first stab at a definition for the class as follows:

```
// Preliminary interface for CRegister
class CRegister
{
    public:
        void DecimalPoint(void);
        void Digit(const int& digit);

        // Plus other functions...

    private:
        double m_Store;                    // Holds value of object

        // Plus other data members...
};
```

There's no reason to put the **m_Store** data member, which will contain the value of a register, in the public domain, so we've put it in the **private** section of the class. Consequently, all references to it, and to operations on it, will be through interface functions in the **public** section. Accepting a digit will involve doing different things with the **CRegister** object, depending on whether the digit precedes or follows a decimal point. We should, therefore, first consider how we handle a decimal point.

Handling a Decimal Point in CRegister

The effect of receiving a decimal point is to change the way that a digit is handled. Before a decimal point is received, processing a digit will involve multiplying the value of the **m_Store** member by 10, to free up the units position in the number, then adding the digit value to **m_Store**. After a decimal point is received, we need to keep track of the current decimal place. For the first digit after the decimal point, we should multiply the digit value by 0.1 before adding it to the member **m_Store**. For the second digit after a decimal point, we multiply the digit by 0.01 before adding it to **m_Store**. For each additional digit after the decimal point, the value that multiplies the digit before adding it to **m_Store**, decreases by a factor of 10.

To implement this process, we can define a data member **m_Factor** in the **CRegister** class, which will act both as an indicator that we have received a decimal point and as a factor by which to multiply a digit once a decimal point has been received. We'll initially set **m_Factor** to zero. As long as it remains zero, we know that no decimal point has been received and, as soon as a decimal point is received, we'll set **m_Factor** to 1.0. For each successive digit received after that, we'll multiply **m_Factor** by 0.1, before using it as a multiplier for the digit received.

We also need to take account of when a decimal point is the first key depression sent to a **CRegister** object. This will necessitate using an indicator that we can call **m_BeginValue**, which will signal when we are starting to enter a new value into a register. We'll also use this to mark when we have come to the end of a value in a register by indicating that a new value is being started. Initially, when the **CRegister** object is created, we'll set it to 1 to indicate that we're starting a new value. The first valid character passed to a register will set the **m_BeginValue** indicator to zero, and the value in **m_Store** to 0.0. When the end of an input value is found, **m_BeginValue** will be set back to 1 again.

We can now write the function to set the data member, **m_Factor**, when a decimal point is keyed, which we called **DecimalPoint()**. Its implementation is:

```
// Function to accept a decimal point
void CRegister::DecimalPoint(void)
{
    if(m_BeginValue)           // Check if we are starting a new number
    {
        m_BeginValue = 0;      // If so, set the indicator to zero
        m_Store = 0.0;         // and reset the value in the member m_Store
    }

    m_Factor = 1.0;            // Set the decimal point indicator
}
```

This function will be called by the **m_LogicUnit** object of type **CLogicUnit** in the **CCalculator** class when a decimal point is signaled to it by the **m_Keyboard** object. The function first checks the **m_BeginValue** flag. This could be set if the decimal point was the first key pressed when entering a number, as would be the case in an expression such as **2*.75**. If so, it sets the **m_BeginValue** flag to zero and resets the member, **m_Store**. In any event, it will set the value of the data member **m_Factor** to **1.0**, which will trigger correct processing of digits to the right of a decimal point in the function **Digit()**.

Handling a Digit in CRegister

We can show the logic for handling a digit in the form of a flow chart. This is shown on the following page:

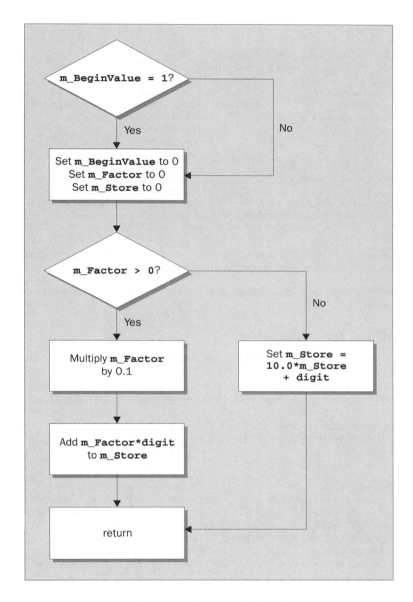

The first action is to test the **m_BeginValue** flag, to check if we are starting a new value. If we are, the flag is reset and the values of **m_Store** and **m_Factor** are reset to zero. Otherwise, we go straight to checking whether **m_Factor** is positive, which would indicate that we have previously received a decimal point. If we have, we're adding the digit as the last decimal place to the left of the decimal point. If we haven't, we're adding the digit as the units position, after multiplying the current value in **m_Store** by 10.

So, from the flowchart, the code for the **Digit()** function in the **CRegister** class will be:

```
// Function to accept a keyed digit
void CRegister::Digit(const int& digit)
{
    if(m_BeginValue)            // Check if we are at the start of a number,
    {                           // if so reset the CRegister components
        m_BeginValue = 0;           // Reset begin flag
        m_Store = 0.0;              // Reset storage
        m_Factor = 0.0;             // Reset decimal point factor
    }

    if(m_Factor > 0.0)          // Test decimal point factor,
    {                           // positive value indicates decimals
        m_Factor *= 0.1;            // Shift decimal place
        m_Store += digit*m_Factor;  // Add digit to storage
    }
    else
        m_Store = 10.0*m_Store + digit;    // Add digit to storage
}
```

This is a straightforward implementation of the logic shown in the flowchart, so we won't spend any more time on it.

Service Functions for a Register

Of course, we'll need interface functions to get and set the value of **m_Store**, as well as a set capability for the **m_BeginValue** flag. We could also include a **Reset()** function to reset the **m_Factor** and **m_BeginValue** members, as well as **m_Store**. A constructor that resets everything will also come in handy. With these capabilities added, the class definition will be:

```
// Preliminary class definition
// Class defining a register for use in CLogicUnit
class CRegister
{
public:
    CRegister();                    // Constructor
    void SetBeginValue(void);       // Function to set m_BeginValue flag
    void Reset(void);           // Function to reset CRegister data members
    double Get(void);               // Function to get m_Store value
    void Set(const double& value);  // Function to set m_Store value
    void DecimalPoint(void);        // Function to accept a decimal point
    void Digit(const int& digit);   // Function to accept a keyed digit

private:
    int m_BeginValue;       // Signals start of a value
    double m_Factor;        // Factor for digits after a decimal point
    double m_Store;         // Storage the register value
};

// Constructor
CRegister::CRegister()
{ Reset(); }

void CRegister::SetBeginValue(void)
{ m_BeginValue = 1; }
```

```
void CRegister::Reset(void)
{
    m_Store = 0.0;
    m_Factor = 0.0;
    m_BeginValue = 1;
}

void CRegister::Set(const double& value)
{ m_Store = value; }

double CRegister::Get(void)
{ return m_Store; }
```

All the new functions that we have added here are very simple. We may need a **Reset()** function to reset all the data members anyway, so this is used to provide the initializing required in the constructor. Since we have no dynamically allocated members, we don't need to worry about the destructor, or about writing a copy constructor.

Arithmetic Operations on Registers

A fundamental capability that we need to consider is arithmetic operations on **CRegister** objects. The arithmetic operations in our calculator will always be between two **CRegister** objects, with the result being placed in one of the **CRegister** objects, so we could implement all of them as overloaded **op=** operators. The **+=** operator function would be:

```
// += operation
CRegister& CRegister::operator+=(const CRegister& rhs)
{
    m_Store += rhs.m_Store;
    return *this;
}
```

This has a **const** reference parameter to avoid copying of the argument and, out of necessity, returns a reference. You'll remember that returning a reference is essential if you want to be able to use the result on the left of another assignment operation. This is a model for all of the **op=** operator functions.

It's not required here but, if you needed to implement a function such as **operator+()** for example, you could use the **operator+=()** function to do it very neatly, as follows:

```
// Addition operator function using += operator function
CRegister operator+(const CRegister& R1, const CRegister& R2)
{
    CRegister Temp(R1);          // Temporary object initialized with R1
    return Temp += R2;           // Return R1+R2
}
```

With the arithmetic operators for **CRegister** objects added, our class will be complete. The complete class, therefore, will be:

```
// CREGISTER.H - Interface of CRegister class
// Class defining a register for use in a logic unit
#ifndef CREGISTER_H
#define CREGISTER_H
```

```
class CRegister
{
public:
    CRegister();                    // Constructor
    CRegister& operator-=(const CRegister& rhs);
    CRegister& operator+=(const CRegister& rhs);
    CRegister& operator/=(const CRegister& rhs);
    CRegister& operator*=(const CRegister& rhs);
    void SetBeginValue(void);       // Function to set m_BeginValue flag
    void Reset(void);            // Function to reset CRegister data members
    double Get(void);               // Function to get m_Store value
    void Set(const double& value); // Function to set m_Store value
    void DecimalPoint(void);        // Function to accept a decimal point
    void Digit(const int& digit);   // Function to accept a keyed digit

private:
    int m_BeginValue;           // Signals start of a value
    double m_Factor;            // Factor for digits after a decimal point
    double m_Store;             // Storage for the register value
};

#endif
```

```
// CREGISTER.CPP - Implementation of CRegister class
#include "CRegister.h"

// Function to accept a keyed digit
void CRegister::Digit(const int& digit)
{
    if(m_BeginValue)            // Check if we are at the start of a number,
    {                          // if so reset the CRegister components
        m_BeginValue = 0;               // Reset begin flag
        m_Store = 0.0;                  // Reset storage
        m_Factor = 0.0;                 // Reset decimal point factor
    }

    if(m_Factor > 0.0)                  // Test decimal point factor,
    {                                   // positive value indicates decimals
        m_Factor *= 0.1;                // Shift decimal place
        m_Store += digit*m_Factor;      // Add digit to storage
    }
    else
        m_Store = 10.0*m_Store + digit;    // Add digit to storage
}

// Function to accept a decimal point
void CRegister::DecimalPoint(void)
{
    if(m_BeginValue)            // Check if we are starting a new number
    {
        m_BeginValue = 0;  // If so, set the indicator to zero
        m_Store = 0.0;     // and reset the value in the member m_Store
    }

    m_Factor = 1.0;            // Set the decimal point indicator
}
```

```
// Constructor
CRegister::CRegister()
{
    Reset();
}

void CRegister::Set(const double& value)
{
    m_Store = value;
}

double CRegister::Get(void)
{
    return m_Store;
}

void CRegister::Reset(void)
{
    m_Store = 0.0;
    m_Factor = 0.0;
    m_BeginValue = 1;
}

void CRegister::SetBeginValue(void)
{
    m_BeginValue = 1;
}

CRegister& CRegister::operator-=(const CRegister& rhs)
{
    m_Store -= rhs.m_Store;
    return *this;
}

// += operation
CRegister& CRegister::operator+=(const CRegister& rhs)
{
    m_Store += rhs.m_Store;
    return *this;
}

CRegister& CRegister::operator/=(const CRegister& rhs)
{
    m_Store /= rhs.m_Store;
    return *this;
}

CRegister& CRegister::operator*=(const CRegister& rhs)
{
    m_Store *= rhs.m_Store;
    return *this;
}
```

Now, we need to come back to the **CLogicUnit** class for our calculator and decide how arithmetic operations are going to be executed.

Handling Arithmetic Operations

The obvious approach to implementing arithmetic operations might seem to be to add a set of interface functions to the **CLogicUnit** class that will do this. But it isn't that straightforward. If we consider what happens when an operation key is pressed, we'll get a better idea of what's required. Look at the position in the diagram below:

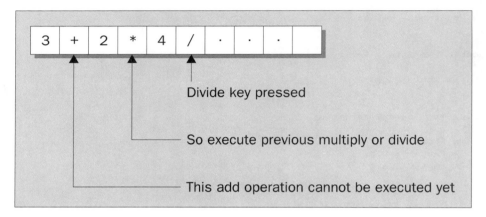

| 3 | + | 2 | * | 4 | / | . | . | . | |

Divide key pressed

So execute previous multiply or divide

This add operation cannot be executed yet

When the divide key is pressed, we can't actually execute a divide, as we haven't yet got the right-hand operand value. At this point, we must execute the previous multiply or divide operation, whichever it was, and then save the operation just entered. Note that we can't execute any previous add or subtract at this time. This can only be triggered by the user pressing another add or subtract key, or the *Enter* key. This position is illustrated below:

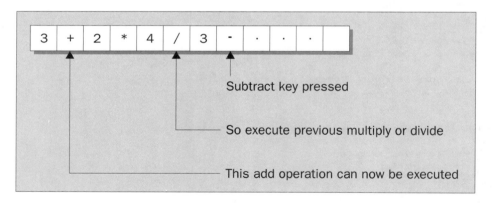

| 3 | + | 2 | * | 4 | / | 3 | . | . | . | |

Subtract key pressed

So execute previous multiply or divide

This add operation can now be executed

A simple set of functions won't really hack it, since an operation is always deferred. There's more than one way to deal with this, but we could use inheritance. If we adopt the approach of defining an operation as an object of a derived class, we could save the current operation in a pointer, ready to be executed when the next triggering operation comes along. Since, when we trigger an operation we won't know what it was, we can use a virtual function call through a pointer to sort it out when the operation is ultimately executed. We'll need to add two data members to the **CLogicUnit** class - one to be used to queue an add or subtract operation and the other a multiply or divide operation. But let's first look at the classes that we need to define the operations.

Defining a Base Class for Arithmetic Operations

The classes will represent arithmetic operations as objects. A base class for arithmetic operations really only needs a virtual member function to execute an operation. Since the operation will act on **CRegister** objects, an operation class won't need any data members at all. The function to execute an operation will be redefined in each of the derived classes, corresponding to a specific operation in each case. Therefore, the base class definition will be:

```
// COPERATION.H - Interface of COperation class
// Abstract base class definition for arithmetic operations
#ifndef COPERATION_H
#define COPERATION_H
#include "CLogicUnit.h"

class COperation
{
   public:
      // Pure virtual function
      virtual void DoOperation(CLogicUnit* pLogicUnit)=0;
      // Virtual destructor
      virtual ~COperation();
};

#endif
```

```
// COPERATION.CPP - Implementation of COperation class
#include "COperation.h"

COperation::~COperation()
{
}
```

A basic assumption is that an operation acts on a **CLogicUnit** object, although, internally to the **DoOperation()** functions, it will only involve the **CRegister** members of the **CLogicUnit** class.

The **DoOperation()** function will be used by the relevant interface function in the **CLogicUnit** class (**AddOperation()**, **DivideOperation()**, etc.) when an arithmetic operation is actually carried out. Since it's declared as **virtual**, the derived class versions can be selected through a pointer to this base class. The pointer will contain the address of an object of one of the derived classes. This will allow us to save an operation in a pointer and execute it properly later, without remembering explicitly what it was. Since the **DoOperation()** function is specified as pure, it must be redefined in the derived classes. They would otherwise be abstract, which would prevent objects being created from them. Since the function **DoOperation()** will be the only member of each derived class, we're unlikely to overlook it.

The destructor in the **COperation** class is declared as **virtual** to ensure that the correct derived class destructor is called when dynamically created objects of the derived classes are deleted.

Deriving Classes for Arithmetic Operations

The derived classes are going to be very simple. They will each just define their version of the virtual function **DoOperation()**. Let's start with multiply:

401

```
// Class defining a multiply operation
class CMultiply : public COperation
{
public:
    virtual void DoOperation(CLogicUnit* pLogicUnit);
};
```

```
// Function to execute multiply operation
void CMultiply::DoOperation(CLogicUnit* pLogicUnit)
{
    // Multiply m_MultiplyRegister by m_DisplayRegister
    pLogicUnit->m_MultiplyRegister *= pLogicUnit->m_DisplayRegister;
    // Put result in display register
    pLogicUnit->m_DisplayRegister = pLogicUnit->m_MultiplyRegister;
    return;
}
```

The **DoOperation()** function is passed a pointer to the **CLogicUnit** object belonging to a calculator. The right operand for the multiply will have been stored in the display register **m_DisplayRegister**. This could be the last numeric value entered, or the result of a parenthesized expression. The left operand will be in the register **m_MultiplyRegister**. This could be the result of a previous line of input, a parenthesized expression, or a numeric value that was keyed in.

Because the register **m_DisplayRegister** always holds the last value generated, the product of the values in the two registers is generated in **m_MultiplyRegister**, and then copied to the display register, **m_DisplayRegister**. We could generate the result directly in **m_DisplayRegister**, but we still need to maintain a copy of the result in case another multiply or divide operation is following. The left operand of another multiply or divide operation will be assumed to be in **m_MultiplyRegister**, and the next value entered or calculated will replace the value in **m_DisplayRegister**.

Note that the DoOperation() function requires access to the **private** members of the **CLogicUnit** class. To enable this, we'll need to declare the operation classes as friends of class **CLogicUnit** in its class definition.

The derived class for division is almost identical to the **CMultiply** class. The only difference is that the divide operation is used instead of multiply. The derived classes for addition and subtraction operations are also very similar to one another and to those for multiplication and division but, this time, we combine the **m_AddRegister** member with **m_DisplayRegister**. A separate register is used to keep the left operand for an add or subtract operation, since the triggering of add or subtract is separate from that of multiply and divide and it's quite possible to have a situation where left operands for both multiply/divide and add/subtract operations are stored simultaneously.

Here, you can see the complete class definitions for all these classes:

```
// OPCLASSES.H - Interface of CCMultiply, CDivide, CAdd, CSubtract classes
#ifndef OPCLASSES_H
#define OPCLASSES_H
#include "COperation.h"
#include "CLogicUnit.h"

// Class defining a multiplication operation
```

```cpp
class CMultiply : public COperation
{
   public:
      virtual void DoOperation(CLogicUnit* pLogicUnit);
};

// Class defining a division operation
class CDivide : public COperation
{
   public:
      virtual void DoOperation(CLogicUnit* pLogicUnit);
};

// Class defining a addition operation
class CAdd : public COperation
{
   public:
      virtual void DoOperation(CLogicUnit* pLogicUnit);
};

// Class defining a subtraction operation
class CSubtract : public COperation
{
   public:
      virtual void DoOperation(CLogicUnit* pLogicUnit);
};

#endif
```

```cpp
// OPCLASSES.CPP - Implementation of CMultiply, CDivide, CAdd, CSubtract
#include "OpClasses.h"

void CMultiply::DoOperation(CLogicUnit* pLogicUnit)
{
    pLogicUnit->m_MultiplyRegister *= pLogicUnit->m_DisplayRegister;
    pLogicUnit->m_DisplayRegister = pLogicUnit->m_MultiplyRegister;
    return;
}

void CDivide::DoOperation(CLogicUnit* pLogicUnit)
{
    pLogicUnit->m_MultiplyRegister /= pLogicUnit->m_DisplayRegister;
    pLogicUnit->m_DisplayRegister = pLogicUnit->m_MultiplyRegister;
    return;
}

void CAdd::DoOperation(CLogicUnit* pLogicUnit)
{
    pLogicUnit->m_AddRegister += pLogicUnit->m_DisplayRegister;
    pLogicUnit->m_DisplayRegister = pLogicUnit->m_AddRegister;
    return;
}

void CSubtract::DoOperation(CLogicUnit* pLogicUnit)
{
    pLogicUnit->m_AddRegister -= pLogicUnit->m_DisplayRegister;
    pLogicUnit->m_DisplayRegister = pLogicUnit->m_AddRegister;
    return;
}
```

Completing the CLogicUnit Class

We'll need data members in the **CLogicUnit** class to store the operations. These will need to be pointers to base class objects, because a pointer to the base class, **COperation**, can store the address of any derived class object. We can define them within the class as:

```
COperation* m_pMultiplyDivide;     // Pointer to CMultiply or CDivide
COperation* m_pAddSubtract;        // Pointer to CAdd or CSubtract
```

We'll be able to use these pointers to call the corresponding version of the virtual function **DoOperation()**. The function member of the **CAdd** class will be called for a **CAdd** object, the function member for the **CMultiply** class being called for a **CMultiply** object, and so on.

Processing Keystrokes in the CLogicUnit Class

We've already seen that the **CLogicUnit** class needs a member function to process each kind of keystroke that is meaningful to the object. We've already written the functions **Digit()** and **DecimalPoint()** for the **CLogicUnit** class. Now we need to add the functions for each of the arithmetic operations we are supporting and a function to deal with the *Enter* key.

Handling Multiply and Divide

As we said earlier, when the user presses a key for a multiply or divide operation, two things must be done. Any queued multiply or divide needs to be executed, and the current operation should be saved so that it can be executed when the right-hand operand has been received. We can implement the multiply operation as follows:

```
// Process a multiply message
void CLogicUnit::MultiplyOperation(void)
{
    if(m_pMultiplyDivide)          // Check for previous multiply/divide
    {
        m_pMultiplyDivide->DoOperation(this);        // If so, do it
        delete m_pMultiplyDivide;    // Now delete the operation object
    }
    else
        // No previous operation queued so save the display register
        m_MultiplyRegister = m_DisplayRegister;

    m_pMultiplyDivide = new CMultiply;          // Queue a new operation
    // Signal start of value in display
    m_DisplayRegister.SetBeginValue();
    return;
}
```

The first check is for a previous operation stored in the pointer **m_pMultiplyDivide**. If the pointer is not **NULL**, the pointer is used to call the corresponding **DoOperation()** function member of the derived operation class object. This will carry out the operation on the register of the **CLogicUnit** object. The pointer **this** contains the address of the current object, so it is passed to **DoOperation()** to identify the **CLogicUnit** object. The **DoOperation()** function will store the result in the **m_MultiplyRegister** data member, as the left operand for the operation just received. When execution is complete, the queued operation is deleted.

If there is no operation waiting, the display register **m_DisplayRegister** must contain the left operand for the operation just received, so this is saved in **m_MultiplyRegister**. We need to free up the display register, since it will be used to store the next operand value.

Finally, a new **CMultiply** object is created in the free store and its address is saved in **m_pMultiplyDivide** for next time around. Since receiving any operation key indicates the end of an input value, the flag is set for the display register to record that this is the case.

The function to process division is virtually identical to the function above, so we won't explain it again. You'll find it in the complete listing for the **CLogicUnit** class a little later in the chapter.

Handling Add and Subtract

Processing addition is slightly more complicated than dealing with a multiply operation, because it's possible that two previous operations may be queued. The code for the function to handle an addition operator is as follows:

```
// Process an add message
void CLogicUnit::AddOperation(void)
{
    if(m_pMultiplyDivide)          // m_pMultiplyDivide is a pointer to any
    {                              // previous * or / object
        // Execute * or / first if it exists
        m_pMultiplyDivide->DoOperation(this);
        delete m_pMultiplyDivide;          // Now delete the object
        m_pMultiplyDivide = 0;             // and set pointer in LU to null
    }

    if(m_pAddSubtract)    // m_pAddSubtract is a pointer to any previous
    {                     // + or - object
        m_pAddSubtract->DoOperation(this);   // Execute previous + or -
        delete m_pAddSubtract;               // Now delete object
    }
    else
        // If there was none, save m_DisplayRegister
        m_AddRegister = m_DisplayRegister;

    // Create a new operation object & signal start of value in display
    m_pAddSubtract = new CAdd;
    m_DisplayRegister.SetBeginValue();
    return;
}
```

Here, we check for a queued multiply or divide operation as with the previous function, and, if we find one, we set the pointer **m_pMultiplyDivide** to zero after the operation has been executed. We then look for a previous add or subtract operation, and, if one is queued, we execute that too. We don't need to set the pointer **m_pAddSubtract** to zero, because we will store the address of the new operation to be queued in it. We finally set the flag in **m_DisplayRegister** to indicate the end of an input value, as we did in the previous member function.

Again, the process for handling subtraction is almost identical to that for addition, so we won't go through it here.

Handling the Enter Key

The last key of interest to the **CLogicUnit** class is the *Enter* key. This will be transmitted at the end of an input line. You will see the code for this on the next page.

```
// Process an Enter message
void CLogicUnit::EnterOperation(void)
{
    if(m_pMultiplyDivide)          // m_pMultiplyDivide is a pointer
    {                              // to any previous * or / object
        m_pMultiplyDivide->DoOperation(this);// Execute previous * or /
        delete m_pMultiplyDivide;      // Now delete the object
        m_pMultiplyDivide = 0;         // and set pointer in LU to null
    }

    if(m_pAddSubtract)             // m_pAddSubtract is a pointer to
    {                              // any previous + or - object
        m_pAddSubtract->DoOperation(this);    // Execute previous + or -
        delete m_pAddSubtract;         // Now delete object
        m_pAddSubtract = 0;            // Set pointer to null
    }

    // Show result in display
    m_pDisplay->ShowRegister(m_DisplayRegister.Get());
    m_DisplayRegister.SetBeginValue();         // Set start of value flag
    return;
}
```

When the *Enter* key is received, all outstanding operations need to be executed and the final result displayed on the screen. The function checks the pointers **m_pMultiplyDivide** and **m_pAddSubtract**, performs any queued operation through the **DoOperation()** function and ensures the pointers are reset to **NULL**.

The message signaling that the *Enter* key was pressed is the only way that output is generated. The value in the display register, **m_DisplayRegister**, is output to the screen by sending it to the **CDisplay** object using the function **ShowRegister()**. The function is called using the pointer, **m_pDisplay** that was initialized by a call to the **DisplayConnect()** member function in the **CCalculator** class constructor. Finally, the flag in **m_DisplayRegister** is set to indicate the start of a new input value.

Of course, the value displayed will still be retained in **m_DisplayRegister** so that the next line entered can be applied to this value.

Just to make sure that we understand what happens between registers when the calculator operates, let's look at how a simple expression, 1+2*3+4, affects the contents of the registers one step at a time. We can best understand this with a table as shown below:

Key Press	Action	Contents of m_DisplayRegister	Contents of m_AddRegister	Contents of m_MultiplyRegister
1	Store in **m_DisplayRegister**	1	-	-
+	Copy **m_DisplayRegister** to **m_AddRegister**	1	1	-

Table Continued on Following Page

Key Press	Action	Contents of m_DisplayRegister	Contents of m_AddRegister	Contents of m_MultiplyRegister
2	Store in **m_DisplayRegister**	2	1	-
*	**m_DisplayRegister** to **m_MultiplyRegister**	2	1	2
3	Store in **m_DisplayRegister**	3	1	2
+	**m_DisplayRegister** * **m_MultiplyRegister**	6	1	2
	Copy **m_DisplayRegister** to **m_MultiplyRegister**	6	1	6
	m_DisplayRegister + **m_AddRegister**	7	1	6
	Copy **m_DisplayRegister** to **m_AddRegister**	7	7	6
4	Store in **m_DisplayRegister**	4	7	6
Enter	**m_DisplayRegister** + **m_AddRegister**	11	7	6

The arrows from each character in the expression point to the line representing the action taken. Each of the numeric values are just stored in the display register, **m_DisplayRegister**. You should be able to relate the **CLogicUnit** function members that we've just discussed to the actions corresponding to the arithmetic operators. You can see how the receipt of each operator frees up the display register for the next operand.

Completing the CLogicUnit Class

To complete the class definition, we need to add the pointers **m_pAddSubtract** and **m_pMultiplyDivide** which store objects representing arithmetic operations. We also need to add the key processing functions that we've just completed and to declare the operation classes (**CMultiply**, etc.) as friends of the class.

407

We also need to add a few functions to support other service operations that we've alluded to along the way, but they're all very simple, so let's look at the complete class:

```
// CLOGICUNIT.H - Interface of CLogicUnit class
#ifndef CLOGICUNIT_H
#define CLOGICUNIT_H
#include "CRegister.h"
#include "CDisplay.h"

class CLogicUnit
{
    friend class COperation;
    friend class CMultiply;
    friend class CDivide;
    friend class CAdd;
    friend class CSubtract;

  public:
      CLogicUnit();
      double GetDisplay(void);
      void SetDisplay(const double& value);
      void Reset(void);
      void EnterOperation(void);
      void AddOperation(void);
      void SubtractOperation(void);
      void DivideOperation(void);
      void MultiplyOperation(void);
      void DecimalPoint(void);
      void Digit(const int& digit);
      void DisplayConnect(CDisplay* pDisplay);

  private:
      CRegister m_DisplayRegister;
      CRegister m_AddRegister;
      CRegister m_MultiplyRegister;
      CDisplay* m_pDisplay;
      COperation* m_pAddSubtract;
      COperation* m_pMultiplyDivide;
};

#endif
```

The class **COperation** and its derived versions are all declared as friends of the **CLogicUnit** class to allow the **DoOperation()** data members to access the **CRegister** members of **CLogicUnit**. We also have a constructor which makes sure all the data members are set to zero, by using the **Reset()** function.

```
// CLOGICUNIT.CPP - Implementation of CLogicUnit class
#include "CLogicUnit.h"
#include "OpClasses.h"

// Connect the display to the logic unit
void CLogicUnit::DisplayConnect(CDisplay* pDisplay)
{
    m_pDisplay = pDisplay;
    return;
}
```

```cpp
// Send a digit to display register
void CLogicUnit::Digit(const int& digit)
{
    m_DisplayRegister.Digit(digit);
}

// Send a point to display register
void CLogicUnit::DecimalPoint(void)
{
    m_DisplayRegister.DecimalPoint();
}

// Process a multiply message
void CLogicUnit::MultiplyOperation(void)
{
    if(m_pMultiplyDivide)               // Check for previous multiply/divide
    {
        m_pMultiplyDivide->DoOperation(this);    // If so, do it
        delete m_pMultiplyDivide;    // Now delete the operation object
    }
    else
        // No previous operation queued, so save the display register
        m_MultiplyRegister = m_DisplayRegister;

    m_pMultiplyDivide = new CMultiply;              // Queue a new operation
    // Signal start of value in display
    m_DisplayRegister.SetBeginValue();
    return;
}

void CLogicUnit::DivideOperation(void)
{
    if(m_pMultiplyDivide)               // Check for previous multiply/divide
    {
        m_pMultiplyDivide->DoOperation(this);    // If so, do it
        delete m_pMultiplyDivide;    // Now delete the operation object
    }
    else
        // No previous operation queued so save the display register
        m_MultiplyRegister = m_DisplayRegister;

    m_pMultiplyDivide = new CDivide;                // Queue a new operation
    // Signal start of value in display
    m_DisplayRegister.SetBeginValue();
    return;
}

// Process an add message
void CLogicUnit::AddOperation(void)
{
    if(m_pMultiplyDivide)           // m_pMultiplyDivide is a pointer to
    {                               // any previous * or / object
        // Execute * or / first if it exists
        m_pMultiplyDivide->DoOperation(this);
        delete m_pMultiplyDivide;        // Now delete the object
        m_pMultiplyDivide = 0;           // and set pointer in LU to null
    }
```

```
        if(m_pAddSubtract)                   // m_pAddSubtract is a pointer to
        {                                     // any previous + or - object
            m_pAddSubtract->DoOperation(this);   // Execute previous + or -
            delete m_pAddSubtract;               // Now delete object
        }
        else
            // If there was none, save m_DisplayRegister
            m_AddRegister = m_DisplayRegister;

        // Create a new operation object & signal start of value in display
        m_pAddSubtract = new CAdd;
        m_DisplayRegister.SetBeginValue();
        return;
    }

    void CLogicUnit::SubtractOperation(void)
    {
        if(m_pMultiplyDivide)                 // m_pMultiplyDivide is a pointer to
        {                                     // any previous * or / object
            // Execute * or / first if it exists
            m_pMultiplyDivide->DoOperation(this);
            delete m_pMultiplyDivide;          // Now delete the object
            m_pMultiplyDivide = 0;             // and set pointer in LU to null
        }

        if(m_pAddSubtract)                    // m_pAddSubtract is a pointer to
        {                                     // any previous + or - object
            m_pAddSubtract->DoOperation(this);   // Execute previous + or -
            delete m_pAddSubtract;               // Now delete object
        }
        else
            // If there was none, save m_DisplayRegister
            m_AddRegister = m_DisplayRegister;

        m_pAddSubtract = new CSubtract;      // Create a new operation object
        // Signal start of value in m_DisplayRegister
        m_DisplayRegister.SetBeginValue();
        return;
    }

    // Process an Enter message
    void CLogicUnit::EnterOperation(void)
    {
        if(m_pMultiplyDivide)                 // m_pMultiplyDivide is a pointer to
        {                                     // any previous * or / object
            m_pMultiplyDivide->DoOperation(this);// Execute previous * or /
            delete m_pMultiplyDivide;          // Now delete the object
            m_pMultiplyDivide = 0;             // and set pointer in LU to null
        }

        if(m_pAddSubtract)                    // m_pAddSubtract is a pointer to
        {                                     // any previous + or - object
            m_pAddSubtract->DoOperation(this);   // Execute previous + or -
            delete m_pAddSubtract;               // Now delete object
            m_pAddSubtract = 0;                  // Set pointer to null
        }

        // Show result in display
```

410

```
        m_pDisplay->ShowRegister(m_DisplayRegister.Get());
        m_DisplayRegister.SetBeginValue();        // Set start of value flag
        return;
}

// Constructor
CLogicUnit::CLogicUnit()
{
    m_pDisplay = 0;                               // Set pointer to display
    Reset();
}

void CLogicUnit::Reset(void)
{
    m_MultiplyRegister.Reset();        // Set Registers to 0
    m_AddRegister.Reset();
    m_DisplayRegister.Reset();
    m_pMultiplyDivide = 0;             // Set pointers to null
    m_pAddSubtract = 0;
    return;
}

void CLogicUnit::SetDisplay(const double& value)
{
    m_DisplayRegister.Set(value);
}

double CLogicUnit::GetDisplay(void)
{
    return m_DisplayRegister.Get();
}
```

The main() Function

Now that we've fully defined all the classes, all that's left is to write a **main()** function to instantiate a **CCalculator** and run it. This is very simple:

```
// EX11_01.CPP - the main() function
#include "CCalculator.h"

int CDisplay::m_DisplayCount=0;  // Initialize count of display objects

int main(void)
{
    CCalculator myCalculator;                    // Create a CCalculator
    myCalculator.Run();                          // ...then run it
    return 0;
}
```

How It Works

The line following the **#include** statement initializes the static data member of the **CDisplay** class. Remember that the keyword **static** isn't used when initializing static data members of a class, only when declaring them.

The function **main()** simply instantiates a **CCalculator** object and runs it. It continues to run until you enter **'Q'** or **'q'** to quit the calculator. I got the following output from exercising it:

```
Ex11_01                                                        _ □ X
2.5-(1.25/17+2.65*7.3)*(1+3.5/14.5*.0023-7/15)/2
      -2.68366
*15/100
      -0.40255
c
          0
1+1/(1+1/(1+1/(1+1/(1+1))))
       1.625
Q
Press any key to continue_ .
```

The organization of this version of a calculator is quite different to that of our procedural programming example. It seems like a lot more code too, but much of it's concerned with class definitions and the house keeping around that. Generally, object-based programs may well involve more lines of code than a procedural approach but, if the classes have been properly designed, the program should be easier to extend to include new capability. Once you've built the classes as a base for the kind of problem you want to solve, applying them to a variety of problems should then be very easy.

Extending the Calculator

This example provides a lot of opportunities for you to exercise your C++ skills further if you think you need it, or even just for fun. The first thing you might try is to build in some error detection and recovery. Don't forget the possibility of a zero divisor. You could also add other operators, such as remainder and exponentiation. Adding trigonometric function capability would also be interesting.

Summary

In this chapter, we've exercised some of the principle ideas involved in using inheritance. The discussion of the problem solution here isn't a very precise reflection of how you would work in practice. You wouldn't usually write all the code and then attempt to execute it. Building the classes in an incremental fashion, adding and testing member functions one at a time would be a more practical and productive approach.

As we said at the end of the last chapter, the fundamentals that you should keep in mind about using inheritance are:

> A derived class inherits all the members of a base class, except for constructors, the destructor and the overloaded assignment operator.

> Members of a base class that are declared as **private** in the base class are not accessible in any derived class. To obtain the effect of the keyword **private**, but allow access in a derived class, you should use the keyword **protected** in place of **private**.

▶ A base class can be specified for a derived class with the keywords **public**, **private**, or **protected**. If none is specified, the default is **private**. Depending on the keyword specified for a base class, the access level of the inherited members may be modified.

▶ If you write a derived class constructor, you must arrange for data members of the base class to be initialized properly, as well as those of the derived class.

▶ A function in a base class may be declared as **virtual**. This allows other definitions of the function appearing in derived classes to be selected at execution time, depending on the type of object for which the function call is made.

▶ You should declare the destructor in a base class containing a virtual function as **virtual**. This will ensure correct selection of a destructor for dynamically created derived class objects.

▶ A virtual function in a base class can be specified as pure, by placing **=0** in the function declaration. The class will then be an abstract class for which no objects can be created. In any derived class, all the pure virtual functions must be defined. If not, it too becomes an abstract class.

▶ A class may be derived from multiple base classes, in which case it inherits members from all of its bases, with the exception of destructors, constructors and overloaded assignment operator functions.

▶ An indirect base class may be specified as **virtual** for derived classes in order to avoid possible multiple occurrences of its members in a class with multiple bases, two or more of which are derived from the indirect base.

Also remember that if you allocate space for members of a class dynamically, to avoid problems, you must provide a copy constructor, a destructor and the assignment operator.

If you have followed along with the example in this chapter without major difficulty, you are ready to try your hand at Windows programming. The programs in the remainder of the book get a bit larger, but none of them are more difficult than the example we have just completed. Windows programming is our ultimate objective, so let's get to it.

Understanding Windows Programming

This chapter is an overview of using Developer Studio for Windows programming. We'll look at how we use Visual C++ to generate a Windows program and how that program is organized. By the end of this chapter, you will understand:

- What the Microsoft Foundation Classes are
- The basic elements of an MFC based program
- Single Document Interface (SDI) applications and Multiple Document Interface(MDI) applications
- What the AppWizard is and how to use it to generate SDI and MDI programs
- What files are generated by the AppWizard and what their contents are
- How an AppWizard-generated program is structured
- The key classes in an AppWizard-generated program and how they are interconnected
- What the principal source files in an AppWizard program contain
- The general approach to customizing an AppWizard-generated program

We'll expand the AppWizard programs that we generate in this chapter by adding features and code incrementally in subsequent chapters. By the end of the book, you should end up with a sizable working Windows program that incorporates the basic user interface programming techniques.

The Essentials of a Windows Program

In Chapter 7, we saw an elementary Windows program to display a short quote from the Bard. It was unlikely to win any awards, being completely free of any useful functionality, but it did serve to illustrate the two essential components of a Windows program - one providing initialization and setup and the other servicing Windows messages. This is illustrated on the next page.

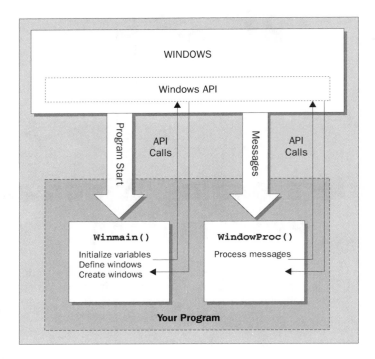

This structure is at the heart of all Windows programs. Here, you can see the two essential pieces of a Windows program: the function **WinMain()** - called by Windows at the start of execution of the program - and a window procedure for each window class you have defined, often referred to as **WndProc()** or **WindowProc()**, which will be called by the operating system whenever a message is to be passed to your application's window.

The function **WinMain()** does any initialization that is necessary and sets up the window or windows that will be the primary interface to the user. It also contains the message loop for retrieving messages that have been queued for the application. The function **WindowProc()** handles all the messages that are not queued, which will include those initiated in the message loop in **WinMain()**. This is where you would code your application-specific response to each Windows message. This code should handle all the communications with the user by processing the Windows messages generated by user actions, such as moving or clicking the mouse or entering information from the keyboard.

The Windows API

The example that you saw in Chapter 7 used the **Windows Application Programming Interface**, abbreviated to the **Windows API**. The Windows API comes as part of every copy of Windows and consists of a large set of functions that provide all the services and communications with Windows that are necessary for producing an application that is to run in the Windows environment. The API actually contains over a thousand functions.

All the interactions between a program and the user are handled by Windows. Your program will receive information from the user secondhand, through Windows messages. Every Windows program uses the Windows API, regardless of how it is produced. All the programs we will write using Visual C++ will ultimately use the Windows API, so there is no getting away from it. Fortunately, we don't need to know very much about the Windows API in detail, as MFC does such a terrific job of packaging it up in a much more organized and friendly form.

Visual C++ and the Windows API

Remember that the Windows API was not written with Visual C++ in mind, or even considering C++ in general, since it was written before C++ became widely used. Naturally, it needs to be usable in programs written in a variety of languages, most of which are not object oriented. The API functions do not handle or recognize class objects but, as we shall soon see, MFC encapsulates the API in a way that makes using it a piece of cake.

Visual C++ lets you develop a Windows program in two stages. First, you use Visual C++'s set of tools to generate code for a program automatically, then you modify and extend the code to suit your needs. As the basis for doing this, Visual C++ uses a hierarchy of classes called the **Microsoft Foundation Classes**. These can be used independently of the development tools in Visual C++.

The Microsoft Foundation Classes

The **Microsoft Foundation Classes**, usually abbreviated to **MFC**, are a set of predefined classes upon which Windows programming with Visual C++ is built. These classes represent an object oriented approach to Windows programming that encapsulates the Windows API. The process of writing a Windows program involves creating and using MFC objects, or objects of classes derived from MFC. In the main, we'll derive our own classes from MFC, with considerable assistance from the specialized tools in Visual C++ to make this even easier. The objects created will incorporate member functions for communicating with Windows, for processing Windows messages and for sending messages to each other.

These derived classes will, of course, inherit all of the members of their base classes. These inherited functions do practically all of the general grunt work necessary for a Windows application to work. All we need to do is to add data and function members to customize the classes to provide the application-specific functionality that we need in our program. In doing this, we'll be applying most of the techniques that we have been grappling with in the preceding chapters, particularly those involving class inheritance and virtual functions.

MFC Notation

All the classes in MFC have names beginning with **C**, such as **CDocument** or **CView**. If you use the same convention when defining your own classes or deriving them from those in the MFC library, your programs will be easier to follow. Data members of an MFC class are prefixed with **m_**. We'll also follow this convention in the examples, just as we have been doing throughout the book.

You'll find that MFC uses Hungarian notation for many variable names, particularly those that originate in the Windows API. As you will recall, this involves using a prefix of **p** for a pointer, **n** for an **int**, **l** for **long**, **h** for a handle, and so on. The name **m_lpCmdLine**, for example, would refer to a data member of a class (because of the **m_** prefix) that is of type pointer to

417

long. This approach of explicitly showing the type of a variable in its name was important in the C environment because of the lack of type checking. Since you could determine the type from the name, you had a fair chance of not using or interpreting its value incorrectly. The downside is that the variable names can become quite cumbersome, making the code look more complicated than it really is. As C++ has strong type checking which will pick up the sort of misuse that used to happen regularly in C, this kind of notation is not essential, so we won't use it for our own variables in our examples in the book. However, we will retain the **p** prefix for pointers, since this helps to make the code more readable.

How an MFC Program is Structured

We know from Chapter 1 that we can produce a Windows program using the AppWizard without writing a single line of code. Of course, this uses the MFC library, but it's quite possible to write a Windows program which uses MFC without using AppWizard. If we first scratch the surface by constructing the minimum MFC based program, we can get a clear idea of the fundamental elements involved.

The simplest program that we can produce using MFC is slightly less sophisticated than the example that we wrote in Chapter 7, using the raw Windows API. The example we'll produce here will have a window but no text displayed in it. This will be sufficient to show the fundamentals, so let's try it out.

TRY IT OUT - An MFC Application without AppWizard

First, create a new project workspace using the File/ New... menu option as you've done many times before. We won't use AppWizard here, so select the type of project as Application as shown here:

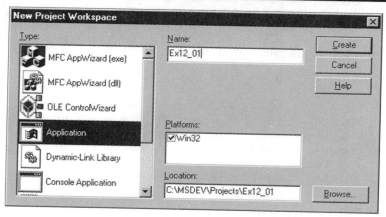

With this choice of project type, we must ensure that the linker knows that we intend to use MFC classes. If we don't do this, the wrong link options will be set and we'll get some obscure linker errors. Use the Build/Settings... menu item to bring up the Project Settings dialog. Go to the General tab and make sure that the Microsoft Foundation Classes: option is showing Use MFC in a Shared DLL. Now, you can create a new source file and insert it in to the project as **Ex12_01.cpp**.

To begin with, add a statement to include the header file **afxwin.h** as this contains definitions for many MFC classes. This will allow us to derive our own classes from MFC.

```
#include <afxwin.h>                    // For the class library
```

To produce the complete program, we will only need to derive two classes from MFC: an **application class** and a **window class**. We won't need to write a `WinMain()` function, as we did in the example in Chapter 7, as this is automatically provided by the MFC library behind the scenes. Let's look at how the two classes that we need are defined.

The Application Class

A class that is fundamental to any Windows program written using MFC is called `CWinApp`. An object of this class includes everything necessary for starting, initializing, running and closing the application. The first thing that we need to do to produce our application is to derive our own application class from `CWinApp`. We'll be defining a specialized version of the MFC class `CWinApp` to suit our application needs. The code for this is as follows:

```
class COurApp : public CWinApp
{
   public:
       virtual BOOL InitInstance();
};
```

There is not a great deal of specialization necessary in this case. We have only included one member in the definition of our class - the function `InitInstance()`. This function is defined as a virtual function in the base class, so this is not a new function in our derived class. We are redefining the base class function for our application class. All the other data and function members that we need in our class we will inherit from `CWinApp` unchanged. Our application class will be endowed with quite a number of data members that are defined in the base class, `CWinApp`. Many of these correspond to variables used as arguments in Windows API functions. For example, the member `m_pszAppName` stores a pointer to a string that defines the name of the application. The member `m_nCmdShow` specifies how the application window is to be shown when the application starts up. We don't need to go into the inherited data members now. We'll see how they are used as the need arises in developing our application-specific code.

In deriving our own application class from `CWinApp`, we must override the virtual function `InitInstance()`. Our version of `InitInstance()` will be called by the version of `WinMain()` that is provided for us, and we'll include code in the function to create and display our application window. However, before we write `InitInstance()`, we need to look at a class in the MFC library which defines a window.

Defining a Window Class

Our MFC application will need a window as the interface to the user, referred to as a **frame window**. We will derive a window class for our application from the MFC class `CFrameWnd` which is designed specifically for this purpose. Since `CFrameWnd` provides everything for creating and managing a window for our application, all we need to add to our derived window class is a constructor. This will allow us to specify a title bar for our window to suit the application context :

```
class COurWnd : public CFrameWnd
{
   public:
       // Class constructor
       COurWnd()
       {
           Create(0, "Our Dumb MFC Application");
```

419

```
        }
};
```

The **Create()** function, which we call in our class constructor, is inherited from the base class and will create the window and attach it to the **COurWnd** object being created. Note that the **COurWnd** object is not the same thing as the window that will be displayed by Windows. The class object and the physical window are distinct entities. The **Create()** function will create the window which is to be displayed and attach it to the **COurWnd** object.

The first argument value for the **Create()** function, **0**, specifies that we want to use the base class default attributes for the window - you will recall that we needed to define window attributes in our example in Chapter 7. The second argument specifies the window name which will be used in the window title bar. There are other parameters to the function **Create()**, but they all have default values which will be quite satisfactory, so we can afford to ignore them here.

Completing the Program

Having defined a window class for our application, we can write the **InitInstance()** function in our **COurApp** class:

```
BOOL COurApp::InitInstance(void)
{
    // Construct a window object in the free store
    m_pMainWnd = new COurWnd();
    m_pMainWnd->ShowWindow(m_nCmdShow);         // ...and display it
    return TRUE;
}
```

This will override the virtual function defined in the base class **CWinApp**, and as we said previously, will be called by the **WinMain()** function that is automatically supplied by the MFC library. The function **InitInstance()** constructs a main window object for our application in the free store by using the operator **new**. We store the address returned in the variable **m_pMainWnd**, which is a member of our class, **COurApp**, since it is inherited from the base class. The effect of this is that the window object will be owned by the application object.

The only other item we need for a complete, albeit rather limited program, is to define an application object. An instance of our application class, **COurApp**, must exist before **WinMain()** is executed, so we should declare it at global scope with the statement:

```
COurApp AnApplication;        // Define an application object
```

The reason that the object needs to exist at global scope is that it is the application and needs to exist before the application can start executing. The **WinMain()** provided by MFC calls the **InitInstance()** function member of the application object to construct the window object and, thus, implicitly assumes the application object already exists.

The Finished Product

Now that you've seen all the code, you can add it to the project. Usually with a Windows program, the classes are defined in **.h** files, and the member functions not appearing within the class definitions are defined in **.cpp** files, but our application is so short that you may as well put it all in a single **.cpp** file. This is structured as follows:

```
// EX12_01.CPP
// An elementary MFC program
#include <afxwin.h>                    // For the class library

// Application class definition
class COurApp:public CWinApp
{
   public:
      virtual BOOL InitInstance();
};

// Window class definition
class COurWnd:public CFrameWnd
{
   public:
      // Class constructor
      COurWnd()
      {
         Create(0, "Our Dumb MFC Application");
      }
};

// Function to create an instance of the main window
BOOL COurApp::InitInstance(void)
{
   // Construct a window object in the free store
   m_pMainWnd = new COurWnd();
   m_pMainWnd->ShowWindow(m_nCmdShow); // ...and display it
   return TRUE;
}

// Application object definition at global scope
COurApp AnApplication;        // Define an application object
```

That's all we need. It looks a bit odd because no **WinMain()** function appears but, as we noted above, the **WinMain()** function is supplied by the MFC library.

Now we're ready to roll, so build and run the application. Select the Build/Build Ex12_01.exe menu item or just press *F7* to build the project. You should end up with a clean compile and link, in which case you can select Build/Execute Ex12_01.exe or press *Ctrl+F5* to run it. Our minimum MFC program will appear as shown:

We can resize the window by dragging the border, we can move the whole thing around and we can also minimize or maximize it in the usual way. The only other function that the program supports is close, for which you can use the system menu, the close button at the top right, or just key *Alt-F4*. It doesn't look like much but, considering that there are so few lines of

421

code, it's quite impressive, particularly if you think of how much code you would need to do this in the old DOS world.

 FYI If you find that the linker throws some errors about the symbols __beginthreadex and __endthreadex, change the **Microsoft Foundation Classes:** list box on the **General** tab of the **Project Settings** dialog to use MFC, either statically or with the DLL. The **Project Settings** dialog is accessed by selecting the **Build/Settings...**menu item.

The Document/View Concept

When you write applications using MFC, it implies acceptance of a specific structure for your program, with application data being stored and processed in a particular way. This may sound restrictive, but it really isn't for the most part, and the benefits in speed and ease of implementation you gain from this far outweigh any conceivable disadvantage. The structure of an MFC program incorporates two application oriented entities - a document and a view - so let's look at what they are and how they are used.

What is a Document?

A **document** is the name given to the collection of data in your application with which the user interacts. Although the word 'document' seems to imply something of a textual nature, it isn't limited to text. It could be the data for a game, a geometric model, a text file, a collection of data on the distribution of orange trees in California or, indeed, anything you want. The term 'document' is just a convenient label for the collection of application data in your program, treated as a unit.

You won't be surprised to hear that a document in your program will be defined as an object of a document class. Your document class will be derived from the class **CDocument** in the MFC library, and you will add your own data members to store items that your application requires and member functions to support processing of that data.

Handling application data in this way enables standard mechanisms to be provided within MFC for managing a collection of application data as a unit and for storing and retrieving data contained in document objects to or from disk. These mechanisms will be inherited by your document class from the base class defined in the MFC library, so you will get a broad range of functionality built in to your application automatically, without having to write any code.

Document Interfaces

You have a choice as to whether your program deals with just one document at a time, or with several. The **Single Document Interface**, referred to as **SDI**, is supported by the MFC library for programs that only require one document to be open at a time. A program using this is referred to as an **SDI application**.

For programs needing several documents to be open at one time, you use the **Multiple Document Interface**, which is usually referred to as **MDI**. With the MDI, as well as being able to open multiple documents of one type, your program can also be organized to handle documents of different types simultaneously. Of course, you will need to supply the code to deal with processing whatever different kinds of documents you intend to support.

What is a View?

A **view** always relates to a particular document object. As we have seen, a document contains a set of application data in your program and a **view** is an object which provides a mechanism for displaying some or all of the data stored in a document. It defines how the data is to be displayed in a window and how the user can interact with it. Similar to the way that you define a document, you will define your own view class by deriving it from the MFC class **CView**. Note that a view object and the window in which it is displayed are distinct. The window in which a view appears is called a **frame window**. A view is actually displayed in its own window that exactly fills the client area of a frame window. The general relationship between a document, a view and a frame window is illustrated below:

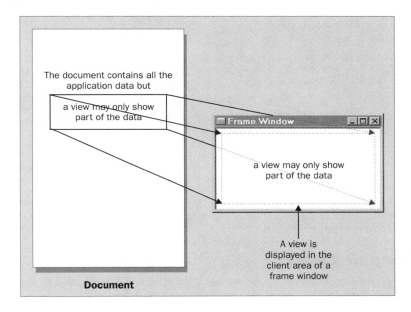

In this illustration, the view displays only part of the data contained in the document although, of course, a view can display all of the data in a document if that is required.

A document object can have multiple view objects associated with it. Each view object can provide a different presentation or subset of the same document data. If you were dealing with text, for example, different views could be displaying independent blocks of text from the same document. For a program handling graphical data, you could display all of the document data at different scales in separate windows, or different formats, such as textual representation of the elements that form the image.

Linking a Document and its Views

MFC incorporates a mechanism for integrating a document with its views and each frame window with a currently active view. A document object automatically maintains a list of pointers to its associated views and a view object has a data member holding a pointer to the document that it relates to. Also, each frame window stores a pointer to the currently active view object. The coordination between a document, a view and a frame window is established by another MFC class of objects that are called **document templates**.

Document Templates

A **document template** manages the document objects in your program and the windows and views associated with each of them. There will be one document template for each different kind of document that you have in your program. To be more specific, document objects and frame window objects are created by a document template object. A view is created by a frame window object. The document template object itself is created by the application object that is fundamental to any MFC application, as we saw in the last example. You can see a graphical representation of these interrelationships here:

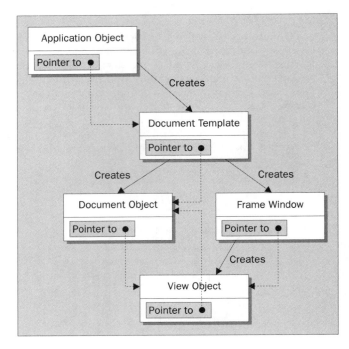

The diagram uses dashed arrows to show how pointers are used to relate objects. These pointers enable function members of one class object to access the **public** data members or functions in the **public** interface of another object.

Document Template Classes

MFC has two classes for defining document templates. For SDI applications, the MFC library class **CSingleDocTemplate** is used. This is relatively straightforward, since an SDI application will have only one document and usually just one view. MDI applications are rather more complicated. They have multiple documents active at one time, so a different class, **CMultiDocTemplate**, is needed to define the document template. We will see more of these classes as we progress into developing application code.

Your Application and MFC

MFC covers a lot of ground and involves a lot of classes. It provides classes that, taken together, are a complete framework for your applications, only requiring the customization necessary to make the programs do what you want them to do. It would be fruitless to try to go through a laundry list of all the classes that are provided. We can learn about them much more easily and naturally by exploring their capabilities as we use them.

However, it's worth taking a look at how the fundamental classes in an SDI application relate to MFC. This is illustrated in the next diagram.

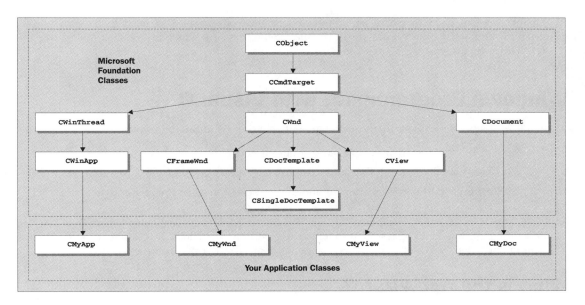

This shows the four basic classes that are going to appear in virtually all your Windows applications

➤ The application class **CMyApp.**

➤ The document class **CMyDoc** defining a document to contain the application data.

➤ The frame window class **CMyWnd.**

➤ The view class **CMyView** which will define how data contained in **CMyDoc** is to be displayed in the client area of a window created by a **CMyWnd** object.

The names for these classes will be specific to a particular application, but the derivation from MFC will be much the same, although there can be alternative base classes, particularly with the view class. As we'll see a bit later, MFC provides several variations of the view class that provide a lot of functionality pre-packaged for you, saving you lots of coding. The class defining a document template for your application will not typically need to be extended, so the standard MFC class **CSingleDocTemplate** will usually suffice in an SDI program. When you are creating an MDI program, your document template class will be **CMultiDocTemplate**, which is also derived from **CCmdTarget**.

The arrows in the diagram point from a base class to a derived class. The MFC library classes shown here form quite a complex inheritance structure but, in fact, these are just a very small part of the complete MFC structure. You need not be concerned about the detail of the complete MFC hierarchy in the main, but it is important to have a general appreciation of it if you want to understand what the inherited members of your classes are. You will not see any of the definitions of the base classes in your program, but the inherited members of a derived class in your program will be accumulated from the direct base class, as well as each of the indirect base classes in the MFC hierarchy. To determine what members one of your program classes has, you, therefore, need to know from which classes it inherits. Once you know that, you can look up its members using the Help facility.

Neither do you need to worry about remembering which classes you need to have in your program and what base classes to use in their definition. As you will see next, all of this is taken care of for you by Visual C++.

Windows Programming with Visual C++

You'll be using three tools in the development of your Windows programs:

▶ **AppWizard** for creating the basic program code.

▶ **ClassWizard** for extending and customizing the classes in your program.

▶ **Resource Editor** for creating or modifying such things as menus and toolbars.

There are, in fact, several resource editors; the one used in any particular situation is selected depending on the kind of resource that you are editing. We'll look at editing resources in the next chapter. For now, let's take a look at what AppWizard can do for us.

What is the AppWizard?

AppWizard is a programming tool that creates a complete skeleton Windows program using the MFC library. We'll be using AppWizard for the rest of the examples in the book. It's an extraordinarily powerful aid to Windows programming, since all you have to do to produce your application is to customize a ready-made program. AppWizard automatically defines all of the classes needed by your program that we have discussed. It even provides hooks and explanations for where you should add your application-specific code.

As we've already seen, you can invoke AppWizard when you create a new project workspace by selecting MFCAppWizard (exe) as the project type. Do this now and name the project TextEditor as shown here:

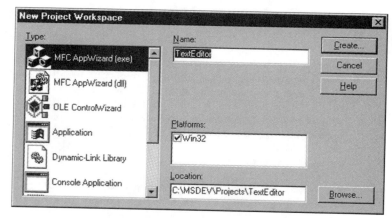

As you know, the name that you assign to the project, TextEditor in this case, will be used as the name of the folder which will contain all the project files, but it will also be used as a basis for creating names for classes generated in the application by AppWizard. When you click on Create... you will be at the first step in the AppWizard dialog to create the application. Initially, AppWizard allows you to choose an SDI, an MDI or a dialog based application. Let's concentrate on the first two options. We will generate both an SDI and an MDI application and see what the resulting programs look like.

Using AppWizard to Create an SDI Application

When you are in the AppWizard dialog, you can always go back to the previous step by clicking on the button labeled < Back. Try it out. If you felt like it, you could now rename the project and then click on Create again to return to Step 1 of the AppWizard dialog.

Step 1

The default option selected is MDI, and the appearance of an MDI application is shown so that you'll know what to expect. Select the SDI option and the representation for the application shown top left will change to a single window, as shown here:

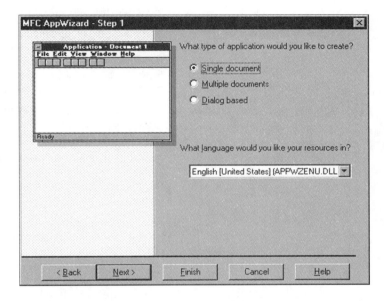

The drop-down list box shows the default language supported. Other languages will only appear in the list if your Visual C++ installation has been set up to support them.

Step 2

To move on to the next step in the dialog, you should click on Next >. Step 2 gives you choices about the database support in your application. We don't need any in this application, so click on Next > once again to move on.

Step 3

This step gives you a range of choices relating to OLE (Object Linking and Embedding). OLE enables you to write programs that can import objects from other programs, or import your program into another application. We'll see more about this in Chapter 20. For now, we'll accept the default selection of no OLE support and move to the next step.

Step 4

This step offers you a range of functions that can be included in your application by the AppWizard. The first group relate to menu and toolbar options. Let's take a brief look through them.

Feature	Meaning
Docking toolbar	The toolbar provides a standard range of buttons that are alternatives to using menu options. A docking toolbar can be dragged to the sides or the bottom of the application window, so you can put it wherever is most convenient. We'll see how to add buttons to the toolbar in Chapter 13.
Initial status bar	The status bar appears at the bottom of the application window. It comes with fully implemented standard functions including indicators for the *NUM LOCK*, *CAPS LOCK*, and *SCROLL LOCK* keys, as well as a message line to display prompts for menu options and toolbar selections.
Printing and print preview	This adds the standard Page Setup..., Print Preview, and Print... options to the File menu. The AppWizard will also provide code to support these functions.
Context-sensitive Help	Enabling this option results in a basic set of facilities to support context sensitive help. You'll obviously need to add the specific contents of the help files if you want to use this feature.
3D controls	This option results in controls that appear in the application, such as buttons, being shaded to give them a 3D appearance.

All these, except Context-Sensitive Help, are default selections and we will keep the default set of options in our example. The second group of choices concern **WOSA**, which is **W**indows **O**pen **S**ervices **A**rchitecture. This is only relevant if your program is to implement communications with other computers. It provides two options for communications support in your program:

Feature	Meaning
MAPI(Messaging API)	This option will cause AppWizard to include support that allows you to send and receive messages.
Windows Sockets	This provides you with the ability to implement TCP/IP capability within your program. This is particularly applicable to applications that support the transfer of files on the Internet.

We will not be getting into either of these options, as they are beyond the scope of this book, so we will leave them unchecked.

Towards the bottom of the dialog, you can vary the number of previously referenced file entries that will appear in the list at the end of the File menu. You can set this to any value from 0 to 16.

Clicking the <u>A</u>dvanced... button brings up a range of options for your application, grouped under two tabs as shown here:

The tab shown allows you to choose the file extension which will identify files that are generated by your application and are to be associated with it. In this instance, we've associated **.ted** with our application. You'll notice that, when you fill in the file extension, the <u>F</u>ilter name: box is automatically filled in for you. From this tab, you can also modify the File Type <u>I</u>D: which is used to label the file type for your application in the system registry. The registry associates files with a given unique extension with a particular application.

AppWizard has already decided on a caption for the title bar in your application window but, like all the strings shown here, you can change this if you don't like it. For example, it would be better with a space between Text and Editor, or you might want to personalize it in some way.

The Doc <u>t</u>ype name: entry is a default name for a document. When you create a new document, MFC will use what is entered here as a basis for naming it. The <u>F</u>ilter name: will be used to describe files associated with your application in the List Files of <u>T</u>ype: box in the <u>F</u>ile/<u>O</u>pen... and <u>F</u>ile/Save <u>A</u>s... menu dialogs although, if you have not specified a file extension for files produced by your application, this will do nothing. If you want to specify the filter name entry, you should put something descriptive to clearly identify the particular document type.

The option headed File <u>n</u>ew name(OLE short name): is important if your application will support more than one type of document. This would mean that you had more than one document template implemented in your program. In this case, what you put here will be used to identify the document template in the <u>F</u>ile/<u>N</u>ew... menu dialog. Along with the option adjacent to it, it's also applicable if you are writing a program which is an OLE server. We'll see a little more about this towards the end of the book.

429

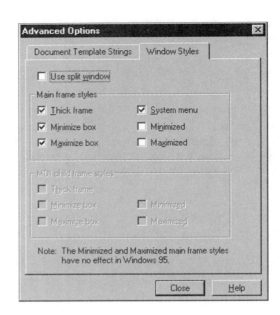

The Windows Styles tab is shown here:

The bottom area is grayed out because the options here only apply to MDI applications. The Main frame styles area enables you to tailor your application window. Here, the Thick frame option is checked by default. It provides you with a window border that can be dragged to resize the window. The Minimize box, Maximize box, and System menu options, which are also checked by default, provide the three standard buttons that appear at the top of a window. The two unchecked options for Maximized and Minimized frame styles do not apply to Windows 95 programs, so you can ignore these.

We can now move to Step 5 by closing the Advanced Options dialog and clicking on Next >.

Step 5

This step offers two options for your consideration. The first is whether or not comments are included in the source code generated by AppWizard. In most instances, you will want to keep the default option of having them included so that you can better understand the code generated for you.

The second option relates to how MFC library code is used in your program. The default choice of using the MFC library as a shared DLL (Dynamic Link Library) means that your program will link to MFC library routines at run time. This can reduce the size of the executable file that you'll generate, but requires the MFC DLL to be on the machine that's running it. The two programs together (`.exe` and `.dll`) may be bigger than if you had statically linked the MFC library. If you opt for static linking, the routines will be included in the executable module for your program when it is built. Generally, it's preferable to keep the default option of using MFC as a shared DLL. With this option, several programs running simultaneously using the dynamic link library can all share a single copy of the library in memory.

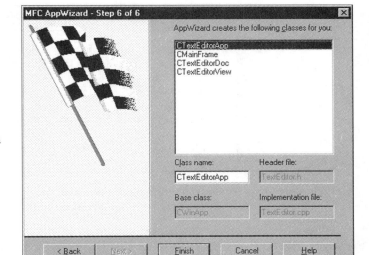

Step 6

The last step presents you with a list of the classes that AppWizard will be generating in your program code, as shown here:

For the highlighted class, the boxes below show the name given to the class, the name of the header file in which the definition will be stored, the base class used and the name of the file containing the implementation of member functions in the class. The class definition is always contained in a **.h** file and the member function source code is always included in a **.cpp** file.

In the case of the class, **CTextEditorApp**, shown above, the only thing that you can alter is the class name and, since it's already a good choice, we'll leave it as it is. Try clicking on the other classes in the list. For **CMainFrame** and **CTextEditorDoc**, you can alter everything except the base class and, for the class **CTextEditorView**, you can change the base class as well. Click on the down arrow to display the list of other classes that you can have as a base class. Since we have called the application TextEditor with the notion that it will be able to edit text, choose **CEditView** to get basic editing capability provided automatically.

If you click on Finish, you will see a summary of what AppWizard will include in your project. Just click on OK to have the program files containing a fully working base program generated by AppWizard using the options you have chosen.

The Output from AppWizard

All the output from AppWizard is stored in the folder **TextEditor**. Developer Studio provides several ways for you to view the information in the project folder.

Tab	View	How project viewed
	ClassView	Viewed by class and function member name, plus the global entities in your program.
	ResourceView	Viewed by resource type.
	FileView	Viewed by file name.
	InfoView	Provides access to books online.

Each of these is selected using the appropriate tab at the bottom of the Project Workspace window in Developer Studio. The fourth tab provides access to all of the documentation available online with Visual C++.

Viewing Project Files

If you select FileView by clicking on the third and expand the list by clicking on the + for TextEditor files then the + for Dependencies, you'll see the complete list of files for the project, as shown opposite:

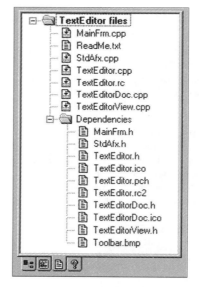

As you can see, there are a total of 17 files in the list. You can view any of the files simply by double-clicking on the file name. The contents of the file selected will be displayed in the right-hand window. Try it out with the **ReadMe.txt** file. You'll see that it contains a brief explanation of the contents of each of the files that make up the project. We won't repeat descriptions of the files here, as they are very clearly summarized in the file.

If you are viewing a **.cpp** file containing the implementation of a class, note that you get an extra toolbar button to enable you to switch directly to the corresponding **.h** file to see the class definition. There are also a couple of drop-down list boxes relating to the class implementation which we'll be using later on.

Viewing Classes

As you may have started to see in the last chapter, ClassView is often much more convenient than FileView, since classes are the basis for the organization of the application. When you want to look at the code, you typically will want to look at the definition of a class or at the implementation of a member function of a class although, as you'll see as we progress through the development of our examples, most of the additions and modifications that you'll want to make can best be done using the ClassWizard. ClassWizard is another standard development tool provided by Visual C++ that we'll start to look at later in this chapter.

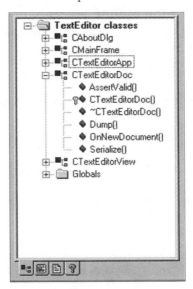

If you click the ClassView tab, you can expand the TextEditor classes folder to show the classes defined for the application. Clicking on + for any of the classes will expand the class to show the members of that class. In the window shown below, the **CTextEditorDoc** class has been expanded.

The icons simply code the various kinds of things that you can display.

 Classes are dark blue.

 Function members are purple.

 Data members are light blue.

 Keys indicate that the member is **private** or **protected**.

You can see that we have the four classes that we discussed earlier that are fundamental to an MFC application: **CTextEditorApp** for the application, **CMainFrame** for the application frame window, **CTextEditorDoc** for the document and **CTextEditorView** for the view. We also have a class **CAboutDlg** which defines objects that support the dialog that appears when you select the menu item Help/About... in the application. If you expand Globals, you'll see that it only contains one definition: the application object **theApp**.

You'll remember from the last chapter that to view the code for a class definition you just double-click the class name in the tree. To view the code for a member function, double-click the function name. Note that you can drag the edge of the Project Workspace window to the left or the right in order to view its contents or your code more easily.

However, it's usually convenient to leave the left window fairly narrow since, if you leave the cursor over any line that is partially obscured, the complete contents of the line will be shown. You can hide or show the Project Workspace window by clicking the button at the right-hand end of the Standard toolbar.

The Class Definitions

We won't examine the classes in complete detail here - we'll just get a feel for how they look and pick out a few important aspects. If you double-click the name of a class in the Class View, the code defining the class will be displayed. Take a look at the application class, **CTextEditorApp** first. The definition for this class is shown below:

```
class CTextEditorApp : public CWinApp
{
    public:
        CTextEditorApp();
// Overrides
        // ClassWizard generated virtual function overrides
        //{{AFX_VIRTUAL(CTextEditorApp)
        public:
        virtual BOOL InitInstance();
        //}}AFX_VIRTUAL

// Implementation

        //{{AFX_MSG(CTextEditorApp)
        afx_msg void OnAppAbout();
        // NOTE - the ClassWizard will add and remove member functions here.
        //    DO NOT EDIT what you see in these blocks of generated code !
          //}}AFX_MSG
            DECLARE_MESSAGE_MAP()
};
```

It may look complicated at first sight but there isn't much to it. It is derived from **CWinApp** and includes a constructor, a virtual function **InitInstance()**, a function **OnAppAbout()**, and a macro **DECLARE_MESSAGE_MAP()**. This last macro is concerned with defining which Windows messages are handled by which function members of the class. This macro will appear in the definition of any class that may process Windows messages. Of course, our application class will inherit a lot of functions and data members from the base class, and we will be looking further into these as we expand our program examples.

The rest of the **CTextEditorApp** class definition is comments. However, they are very important comments. They include a note indicating where the ClassWizard will make changes to the code. Don't be tempted to delete or alter any of the comments because some will be used as markers to enable the ClassWizard to find where changes to the class definition should be made. Modifying them may prevent ClassWizard from working properly with this project ever again.

The application frame window for our SDI program will be created by an object of the class **CMainFrame** that is defined by the code shown opposite:

```
class CMainFrame : public CFrameWnd
{
protected: // create from serialization only
     CMainFrame();
     DECLARE_DYNCREATE(CMainFrame)

// Attributes
public:

// Operations
public:

   // Overrides
   // ClassWizard generated virtual function overrides
   //{{AFX_VIRTUAL(CMainFrame)
       virtual BOOL PreCreateWindow(CREATESTRUCT& cs);
   //}}AFX_VIRTUAL

// Implementation
public:
   virtual ~CMainFrame();
   #ifdef _DEBUG
    virtual void AssertValid() const;
    virtual void Dump(CDumpContext& dc) const;
   #endif

protected:  // control bar embedded members
   CStatusBar   m_wndStatusBar;
   CToolBar     m_wndToolBar;

// Generated message map functions
protected:
   //{{AFX_MSG(CMainFrame)
   afx_msg int OnCreate(LPCREATESTRUCT lpCreateStruct);
   // NOTE - the ClassWizard will add and remove member functions here.
   //    DO NOT EDIT what you see in these blocks of generated code!
   //}}AFX_MSG
   DECLARE_MESSAGE_MAP()
};
```

This class is derived from **CFrameWnd** which provides most of the functionality required for our application frame window. The derived class includes two protected data members, **m_wndStatusBar** and **m_wndToolBar** which are instances of the MFC classes **CStatusBar** and **CToolBar** respectively. These objects will create and manage the status bar that will appear at the bottom of the application window, and the toolbar which will provide buttons to access standard menu functions.

The definition of the **CTextEditorDoc** class supplied by AppWizard is:

```
class CTextEditorDoc : public CDocument
{
protected: // create from serialization only
     CTextEditorDoc();
     DECLARE_DYNCREATE(CTextEditorDoc)

// Attributes
public:
```

```
        // Operations
        public:

        // Overrides
            // ClassWizard generated virtual function overrides
            //{{AFX_VIRTUAL(CTextEditorDoc)
        public:
            virtual BOOL OnNewDocument();
            virtual void Serialize(CArchive& ar);
            //}}AFX_VIRTUAL

        // Implementation
        public:
            virtual ~CTextEditorDoc();
            #ifdef _DEBUG
             virtual void AssertValid() const;
             virtual void Dump(CDumpContext& dc) const;
            #endif

        protected:

        // Generated message map functions
        protected:
            //{{AFX_MSG(CTextEditorDoc)
            // NOTE - the ClassWizard will add and remove member functions here.
            //     DO NOT EDIT what you see in these blocks of generated code !
            //}}AFX_MSG
            DECLARE_MESSAGE_MAP()
    };
```

As in the case of the previous classes, most of the meat comes from the base class and is therefore not apparent here. There are also a lot of comments, some of which are for you, and some are to help ClassWizard out.

The macro **DECLARE_DYNCREATE()** which appears after the constructor (and was also used in the **CMainFrame** class) enables an object of the class to be created dynamically by synthesizing it from data read from a file. Reading and writing a document object to a file is supported by a process called **serialization**. We'll be seeing in the examples we will develop how to write our own documents to file using serialization, and then reconstruct them from the file data.

The document class also includes the macro **DECLARE_MESSAGE_MAP()** in its definition to enable Windows messages to be handled by class member functions if necessary.

The view class in our SDI application is defined as:

```
class CTextEditorView : public CEditView
{
    protected: // create from serialization only
        CTextEditorView();
        DECLARE_DYNCREATE(CTextEditorView)

    // Attributes
    public:
        CTextEditorDoc* GetDocument();
```

```
        // Operations
        public:

        // Overrides
            // ClassWizard generated virtual function overrides
            //{{AFX_VIRTUAL(CTextEditorView)
        public:
            virtual void OnDraw(CDC* pDC);   // overridden to draw this view
            virtual BOOL PreCreateWindow(CREATESTRUCT& cs);
        protected:
            virtual BOOL OnPreparePrinting(CPrintInfo* pInfo);
            virtual void OnBeginPrinting(CDC* pDC, CPrintInfo* pInfo);
            virtual void OnEndPrinting(CDC* pDC, CPrintInfo* pInfo);
            //}}AFX_VIRTUAL

        // Implementation
        public:
            virtual ~CTextEditorView();
            #ifdef _DEBUG
             virtual void AssertValid() const;
             virtual void Dump(CDumpContext& dc) const;
            #endif

        protected:

        // Generated message map functions
        protected:
            //{{AFX_MSG(CTextEditorView)
            // NOTE - the ClassWizard will add and remove member functions here.
            //    DO NOT EDIT what you see in these blocks of generated code !
            //}}AFX_MSG
            DECLARE_MESSAGE_MAP()
    };
```

As we specified in the AppWizard dialog, the view class is derived from the class **CEditView**, which already includes basic text handling facilities. The **GetDocument()** function returns a pointer to the document object corresponding to the view, and you will be using this to access data in the document object when you add your own extensions to the view class.

There are two implementations of the **GetDocument()** function in the code. The one that appears in the **.cpp** file for the class is used for the debug version of the program. You will normally use this during program development, since it provides validation of the pointer value stored for the document (stored in the inherited data member **m_pDocument** in the view class). The version that applies to the release version of your program appears after the class definition in the **.h** file.

Creating an Executable Module

To compile and link the program, click on Build/Build TextEditor.exe, press *Shift+F8* or click on the Build icon.

By default, you will have debug capability included in your program. As well as the special version of **GetDocument()**, there are lots of checks in the MFC code that are included in this case. If you want to change this, you can use the drop-down list box in the Project toolbar to choose the release configuration that doesn't contain all the debug code.

FYI When compiling your program with debug switched on, the compiler does not detect uninitialized variables, so it can be helpful to do the occasional release build, even while you are still testing your program.

Precompiled Header Files

The first time you compile and link a program, it will take some time. The second and subsequent times it should be quite a bit faster because of a feature of Visual C++ called precompiled headers. During the initial compilation, the compiler saves the output from compiling header files in a special file with the extension **.pch**. On subsequent builds this file is reused if the source in the headers has not changed, thus saving the compilation time for the headers.

You can determine whether or not precompiled headers are used, and control how they are handled. Choose Build/ Settings... and then select the C/C++ tab. From the Category: drop-down list box, select Precompiled Headers, and you'll see the dialog shown here:

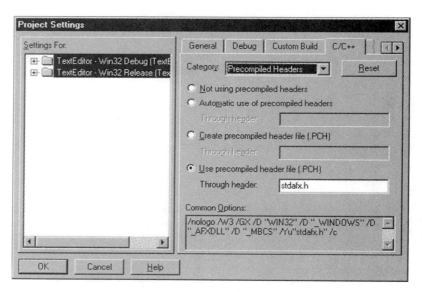

The option for automatic use of precompiled headers shown here is the easiest to apply. The **.pch** file will be generated if there isn't one, and if there is one it will be used. The option to create a **.pch** file does exactly that. The ability to specify the last header file to be included allows you to control what is included in the precompiled header. The option to use a precompiled header file presumes that one already exists. You can get more information on this through the Help button in the dialog.

Running the Program

To execute the program press *Ctrl+F5*, or select the Execute option in the Build menu. Because we chose **CEditView** as the base class for our class **CTextEditorView**, the program is a fully functioning, simple text editor. You can enter text in the window as shown opposite:

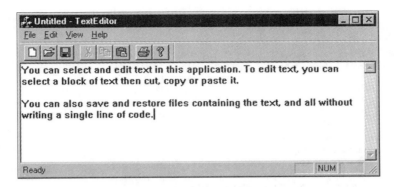

Note that the application has scroll bars for viewing text outside the visible area within the window and, of course, you can resize the window by dragging the boundaries. When you save a document, it will automatically be given the extension **.ted**. All the options under the File menu are fully operational. As you move the cursor over the toolbar buttons or the menu options, prompts appear in the status bar describing the function that will be invoked, and if you let the cursor linger on a toolbar button, a tooltip will be displayed showing its purpose.

How the Program Works

As in our trivial MFC example that we looked at earlier in this chapter, the application object is created at global scope in our SDI program. You can see this if you expand the Globals item in the Class View and then double-click on **theApp**. In the right part of the project workspace window you will see the statement:

```
CTextEditorApp theApp;
```

This declares the object **theApp** as an instance of our application class **CTextEditorApp**. This statement is in the file **TextEditor.cpp**, which also contains member function definitions for the application class, and the definition of the **CAboutDlg** class.

Once the object **theApp** has been created, the MFC-supplied **WinMain()** function is called. This calls two member functions of **theApp** object. First it calls **InitInstance()** which provides for any initialization of the application that is necessary and then **Run()** which provides initial handling for Windows messages.

The Function InitInstance()

You can access the code for this function by double-clicking its entry in the ClassView after expanding the **CTextEditorApp** class in the left pane of the Project Workspace window. The version created by AppWizard is as follows:

```
BOOL CTextEditorApp::InitInstance()
{
    // Standard initialization
    // If you are not using these features and wish to reduce the size
    // of your final executable, you should remove from the following
    // the specific initialization routines you do not need.

    #ifdef _AFXDLL
     Enable3dControls();    // Call this when using MFC in a shared DLL
```

```
#else
  Enable3dControlsStatic();    // Call this when linking to MFC statically
#endif

  LoadStdProfileSettings();// Load stndrd INI file options(including MRU)

  // Register the application's document templates.  Document templates
  //  serve as the connection between documents, frame windows and views.

  CSingleDocTemplate* pDocTemplate;
  pDocTemplate = new CSingleDocTemplate(
      IDR_MAINFRAME,
      RUNTIME_CLASS(CTextEditorDoc),
      RUNTIME_CLASS(CMainFrame),          // main SDI frame window
      RUNTIME_CLASS(CTextEditorView));
  AddDocTemplate(pDocTemplate);

  // Enable DDE Execute open
  EnableShellOpen();
  RegisterShellFileTypes(TRUE);

  // Parse command line for standard shell commands, DDE, file open
  CCommandLineInfo cmdInfo;
  ParseCommandLine(cmdInfo);

  // Dispatch commands specified on the command line
  if (!ProcessShellCommand(cmdInfo))
     return FALSE;

  // Enable drag/drop open
  m_pMainWnd->DragAcceptFiles();

  return TRUE;
}
```

A document template object is created dynamically within this function by the statement:

```
pDocTemplate = new CSingleDocTemplate(
    IDR_MAINFRAME,
    RUNTIME_CLASS(CTextEditorDoc),
    RUNTIME_CLASS(CMainFrame),          // main SDI frame window
    RUNTIME_CLASS(CTextEditorView));
```

The first parameter to the **CSingleDocTemplate** constructor is a symbol, **IDR_MAINFRAME**, which defines the menu and toolbar to be used with the document type. The following three parameters define the document, main frame window and view class objects that are to be bound together within the document template. Since we have an SDI application here, there will only ever be one of each in the program, managed through one document template object. **RUNTIME_CLASS()** is a macro that enables the type of a class object to be determined at runtime.

There's a lot of other stuff here for setting up the application instance that we need not worry about. You can add any initialization of your own that you need for the application to the **InitInstance()** function.

The Function Run()

The function **Run()** in the class **CTextEditorApp** is inherited from the application base class **CWinApp**. Because it is declared as **virtual**, you can replace the base class version of the function **Run()** with one of your own, but this is not usually necessary so you don't need to worry about it.

The function **Run()** acquires all the messages from Windows destined for the application and ensures that each message is passed to the function in the program designated to service it, if one exists. Therefore, this function continues executing as long as the application is running. It terminates when you close the application.

You can, thus, boil the operation of the application down to four steps:

▶ Creating an application object, **theApp**.

▶ Executing **WinMain()**, which is supplied by MFC.

▶ **WinMain()** calling **InitInstance()**, which creates the document template, the main frame window, the document and the view.

▶ **WinMain()** calling **Run()**, which executes the main message loop to acquire and dispatch Windows messages.

Using AppWizard to Create an MDI Application

Now, let's create an MDI application using AppWizard. Let's give it the project name Sketcher, as we'll be expanding it into a sketching program during subsequent chapters. You should have no trouble with this as there are only three things that we need to do differently from the process that we have just gone through for the SDI application. On Step 1 you should leave the default option, MDI, rather than changing to the SDI option under the Advanced... button. In Step 4, you can specify the file extension as ske, and on Step 6, leave the base class for the class **CSketcherView** as **CView**.

In Step 6, which is shown here, we get an extra class derived from the MFC for our application:

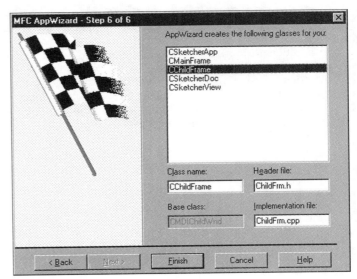

441

The extra class is **CChildFrame** which is derived from the MFC class **CMDIChildWnd**. This class provides a frame window for a view of the document that will appear inside the application window created by a **CMainFrame** object. With an SDI application, there is a single document with a single view, so the view is displayed in the client area of the main frame window. In an MDI application, we can have multiple documents open, each having multiple views. To accomplish this, each view of a document in our program will have its own child frame window created by an object of the class **CChildFrame**. As we saw earlier, a view will be displayed in what is actually a separate window, which exactly fills the client area of a frame window.

Running the Program

You can build the program in exactly the same way as the previous example. Then, if you execute it, you will get the application window shown below:

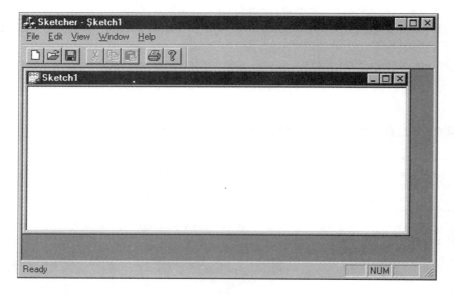

In addition to the main application window, we have a separate document window with the caption Sketch1. **Sketch1** is the default name for the initial document and it will have the extension **.ske** if you save it. You can create additional views for the document by selecting the Window/New Window menu option. You can also create a new document by selecting File/New, so that there will be two active documents in the application. The situation with two documents active each with two views is shown opposite:

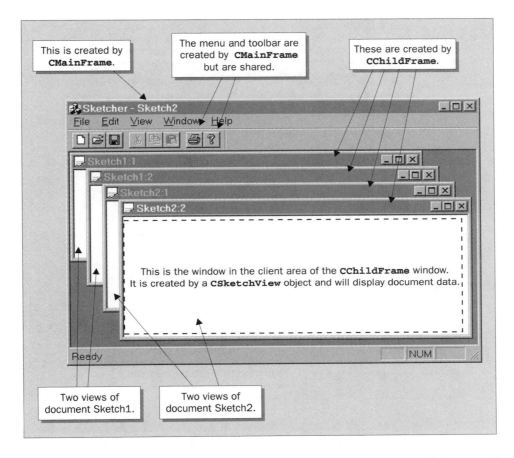

Figure callouts:
- This is created by **CMainFrame**.
- The menu and toolbar are created by **CMainFrame** but are shared.
- These are created by **CChildFrame**.
- This is the window in the client area of the **CChildFrame** window. It is created by a **CSketchView** object and will display document data.
- Two views of document Sketch1.
- Two views of document Sketch2.

You can't yet actually create any data in the application, since we haven't added any code to do that, but all the code for creating documents and views has already been included by AppWizard.

What is the ClassWizard?

We've mentioned the ClassWizard several times in this chapter, so it's about time we took a peek at how it works. Most of the rest of the book will be concerned with using the ClassWizard in various ways, so here we'll just introduce it. Once the AppWizard has generated the initial application code, you'll be able to use the ClassWizard to implement most of the additional code necessary to support your specific application needs, so you'll be able to learn how to use it in practical situations.

You can start the ClassWizard by selecting the View/ClassWizard... menu option, by pressing *Ctrl+W*, or easiest of all, by clicking on the toolbar button.

Let's try it out with the Sketcher Application. You'll get the ClassWizard dialog displayed for the current project. The dialog below shows the Sketcher project with the **CSketcherDoc** class selected in the right-hand drop-down list.

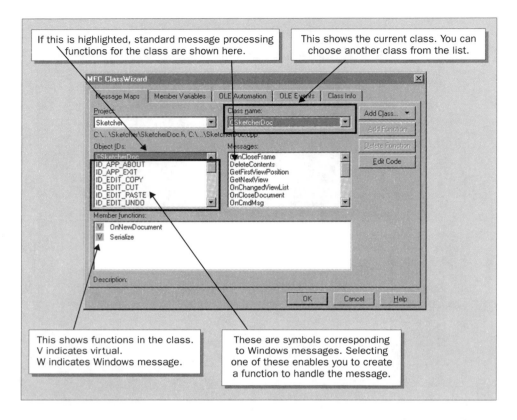

Here you can see the **Message Maps** tab, where you can add functions to the classes in your application to process specific Windows messages. You can also edit or delete any of the existing functions in a class. Highlighting one of the existing member functions will enable the grayed out button for **Delete Function**.

The **Add Class...** button enables you to derive a new class in your application. The other tabs provide a wealth of other facilities for extending your program. We'll be going further into how we actually use the ClassWizard, starting in the very next chapter.

Summary

In this chapter, we've been concerned mainly with the mechanics of using the AppWizard. We've looked at how a Windows program is structured, and we've taken a peek at MFC. We have also seen the basic components of MFC programs generated by the AppWizard. All our examples will be AppWizard-based, so it's a good idea to keep the general structure and broad class relationships in mind. You probably won't feel too comfortable with the detail at this point. Don't worry about that now. You will find that it becomes much clearer once we have applied the ClassWizard and other Developer Studio tools a few times in the succeeding chapters. They'll be taking care of most of the detail automatically and, an appreciation of what fits where, will become quite obvious after a bit of practice.

The key points that we have discussed in this chapter are:

▶ The AppWizard generates a complete, working framework Windows application for you to customize to your requirements.

▶ The AppWizard can generate single document interface (SDI) applications which work with a single document and a single view, or multiple document interface (MDI) programs which can handle multiple documents and views simultaneously.

▶ The four essential classes in an SDI application that are derived from the foundation classes are:
>> the application class
>> the frame window class
>> the document class
>> the view class

▶ A program can have only one application object. This is defined automatically by the AppWizard at global scope.

▶ A document class object stores application specific data and a view class object displays the contents of a document object.

▶ A document template class object is used to tie together a document, a view and a window. For an SDI application, a **CSingleDocTemplate** class does this and, for an MDI application, the **CDocTemplate** class is used. These are both foundation classes and application specific versions do not normally need to be derived.

Working with Menus and ToolBars

In the last chapter, we saw how a simple framework application generated by AppWizard is made up and how the parts interrelate. In this chapter, we'll start customizing the MDI framework application, Sketcher, with a view to making it into a useful program. The first step in this process is to understand how menus are defined in Visual C++, and how functions are created to service the application-specific menu items that we add to our program. We'll also see how to add toolbar buttons to the application. By the end of this chapter you'll have learned:

- How an MFC-based program handles messages
- What menu resources are, and how you can create and modify them
- What menu properties are, and how you can create and modify them
- How to create a function to service the message generated when a menu item is selected
- How to add handlers to update menu properties
- How to add toolbar buttons and associate them with existing menu items

Communicating with Windows

As we saw in Chapter 7, Windows communicates with your program by sending messages to it. Most of the drudgery of message handling in a Visual C++ program is taken care of by MFC, so you don't have to worry about providing a **WndProc()** function at all. MFC enables you to provide functions to handle the individual messages that you are interested in and to ignore the rest. These functions are referred to as **message handlers** or just **handlers**. Since your application is MFC-based, a message handler is always a member function of one of your application's classes.

The association between a particular message and the function in your program that is to service it is established by a **message map**, so let's look into how a message map operates.

Understanding Message Maps

A message map is established by AppWizard for each of the four main classes in your program. The message map for each class appears in the **.cpp** file containing the implementation of the class, but the functions that are included in the message map also need to be declared in the class definition. Look at the definition for the **CSketcherApp** class shown below:

```
class CSketcherApp : public CWinApp
{
public:
    CSketcherApp();

// Overrides
    // ClassWizard generated virtual function overrides
    //{{AFX_VIRTUAL(CSketcherApp)
    public:
    virtual BOOL InitInstance();
    //}}AFX_VIRTUAL

// Implementation

    //{{AFX_MSG(CSketcherApp)
    afx_msg void OnAppAbout();
    // NOTE - the ClassWizard will add and remove member functions here.
    //    DO NOT EDIT what you see in these blocks of generated code !
    //}}AFX_MSG
    DECLARE_MESSAGE_MAP()
};
```

You can see the comments that indicate the start (**//{{AFX_MSG(CSketcherApp)**) and end (**// }}AFX_MSG**) of the lines in the class definition where ClassWizard will add declarations for the message handlers that you define in the class. The functions appearing here will also appear in a message map in the class implementation in the **.cpp** file for the class. In **CSketcherApp**, only one message handler, **OnAppAbout()**, is declared. The word **afx_msg** at the beginning of the line is just to distinguish a message handler from other member functions in the class. It will be converted to whitespace by the preprocessor, so it has no effect when the program is compiled.

The macro, **DECLARE_MESSAGE_MAP()**, indicates that the class can contain function members that are message handlers. In fact, any class that you derive from the MFC class **CCmdTarget** can potentially have message handlers, so such classes will have this macro included as part of the class definition by AppWizard or ClassWizard, depending on which was responsible for creating it. The diagram on the following page shows the MFC classes derived from **CCmdTarget** that have been used in our examples so far:

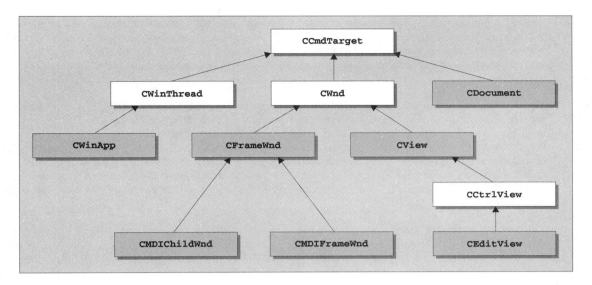

The classes that have been used directly, or as a direct base for our own application classes, are shown shaded. Thus, our class **CSketcherApp** has **CCmdTarget** as an indirect base class and, therefore, will always include the **DECLARE_MESSAGE_MAP()** macro. All of the view classes and classes derived from **CWnd** will also have it.

If you are adding your own members to a class, it's best to leave the **DECLARE_MESSAGE_MAP()** macro as the last line in the class definition, as it contains access specifiers. If you do add members after the **DECLARE_MESSAGE_MAP()** you'll also need to include an access specifier for them - **public**, **protected**, or **private**.

Message Handler Definitions

If a class definition includes the macro **DECLARE_MESSAGE_MAP()**, the class implementation must include the macros **BEGIN_MESSAGE_MAP()** and **END_MESSAGE_MAP()**. If you look in **Sketcher.cpp**, you'll see the following code as part of the implementation of **CSketcherApp**:

```
BEGIN_MESSAGE_MAP(CSketcherApp, CWinApp)
   //{{AFX_MSG_MAP(CSketcherApp)
   ON_COMMAND(ID_APP_ABOUT, OnAppAbout)
     // NOTE - the ClassWizard will add and remove mapping macros here.
     //    DO NOT EDIT what you see in these blocks of generated code!
   //}}AFX_MSG_MAP
   // Standard file based document commands
   ON_COMMAND(ID_FILE_NEW, CWinApp::OnFileNew)
   ON_COMMAND(ID_FILE_OPEN, CWinApp::OnFileOpen)
   // Standard print setup command
   ON_COMMAND(ID_FILE_PRINT_SETUP, CWinApp::OnFilePrintSetup)
END_MESSAGE_MAP()
```

This is a message map. The **BEGIN_MESSAGE_MAP()** and **END_MESSAGE_MAP()** macros define the boundaries of the message map and each of the message handlers in the class will appear between these macros. In the case above, the code is only handling one message: the **WM_COMMAND** message. This message is generated when the user selects a menu option or accelerator keys.

The message map knows which menu or key is pressed by the identifier (ID) that is included in the message. This is why there are four **ON_COMMAND** macros in the code above. The first argument to this macro is an ID which is associated with one particular command and the **ON_COMMAND()** macro ties the function name to the command specified. Thus, when a message corresponding to the identifier **ID_APP_ABOUT** is received, the function **OnAppAbout()** will be called. Similarly, for a message corresponding to the **ID_FILE_NEW** identifier, the function **OnFileNew()** will be called. This last handler is actually defined in the base class, **CAppWin**, as are all the remaining handlers.

The **BEGIN_MESSAGE_MAP()** macro has two arguments. The first argument identifies the current class name for which the message map is defined and the second provides a connection to the base class for finding a message handler. If a handler is not found in the class defining the message map, the message map for the base class is then searched.

Note that command IDs such as **ID_APP_ABOUT** are standard IDs defined in MFC. These correspond to messages from standard menu items and toolbar buttons. The prefix **ID_** is used to identify a command associated with a menu item or a toolbar button, as we'll see when we discuss resources later. For example, **ID_FILE_NEW** is the ID that corresponds to the File/New menu item being selected and **ID_APP_ABOUT** corresponds to the Help/About menu option.

There are more symbols besides **WM_COMMAND** that Windows uses to identify standard messages. Each of them are prefixed with **WM_** for Windows Message. These symbols are defined in **Winuser.h**, which is included in **Windows.h**. If you want to look at these, you'll find **Winuser.h** in the **Include** folder in the **MSDEV** folder containing your Visual C++ system. Windows messages often have additional data values that are used to refine the identification of a particular message specified by a given ID. The message **WM_COMMAND**, for instance, is sent for a whole range of commands, including those originating from selecting a menu item or a toolbar button.

Note that you should not map a message (or in the case of command messages, a command ID) to more than one message handler in a class. If you do, it won't break anything, but the second message handler will never be called. Since one of the major uses of the ClassWizard is to define message handlers and make appropriate entries in the message maps in your program, this situation should not arise if you stick to using the ClassWizard. Only when you need to make message map entries manually will you need to take care not to assign more than one handler to a message.

Message Categories

There are three categories of messages that your program may be dealing with, and the category to which it belongs will determine how a message is handled. The message categories are:

Message category	Explanation
Windows messages	These are standard Windows messages that begin with the **WM_** prefix, with the exception of **WM_COMMAND** messages which we will come to in a moment. Examples of Windows messages are **WM_PAINT** which indicates that you need to redraw the client area of a window, and **WM_LBUTTONUP** which signals that the left mouse button has been released.
Control notification messages	These are **WM_COMMAND** messages which are sent from controls, such as a list box, for instance, to the window that created the control, or from a child window to a parent window. Parameters associated with a **WM_COMMAND** message enable messages from the controls in your application to be differentiated.
Command messages	These are also **WM_COMMAND** messages that originate from the user interface elements, such as menu items and toolbar buttons. MFC defines unique identifiers for standard menu and toolbar command messages.

The standard Windows messages in the first category will be identified by the **WM_** prefixed IDs that Windows defines. We'll be writing handlers for some of these messages in the next chapter. The messages in the second category are a particular group of **WM_COMMAND** messages that we'll see in Chapter 16 when we work with dialogs. We'll deal with the last category, messages originating from menus and toolbars, in this chapter. In addition to the message IDs defined by MFC for the standard menus and toolbars, you can define your own message IDs for the menus and toolbar buttons that you add to your program. If you don't supply IDs for these items, MFC will automatically generate IDs for you, based on the menu text.

Handling Messages in Your Program

You cannot put a handler for a message anywhere you like. The permitted sites for a handler depend on what kind of message is to be processed. The first two categories of message that we saw above, that is, standard Windows messages and control notification messages, are always handled by objects of classes derived from **CWnd**. Frame window classes and view classes are derived from **CWnd**, for example, so they can have member functions to handle Windows messages and control notification messages, but application classes, document classes and document template classes are not, so they cannot handle these messages.

Using the ClassWizard solves the headache of remembering where to place handlers, as it will only give you the options that are allowed. For example, selecting **CSketcherDoc** as the Class name: will not give you any of the **WM_** Messages:.

For standard Windows messages, the class **CWnd** provides default message handling. Thus, if your derived class does not include a handler for a standard Windows message, it will be processed by the default handlers defined in the base class. If you do provide a handler in your class, you'll sometimes still need to call the base class handler as well, so that the message will be processed properly. When you are creating your own handler, ClassWizard will provide a skeleton implementation of it, which will include a call to the base handler where necessary.

Handling command messages is much more flexible. You can put handlers for these in the application, the document and document template classes and, of course, in the window and view classes in your program. So what happens when a command message is sent to your application, bearing in mind there are a lot of options as to where it is handled?

How Command Messages are Processed

All command messages are sent to the main frame window for the application. The main frame window then tries to get the message handled by routing it in a specific sequence to the classes in your program. If one class cannot process the message, it passes on to the next.

For an SDI program, the sequence in which classes are offered an opportunity to handle a command message is:

1 The view object

2 The document object

3 The document template object

4 The main frame window object

5 The application object

The view object is given the opportunity to handle a command message first and, if no handler has been defined, the next class object has a chance to process it. If none of the classes has a handler defined, default Windows processing takes care of it, essentially throwing the message away.

For an MDI program, things are only a little more complicated. Although we have the possibility of multiple documents, each with multiple views, only the active view and its associated document is involved in the routing of a command message. The sequence for routing a command message in an MDI program is:

1 The active view object

2 The document object associated with the active view

3 The document template object for the active document

4 The frame window object for the active view

5 The application object

6 The main frame window object

It's possible to alter the sequence for routing messages, but this is so rarely necessary that we won't go into it in this book.

Extending the Sketcher Program

We are going to add code to the Sketcher program created in the last chapter to implement the functionality we need to create sketches. We'll provide code for drawing lines, circles, rectangles and curves with various colors and line thickness, and for adding annotations to a sketch. The data for a sketch will be stored in a document and we'll also allow multiple views of the same document at different scales.

It will take us several chapters to add everything we need, but a good starting point would be to add menu items to deal with the types of elements that we want to be able to draw and to select a color for drawing. We'll make both the element type and color selection persistent in the program, meaning that, having selected a color and an element type, both of these will remain in effect until we change one or other of them.

The steps that we will work through to add menus to Sketcher are:

> Define the menu items to appear on the main menu bar and in each of the menus.

> Decide which of the classes in our application should handle the message for each menu item.

> Add message handling functions to the classes for our menu messages.

> Add functions to the classes to update the appearance of the menus to show the current selection in effect.

> Add a toolbar button complete with tooltips for each of our menu items.

Elements of a Menu

We will be looking at two aspects of dealing with menus in Visual C++: the creation and modification of the menu as it appears in your application and the processing that is necessary when a particular menu item is selected - the definition of a message handler for it. We can look at creating the menu items first.

Creating and Editing Menu Resources

Menus are defined external to the program code in a **resource file** and the specification of the menu is referred to as a **resource**. There are several other kinds of resources that you can include in your application, such as dialogs, toolbars and icons. You will be seeing more on these as we extend our application.

Having a menu defined in a resource allows the physical appearance of the menu to be changed without affecting the code that processes menu events. For example, you could change your menu items from English to French, Norwegian, or whatever, without having to modify or recompile the program code. The code to handle the message created when the user selects a menu item does not need to be concerned with how the menu looks, only with the fact that it was selected. Of course, if you add items to the menu, you will need to add some code for each of them to ensure that they actually do something!

The Sketcher program already has a menu, which means that it already has a resource file. We can access the resource file contents for the Sketcher program by selecting the ResourceView in the workspace window, or if you are have the FileView displayed, by double-clicking **Sketcher.rc**. This will switch you to the ResourceView and display the resources. If you expand the menu resource, you'll see that there are two menus defined, indicated by the identifiers **IDR_MAINFRAME** and **IDR_SKETCHTYPE**. The first of these applies when there are no documents open in the application and the second when we have one or more documents open. MFC uses the prefix **IDR_** to identify a menu resource for a complete menu.

We are only going to be modifying the second menu which has the identifier **IDR_SKETCHTYPE**. We don't need to look at **IDR_MAINFRAME** as our new menu items will only be relevant when a document is open. You can invoke a resource editor for the menu by double-clicking its menu ID. If you do this for **IDR_SKETCHTYPE**, you'll see the window shown below:

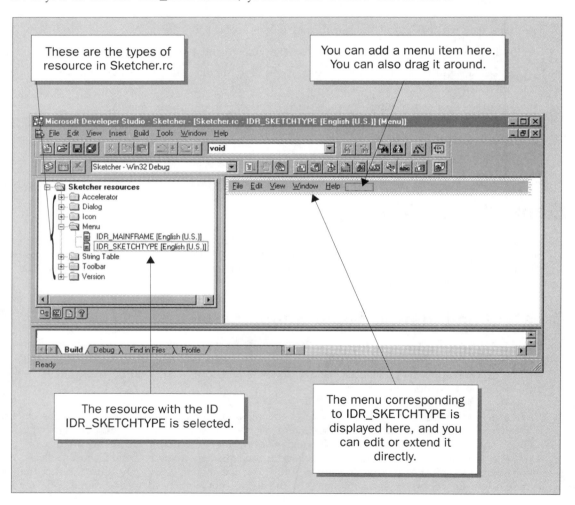

Adding a Menu Item to the Menu Bar

To add a new menu item, you can just click on the empty menu box to select it and type in the menu name. If you insert **&** in front of a letter in the menu item, the letter will be identified as a shortcut key to invoke the menu from the keyboard. Type the first menu item as E&lement. This will select l as the shortcut letter, so we can invoke the menu item by typing *Alt-l*. We can't use E because it's already used by Edit. As soon as you begin typing, the menu item properties box will appear as shown below:

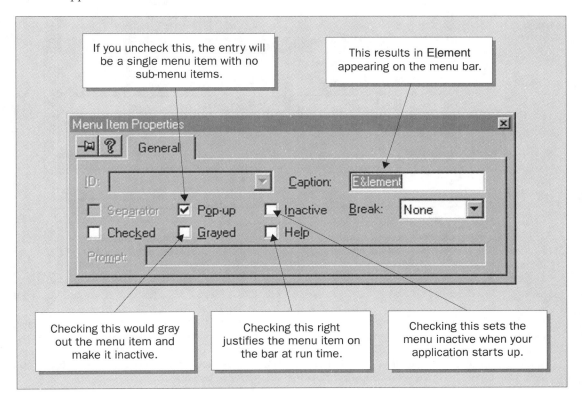

If you uncheck this, the entry will be a single menu item with no sub-menu items.

This results in Element appearing on the menu bar.

Checking this would gray out the menu item and make it inactive.

Checking this right justifies the menu item on the bar at run time.

Checking this sets the menu inactive when your application starts up.

Properties are simply parameters that determine how the menu item will appear and behave. Since we want to create a menu containing the list of elements that we'll have in our program, we can leave everything as it is, so you can just press *Enter*. No ID is necessary for a pop-up menu item, since selecting it just displays the menu beneath. Note that you get a new blank menu box for the first item of the new menu, as well as one on the main menu bar.

It would be better if the Element menu appeared between the View and Window items, so place the cursor on the Element menu item and, with the left mouse button pressed, drag it to a position between the View and Window items. Then release the left mouse button. After positioning the new Element menu item, the next step is to add items on the menu beneath it.

Adding Items to the Element Menu

Select the first, currently empty, item in the Element menu by clicking on it, then type &Line as the Caption: in the Menu Item Properties dialog, as shown below:

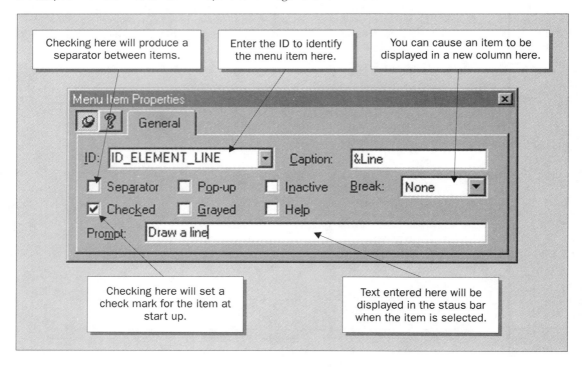

The properties modify the appearance of the menu item and also specify the ID of the message that will be passed to your program when the menu item is selected. Because this item is part of a pop-up menu, it is not identified as a pop-up item by default, although you could make it another pop-up with a further list of items, in which case you would need to check the Pop-up box. Don't you love the way pop-ups pop up all over the place!

Defining Menu Item Properties

You can enter an ID for the menu item in the ID: box, as shown above. If you don't, one will be generated for you automatically, based on the menu item name. Sometimes, though, it's convenient to specify the ID yourself, such as when the generated ID is too long or its meaning is unclear. If you do choose to define your own ID, you should use the MFC convention of prefixing it with **ID_** to indicate that it's a command ID for a menu item. We can use the same format for each of the Element menu item IDs, in this case, starting the ID with **ID_ELEMENT_**. The ID will identify the message created when the user selects the menu item, so you'll see it as an entry in the message map for the class handling the messages from the Element menu items.

In the Prompt: box, you can enter a text string that will appear in the status bar of your application when the menu item is highlighted. If you leave it blank, nothing is displayed in the status bar. We want the default element, selected in the application at start up, to be a line, so we can check the Checked box to get a check mark against the menu item to indicate this. We'll have to remember to add code to update check marks for the menu items when a different selection is made. The Break: entry can alter the appearance of the pop-up by shifting the item into a new column. We don't need that here, so leave it as it is. Press *Enter* to move to the next menu item.

Modifying Existing Menu Items

If you think that you may have made a mistake and want to change an existing menu item, or even if you just want to verify that you set the properties correctly, it's very easy to go back to an item. Just double-click the item you are interested in and the properties box for that item will be displayed. You can then change the properties in any way that you want and press *Enter* when you are done. If the item you want to access is in a menu that is not displayed, just click on the item on the menu bar for the pop-up to be displayed.

Completing the Menu

Now go through the remaining Element menu items we need, &Rectangle, &Circle and Cur&ve. Of course, none of these should have the Checked box checked. We can't use C as the hotkey for the last item, as hotkeys must be unique and we have already assigned C to the menu item for a circle. You can use the default IDs **ID_ELEMENT_RECTANGLE**, **ID_ELEMENT_CIRCLE** and **ID_ELEMENT_CURVE** for these.

We also need a Color menu on the menu bar, with items for Black, Red, Green and Blue. You can create these, starting at the empty menu entry on the menu bar, using the same procedure that we just went through. Set Black as checked, as that will be the default color. You can use the default IDs **ID_COLOR_BLACK**, etc., as the IDs for the menu items. You can also add the status bar prompt for each. Once you have finished that, if you drag Color so that it just to the right of Element, the menu should appear as shown below:

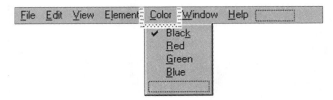

Note that you need to take care not to use the same letter more than once as a shortcut in the pop-up, or in the main menu for that matter. There is no check made as you create new menu items, but if you click the right mouse button with the cursor on the menu when you have edited it, you'll get a pop-up which contains an item Check Mnemonics. Selecting this will verify that you have no duplicate shortcut keys. It's a good idea to do this every time you edit a menu because it's very easy to create duplicates by accident.

That completes extending the menu for elements and colors. Don't forget to save the file to make sure that the additions are safely stored away. Next, we need to decide in which classes we want to deal with messages from our menu items and add member functions to handle each of the messages. For that, we'll use the ClassWizard.

457

Using ClassWizard for Menu Messages

You're spoilt for choice for starting ClassWizard. You can invoke ClassWizard from where we are in the Resource Editor for menus by right-clicking in the right-hand pane and selecting ClassWizard... from the pop-up. Alternatively, you can enter *Ctrl+W* from the keyboard, or you can click on the icon shown above, as we saw in Chapter 12. You'll see the ClassWizard window as shown below:

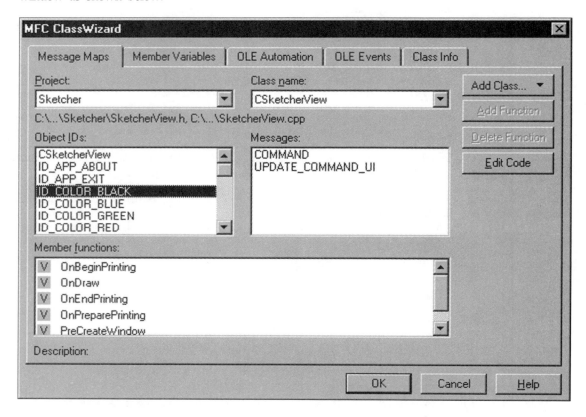

We'll concentrate on **Message Maps**, so ignore the other tabs for the moment. The contents of the five boxes on this tab are fairly self-explanatory:

Control	Use
Projects:	Identifies the current project.
Class name:	Identifies the class that we are currently working on.
Object IDs:	Lists the IDs for which we can add handlers to the current class.

Table Continued on Following Page

Control	Use
Messages:	Identifies the message types available for a particular object ID. (In the screenshot opposite, as we have selected a command ID, we have the option of choosing COMMAND or UPDATE_COMMAND_UI. We'll see the difference between these two message types later in this chapter.)
Member functions:	Lists the message handlers already defined in the current class.

You can see that the IDs we assigned to our menu items appear in the Object IDs: box. If you change to any of the other classes in the program by selecting from the drop-down list in the Class name: box, you'll see that the IDs for our new menu items appear there too. Because the menu items result in command messages, we can choose to handle them in any of the classes that are currently defined in the application. So how do we decide where we should process the messages?

Choosing a Class to Handle Menu Messages

Before we can decide which class should handle the messages for the menu items we have added, we must know what we want to do with the messages, so let's consider that.

We have two basic possibilities for handling the setting of a color and the selection of an element type - setting them by view or by document. We could set them by view, in which case, if there is more than one view of a document, each view will have its own color and element set. This would mean that we might draw a red circle in one view and when we switch to another view we could find that we are drawing a blue rectangle. This could be rather confusing. It would be better, perhaps, to have the color and element selection apply per document. We can then switch from one view to another and continue drawing the same elements in the same color. The only difference between the views may be the scale at which the document is displayed.

This suggests that we should store the current color and element in the document object. These could then be accessed by any view object associated with the document object. Of course, if we had more than one document active, each document would have its own color and element type settings. It would, therefore, be sensible to handle the messages for our new menu items in the **CSketcherDoc** class and to store information about the current selections in an object of this class.

Creating Menu Message Functions

Switch the class shown in the ClassWizard Class name: box to CSketcherDoc and click on ID_COLOR_BLACK in the Object IDs: list. The window should appear as shown on the following page.

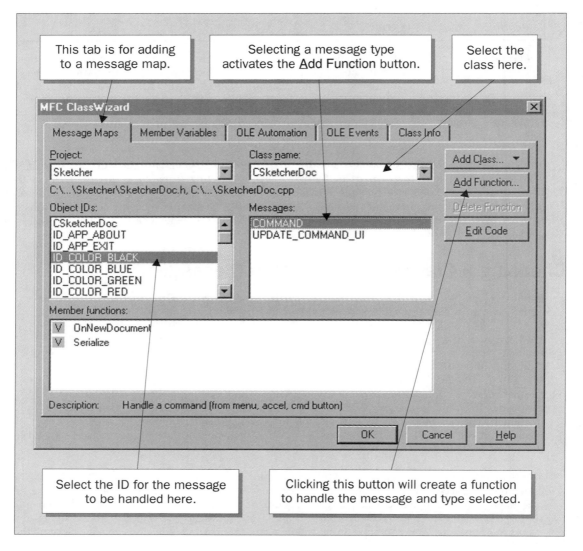

This tab is for adding to a message map.

Selecting a message type activates the Add Function button.

Select the class here.

Select the ID for the message to be handled here.

Clicking this button will create a function to handle the message and type selected.

The Messages: box in the window above shows the two kinds of message that can arise, associated with a particular menu ID. They serve distinct purposes in dealing with a menu item:

Message	Issued
COMMAND	When a particular menu item has been selected. The handler should provide the action appropriate to the menu item being selected, for example, setting the current color in the document object.
UPDATE_COMMAND_UI	When the menu should be updated, for example, checked or unchecked, depending on its status. This message occurs before a pop-up menu is displayed.

The way these work is quite simple. When you click on a menu item in the menu bar, an UPDATE_COMMAND_UI message is sent for each item in that menu before the menu is displayed. This provides the opportunity to do any necessary updating of the menu items' properties. When these messages have been handled and any changes to the items' properties have been completed, the menu is drawn. When you then click on one of the items in the menu, a COMMAND message for that menu item is sent. We'll deal with the COMMAND messages for now, and come back to the UPDATE_COMMAND_UI messages a little later in this chapter.

With the ID_COLOR_BLACK object highlighted and COMMAND selected in the Messages: box, click on the button Add Function.... The window will be as shown below:

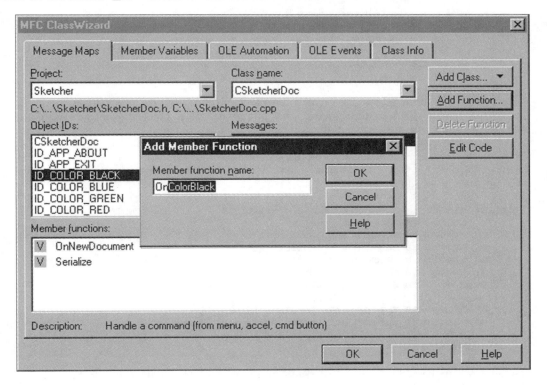

Here, the ClassWizard is about to generate a handler function in the class `CSketcherDoc` with the name shown. You have an opportunity to alter the function name, but this is a good choice so click on the OK button to accept it. This function will be added to the Member functions: box and the message ID and the type of message that this handler will deal with will also be shown.

In the same way, add COMMAND message handlers for the other color menu IDs and all the element menu IDs. You can create each of the handler functions for the menu items with just four mouse clicks.

ClassWizard will have added the handlers to the class definition, which will now look as you will see on the next page.

```
class CSketcherDoc : public CDocument
{
...
    protected:

    // Generated message map functions
    protected:
        //{{AFX_MSG(CSketcherDoc)
        afx_msg void OnColorBlack();
        afx_msg void OnColorBlue();
        afx_msg void OnColorGreen();
        afx_msg void OnColorRed();
        afx_msg void OnElementCircle();
        afx_msg void OnElementCurve();
        afx_msg void OnElementLine();
        afx_msg void OnElementRectangle();
        //}}AFX_MSG
        DECLARE_MESSAGE_MAP()
};
```

A declaration has been added for each of the handlers that we have specified in the ClassWizard dialog. Each of the function declarations has been prefixed with **afx_msg** to indicate that they are message handlers.

The ClassWizard also automatically updates the message map in your **CSketcherDoc** class with the new message handlers. If you take a look in the file **SketcherDoc.cpp**, you'll see the message map is as shown below:

```
BEGIN_MESSAGE_MAP(CSketcherDoc, CDocument)
    //{{AFX_MSG_MAP(CSketcherDoc)
    ON_COMMAND(ID_COLOR_BLACK, OnColorBlack)
    ON_COMMAND(ID_COLOR_BLUE, OnColorBlue)
    ON_COMMAND(ID_COLOR_GREEN, OnColorGreen)
    ON_COMMAND(ID_COLOR_RED, OnColorRed)
    ON_COMMAND(ID_ELEMENT_CIRCLE, OnElementCircle)
    ON_COMMAND(ID_ELEMENT_CURVE, OnElementCurve)
    ON_COMMAND(ID_ELEMENT_LINE, OnElementLine)
    ON_COMMAND(ID_ELEMENT_RECTANGLE, OnElementRectangle)
    //}}AFX_MSG_MAP
END_MESSAGE_MAP()
```

The ClassWizard has added an **ON_COMMAND()** macro for each of the handlers that you have identified. This associates the handler name with the message ID, so, for example, the member function **OnColorBlack()** will be called to service a COMMAND message for the menu item with the ID **ID_COLOR_BLACK**.

Each of the handlers generated by ClassWizard is just a skeleton. For example, take a look at the code provided for **OnColorBlack()**. This is also defined in the file **SketcherDoc.cpp**, so you can scroll down to find it, or go directly to it by switching to the ClassView, and double-clicking the function name after expanding the tree for the class **CSketcherDoc** (make sure that the file is saved first):

```
void CSketcherDoc::OnColorBlack()
{
    // TODO: Add your command handler code here
}
```

As you can see, the handler takes no arguments and returns nothing. It also does nothing at the moment, but this is hardly surprising since ClassWizard has no way of knowing what you want to do with these messages.

Coding Menu Message Functions

Let's consider what we should do with the COMMAND messages for our new menu items. We said earlier that we want to record the current element and current color in the document, so we need a data member added to the **CSketcherDoc** class for each of these.

Adding Members to Store Color and Element Mode

You can add the data members that we need to the Attributes section of the class definition, just by editing the class definition directly. Display the class definition by double-clicking the class name in the ClassView, then insert the code shown below:

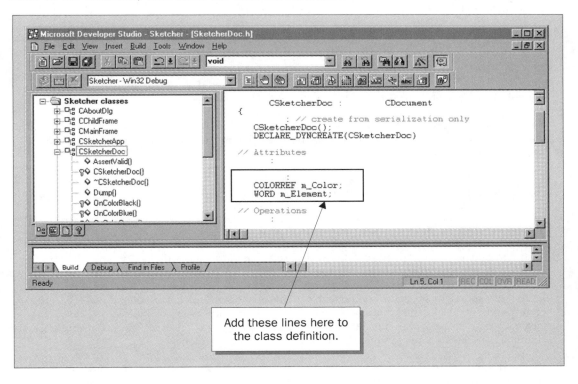

Add these lines here to
the class definition.

The three additional lines are shown in the box. The new data members are **m_Color** and **m_Element**. We have prefixed their names with **m_** to show that they are members of a class. **m_Element** is declared to be of type **WORD**, which is equivalent to **unsigned int**. We'll see why this is a good choice when we come to look into how to save a document in a file. The type for **m_Color** is **COLORREF**, a Windows defined type that is used to represent color values. It is a 32-bit integer. We'll be able to use this value directly to set the color when we get to draw elements in a view. Both the new data members are **protected** because there is no need for them to be **public**. As we saw when we discussed classes, data members should not be declared as **public** unless it is absolutely necessary, as this undermines the security of the class.

You could also have added these data members by right-clicking the class name in ClassView and selecting Add Variable... from the pop-up. You can add the information necessary to define these data members in the dialog box that is displayed. Of course, if you want to add comments - and it's a good idea to do so - you must still go back to the class definition to insert them.

Initializing the New Class Data Members

We need to decide how to represent a color and an element. We could just set them to numeric values, but this would introduce 'magic numbers' into the program, the significance of which would be less than obvious to anyone else looking at the code. A better way would be to define a set of constants that we can use to set values for the two member variables we have added. In this way, we can use a standard mnemonic to refer to a given type of element. We could define the element types with the following statements:

```
// Element type definitions
// Each type value must be unique
const WORD LINE = 101U;
const WORD RECTANGLE = 102U;
const WORD CIRCLE = 103U;
const WORD CURVE = 104U;
```

The constants initializing the element types are arbitrary unsigned integers. You can choose different values if you like, as long as they are all distinct. If we want to add further types in the future, it will obviously be very easy to add definitions here.

For the color values, it would be a good idea if we used constant variables that are initialized with the values that Windows uses to define the color in question. We can do this with the following lines of code:

```
// Color values for drawing
const COLORREF BLACK = RGB(0,0,0);
const COLORREF RED = RGB(255,0,0);
const COLOREF GREEN = RGB(0,255,0);
const COLOREF BLUE = RGB(0,0,255);
```

Each constant is initialized by **RGB()**, which is a standard macro defined in the file **Wingdi.h** included as part of **Windows.h**. The three arguments define the red, green and blue components of the color value, respectively. Each parameter is an integer between 0 and 255, where these limits correspond to no color component and the maximum color component. **RGB(0,0,0)** corresponds to black, since there are no components of red, green, or blue. **RGB(255,0,0)** create a color value with a maximum red component, and no green or blue contribution. Other colors can be created by combining red, blue and green components.

We need somewhere to put these constants, so let's create a new header file and call it **OurConstants.h**. You can create a new file by using the File/New menu option in Developer Studio, then entering the constant definitions as shown below:

```
//Definitions of constants

#ifndef OurConstants_h
#define OurConstants_h

    // Element type definitions
    // Each type value must be unique
```

```
        const WORD LINE = 101U;
        const WORD RECTANGLE = 102U;
        const WORD CIRCLE = 103U;
        const WORD CURVE = 104U;
        /////////////////////////////////

        // Color values for drawing
        const COLORREF BLACK = RGB(0,0,0);
        const COLORREF RED = RGB(255,0,0);
        const COLORREF GREEN = RGB(0,255,0);
        const COLORREF BLUE = RGB(0,0,255);
        /////////////////////////////////

    #endif
```

As you will recall, the preprocessor **#ifndef** is there to ensure that the definitions are not included more than once. The block of statements down to **#endif** will only be included if **OurConstants_h** has not been defined previously.

After saving the file, you can add the following **#include** statement to the beginning of the file **Sketcher.h**:

```
    #include "OurConstants.h"
```

Sketcher.h is included into the other **.cpp** files in the program so our constants will be available to any of them. You can verify that our new constants are now part of the project by expanding Globals in the ClassView. You'll see the names of the color and element types that have been added, along with the global variable, **theApp**.

Modifying the Class Constructor

It's important that we make sure that the data members we have added to the **CSketcherDoc** class are initialized when a document is created. You can add the code to do this to the class constructor as shown below:

```
    CSketcherDoc::CSketcherDoc()
    {
        // TODO: add one-time construction code here
        m_Element = LINE;     // Set initial element type
        m_Color = BLACK;      // Set initial drawing color
    }
```

The element type is initialized with **LINE**, and the color with **BLACK**, consistent with the initial check marks that we specified for the menus.

Now we are ready to add the code for the handler functions that we created. We can do this with the ClassView. Just click on the name of the first handler function, OnColorBlack(). We just need to add one line to the function, so the code for it becomes:

```
    void CSketcherDoc::OnColorBlack()
    {
        m_Color = BLACK;             // Set the drawing color to black
    }
```

The only job that the handler has to do is to set the appropriate color. In the interests of conciseness, the new line replaces the comment provided by ClassWizard. You can go through and add one line to each of the Color menu handlers. The element menu handlers are much the same. The handler for the Element/Line menu item will be:

```
void CSketcherDoc::OnElementLine()
{
    m_Element = LINE;            // Set element type as a line
}
```

With this model, it's not too difficult to write the other handlers for the Element menu. That's eight message handlers completed. Let's rebuild the example and see how it works.

Running the Extended Example

Assuming that there are no typos, the compile and link should run without error. When you run the program you should see the window shown below:

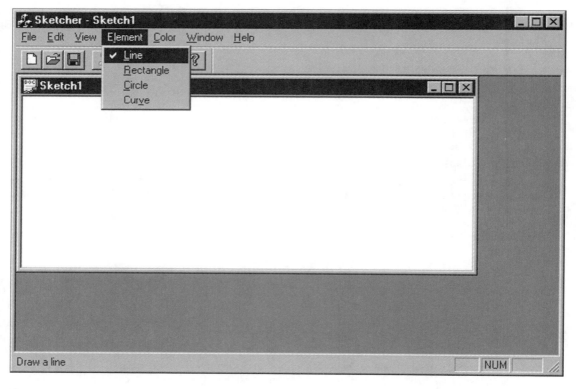

Our new menus are in place on the menu bar and you can see that the items we have added in the Element menu are all there, as is the message in the status bar that we provided in the properties box. You could also verify that *Alt+C* and *Alt+I* work as well. The thing that doesn't work is the check mark for the currently selected color and element. It remains firmly stuck to the initial default. Let's look at how we can fix that.

Adding Message Handlers to Update the User Interface

To set the check mark correctly for the new menus, we need to add the second kind of message handler, UPDATE_COMMAND_UI or update command user interface message handlers for each of the new menu items. This sort of message handler is specifically aimed at updating the menu item properties before the item is displayed.

Let's go back to the ClassWizard by clicking the icon. Make sure that the Class name: box shows CSketcherDoc first then select ID_COLOR_BLACK in the Object IDs: box and UPDATE_COMMAND_UI in the Messages: box. You'll be able to click on the Add Function... button and see the window shown below:

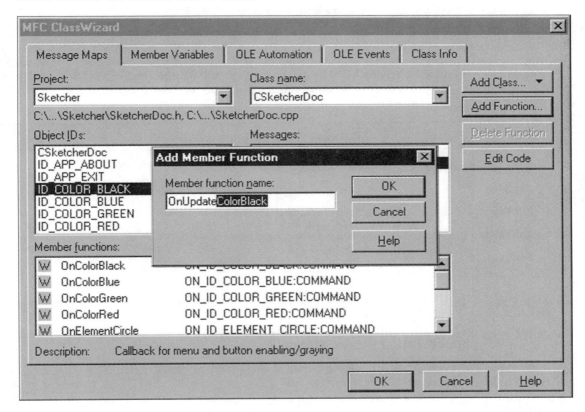

You can see the description of the purpose of the function below the Member functions: box. This description fits our requirement precisely. The name for an update function has been generated, **OnUpdateColorBlack()** and, since this seems a reasonable name for the function we want, click on the OK button and have ClassWizard generate it. As well as generating the skeleton function definition in **SketcherDoc.cpp**, its declaration will be added to the class definition. An entry for it will also be made in the message map:

```
ON_UPDATE_COMMAND_UI(ID_COLOR_BLACK, OnUpdateColorBlack)
```

467

This uses the macro **ON_UPDATE_COMMAND_UI()** which identifies the function you have just generated as the handler to deal with update messages corresponding to the ID shown. You can now add command update handlers for each of the other menu items.

Coding a Command Update Handler

You can access the code for the handler, **OnUpdateColorBlack()**, by selecting the appropriate line in the Member functions: box, and then clicking the Edit Code button. This is the skeleton code for the function:

```
void CSketcherDoc::OnUpdateColorBlack(CCmdUI* pCmdUI)
{
    // TODO: Add your command update UI handler code here
}
```

The argument passed to the handler is a pointer to an object of the **CCmdUI** class. This is an MFC class that is only used with update handlers. The pointer points to an object that identifies the particular menu item originating the update message and can be used to access members of the class object. The class has five member functions that act on user interface items. The purpose of each of these are:

Method	Purpose
ContinueRouting()	Pass the message on to the next priority handler.
Enable()	Enable or disable the relevant interface item.
SetCheck()	Set a check mark for the relevant interface item.
SetRadio()	Set a button in a radio group on or off.
SetText()	Set the text for the relevant interface item.

We'll use the third function, **SetCheck()** as that seems to do what we want. The function is declared in the **CCmdUI** class as:

```
virtual void SetCheck(int nCheck = 1);
```

This function will set a menu item as checked if the argument passed is **1** and set it unchecked if the argument passed is **0**. The parameter has a default value of **1**, so if you just want to set a check mark for a menu item regardless, you just call this function without specifying an argument.

In our case, we want to set a menu item as checked if the current color is the color that corresponds to the menu item. We can, therefore, write the update handler for **OnUpdateColorBlack()** as:

```
void CSketcherDoc::OnUpdateColorBlack(CCmdUI* pCmdUI)
{
    // Set menu item Checked if the current color is black
    pCmdUI->SetCheck(m_Color==BLACK);
}
```

The first part of the statement, **pCmdUI->SetCheck**, calls the **SetCheck()** function of the Color/Black menu item, while the comparison, **m_Color==BLACK** results in either **1**, if **m_Color** is **BLACK**, or **0** otherwise. The effect, therefore, is to check the menu item only if the current color stored in **m_Color** is **BLACK**, which is precisely what we want.

Since the update handlers for all the menu items in a menu are always called before the menu is displayed, you can code the other handlers in the same way to ensure that only the item corresponding to the current color (or the current element) will be checked:

```
void CSketcherDoc::OnUpdateColorRed(CCmdUI* pCmdUI)
{
    // Set menu item Checked if the current color is red
    pCmdUI->SetCheck(m_Color==RED);
}

void CSketcherDoc::OnUpdateColorGreen(CCmdUI* pCmdUI)
{
    // Set menu item Checked if the current color is green
    pCmdUI->SetCheck(m_Color==GREEN);
}

void CSketcherDoc::OnUpdateColorBlue(CCmdUI* pCmdUI)
{
    // Set menu item Checked if the current color is blue
    pCmdUI->SetCheck(m_Color==BLUE);
}
```

A typical Element menu item update handler will be coded as:

```
void CSketcherDoc::OnUpdateElementCircle(CCmdUI* pCmdUI)
{
    // Set Checked if the current element is a circle
    pCmdUI->SetCheck(m_Element==CIRCLE);
}
```

You can now code all the other update handlers in a similar manner:

```
void CSketcherDoc::OnUpdateElementLine(CCmdUI* pCmdUI)
{
    // Set Checked if the current element is a line
    pCmdUI->SetCheck(m_Element==LINE);
}
```

```
void CSketcherDoc::OnUpdateElementRectangle(CCmdUI* pCmdUI)
{
    // Set Checked if the current element is a rectangle
    pCmdUI->SetCheck(m_Element==RECTANGLE);
}

void CSketcherDoc::OnUpdateElementCurve(CCmdUI* pCmdUI)
{
    // Set Checked if the current element is a curve
    pCmdUI->SetCheck(m_Element==CURVE);
}
```

Once you get the idea, it's easy, isn't it?

Exercising the Update Handlers

When you've added the code for all the update handlers, you can build and execute the Sketcher application again. Now, when you change a color or an element type selection, this will be reflected in the menu, as shown below:

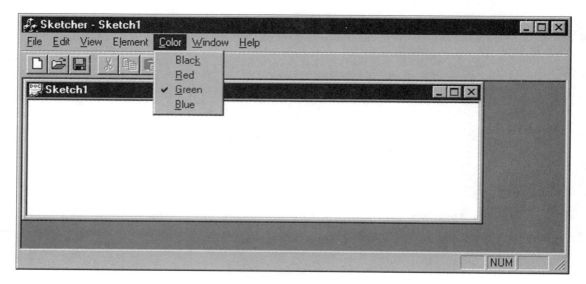

We have completed all the code that we need for our menu items. Make sure that you have saved everything. These days, toolbars are a must in any Windows program of consequence, so we should now take a look at how we can add toolbar buttons to support our new menu.

Adding Toolbar Buttons

Select the ResourceView and extend the toolbar resource. You'll see that it has the same ID as the main menu, **IDR_MAINFRAME**. If you double-click this ID, the Resource Editor window will be as shown on the following page:

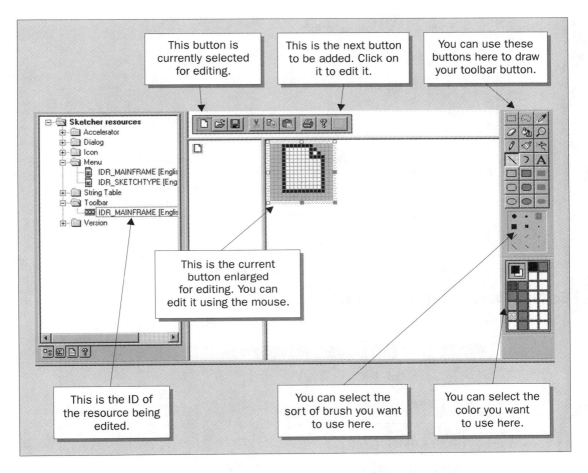

A toolbar button is a 16x16 array of pixels which contains a pictorial representation of the function it represents. You can see above that the resource editor provides an enlarged view of a toolbar button so that you can see and manipulate individual pixels. If you click on the new button at the left-hand end of the row as indicated, you'll be able to draw this button. Before starting the editing, drag the new button about half a button width to the right. It will separate from its neighbor on the left to start a new block.

We should keep the toolbar button blocks in the same sequence as the items on the menu bar, so we'll create the element type selection buttons first. We'll be using the following editing buttons provided by the resource editor:

 Pencil for drawing individual pixels

 Eraser for erasing individual pixels

 Fill an area with the current color

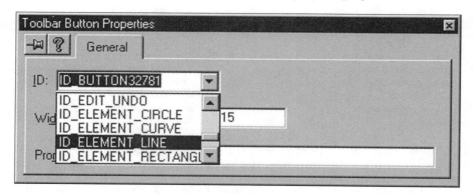	Zoom the view of the button
	Draw a rectangle
	Draw an ellipse
	Draw a curve

Make sure that the black color is selected and use the pencil tool to draw a diagonal line in the enlarged image of the new toolbar button. In fact, if you want it a bit bigger, you can use the zoom editing button to enlarge it up to eight times its actual size. If you make a mistake, you can change to the eraser editing button, but you need to make sure that the color selected corresponds to the background color for the button you are editing. You can also erase individual pixels by clicking on them using the right mouse button, but again you need to be sure that the background color is set correctly when you do this. To set the background color, just click on the appropriate color using the right mouse button. Once you are happy with what you have drawn, the next step is to edit the toolbar button properties.

Editing Toolbar Button Properties

Double-clicking your new button in the toolbar will bring up its properties window:

The properties box will show a default ID for the button, but we want to associate the button with the menu item Element/Line that we have already defined, so select ID_ELEMENT_LINE from the drop-down box. You will find that this will also add the same prompt to appear in the status bar because the prompt is recorded along with the ID. You can press *Enter* to complete the button definition.

You can now go on to designing the other three element buttons. You can use the rectangle editing button to draw a rectangle and the ellipse button to draw a circle. You can draw a curve using the pencil to set individual pixels, or use the curve button. You need to associate each button with the ID corresponding to the equivalent menu item that we defined earlier.

Now add the buttons for the colors. You should also drag the first button for selecting a drawing color to the right, so that it starts a new group of buttons. You could keep the color buttons very simple and just color the whole button with the color it selects. You can do this by selecting the appropriate foreground color, then selecting the fill editing button and clicking on the enlarged button image. Again you need to use **ID_COLOR_BLACK**, **ID_COLOR_RED** etc. as IDs for the buttons. The toolbar editing window should look like that shown below:

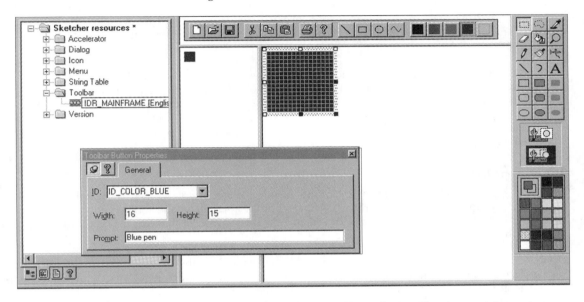

That's all we need for the moment, so save the resource file and give Sketcher another spin.

Exercising the Toolbar Buttons

Build the application once again and execute it. You should see the application window shown below:

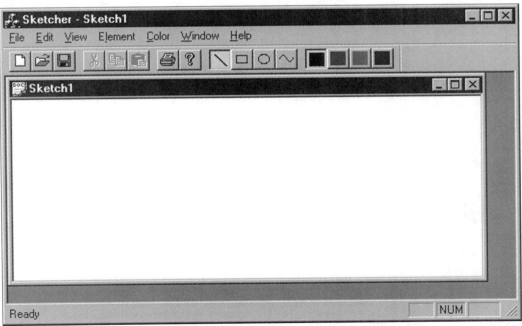

473

There are some amazing things happening here. The toolbar buttons that we added already reflect the default settings that we defined for the new menu items. If you let the cursor linger over one of the new buttons, the prompt for the button will appear in the status bar. The new buttons work as a complete substitute for the menu items and any new selection made, using either the menu or the toolbar, is reflected by showing the toolbar button depressed, as well as the check against the menu item.

If you close the document view window, Sketch1, you'll see that our toolbar buttons are automatically grayed and disabled. If you open a new document window, they will be automatically enabled once again. You can also try dragging the toolbar with the cursor. You can move it to either side of the application window, or have it free floating. You can also enable or disable it through the View/Toolbar menu option. We got all this without writing a single additional line of code.

Adding Tooltips

There is one further tweak that we can add to our toolbar buttons which is remarkably easy - adding **tooltips**. A tooltip is a small box that appears adjacent to the toolbar button when you let the cursor linger on the button. The tooltip contains a text string which is an additional clue as to the purpose of the toolbar button.

To add tooltips, select the ResourceView and, after expanding the resource list, double-click on the String Table resource. This contains the IDs and prompt strings associated with menu items and toolbar buttons. You should see the IDs for the menus that we added earlier. Double-click on ID_ELEMENT_LINE to cause the String Properties dialog to be displayed. To add a tooltip, you just need to add \n followed by the tooltip text to the end of the prompt text. For this ID, you could add \nLine, for example.

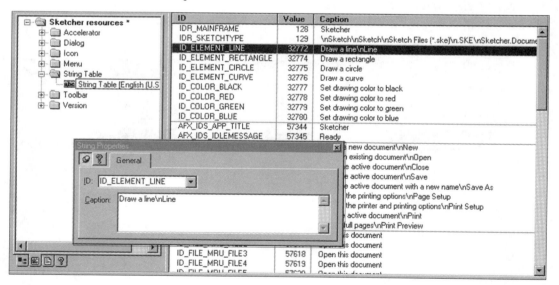

If you press *Enter*, the new prompt string with the tooltip text appended will be recorded against the ID. You can now go through the other menu IDs for elements and colors adding similar tooltips.

That's all you have to do. After saving the String Table resource, you can now rebuild the application and execute it. Placing the cursor over one of the new toolbar buttons will cause the tooltip to be displayed after a second or two.

Summary

In this chapter, you've learned how MFC connects a message with a class member function to process it, and you have written your first message handlers. Much of the work in writing a Windows program is writing message handlers, so it's important to have a good grasp of what happens in the process. When we get to consider other message handlers, you'll see that the process for adding them is the same.

You have also extended the standard menu and the toolbar in the AppWizard-generated program which provides a good base for the application code that we will add in the next chapter. Although there is no functionality under the covers yet, the menu and toolbar operation looks very professional, courtesy of the AppWizard-generated framework and ClassWizard.

The important points that we have seen in this chapter are:

> ▶ MFC defines the message handlers in a class in a message map which appears in the **.cpp** file for the class.

> ▶ Command messages which arise from menus and toolbars can be handled in any class that is derived from **CCmdTarget**. This includes the application class, the frame and child frame window classes, the document class and the view class.

> ▶ Messages other than command messages can only be handled in a class derived from **CWnd**. This includes frame window and view classes, but not application or document classes.

> ▶ MFC has a predefined sequence for searching the classes in your program to find a message handler for a command message.

> ▶ You should always use ClassWizard to add message handlers to your program.

> ▶ The physical appearance of menus and toolbars are defined in resource files, which are edited by the built-in resource editor within the Developer Studio.

> ▶ Items in a menu that can result in command messages are identified by a symbolic constant with the prefix **ID_**. These IDs are used to associate a handlers with the message from the menu item.

> ▶ To associate a toolbar button with a particular menu item, you give it the same ID as that of the menu item.

> ▶ To add a tooltip for a toolbar button corresponding to a menu item, you add the tooltip text to the entry for the ID for the menu item in the string table resource. The tooltip text is separated from the menu prompt text by **\n**.

In the next chapter, you'll be adding the necessary code to draw elements in a view and using the menus and toolbar buttons that we have created here to select what is to be drawn and in which color. This is where the Sketcher program begins to live up to its name.

Drawing in a Window

In this chapter, we'll add some meat to our Sketcher application. We'll concentrate on understanding how you get graphical output displayed in the application window. Although we'll be able to draw all but one of the elements for which we have added menu items, we'll leave the problem of how to store them in a document until the next chapter. In this chapter, you will learn:

- What coordinate systems Windows provides for drawing in a window
- What a device context is and why it is necessary
- How and when your program draws in a window
- How to define handlers for mouse messages
- How to define your own shape classes
- How to program the mouse to draw your shapes in a window
- How to get your program to capture the mouse

Basics of Drawing in a Window

Before we go into drawing using MFC, it's useful to get an idea of what is happening under the covers of the Windows operating system. Like any other operation under Windows, writing to a window on your display screen is achieved through using Windows API functions. There is slightly more to it than that though - the way Windows works does complicate the situation somewhat.

For a start, you can't just write to a window and forget it. There are many events that occur which mean that you must redraw the window, for instance, if the user resizes the window that you are drawing in, or if part of your window is exposed by the user moving another one

Fortunately, you don't need to worry about the details of such occurrences because Windows actually manages all these events for you, but it does mean that you can only write permanent data to a window when your application receives a specific Windows message requesting that you do so. It also means that you need to be able to reconstruct everything that you have drawn in the window at any time.

When all, or part of a window needs to be redrawn, Windows sends a **WM_PAINT** message to your application. This is intercepted by MFC, which will then pass the message to a function member of one of your classes. You'll see how to handle this a little later in this chapter.

The Window Client Area

Of course, a window does not have a fixed position on the screen, or even a fixed visible area, because a window can be dragged around using the mouse and resized by dragging its borders, so how do you know where to draw on the screen?

Fortunately, you don't. Because Windows provides you with a consistent way of drawing in a window, you don't have to worry about where it is on the screen, otherwise drawing in a window would be inordinately complicated. Windows does this by maintaining a coordinate system for the client area of a window that is local to the window. It always uses the top left corner of the client area as its reference point. All points within the client area are defined relative to this point, as shown below:

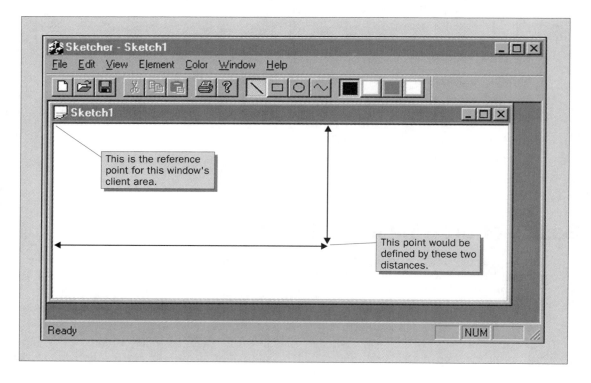

The horizontal and vertical distances of a point from the top left corner of the client area will always be the same, regardless of where the window is on the screen. Of course, Windows will need to keep track of where the window is, and when you draw something at a point in the client area, it will need to figure out where that actually is on the screen.

The Windows Graphical Device Interface

The final constraint that Windows imposes is that you don't actually write data to the screen in any direct sense. All output to your display screen is graphical, regardless of whether it is lines and circles, or text. Windows insists that you define this output using the **Graphical Device Interface** (**GDI**). The GDI enables you to program graphical output independently of the hardware on which it will be displayed, which means that your program will work on different machines with different display hardware. In addition to display screens, the Windows GDI also supports printers and plotters, so outputting data to a printer or a plotter involves essentially the same mechanisms as displaying information on the screen.

What is a Device Context?

When you want to draw something on a graphical output device such as the display screen, you must use a **device context**. A device context is a data structure that is defined by Windows and which contains information that allows Windows to translate your output requests, which are in the form of device independent GDI function calls, into actions on the particular physical output device being used. A pointer to a device context is obtained by calling a Windows API function.

A device context provides you with a choice of coordinate systems called **mapping modes**, which will be automatically converted to client coordinates. You can also alter many parameters that affect the output to a device context by calling GDI functions. Such parameters are called **attributes**. Examples of attributes that you can change are the drawing color, the background color, the line thickness to be used when drawing and the font for text output. There are also GDI functions that will provide information about the physical device you are working with. For example, you may need to be certain that the display on the computer executing your program can support 256 colors, or that a printer can support the output of bitmaps.

Mapping Modes

Each **mapping mode** in a device context is identified by an ID in a similar manner to what you have seen with Windows messages. Each symbol has the prefix **MM_** to indicate that it defines a mapping mode. The mapping modes provided by Windows are:

Mapping Mode	Definition
MM_TEXT	A logical unit is one device pixel with positive x from left to right, and positive y from top to bottom of the window client area.
MM_LOENGLISH	A logical unit is 0.01 inches with positive x from left to right, and positive y from the top of the client area upwards.
MM_HIENGLISH	A logical unit is 0.001 inches with the x and y directions as in MM_LOENGLISH.
MM_LOMETRIC	A logical unit is 0.1 millimeters with the x and y directions as in MM_LOENGLISH.

Table Continued on Following Page

Mapping Mode	Definition
MM_HIMETRIC	A logical unit is 0.01 millimeters with the *x* and *y* directions as in **MM_LOENGLISH**.
MM_ISOTROPIC	A logical unit is of arbitrary length but the same along both the *x* and *y* axes. The *x* and *y* directions are as in **MM_LOENGLISH**.
MM_ANISOTROPIC	This mode is similar to **MM_ISOTROPIC** but allows the length a logical unit on the *x* axis to be different from that of a logical unit on the *y* axis.
MM_TWIPS	A logical unit is 0.05 of a point which is $6.9*10^{-4}$ of an inch. (A **point** is a unit of measurement for fonts). The *x* and *y* directions are as in **MM_LOENGLISH**.

We're not going to be using all of these mapping modes in this book. However, the ones we will be using are a good cross section of those available, so you won't have any problem using the others when you need to.

MM_TEXT is the default mapping mode for a device context. If you need to use a different mapping mode, you'll have to take steps to change it. Note that the direction of the positive *y* axis in the **MM_TEXT** mode is opposite to what you will have seen in high school coordinate geometry, as you can see in the following drawing:

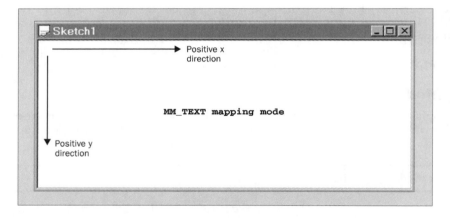

By default, the point at the top left corner of the client area has the coordinates (0,0) in each mapping mode, although it's also possible to move the origin point away from the top left corner of the client area. With the origin at the top left corner in **MM_TEXT** mode, a point 50 pixels from the left border and 100 pixels down from the top of the client area will have the coordinates (50,100). Of course, since the units are pixels, this latter point will be nearer the top left corner of the client area if your monitor is using 800x600 SVGA resolution than if your monitor was working with 640x480 VGA resolution. An object drawn in this mapping mode will be smaller at the SVGA resolution than it is at the VGA resolution.

Coordinates are always 16-bit signed integers in Windows 95, which is the same as in earlier 16-bit versions of Windows. (It's slightly different under Windows NT, but we won't go into that here). This limits the *x* and *y* values to ±32K. The maximum physical size of the total drawing varies with the physical length of a coordinate unit which is determined by the mapping mode.

The directions of the x and y coordinate axes in the **MM_LOENGLISH** mapping mode are the same as in the remaining mapping modes. While positive y is consistent with what you learned in high school, that is y values increase as you move up the screen, **MM_LOENGLISH** is still slightly odd because the origin is at the top left corner of the client area, so for points within the visible client area, y is always negative.

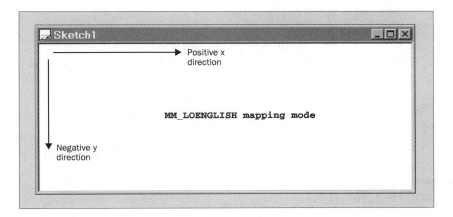

With the **MM_LOENGLISH** mapping mode, the units along the axes are now 0.01 inches, so a point at the position (50,-100) will be half an inch from the left border and one inch down from the top of the client area. An object will be the same size in the client area, regardless of the resolution of the monitor on which it is displayed. If you draw anything in the **MM_LOENGLISH** mode with negative x or positive y coordinates, they will be outside the client area and therefore invisible, since the reference point (0,0) is the top left hand corner by default. It's possible to move the position of the reference point though, by calling the **SetViewportOrg()** Windows API function (or the **SetViewportOrg()** member of the **CDC** MFC class which we will come to shortly).

The Drawing Mechanism in Visual C++

MFC encapsulates the Windows interface to your screen and printer and relieves you of the need to worry about much of the detail involved in programming graphical output. As we saw in the last chapter, your AppWizard generated application will already contain a class derived from the MFC class **CView** that is specifically designed to display document data on the screen.

The View Class in Your Application

AppWizard generated the class **CSketcherView** to display information from a document in the client area of a document window. The class definition includes overrides for several virtual functions, but the one we are particularly interested in here is the function **OnDraw()**, because this: function will be called whenever the client area of the document window needs to be redrawn. This is the function that is called by the application framework when a **WM_PAINT** message is received in your program.

The OnDraw() Member Function

The implementation of the **OnDraw()** member function that is created by AppWizard looks like this:

```
void CSketcherView::OnDraw(CDC* pDC)
{
   CSketcherDoc* pDoc = GetDocument();
   ASSERT_VALID(pDoc);

   // TODO: add draw code for native data here
}
```

A pointer to an object of the class **CDC** is passed to the **OnDraw()** member of the view. This object has member functions that call the Windows API functions that allow you to draw in a device context.

Since you will put all the code to draw the document in this function, the AppWizard has included a declaration for the pointer **pDoc** and initialized it using the function **GetDocument()**, which returns the address of the document object related to the current view:

```
CSketcherDoc* pDoc = GetDocument();
```

GetDocument() actually retrieves the pointer to the document from an inherited data member of the view object, **m_pDocument**, and the function simply casts the pointer stored in this data member to the type corresponding to the document class in the application, **CSketcherDoc**. This is important so that the compiler will have access to the members of the document class that you have defined. Otherwise, the compiler would only be able to access the members of the base class. Thus, **pDoc** will point to the document object in your application associated with the current view and you will be using this to access the data that you will store in the document object when you want to draw it.

The following line,

```
ASSERT_VALID(pDoc);
```

just makes sure that the pointer **pDoc** contains a valid address.

The object of the **CDC** class pointed to by the **pDC** argument that is passed to the **OnDraw()** function is the key to drawing in a window. It provides a device context, plus the tools we need to write graphics and text to it, so we need to look at this in more detail.

The CDC Class

You should do all the drawing in your program using members of the **CDC** class. All objects of this class contain a device context and the member functions you need for sending graphics and text to your display and your printer. There are also member functions for retrieving information about the physical output device that you are using.

Because **CDC** class objects can provide almost everything you are likely to need by way of graphics output, there are a lot of member functions of this class, in fact well over a hundred. Therefore, we'll only look at those we are going to use in the Sketcher program here in this chapter, and go into others as we need them later on.

Note that MFC includes some more specialized classes for graphics output that are derived from **CDC**. We'll also be using objects of **CClientDC** for example, which contains all the members that we'll discuss at this point, because it is derived from **CDC**.

Displaying Graphics

You draw entities such as lines, circles and text in a device context, relative to a **current position**. A current position is a point in the client area that was set either by the previous entity that was drawn, or by calling a function to set it. For example, we could extend the **OnDraw()** function to set the current position as follows:

```
void CSketcherView::OnDraw(CDC* pDC)
{
    CSketcherDoc* pDoc = GetDocument();
    ASSERT_VALID(pDoc);

    pDC->MoveTo(50, 50);     // Set the current position as 50,50
}
```

The shaded line calls the function **MoveTo()** for the **CDC** object pointed to by **pDC**. This member function simply sets the current position to the x and y coordinates specified as arguments. As we saw earlier, the default mapping mode is **MM_TEXT**, so the coordinates are in pixels and the current position will be set to a point 50 pixels from the inside left border of the window and 50 pixels down from the top of the client area.

The **CDC** class overloads the **MoveTo()** function to provide flexibility in how you specify the position that you want to set as the current position. There are two versions of the function, declared in the **CDC** class as:

```
CPoint MoveTo(int x, int y);     // Move to position x,y
CPoint MoveTo(POINT aPoint);     // Move to position defined by aPoint
```

The first version accepts the x and y coordinates as separate arguments. The second accepts one argument of type **POINT**, which is a structure defined as:

```
typedef struct tagPOINT
{
    LONG x;
    LONG y;
} POINT;
```

The coordinates are members of the **struct** and are of type **long**. You may prefer to use a class, instead of a structure, for a point. You can use objects of the class **CPoint** anywhere that a **POINT** object can be used. The class **Point** has data members **x** and **y**, and using **CPoint** objects has the advantage that the class also defines member functions that operate on **CPoint** and **POINT** objects. We'll use **CPoint** objects in our examples, so you'll have an opportunity to see some of the member functions in action.

The return value from the **MoveTo()** function is a **CPoint** object that specifies the current position as it was before the move.

Drawing Lines

We can follow the call to **MoveTo()** in the **OnDraw()** function with a call to the function **LineTo()**, which will then drawn a line in the client area from the current position to the point specified by the arguments to the **LineTo()** function, as illustrated in the following diagram:

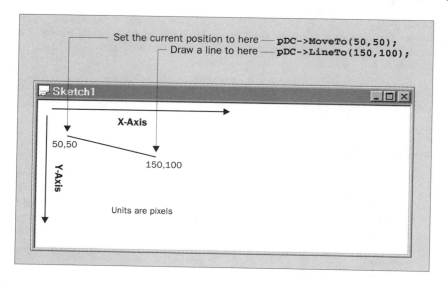

The class **CDC** also defines two versions of the **LineTo()** function with the prototypes:

```
BOOL LineTo(int x, int y); // Draw a line to position x,y
BOOL LineTo(POINT aPoint); // Draw a line to position defined by aPoint
```

This offers you the same flexibility in specifying the argument to the function as **MoveTo()**. You can use a **CPoint** object as an argument to the second version of the function. The function returns **1** if the line was drawn, and **0** otherwise.

When the **LineTo()** function is executed, the current position is changed to the point specifying the end of the line. This allows you to draw a series of connected lines by just calling the **LineTo()** function for each line. Look at the following version of the **OnDraw()** function:

```
void CSketcherView::OnDraw(CDC* pDC)
{
    CSketcherDoc* pDoc = GetDocument();
    ASSERT_VALID(pDoc);

    pDC->MoveTo(50,50);          // Set the current position
    pDC->LineTo(50,200);         // Draw a vertical line down 150 units
    pDC->LineTo(150,200);        // Draw a horizontal line right 100 units
    pDC->LineTo(150,50);         // Draw a vertical line up 150 units
    pDC->LineTo(50,50);          // Draw a horizontal line left 100 units
}
```

If you plug this into the Sketcher program and execute it, it will display the document window shown opposite:

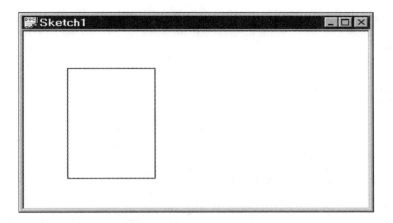

The four calls to the **LineTo()** function draw the rectangle shown counterclockwise, starting with the top left corner. The first call uses the current position set by the **MoveTo()** function. The succeeding calls use the current position set by the previous **LineTo()** function call. You can use this to draw any figure consisting of a sequence of lines each connected to the previous line. Of course, you are also free to use **MoveTo()** to change the current position at any time.

Drawing Circles

You have a choice of several function members in the class **CDC** for drawing circles, but they are all designed to draw ellipses. As you will know from a high school geometry, a circle is a special case of an ellipse with the major and minor axes equal. You can, therefore, use the member function **Ellipse()** to draw a circle. Like other closed shapes supported by the **CDC** class, the **Ellipse()** function fills the interior of the shape with a color that you set. The interior color is determined by a **brush** that is selected into the device context. The current brush in the device context determines how any closed shape will be filled.

MFC provides a class **CBrush** which you can use to define a brush. You can set the color of a **CBrush** object and also define a pattern to be produced when filling a closed shape. If you want to draw a closed shape that is not filled, you can use a null brush which leaves the interior of the shape empty. We'll come back to brushes a little later in this chapter.

If you want to draw circles that are not filled, you can do this without involving brushes by using the **Arc()** function. This has the advantage that you can draw any arc of an ellipse, not just the complete curve. There are two versions of this function declared in the **CDC** class as:

```
BOOL Arc(int x1, int y1, int x2, int y2,
         int x3, int y3, int x4, int y4);
BOOL Arc( LPCRECT lpRect, POINT StartPt, POINT EndPt );
```

In the first version, (**x1,y1**) and (**x2,y2**) define the top left and bottom right corners of a rectangle enclosing the complete curve. If you make these coordinates into the corners of a square, the curve drawn will be a segment of a circle. The points (**x3,y3**) and (**x4,y4**) define the start and end points of the segment to be drawn. The segment is drawn counterclockwise. If you make (**x4,y4**) identical to (**x3,y3**), you will generate a complete, apparently closed curve.

In the second version of **Arc()**, the enclosing rectangle is defined by a **RECT** object and a pointer to this object is passed as the first argument. The function will also accept a pointer to

485

an object of the class **CRect**, which has four public data members **left**, **top**, **right**, and **bottom**. These correspond to the *x* and *y* coordinates of the top left and bottom right points of the rectangle respectively. The class also provides a range of function members which operate on **CRect** objects and we shall be using some of these later.

The **POINT** objects **StartPt** and **EndPt** in the second version of **Arc()** define the start and end of the arc to be drawn.

Here's some code that exercises both versions of the **Arc()** function:

```
void CSketcherView::OnDraw(CDC* pDC)
{
    CSketcherDoc* pDoc = GetDocument();
    ASSERT_VALID(pDoc);

    pDC->Arc(50,50,150,150,100,50,150,100);   // Draw the 1st (large) circle

    // Define the bounding rectangle for the 2nd (smaller) circle
    CRect* pRect = new CRect(250,50,300,100);
    CPoint Start(275,100);                    // Arc start point
    CPoint End(250,75);                       // Arc end point
    pDC->Arc(pRect,Start, End);               // Draw the second circle
    delete pRect;
}
```

Note that we used a **CRect** class object instead of a **RECT** structure to define the bounding rectangle, and that we used **CPoint** class objects instead of **POINT** structures. We'll also be using **CRect** objects later, but they have some limitations, as you will see. The **Arc()** function does not require a current position to be set, as the position and size of the arc are completely defined by the arguments you supply. Although coordinates can be ±32K, the maximum width or height of the rectangle bounding a shape is 32,767 because this is the maximum positive value that can be represented in a signed 16-bit integer.

Now try running Sketcher with this code in the **OnDraw()** function. You should get the results shown:

Try re-sizing the borders. The client area is automatically redrawn as you cover or uncover the arcs in the picture. Remember that screen resolution will affect the scale of what is displayed. If you are using a VGA screen at 640x480 resolution, the arcs will be larger and further from the top left corner of the client area.

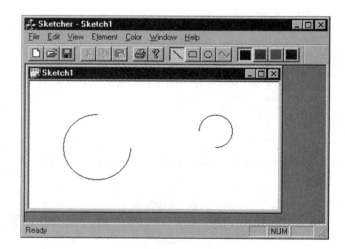

Drawing in Color

Everything that we have drawn so far has appeared on the screen in black. Drawing implies using a **pen object** which has a color and a thickness, and we have been using the default pen object that is provided in a device context. You are not obliged to do this, of course, - you can create your own pen with a given thickness and color. MFC defines the class **CPen** to help you do this.

All closed curves that you draw are filled with the current brush in the device context. As we said, you can define a brush as an instance of the class **CBrush**. Let's take a look at some of the features of **CPen** and **CBrush** objects.

Creating a Pen

The simplest way to create a pen object is to first declare an object of the **CPen** class:

```
CPen aPen;                     // Declare a pen object
```

This object now needs to be initialized with the properties you want. You do this using the class member function **CreatePen()** which is declared in the **CPen** class as:

```
BOOL CreatePen (int aPenStyle, int aWidth, COLORREF aColor);
```

The function returns **TRUE** as long as the pen is successfully initialized, and **FALSE** otherwise. The first argument defines the line style that you want to use when drawing. You must specify it by one of the following symbolic values:

Pen Style	Meaning
PS_SOLID	The pen draws a solid line.
PS_DASH	The pen draws a dashed line. This line style is valid only when the pen width is specified as 1.
PS_DOT	The pen draws a dotted line. This line style is valid only when the pen width is specified as 1.
PS_DASHDOT	The pen draws a line with alternating dashes and dots. This line style is valid only when the pen width is specified as 1.
PS_DASHDOTDOT	The pen draws a line with alternating dashes and double dots. This line style is valid only when the pen width is specified as 1.
PS_NULL	The pen does not draw anything.

Table Continued on Following Page

487

Pen Style	Meaning
PS_INSIDEFRAME	The pen draws a solid line, but unlike PS_SOLID, the points that specify the line occur on the edge of the pen rather than in the center, so that the drawn object never extends beyond the enclosing rectangle.

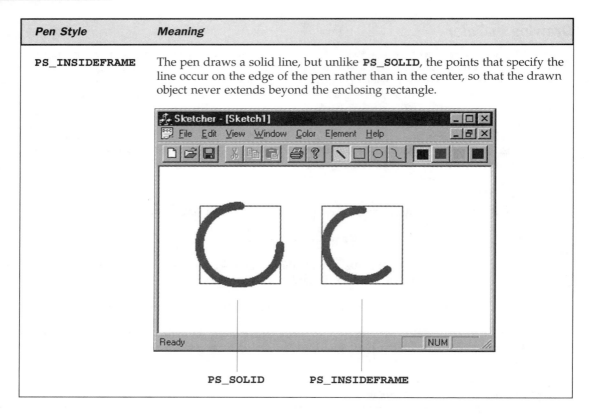

PS_SOLID   PS_INSIDEFRAME

The second argument to the **CreatePen()** function defines the line width. If **aWidth** has the value **0**, the line drawn will be 1 pixel wide, regardless of the mapping mode in effect. For values of **1** or more, the pen width is in the units determined by the mapping mode, for example, a value of **2** in **MM_TEXT** mode will be 2 pixels, and in **MM_LOENGLISH** mode the pen width will be 0.02 millimeters.

The last argument specifies the color to be used when drawing with the pen, so we could initialize a pen with the statement:

```
aPen.CreatePen(PS_SOLID, 2, RGB(255, 0, 0));  // Create a red solid pen
```

Assuming that the mapping mode is **MM_TEXT**, this pen will draw a red solid line which is 2 pixels wide.

Using a Pen

In order to use a pen, you must select it in to the device context in which you are drawing. To do this, you use a **CDC** class member function **SelectObject()**. To select the pen that you want to use, you call this function with a pointer to the pen object as an argument. The function returns a pointer to the previous pen object being used, so that you can save it and restore the old pen when you have finished drawing. A typical statement selecting a pen is:

```
CPen* pOldPen = pDC->SelectObject(&aPen);    // Select aPen as the pen
```

To restore the old pen when you are done, you simply call the function again passing the pointer returned from the original call:

```
pDC->SelectObject(pOldPen);         // Restore the old pen
```

We can demonstrate this in action by amending the previous version of the **OnDraw()** function in our view class to:

```
void CSketcherView::OnDraw(CDC* pDC)
{
    CSketcherDoc* pDoc = GetDocument();
    ASSERT_VALID(pDoc);

    // Declare a pen object and initialize it as
    // a red solid pen drawing a line 2 pixels wide
    CPen aPen;
    aPen.CreatePen(PS_SOLID, 2, RGB(255, 0, 0));

    CPen* pOldPen = pDC->SelectObject(&aPen); // Select aPen as the pen

    pDC->Arc(50,50,150,150,100,50,150,100);    // Draw the 1st circle

    // Define the bounding rectangle for the 2nd circle
    CRect* pRect = new CRect(250,50,300,100);
    CPoint Start(275,100);                     // Arc start point
    CPoint End(250,75);                        // Arc end point
    pDC->Arc(pRect,Start, End);                // Draw the second circle
    delete pRect;

    pDC->SelectObject(pOldPen);                // Restore the old pen

}
```

If you build and execute the Sketcher application with this version of the **OnDraw()** function, you will get the same arcs drawn as before, but this time the lines will be thicker and they will be red. You could usefully experiment with this example by trying different combinations of arguments to the **CreatePen()** function and seeing their effects. Note that we have ignored the value returned from the **CreatePen()** function, so we run the risk of the function failing and not detecting it in the program. It doesn't matter here as the program is still trivial, but as we develop the program, it will be important to check for failures of this kind.

Creating a Brush

An object of the **CBrush** class encapsulates a Windows brush. You can define a brush to be solid, hatched, or patterned. A brush is actually an 8x8 block of pixels that is repeated over a region that is to be filled.

To define a brush with a solid color, you can specify the color when you create the brush object. For example:

```
CBrush aBrush(RGB(255,0,0));      // Define a red brush
```

This defines a red brush. The value passed to the constructor must be of type **COLORREF**, which is the type returned by the **RGB()** macro, so this is a good way to specify the color.

Another constructor is available to define a hatched brush. It requires two arguments to be specified, the first defining the type of hatching, and the second specifying the color, as before. The hatching argument can be any of the following symbolic constants:

HS_HORIZONTAL	Horizontal hatching
HS_VERTICAL	Vertical hatching
HS_BDIAGONAL	Downward hatching from left to right at 45 degrees
HS_FDIAGONAL	Upward hatching from left to right at 45 degrees
HS_CROSS	Horizontal and vertical crosshatching
HS_DIAGCROSS	Crosshatching at 45 degrees

So, to obtain a red, 45 degree crosshatched brush, you can define the **CBrush** object with the statement:

```
CBrush aBrush(HS_DIAGCROSS, RGB(255, 0, 0));
```

You can also initialize a **CBrush** object in a similar manner to that of a **CPen** object, by using the **CreateSolidBrush()** member function of the class for a solid brush, and the **CreateHatchBrush()** member for a hatched brush. They require the same arguments as the equivalent constructors. For example, we could create the same hatched brush as previously, with the statements:

```
CBrush aBrush;                  // Define a brush object
aBrush.CreateHatchBrush(HS_DIAGCROSS, RGB(255, 0, 0));
```

Using a Brush

To use a brush, you select the brush into the device context by calling the **SelectObject()** member of the CDC class in a parallel fashion to that used for a pen. This member function is overloaded to support selecting brush objects into a device context. To select the brush we defined previously, you would simply write:

```
SelectObject(aBrush);      // Select the brush into the device context
```

There are a number of standard brushes available. Each of the standard brushes is identified by a predefined symbolic constant, and there are seven that you can use. They are the following:

GRAY_BRUSH	**LTGRAY_BRUSH**	**DKGRAY_BRUSH**
BLACK_BRUSH	**WHITE_BRUSH**	
HOLLOW_BRUSH	**NULL_BRUSH**	

The names of these are quite explanatory. To use one of these brushes, you call the **SelectStockObject()** member of the **CDC** class, passing the symbolic name for the brush that you want to use as an argument. To select the null brush, which will leave the interior of a closed shape unfilled, you could write:

```
SelectStockObject(NULL_BRUSH);
```

You can also use one of a range of standard pens through this function. The symbols for standard pens are **BLACK_PEN**, **NULL_PEN** which doesn't draw anything, and **WHITE_PEN**.

Drawing Graphics in Practice

We now know how to draw lines and arcs, so it's about time we considered how the user is going to define what he wants drawn. In other words, we need to decide how the user interface is going to work.

Since this program is to be a sketching tool, we don't want the user to worry about coordinates. The easiest mechanism for drawing is using just the mouse. To draw a line, for instance, the user could position the cursor and press the left mouse button where he wants the line to start and then define the end of the line by moving the cursor with the left button held down. It would be ideal if we could arrange that the line was continuously drawn as the cursor was moved with the left button down (this is known as rubber-banding to graphic designers). The line would be fixed when the left mouse button was released. This process is illustrated in the diagram below:

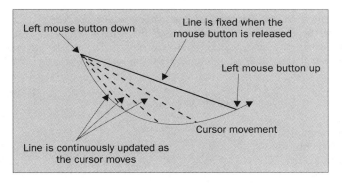

We could allow circles to be drawn in a similar fashion. The first press of the left mouse button would define the center and, as the cursor was moved with the button down, the program would track it, the circle being continuously redrawn with the current cursor position defining a point on the circumference of the current circle. As with drawing a line, the circle would be fixed when the left mouse button was released. We can see this in the diagram opposite:

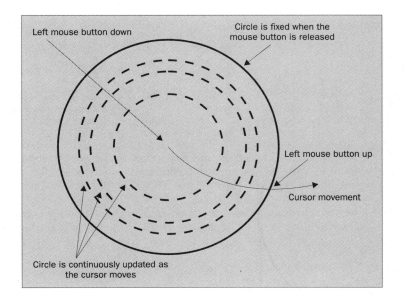

We can draw a rectangle as easily as we draw a line, as illustrated here:

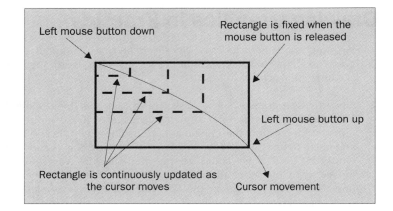

The first point is defined by the position of the cursor when the left mouse button is pressed. This is one corner of the rectangle. The position of the cursor when the mouse is moved with the left button held down defines the diagonal opposite corner of the rectangle. The rectangle actually stored is the last one defined when the left mouse button is released.

A curve will be somewhat different. An arbitrary number of points may define a curve. The mechanism that we'll use is illustrated here:

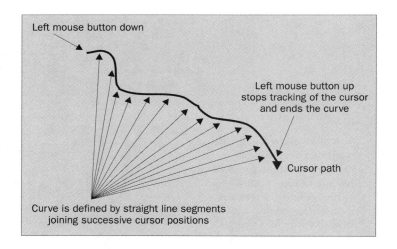

As with the other shapes, the first point is defined by the cursor position when the left mouse button is pressed. Successive positions recorded when the mouse is moved are connected by straight line segments to form the curve, so the mouse track defines the curve to be drawn.

Now that we know how the user is going to define an element, clearly our next step in understanding how to implement this is to get a grip on how the mouse is programmed.

Programming the Mouse

To be able to program the drawing of shapes in the way we have discussed, there are various things we need to know about the mouse:

> When a mouse button is pressed, since this signals the start of a drawing operation.

> Where the cursor is when a button is pressed, because this defines a reference point for the shape.

> When the mouse moves and where the cursor moves to when it does, as a mouse movement after detecting that a mouse button has been pressed is a cue to draw a shape, and the cursor position provides a defining point for the shape.

> When the mouse button is released, and the cursor position at that instant, because this signals that the final version of the shape should be drawn.

As you may have guessed, all this information is provided by Windows in the form of messages sent to your program. The implementation of the process for drawing lines and circles will consist almost entirely of writing message handlers.

Messages from the Mouse

When the user of our program is drawing a shape, they will be interacting with a particular document view. The view class is, therefore, the obvious place to put the message handlers for the mouse. Fire up the ClassWizard and take a look at the Message Maps tab for the **CSketcherView** class. We don't want the messages associated with **ID_** specified objects. We need to get to the standard Windows messages sent to the class which have IDs prefixed with **WM_**. You can see these if you select the class name in the Object IDs: box and scroll down the Messages: list, as shown below:

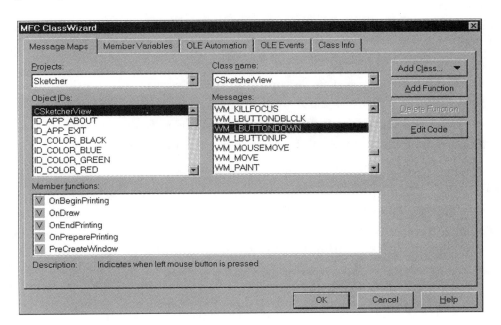

We are interested in three mouse messages at the moment:

Message	Occurs...
WM_LBUTTONDOWN	when the left mouse button is pressed.
WM_LBUTTONUP	when the left mouse button is released.
WM_MOUSEMOVE	when the mouse is moved.

These messages are quite independent of one another and are being sent to the document views in your program, even if you don't supply handlers for them. It's quite possible for a window to receive a **WM_LBUTTONUP** message without having previously received a **WM_LBUTTONDOWN** message. This can happen if the button is pressed with the cursor over another window and then moved to your view window before being released.

If you scroll the Messages: box, you'll see there are other mouse messages that occur. You can choose to process any or all of the messages, depending on your application requirements. Let's define in general terms what we want to do with the three messages that we are currently interested in, based on the process for drawing shapes that we saw earlier:

WM_LBUTTONDOWN

This starts the process of drawing an element. So we will:

- Note that the element drawing process has started.
- Record the current cursor position as the first point for defining an element.

WM_MOUSEMOVE

This is an intermediate stage where we want to create and draw a temporary version of the current element, but only if the left mouse button is down, so:

- Check that the left button is down.
- If it is, delete any previous version of the current element that was drawn.
- If it isn't, then exit.
- Record the current cursor position as the second defining point for the current element.
- Cause the current element to be drawn using the two defining points.

WM_LBUTTONUP

This indicates that the process for drawing an element is finished, so all we need to do is:

- Store the final version of the element defined by the first point recorded plus the position of the cursor when the button is released for the second point.
- Record the end of the process of drawing an element.

Let's now use ClassWizard to generate handlers for these three mouse messages.

Mouse Message Handlers

You create the handlers for the mouse messages in the same way as you created the menu message handlers. Just click on the <u>A</u>dd Function button with the message highlighted. The functions generated will be **OnLButtonDown()**, **OnLButtonUp()** and **OnMouseMove()**. You don't get the option of changing the names of these functions because you are replacing versions that are already defined in the base class for your **CSketcherView** class. Let's look at how we implement these handlers.

The ClassWizard Generated Code

We can start by looking at the **WM_LBUTTONDOWN()** handler. Make sure that it is highlighted in the Member <u>f</u>unctions: box and click on the <u>E</u>dit Code button. This is the skeleton code that is generated:

```
void CSketcherView::OnLButtonDown(UINT nFlags, CPoint point)
{
    // TODO: Add your message handler code here and/or call default

    CView::OnLButtonDown(nFlags, point);
}
```

You can see that ClassWizard has put a call to the base class handler in the skeleton version. This ensures that the base handler is called if you don't add any code here. In this case, you don't need to call the base class handler when you handle the message yourself, although you can if you want to. Whether you need to call the base class handler for a message depends on the circumstances. Generally, the comment indicating where you should add your own code is a good guide. Where it suggests, as in the present instance, that calling the base class handler is optional, you can omit it when you add your own message handling code. Note that the position of the comment in relation to the call of the base class handler is also important, as sometimes you must call the base class message handler before your code, and other times afterwards. The comment indicates where your code should appear in relation to the base class message handler call.

The handler in your class is passed two arguments: **nFlags** which is of type **UINT**, and contains a number of status flags indicating whether various keys are down, and the **CPoint** object, **point**, which defines the cursor position when the left mouse button was pressed. The type **UINT** is a portable unsigned integer which corresponds to a 32-bit unsigned integer in Windows 95.

The value of **nFlags** which is passed to the function can be any combination of the following symbolic values:

Flag	Meaning
MK_CONTROL	Corresponds to the *Ctrl* key being pressed.
MK_LBUTTON	Corresponds to the left mouse button being down.
MK_MBUTTON	Corresponds to the middle mouse button being down.
MK_RBUTTON	Corresponds to the right mouse button being down.
MK_SHIFT	Corresponds to the *Shift* key being pressed.

Being able to detect if a key is down in the message handler allows you to support different actions, depending on what you find. The value of **nFlags** may contain more than one of these indicators, each of which corresponds to a particular bit in the word, so you can test for a particular key using the bitwise AND operator. For example, to test for the *Ctrl* key being pressed, you could write:

```
if(nFlags & MK_CONTROL)
    // Do something...
```

The expression **nFlags & MK_CONTROL** will only have the value **TRUE** if the **nFlags** variable has the bit defined by **MK_CONTROL** set. In this way, you can have different actions when the left mouse button is pressed, depending on whether the *Ctrl* key was also pressed.

The arguments passed to the other two message handlers are the same as those for the **OnLButtonDown()** function. The code generated by the ClassWizard for them is:

```
void CSketcherView::OnLButtonUp(UINT nFlags, CPoint point)
{
    // TODO: Add your message handler code here and/or call default

    CView::OnLButtonUp(nFlags, point);
}
```

```
void CSketcherView::OnMouseMove(UINT nFlags, CPoint point)
{
    // TODO: Add your message handler code here and/or call default

    CView::OnMouseMove(nFlags, point);
}
```

Apart from the function names, the skeleton code is the same for each with the same arguments passed. With an understanding of the information passed to the message handlers, we can start adding our own code.

Drawing Using the Mouse

For the **WM_LBUTTONDOWN** message, we want to record the cursor position as the first point defining an element. We also want to record the position of the cursor after a mouse move. The obvious place to store these is in the **CSketcherView** class, so we can add data members to the attributes section of the class for these as follows:

```
class CSketcherView : public CView
{
    protected: // create from serialization only
        CSketcherView();
        DECLARE_DYNCREATE(CSketcherView)

    // Attributes
    public:
        CSketcherDoc* GetDocument();

    protected:
        CPoint m_FirstPoint;      // First point recorded for an element
        CPoint m_SecondPoint;     // Second point recorded for an element
```

```
...

// Generated message map functions
protected:
    //{{AFX_MSG(CSketcherView)
    afx_msg void OnLButtonDown(UINT nFlags, CPoint point);
    afx_msg void OnLButtonUp(UINT nFlags, CPoint point);
    afx_msg void OnMouseMove(UINT nFlags, CPoint point);
    //}}AFX_MSG
    DECLARE_MESSAGE_MAP()
};
```

As you saw in previous chapters, another way of adding a new variable to a class is to right-click on the class name in the ClassView and select **Add Variable...** from the context menu. You can then fill in the details of the variable in the dialog. However, there will be no comments explaining the new data member unless you add them separately.

The declarations for the handlers function that were added by the ClassWizard are highlighted, as well as the declarations for the additional data members we need. The new data members are **protected** to prevent direct modification of them from outside the class. Both the data members need to be initialized, so you should add code to the class constructor to do this, as follows:

```
// CSketcherView construction/destruction
CSketcherView::CSketcherView()
{
    // TODO: add construction code here
    m_FirstPoint = CPoint(0,0);          // Set 1st recorded point to 0,0
    m_SecondPoint = CPoint(0,0);         // Set 2nd recorded point to 0,0
}
```

We can now implement the handler for the **WM_LBUTTONDOWN** message as:

```
void CSketcherView::OnLButtonDown(UINT nFlags, CPoint point)
{
    // TODO: Add your message handler code here and/or call default
    m_FirstPoint = point;                // Record the cursor position
}
```

All it does is to note the coordinates passed by the second argument. We can ignore the first argument in this situation altogether.

We can't complete this function yet, but we can have a stab at writing the code for the **WM_MOUSEMOVE** message handler in outline:

```
void CSketcherView::OnMouseMove(UINT nFlags, CPoint point)
{
    // TODO: Add your message handler code here and/or call default
    if(nFlags & MK_LBUTTON)
    {
        m_SecondPoint = point;       // Save the current cursor position
```

497

```
            // Test for a previous temporary element
        {
            // We get to here if there was a previous mouse move
            // so add code to delete the old element
        }

        // Add code to create new element
        // and cause it to be drawn
    }
}
```

The first thing that the handler does after verifying the left mouse button is down is to save the current cursor position. This will be used as the second defining point for an element. The rest of the logic is clear in general terms, but there are major gaps in our knowledge of how to complete the function. We have no means of defining an element - in other words we need to be able to define an element as an object of a class. Even if we could, we don't know how to delete an element or get one drawn when we have a new one. A brief digression is called for.

Getting the Client Area Redrawn

As you know, the client area gets drawn by the **OnDraw()** member function of the **CSketcherView** class, which is called when a **WM_PAINT** message is received. Along with the basic message to repaint the client area, Windows supplies information about the part of the client area that needs to be redrawn. This can save a lot of time when you are displaying complicated images, because only the area specified actually needs to be redrawn, which may be a very small proportion of the total area.

You can tell Windows that a particular area should be redrawn by calling the **InvalidateRect()** function, which is a member of your view class. The function accepts two arguments. The first argument is a pointer to a **RECT** or **CRect** object that defines the rectangle in the client area to be redrawn. Passing **NULL** for this parameter causes the whole client area to be redrawn. The second is a **BOOL** value which is **TRUE** if the background to the rectangle is to be erased, and **FALSE** otherwise. This argument has a default value of **TRUE**, so you can ignore it most of the time.

The area specified in calls to **InvalidateRect()** is accumulated and then passed to all windows along with the next **WM_PAINT** message. Thus, all you have to do to get a newly created shape drawn is:

▶ Make sure that the **OnDraw()** function in your view includes the newly created item when it redraws the window.

▶ Call **InvalidateRect()** with a pointer to the rectangle bounding the shape to be redrawn passed as the first argument.

Similarly, if you want a shape removed from the client area of a window, you need to do the following:

▶ Remove the shape from the items that the **OnDraw()** function will draw.

▶ Call **InvalidateRect()** with the first argument pointing to the rectangle bounding the shape that is to be removed.

498

Since the background to the rectangle specified is automatically erased, as long as the **OnDraw()** function does not draw the shape again, the shape will disappear. Of course, this means that we need to be able to obtain the rectangle bounding any shape that we create, so we'll include a function to provide this as a member of our classes that define the elements that can be drawn by Sketcher.

Defining Classes for Elements

Thinking ahead a bit, we are going to want to store elements in a document in some way, and to be able to perform file operations with them. We'll deal with the details of file operations later on, but the MFC class **CObject** includes the tools for us to do this, so we'll use **CObject** as a base class for our element classes.

We'll also have the problem of not knowing in advance what sequence of element types the user will create. This suggests that using a base class pointer for selecting a particular element class function will simplify things a bit. For example, we won't need to know what an element is in order to draw it. As long as we are accessing the element through a base class pointer, we can always get an element to draw itself by using a virtual function. This is called polymorphism, as you saw when we discussed virtual functions. All we need to do to achieve this is to make sure that the classes defining specific elements share a common base class, and that, in this class, we declare as virtual all the functions we want to have selected automatically at run time. This indicates that our class structure should be like that shown in the diagram below:

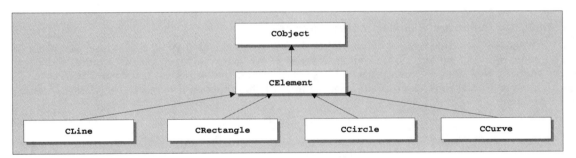

The arrows in the diagram point towards the base class in each case. If we need to add another element type, all we need to do is to derive another class from **CElement**. We'll be putting the definitions for these classes in a new **.h** file that we can call **Elements.h**. Create a new source file and add the following skeleton code:

```
#ifndef Elements_h
#define Elements_h

// Generic element class
class CElement:public CObject
{
    // Add virtual function declarations here
};

// Class defining a line object
class CLine:public CElement
{
    // Add class definition here
```

```
};

// Class defining a rectangle object
class CRectangle:public CElement
{
   // Add class definition here
};

// Class defining a circle object
class CCircle:public CElement
{
   // Add class definition here
};

// Class defining a curve object
class CCurve:public CElement
{
   // Add class definition here
};

#endif
```

You can save the file in the Sketcher folder as **Elements.h**. We have added the standard **#ifndef** command to protect against having the definitions for our element classes included more than once.

Storing a Temporary Element in the View

When we saw how shapes would be drawn, it was evident that, as the mouse was dragged after pressing the left mouse button, a series of temporary element objects would be created and drawn. Now that we know that the base class for all the shapes is **CElement**, we can add a pointer to the view class to store the address of the temporary element. The class definition will become:

```
class CSketcherView : public CView
{
   // other bits of the class definition as before...

   // Attributes
   public:
      CSketcherDoc* GetDocument();

   protected:
      CPoint m_FirstPoint;        // First point recorded for an element
      CPoint m_SecondPoint;       // Second point recorded for an element
      CElement* m_pTempElement; // Pointer to temporary element

   // other bits of the class definition as before...
};
```

Of course, we should ensure that this is initialized when the view object is constructed, so we need to add the following line to the **CSketcherView** class constructor:

```
   m_pTempElement = 0;        // Set temporary element pointer to 0
```

We'll be able to use this pointer as a test for previous temporary elements in the **WM_MOUSEMOVE** message handler.

Since we are now creating **CElement** class objects in the view class, we need to ensure that the definition of the **CElement** class is included before the **CSketcherView** class definition. You can do this by adding an include statement to the **SketchView.h** file before the **CSketcherView** definition:

```
#include "Elements.h"
```

The CElement Class

We need to fill out the element class definitions. We'll be doing this incrementally as we add functionality to the Sketcher application, but what do we need now? We'll put some data elements, such as element color, that are clearly common to all types of elements in the **CElement** class but, since the data elements in the classes which define specific elements may be quite disparate, it will be easier to understand if we keep the complete set of defining data elements together in the particular class to which they belong. The **CElement** class will then only contain virtual functions that will be replaced in the derived classes, plus data and function members which are the same in all the derived classes. The virtual functions will be those that are selected automatically for a particular object through a pointer. For now, we can define the **CElement** class as:

```
class CElement:public CObject
{
protected:
    COLORREF m_Color;                        // Color of an element

public:
    virtual ~CElement(){}                    // Virtual destructor
    virtual void Draw(CDC* pDC) {}           // Virtual draw operation

    CRect GetBoundRect();    // Get the bounding rectangle for an element

protected:
    CElement(){}                             // Default constructor
};
```

The members to be inherited by the derived classes are a data member storing the color, **m_Color**, and a function member to calculate the rectangle bounding an element, **GetBoundRect()**. This function returns a value of type **CRect** which will be the rectangle bounding the shape.

We also have a virtual destructor - necessary to ensure that derived class objects are destroyed properly - and a virtual **Draw()** function which, in the derived classes, will draw the particular object in question. The default constructor is in the protected section of the class to ensure that it can't be used externally. The **Draw()** function will need a pointer to a **CDC** object passed to it in order to provide access to the drawing functions that we saw earlier.

You may wonder why we don't declare the **Draw()** member as a pure virtual function in the **CElement** class - after all it can have no meaningful content in this class. This would also force its definition in any derived class. Normally you would do this, but the facilities we will use later that are inherited from **CObject** require an instance of the class to be created. A class with a pure virtual function member is an abstract class, and instances of an abstract class cannot be created.

You might be tempted to declare the `GetBoundRect()` function as returning a pointer to a `CRect` object - after all, we're going to pass a pointer to the `InvalidateRect()` member function in the view class. This could lead to problems. You will be creating the `CRect` object as local to the class, so the pointer would be pointing to a non-existent object on return from `GetBoundRect()` the function. You could get around this by creating the `CRect` object on the heap, but then you need to take care that it is deleted after use, otherwise you'll be filling the heap with `CRect` objects - a new one for every call of `GetBoundRect()`.

The CLine Class

We'll define the `CLine` class as:

```
class CLine: public CElement
{
public:
    virtual void Draw(CDC* pDC);   // Function to display a line

    // Constructor for a line object
    CLine(CPoint Start, CPoint End, COLORREF aColor);

protected:
    CPoint m_StartPoint;            // Start point of line
    CPoint m_EndPoint;              // End point of line

    CLine(){}                       // Default constructor - should not be used
};
```

The data members that define a line are **m_StartPoint** and **m_EndPoint** both of which are **protected**. The class has a public constructor which has parameters for the values that define a line, and a default constructor declared as protected to prevent its use externally.

Implementing the CLine Class

We can place the implementation of the member functions in a new file **Elements.cpp** that we can define in outline as:

```
// Implementations of the element classes
#include "stdafx.h"

#include "OurConstants.h"
#include "Elements.h"

// Add definitions for member functions here
```

We need the file **stdafx.h** to be included into this file to gain access to the definitions of the standard system header files. The other two files we have included are the ones that we created containing definitions for our constants and for the classes we are implementing here. We may need to add **#include** statements for the files containing definitions for AppWizard generated classes if we use any in our code.

We also need to add the **Elements.cpp** file to the Sketcher project, so once you have saved this file, you need to select the Insert/Files into Project... menu item and add the file to the project. If you now have a look at the project in the ClassView, you'll find that the file **Elements.h** has been automatically added to the list of dependencies.

We're now ready to add the constructor for the **CLine** class to the **Elements.cpp** file.

The CLine Class Constructor

The code for this will be:

```
// CLine class constructor
CLine::CLine(CPoint Start, CPoint End, COLORREF aColor)
{
   m_StartPoint = Start;      // Set line start point
   m_EndPoint = End;          // Set line end point
   m_Color = aColor;          // Set line color
}
```

There's nothing too intellectually taxing here. We just store each of the values passed to the constructor in the appropriate data member.

Drawing a Line

The **Draw()** function is not too difficult either, although we do need to take account of the color to be used when the line is drawn:

```
// Draw a CLine object
void CLine::Draw(CDC* pDC)
{
   // Create a pen for this object and
   // initialize it to the object color and line width of 1 pixel
   CPen aPen;
   if(!aPen.CreatePen(PS_SOLID, m_Pen, m_Color))
   {                                          // Pen creation failed
      AfxMessageBox("Pen creation failed drawing a line", MB_OK);
      AfxAbort();                             // Abort the program
   }

   CPen* pOldPen = pDC->SelectObject(&aPen);  // Select the pen

   // Now draw the line
   pDC->MoveTo(m_StartPoint);
   pDC->LineTo(m_EndPoint);

   pDC->SelectObject(pOldPen);                // Restore the old pen
}
```

We create a pen as we have seen earlier, only this time we make sure that the creation works. If it doesn't, the most likely cause is that we are running out of memory, which is a serious problem. This will almost invariably be caused by an error in the program, so we have written the function to call **AfxMessage()** which is a global function to display a message box and then call **AfxAbort()** to terminate the program. The first argument to **AfxMessage()** specifies the message that is to appear and the second specifies that it should have an OK button.

After creating a pen, we move the current position to the start of the line, defined in the **m_StartPoint** data member, and then draw the line from this point to the point **m_EndPoint**. Finally, we restore the old pen and we are done.

Creating Bounding Rectangles

At first sight, obtaining the bounding rectangle for a shape looks trivial. For example, a line is always a diagonal of its enclosing rectangle and a circle is defined by its enclosing rectangle, but there are a couple of slight complications. Firstly, the shape must lie completely inside the rectangle, so we must allow for the thickness of the line used to draw the shape when we create the bounding rectangle. Secondly, how you work out adjustments to the coordinates defining the rectangle depends on the mapping mode, so we must take that into account too.

Look at the illustration below, relating to obtaining the bounding rectangle for a line and a circle:

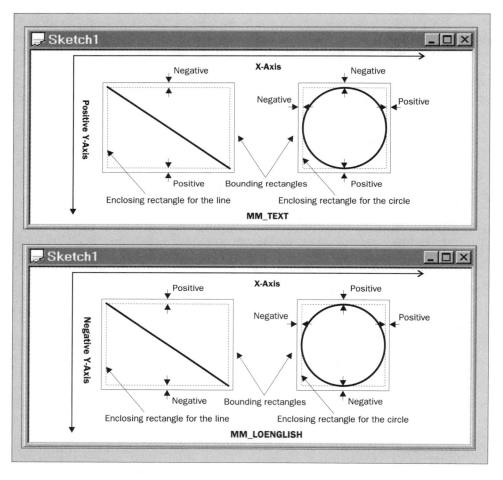

We'll call the rectangle that is used to draw a shape the 'enclosing rectangle', while the rectangle which takes into account the width of the pen we'll call the 'bounding rectangle'. The illustration shows the shapes with their enclosing rectangles, and the bounding rectangle offset by the line thickness. This is obviously exaggerated here so that you can see what's happening. The differences in how you calculate the coordinates for the bounding rectangle in different mapping modes occur with the y coordinates. To get the corners of the bounding rectangle in the **MM_TEXT** mapping mode, subtract the line thickness for the y coordinate of the top left corner of the defining rectangle, and add it to the y coordinate of the bottom right corner. However, in **MM_LOENGLISH**, and in the other mapping modes, the y axis increases in the opposite direction, so you need to *add* the line thickness to the y coordinate for the top left corner of the defining rectangle, and *subtract* it from the y coordinate of the bottom right corner. For all the mapping modes, you subtract the line thickness from the x coordinate of the top left corner defining rectangle, and add it to the x coordinate of the bottom right corner.

To implement our element types as consistently as possible, we could always store an enclosing rectangle for each shape in a data element in the base class. This will need to be calculated when a shape is constructed. The job of the **GetBoundRect()** function in the base class will then be to calculate the bounding rectangle by offsetting the enclosing rectangle by the pen width. We can amend the **CElement** class definition by adding two data members as follows:

```
class CElement:public CObject
{
protected:
    COLORREF m_Color;                      // Color of an element
    CRect m_EnclosingRect;                 // Rectangle enclosing an element
    int m_Pen;                             // Pen width

public:
    virtual ~CElement(){}                  // Virtual destructor
    virtual void Draw(CDC* pDC) {}         // Virtual draw operation

    CRect GetBoundRect();     // Get the bounding rectangle for an element

protected:
    CElement(){}                           // Default constructor
};
```

We must update the **CLine** constructor so that it has the correct pen width:

```
// CLine class constructor
CLine::CLine(CPoint Start, CPoint End, COLORREF aColor)
{
    m_StartPoint = Start;      // Set line start point
    m_EndPoint = End;          // Set line end point
    m_Color = aColor;          // Set line color
    m_Pen = 1;                 // Set pen width
}
```

We can now implement the **GetBoundRect()** member of the base class assuming the **MM_TEXT** mapping mode:

```
// Get the bounding rectangle for an element
CRect CElement::GetBoundRect()
{
    CRect BoundingRect;                    // Object to store the bounding rectangle
    BoundingRect = m_EnclosingRect;        // Store the enclosing rectangle

    // Increase the rectangle by the pen width
    BoundingRect.InflateRect(m_Pen, m_Pen);
    return BoundingRect;                   // Return the bounding rectangle
}
```

This will return the bounding rectangle for any derived class object. We then define the bounding rectangle by modifying the coordinates of the enclosing rectangle stored in the base class data member so that it is enlarged all round by the pen width, using the **InflateRect()** method of the **CRect** class.

The **CRect** class provides an operator **+** for rectangles, which we could have used. For example, we could have written the return statement as:

```
BoundingRect = m_EnclosingRect + CRect(m_Pen, m_Pen, m_Pen, m_Pen);
```

Equally, we could have simply added (or subtracted) the pen width to each of the x and y values that make up the rectangle. We could have replaced the assignment by the following statements:

```
BoundingRect = m_EnclosingRect;
BoundingRect.top -= m_Pen;
BoundingRect.left -= m_Pen;
BoundingRect.bottom += m_Pen;
BoundingRect.right += m_Pen;
```

> The individual data members of a **CRect** object are **left** and **top** (storing the x and y coordinates of the top left corner) and **right** and **bottom** (storing the coordinates of the bottom right corner). These are all **public** members, so we can access them directly. A commonly made mistake, especially by me, is to write the coordinate pair as **(top,left)** instead of in the correct order - **(left,top)**.

The hazard with both this and the previous option is that there is a built-in assumption that the mapping mode is **MM_TEXT**, which means that the positive y axis is assumed to run from top to bottom. If you change the mapping mode, neither of these will work properly, although it's not immediately obvious that they won't.

Normalized Rectangles

The **InflateRect()** function works by subtracting the values that you give it from the **top** and **left** members of the rectangle and adding the values to the **bottom** and **right**. This means that you may find your rectangle actually decreasing in size if you don't make sure that the rectangle is **normalized**. A normalized rectangle has a **left** value that is less than or equal to the **right** value, and a **top** value that is less than or equal to the **bottom** value. You can make sure that a **CRect** object is normalized by calling the **NormalizeRect()** member of the object. Most of the **CRect** member functions will require the object to be normalized in order for them to work as expected, so we need to make sure that when we store the enclosing rectangle in **m_EnclosingRect**, it is normalized.

Calculating the Enclosing Rectangle for a Line

Now, all we need is code in the constructor for a line to calculate the enclosing rectangle:

```
CLine::CLine(CPoint Start, CPoint End, COLORREF Color)
{
   m_StartPoint = Start;          // Set line start point
   m_EndPoint = End;              // Set line end point
```

```
    m_Color = Color;          // Set line color
    m_Pen = 1;                // Set pen width


    // Define the enclosing rectangle
    m_EnclosingRect = CRect(Start, End);
    m_EnclosingRect.NormalizeRect();
}
```

This simply calculates the coordinates of the top left and bottom right points, defining the rectangle from the start and end points of the line. We need to take care, though, that the bounding rectangle has the **top** value less than the **bottom** value, regardless of the relative positions of the start and end points of the line, so we call the **NormalizeRect()** member for the **m_EnclosingRect** object.

The CRectangle Class

Although we'll be defining a rectangle object by the same data that we used to define a line, we don't need to store the defining points. The enclosing rectangle in the data member inherited from the base completely defines the shape, so we don't need any data members:

```
// Class defining a rectangle object
class CRectangle: public CElement
{
   public:
        virtual void Draw(CDC* pDC);   // Function to display a rectangle

        // Constructor for a rectangle object
        CRectangle(CPoint Start, CPoint End, COLORREF aColor);
   protected:
        CRectangle(){}           // Default constructor - should not be used
};
```

The definition of the rectangle becomes very simple - just a constructor, the virtual **Draw()** function, and the default constructor in the **protected** section of the class.

The CRectangle Class Constructor

The code for the class constructor is somewhat similar to that for a **CLine** constructor:

```
// CRectangle class constructor
CRectangle:: CRectangle(CPoint Start, CPoint End, COLORREF Color)
{
   m_Color = Color;           // Set rectangle color
   m_Pen = 1;                 // Set pen width

   // Define the enclosing rectangle
   m_EnclosingRect = CRect(Start, End);
   m_EnclosingRect.NormalizeRect();
}
```

This is cheap code. Some minor alterations to a subset of the **CLine** constructor, fix the comments, and we have a new constructor for **CRectangle**. It just stores the color and pen width and computes the enclosing rectangle from the points passed as arguments.

Drawing a Rectangle

There is a member of the class **CDC** to draw a rectangle, called **Rectangle()**. This draws a closed figure and fills it with the current brush. You may think that this isn't quite what we want, since we want to draw rectangles as outlines only but, by selecting a **NULL_BRUSH**, this is exactly what we'll draw. There is also a function **PolyLine()** to draw shapes consisting of multiple line segments from an array of points, or we could have used **LineTo()** again, but the easiest approach for us is to use the **Rectangle()** function:

```
// Draw a CRectangle object
void CRectangle::Draw(CDC* pDC)
{
  // Create a pen for this object and
  // initialize it to the object color and line width of 1 pixel
  CPen aPen;
  if(!aPen.CreatePen(PS_SOLID, m_Pen, m_Color))
  {                                              // Pen creation failed
    AfxMessageBox("Pen creation failed drawing a rectangle", MB_OK);
    AfxAbort();
  }

  // Select the pen
  CPen* pOldPen = pDC->SelectObject(&aPen);
  // Select the brush
  CBrush* pOldBrush = (CBrush*)pDC->SelectStockObject(NULL_BRUSH);

  // Now draw the rectangle
  pDC->Rectangle(m_EnclosingRect);

  pDC->SelectObject(pOldBrush);                // Restore the old brush
  pDC->SelectObject(pOldPen);                  // Restore the old pen
}
```

After setting up the pen and the brush, we can simply pass the whole rectangle directly to the **Rectangle()** function for it to draw the rectangle. All that then remains to do is to clear up after ourselves and restore the DC's old pen and brush.

The CCircle Class

The interface of the **CCircle** class is no different from that of the **CRectangle** class. We can define a circle solely by its enclosing rectangle, so the class definition will be:

```
// Class defining a circle object
class CCircle: public CElement
{
  public:
    virtual void Draw(CDC* pDC);   // Function to display a circle

    // Constructor for a circle object
    CCircle(CPoint Start, CPoint End, COLORREF aColor);

  protected:
    CCircle(){}                    // Default constructor - should not be used
};
```

We have a public constructor defined and the default constructor is declared as protected for the reason we have already seen.

Implementing the CCircle Class

As we discussed earlier, when you create a circle on screen, the point where you press the left mouse button will be the center of the circle and, after moving the cursor with the left button down, the point where you release the cursor is a point on the circumference of the final circle. The job of the constructor will be to convert these points into the form used in the class to define a circle.

The CCircle Class Constructor

The point at which you release the left mouse button can be anywhere on the circumference, so the coordinates of the points specifying the enclosing rectangle need to be calculated, as illustrated below:

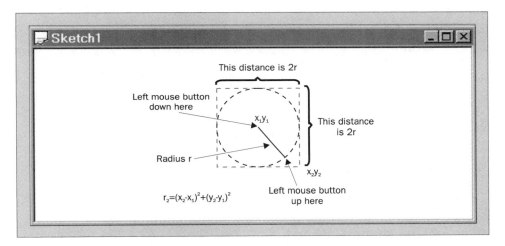

From this diagram, you can see that we can calculate the coordinates of the top left and bottom right points of the enclosing rectangle relative to the center of the circle (x_1, y_1), which is the point we record when the left mouse button is pressed. Assuming that the mapping mode is **MM_TEXT**, we just subtract the radius from each of the coordinates of the center. Similarly, the bottom right point is obtained by adding the radius to the x and y coordinates of the center. We can, therefore, code the constructor as:

```
// Constructor for a circle object
CCircle::CCircle(CPoint Start, CPoint End, COLORREF aColor)
{
    // First calculate the radius
    // We use floating point because that is required by
    // the library function (in math.h) for calculating a square root.
    long Radius = (long) sqrt((double)((End.x-Start.x)*(End.x-Start.x)+
                                       (End.y-Start.y)*(End.y-Start.y)));

    // Now calculate the rectangle enclosing
    // the circle assuming the MM_TEXT mapping mode
    m_EnclosingRect = CRect(Start.x-Radius, Start.y-Radius,
                            Start.x+Radius, Start.y+Radius);

    m_Color = aColor;          // Set the color for the circle
    m_Pen = 1;                 // Set pen width to 1
}
```

509

To use **sqrt()** function, you should add an **#include** statement for **math.h** to the beginning of the file. The maximum coordinate values are 16 bits, and the **CPoint** members **x** and **y** are declared as **long**, so evaluating the argument to the **sqrt()** function can safely be carried out as an integer. The result of the square root calculation will be of type **double**, so we cast it to **long** because we want to use it as an integer.

Drawing a Circle

We've already seen how to draw a circle using the **Arc()** function in the **CDC** class, so let's use the **Ellipse()** function here. The **Draw()** function in the **CCircle** class will be:

```
// Draw a circle
void CCircle::Draw(CDC* pDC)
{
   // Create a pen for this object and
   // initialize it to the object color and line width of 1 pixel
   CPen aPen;
   if(!aPen.CreatePen(PS_SOLID, m_Pen, m_Color))
   {                                           // Pen creation failed
      AfxMessageBox("Pen creation failed drawing a circle", MB_OK);
      AfxAbort();
   }

   CPen* pOldPen = pDC->SelectObject(&aPen);   // Select the pen

   // Select a null brush
   CBrush* pOldBrush = (CBrush*)pDC->SelectStockObject(NULL_BRUSH);

   // Now draw the circle
   pDC->Ellipse(m_EnclosingRect);

   pDC->SelectObject(pOldPen);                 // Restore the old pen
   pDC->SelectObject(pOldBrush);               // Restore the old brush
}
```

After selecting a pen of the appropriate color and a null brush, the circle is drawn by calling the **Ellipse()** function. The only argument is a **CRect** object which encloses the circle to be drawn.

The CCurve Class

The **CCurve** class is different from the others in that it needs to handle a variable number of defining points. This necessitates maintaining a list of some kind, and since we will look at how MFC can help with lists in the next chapter, we'll defer defining the detail of this class until then. For now, we'll include a class definition that provides dummy member functions so we can compile and link code that contains calls to them. In **Element.h**, you should have,

```
class CCurve: public CElement
{
public:
   virtual void Draw(CDC* pDC); // Function to display a curve

   // Constructor for a curve object
   CCurve(COLORREF aColor);

protected:
```

```
    CCurve(){}              // Default constructor - should not be used
};
```

and in **Element.cpp**:

```
void CCurve::Draw(CDC* pDC)
{
}

CCurve::CCurve(COLORREF aColor)
{
    m_Color = aColor;
    m_EnclosingRect = CRect(0,0,0,0);
    m_Pen = 1;
}
```

None of the member functions do anything useful yet, and we have no data members to define a curve. The constructor just sets the color, **m_EnclosingRect** to an empty rectangle and sets the pen width. We'll expand the class into a working version in the next chapter.

Completing the Mouse Message Handlers

We can now come back to the **WM_MOUSEMOVE** message handler and fill out the detail. You can get to it through the ClassWizard or by expanding **CSketcherView** in the ClassView and double-clicking the handler name, **OnMouseMove()**.

This handler will only be concerned with drawing a succession of temporary versions of an element as you move the cursor, as the final element will be created when you release the left mouse button. We can, therefore, treat the drawing of temporary elements to provide rubber-banding as entirely local to this function, leaving the final version of the element being created to be drawn by the **OnDraw()** function member of the view. This approach will result in the drawing of the rubber-banded elements to be reasonably efficient, as we won't involve the **OnDraw()** function, which ultimately will be responsible for drawing the entire document.

We can do this best with the help of a member of the **CDC** class that is particularly effective in rubber-banding operations, **SetROP2()**.

Setting the Drawing Mode

The **SetROP2()** function sets the **drawing mode** for all subsequent output operations in the device context associated with a CDC object. The 'ROP' bit of the function name stands for Raster OPeration, because the setting of drawing modes only applies to raster displays. (There are other kinds of graphic displays, called vector displays or directed beam displays, for which this mechanism does not apply, but you are unlikely to meet them these days since they have been largely rendered obsolete by raster displays.)

The drawing mode determines how the color of the pen that you use for drawing is to combine with the background color to produce the color of the entity you are displaying. You specify the drawing mode with a single argument to the function which can be any of the following values:

Drawing Mode	Effect
R2_BLACK	All drawing is in black.
R2_WHITE	All drawing is in white.
R2_NOP	Drawing operations do nothing.
R2_NOT	Drawing is in the inverse of the screen color. This ensures the output will always be visible since it prevents drawing in the same color as the background.
R2_COPYPEN	Drawing is in the pen color. This is the default drawing mode if you don't set it.
R2_NOTCOPYPEN	Drawing is in the inverse of the pen color.
R2_MERGEPENNOT	Drawing is in the color produced by ORing the pen color with the inverse of the background color.
R2_MASKPENNOT	Drawing is in the color produced by ANDing the pen color with the inverse of the background color.
R2_MERGENOTPEN	Drawing is in the color produced by ORing the background color with the inverse of the pen color.
R2_MASKNOTPEN	Drawing is in the color produced by ANDing the background color with the inverse of the pen color.
R2_MERGEPEN	Drawing is in the color produced by ORing the background color with the pen color.
R2_NOTMERGEPEN	Drawing is in the color that is the inverse of the **R2_MERGEPEN** color.
R2_MASKPEN	Drawing is in the color produced by ANDing the background color with the pen color.
R2_NOTMASKPEN	Drawing is in the color that is the inverse of the **R2_MASKPEN** color.
R2_XORPEN	Drawing is in the color produced by exclusive ORing the pen color and the background color
R2_NOTXORPEN	Drawing is in the color that is the inverse of the **R2_XORPEN** color.

Each of these symbols is predefined and corresponds to a particular drawing mode. There are a lot of options here, but the one that can work some magic for us is the last of these, **R2_NOTXORPEN**.

When we set the mode as **R2_NOTXORPEN**, the first time you draw a particular shape on the default white background, it will be drawn normally in the pen color you specify. If you draw the same shape again, overwriting the first, the shape will disappear, because the color that the shape will be drawn in corresponds to that produced by exclusive ORing the pen color with itself. The drawing color that results from this will be white. You can see this more clearly by working through an example.

White is equal proportions of red, blue, and green which, for simplicity, we can represent as 1,1,1 - the three values being the RGB components of the color. We can represent red as 1,0,0 in the same way. These combine as follows:

	R	G	B	
Background - white	1	1	1	
Pen - red	1	0	0	
XORed	0	1	1	
NOT XOR	1	0	0	which is red

So, the first time we draw a red line on a white background, it comes out red.

If we draw the same line a second time, overwriting the existing line, the background pixels we are writing over are red. The resultant drawing color works out as follows:

	R	G	B	
Background - red	1	0	0	
Pen - red	1	0	0	
XORed	0	0	0	
NOT XOR	1	1	1	which is white

Since the rest of the background is white, the line will disappear.

You need to take care to use the right background color here. You should be able to see that drawing with a white pen on a red background is not going to work too well, as the first time you draw something it will be red, and therefore invisible. The second time it will appear as white. If you draw on a black background, things will appear and disappear, as on a white background, but they won't be drawn in the pen color you choose.

Coding the OnMouseMove() Handler

Let's start by adding the code that creates the element after a mouse move message. Since we are going to draw the element from the handler function, we need to create an object for the device context. The most convenient class to use for this is **CClientDC** which is derived from **CDC**. The advantage of using this class, rather than **CDC** is that it will automatically take care of creating the device context for us and destroying it when we are done. The device context that it creates corresponds to the client area of a window, which is exactly what we want. Add the following code to the outline handler that we defined earlier:

```
void CSketcherView::OnMouseMove(UINT nFlags, CPoint point)
{
    // Define a Device Context object for the view
```

```
        CClientDC aDC(this);
        aDC.SetROP2(R2_NOTXORPEN);   // Set the drawing mode
    if(nFlags & MK_LBUTTON)
    {
        m_SecondPoint = point;       // Save the current cursor position
        // Test for a previous temporary element
        {
            // We get to here if there was a previous mouse move
            // so add code to delete the old element
        }

        // Create a temporary element of the type and color that
        // is recorded in the document object, and draw it
        m_pTempElement = CreateElement();   // Create a new element
        m_pTempElement->Draw(&aDC);         // Draw the element
    }
}
```

The first new line of code creates a local **CClientDC** object. As well as the characteristics we mentioned, this object has all the drawing functions we need, as they are inherited from the class **CDC**. The first member function we use is **SetROP2()**, which sets the drawing mode to **R2_NOTXORPEN**.

To create a new element, we save the current cursor position in the data member **m_SecondPoint**, and then call a view member function **CreateElement()**. (We'll define the **CreateElement()** function as soon as we have finished this handler.) This function should create an element using the two points stored in the current view object, with the color and type specification stored in the document object, and return the address of the element. We save this in **m_pTempElement**.

Using the pointer to the new element, we call its **Draw()** member to get the object to draw itself. The address of the **CClientDC** object is passed as an argument. Since we defined the **Draw()** function as virtual in the base class, **CElement**, the function for whatever type of element **m_pTempElement** is pointing to will automatically be selected. The new element will be drawn normally with the **R2_NOTXORPEN** because we are drawing it for the first time on a white background.

We can use the pointer **m_pTempElement** as an indicator of whether a previous temporary element exists. The code for this part of the handler will be:

```
    void CSketcherView::OnMouseMove(UINT nFlags, CPoint point)
    {
        // Define a Device Context object for the view
        CClientDC aDC(this);
        aDC.SetROP2(R2_NOTXORPEN);   // Set the drawing mode
        if(nFlags&MK_LBUTTON)
        {
            m_SecondPoint = point;       // Save the current cursor position
            if(m_pTempElement)
            {
                // Redraw the old element so it disappears from the view
                m_pTempElement->Draw(&aDC);
                delete m_pTempElement;       // Delete the old element
                m_pTempElement = 0;          // Reset the pointer to 0
            }
```

```
                // Create a temporary element of the type and color that
                // is recorded in the document object, and draw it
                m_pTempElement = CreateElement();  // Create a new element
                m_pTempElement->Draw(&aDC);        // Draw the element
        }
    }
```

A previous temporary element exists if the pointer **m_pTempElement** is not zero. We need to redraw the element it points to in order to remove it from the client area of the view. We then delete the element and reset the pointer to zero. The new element will then be created and drawn by the code that we added previously. This combination will automatically rubber-band the shape being created, so it will appear to be attached to the cursor position as it moves. We must remember to reset the pointer **m_pTempElement** back to 0 in the **WM_LBUTTONUP** message handler after we create the final version of the element.

Creating an Element

We need to add the **CreateElement()** function as a **protected** member to the operations section of the **CSketcherView** class:

```
class CSketcherView : public CView
{

    // Rest of the class definition as before...

    // Operations
    public:

    protected:
        CElement* CreateElement(); // Create a new element on the heap

      // Rest of the class definition as before...

};
```

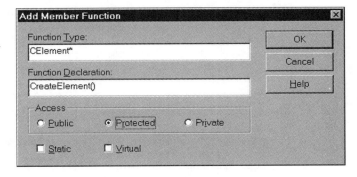

ClassWizard won't help us with this, so right-click on the class name, **CSketcherView**, in ClassView, and select Add Function... from the menu. This will open the following dialog:

Add the specifications of the function, as shown, and click on OK, so that a declaration for the function member will be added to the class definition, and you'll be taken directly to a skeleton for the function in **SketcherView.cpp**. Now add the following implementation to the body of the function.

```
// Create an element of the current type
CElement* CSketcherView::CreateElement()
{
    // Get a pointer to the document for this view
    CSketcherDoc* pDoc = GetDocument();
    ASSERT_VALID(pDoc);                    // Verify the pointer is good

    // Now select the element using the type stored in the document
    switch(pDoc->GetElementType())
    {
        case RECTANGLE:
            return new CRectangle(m_FirstPoint, m_SecondPoint,
                                         pDoc->GetElementColor());
        case CIRCLE:
            return new CCircle(m_FirstPoint, m_SecondPoint,
                                         pDoc->GetElementColor());
        case CURVE:
            return new CCurve(pDoc->GetElementColor());

        case LINE:
            return new CLine(m_FirstPoint, m_SecondPoint,
                                         pDoc->GetElementColor());

        default:                            // Something's gone wrong
            AfxMessageBox("Bad Element code", MB_OK);
            AfxAbort();
            return
    }
}
```

The lines that are not shaded are those that have been supplied automatically when we created the function. The first thing we do here is to get a pointer to the document by calling **GetDocument()**, as we've seen before. For safety, the **ASSERT_VALID()** macro is used to ensure that a good pointer is returned. The **switch** statement selects the element to be created based on the type returned by a function in the document class, **GetElementType()**. Another function in the document class is used to obtain the current element color. We can add the definitions for both these functions directly to the **CSketcherDoc** class definition, because they are very simple:

```
class CSketcherDoc : public CDocument
{

    // Rest of the class definition as before...

    // Operations
    public:
        WORD GetElementType()        // Get the element type
            { return m_Element; }
        COLORREF GetElementColor()   // Get the element color
            { return m_Color; }

    // Rest of the class definition as before...

};
```

Each of the functions returns the value stored in the corresponding data member. Remember that putting a member function definition in the class definition is equivalent to a request to make the function **inline**, so as well as being simple these should be fast.

Dealing with WM_LBUTTONUP Messages

The **WM_LBUTTONUP** message completes the process of creating an element. The job of this handler is to pass the final version of the element that was created to the document object and then clean up the view object data members. You can access and edit the code for the handler in the same way as the previous handler. Add the following lines to the function:

```
void CSketcherView::OnLButtonUp(UINT nFlags, CPoint point)
{
    if(m_pTempElement)
    {
        // Make sure there is an element
        // Call a document class function to store the element
        //  pointed to by m_pTempElement in the document object
        delete m_pTempElement;   // This code is temporary
        m_pTempElement = 0;      // Reset the element pointer
    }
}
```

The **if** statement will test that **m_pTempElement** is not zero. It's always possible that the user could press and release the left mouse button without moving the mouse, in which case no element would have been created. As long as there is an element, the pointer to the element will be passed to the document object. We'll add the code for this in the next chapter. In the meantime, we'll just delete the element here so as not to pollute the heap. Finally, the **m_pTempElement** pointer is reset to **0**, ready for the next time when the user draws an element.

Exercising Sketcher

Before we can run the example with the mouse message handlers, we need to update the **OnDraw()** function in the **CSketcherView** class implementation to get rid of any old code that we added earlier.

To make sure that the **OnDraw()** function is clean, from ClassView double-click on the function name to take you to its implementation in **SketcherView.cpp**. Delete any old code that you added, but leave in the first two lines that AppWizard provided to get a pointer to the document object. We'll need this later to get to the elements when they are stored in the document. The code for the function should now be:

```
void CSketcherView::OnDraw(CDC* pDC)
{
    CSketcherDoc* pDoc = GetDocument();
    ASSERT_VALID(pDoc);
}
```

Since we have no elements in the document as yet, we don't need to add anything to this function at this point. When we start storing data in the document in the next chapter, we'll need to add code here to draw the elements in response to a **WM_PAINT** message. Without it, the elements will just disappear whenever you resize the view, as you'll see.

Running the Example

After making sure that you have saved all the source files, build the program. If you haven't made any mistakes entering the code, you'll get a clean compile and link, so you can execute the program. You can draw lines circles and rectangles in any of the four colors the program supports. A typical window is shown below:

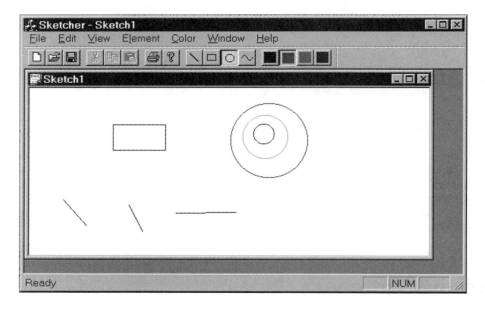

Try experimenting with the user interface. Note that you can move the window around and that the shapes stay in the window as long as you don't move it so far that they're outside the borders of the application window. If you do, the elements do not reappear after you move it back. This is because the existing element is never redrawn. When the client area is covered and uncovered, Windows will send a **WM_PAINT** message to the application which will cause the **OnDraw()** member of the view object to be called. As you know, the **OnDraw()** function for the view doesn't do anything at present. This will get fixed when we use the document to store the elements.

When you resize the view window, the shapes disappear immediately, but, when you move the whole view around, they remain, as long as they don't slide beyond the application window border. How come? Well, when you resize the window, Windows invalidates the whole client area and expects your application to redraw it in response to the **WM_PAINT** message. If you move the view around, Windows takes care of relocating the client area as is. You can demonstrate this by moving the view so that a shape is partially obscured. When you slide it back, you still have a partial shape, with the bit that was obscured erased.

If you try drawing a shape while dragging the cursor outside the view client area, you'll notice some peculiar effects. Outside the view window, we lose track of the mouse, which tends to mess up our rubber-banding mechanism. What's going on?

Capturing Mouse Messages

The problem is caused by the fact that Windows is sending the mouse messages to the window under the cursor. As soon as the cursor leaves the client area of our application view window, the **WM_MOUSEMOVE** messages are being sent elsewhere. We can fix this by using some inherited members of **CSketcherView**.

Our view class inherits a function, **GetCapture()**, which tells Windows that we want our window to get all the mouse messages, until such time as we say we are done by calling another inherited function in our view class, **ReleaseCapture()**. We can capture the mouse as soon as the left button is pressed by modifying the handler for the **WM_LBUTTONDOWN** message:

```
// Handler for left mouse button down message
void CSketcherView::OnLButtonDown(UINT nFlags, CPoint point)
{
    m_FirstPoint = point;              // Record the cursor position
    SetCapture();                      // Capture subsequent mouse messages
}
```

Now, we must call the **ReleaseCapture()** function in the **WM_LBUTTONUP** handler. If we don't do this, other programs won't be able to receive any mouse messages as long as our program continues to run. Of course, we should only release the mouse if we have captured it earlier. The function **GetCapture()** that our view class inherits, will return a pointer to the window that has captured the mouse. There, we just need to add the following:

```
void CSketcherView::OnLButtonUp(UINT nFlags, CPoint point)
{
    if(this == GetCapture())
        ReleaseCapture();              // Stop capturing mouse messages
    if(m_pTempElement)
    {                                  // Make sure there is an element
        // Call a document class function to store the element
        // pointed to by m_pTempElement in the document object
        delete m_pTempElement;         // This code is temporary
        m_pTempElement = 0;            // Reset the element pointer
    }
}
```

If the pointer returned by the **GetCapture()** function is equal to the pointer **this**, our view has captured the mouse, so we release it.

The final alteration we should make is to modify the **WM_MOUSEMOVE** handler so that it only deals with messages that have been captured by our view. We can do this with one small change:

```
void CSketcherView::OnMouseMove(UINT nFlags, CPoint point)
{
    // Rest of the handler as before
    if((nFlags & MK_LBUTTON) && (this == GetCapture()))
    {
        // Rest of the handler as before....
    }
}
```

The handler will only process the message if the left button is down, and the left button down handler for our view has been called so that the mouse has been captured by our view window.

If you rebuild Sketcher with these additions, you'll find that the problems which arose earlier when the cursor was dragged off the client area no longer occur.

Summary

After completing this chapter, you should have a good grasp of how to write message handlers for the mouse and how to organize drawing operations in your Windows programs. The important points that we have covered in this chapter are:

▶ Windows addresses the client area of a window using a client coordinate system with the origin in the top left corner of the client area. The positive x direction is from left to right, and the positive y direction is from top to bottom.

▶ You can only draw in the client area of a window by using a device context.

▶ A device context provides a range of logical coordinate systems called mapping modes for addressing the client area of a window.

▶ The default origin position for a mapping mode is the top left corner of the client area The default mapping mode is **MM_TEXT** which provides coordinates measured in pixels. The positive x axis runs from left to right in this mode, and the positive y axis from top to bottom.

▶ Your program should always draw the permanent contents of the client area of a window in response to a **WM_PAINT** message, although temporary entities can be drawn at other times. All the drawing for your application document should be controlled from the **OnDraw()** member function of a view class. This function is called when a **WM_PAINT** message is received by your application.

▶ You can identify the part in the client area you want to have redrawn by calling the **InvalidateRect()** function member of your view class. The area passed as an argument will be added by Windows to the total area to be redrawn when the next **WM_PAINT** message is sent to your application.

▶ Windows sends standard messages to your application for mouse events. You can create handlers to deal with these messages by using ClassWizard.

▶ You can cause all mouse messages to be routed to your application by calling the **SetCapture()** function in your view class. You must release the mouse when you are finished with it by calling the **ReleaseCapture()** function. If you fail to do this, other applications will be unable to receive mouse messages.

▶ You can implement rubber-banding when creating geometric entities by drawing them in the mouse move message handler.

▶ The **SetROP2()** member of the **CDC** class enables you to set drawing modes. Selecting the right drawing mode greatly simplifies rubber-banding operations.

Creating the Document and Improving the View

In this chapter, we'll look into the facilities offered by MFC for managing collections of data items. We'll use these to complete the class definition and implementation for the curve element that we left open in the last chapter. We'll extend the Sketcher application to store data in a document. We will also make the document view more flexible and introduce several new techniques in the process.

In this chapter, you will learn:

▶ What collections the MFC implements, and what you can do with them

▶ How to use a collection to store point data for a curve

▶ How to use a collection to store document data

▶ How to implement drawing a document

▶ How to implement scrolling in a view

▶ How to create a pop-up menu at the cursor

▶ How to highlight the element nearest the cursor to provide feedback to the user for moving and deleting elements

▶ How to program the mouse to move and delete elements

What are Collection Classes?

By the nature of Windows programming, you'll frequently handle collections of data items where you have no advance knowledge of how many items you will need to manage, or even what particular type they are going to be. This is clearly illustrated by our Sketcher application. The user can draw an arbitrary number of elements which can be lines, rectangles, circles and curves, and in any sequence. MFC provides a group of **collection classes** designed to handle exactly this sort of problem, a collection being an aggregation of an arbitrary number of data items organized in a particular way.

Types of Collections

MFC provides you with a large number of collection classes for managing data. We'll use just a couple of these in practice, but first it would be helpful to understand the types of collections available. MFC supports three kinds of collections, differentiated by the way in which the data items are organized. The way a collection is organized is referred to as the **shape** of the collection. The three types of organization, or shape, are:

Shape	How information is organized
Arrays	An array in this context is just like the array we have seen in the C++ language. It is an ordered arrangement of elements, where any element is retrieved by using an integer index value. An array collection can automatically grow to accommodate more data items. However, one of the other collection types is generally preferred, since array collections can be rather slow in operation.
Lists	A list collection is an ordered arrangement of data items, where each item has two pointers associated with it which point to the next and previous items in the list. We saw a linked list in Chapter 7 when we discussed structures. The list we have here is called a **doubly linked** list because it has backward as well as forward pointing links. It can be searched in either direction and, like an array, a list collection grows automatically when required. A list collection is easy to use, and fast when it comes to adding items. Searching for an item can be slow, though, if there are a lot of data items in the list.
Maps	A map is an unordered collection of data items, where each item is associated with a key that is used to retrieve the item from the map. A key is usually a string, but it can also be a numeric value. Maps are fast in storing data items and in searching, since a key will take you directly to the item you need.

MFC collection classes provide two approaches to implementing each type of collection. One approach is based on the use of class templates and provides you with **type-safe** handling of data in a collection. Type-safe handling means that the data passed to a function member of the collection class will be checked to ensure that it is of a type that can be processed by the function.

 We covered templates for functions back in Chapter 6. Class templates work in a similar way.

The other approach doesn't use templates, but consists of a range of collection classes that you can use and, if you want your collection classes to be type-safe, you have to include code yourself to assure this. These latter classes were available in previous versions of Visual C++ under Windows, but the template collection class were not. We'll concentrate on the template-based versions, since these will provide the best chance of avoiding errors in our application.

The Type-safe Collection Classes

The type-safe collection classes that are template-based support collections of objects of any type and collections of pointers to objects of any type. Collections of objects are supported by the template classes **CArray**, **CList** and **CMap**, and collections to pointers to objects are supported by the template classes **CTypedPtrArray**, **CTypedPtrList** and **CTypedPtrMap**. We won't go into the detail of all of these, just the two that we'll use in the Sketcher program. One will store objects and the other will store pointers to objects, so you'll get a feel for both sorts of collection.

Collections of Objects

The template classes for defining collections of objects are all derived form the MFC class **CObject**. They are defined this way so that they inherit the properties of the **CObject** class which are particularly useful for a number of things, including the file input and output operations (serialization, which we'll look at in Chapter 17).

These template classes can store and manage any kind of object, including all the C++ basic data types, plus any classes or structures that you or any body else may define. Because these classes store objects, whenever you add an element to a list, an array, or a map, the class template object will need to make a copy of your object. Consequently, any class type that you want to store in any of these collections must have a copy constructor. The copy constructor for your class will be used to create a duplicate of the object that you wish to store in the collection.

Let's look at the general properties of each of the template classes providing type-safe management of objects. This is not an exhaustive treatment of all the member functions provided. Rather, it's intended to give you a sufficient flavor of how they work to enable you to decide if you want to use them or not. You can get information on all of the member functions by using Help to get to the template class definition.

The CArray Template Class

You can use this template to store any kind of object in an array and have the array automatically grow to accommodate more elements when necessary. An array collection is illustrated here.

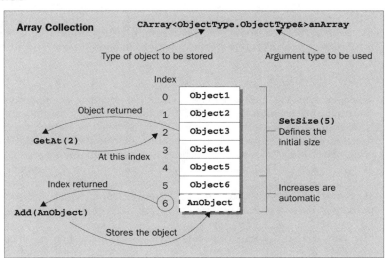

As with the arrays that we've seen in C++, elements in array collections are indexed from 0. The declaration of an array collection takes two arguments. The first argument is the type of the object to be stored so, if your array collection is to store objects of type **Cpoint**, for example, you specify **CPoint** as the first argument. The second argument is the type to be used in member function calls. This is usually a reference to avoid the overhead in copying objects when passed by value, so an example of an array collection declaration to hold **CPoint** objects is:

525

```
CArray<CPoint, CPoint&> PointArray;
```

This defines the array collection class, **PointArray**, which will store **CPoint** objects. When you call function members of this collection class, the argument is a reference, so, to add a **CPoint** object, you would write,

```
PointArray.Add(aPoint);
```

and the argument **aPoint** will be passed as a reference.

If you declare an array collection, it's important to call the **SetSize()** member function to fix the initial number of elements that you require before you use it. It will still work if you don't do this, but the initial allocation of elements and subsequent increments will be small, resulting in inefficient operation and frequent reallocation of memory for the array. The initial number of elements that you should specify depends on the typical size of array you expect to need, and how variable the size is. If you expect the minimum your program will require to be of the order of 400 to 500 elements, for example, but with expansion up to 700 or 800, an initial size of 600 should be suitable.

To retrieve the contents of an element, you can use the **GetAt()** function, as shown in the diagram above. The class also overloads the **[]** operator, so you could retrieve the same element as in the illustration by using **AnArray[2]**. This notation can also be used instead of the **SetAt()** function to set the contents of an existing element. The following two statements are, therefore, equivalent:

```
PointArray.SetAt(3,NewPoint);      // Store NewObject in the 4th element
PointArray.AnArray[3] = NewPoint;  // Same as previous line of code
```

Here, **NewPoint** is an object of the type used to declare the array. In both cases, the element must already exist. You cannot extend the array by this means. To extend the array, you can use the **Add()** function shown in the diagram, which adds a new element to the array. There is also a function **Append()** to add an array of elements to the end of the array.

Helper Functions

Whenever you call the **SetSize()** function member of an array collection, a global function, **ConstructElements()**, is called to allocate memory for the number of elements you want to store initially in the array collection. This is called a **helper function**. The default version of this function sets the contents of the memory allocated to zero and does not call a constructor for your object class, so you may need to supply your own version if this action is not appropriate for your objects. This will be the case if space for data members of objects of your class is allocated dynamically, or if there is other initialization required. **ConstructElements()** is also called by the member function **InsertAt()**, which inserts one or more elements at a particular index position within the array.

Members of the **CArray** collection class also call the helper function, **DestructElements()**. The default version does nothing so, if your object construction allocates any memory on the heap, you must override this function to release the memory properly.

Another helper function, **SerializeElements()**, is used by the array, list and map collection classes, but we'll discuss this when we come to look into how we can write a document to file.

526

The CList Template Class

A list collection is very flexible. You're likely to find yourself using lists more often than you use either arrays or maps. Let's look at the list collection template in some detail, as we'll apply it in our Sketcher program. The parameters to the **CList** collection class template are the same as those for the **CArray** template:

```
CList<ObjectType, ObjectType&> aList;
```

You need to supply two arguments to the template when you declare a list collection: the type of object to be stored and the way an object is to be specified in function arguments. The example shows the second argument as a reference, since this is used most frequently. It doesn't necessarily have to be a reference, though - you could use a pointer, or even the object type, so objects would be passed by value, but this would be slow.

We can use a list to manage a curve in the Sketcher program. We could declare a list collection to store the points specifying a curve object with the statement:

```
CList<CPoint, CPoint&> PointList;
```

This declares a list called **PointList** which stores **CPoint** objects that are passed to functions in the class by reference. We'll come back to this when we fill out more detail of the Sketcher program in this chapter.

Adding Elements to a List

You can add objects at the beginning or at the end of the list by using the **AddHead()** or **AddTail()** member functions, as shown in the following diagram:

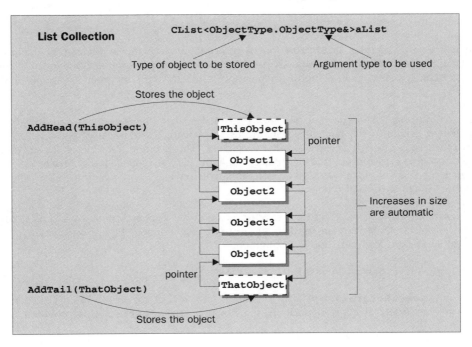

The diagram shows backward and forward pointers for each list element that glue the objects in the list together. These are internal links that you can't access in any direct way, but you can do just about anything you want by using the functions provided in the public interface to the class.

To add the object **aPoint** to the tail of the list **PointList**, you would write:

```
PointList.AddTail(aPoint);      // Add an element to the end
```

As new elements are added, the size of the list will increase automatically.

Both the **AddHead()** and **AddTail()** functions return a value of type **POSITION**, which specifies the position of the inserted object in the list. The way in which a variable of type **POSITION** is used is shown this next diagram:

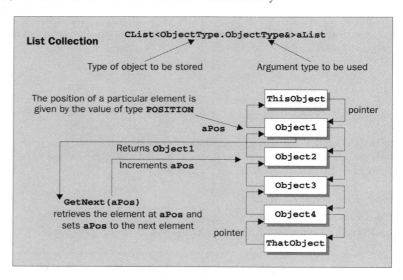

You can use a value of type **POSITION** for an object to retrieve the object at that position in the list by using the **GetNext()** function. Note that you cannot perform arithmetic on values of type **POSITION** - you can only modify a position value through member functions of the list object.

As well as returning the object, the **GetNext()** function increments the position variable passed to it, so that it points to the next object in the list. You can, therefore, use repeated calls to **GetNext()** to step through a list element by element. The position variable is set to **NULL** if you use **GetNext()** to retrieve the last object from the list, so you can use this to control your loop operation. You should always make sure that you have a valid position value when you call member functions of a list object.

You can insert an element in a list at a specific position as long as you have a **POSITION** value. To insert the object **ThePoint** in the list **PointList** immediately before an element at the position **aPosition**, you can use the statement:

```
PointList.InsertBefore(aPosition,  ThePoint)
```

The function **InsertBefore()** will also return the position of the new object. To insert an element after the object at a given position, the function **InsertAfter()** is provided.

When you need to set an existing object in a list to a particular value, you can use the function **SetAt()**, as long as you know the position value for the object:

```
PointList.SetAt(aPosition, aPoint);
```

There is no return value for this function. You must ensure that the **POSITION** value you pass to the function is valid. An invalid value will cause an error. You should, therefore, only pass a **POSITION** value to this function that was returned by one of the other member functions and that you have verified is not **NULL**.

Iterating through a List

If you want to get the **POSITION** value for the beginning or the end of the list, the class provides the member functions **GetHeadPosition()** and **GetTailPosition()**. Starting with the **POSITION** value for the head of the list, you can iterate through the complete list by calling **GetNext()** until the position value is **NULL**. We can illustrate the typical code to do this using the list of **CPoint** objects that we declared earlier:

```
CPoint CurrentPoint(0,0);        // Storage for a point

// Get the position of the first list element
POSITION aPosition = PointList.GetHeadPosition();

while(aPosition)                 // Loop while aPosition is not NULL
{
    CurrentObject = PointList.GetNext(aPosition);
    // Process the current object...
}
```

You can work through the list backwards by using another member function, **GetPrev()**, which retrieves the current object and then decrements the position indicator. Of course, in this case, you would start out by calling **GetTailPosition()**.

Once you know a position value for an object in a list, you can retrieve the object with the member function **GetAt()**. You specify the position value as an argument and the object is returned. An invalid position value will cause an error.

Searching a List

You can find the position of an element that is stored in a list by using the member function **Find()**:

```
POSITION aPosition = PointList.Find(ThePoint);
```

This searches for the object specified as an argument by comparing its address with that of objects in the list. Note that it does not compare objects. If the search is to be successful, the argument must actually be an element in the list, not a copy. If the object is found in the list, the position of the element is returned. If it isn't found, **NULL** is returned. You can specify a second argument to define a position value where the search should begin.

You can also obtain the position of an element in a list by using an index value. The index works in the same way as for an array, with the first element being at index 0, the second at index 1, and so on. The function **FindIndex()** takes an index value of type **int** as an argument and returns a value of type **POSITION** for the object at the index position in the list. If you want to use an index value, you are likely to need to know how many objects there are in a list. The **GetCount()** function will return this for you:

```
int ObjectCount = PointList.GetCount();
```

Here, the integer count of the number of elements in the list will be stored in the variable **ObjectCount**.

Deleting Objects from a List

You can delete the first element in a list using the member function **RemoveHead()**. This function will return the object that is the new head of the list. To remove the last object, you can use the function **RemoveTail()**. Both of these functions require that there should be at least one object in the list, so you should use the function **IsEmpty()** first, to verify that the list is not empty. For example:

```
if(!PointList.IsEmpty())
    PointList.RemoveHead();
```

The function **IsEmpty()** returns **TRUE** if the list is empty, and **FALSE** otherwise.

If you know the position value for an object that you want to delete from the list, you can do this directly:

```
PointList.RemoveAt(aPosition);
```

There is no return value from this function. It's your responsibility to ensure that the position value you pass as an argument is valid.

If you want to delete the entire contents of a list, you use the member function **RemoveAll()**:

```
PointList.RemoveAll();    // Delete all elements
```

This function will also free the memory that was allocated for the elements in the list.

Helper Functions for a List

Both the **ConstructElements()** and **DestructElements()** global helper functions are used by members of a **CList** template class. These are template functions which will be declared using the object type you specify in your **CList** class declaration. For example, the prototypes for the **PointList** class for these will be:

```
void ConstructElements(CPoint* pPoint, int PointCount);
void DestructElements(CPoint* pPoint, int PointCount);
```

As for the **CArray** template class, you need to implement your versions of these functions if the default operation is not suitable for your object class.

The **CList** class also uses another global helper function **CompareElements()**. This is called by the member function **Find()**, so, if you use this, you must implement the **CompareElements()** function to compare objects of your class. This is also a template function using the type of your objects and the way they are referred to in function calls as parameters, so the template is of the form:

```
template< class TYPE, class ARG_TYPE >
BOOL CompareElements(const TYPE* pElement1, const ARG_TYPE* pElement2);
```

If we take the **PointList** class as an example, the prototype of the function would be:

```
BOOL CompareElements(const CPoint* pPoint1, const CPoint* pPoint2);
```

The function should return **TRUE** if the objects pointed to are equal, and **FALSE** otherwise.

We could implement this as:

```
BOOL CompareElements(const CPoint* pPoint1, const CPoint* pPoint2)
{
    return (*CPoint1.x==*CPoint2.x) && (*CPoint1.y==*CPoint2.y);
}
```

The CMap Template Class

Because of the way they work, maps are particularly suited to applications where your objects obviously have a relatively dissimilar key associated with them, such as a customer class where each customer will have an associated customer number, or a name and address class where the name might be used as a key. The organization of a map is shown below:

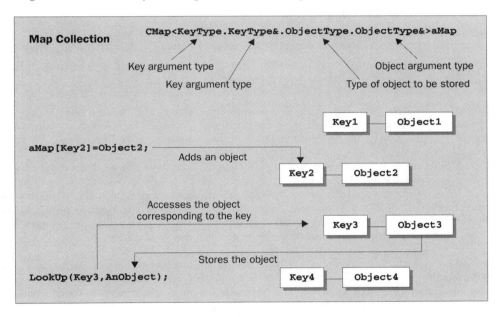

A map stores an object and a key combination. The key is used to determine where in a block of memory allocated to the map the object is to be stored. The key, therefore, provides a means of going directly to an object stored, as long as the key is unique. The process of converting a key to an address of an object is called **hashing**. The hashing process may not produce a unique key, in which case an element will be entered adjacent to whatever element or elements were previously stored with the same hashed key value. Of course, the fewer unique hash values that are generated, the less efficient the retrieval process from your map will be.

There are four arguments necessary when you declare a map:

```
CMap<LONG, LONG&, CPoint, CPoint&> PointMap;
```

The first two specify the key type and how it is passed as an argument. Usually, it will be passed as a reference. The second pair of arguments specify the object type and how the object is passed as an argument, as we have seen previously.

You can store an object in a map by using the **[]** operator as shown in the diagram above. You can also use a member function **SetAt()** to store an object, where you supply the key value and the object as arguments. Note that you cannot use the **[]** operator on the right-hand side of an assignment to retrieve an object, as this version of the operator has not been implemented in the class.

To retrieve an object, you use the **LookUp()** function shown in the diagram. This will retrieve the object corresponding to the key specified; the function returns **TRUE** if the object was found, and **FALSE** otherwise. You can also iterate through all the objects in a map using a variable of type **POSITION**, although the sequence in which objects are retrieved is unrelated to the sequence in which they were added to the map.

Helper Functions Used by CMap

As well as the helper functions that we have discussed in the context of arrays and lists, map collection classes also use a global function **HashKey()** which is defined by the template:

```
template<class ARG_KEY>
    UINT HashKey(ARG_KEY key);
```

This function converts your key value to a key of type **UINT**. The default version does this by simply shifting your key value right by 4 bit positions. You need to implement your own version of this function if the default operation is not suited to your key type.

There are different techniques used for hashing which vary depending on the type of data being used as a key and the number of elements you are likely to want to store in your map. The likely number of elements to be stored indicates the number of unique hash values you need. A common method for hashing a numeric key value is to compute the hash value as the value of the key modulo N, where N is the number of different values you want. For reasons it would take too long to explain here, N needs to be prime for this to work well.

Where a key is a character string, the process is rather more complicated, particularly with long or variable strings. However, a method that is commonly used involves using numerical values derived from characters in the string. This typically involves assigning a numerical value to each character, so if your string was lower case letters plus blank, you could assign each character a value between 0 and 26, with blank as 0, a as 1, b as 2, and so on. The string can then be treated as the representation of a number to some base, 32 say. The value of a key for "fred" for instance would then be

$6*32^3+18*32^2+5*32^1+4*32^0$

and, assuming you expected to store 500 strings, you could calculate the hashed value of the key as:

$6*32^3+18*32^2+5*32^1+4*32^0$ mod 503

The value of 503 for N is the smallest prime greater than the likely number of entries. The base chosen to evaluate a key value for a string is usually a power of 2 that corresponds to the minimum value that is greater than or equal to the number of possible different characters in a string. For long strings, this generates very large numbers, so special techniques are used to compute the value modulo N. Detailed discussion of this is beyond the scope of this book.

The Typed Pointer Collections

The typed pointer collection class templates store pointers to objects, rather than objects themselves. This is the primary difference between these class templates and the template classes we have just discussed. We'll look at how one example is used, the **CTypedPtrList** class template, because we'll use this as a basis for managing elements in our document class, **CSketcherDoc**.

The CTypedPtrList Template Class

You can declare a typed-pointer list class with a statement of the form:

```
CTypedPtrList<BaseClass, Type*> ListName;
```

The first argument specifies a base class that must be one of two pointer-list classes defined in MFC, either **CObList** or **CPtrList**. Your choice will depend on how your object class has been defined. Using the **CObList** class creates a list supporting pointers to objects derived from **CObject**, while **CPtrList** supports lists of **void*** pointers. Since the elements in our Sketcher example have **CObject** as a base class, we'll concentrate on how this is used.

The second argument to the template is the type of the pointers to be stored in the list. In our example, this is going to be **CElement***, since all our shapes have **CElement** as a base and **CElement** is derived from **CObject**. Thus, the declaration of a class for storing shapes is:

```
CTypedPtrList<CObList, CElement*> m_ElementList;
```

We could have used **CObList** to store the pointers to our elements, but then the list could contain an object of any class that has **CObject** as a base. The declaration of **m_ElementList** ensures that only pointers to objects of the class **CElement** can be stored. This provides a greatly increased level of security in the program.

CTypePtrList Operations

The functions provided in the **CTypedPtrList** based classes are similar to those supported by **CList**, except, of course, that all operations are with pointers to objects rather than with objects, so let's tabulate them. They fall into two groups: those that are defined in **CTypedPtrList** and those that are inherited from the base class - **CObList** in this case.

Defined in **CTypedPtrList**:

Function	Remarks
GetHead()	Returns the pointer at the head of the list. You should use **IsEmpty()** to verify that the list is not empty before calling this function.

Table Continued on Following Page

Function	Remarks
`GetTail()`	Returns the pointer at the tail of the list. You should use `IsEmpty()` to verify that the list is not empty before calling this function.
`RemoveHead()`	Removes the first pointer in the list. You should use `IsEmpty()` to verify that the list is not empty before calling this function.
`RemoveTail()`	Removes the last pointer in the list. You should use `IsEmpty()` to verify that the list is not empty before calling this function.
`GetNext()`	Returns the pointer at the position indicated by the variable of type `POSITION` passed as a reference argument. The variable is updated to indicate the next element in the list. When the end of the list is reached, the position variable is set to `NULL`. This function can be used to iterate forwards through all the pointers in the list.
`GetPrev()`	Returns the pointer at the position indicated by the variable of type `POSITION` passed as a reference argument. The variable is updated to indicate the previous element in the list. When the beginning of the list is reached, the position variable is set to `NULL`. This function can be used to iterate backwards through all the pointers in the list.
`GetAt()`	Returns the pointer stored at the position indicated by the variable of type `POSITION` passed as an argument, which is not changed. Since the function returns a reference, as long as the list is not defined as `const`, this function can be used on the left of an assignment operator to modify a list entry.

Inherited from `CObList`:

Function	Remarks
`AddHead()`	Adds the pointer passed as an argument to the head of the list and returns a value of type `POSITION` that corresponds to the new element. There is another version of this function which can add another list to the head of the list.
`AddTail()`	Adds the pointer passed as an argument to the tail of the list and returns a value of type `POSITION` that corresponds to the new element. There is another version of this function which can add another list to the tail of the list.
`RemoveAll()`	Removes all the elements from the list. Note that this does not delete the objects pointed to by elements in the list. You need to take care of this yourself.

Table Continued on Following Page

Function	Remarks
`GetHeadPosition()`	Returns the position of the element at the head of the list.
`GetTailPosition()`	Returns the position of the element at the tail of the list.
`SetAt()`	Stores the pointer specified by the second argument at the position in the list defined by the first argument. An invalid position value will cause an error.
`RemoveAt()`	Removes the pointer from the position in the list specified by the argument of type **POSITION**. An invalid position value will cause an error.
`InsertBefore()`	Inserts a new pointer specified by the second argument before the position specified by the first argument. The position of the new element is returned.
`InsertAfter()`	Inserts a new pointer specified by the second argument after the position specified by the first argument. The position of the new element is returned.
`Find()`	Searches for a pointer in the list that is identical to the pointer specified as an argument. Its position is returned if it is found. **NULL** is returned otherwise.
`FindIndex()`	Returns the position of a pointer in the list specified by a zero-based integer index argument.
`GetCount()`	Returns the number of elements in the list.
`IsEmpty()`	Returns **TRUE** if there are no elements in the list, and **FALSE** otherwise.

We'll see some of these member functions in action a little later in this chapter in the context of implementing the document class for the Sketcher program.

Using the CList Template Class

We can make use of the **CList** collection template in the definition of the curve object in our Sketcher application. A curve is defined by two or more points, so storing these in a list would be a good method of handling them. We first need to define a **CList** collection class object as a member of the **CCurve** class. We'll use this collection to store points. We have looked at the **CList** template class in some detail, so this should be easy.

The **CList** template class has two parameters, so the general form of declaring a collection class of this type is:

```
CList<YourObjectType, FunctionArgType> ClassName;
```

The first argument, **YourObjectType**, specifies the type of object that you want to store in the list. The second argument specifies the argument type to be used in function members of the collection class when referring to an object.

This is usually specified as a reference to the object type to minimize copying of arguments in a function call. So let's declare a collection class object to suit our needs in the **CCurve** class as:

```
class CCurve: public CElement
{
// Rest of the class definition...

protected:
    // CCurve data members to go here
    CList<CPoint, CPoint&> m_PointList;   // Type safe point list

    CCurve(){}              // Default constructor - should not be used
};
```

The rest of the class definition is omitted here, since we're not concerned with it for now. The collection declaration is shaded. It declares the collection **m_PointList** which will store **CPoint** objects in the list, and its functions will use reference arguments to **CPoint** objects.

The **CPoint** class doesn't allocate memory dynamically, so we won't need to implement **ConstructElements()** or **DestructElements()**, and we don't need to use the **Find()** member function, so we can forget about the **CompareElements()** function.

Drawing a Curve

Drawing a curve is different from drawing a line or a circle. With a line or a circle, as we move the cursor with the left button down, we are creating a succession of different line or circle elements that share a common reference point - the point where the left mouse button was pressed. This is not the case when we draw a curve, as shown in the diagram below:

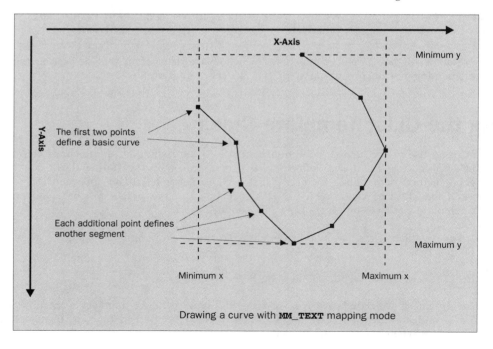

Drawing a curve with **MM_TEXT** mapping mode

When we move the cursor while drawing a curve, we're not creating a sequence of new curves, but extending the same curve, so each successive point adds another segment to the definition of the curve. We, therefore, need to create a curve object as soon as we have the two points from the **WM_LBUTTONDOWN** message and the first **WM_MOUSEMOVE** message. Points defined with subsequent mouse move messages then define additional segments to the existing curve object. We'll need to add a function **AddSegment()** to the **CCurve** class to extend the curve once it has been created by the constructor.

A further point to consider is how we are to calculate the enclosing rectangle. This is defined by getting the minimum x and minimum y pair from all the defining points for the top left corner of the rectangle, and the maximum x and maximum y pair for the bottom right. This involves going through all the points in the list. We will, therefore, compute the enclosing rectangle incrementally in the **AddSegment()** function as points are added to the curve.

Defining the CCurve Class

With these features added, the complete definition of the **CCurve** class will now be:

```
class CCurve: public CElement
{
public:
    virtual BOOL Draw(CDC* pDC);                    // Function to display a curve

    // Constructor for a curve object
    CCurve(CPoint FirstPoint, CPoint SecondPoint, COLORREF aColor);

    void AddSegment(CPoint& aPoint);               //Add a segment to the curve

protected:
    // CCurve data members to go here
    CList<CPoint, CPoint&> m_PointList;            // Type safe point list

    CCurve(){}                                      // Default constructor - should not be used
};
```

You should modify the definition of the class in **Elements.h** to correspond with the above. The constructor has the first two defining points and the color as parameters, so it only defines a curve with one segment. This will be called in the **CreateElement()** function invoked by the **OnMouseMove()** function in the view class the first time a **WM_MOUSEMOVE** message is received for a curve, so don't forget to modify the **CreateElement()** function to call the constructor with the correct arguments. The statement using the **CCurve** constructor in the **switch** in this function should be changed to:

```
case CURVE:
    return new CCurve(m_FirstPoint, m_SecondPoint, pDoc->GetElementColor());
```

After the constructor has been called, all subsequent **WM_MOUSEMOVE** messages will result in the **AddSegment()** function being called to add a segment to the existing curve, as shown in the diagram on the following page.

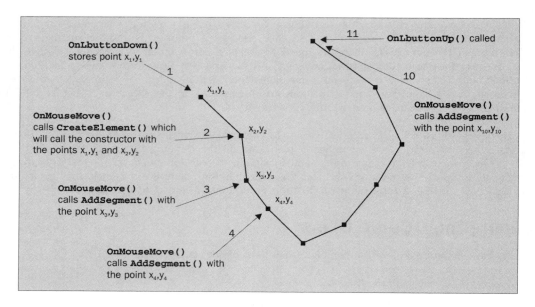

This shows the complete sequence of message handler calls for a curve comprised of nine segments. The sequence is indicated by the numbered arrows. The code for the **OnMouseMove()** function in **CSketcherView** needs to be updated as follows:

```
void CSketcherView::OnMouseMove(UINT nFlags, CPoint point)
{
    CClientDC aDC(this);                        // Device context for the current view
    aDC.SetROP2(R2_NOTXORPEN);                  // Set drawing mode
    if((nFlags&MK_LBUTTON)&&(this==GetCapture()))
    {

        m_SecondPoint = point;      // Save the current cursor position

        if(m_pTempElement)
        {
            // Redraw the old element so it disappears from the view
            m_pTempElement->Draw(&aDC);
            if(CURVE == GetDocument()->GetElementType())    // Is it a curve?
            {   // We are drawing a curve
                // so add a segment to the existing curve
                ((CCurve*)m_pTempElement)->AddSegment(m_SecondPoint);
                m_pTempElement->Draw(&aDC);    // Now redraw it
                return;                        // We are done
            }
            delete m_pTempElement;              // Delete the old element
            m_pTempElement = 0;                 // Reset the pointer to 0
        }
        // Create an element of the type and color
        // recorded in the document object
        m_pTempElement = CreateElement();
        m_pTempElement->Draw(&aDC);
    }
}
```

We have to treat an element of type **CURVE** as a special case once it has been created, because on all subsequent calls of the **OnMouseMove()** handler we want to call the **AddSegment()** function for the existing element, rather than construct a new one in place of the old. Note that we need to cast the **m_pTempElement** pointer to type **CCurve** in order to use it to call **AddSegment()** for the old element, because **AddSegment()** is not a virtual function. If we don't add the cast, we'll get an error, because the compiler will try to resolve the call statically to a member of the **CElement** class.

After adding the new segment, we just redraw the curve. The previous version will already have been erased by the call to the **Draw()** function immediately preceding the check for an element of type **CURVE**.

Implementing the CCurve Class

Let's first write the code for the constructor. This should be added to the **Elements.cpp** in place of the temporary constructor that we used in the last chapter. It needs to store the two points passed as arguments in the **CList** data member, **m_PointList**:

```
CCurve::CCurve(CPoint FirstPoint,CPoint SecondPoint, COLORREF aColor)
{
    m_PointList.AddTail(FirstPoint);      // Add the 1st point to the list
    m_PointList.AddTail(SecondPoint);     // Add the 2nd point to the list
    m_Color = aColor;                     // Store the color
    m_Pen = 1;                            // Set the pen width

    // Construct the enclosing rectangle assuming MM_TEXT mode
    m_EnclosingRect = CRect(FirstPoint, SecondPoint);
    m_EnclosingRect.NormalizeRect();
}
```

The points are added to the list, **m_PointList**, by calling the **AddTail()** member of the **CList** template class. This function adds a copy of the point passed as an argument to the end of the list. The enclosing rectangle is defined in exactly the same way that we defined it for a line.

The next function we should add to **Elements.cpp** is **AddSegment()**. This function will be called when additional curve points are recorded, after the first version of a curve object has been created. This member function is very simple:

```
void CCurve::AddSegment(CPoint& aPoint)
{
    m_PointList.AddTail(aPoint);                          //Add the point to the end

    // Modify the enclosing rectangle for the new point
    m_EnclosingRect = CRect(
        min(aPoint.x, m_EnclosingRect.left),
        min(aPoint.y, m_EnclosingRect.top),
        max(aPoint.x, m_EnclosingRect.right),
        max(aPoint.y, m_EnclosingRect.bottom));
}
```

The new point is added to the tail of the list in the same way as in the constructor. It's important that each new point is added to the list in a way that is consistent with the constructor, because we'll draw the segments using the points in sequence, from the beginning to the end of the list. Each line segment will be drawn from the end point of the previous line to the new point. If the points are not in the right sequence, the line segments won't be drawn correctly. After adding the new point, the enclosing rectangle for the curve is redefined, taking account of the new point.

The last member function we need to define for the interface to the **CCurve** class is **Draw()**:

```
void CCurve::Draw(CDC* pDC)
{
    // Create a pen for this object and
    // initialize it to the object color and line width of 1 pixel
    CPen aPen;
    if(!aPen.CreatePen(PS_SOLID, m_Pen, m_Color))
    {                                          // Pen creation failed
        AfxMessageBox("Pen creation failed drawing a curve", MB_OK);
        AfxAbort();                            // Closing the program
    }

    CPen* pOldPen = pDC->SelectObject(&aPen);  // Select the pen

    // Now draw the curve
    // Get the position in the list of the first element
    POSITION aPosition = m_PointList.GetHeadPosition();

    // As long as it's good, move to that point
    if(aPosition)
        pDC->MoveTo(m_PointList.GetNext(aPosition));

    // Draw a segment for each of the following points
    while(aPosition)
        pDC->LineTo(m_PointList.GetNext(aPosition));

    pDC->SelectObject(pOldPen);                // Restore the old pen
}
```

To draw the **CCurve** object, we need to iterate through all the points in the list from the beginning, drawing each segment as we go. We get a **POSITION** value for the first element by using the function **GetHeadPosition()** and then use **MoveTo()** to set the first point as the current position in the device context. We then draw line segments in the **while** loop as long as **aPosition** is not **NULL**. The **GetNext()** function, which appears as the argument to the **LineTo()** function, returns the current point and simultaneously increments **aPosition** to refer to the next point in the list.

Exercising the CCurve Class

With the changes we've just discussed added to the Sketcher program, we've implemented all the code necessary for the element shapes in our menu. In order to make use of the collection class templates, though, we must include the file **Afxtempl.h**. The best place to put the **#include** statement would be in **Stdafx.h**, so that it will be added to the precompiled header file. Go to **Stdafx.h** in file mode and add the line shown next:

```
// stdafx.h : include file for standard system include files,
//   or project specific include files that are used frequently, but
//      are changed infrequently
//

#define VC_EXTRALEAN       // Exclude rarely-used stuff from Windows headers

#include <afxwin.h>        // MFC core and standard components
#include <afxext.h>        // MFC extensions
#include <afxtempl.h>      // Collection templates

#ifndef _AFX_NO_AFXCMN_SUPPORT
#include <afxcmn.h>             // MFC support for Windows 95 Common Controls
#endif  // _AFX_NO_AFXCMN_SUPPORT
```

With the file included here, it will also be available to the implementation of **CSketcherDoc** when we get to use a collection class template there.

You can now build the Sketcher program once more, and execute it. You should be able to create curves in all four colors. A typical application window is shown here:

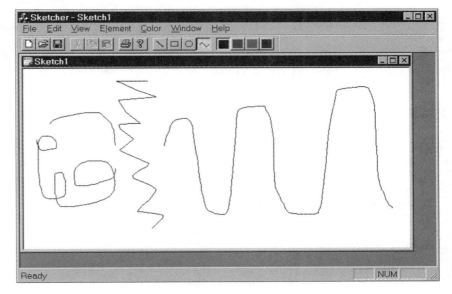

Of course, like the other elements you can draw, the curves are not persistent. As soon as you cause a **WM_PAINT** message to be sent to the application, by resizing the view for instance, they will disappear. Once we can store them in the document object for the application, though, they will be a bit more permanent, so let's take a look at that next.

Creating the Document

The document in the Sketcher application needs to be able to store an arbitrary collection of lines, rectangles, circles and curves in any sequence, and an excellent vehicle for handling this is a list. Because all the element classes that we have defined include the capability for the objects to draw themselves, drawing the document is easily accomplished by stepping through the list.

Using a CTypedPtrList Template

We can declare a **CTypedPtrList** that will store pointers to instances of our shape classes as **CElement** pointers. We just need to add the list declaration as a data member in the **CSketcherDoc** class definition:

```
class CSketcherDoc : public CDocument
{
protected: // create from serialization only
    CSketcherDoc();
    DECLARE_DYNCREATE(CSketcherDoc)

// Attributes
public:

protected:
    COLORREF m_Color;                       // Current drawing color
    WORD m_Element;                         // Current element type
    CTypedPtrList<CObList, CElement*> m_ElementList; // Element list

// Operations
public:
    WORD GetElementType(){return m_Element;}    // Get the element type
    COLORREF GetElementColor(){return m_Color;}// Get the element color

// Rest of the class as before...

};
```

Of course, we'll also need a member function to add an element to the list. **AddElement()** would be a good, if unoriginal, name for this function. We create shape objects on the heap, so we can just pass a pointer to the function and, since all it does is add an element, we might just as well put the implementation in the class definition:

```
class CSketcherDoc : public CDocument
{
protected: // create from serialization only
    CSketcherDoc();
    DECLARE_DYNCREATE(CSketcherDoc)

// Attributes
public:

protected:
    COLORREF m_Color;                                   // Current drawing color
    WORD m_Element;                                     // Current element type
    CTypedPtrList<CObList, CElement*> m_ElementList;   // Element list

// Operations
public:
    WORD GetElementType(){return m_Element;}    // Get the element type
    COLORREF GetElementColor(){return m_Color;} // Get the element color

    void AddElement(CElement* pElement) // Add an element to the list
        { m_ElementList.AddTail(pElement); }
```

```
// Rest of the class as before...

};
```

Adding an element to the list only requires one statement which calls the **AddTail()** member function. That's all we need to create the document, but we need to consider what happens when a document is closed. We need to make sure that the list of pointer and all the elements they point to are destroyed properly. To do this, we need to add code to the destructor for **CSketcherDoc** objects.

Implementing the Document Destructor

In the destructor, we'll need to go through the list deleting the element pointed to by each entry. Once that is complete, we must delete the pointers from the list. The code to do this will be:

```
CSketcherDoc::~CSketcherDoc()
{
    // Get the position at the head of the list
    POSITION aPosition = m_ElementList.GetHeadPosition();

    // Now delete the element pointed to by each list entry
    while(aPosition)
        delete m_ElementList.GetNext(aPosition);

    m_ElementList.RemoveAll();    // Finally delete all pointers
}
```

We use the **GetHeadPosition()** function to obtain the position value for the entry at the head of the list and initialize the variable **aPosition** with this value. We then use **aPosition** in the **while** loop to walk through the list and delete the object pointed to by each entry. The function **GetNext()** returns the current pointer entry and updates the **aPosition** variable to refer to the next entry. When the last entry is retrieved, **aPosition** will be set to **NULL** by the **GetNext()** function and the loop will end.

You should add this code to the definition of the destructor in **SketcherDoc.cpp**. You can go directly to the code for the destructor through the ClassView.

Drawing the Document

As the document owns the list of elements and the list is **protected**, we can't use it directly from the view. The **OnDraw()** member of the view does need to be able to call the **Draw()** member for each of the elements in the list, though, so we need to consider how best to do this. Let's look at our options:

- We could make the list **public**, but this would rather defeat the object of maintaining protected members of the document class, as it would expose all the function members of the list object.

- We could add a member function to return a pointer to the list, but this would effectively make the list **public** and also incur overhead in accessing it.

- We could add a **public** function to the document which would call the **Draw()** member for each element. We could then call this member from the **OnDraw()** function in the view. This would not be a bad solution, as it would produce what we want and would still maintain the privacy of the list. The only thing against it is that the function would need access to a device context, and this is really the domain of the view.

> We could add a function to provide a **POSITION** value for the first list element, and a member to iterate through the list elements. This would not expose the list, but would make the element pointers available.

The last option looks to be the best choice, so let's go with that. We can extend the document class definition to:

```
class CSketcherDoc : public CDocument
{
protected: // create from serialization only
    CSketcherDoc();
    DECLARE_DYNCREATE(CSketcherDoc)

// Attributes
public:

protected:
    COLORREF m_Color;                       // Current drawing color
    WORD m_Element;                         // Current element type
    CTypedPtrList<CObList, CElement*> m_ElementList;  // Element list

// Operations
public:
    WORD GetElementType(){return m_Element;}    // Get the element type
    COLORREF GetElementColor(){return m_Color;} // Get the element color

    void AddElement(CElement* pElement)     // Add an element to the list
    { m_ElementList.AddTail(pElement); }

    POSITION GetListHeadPosition()          // return list head POSITION value
    { return m_ElementList.GetHeadPosition(); }

    CElement* GetNext(POSITION& aPos)       // Return current element pointer
    { return m_ElementList.GetNext(aPos); }

// Rest of the class as before...

};
```

By using the two functions that we have added to the document class, the **OnDraw()** function for the view will be able to iterate through the list, calling the **Draw()** function for each element. The implementation of **OnDraw()** to do this will be:

```
void CSketcherView::OnDraw(CDC* pDC)
{
    CSketcherDoc* pDoc = GetDocument();
    ASSERT_VALID(pDoc);

    // TODO: add draw code for native data here
    POSITION aPos = pDoc->GetListHeadPosition();
    while(aPos)                    // Loop while aPos is not null
    {
        pDoc->GetNext(aPos)->Draw(pDC);    // Draw the current element
    }
}
```

If we implement it like this, the function will always draw all the elements the document contains. It plows through the list from beginning to end. We can do it better, though, and make our program more efficient.

Frequently, when a **WM_PAINT** message is sent to your program, only part of the window needs to be redrawn. When Windows sends the **WM_PAINT** message to a window, it also defines an area in the client area of the window, and only this area needs to be redrawn. The **CDC** class provides a member function, **RectVisible()**, which checks whether a rectangle that you supply to it as an argument overlaps the area that Windows requires to be redrawn. We can use this to make sure we only draw the elements that are in the area Windows wants redrawn, thus improving the performance of the application:

```
void CSketcherView::OnDraw(CDC* pDC)
{
    CSketcherDoc* pDoc = GetDocument();
    ASSERT_VALID(pDoc);

    // TODO: add draw code for native data here
    POSITION aPos = pDoc->GetListHeadPosition();
    CElement* pElement = 0;        // Store for an element pointer
    while(aPos)                    // Loop while aPos is not null
    {
        pElement = pDoc->GetNext(aPos);      // Get the current element pointer
        // If the element is visible...
        if(pDC->RectVisible(pElement->GetBoundRect()))
            pElement->Draw(pDC);                 // ...draw it
    }
}
```

We get the position for the first entry in the list and store it in **aPos**. This controls the loop which retrieves each pointer entry in turn. The bounding rectangle for each element is obtained using the **GetBoundRect()** member of the object and is passed to the **RectVisible()** function in the **if** statement. As a result, only elements that overlap the area that Windows has identified as invalid will be drawn. Drawing on the screen is a relatively expensive operation in terms of time, so checking for just the elements that need to be redrawn, rather than drawing everything each time, will improve performance considerably.

Adding an Element to the Document

The last thing we need to do to have a working document in our program is to add the code to the **OnLButtonUp()** handler in **CSketcherView** class to add the temporary element to the document:

```
void CSketcherView::OnLButtonUp(UINT nFlags, CPoint point)
{
    if(this == GetCapture())
        ReleaseCapture();        // Stop capturing mouse messages

    // If there is an element, add it to the document
    if(m_pTempElement)
    {
        GetDocument()->AddElement(m_pTempElement);
        InvalidateRect(0);           // Redraw the current window
        m_pTempElement = 0;          // Reset the element pointer
    }
}
```

Of course, we do need to check that there really is an element before we add it to the document. The user might just have clicked the left mouse button without moving the mouse. After adding the element to the list in the document, we call **InvalidateRect()** to get the client area for the current view redrawn. The argument of **0** invalidates the whole of the client area in the view. Because of the way the rubber-banding process works, some elements may not be displayed properly if we don't do this. If you draw a horizontal line, for instance, and then rubber-band a rectangle with the same color, so that its top or bottom edge overlaps the line, the overlapped bit of line will disappear. This is because the edge being drawn is XORed with the line underneath, so you get the background color back. We also must reset the pointer **m_pTempElement** to avoid confusion when another element is created.

Exercising the Document

Because we now use **CElement** class objects in the **CSketcherDoc** class, we must add **#include** statements for **Elements.h** to the beginning of **SketcherDoc.h**. After saving all the modified files, you can build the latest version of Sketcher and execute it. You'll now be able to produce art such as 'the happy programmer' shown here:

The program is now working more realistically. It stores a pointer to each element in the document object, so they are all automatically redrawn as necessary. The program also does a proper clean up of the document data when it's deleted.

There are still some limitations in the program that we need to address. For instance:

▶ You can open another view window by using the Window/New Window menu option in the program. This capability is built in to an MDI application and opens a new view to an existing document, not a new document. However, if you draw in one window, the elements are not drawn in the other window. Elements never appear in windows other than the one where they were drawn, unless the area they occupy needs to be redrawn for some other reason.

▶ We can only draw in the client area that we can see. It would be nice to be able to scroll the view and draw over a bigger area.

▶ Neither can we delete an element, so, if you make a mistake, you either live with it or start over with a new document.

These are all quite serious deficiencies which, together, make the program fairly useless as it is. We'll overcome all of them before the end of this chapter.

Improving the View

The first item that we can try to fix is the updating of all the document windows that are displayed when an element is drawn. The problem arises because only the view in which an element is drawn knows about the new element. Each view is acting independently of the others and there is no communication between them. We need to arrange for any view that adds an element to the document to let all the other views know about it and they need to take the appropriate action.

Updating Multiple Views

The document class conveniently contains a function **UpdateAllViews()** to help with this particular problem. This function essentially provides a means for the document to send a message to all its views. We just need to call it from the **OnLButtonUp()** function in the **CSketcherView** class, whenever we have added a new element to the document:

```
void CSketcherView::OnLButtonUp(UINT nFlags, CPoint point)
{
    if(this == GetCapture())
        ReleaseCapture();          // Stop capturing mouse messages

    // If there is an element, add it to the document
    if(m_pTempElement)
    {
        GetDocument()->AddElement(m_pTempElement);
        GetDocument()->UpdateAllViews(0,0,m_pTempElement);    // Tell all the views
        m_pTempElement = 0;        // Reset the element pointer
    }
}
```

When the **m_pTempElement** pointer is not **NULL**, the specific action of the function has been extended to call the **UpdateAllViews()** member of our document class. This function communicates with the views by causing the **OnUpdate()** member function in each view to be called. The three arguments to **UpdateAllViews()** are described below:

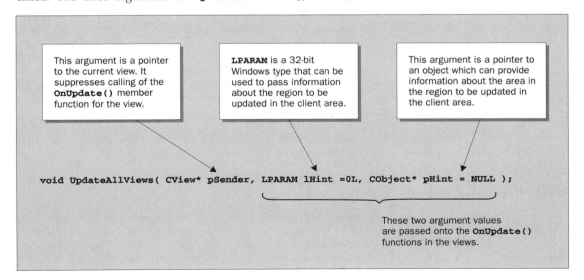

This argument is a pointer to the current view. It suppresses calling of the **OnUpdate()** member function for the view.

LPARAM is a 32-bit Windows type that can be used to pass information about the region to be updated in the client area.

This argument is a pointer to an object which can provide information about the area in the region to be updated in the client area.

```
void UpdateAllViews( CView* pSender, LPARAM lHint =0L, CObject* pHint = NULL );
```

These two argument values are passed onto the **OnUpdate()** functions in the views.

The first argument to the **UpdateAllViews()** function call will often be the **this** pointer for the current view. This suppresses the call of the **OnUpdate()** function for the current view. This is a useful feature when the current view is already up to date. In our case, because we are rubber- banding, we want to get the current view redrawn as well, so, by specifying the first argument as **0**, we get the **OnUpdate()** function called for all the views, including the current view. This removes the need to call **InvalidateRect()** as we did before.

We don't use the second argument to **UpdateAllViews()** here, but we do pass the pointer to the new element through the third argument. Passing a pointer to the new element will allow the views to figure out which bit of their client area needs to be redrawn.

In order to catch the information passed to the **UpdateAllViews()** function, we need to add the **OnUpdate()** member function to our view class. You can do this by opening ClassWizard and looking at the Message Maps tab for **CSketcherView**. If you select **CSketcherView** in the Object IDs: box, you'll be able to find **OnUpdate** in the Messages: box. Click on the Add Function button, then the Edit Code button. You only need to add the highlighted code below to the function definition:

```
void CSketcherView::OnUpdate(CView* pSender, LPARAM lHint, CObject* pHint)
{
    // Invalidate the area corresponding to the element pointed to
    // if there is one, otherwise invalidate the whole client area
    if(pHint)
        InvalidateRect(((CElement*)pHint)->GetBoundRect());
    else
        InvalidateRect(0);
}
```

The three arguments passed to the **OnUpdate()** function in the view correspond to the arguments that we passed in the **UpdateAllViews()** function call. Thus, **pHint** will contain the address of the new element. However, we cannot assume that this is always the case. The **OnUpdate()** function is also called when a view is first created, but with a **NULL** pointer for the third argument. Therefore, the function checks that the **pHint** pointer is not **NULL** and only then gets the bounding rectangle for the element passed as the third argument. It invalidates this area in the client area of the view by passing the rectangle to the **InvalidateRect()** function. This area will be redrawn by the **OnDraw()** function in this view when the next **WM_PAINT** message is sent to the view. If the **pHint** pointer is **NULL**, the whole client area is invalidated.

You might be tempted to consider redrawing the new element in the **OnUpdate()** function. This is not a good idea. You should only do any permanent drawing in response to the Windows **WM_PAINT** message. This means that the **OnDraw()** function in the view should be the only place that is initiating any drawing operations for document data. This ensures that the view is drawn correctly whenever Windows deems it necessary.

If you build and execute Sketcher with the new modifications included, you should find that all the views will be updated to reflect the contents of the document.

Scrolling Views

Adding scrolling to a view looks remarkably easy at first sight; the water is in fact deeper and murkier that it at first appears, but let's jump in anyway. Your first step is to change the base class for **CSketcherView** from **CView** to **CScrollView**. This new base class has the scrolling functionality built in, so you can alter the definition of the **CSketcherView** class to:

```
class CSketcherView : public CScrollView
{
    // Class definition as before...
};
```

You must also modify two lines of code at the beginning of the **SketcherView.cpp** file which refer to the base class for **CSketcherView**. You need to replace **CView** with **CScrollView** as the base class :

```
IMPLEMENT_DYNCREATE(CSketcherView, CScrollView)

BEGIN_MESSAGE_MAP(CSketcherView, CScrollView)
```

However, this is still not quite enough. The new version of our view class needs to know some things about the area we are drawing on, such as the size and how far the view is to be scrolled when you use the scroller. This information has to be supplied before the view is first drawn. We can put the code to do this in the **OnInitialUpdate()** function in our view class.

We supply the information that is required by calling a function inherited from the **CScrollView** class - **SetScrollSizes()**. The arguments to this function are shown in the following diagram:

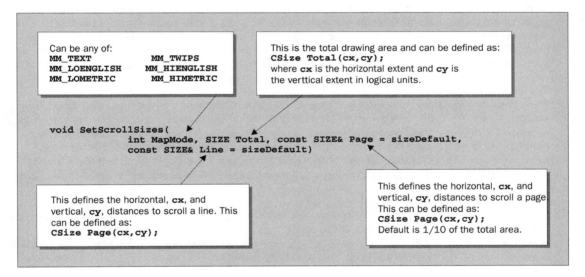

We have an opportunity to change the mapping mode here. **MM_LOENGLISH** would be a good choice for our application, but let's first get scrolling working in **MM_TEXT**, as there are still some difficulties to be uncovered.

To add the code to call **SetScrollSizes()**, you need to override the default version of the **OnInitialUpdate()** function in the view. Use ClassWizard to add the function to **CSketcherView** by selecting **OnInitialUpdate** in the Messages: box and clicking Edit Code. The version generated will call the default version in **CView**. We just add our code to the function where indicated by the comment:

```
void CSketcherView::OnInitialUpdate()
{
    CScrollView::OnInitialUpdate();
    // Define document size
    CSize DocSize(20000,20000);

    // Set mapping mode and document size.
    SetScrollSizes(MM_TEXT,DocSize);
}
```

This maintains the mapping mode as **MM_TEXT** and defines the total extent that we can draw on as 20000 pixels in each direction.

This is enough to get the scrolling mechanism working. Build the program and execute it with these additions and you'll be able to draw a few elements and then scroll the view. However, although the window scrolls OK, if you try to draw more elements with the view scrolled, things don't work as they should. The elements appear in a different position from where you draw them and they're not displayed properly, so what is going on?

Logical Coordinates and Client Coordinates

The problem is the coordinate systems that we are using. Note the plural. We have actually been using two coordinate systems in all our examples up to now, although you may not have noticed. As we saw in the previous chapter, when we call a function such as **LineTo()**, it assumes that the arguments passed are **logical coordinates**. The function is a member of the **CDC** class which defines a device context, and the device context has its own system of logical coordinates. The mapping mode, which is a property of the device context, determines what the unit of measure is for the coordinates when you draw something.

The coordinate data that we receive, along with the mouse messages, on the other hand, has nothing to do with the device context or the **CDC** object and outside of a device context, logical coordinates don't apply. The points passed to our **OnLButtonDown()** and **OnMouseMove()** handlers have coordinates that are always in device units, that is pixels, and are measured relative to the top left corner of the client area. These are referred to as **client coordinates**. Similarly, when we call **InvalidateRect()**, the rectangle is assumed to be defined in client coordinates.

In **MM_TEXT** mode, the client coordinates, and the logical coordinates in the device context, are both in units of pixels, so are the same - *as long as you don't scroll the window*. In all our previous examples there was no scrolling, so everything worked without any problems. With the latest version, it all works fine until you scroll the view, whereupon the logical coordinates origin (the 0,0 point) is moved by the scrolling mechanism, so is no longer in the same place as the client coordinates origin. The units for logical coordinates and client coordinates are the same here, but the origins for the two coordinates systems are not in the same place. This situation is illustrated next:

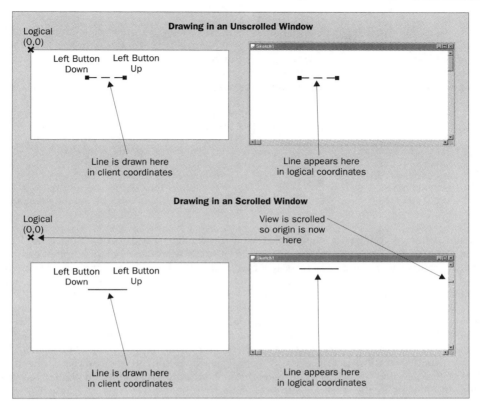

The left-hand side shows the position in the client area where you draw and the points that are the mouse positions defining the line. These are recorded in client coordinates. The right-hand side shows where the line will actually be drawn. Drawing is in logical coordinates, but we have been using client coordinate values. In the case of the scrolled window, the line appears displaced, due to the logical origin being relocated.

This means that we are using the wrong values to define elements in our program, and when we invalidate areas of the client area to get them redrawn, the rectangles passed to the function are also wrong. Hence, the weird behavior of our program. With other mapping modes it gets worse because, not only are the units of measure in the two coordinate systems different, but the *y* axes may also be in opposite directions.

Dealing with Client Coordinates

Let's consider what we need to do to fix the problem. There are two things we may have to address:

> First, we would need to convert the client coordinates that we got with mouse messages to logical coordinates before we could use them to create our elements.

> Second, we would need to convert bounding rectangles that we created in logical coordinates back to client coordinates if we were to call **InvalidateRect()**.

This amounts to making sure that we always use client coordinates when using device context functions, and always use client coordinates for other communications about the window.

The functions that we'll have to apply to do the conversions are associated with a device context, so we need to obtain a device context whenever we want to convert from logical to client coordinates, or vice versa. We can use the coordinate conversion functions of the **CDC** class that are inherited by **CClientDC** to do the work. The new version of the **OnLButtonDown()** handler incorporating this will be:

```
// Handler for left mouse button down message
void CSketcherView::OnLButtonDown(UINT nFlags, CPoint point)
{
    CClientDC aDC(this);                // Create a device context
    OnPrepareDC(&aDC);                  // Get origin adjusted
    aDC.DPtoLP(&point);                 // convert point to Logical
    m_FirstPoint = point;               // Record the cursor position
    SetCapture();                       // Capture subsequent mouse messages
}
```

We obtain a device context for the current view by creating a **CClientDC** object and passing the pointer **this** to the constructor. The advantage of **CClientDC** is that it automatically releases the device context when the object goes out of scope. It's important that device contexts are not retained, as there are a limited number available from Windows and you could run out of them. If you use **CClientDC**, you're always safe.

As we're using **CScrollView**, the **OnPrepareDC()** member function inherited from that class must be called to set the origin for the logical coordinate system in the device context to correspond with the scrolled position. Once the origin is set, the function **DPtoLP()**, which converts from **D**evice **P**oints to **L**ogical **P**oints, is used to convert the **point** value that is passed to the handler to logical coordinates. We then store the converted value, ready for creating an element in the **OnMouseMove()** handler.

The new code for the **OnMouseMove()** handler will be as follows:

```
void CSketcherView::OnMouseMove(UINT nFlags, CPoint point)
{
    CClientDC aDC(this);                       // Device context for the current view
    aDC.SetROP2(R2_NOTXORPEN);                 // Set drawing mode
    OnPrepareDC(&aDC);                         // Get origin adjusted
    aDC.DPtoLP(&point);                        // convert point to Logical

    if((nFlags&MK_LBUTTON) && (this==GetCapture()))
    {

        m_SecondPoint = point;      // Save the current cursor position

        if(m_pTempElement)
        {
            m_pTempElement->Draw(&aDC);                 // Erase the previous element
            if(CURVE == GetDocument()->GetElementType())// Is it a curve?
            {   // We are drawing a curve
                // so add a segment to the existing curve
                ((CCurve*)m_pTempElement)->AddSegment(m_SecondPoint);
                m_pTempElement->Draw(&aDC);  // Now redraw it
                return;                      // We are done
            }
            delete m_pTempElement;               // Delete the old element
            m_pTempElement = 0;                  // Reset the pointer to 0
```

```
        }
        // Create an element of the type and color
        // recorded in the document object
        m_pTempElement = CreateElement();
        m_pTempElement->Draw(&aDC);
    }
```

The code for the conversion of the point value passed to the handler is exactly the same as in the previous handler, and that's all we need here for the moment.

The last function that we must change is easy to overlook - the **OnUpdate()** function in the view class. This needs to be modified to:

```
void CSketcherView::OnUpdate(CView* pSender, LPARAM lHint, CObject* pHint)
{
    // Invalidate the area corresponding to the element pointed to
    // if there is one, otherwise invalidate the whole client area
    if(pHint)
    {
    CClientDC aDC(this);            // Create a device context
    OnPrepareDC(&aDC);              // Get origin adjusted
    // Get the enclosing rectangle and convert to client coordinates
    CRect aRect=((CElement*)pHint)->GetBoundRect();
    aDC.LPtoDP(aRect);
    InvalidateRect(aRect);          // Get the area redrawn
    }
    else
        InvalidateRect(0);                  // Invalidate the client area
}
```

The modification here just creates a **CClientDC** object and uses the **LPtoDP()** function member to convert the rectangle for the area that is to be redrawn to client coordinates.

If you now compile and execute Sketcher with the modifications we have discussed and are lucky enough not to have introduced any typos, it will work correctly, regardless of the scroller position.

Using MM_LOENGLISH Mapping Mode

Let's now look into what we need to do to use the **MM_LOENGLISH** mapping mode. This will provide drawings in logical units of 0.01 inches and will also ensure that the drawing size is consistent on displays at different resolutions. This will make the application much more satisfactory from the user's point of view.

We can set the mapping mode in the call to **SetScrollSizes()** made from the **OnInitialUpdate()** function in the view class. We also need to specify the total drawing area, so, if we define it as 4000 by 4000, this will provide a drawing area of 40 inches by 40 inches, which should be adequate for our needs. The default scroll distances for a line and a page will be satisfactory, so we don't need to specify those. You can use ClassView to get to the **OnInitialUpdate()** function and then change it to that shown below:

```
void CSketcherView::OnInitialUpdate()
{
```

```
        CView::OnInitialUpdate();
        // Define document size as 40x40ins in MM_LOENGLISH
        CSize DocSize(4000,4000);

        // Set mapping mode and document size.
        SetScrollSizes(MM_LOENGLISH,DocSize);
    }
```

We just alter the arguments in the call to **SetScrollSizes()** for the mapping mode and document the size that we want. That's all we need to enable the view to work in **MM_LOENGLISH**, but we still need to fix our dealings with rectangles.

Note that you are not limited to setting the mapping mode once and for all. You can change the mapping mode in a device context at any time and draw different parts of the image to be displayed, using different mapping modes. A function **SetMapMode()** is used to do this, but we won't be going into this further. We'll stick to getting our application working just using **MM_LOENGLISH**. Whenever we create a **CClientDC** object for the view and call **OnPrepareDC()**, the device context that it owns will have the mapping mode we have set for the view.

The problem we have with rectangles is that our element classes all assume **MM_TEXT** and, in **MM_LOENGLISH**, these will be upside-down from an **MM_LOENGLISH** perspective because of the reversal of the *y* axis. As a consequence, when we apply **LPtoDP()** to a rectangle, it is assumed to be oriented properly with respect to the **MM_LOENGLISH** axes. Therefore, because ours are not, the function will invert our rectangles. This creates a problem when we call **InvalidateRect()** to invalidate an area of a view, as the inverted rectangle in device coordinates will not be recognized by Windows as inside the visible client area.

We have two options for dealing with this. We can modify the element classes so that the enclosing rectangles are the right way up for **MM_LOENGLISH**, or we can re-normalize the rectangle that we intend to pass to the **InvalidateRect()** function. The easiest course is the latter, since we only need to modify one member of the view class, **OnUpdate()**:

```
void CSketcherView::OnUpdate(CView* pSender, LPARAM lHint, CObject* pHint)
{
    // Invalidate the area corresponding to the element pointed to
    // if there is one, otherwise invalidate the whole client area
    if(pHint)
    {
        CClientDC aDC(this);              // Create a device context
        OnPrepareDC(&aDC);                // Get origin adjusted

        // Get the enclosing rectangle and convert to client coordinates
        CRect aRect=((CElement*)pHint)->GetBoundRect();
        pDC->LPtoDP(aRect);
        aRect.NormalizeRect();
        ReleaseDC(pDC);

        InvalidateRect(aRect);            // Get the area redrawn
    }
    else
        InvalidateRect(0);
}
```

That should do it for the program as it is. If you rebuild Sketcher, you should have scrolling working, with support for multiple views. We'll need to remember to re-normalize any rectangle that we convert to device coordinates for use in **InvalidateRect()** in the future. Any reverse conversion will also be affected.

Deleting and Moving Shapes

Being able to delete shapes is a fundamental requirement in a drawing program. One question relating to this that we'll need to find an answer for is how you are to select the element you want to delete. Of course, once we decide how to select an element, this will apply equally well if you want to move an element, so we can treat moving and deleting elements as related problems. But let's first consider how we're going to bring move and delete operations into the program.

A neat way of providing move and delete functions would be to have a pop-up context menu appear at the cursor position when you click the right mouse button. We could then put Move and Delete as menu items on the menu. A pop-up that works like this is a very handy facility that you can use in lots of different situations.

How should the pop-up be used? The standard way that context menus work is that the user moves the mouse over a particular object and right-clicks on it. This selects the object and pops up a menu containing a list of items which relate to actions that can be performed on that object. This means that different objects can have different menus. You can see this in action in Developer Studio itself. When you right-click on a class icon in ClassView, you get a menu that's different to the one you get if you right-click on the icon for a member function. The menu that appears is sensitive to the context of the cursor, hence the term *context menu*.

So, how will we implement this functionality in the Sketcher application? We can do this simply by creating two menus - one for all drawing elements and one if no element is found under the cursor. We can determine if there is an element under the cursor when the user presses the right mouse button. If there is an element under the cursor, we can highlight the element so that the user knows exactly which element the context pop-up is referring to.

Let's first take a look at how we can create a pop-up at the cursor and, once that works, come back to how we are going to implement the detail of the move and delete operations.

Implementing a Context Menu

The first step is to create two new menus - one containing Move and Delete as items, the other a combination of the Element and Color menus. So change to ResourceView and expand the list of resources. Right-click on the Menu folder to bring up a context menu - another demonstration of what we are trying to create in our application. Select Insert Menu to create a new menu. This will have a default name **IDR_MENU1** assigned, but you can change this by right-clicking the new menu name and selecting Properties. You could change it to something more suitable, such as **IDR_CURSOR_MENU** in the properties box.

To add menu items to the menu, double-click **IDR_CURSOR_MENU**. Now create two new items on the menu bar. These can have any old caption, since they won't actually be seen by the user. They will represent the two context menus that we will provide with Sketcher, so we have named them element and no element, according to the situation in which the context menu will be used. Now you can add the Move and Delete items to the element pop-up.

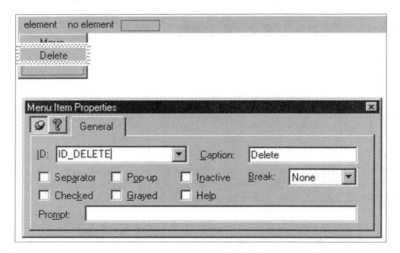

Make sure that you type sensible IDs rather than allowing the default, using the junk name on the menu bar. Here, we have entered **ID_MOVE** and **ID_DELETE** as the IDs for the two items in the pop-up. The illustration shows the properties box for the Delete menu item.

The second menu contains the list of available elements and colors separated by a Separator. The IDs used are the same as we applied to the **IDR_SKETCHTYPE** menu.

Close the properties box and save the resource file. At the moment, all we have is the definition of the menu in a resource file. It's not connected to the code in the Sketcher program. We now need to associate this menu and its ID, **IDR_CURSOR_MENU**, with our view class. This will enable us to create command handlers for the menu items in the pop-up corresponding to the IDs **ID_MOVE** and **ID_DELETE**.

Associating a Menu with a Class

To associate the new menu with the view class in Sketcher, you can use ClassWizard. With the cursor on the menu bar of our new menu, click the right mouse button and select ClassWizard from the pop-up. This will bring up a dialog which will ask whether you want to Create, Import, or Select a class. We want to Select an existing class, which is the default option, so just click OK. This will bring up a second dialog with a list of available classes to associate with the menu. Select CSketcherView from the Class list: and click the Select button.

Once you've done that, you'll be back to ClassWizard's standard window. Now, select ID_MOVE in the Object IDs: box, and COMMAND in the Messages: box and click the Add Function button to create a handler for the menu item. Do the same for ID_DELETE and then close the ClassWizard dialog.

We don't have to do anything for the second context menu, as we already have handlers written for them. We're now ready to write the code to allow the pop-up to be displayed.

Displaying a Pop-up at the Cursor

MFC provides a class, **CMenu**, for managing and processing menus. Whenever you want to do something with a new menu, you can create a local object of this class and use its member functions to do what you want. We want to be able to display the pop-up menu when the user presses the right mouse button, so clearly, we need to add the code to do this to the handler for **WM_RBUTTONUP** in **CSketcherView**. You can add the handler for this message using ClassWizard in the same way that you added the handlers for the other mouse messages. Just fire up ClassWizard again and select the WM_RBUTTONUP message in the Messages: box for **CSketcherView**. Then create the handler and click the Edit Code button. The code you need to add is:

```
// Handler for right mouse button down messages
void CSketcherView::OnRButtonDown(UINT nFlags, CPoint point)
{
    // Create the cursor menu
    CMenu aMenu;
    aMenu.LoadMenu(IDR_CURSOR_MENU);      // Load the cursor menu
    ClientToScreen(&point);                // Convert to screen coordinates

    // Display the pop-up at the cursor position
    aMenu.GetSubMenu(0)->TrackPopupMenu(TPM_LEFTALIGN|TPM_RIGHTBUTTON,
                                        point.x, point.y, this);
}
```

We don't need to keep the call to the handler in the base class **CScrollView** that ClassWizard supplies. That was there to ensure that the message would be handled in the base class, even if you didn't add code to deal with it. As we said before, the comment left by ClassWizard, indicating where you should add your code, is a clue to the fact that you can omit it in this case.

The handler first creates a local **CMenu** object, **aMenu**, then uses its member function **LoadMenu()** to load the menu that we have just created. The cursor position when the user presses the right button is passed to the handler in the argument **point**, which is in client coordinates. When we display the menu, we must supply the coordinates of where the menu is to appear in **screen coordinates**. Screen coordinates are in pixels and have the top left corner of the screen as position 0,0. As in the case of client coordinates, the positive y axis is from top to bottom. The inherited function **ClientToScreen()** in **CSketcherView** does the conversion for us.

To display the menu, we call two functions. The **GetSubMenu()** member of the object **aMenu** returns a pointer to a **CMenu** object. This object contains the pop-up from the menu owned by **aMenu**, which is the **IDR_CURSOR_MENU** menu that we loaded previously. The argument to **GetSubMenu()** is an integer index specifying the pop-up, with index 0 referring to the first pop-up. The function **TrackPopupMenu()** for the **CMenu** object returned is then called. The arguments to **TrackPopupMenu()** are shown on the following page.

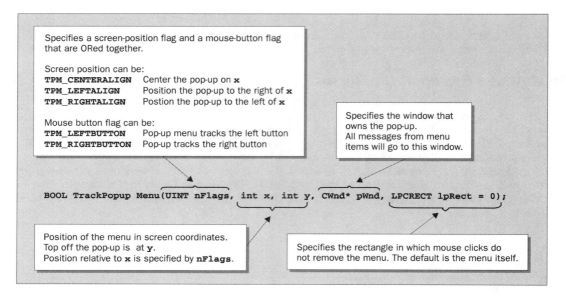

In our case, we have specified the pop-up as being associated with the right mouse button and displayed with the left side of the pop-up at the x coordinate passed to the function. The coordinates are the x and y coordinates of the cursor position specified by the **point** object after conversion to screen coordinates. The **this** pointer is used to specify the current view as the owning window.

We don't specify the fourth argument, so it defaults to **0**. The rectangle is, therefore, the pop-up itself, so, if you click outside the pop-up, it will close the menu without selecting an item or causing a message to be sent to the view. Of course, if you click on a menu item, it will also close, but will also send a message to the view corresponding to the item clicked.

However, this will only display the first context pop-up, no matter where the right button is clicked. This is not what we want to do. Instead, we want to find out if there are any elements under the cursor. If there are, we need to display the first menu. If there aren't, we display the second.

```
void CSketcherView::OnRButtonDown(UINT nFlags, CPoint point)
{
    // Find the element under the cursor
    m_pSelected = SelectElement(point);
    // Create the cursor menu
    CMenu aMenu;
    aMenu.LoadMenu(IDR_CURSOR_MENU);        // Load the cursor menu
    ClientToScreen(&point);                 // Convert to screen coordinates

    // Display the pop-up at the cursor position
    if(m_pSelected)
        aMenu.GetSubMenu(0)->TrackPopupMenu(TPM_LEFTALIGN|TPM_RIGHTBUTTON,
                                                point.x, point.y, this);
    else
        aMenu.GetSubMenu(1)->TrackPopupMenu(TPM_LEFTALIGN|TPM_RIGHTBUTTON,
                                                point.x, point.y, this);
}
```

We have used the function **SelectElement()** which we haven't written yet. This will return a pointer to the element under the cursor, or **NULL** if there is none. Then, depending on this value, we display one or the other of the context menus.

In order to keep the highlighting process local to the view, we'll store the value returned by **SelectElement()** in a protected member of the view. We need to add the data member **m_pSelected** to **CSketcherView**. You can do this by adding a line directly to the **protected** section of the class definition:

```
class CSketcherView : public CScrollView
{
    // Rest of the class as before...

    protected:
        CPoint m_FirstPoint;                // First point recorded for an element
        CPoint m_SecondPoint;               // Second point recorded for an element
        CElement* m_pTempElement;           // Pointer to temporary element
        CElement* m_pSelected;              // Currently selected element

    // Rest of the class as before...
};
```

Alternatively, you can right-click on the class name and select Add Variable... from the pop-up to open the dialog for adding a data member. It's usually a good idea to go back and add some comments, though.

You also need to initialize this element in the class constructor, so add the shaded code shown below:

```
CSketcherView::CSketcherView()
{
    // TODO: add construction code here
    m_FirstPoint = CPoint(0,0);           // Set 1st recorded point to 0,0
    m_SecondPoint = CPoint(0,0);          // Set 2nd recorded point to 0,0
    m_pTempElement = 0;                   // Set temporary element pointer to 0
    m_pSelected = 0;                      // No elements should be selected initially
}
```

Identifying a Selected Element

To find which element is selected, we can use the functions that we added to the document class to iterate through the list of elements. As we retrieve the pointer to each element, we can check whether the current cursor position is within any of the bounding rectangles. Add the declaration of **SelectElement()** to the **protected** section of **CSketcherView** as follows:

```
CElement* SelectElement(CPoint aPoint);                    // Select an element
```

You can add the implementation of the function to **SketcherView.cpp**, like this:

```
CElement* CSketcherView::SelectElement(CPoint aPoint)
{
    // Convert the passed point to logical coordinates
    CClientDC aDC(this);
    OnPrepareDC(&aDC);
    aDC.DPtoLP(&aPoint);
```

```
        CSketcherDoc* pDoc=GetDocument();              // Get a pointer to the document
        CElement* pElement = 0;                        // Store an element pointer
        CRect aRect(0,0,0,0);                          // Store a rectangle
        POSITION aPos = pDoc->GetListHeadPosition();   // Get the 1st element position

        while(aPos)                                    // Iterate through the list
        {
            pElement = pDoc->GetNext(aPos);
            aRect = pElement->GetBoundRect();
            // Select the first element that appears under the cursor
            if(aRect.PtInRect(aPoint))
              return pElement;
        }

        return 0;
    }
```

We first get a device context and use this to convert the passed **CPoint** from client coordinates to logical coordinates. We then get a pointer to the document and declare local variables to store an element pointer, **pElement**, and a **CRect** object, **aRect**. We get the **POSITION** value, corresponding to the first element in the element list in the document, and store it in **aPos**. We then run through the elements in the list, checking whether the bounding rectangle for each element encloses the current cursor position passed in the parameter **aPoint**. This is done in the **if** statement using the **PtInRect()** member of the **CRect** class. This function requires the rectangle to be normalized, which, of course, all ours are because we created them to be so. The function returns **TRUE** if the **CPoint** value passed as an argument is within the **CRect** object owning the function, and **FALSE** otherwise. As soon as we find one, we exit the function, returning the pointer to that element. If we manage to walk through the entire list without finding an element, which occurs when the cursor is not over an element, we return **0**.

The code is now in a state where we can test the context menus.

Exercising the Pop-ups

We have added all the code we need to make the pop-ups operate. So you can build and execute Sketcher to try it out. If there are no elements under the cursor, the second context pop-up appears, allowing you to change the element type and color. These options work because they generate exactly the same messages as the main menu options and because we have already written handlers for them.

If there is an element under the cursor, the first context menu will appear with Move and Delete. It won't do anything yet, as we have yet to handle the message generated. Try right button clicks outside of the view window. Messages for these are not passed to the document view window in our application, so the pop-up is not displayed.

Highlighting Elements

To show precisely which element it is that the user has selected, we need to highlight the element in some way. We'll do this in the **Draw()** member function for an element. They will all work in the same way, so we'll take the **CLine** member as an example. You can add the same code for each of the other element types. Before we start changing **CLine**, we must first amend the definition of the base class **CElement**:

```
class CElement:public CObject
{
    protected:
        COLORREF m_Color;                    // Color of an element
        CRect m_EnclosingRect;               // Rectangle enclosing an element
        int m_Pen;                           // Pen width

    public:
        virtual ~CElement(){}                // Virtual destructor
        virtual void Draw(CDC* pDC, BOOL Select=FALSE){}// Virtual draw operation

        CRect GetBoundRect();                // Get the bounding rectangle for an element

    protected:
        CElement(){}                         // Default constructor
};
```

The only change is to add the second parameter to the virtual **Draw()** function. When a value **TRUE** is passed as a second argument, the member function should draw an element in a highlight color. By assigning a default value of **FALSE** to this parameter, the function will draw normally if the second argument is omitted, so all our existing calls will continue to work without modification.

You need to modify the declaration of the **Draw()** function in each of the classes derived from **CElement** in exactly the same way. For example, you should change the **CLine** class definition to:

```
class CLine: public CElement
{
    public:
        // Function to display a line
        virtual void Draw(CDC* pDC, BOOL Select = FALSE);

        // Constructor for a line object
        CLine(CPoint Start, CPoint End, COLORREF aColor);

    protected:
        CPoint m_StartPoint;            // Start point of line
        CPoint m_EndPoint;              // End point of line

        CLine(){}                // Default constructor - should not be used
};
```

The implementation for each of the **Draw()** functions for the classes derived from **CElement** all need to be extended in the same way. The function for the **CLine** class will be:

```
void CLine::Draw(CDC* pDC, BOOL Select)
{
    // Create a pen for this object and
    // initialize its color and set line width of 1 pixel
    CPen aPen;
    COLORREF Color = m_Color;                       // Initialize with element color

    if(Select)
        Color = SELECT_COLOR;                       // Set selected color
    if(!aPen.CreatePen(PS_SOLID, m_Pen, Color))
```

561

```
    {                                                    // Pen creation failed
        AfxMessageBox("Pen creation failed drawing a line", MB_OK);
        AfxAbort();
    }

    CPen* pOldPen = pDC->SelectObject(&aPen);   // Select the pen

    // Now draw the line
    pDC->MoveTo(m_StartPoint);
    pDC->LineTo(m_EndPoint);

    pDC->SelectObject(pOldPen);                          // Restore the old pen
}
```

This is a very simple change. We have added the additional parameter, **Select**, to the function header, and an **if** statement to set the value of **aColor** to **SELECT_COLOR** when **Select** is **TRUE**. You also need to add the definition for **SELECT_COLOR** to the **OurConstants.h** file:

```
#ifndef OurConstants_h
#define OurConstants_h

    // Element type definitions
    // Each type value must be unique
    const WORD LINE = 101U;
    const WORD RECTANGLE = 102U;
    const WORD CIRCLE = 103U;
    const WORD CURVE = 104U;
    ///////////////////////////////////

    // Color values for drawing
    const COLORREF BLACK = RGB(0,0,0);
    const COLORREF RED = RGB(255,0,0);
    const COLORREF GREEN = RGB(0,255,0);
    const COLORREF BLUE = RGB(0,0,255);
    const COLORREF SELECT_COLOR = RGB(255,0,180);
    ///////////////////////////////////

#endif
```

We have nearly implemented the highlight. The derived classes of the **CElement** class are now able to draw themselves as selected, we just need a mechanism to tell the selected element to do so. The best place for this code is then in the **SelectElement()** function. The amendments to this function appear highlighted below:

```
CElement* CSketcherView::SelectElement(CPoint aPoint)
{
    // Convert the passed point to logical coordinates
    CClientDC aDC(this);
    OnPrepareDC(&aDC);
    aDC.DPtoLP(&aPoint);

    // If there is already a selected element, redraw it unselected
    if(m_pSelected)
        m_pSelected->Draw(&aDC);

    CSketcherDoc* pDoc=GetDocument();                    // Get a pointer to the document
```

```
        CElement* pElement = 0;                      // Store an element pointer
        CRect aRect(0,0,0,0);                        // Store a rectangle
        POSITION aPos = pDoc->GetListHeadPosition(); // Get the 1st element position

        while(aPos)                                  // Iterate through the list
        {
            pElement = pDoc->GetNext(aPos);
            aRect = pElement->GetBoundRect();
            // Select the first element that appears under the cursor
            if(aRect.PtInRect(aPoint))
            {
                pElement->Draw(&aDC, TRUE);          // Draw element with highlight
                return pElement;
            }
        }

        return 0;
    }
```

Exercising the Highlights

This is all that's required for the highlighting to work. You can build and execute Sketcher to try it out. When there is an element under the cursor when the user presses the right mouse, the element is drawn in magenta. This makes it obvious which element the context menu is going to act on.

Servicing the Menu Messages

The next step is to provide handlers for the Move and Delete menu items. Both of these need the handlers to be in the view, so use ClassWizard to add COMMAND handlers for ID_DELETE and ID_MOVE in CSketcherView, accepting the default names for the functions.

We'll add the code for Delete first, as that is the simpler of the two.

Deleting an Element

The code that you need to delete a selected element is very simple:

```
void CSketcherView::OnDelete()
{
    if(m_pSelected)
    {
        CSketcherDoc* pDoc = GetDocument();       // Get the document pointer
        pDoc->DeleteElement(m_pSelected);         // Delete the element
        pDoc->UpdateAllViews(0);                  // Redraw all the views
        m_pSelected = 0;                          // Reset selected element pointer
    }
}
```

The code to delete an element is only executed if **m_pSelected** contains a valid address, indicating that there is an element to be deleted. We get a pointer to the document and call the function **DeleteElement()** for the document object. We'll add this member to the **CSketcherDoc** class in a moment. When the element has been removed from the document, we call **UpdateAllViews()** to get all the views redrawn without the deleted element. Finally, we set **m_pSelected** to zero to indicate that there isn't an element selected.

You should add a declaration for **DeleteElement()** as a **public** member of the **CSketcherDoc** class:

```
void DeleteElement(CElement* pElement);   // Delete an element
```

It accepts a pointer to the element to be deleted as an argument and returns nothing. You can implement it as:

```
void CSketcherDoc::DeleteElement(CElement* pElement)
{
   if(pElement)
   {  // If the  element pointer is valid
      // Find the pointer in the list and delete it
      POSITION aPosition = m_ElementList.Find(pElement);
      m_ElementList.RemoveAt(aPosition);
      delete pElement;               // Delete the element from the heap
   }
}
```

You shouldn't have any trouble with this. After making sure that we have a non-null pointer, we find the **POSITION** value for the pointer in the list using the **Find()** member of the list object. We use this with the **RemoveAt()** member to delete the pointer from the list, then we delete the element pointed to by the parameter, **pElement**, from the heap.

That's all we need to delete elements. You should now have a Sketcher program in which you can draw in multiple scrolled views and delete any of the elements in your sketch from any of the views.

Moving an Element

Moving the selected element is a bit more involved. As the element must move along with the mouse cursor, we must add code to the **OnMouseMove()** method to account for this behavior. As this function is also used to draw elements, we must have a mechanism for indicating when we are in move mode. The easiest way to do this is to have a flag in the view class. We can do this by adding a data member to the view class definition, as follows:

```
class CSketcherView : public CScrollView
{
   // Rest of the class as before...

   protected:
      CPoint m_FirstPoint;        // First point recorded for an element
      CPoint m_SecondPoint;       // Second point recorded for an element
      CElement* m_pTempElement;   // Pointer to temporary element
      CElement* m_pSelected;      // Currently selected element
      BOOL m_MoveMode;            // Move element flag

   // Rest of the class as before...
};
```

This just adds a data member of type **BOOL** which will act as a flag indicating whether the move mode is on or off. We'll set the flag to **TRUE** when move mode is on, and set it to **FALSE** to turn the mode off. We need to initialize the flag in the constructor for **CSketcherView** by adding the following statements:

```
CSketcherView::CSketcherView()
{
    m_FirstPoint = CPoint(0,0);         // Set 1st recorded point to 0,0
    m_SecondPoint = CPoint(0,0);        // Set 2nd recorded point to 0,0
    m_pTempElement = 0;                 // Set temporary element pointer to 0
    m_pSelected = 0;                    // No elements should be selected initially
    m_MoveMode = FALSE;                 // Set move mode off
}
```

Now we can add the code for the message handler for the Move item:

```
void CSketcherView::OnMove()
{
    CClientDC aDC(this);
    OnPrepareDC(&aDC);      // Set up the device context

    // Find the center of the bounding rectangle for the selected element
    CPoint center(0,0);
    center = m_pSelected->GetBoundRect().TopLeft();
    center.x += m_pSelected->GetBoundRect().Width() / 2;
    center.y += m_pSelected->GetBoundRect().Height() / 2;

    m_MoveMode = TRUE;               // Start move mode
    m_FirstPoint = center;           // Set this for the initial starting point
    m_SecondPoint = m_FirstPoint;    // Set this so that we can undo the move

    // Move the cursor to the center of the bounding rectangle
    aDC.LPtoDP(&center);
    ClientToScreen(&center);
    SetCursorPos(center.x, center.y);
}
```

As you can see, we need to do a lot more than simply set the flag. The first task is to get a device context by creating an object of class **CClientDC** then prepare it for use by calling the **OnPrepareDC()** function of the base class as we've done before.

The next four lines find the center of the bounding rectangle of the selected element. We have used the top-left corner of the rectangle and added half the width and height to it. This works whether the rectangle is normalized or not.

We then turn on the move mode by setting the flag to **TRUE**. The flag will be reset when the processing of the move mode has been completed, at least it will be as soon we write the code to do that. We also set **m_FirstPoint** and **m_SecondPoint** to the center of the bounding rectangle. We need to do this as we'll be using **m_FirstPoint** to determine how far to move the element. **m_SecondPoint** is used if the user decides to cancel the move, in which case we need to know the original position of the element.

Finally, we convert the center of the bounding rectangle to device coordinates, and then to screen coordinates. We then call the **SetCursorPos()** API function, passing it the center of the bounding rectangle. This causes Windows to reposition the mouse cursor at the indicated place. We do this so that when the user starts moving the element, the mouse cursor is in a sensible place in relation to the element being moved.

If we had missed out this last step, the element would suddenly jump to the cursor when the mouse is moved. This is a bit annoying if you are trying to make a fine adjustment to the position of the element.

Now we have set the move mode flag, it's time to handle the mouse move message, or rather make amendments to the handler we already have.

Modifying the WM_MOUSEMOVE Handler

Moving an element only occurs when move mode is on and the cursor is being moved. We must, therefore, implement the move operation in the **OnMouseMove()** handler. The new code to do this is as follows:

```
void CSketcherView::OnMouseMove(UINT nFlags, CPoint point)
{
    // Define a Device Context object for the view
    CClientDC aDC(this);
    aDC.SetROP2(R2_NOTXORPEN);   // Set the drawing mode
    OnPrepareDC(&aDC);           // Get origin adjusted
    aDC.DPtoLP(&point);          // convert point to Logical


    // If we are in move mode, move the selected element and return
    if(m_MoveMode)
    {
        MoveElement(aDC, point);
        return;
    }

    // Rest of the mouse move handler as before...
}
```

This addition doesn't need much explaining really, does it? The **if** verifies that we are in move mode and then calls a function **MoveElement()**, which does the necessary drawing. All we need to do now is to implement this function.

Add the declaration for **MoveElement()** as a **protected** member of the **CSketcherView** class by adding the following at the appropriate point in the class definition:

```
void MoveElement(CClientDC& aDC, CPoint& point);   // Move an element
```

As always, you can also right-click on the class name in ClassView to do this if you want. The function will need access to the object owning a device context for the view, **aDC**, and the current cursor position, **point**, so both of these are reference parameters. The implementation of the function in the **.cpp** file will be:

```
void CSketcherView::MoveElement(CClientDC& aDC, CPoint& point)
{
    CSize aSize = point - m_FirstPoint;
    m_FirstPoint = point;                     // Set current point as 1st for next time

    // If there is an element, selected, move it
    if(m_pSelected)
    {
        aDC.SetROP2(R2_NOTXORPEN);
```

```
            m_pSelected->Draw(&aDC,TRUE); // Draw over the element to erase it
            m_pSelected->Move(aSize);       // Now move the element
            m_pSelected->Draw(&aDC,TRUE); // Draw the moved element
        }
    }
```

The distance to move the element currently selected is stored as a **CSize** object. The **CSize** class is specifically designed to represent a relative coordinate position and has two public data members, **cx** and **cy**, which correspond to the *x* any *y* increments. These are calculated as the difference between the position saved in **m_FirstPoint**, and the current cursor position stored in **point**. This uses the **-** operator, which is overloaded in the **CPoint** class. The version we are using here returns a **CSize** object, but there is also a version which returns a **CPoint** object. You can usually operate on **CSize** and **CPoint** objects combined. We save the current cursor position in **m_FirstPoint** for use the next time this function is called, which will occur if there is a further mouse move message during the current move operation.

Moving an element in the view is going to be implemented using the **R2_NOTXORPEN** drawing mode, because it is easy and fast. We redraw the selected element as highlighted to reset it to the background color and then call the function **Move()** to relocate the selected element by the distance specified by **aSize**. We'll add this function to the element classes in a moment. When the element has moved itself, we simply draw the function once more to display it highlighted at the new position. The color of the element will revert to normal when the move operation ends, as the **OnLButtonUp()** handler will redraw all the windows normally, by calling **UpdateAllViews()**.

Getting the Elements to Move Themselves

We need to add the **Move()** function as a virtual member of the base class, **CElement**. Modify the class definition to:

```
class CElement:public CObject
{
    protected:
        COLORREF m_Color;             // Color of an element
        CRect m_EnclosingRect;        // Rectangle enclosing an element
        int m_Pen;                    // Pen width

    public:
        virtual ~CElement(){}                                // Virtual destructor
        virtual void Draw(CDC* pDC, BOOL Select=FALSE) {}  // Virtual draw operation
        virtual void Move(CSize& aSize){}                    // Move an element
        CRect GetBoundRect();                  // Get the bounding rectangle for an element

    protected:
        CElement(){}                          // Default constructor
};
```

As we discussed before in relation to the **Draw()** member, although an implementation of the **Move()** function here has no meaning, we cannot make it a pure virtual function because of the requirements of serialization.

We need to add a declaration for the **Move()** function as a **public** member of each of the classes derived from **CElement**. It will be the same in each:

```
    virtual void Move(CSize& aSize);              // Move an element
```

567

Now we can look at how we implement the **Move()** function in the **CLine** class:

```
void CLine::Move(CSize& aSize)
{
   m_StartPoint += aSize;              // Move the start point
   m_EndPoint += aSize;                // and the end point
   m_EnclosingRect += aSize;           // Move the enclosing rectangle
}
```

This is very easy because of the overloaded **+=** operators in the **CPoint** and **CRect** classes. They all work with **CSize** objects, so we just add the relative distance specified by **aSize** to the start and end points for the line, and to the enclosing rectangle.

Moving a **CRectangle** object is even easier:

```
void CRectangle::Move(CSize& aSize)
{
   m_EnclosingRect+= aSize;             // Move the rectangle
}
```

Because the rectangle is defined by the **m_EnclosingRect** member, that's all we need to move it.

The **Move()** member of **CCircle** is identical:

```
void CCircle::Move(CSize& aSize)
{
   m_EnclosingRect+= aSize;                  // Move rectangle defining the circle
}
```

Moving a **CCurve** object is a little more complicated because it is defined by an arbitrary number of points. You can implement the function as follows:

```
void CCurve::Move(CSize& aSize)
{
   m_EnclosingRect+= aSize;                          // Move the rectangle

   // Get the 1st element position
   POSITION aPosition = m_PointList.GetHeadPosition();

   while(aPosition)
      m_PointList.GetNext(aPosition)+= aSize;     // Move each point in the list
}
```

There's still not a lot to it. We first move the enclosing rectangle stored in **m_EnclosingRect**, using the overloaded **+=** operator for **CRect**. We then iterate through all the points defining the curve, moving each one in turn with the overloaded **+=** operator in **CPoint**.

Dropping the Element

All that remains is to drop the element once the user has finished moving it. There are two different situations to handle. The first is to drop the element at the current cursor position. The second is to drop the cursor back where it started. We want to offer this second option so that the user can cancel the move if they want to.

We'll differentiate between the two by the mouse button that the user uses to drop the element. The left button will drop the element at the current location, while the right button will cancel the move.

This means that the handlers for the **WM_LBUTTONDOWN** and **WM_RBUTTONDOWN** need modifying to do this work. Let's deal with the left mouse button first. This means modifying the **OnLButtonDown()** function. The changes are highlighted below:

```
void CSketcherView::OnLButtonDown(UINT nFlags, CPoint point)
{
    CClientDC aDC(this);            // Create a device context
    OnPrepareDC(&aDC);              // Get origin adjusted
    aDC.DPtoLP(&point);             // convert point to Logical

    // In moving mode, so drop the element
    if(m_MoveMode)
    {
        m_MoveMode = FALSE;             // Kill move mode
        m_pSelected = 0;                // De-select element
        GetDocument()->UpdateAllViews(0);   // Redraw all the views
    }
    else
    {
        m_FirstPoint = point;           // Record the cursor position
        SetCapture();                   // Capture subsequent mouse messages
    }
}
```

The code is pretty simple. We must first make sure that we are in move mode. If this is the case, we just set the move mode flag back to **FALSE** and then de-select the element. This is all that's required because we have been tracking the element with the mouse, so it's already in the right place. Finally, to tidy up all the views of the document, we call the document's **UpdateAllViews()** function, causing all the views to be redrawn.

The amendments to the **OnRButtonDown()** function require a few more steps than the left button. This is because we have to move the element from it's current position under the cursor back to where it originated. The code is as follows:

```
void CSketcherView::OnRButtonDown(UINT nFlags, CPoint point)
{
    // In moving mode, so drop element back in original position
    if(m_MoveMode)
    {
        CClientDC aDC(this);
        OnPrepareDC(&aDC);                          // Get origin adjusted
        MoveElement(aDC, m_SecondPoint);  // Move element back to orginal position
        m_MoveMode = FALSE;                         // Kill move mode
        m_pSelected = 0;                            // De-select element
        GetDocument()->UpdateAllViews(0);// Redraw all the views
        return;                                     // Don't want context pop-up so exit
    }

    // Find the element under the cursor
    m_pSelected = SelectElement(point);
    // Create the cursor menu
```

```
CMenu aMenu;
aMenu.LoadMenu(IDR_CURSOR_MENU);       // Load the cursor menu
ClientToScreen(&point);                // Convert to screen coordinates

// Display the pop-up at the cursor position
if(m_pSelected)
    aMenu.GetSubMenu(0)->TrackPopupMenu(TPM_LEFTALIGN|TPM_RIGHTBUTTON,
                                            point.x, point.y, this);
else
    aMenu.GetSubMenu(1)->TrackPopupMenu(TPM_LEFTALIGN|TPM_RIGHTBUTTON,
                                            point.x, point.y, this);
}
```

The code does the same as for the left mouse button, namely setting the move mode flag to **FALSE**, de-selecting the element and updating all the views. However, before this, we have to move the element back to its original place. We can do this as we had the foresight to store the original location of the element in the **m_SecondPoint** member. We pass this to the **MoveElement()** function along with a device context. We have already written this function to handle moving the element with the mouse.

After doing this work, we return from the handler as we don't want a new context menu to appear after canceling the move.

Exercising the Application

Everything is now complete for the context pop-ups to work. If you build Sketcher, you can select the element type and color from one context menu, or if you are over an element, then you can move or delete that element from the other context menu.

Summary

In this chapter, you have seen how to apply MFC collection classes to managing objects and managing pointers to objects. Collections are a real asset in programming for Windows because the application data that you store in a document often originates in an unstructured and unpredictable way, and you need to be able traverse the data whenever a view needs to be updated.

You have also seen how to create document data and manage it in a pointer list in the document, and in the context of the Sketcher application, how the views and the document communicate with each other.

We have improved the view capability in Sketcher in several ways. We've added scrolling to the views using the MFC class **CScrollView**, and we have introduced a pop-up at the cursor for moving and deleting elements. We've also implemented an element highlighting feature to provide the user with feedback when moving or deleting elements.

We have covered quite a lot of ground in this chapter, and some of the important points you need to keep in mind are:

▶ If you need a collection class to manage your objects or pointers, the best choice is the template-based collection classes, since they provide type-safe operation in most cases.

▶ When you draw in a device context, coordinates are in logical units that depend on the mapping mode set. Points in a window that are supplied along with Windows mouse messages are in client coordinates. The two coordinate system are usually not the same.

▶ Functions to convert between client coordinates and logical coordinates are available in the **CDC** class.

▶ Windows requests that a view is redrawn by sending a **WM_PAINT** message to your application. This causes the **OnDraw()** member of the affected view to be called.

▶ You should always do any permanent drawing of a document in the **OnDraw()** member of the view class. This will ensure that the window is drawn properly when required by Windows.

▶ You can make your **OnDraw()** implementation more efficient by calling the **RectVisible()** member of the **CDC** class to check whether an entity needs to be drawn.

▶ To get multiple views updated when you change the document contents, you can call the **UpdateAllViews()** member of the document object. This causes the **OnUpdate()** member of each view to be called.

▶ You can pass information to the **UpdateAllViews()** function to indicate which area in the view needs to be redrawn. This will make redrawing the views faster.

▶ You can display a context menu at the cursor position in response to a right mouse click. This menu is created as a normal pop-up.

Working with Dialogs and Controls

Dialogs and controls are basic tools for user communications in the Windows environment. In this chapter, you'll learn how to implement dialogs and controls by applying them to extend the Sketcher program. As you do so, you'll see:

▶ What a dialog is and how you can create dialog resources

▶ What controls are and how to add them to a dialog

▶ What basic varieties of controls are available to you

▶ How to create a dialog class to manage a dialog

▶ How to program the creation of a dialog box and how to get information back from the controls in it

▶ What is meant by modal and modeless dialogs

▶ How to implement and use direct data exchange and validation with controls

Understanding Dialogs

Of course, dialogs are not new to you. Most Windows programs of consequence use dialogs to manage some of their data input. You click a menu item and up pops a **dialog box** with various **controls** that you use for entering information. Just about everything that appears in a dialog box is a control. A dialog box is actually a window and, in fact, each of the controls in a dialog are also specialized windows. Come to think of it, most things you see on the screen under Windows are windows!

Although controls have a particular association with dialog boxes, if you want, you can also create and use them in other windows. A typical dialog box is illustrated below:

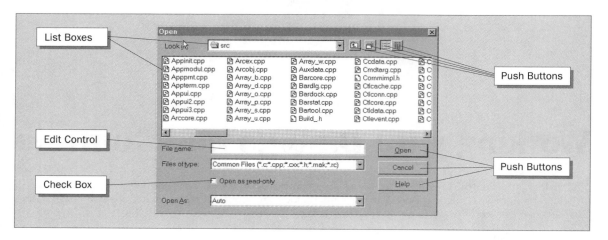

This is the File/Open... dialog in Visual C++. The annotations show the variety of controls that are used, which combine to provide a very intuitive interface for selecting a file to be opened. This makes the dialog very easy to use, even though there's a whole range of possibilities here.

There are two things needed to create and use a dialog box in an MFC program. The physical appearance of the dialog box which is defined in a resource file, and a dialog class object that is used to manage the operation of the dialog and its controls. MFC provides a class **CDialog** for you to use, once you have defined your dialog resource.

Understanding Controls

There are many different controls available to you in Windows and, in most cases, there's quite a bit of flexibility in how they look and operate. Most of them fall into one of six categories. We'll take a look at these and, for each category, see what a typical control looks like and what it does.

Type	Appearance	What they do
Static Controls	This is a static control	These provide static information, such as titles or instructions, or simply provide decoration in a dialog in the form of an icon or a filled rectangle.
Button Controls	A check box A radio button A push button	Buttons allow communication to the application with a single mouse button click. Radio buttons, named after the old car radios which used push buttons to select predefined stations, are usually grouped so that if one is checked, the others are unchecked. Check boxes can be individually checked so more than one can be checked at one time. Push buttons, such as OK and Cancel buttons, are typically used to close a dialog.

574

Table Continued on Following Page

Type	Appearance	What they do
Scroll Bars		We have already seen scroll bars attached to the edge of our view window. They can also be free standing controls.
List Boxes	Items / Listbox / Sample	This presents a list from which you can choose predefined items The scroll bar need not appear in a short list. The list can also have multiple columns and can be scrolled horizontally. A version of the list box is available that can display icons instead of text.
Edit Controls	You can edit this	In its simplest form, you can enter and edit a line of text. An edit control can be extended to allow sophisticated editing of multiple lines of text.
Combo Boxes	Choose this item / Or choose this item / Or enter one yourself	These combine the capability of a list box with the option of modifying a line or entering a complete line yourself. This is used to present a list of files in the Save As dialog.

A control may or may not be associated with a class object. Static controls don't do anything directly, so an associated class object may seem superfluous, but there's an MFC class, **CStatic**, that provides functions to enable you to alter the appearance of static controls. Button controls can also be handled by the dialog object in many cases, but MFC does provide the **CButton** class for use in situations where you do need a class object to manage a control. MFC also provides a full complement of classes to support the other controls. Since a control is a window, they are all derived from **CWnd**.

Common Controls

The set of standard controls that are supported by MFC and the Resource Editor under Windows 95 and Windows NT 3.51 are called **common controls**. Common controls include all of the controls we have just seen, as well as other more complex controls such as the **animate control**, for example, which has the capability to play an **AVI** (Audio Video Interleaved) file, and the **tree control** which can display a hierarchy of items in a tree. The tree control is used in Explorer in Windows 95 to display your files and folders in a hierarchy, but it can be used to display anything you like that can be represented by a tree.

Another useful control in the set of common controls is the **spin button**. You can use this to increment or decrement values in an associated edit control. To go into all of the possible controls that you might use is beyond the scope of this book, so we'll just take a few illustrative examples, including an example that uses a spin button, and implement them in the Sketcher program.

Creating a Dialog Resource

Let's take a concrete example. We can add a dialog to Sketcher to provide a choice of pen widths for drawing elements. This will ultimately involve modifying the current pen width in the document, as well as in **CElement**, and adding or modifying functions to deal with pen widths. We'll deal with all that, though, once we've got the dialog together.

575

First, change to the ResourceView, expand the resource tree for Sketcher and right-click on the Dialog folder in the tree. You will see the pop-up shown here:

If you click on Insert Dialog, a new dialog resource is displayed with a default ID assigned. You can edit the ID by right-clicking on it and selecting properties from the pop-up. Change the ID to something more meaningful, such as **IDD_PENWIDTH_DLG**. To the right of the ResourceView, you'll see a basic dialog box which already has an OK button and a Cancel button. There is a Controls palette from which you can select the controls to be added. The palette includes 21 different controls, all of which are Windows 95 common controls.

Adding Controls to a Dialog Box

To provide a mechanism for entering a pen width, we're going to modify the basic dialog that's initially displayed to that shown below:

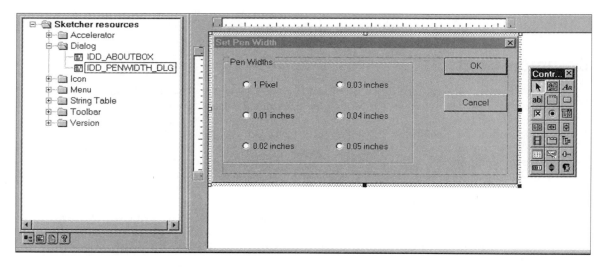

The dialog has six **radio buttons** which provide the pen width options. These are enclosed within a **group box** with the caption Pen Widths. Each radio button has an appropriate label to identify it.

The first step is to change the text in the title bar of the dialog box:

Make sure that the select button is active in the Controls window, as shown on the left. You can now double-click on the dialog box to display its properties box and modify the caption text to Set Pen Width, as shown above. Each of the controls in a dialog will have their own set of properties that you can access and modify in the same way as for the dialog box.

The next step is to add the **group box**:

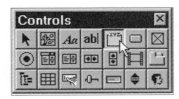

We'll use the group box to enclose the radio buttons that will be used to select a pen width. The group box serves to associate the radio buttons in a group from an operational standpoint and to provide a caption and a boundary for the group of buttons. Where you need more than one set of radio buttons, a means of grouping them is essential if they are to work properly. Select the button corresponding to the group box from the common controls palette as shown on the left by clicking it with the left mouse button. Then move the cursor to the approximate position in the dialog box where you want the center of the group box to be and press the left mouse button once more. This will place a group box of default size on to the dialog. You can then drag the borders of the group box to enlarge it to accommodate the six radio buttons that we will add. To set the caption for the group box, you can just type the caption you want. In this case, type Pen Widths. The properties box will open automatically.

The last step is to add the radio buttons:

Select the radio button control, as shown on the left. You can now position the mouse cursor at the point where you want to position a radio button within the group box and click the left mouse button. Do the same for all six radio buttons. For each radio button, just type in the caption to change it. This will open the properties box as before. The width of the radio button will increase to accommodate the text. You can also drag the border of the button to set its size. You can change the ID for each radio button in the properties dialog to correspond better with its purpose - **IDC_PENWIDTH0** for the 1 pixel pen width, **IDC_PENWIDTH1** for the 0.01 inch width pen, **IDC_PENWIDTH2** for the 0.02 inch pen, and so on.

You can position individual controls by dragging them around with the mouse when the selection tool is active in the Controls window. You can also select a group of controls by selecting successive controls with the *Shift* key pressed, or by dragging the cursor with the left button pressed to create a rectangle enclosing them. To align a group of controls, select an item from the <u>L</u>ayout menu pop-up on the main menu, or press the right mouse button and select from the pop-up at the cursor.

577

Testing the Dialog

The dialog resource is now complete. You can test it by selecting the Layout/Test menu option, pressing *Ctrl+T*, or by using the leftmost dialog edit toolbar button that appears at the bottom of the Developer Studio window. This will display a dialog window with the basic operations of the controls available, so you can try clicking on the radio buttons. When you have a group of radio buttons, only one can be selected, so, as you select one, any other that was previously selected is reset. Click on the OK or Cancel button in the dialog to end the test. Once you have saved the dialog resource, we're ready to add some code to support it.

Programming for a Dialog

There are two aspects to programming for a dialog: getting it displayed and handling the effects of its controls. Before we can display the dialog corresponding to the resource we've just created, we first need to define a dialog class for it. Class Wizard will help us with this.

Adding a Dialog Class

With the cursor on the dialog box that we've just created, press the right mouse button and select ClassWizard from the pop-up at the cursor. ClassWizard will then take you through a process to associate a class with the dialog. The first ClassWizard dialog will ask if you want to associate the new resource with a new class, an existing class or import a class to associate with it. We'll define a new dialog class derived from the MFC class **CDialog**, which you can call **CPenDialog** in the following dialog. Just click OK to bring it up.

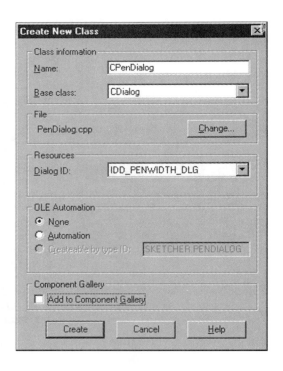

In the Create New Class dialog, type in CPenDialog in the Name: box. The Base Class: drop-down list will automatically show CDialog, which is fine for us. You may have to select the Dialog ID: - just make sure that it shows **IDD_PENWIDTH_DLG**. Finally, you may want to turn off the Add to Component Gallery checkbox so that you don't clutter it up with new dialogs. You can now click Create to create the new class.

The **CDialog** class is a window class (derived from the MFC class **CWnd**) that is specifically for displaying and managing dialogs. The dialog resource that we've created will automatically be associated with an object of our **CPenDialog** class, since the class definition includes a definition of a member **IDD** which is initialized with the ID of the dialog resource:

```
class CPenDialog : public CDialog
{
// Construction
public:
    CPenDialog(CWnd* pParent = NULL);   // standard constructor

// Dialog Data
    //{{AFX_DATA(CPenDialog)
        enum { IDD = IDD_PENWIDTH_DLG };
        // NOTE: the ClassWizard will add data members here
    //}}AFX_DATA

// Plus the rest of the class definition...
};
```

The highlighted statement defines **IDD** as a symbolic name for the dialog ID in the enumeration. Incidentally, using an enumeration is the only way you can get an initialized data member into a class definition. It works because an **enum** defines a symbolic name for an **int**. Unfortunately, you can only define values of type **int** in this way. It's not strictly necessary here, since the initialization for **IDD** could be done in the constructor, but this is how ClassWizard chose to do it. This technique is more commonly used to define a symbol for the dimension of an array which is a member of a class, in which case using an enumeration is your only option.

Having our own dialog class derived from **CDialog** also enables us to customize the dialog class by adding data members and functions to suit our particular needs. You'll often want to handle messages from controls within the dialog class, although you can also choose to handle them in a view or a document class if this is more convenient.

Modal and Modeless Dialogs

There are two quite distinct ways in which a dialog can operate. These are termed a **modal** dialog and a **modeless** dialog. While a modal dialog remains in effect, all operations in the other windows in the application are suspended until the dialog box is closed, usually by clicking on an OK or Cancel button. With a modeless dialog, you can move the focus back and forth between the dialog box and other windows in your application just by clicking on them with the mouse and you can continue to use the dialog box at any time until you close it. ClassWizard is an example of a modal dialog, while the properties window is modeless.

A modeless dialog box is created by calling the **Create()** function defined in the **CDialog** class but as we'll be using only modal dialogs in our example, we call the **DoModal()** function in the dialog object, as you'll see shortly.

Displaying a Dialog

Where you put the code to display a dialog in your program depends on the application. In the Sketcher program, we need to add a menu item which, when it's selected, will result in the pen widths dialog being displayed. We'll put this in the **IDR_SKETCHTYPE** menu bar.

As both the width and the color are associated with a pen, we'll rename the Color menu as Pen. You do this just by double-clicking the Color menu item to open its properties box and changing the Caption: entry to &Pen.

When we add the menu item Width... to the Pen menu, we should separate it from the colors in the menu. You can add a separator after the last color menu item by double-clicking the last empty menu item in the menu and selecting the Separator check box. If you close the properties box, you can then enter the new Width... item as the next menu item after the separator. Double-click on the menu ID to display the menu properties for modification, as shown below:

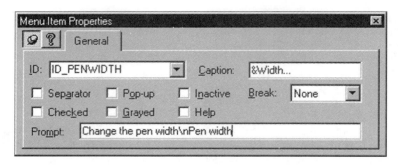

Enter **ID_PENWIDTH** as the ID for the menu item, Width.... You can also add a status bar prompt for it and, since we'll also add a toolbar button, you can include text for the tool tip as well. The menu will look like this:

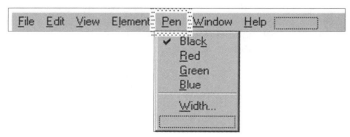

To add the toolbar button, open the toolbar resource by extending Toolbar in the ResourceView and double-clicking on **IDR_MAINFRAME**. You can add a toolbar button to represent a pen width. The one shown below tries to represent a pen drawing a line:

To associate the new button with the menu item that we just added, open the properties box for the button and specify its ID as **ID_PENWIDTH**, the same as that for the menu item.

Code to Display the Dialog

The code to display the dialog will go in the handler for the Pen/Width... menu item, so in which class should we implement this handler? We could consider the view class as a candidate for dealing with pen widths, but following our previous logic with colors and elements, it would be sensible to have the current pen width selection in the document, so we'll put the handler in the **CSketcherDoc** class. Open ClassWizard and create a function for the Command message handler corresponding to **ID_PENWIDTH** in the **CSketcherDoc** class. Now edit this handler and enter the following code:

```
// Handler for the pen width menu item
void CSketcherDoc::OnPenwidth()
{
   CPenDialog aDlg;                     // Create a local dialog object

   // Display the dialog as modal
   aDlg.DoModal();
}
```

There are just two statements in the handler at the moment. The first creates a dialog object which is automatically associated with our dialog resource. We then display the dialog by calling the function **DoModal()** in the **aDlg** object. When the dialog box is closed, the function returns a value corresponding to the button used to close it. In our dialog, the value returned can be **IDOK** if the OK button is selected to close the dialog, or **IDCANCEL** if the dialog is closed using the Cancel button. We'll add code to use this a little later.

Because the handler declares a **CPenDialog** object, you must add an **#include** statement for **PenDialog.h** to the beginning of **SketcherDoc.cpp** (after the **#include**s for **stadafx.h** and **sketcher.h**), otherwise you'll get compilation errors when you build the program. Once you have done that, you can build Sketcher and try out the dialog. It should appear when you click the toolbar button or the Pen/Width... menu item. Of course, if the dialog is to do anything, we still have to add the code to support the operation of the controls.

Supporting the Dialog Controls

For our pen dialog, we'll store the selected pen width in a data member, **m_PenWidth**, of the **CPenDialog** class. You can either add the data member by right-clicking the **CPenDialog** class name, or you can add it directly to the class definition as follows:

```
class CPenDialog : public CDialog
{
// Construction
public:
   CPenDialog(CWnd* pParent = NULL);   // standard constructor

// Dialog Data
   //{{AFX_DATA(CPenDialog)
   enum { IDD = IDD_PENWIDTH_DLG };
   //}}AFX_DATA

// Data stored in the dialog
public:
   int m_PenWidth;                     // Record the pen width

// Plus the rest of the class definition....

};
```

If you do use the context menu for the class to add **m_PenWidth**, be sure to add a comment to the class definition. This is a good habit to get into - even when the member name looks self-explanatory.

We'll use the data member **m_PenWidth** to set the radio button corresponding to the current pen width in the document as checked. We'll also arrange that the pen width selected in the dialog is stored in this member, so that we can retrieve it when the dialog closes.

Initializing the Controls

We can initialize the radio buttons by overriding the function **OnInitDialog()** which is defined in the base class, **CDialog**. This function is called in response to a **WM_INITDIALOG** message which is sent during the execution of **DoModal()** just before the dialog box is displayed. You can add the function to the class by selecting **WM_INITDIALOG** in the Messages: box in ClassWizard, or by selecting from the Messages: drop-down list at the top of the window when you have the **CPenDialog.cpp** file displayed. The implementation for our version of **OnInitDialog()** will be:

```
BOOL  CPenDialog::OnInitDialog()
{
    CDialog::OnInitDialog();
    // Check the radio button corresponding to the pen width
    switch(m_PenWidth)
    {
        case 1:
            CheckDlgButton(IDC_PENWIDTH1,1);
            break;
        case 2:
            CheckDlgButton(IDC_PENWIDTH2,1);
            break;
        case 3:
            CheckDlgButton(IDC_PENWIDTH3,1);
            break;
        case 4:
            CheckDlgButton(IDC_PENWIDTH4,1);
            break;
        case 5:
            CheckDlgButton(IDC_PENWIDTH5,1);
            break;
        default:
            CheckDlgButton(IDC_PENWIDTH0,1);
    }
    return TRUE;   // return TRUE unless you set the focus to a control
                   // EXCEPTION: OCX Property Pages should return FALSE
}
```

You should leave the call to the base class function there, as it does some essential setup for the dialog. The **switch** statement will check one of the radio buttons, depending on the value set in the **m_PenWidth** data member. This implies that we must arrange to set **m_PenWidth** before we execute **DoModal()**, since the **DoModal()** function causes the **WM_INITDIALOG** message to be sent and our version of **OnInitDialog()** to be called.

The **CheckDlgButton()** function is inherited indirectly from **CWnd** through **CDialog**. If the second argument is **1**, it checks the button corresponding to the ID specified in the first argument. If the second argument is **0**, the button is unchecked. This works with both check boxes and radio buttons.

Handling Radio Button Messages

Once the dialog box is displayed, every time you click on one or other of the radio buttons, a message will be generated and sent to the application. To deal with these messages, we can add handlers to our **CPenDialog** class. Open ClassWizard and create a function for the **BN_CLICKED** message for each of the radio button IDs, **IDC_PENWIDTH0** through **IDC_PENWIDTH5**. The implementation of all of these are very similar, since they each just set the pen width in the dialog object. As an example, the handler for **IDC_PENWIDTH0** will be:

```
void CPenDialog::OnPenwidth0()
{
    m_PenWidth = 0;
}
```

You need to add the code for all six handlers to the **CPenDialog** class implementation, setting **m_PenWidth** to 1 in **OnPenWidth1()**, 2 in **OnPenWidth2()**, and so on.

Completing Dialog Operations

We need to modify the **OnPenwidth()** handler in **CSketcherDoc** to make the dialog effective. Add the following code to the function:

```
// Handler for the pen width menu item
void CSketcherDoc::OnPenwidth()
{
        CPenDialog aDlg;        // Create a local dialog object

    // Set the pen width in the dialog to that stored in the document
    aDlg.m_PenWidth = m_PenWidth;

    // Display the dialog as modal
    // When closed with OK, get the pen width
        if(aDlg.DoModal() == IDOK)
            m_PenWidth = aDlg.m_PenWidth;
}
```

The **m_PenWidth** member of the **aDlg** object is passed a pen width stored in the **m_PenWidth** member of the document. We have still to add this member to **CSketcherDoc**. The call of the **DoModal()** function now occurs in the condition of the **if** statement, which will be **TRUE** if the **DoModal()** function returns **IDOK**. In this case, we retrieve the pen width stored in the **aDlg** object and store it in the **m_PenWidth** member of the document. If the dialog box is closed using the Cancel button, **IDOK** will not be returned by **DoModal()** and the value of **m_PenWidth** in the document will not be changed.

Note that even though the dialog box is closed when **DoModal()** returns a value, the **aDlg** object still exists, so we can call its member functions without any problem. The object **aDlg** is destroyed automatically on return from **OnPenwidth()**.

All that remains to do to support variable pen widths in our application is to update the affected classes, **CSketcherDoc**, **CElement**, and the four shape classes derived from **CElement**.

Adding Pen Widths to the Document

We need to add the member **m_PenWidth** to the document, and the function **GetPenWidth()** to allow external access to the value stored. You should add the shaded statements below to the **CSketcherDoc** class definition:

```
class CSketcherDoc : public CDocument
{
// the rest as before...

protected:
// the rest as before...
    int m_PenWidth;                             // Current pen width

// Operations
public:
// the rest as before...
    int GetPenWidth(){ return m_PenWidth; }     // Get the current pen width

// the rest as before...
};
```

Because it is trivial, we can define the **GetPenWidth()** function in the definition of the class and we gain the benefit of it being implicitly **inline**. We do need to add initialization for **m_PenWidth** to the constructor for **CSketcherDoc**, so add the line,

```
    m_PenWidth = 0;        // Set 1 pixel pen
```

to the constructor definition in **SketchDoc.cpp**.

Adding Pen Widths to the Elements

We have a little more to do to the **CElement** class and the shape classes derived from it. We already have a member **m_Pen** in the **CElement** to store the width to be used when drawing an element, and we must extend each of the constructors for elements to accept a pen width as an argument and set the member in the class accordingly. The **GetBoundRect()** function in **CElement** must be altered to deal with a pen width of zero. Let's deal with **CElement** first. The new version of **GetBoundRect()** in the **CElement** class will be:

```
// Get the bounding rectangle for an element
CRect CElement::GetBoundRect()
{
    CRect BoundingRect;                    // Object to store the bounding rectangle
    BoundingRect = m_EnclosingRect;        // Initialize with the enclosing rectangle

    //Increase bounding rectangle by the pen width
    int Offset = m_Pen == 0? 1: m_Pen;     // Width must be at least 1
    BoundingRect.InflateRect(Offset, Offset);
    return BoundingRect;
}
```

> *Since the* `InflateRect()` *function doesn't like to inflate rectangles by zero, we use the local variable* `Offset` *to ensure that we pass the function a value of* `1` *if the pen width is* `0` *and we pass the actual pen width in all other cases.*

Each of the constructors for `CLine`, `CRectangle`, `CCircle` and `CCurve` need to be modified to accept a pen width as an argument and to store it in the `m_PenWidth` member of the class. The declaration for the constructor in each class definition needs to be modified to add the extra parameter. For example, in the `CLine` class, the constructor declaration will become,

```
CLine(CPoint Start, CPoint End, COLORREF aColor, int PenWidth);
```

and the constructor implementation should be modified to:

```
CLine::CLine(CPoint Start, CPoint End, COLORREF Color, int PenWidth)
{
    m_StartPoint = Start;                  // Set line start point
    m_EndPoint = End;                      // Set line end point
    m_Color = Color;                       // Set line color
    m_Pen = PenWidth;                      // Set pen width

    // Define the enclosing rectangle
    m_EnclosingRect = CRect(Start, End);
    m_EnclosingRect.NormalizeRect();
}
```

You should modify each of the class definitions and constructors for the shapes in the same way.

Creating Elements in the View

The last change we need to make is to the `CreateElement()` member of `CSketcherView`. Since we've added the pen width as an argument to the constructors for each of the shapes, we must update the calls to the constructors to reflect this. Change the definition of `CSketcherView::CreateElement()` to:

```
CElement* CSketcherView::CreateElement()
{
    // Get a pointer to the document for this view
    CSketcherDoc* pDoc = GetDocument();
    ASSERT_VALID(pDoc);                              // Verify the pointer is good

    // Now select the element using the type stored in the document
    switch(pDoc->GetElementType())
    {
    case RECTANGLE:
        return new CRectangle(m_FirstPoint, m_SecondPoint,
                    pDoc->GetElementColor(), pDoc->GetPenWidth());
    case CIRCLE:
        return new CCircle(m_FirstPoint, m_SecondPoint,
                    pDoc->GetElementColor(), pDoc->GetPenWidth());
    case CURVE:
        return new CCurve(m_FirstPoint, m_SecondPoint,
                    pDoc->GetElementColor(), pDoc->GetPenWidth());
```

```
        case LINE:                          // Always default to a line
            return new CLine(m_FirstPoint, m_SecondPoint,
                             pDoc->GetElementColor(), pDoc->GetPenWidth());
        default:                            // Something's gone wrong
            AfxMessageBox("Bad Element code", MB_OK);
            AfxAbort();
    }
}
```

Each constructor call now passes the pen width as an argument. This is retrieved from the document using the **GetPenWidth()** function that we added to the document class.

Exercising the Dialog

You can now build and run the latest version of Sketcher to see how our dialog works out. Selecting the Pen/Width... menu option will display the dialog box so that you can select the pen width. The following screen is typical of what you might see when the program is executing:

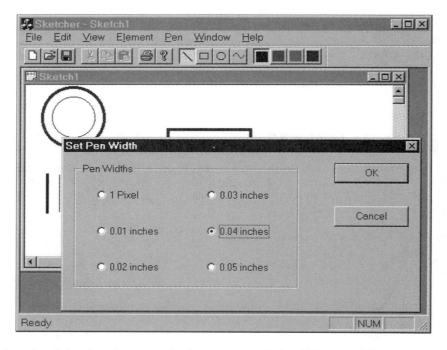

Note that the dialog box is a completely separate window. You can drag it around to position it where you want. You can even drag it outside the Sketcher application window.

Using a Spin Button Control

Now let's move on to looking at how the spin button can help us in the Sketcher application. The spin button is particularly useful when you want to constrain an input within a given integer range. It's normally used in association with another control, called a **buddy control**, which displays the value that the spin button modifies. The associated control is usually an edit control, but it doesn't have to be. We could apply the spin control to managing scaling in a document view. A drawing scale would be a view-specific property and we would want the element draw functions to take account of the current scale for a view.

Altering the existing code to deal with view scaling will require rather more work than setting up the control, so let's first look at how we can create a spin button and make it work.

Creating the Spin Button

We'll be invoking the scale dialog through a new menu item Scale..., so add this to the **IDR_SKETCHTYPE** menu under View. Make sure you uncheck the pop-up property. The default ID for the item will be **ID_SCALE**, which is fine. You can also add a toolbar button if you want.

Now we can add a dialog to set the view scale. In ResourceView, add a new dialog by right-clicking the Dialog folder of the tree and selecting Insert Dialog. Change the ID to **IDD_SCALE_DLG**.

Click on the spin control in the palette, as shown on the left, and then click on the position in the dialog where you want it to be placed. Next, double-click on the spin control to display its properties. Changes its ID to something more meaningful than the default, such as **IDC_SPIN_SCALE**. Now take at look at the Styles page in the spin button properties. It is shown below:

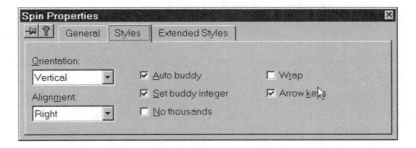

The Arrow keys check box will be automatically selected enabling you to operate the spin button by using arrow keys on the keyboard. You should also check the box Set buddy integer, which specifies the buddy control value as integer, and Auto buddy, which provides for automatic selection of the buddy control. The control selected automatically as the buddy will be the previous control defined in the dialog. At the moment, this is the Cancel button which is not exactly ideal, but we'll see how to change this in a moment. The Alignment: list determines how the spin button will be displayed in relation to its buddy. You should set this to Right so that the spin button is attached to the right edge of its buddy.

Next, add an edit control at the side of the spin button by selecting the edit control from the palette, as shown on the left, and clicking in the dialog where you want it positioned. Change the ID for the edit control to **IDC_SCALE**.

To make the contents of the edit control quite clear, you could add a static control - just to the left of the edit control in the palette - and enter View Scale: as the caption. You can select all three controls by clicking on them while holding down the *Shift* key. Clicking the right mouse button will pop up a menu at the cursor with options you can use for aligning the controls tidily.

The Controls' Tab Sequence

Controls in a dialog have what is called a **tab sequence**. This is the sequence in which the focus shifts from one control to the next. This is initially determined by the sequence in which controls are added to the dialog. You can see the tab sequence for the current dialog box by selecting Layout/Tab Order from the main menu, or by pressing *Ctrl+D*.

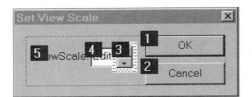

The tab order will be displayed as shown on the left. Because the Cancel button immediately precedes the spin button in sequence, the Auto buddy property for the spin button will select it as the buddy control. We want the edit control to precede the spin button in the tab sequence, so you need to select the controls by clicking on them with the left mouse button in the sequence: OK button; Cancel button; edit control; spin button; and finally the static control. Now, the edit control will be selected as the buddy to the spin button.

Generating the Scale Dialog Class

After saving the resource file, you can click the right mouse button on the dialog and select ClassWizard from the pop-up at the cursor. This will take you through a dialog to define the new class associated with the dialog resource that you have created. You should name the class **CScaleDialog**.

We need to define a variable in the dialog class that will store the value returned from the edit control, so switch to the Member Variables tab in ClassWizard and select the **IDC_SCALE** ID which identifies the edit control. Click on Add Variable... and enter the variable name as **m_Scale**. We'll be storing an integer scale value, so select **int** as the variable type and click OK.

The ClassWizard will display boxes at the bottom of the Member Variables tab where you can enter maximum and minimum values for the variable **m_Scale**. For our application, a minimum of 1 and a maximum of 8 would be good values. The definition which ClassWizard will produce when you click on the OK button is as follows:

```
class CScaleDialog : public CDialog
{
    // Construction
    public:
        CScaleDialog(CWnd* pParent = NULL);   // standard constructor

    // Operations
    public:
```

```
    // Dialog Data
      //{{AFX_DATA(CScaleDialog)
      enum { IDD = IDD_SCALE_DLG };
      int      m_Scale;
      //}}AFX_DATA


   // Overrides
      // ClassWizard generated virtual function overrides
      //{{AFX_VIRTUAL(CScaleDialog)
      protected:
         virtual void DoDataExchange(CDataExchange* pDX);// DDX/DDV support
      //}}AFX_VIRTUAL


   // Implementation
   protected:
         // Generated message map functions
         //{{AFX_MSG(CScaleDialog)
         virtual BOOL OnInitDialog();
         //}}AFX_MSG
         DECLARE_MESSAGE_MAP()};
```

The interesting bits are shaded. The class is associated with the dialog resource through the **enum** statement initializing **IDD** with the ID of the resource. It contains the variable **m_Scale**, which is specified as a **public** member of the class, so we can set it and retrieve its value directly.

Two virtual functions have been included in the class, **DoDataExchange()** and **OnInitDialog()**. Let's look at each of these in turn.

Dialog Data Exchange and Validation

The **DoDataExchange()** function has been implemented by ClassWizard as:

```
void CScaleDialog::DoDataExchange(CDataExchange* pDX)
{
   CDialog::DoDataExchange(pDX);
   //{{AFX_DATA_MAP(CScaleDialog)
   DDX_Text(pDX, IDC_SCALE, m_Scale);
   DDV_MinMaxInt(pDX, m_Scale, 1, 8);
   //}}AFX_DATA_MAP
}
```

This function is called by the framework to carry out the exchange of data between variables in a dialog and the dialog's controls. This mechanism is called **Dialog Data Exchange**, usually abbreviated to **DDX**. This is a very powerful mechanism that can provide automatic transfer of information between a dialog and its controls in most circumstances, thus saving you the effort of programming to get the data yourself, as we did with the radio buttons in the pen width dialog.

In our scale dialog, DDX handles data transfers between the edit control and the variable **m_Scale** in the **CScaleDialog** class. The variable **pDX** passed to the function controls the direction in which data is transferred. After calling the base class **DoDataExchange()** function, the **DDX_Text()** function is called, which actually moves data between the variable, **m_Scale**, and the edit control.

589

The call to the **DDV_MinMaxInt()** function verifies that the value transferred is within the limits specified. This mechanism is called **Dialog Data Validation**, or **DDV**. The **DoDataExchange()** function will be called automatically before the dialog is displayed, to pass the value stored in **m_Scale** to the edit control. When the dialog is closed with the OK button, it will be automatically called again to pass the value in the control back to the variable **m_Scale** in the dialog object. All this is taken care of for you. You only need to ensure that the right value is stored in **m_Scale** before the dialog box is displayed and arrange to collect the result when the dialog box closes.

Initializing the Dialog

OnInitDialog() is the handler for the **WM_INITDIALOG** message, as we saw when we implemented the pen width dialog. As it's called just before the dialog is displayed, you can use this function to do any initialization required. We'll use it to set up the spin control. We'll initialize the **m_Scale** member of the dialog when we create the dialog in the handler for a Scale... menu item, because we will want to set it to the value of the scale stored in the view. Add the handler for the **WM_INITDIALOG** message to the **CScaleDialog** class, using the same mechanism that you used for the previous dialog, and add code to initialize the spin control as follows:

```
BOOL CScaleDialog::OnInitDialog()
{
    CDialog::OnInitDialog();

    // First get a pointer to the spin control
    CSpinButtonCtrl* pSpin;
    pSpin = (CSpinButtonCtrl*)GetDlgItem(IDC_SPIN_SCALE);

    // If you have not checked the auto buddy option in
    // the spin control's properties, set the buddy control here

    // Set the spin control range
    pSpin->SetRange(1, 8);

    return TRUE;   // return TRUE unless you set the focus to a control
                   // EXCEPTION: OCX Property Pages should return FALSE
}
```

There are only three lines of code added, along with four lines of comments. The first line of code creates a pointer to an object of the MFC class **CSpinButtonCtrl**. This class is specifically for managing spin buttons and is initialized in the next statement to point to the control in our dialog. The function **GetDlgItem()** is inherited from **CWnd** via **CDialog**, and it will retrieve the address of any control from the ID passed as an argument. Since, as we saw earlier, a control is just a specialized window, the pointer returned is of type **CWnd***, so we have to cast it to the type appropriate to the particular control, which is **CSpinButtonCtrl*** in this case. The third statement that we have added sets the upper and lower limits for the spin button by calling the **SetRange()** member of the spin control object.

If you want to set the buddy control using code rather than using the Auto buddy option in the spin button's properties, the **CSpinButtonCtrl** class has a function member to do this. You would need to add the statement,

```
pSpin->SetBuddy(GetDlgItem(IDC_SCALE));
```

at the point indicated by the comments.

Adding the Scale Menu and Toolbar

Now would be a good time to provide a means of actually displaying the scale dialog, so go to
ResourceView and open the **IDR_SKETCHTYPE** menu. We'll add a S̲cale... menu item to the end
of the V̲iew menu. First, add a separator to the end of that menu by checking the Separator
check box in the properties window for a new item. Now fill in the properties window for the
next item, as shown below. This item will bring up the scale dialog, so we end the caption with
an ellipsis (three periods) to indicate that the menu item displays a dialog. This is a standard
Windows convention.

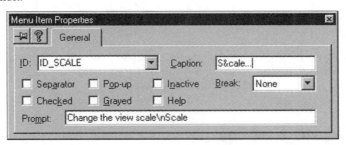

The menu should now look like this:

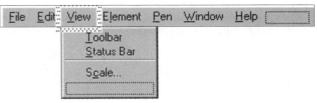

You can also add a toolbar button for this menu item. All you need to do is make sure that the
ID for this button is also set to **ID_SCALE**.

Displaying the Spin Button

The dialog will be displayed when the S̲cale... menu option or its associated toolbar button is
selected, so you need to use ClassWizard's Message Maps tab to add a COMMAND handler to
the **CSketcherView** class corresponding to the **ID_SCALE** message. Then you can select the
E̲dit Code button and add code as follows:

```
void CSketcherView::OnViewScale()
{
   CScaleDialog aDlg;           // Create a dialog object
   aDlg.m_Scale = m_Scale;      // Pass the view scale to the dialog
   if(aDlg.DoModal() == IDOK)
   {
      m_Scale = aDlg.m_Scale;   // Get the new scale
      InvalidateRect(0);        // Invalidate the whole window
   }
}
```

The dialog is created as modal, in the same way as the pen widths dialog. Before the dialog box
is displayed by the **DoModal()** call, we store the scale value provided by the **CSketcherView**
member, **m_Scale**, in the dialog member with the same name, which ensures that the control
will display the current scale value when the dialog is displayed.

If the dialog is closed with the OK button, we store the new scale from the dialog member **m_Scale**, in the view member **m_Scale**.

Of course, we must add **m_Scale** to the definition of **CSketcherView**, so add the following line at the end of the other data members in the class definition:

```
int m_Scale;          // Current view scale
```

You should also add a line to the **CSketcherView** constructor to initialize **m_Scale** to 1. This will result in a view always starting out with a scale of one to one. If you forget to do this, it's unlikely that your program will work properly.

As we're using the **CScaleDialog** class, we need to add an include statement for **ScaleDialog.h** to the beginning of the **SketcherView.cpp** file. That's all we need to get the scale dialog and its spin control operational. You can build and run Sketcher to give it a trial spin before we add the code to use a view scale factor.

Using the Scale Factor

Scaling with Windows usually involves using one of the scaleable mapping modes **MM_ISOTROPIC** or **MM_ANISOTROPIC**. By using one or other of these mapping modes, you can get Windows to do most of the work. Unfortunately, it's not as simple as just changing the mapping mode, because neither of these mapping modes are supported by **CScrollView**. However, if we can get around that, we're home and dry. We'll use **MM_ANISOTROPIC**, so let's first understand what's involved in using this mapping mode.

Scaleable Mapping Modes

There are two mapping modes that allow the mapping between logical coordinates and device coordinates to be altered. These are **MM_ISOTROPIC** and **MM_ANISOTROPIC**. **MM_ISOTROPIC** has the property that Windows will force the scaling factor for both the x and y axes to be the same, which has the advantage that your circles will always be circles, but you can't map a document to fit into a rectangle of a different shape. **MM_ANISOTROPIC**, on the other hand, permits scaling of each axis independently. Because it's the most flexible, we'll use **MM_ANISOTROPIC** for scaling operations in Sketcher.

The way in which logical coordinates are transformed to device coordinates is dependent on the following parameters which you can set:

Parameter	Description
Window Origin	The logical coordinates of the top left corner of the window. This is set by calling the function **CDC::SetWindowOrg()**.
Window Extent	The size of the window specified in logical coordinates. This is set by calling the function **CDC::SetWindowExt()**.

Table Continued on Following Page

Parameter	Description
Viewport Origin	The coordinates of the top left corner of the window in device coordinates(pixels). This is set by calling the function `CDC::SetViewportOrg()`.
Viewport Extent	The size of the window in device coordinates(pixels). This is set by calling the function `CDC::SetViewportExt()`.

The viewport referred to here has no physical significance by itself. It only serves as a parameter for defining how coordinates are transformed from logical coordinates to device coordinates. The formulae that are used by Windows to convert from logical coordinates to device coordinates are:

$$xDevice = (xLogical - xWindowOrg) * \frac{xViewPortExt}{xWindowExt} + xViewportOrg$$

$$yDevice = (yLogical - yWindowOrg) * \frac{yViewPortExt}{yWindowExt} + yViewportOrg$$

With coordinate systems other than **MM_ISOTROPIC** and **MM_ANISOTROPIC**, the window extent and the viewport extent are fixed by the mapping mode and you can't change them. Calling the functions **SetWindowExt()** or **SetViewportExt()** in the **CDC** object to change them will have no effect, although you can still move the position of (0,0) in your logical reference frame by calling **SetWindowOrg()** or **SetViewportOrg()**. However, for a given document size which will be expressed by the window extent in logical coordinate units, we can adjust the scale at which elements are displayed by setting the viewport extent appropriately. By using and setting the window and viewport extents, we can get the scaling done automatically.

Setting the Document Size

We need to maintain the size of the document in logical units in the document object. Add a **protected** data member, **m_DocSize**, to the **CSketcherDoc** class definition:

```
CSize m_DocSize;                          // Document size
```

We will also need to access this data member from the view class, so add a **public** function to the **CSketcherDoc** class definition as follows:

```
CSize GetDocSize(){ return m_DocSize; }   // Retrieve the document size
```

We must initialize the **m_DocSize** member in the constructor for the document, so modify the implementation of **CSketcherDoc()** as follows:

```
CSketcherDoc::CSketcherDoc()
{
   // TODO: add one-time construction code here
   m_Element = LINE;               // Set initial element type
   m_Color = BLACK;                // Set initial drawing color
   m_PenWidth = 0;                 // Set 1 pixel pen
   m_DocSize = CSize(4000,4000);   // Set initial document size 40x40 inches
}
```

We'll be using notional **MM_LOENGLISH** coordinates, so we can treat the logical units as 0.01 inches, so the value set will give an area of 40 inches square to draw on.

Setting the Mapping Mode

We'll set the mapping mode to **MM_ANISOTROPIC** in the **OnPrepareDC()** member of **CSketcherView**. This is always called for any **WM_PAINT** message, and we have arranged to call it when we draw temporary objects in the mouse message handlers. However, we must do a little more than just set the mapping mode. The implementation of **OnPrepareDC()** will be:

```
void CSketcherView::OnPrepareDC(CDC* pDC, CPrintInfo* pInfo)
{
    CScrollView::OnPrepareDC(pDC, pInfo);
    CSketcherDoc* pDoc = GetDocument();
    pDC->SetMapMode(MM_ANISOTROPIC);            // Set the map mode
    CSize DocSize = pDoc->GetDocSize();         // Get the document size

    // y extent must be negative because we want MM_LOENGLISH
    DocSize.cy = -DocSize.cy;                    // Change sign of y
    pDC->SetWindowExt(DocSize);                  // Now set the window extent

    // Get the number of pixels per inch in x and y
    int xLogPixels = pDC->GetDeviceCaps(LOGPIXELSX);
    int yLogPixels = pDC->GetDeviceCaps(LOGPIXELSY);

    // Calculate the viewport extent in x and y
    long xExtent = (long)DocSize.cx*m_Scale*xLogPixels/100L;
    long yExtent = (long)DocSize.cy*m_Scale*yLogPixels/100L;

    pDC->SetViewportExt((int)xExtent, (int)-yExtent); // Set viewport extent
}
```

You'll need to create the handler for this before you can add the code. The easiest way is to open **SketcherView.cpp** and select OnPrepareDC from the Messages drop-down list, or you could achieve the same thing using ClassWizard.

After setting the mapping mode and obtaining the document extent, we set the window extent with the *y* extent negative. This is just to be consistent with the **MM_LOENGLISH** mode that we were using previously.

The **CDC** member function, **GetDeviceCaps()**, supplies information about the device that the device context is associated with. You can get various kinds information about the device, depending on the argument you pass to the function. In our case, the arguments **LOGPIXELSX** and **LOGPIXELSY** return the number of pixels per logical inch in the *x* and *y* directions. These values will be equivalent to 100 units in our logical coordinates.

We use these values to calculate the *x* and *y* values for the viewport extent which we store in the local variables **xExtent** and **yExtent**. The document extent along an axis in logical units, divided by 100, gives the document extent in inches. If this is multiplied by the number of logical pixels per inch for the device, we get the equivalent number of pixels for the extent. If we use this value as the viewport extent, we will get the elements displayed at a scale of 1 to 1. If we multiply this value by the scale, in **m_Scale**, the elements will be drawn according to the value of **m_Scale**. This is exactly the expressions for the *x* and *y* viewport extents.

That's all we need to scale the view. Unfortunately, at the moment the scrolling won't work, so let's take a look at that.

Implementing Scrolling with Scaling

CScrollView just won't work with **MM_ANISOTROPIC**, so clearly we must use another mapping mode to set up the scrollbars. The easiest way to do this is to use **MM_TEXT**, because, in this case, the logical coordinates are the same as the client coordinates - that is pixels. All we need to do, then, is to figure out how many pixels are equivalent to our logical document extent for the scale at which we are drawing. This is easier than you might think. We can add a function to **CSketcherView** to take care of the scrollbars and implement everything in there. Right-click on the **CSketcherView** class name and add a **public** function **ResetScrollSizes()** with a **void** return type. Add the code to the implementation, as follows:

```
void CSketcherView::ResetScrollSizes()
{
    CClientDC aDC(this);
    OnPrepareDC(&aDC);                              // Set up the device context
    CSize DocSize = GetDocument()->GetDocSize();    // Get the document size
    aDC.LPtoDP(&DocSize);                           // Get the size in pixels
    SetScrollSizes(MM_TEXT, DocSize);               // Set up the scrollbars
}
```

After creating a local **CClientDC** object for the view, we call **OnPrepareDC()** to set up the **MM_ANISOTROPIC** mapping mode. Because this takes account of the scaling, the **LPtoDP()** member of **aDC** will convert the document size stored in the local variable **DocSize** to the correct number of pixels for the current logical document size and scale. We can then get the **SetScrollSizes()** member of **CScrollView** to set up the scrollbars based on this by specifying **MM_TEXT** as the mapping mode. Simple really, when you know how.

Setting Up the Scrollbars

We must set up the scrollbars initially for the view in the **OnInitialUpdate()** member of **CSketcherView**. Change the previous implementation of the function to:

```
void CSketcherView::OnInitialUpdate()
{
    ResetScrollSizes();                     // Set up the scrollbars
    CScrollView::OnInitialUpdate();
}
```

All we need to do is call the function that we just added to the view. This takes care of everything - well, almost. The **CScrollView** needs an initial extent to be set for **OnPrepareDC()** to work properly, so we need to add one statement to the **CSketcherView** constructor:

```
CSketcherView::CSketcherView()
{
// TODO: add construction code here
    m_FirstPoint = CPoint(0,0);         // Set 1st recorded point to 0,0
    m_SecondPoint = CPoint(0,0);        // Set 2nd recorded point to 0,0
    m_pTempElement = 0;                 // Set temporary element pointer to 0
    m_pSelected = 0;                    // No elements should be selected initially
    m_MoveMode = FALSE;                 // Set move mode off
    m_Scale = 1;                        // Set initial scale
    SetScrollSizes(MM_TEXT, CSize(0,0)); // Set arbitrary scrollers
}
```

This just calls **SetScrollSizes()** to an arbitrary extent to get the scrollbars initialized before the view is drawn. When the view is drawn for the first time, the **ResetScrollSizes()** function call in **OnInitialUpdate()** will set up the scrollbars properly.

Of course, each time the view scale changes, we need to update the scrollbars before the view is redrawn. We can take care of this in the **OnScale()** handler in **CSketcherView**:

```
void CSketcherView::OnScale()
{
   CScaleDialog aDlg;              // Create a dialog object
   aDlg.m_Scale = m_Scale;        // Pass the view scale to the dialog
   if(aDlg.DoModal() == IDOK)
   {
      m_Scale = aDlg.m_Scale;     // Get the new scale
      ResetScrollSizes();         // Adjust scrolling to the new scale
      InvalidateRect(0);          // Invalidate the whole window
   }
}
```

Using our function **ResetScrollSizes()**, taking care of the scrollbars isn't complicated. Everything is taken care of by the one additional line of code.

Now, you can build the project and run the application. You'll see that the scrollbars work just as they should. Note that each view maintains its own scale factor, independently of the other views.

Creating a Status Bar

With each view now being scaled independently, it becomes necessary to have some indication of what the current scale in a view is. A convenient way to do this would be to display the scale in a status bar. The Windows 95 style indicates that the status bar should appear at the bottom of the window, below the scroll bar if there is one. Also, there tends to be only one status bar attached to the main application window, which you can see in the following screen showing Sketcher at its current stage of development:

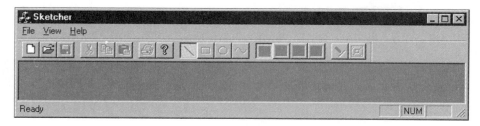

The status bar is divided into segments, called **panes**. The status bar in the previous screen has four panes. One on the left contains the text Ready, and the other three are the recessed areas on the right. It's possible for you to write to this status bar, but you need to get access to the **m_wndStatusBar** member of **CMainFrame**. As this is a **protected** member of the class, you must add a member function to modify the status bar. You could add a **public** function member to **CMainFrame** as follows:

```
      void CMainFrame::SetPaneText(int Pane, LPCTSTR Text)
      {
         m_wndStatusBar.SetPaneText(Pane, Text);
      }
```

This function sets the text in pane selected by **Pane** in the status bar represented by **m_wndStatusBar** to the text, **Text**. The status bar panes are indexed from the left starting at 0.

Now we could write from anywhere outside the **CMainFrame** class:

```
      CMainFrame* pFrame = (CMainFrame*) AfxGetApp()->m_pMainWnd;
      pFrame->SetPaneText(0, "Goodbye cruel World");
```

This gets a pointer to the main window of the application and outputs the text string you see to the leftmost pane in the status bar. This is fine, but the main application window is no place for a view scale. We may well have several views, so we really want to associate displaying the scale with each view. The answer is to give each child window its own status bar. The **m_wndStatusBar** in **CMainFrame** is an instance of the **CStatusBar** class. We can use the same class to implement our own status bars.

Adding a Status Bar to a Frame

The **CStatusBar** class is built upon the Windows Common Controls version of the status bar, **CStatusBarCtrl**, and also allows direct access to this class to provide extra functionality. The first step to utilizing it is to add a data member for the status bar to the definition of **CChildFrame**, which is the frame window for a view, so add the following declaration to the **public** section of the class:

```
      CStatusBar m_StatusBar;      // Status bar object
```

A word of warning is required at this point. Status bars should be part of the frame, not part of the view. We don't want to be able to scroll the status bars or draw over them. They should just remain anchored to the bottom of the window. If you added a status bar to the view, it would appear inside the scrollbars and would be scrolled whenever we scrolled the view. Any drawing over the part of the view containing the status bar would cause the bar to be redrawn, leading to an annoying flicker. Having the status bar as part of the frame avoids these problems.

We need to initialize this data member just before the visible view window is displayed. So, using ClassWizard, add a function to the class that will be called in response to the **WM_CREATE** message which is sent to the application when the window is to be created. Add the following code to the **OnCreate()** handler:

```
      int CChildFrame::OnCreate(LPCREATESTRUCT lpCreateStruct)
      {
         if (CScrollView::OnCreate(lpCreateStruct) == -1)
            return -1;

         // Create the status bar.
         m_StatusBar.Create(this);
```

```
    // Work out the width of the text we want to display
    CRect textRect;
    CClientDC aDC(&m_StatusBar);
    aDC.SelectObject(m_StatusBar.GetFont());
    aDC.DrawText("View Scale:99", -1, textRect, DT_SINGLELINE | DT_CALCRECT);

    // Setup a part big enough to take the text
    int width = textRect.Width();
    m_StatusBar.GetStatusBarCtrl().SetParts(1, &width);

    // Initialize the text for the status bar
    m_StatusBar.GetStatusBarCtrl().SetText("View Scale:1", 0, 0);

    return 0;
}
```

The ClassWizard generated the code that isn't shaded. It has inserted a call to the base class version of the **OnCreate()** function, which takes care of creating the definition of the view window. It's important not to delete this function call, otherwise the window will not be created.

The actual creation of the status bar is done with the **Create()** function. The **this** pointer for the current **CChildFrame** object is passed to the **Create()** function, setting up a connection between the status bar and the window that owns it.

Defining the Status Bar Parts

A status bar has an associated **CStatusBarCtrl**, with one or more **parts**. You can display a separate item of information in each part. We define the number of parts and their widths by a call to the **SetParts()** member of the status bar control object. The first argument is the number of parts in the status bar and the second is an array specifying the right-hand edge of each part in client coordinates. If you omit the call to **SetParts()**, the status bar will have one part by default, which stretches across the whole bar. We could use this, but it looks untidy. A better design is to size the part so that the text to be displayed fits nicely. This is what the code does.

We first create a temporary **CRect** in which we'll store the enclosing rectangle for the text. We then create a **CClientDC** object which will contain a device context with the same extent as the status bar. This is possible because the status bar, like other controls, is a window.

The font used in the status bar (set up as part of the desktop properties) is then selected into the device context by calling the **SelectObject()** function, and the **DrawText()** member of the **CClientDC** object is called. This function has four arguments:

▶ The text string to be drawn in the rectangle pointed to by the third argument.

▶ The count of the number of characters in the string. If this is **-1**, it indicates a **\0** terminated string, so the function will work out the character count.

▶ A pointer to a rectangle, defined in logical coordinates, in which the string is to be drawn.

▶ One or more flags controlling the operation of the function.

We have specified with the flags that the text is to be on a single line (**DT_SINGLELINE**), and that we want the function to calculate the size of the rectangle required to display the string

(**DT_CALCRECT**) and store it in the rectangle pointed to by the second argument. The **DT_CALCRECT** flag also stops the function from actually drawing the string. There are a range of other flags that you can specify. You can find details of these by looking up this function with <u>H</u>elp.

We have passed a string containing the maximum number of characters we would ever want to display, **"View Scale:99"**. The extent of this string in logical coordinates will be stored in **textRect**, and we use the width of this rectangle to define the width of the status bar part in which we are going to display details of the current view scale.

The statement,

```
m_StatusBar.GetStatusBarCtrl().SetParts(1, &width);
```

retrieves a **CStatusBarCtrl** object that belongs to **m_StatusBar**. This contains the function **SetParts()** which defines the number of parts for the status bar in the first argument, and a pointer to the widths corresponding to the number of parts in the second argument. When there is more than one part, the second argument points to an array of type **int**.

We set the initial text in the status bar with the call to the **SetText()** member. The first argument is the text string to be written, the second is the index position of the part which is to contain the text string, and the third argument specifies the appearance of the part on the screen. The third argument can be any of the following:

Style code	Appearance
0	The text will have a border, so it appears recessed into the status bar.
SBT_NOBORDERS	The text is drawn without borders.
SBT_OWNERDRAW	The text is drawn by the parent window.
SBT_POPOUT	The text will have a border, so it appears stand out from the status bar.

In our code, we specify the text with a border so that it appears recessed into the status bar. You could try the other options to see how they look.

Updating the Status Bar

If you build and run the code now, the status bars will appear but they will only show a scale factor of 1, no matter what scale factor is actually being used. Not very useful really. What we need to do is to change the text each time a different scale is chosen. This means modifying the **OnScale()** handler in **CSketcherView** to change the status bar for the frame. We need to add only four lines of code:

```
void CSketcherView::OnScale()
{
   CScaleDialog aDlg;              // Create a dialog object
   aDlg.m_Scale = m_Scale;        // Pass the view scale to the dialog
   if(aDlg.DoModal() == IDOK)
   {
      m_Scale = aDlg.m_Scale;     // Get the new scale
```

```
        // Get the frame window for this view
        CChildFrame* childFrame = (CChildFrame*)GetParentFrame();

        // Build the message string
        CString StatusMsg("View Scale:");
        StatusMsg += (char)('1' + m_Scale - 1);

        // Write the string tothe status bar
        childFrame->m_StatusBar.GetStatusBarCtrl().SetText(StatusMsg, 0, 0);

    ResetScrollSizes();        // Adjust scrolling to the new scale
    InvalidateRect(0);         // Invalidate the whole window
    }
}
```

As we refer to **CChildFrame** object here, you must add an **#include** directive for **ChildFrm.h** to the beginning of **SketcherView.cpp** after the **#include** for **Sketcher.h**.

The first line calls the **GetParentFrame()** member of **CSketcherView** that is inherited from the **CView** class. This returns a pointer to a **CFrameWnd** object to correspond to the frame window, so it has to be cast to a **CChildFrame** for it to be of any use to us.

The next two lines build the message that is to be displayed in the status bar. The **CString** class is used simply because it is more flexible than using a **char** array. **CString**s will be discussed in greater depth a bit later when we add a new element type to Sketcher. Notice the loops we have to jump through, though, to add the digit to the string. The reason for this is that **m_Scale** is in the range 1 to 8, and we can't use **'0' + m_Scale**, as **'0'** is the character after **'9'**.

Finally, we use the pointer to the child frame to get at the **m_StatusBar** member that we added earlier. We can then get its status bar control and use the **SetText()** member of the control to change the displayed text. The rest of the **OnScale()** function remains unchanged.

That's all we need for the status bar. If you build Sketcher again, you should have multiple, scrolled windows, each at different scales, with the scale displayed in a status bar in each view.

Using a List Box

Of course, you don't have to use a spin button to set the scale. You could also use a list box, for example. The logic for handling a scale factor would be exactly the same and only the dialog box and the code to extract the value for the scale factor from the dialog box would change. If you want to try this out without messing up the development of the Sketcher program, you can copy the complete Sketcher project to another folder and make the modifications to the copy. You first need to delete the definition and implementation of **CScaleDialog** from the new Sketcher project, as well as the resource for the scale dialog.

To do this, go to FileView, select **ScaleDialog.cpp** and press *Delete* to remove it from the project. Then go to ResourceView, expand the Dialog folder, click on IDD_SCALE_DIALOG and hit *Delete* to remove the dialog resource. Now, delete the **#include** statement for **CScaleDialog.h** from **CSketcherView.cpp**. At this stage, all references to the original dialog class will have been removed from the project, but ClassWizard will still think that the **CScaleDialog** class exists.

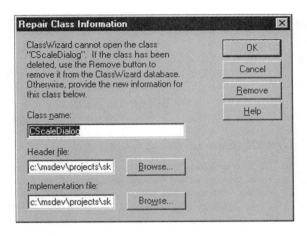

To get around this, you need to remove or delete the files **ScaleDialog.h** and **ScaleDialog.cpp** from the project directory, then start ClassWizard and attempt to choose CScaleDialog as the Class name:. You'll see the following dialog:

You should select Remove to completely remove the class from the project. You'll need to go through this rigmarole every time that you want to delete a class from an AppWizard-generated project. Once that's done, we can start by recreating the dialog resource for entering a scale value.

Creating a List Box Control

Right-click on Dialog in ResourceView and add a new dialog with a suitable ID and caption. You could use the same ID as before, **IDD_SCALE_DLG**.

Select the list box button in the controls palette as shown, and click on where you want the list box positioned in the dialog box. You can enlarge the list box and adjust its position in the dialog by appropriately dragging it.

Right-click on the list box and select Properties from the pop-up. You can set the ID to something suitable, such as **IDC_SCALELIST**. Next, select the Styles tab and set it to the options shown below:

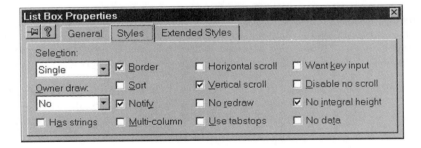

The Sort option box will be checked by default, so make sure you uncheck it. This will mean that strings that we add to the list box will not be automatically sorted. Instead, they'll be appended to the end of the list in the box, and so will be displayed in the sequence in which they are entered.

Since we'll use the position of the selected list item to indicate the scale, it's important not to have the sequence changed. The list box will have a vertical scroll bar for the list entries by default, which is very useful, and we can ignore the other options. If you want to look into the effects of the other options, you can click the question mark button to display a help screen explaining them.

Now that the dialog is complete you can save it, and you're ready to create the class for the dialog.

Creating the Dialog Class

Right-click on the dialog and select ClassWizard... from the pop-up. Again, you'll be taken through the dialog to create a new class. Give it an appropriate name, such as the one we used before - **CScaleDialog**. Once you've completed that, all you need to do is add a member variable form ClassWizard's Member Variables tab, called **m_Scale**, corresponding to the list box ID, **IDC_SCALELIST**. The default type will be **int**, which is fine. ClassWizard will implement DDX for this data member and store an index to the selected entry in the list box in it.

We need to add some code to the **OnInitDialog()** member of **CScaleDialog** to initialize the list box, so you'll have to create a handler for **WM_INITDIALOG**, either through ClassWizard or through the drop-down Messages list when you're looking at the **ScaleDialog.cpp** file. Add code as follows:

```
BOOL CScaleDialog::OnInitDialog()
{
    CDialog::OnInitDialog();

    CListBox* pListBox = (CListBox*)GetDlgItem(IDC_SCALELIST);
    pListBox->AddString("Scale 1");
    pListBox->AddString("Scale 2");
    pListBox->AddString("Scale 3");
    pListBox->AddString("Scale 4");
    pListBox->AddString("Scale 5");
    pListBox->AddString("Scale 6");
    pListBox->AddString("Scale 7");
    pListBox->AddString("Scale 8");

    return TRUE;  // return TRUE unless you set the focus to a control
                  // EXCEPTION: OCX Property Pages should return FALSE
}
```

The first line that we have added obtains a pointer to the list box control by calling the **GetDlgItem()** member of the dialog class. This is inherited from the MFC class **CWnd**. It returns a pointer of type **CWnd***, so we need to cast this to the type **CListBox***, which is a pointer to the MFC class defining a list box.

Using the pointer to our control's **CListBox** object, we then use the **AddString()** member to add the lines defining the list of scale factors. These will appear in the list box in the order that we enter them, so that the dialog will be displayed as shown on the following page:

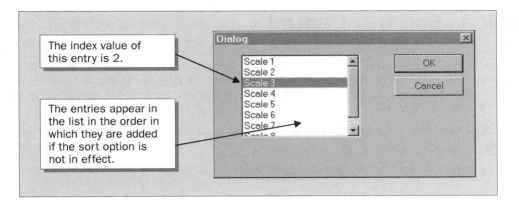

Each entry is associated with a zero-based index value that will be automatically stored in the **m_Scale** member of **CScaleDialog** through the DDX mechanism. Thus, if the third entry in the list is selected, **m_Scale** will be set to 2.

Displaying the Dialog

The dialog will be displayed by the **OnScale()** handler that we added to **CSketcherView** in the previous version of Sketcher. You just need to amend this to deal with the new dialog using a list box. The code for it will be as follows:

```
void CSketcherView::OnScale()
{
    CScaleDlg aDlg;              // Create a dialog object
    aDlg.m_Scale = m_Scale;     // Pass the view scale to the dialog
    if(aDlg.DoModal() == IDOK)
    {
        m_Scale = 1 + aDlg.m_Scale;   // Get the new scale

        // Get the frame that wraps this view
        CChildFrame* childFrame = (CChildFrame*)GetParentFrame();

        // Build the message string
        CString StatusMsg("View Scale:");
        StatusMsg += (char)('1' + m_Scale - 1);
        // Set the status bar
        childFrame->m_StatusBar.GetStatusBarCtrl().SetText(StatusMsg, 0, 0);

        ResetScrollSizes();           // Adjust scrolling to the new scale
        InvalidateRect(0);            // Invalidate the whole window
    }
}
```

Because the index value for the entry selected from the list is zero-based, we just need to add 1 to it to get the actual scale value to be stored in the view. The code to display this value in the view's status bar is exactly as before. The rest of the code to handle scale factors is already complete and requires no changes. Once you've added back the **#include** statement for **ScaleDialog.h**, you can build and execute this version of Sketcher to see the list box in action.

Using an Edit Box Control

We could use an edit box control to add annotations in Sketcher. We'll need a new element type, **CText**, that will correspond to a text string, and an extra menu item to set a **TEXT** mode for creating elements. Since a text element will only need one reference point, we can create it in the **OnLButtonDown()** handler. We'll also need a new menu item in the Element pop-up to set the **TEXT** mode. We'll add this text capability to Sketcher in the following sequence:

▶ Create the dialog box resource and its associated class.

▶ Add the new menu item.

▶ Add the code to open the dialog for creating an element.

▶ Add the support for a **CText** class.

Creating an Edit Box Resource

Create a new dialog resource in ResourceView by right-clicking the Dialog folder and selecting Insert Dialog from the pop-up. Change the ID for the new dialog to **IDD_TEXT_DLG** and the caption text to Enter Text.

To add an edit box, select the edit box icon from the control palette as shown on the left, and then click the position in the dialog where you want to place it. You can adjust the size of the edit box by dragging its borders and you can alter its position in the dialog by dragging the whole thing around.

You can display the properties for the edit box by double-clicking it when it's selected (its border is highlighted to indicate this) or by right-clicking it and selecting Properties from the pop-up. You could first change its ID to **IDC_EDITTEXT**, then select the Styles tab which is shown below:

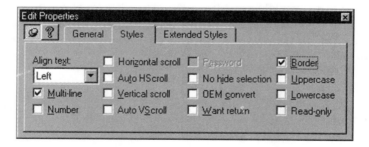

Some of the options here are of interest at this point. First select the Multi-line option. This creates a multi-line edit box where the text entered can span more than one line. This enables quite a long line of text to be entered and still remain visible in its entirety in the edit box.

The Align text: option determines how the text is to be positioned in the multi-line edit box. Left is fine for us, since we'll be displaying the text as a single line anyway, but you also have the options for Center and Right.

If you select the Want return option, pressing *Enter* on the keyboard would enter a return character in the text string. This would allow you to analyze the string if you wanted to break it into multiple lines for display. We don't want this effect, so leave it unselected. In this state, pressing *Enter* has the effect of the default control being selected which is the OK button, so pressing *Enter* will close the dialog.

If Auto HScroll is unselected, there will be an automatic spill to the next line in the list box when you reach the end of a line of text. This is just for visibility in the edit box, however. It has no effect on the contents of the string.

When you've finished setting the styles for the edit box, you can press *Enter* to close it. You should make sure that the edit box is first in the tab order by selecting the Tab Order menu item from the Layout pop-up. You can then test the dialog by selecting the Test menu item. The dialog is shown here:

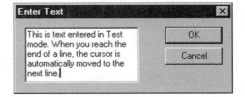

You can even enter text into the dialog in test mode to see how it works. Pressing *Enter* or clicking on the OK button will close the dialog.

Creating the Dialog Class

After saving the dialog resource, you can go to ClassWizard to create a suitable dialog class corresponding to the resource, which you could call **CTextDialog**. Then switch to the Member Variables tab in ClassWizard, select the **IDC_EDITTEXT** control ID and click the Add variable... button. Call the new variable **m_TextString** string and select its type as **CString** - we'll take a look at this class once we've finished the dialog class. Having added the variable **m_TextString** corresponding to the edit control, you can also specify a maximum length for it as shown here:

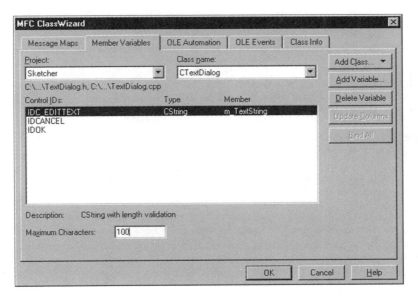

A length of 100 will be more than adequate for our needs. The variable that we have added here will be automatically updated from the data entered into the control by the DDX mechanism. You can click on OK to save the dialog class and close ClassWizard.

The CString Class

The **CString** class provides a very convenient and easy-to-use mechanism for handling strings that you can use just about anywhere a string is required. To be more precise, you can use a **CString** object in place of strings of type **const char***, which is the usual type for a character string in C++, or of type **LPCTSTR**, which is a type that comes up frequently in Windows API functions.

The **CString** class provides several overloaded operators which makes it easy to process strings:

Operator	Usage

=	Copies one string to another, as in:
	
	`Str1 = Str2;           // Copies contents of Str1 to Str2`
	`Str1 = "A normal string"; // Copies the RHS string to Str1`

+	Concatenates two or more strings, as in: `Str1 = Str2+Str3+" more"; // Forms a Str1 from 3 strings`
+=	Appends a string to an existing **CString** object

==	Compares two strings for equality, as in:
	
	`if(Str1 == Str2)`
	`        // do something`

< <=	Tests if one string is less than, or less than or equal to, another.
> >=	Tests if one string is greater than, or greater than or equal to, another.

The variables **Str1** and **Str2** above are **CString** objects. **CString** objects automatically grow as necessary, such as when you add an additional string to the end of an existing object. For example, in the statements,

```
CString Str = "A fool and your money ";
Str += "are soon partners";
```

the first statement declares and initializes the object **Str**. The second statement appends an additional string to **Str,** so the length of **Str** will automatically increase.

FYI   Generally, you should avoid creating **CString** objects on the heap as far as possible, as operations will be rather slow because of the memory management necessary for growing them.

Adding the Text Menu Item

Adding a new menu item should be easy by now. You just need to open the menu resource with the ID **IDR_SKETCHTYPE** by double-clicking it, and add a new menu item Text to the Element menu. The default ID, **ID_ELEMENT_TEXT**, will be fine so you can accept that. You can add a prompt to be displayed on the status bar corresponding to the menu item, and since we will also want add an additional toolbar button corresponding to this menu item, you can add a tool tip to the end of the prompt line, using a \n to separate the prompt and the tool tip.

Add the toolbar button to the **IDR_MAINFRAME** toolbar and set its ID to the same as that for the menu item, **ID_ELEMENT_TEXT**. You can drag the new button so that it's positioned at the end of the block defining the other types of element. When you have saved the resources, we need to add a handler for the menu item.

Go to ClassWizard and add a COMMAND handler to **CSketcherDoc** corresponding to **ID_ELEMENT_TEXT**. Click the Edit Code button and add code as follows:

```
void CSketcherDoc::OnElementText()
{
    m_Element = TEXT;
}
```

Only one line of code is necessary to set the element type in the document to **TEXT**. You must also add a line to the **OurConstants.h** file:

```
const WORD TEXT = 105U;
```

This statement can be added at the end of the other element type definitions. You also need to add a function to check the menu item if it is the current mode, so use ClassWizard to add an **UPDATE_COMMAND_UI** handler corresponding to the **ID_ELEMENT_TEXT** ID, and implement the code for it as follows:

```
void CSketcherDoc::OnUpdateElementText(CCmdUI* pCmdUI)
{
    // Set checked if the current element is text
    pCmdUI->SetCheck(m_Element == TEXT);
}
```

This operates in the same way as the other Element pop-up menu items. We can now define the **CText** class for an object of type **TEXT**.

Defining a Text Element

We can derive the class **CText** from the **CElement** class as follows:

```
class CText:public CElement
{
    public:
        // Function to display a text element
        virtual void Draw(CDC* pDC, BOOL Select = FALSE);

        // Constructor for a text element
        CText(CPoint Start, CPoint End, CString aString, COLORREF aColor);
```

```
        virtual void Move(CSize aSize);            // Move a text element

    protected:
        CPoint m_StartPoint;                        // position of a text element
        CString m_String;                           // Text to be displayed
        CText(){}                                   // Default constructor
};
```

You can put this definition at the end of the **Elements.h** file (but before the **#endif** statement, of course). This class definition has some similarities with other element classes: the data member **m_String** of type **CString** stores the text and **m_StartPoint** specifies the position of the string in the client area of a view. We should now look at the constructor declaration in a little more detail.

The **CText** constructor declaration defines five parameters which provide the following essential information:

Argument	Defines
CPoint Start	The position of the text in logical coordinates.
CPoint End	The corner opposite **Start** that defines the rectangle enclosing the text.
CString aString	The text string to be displayed as a **CString** object.
COLORREF aColor	The color of the text.
int PenWidth	This is included for consistency with other elements and will be used in the **GetBoundRect()** function inherited from the base class.

Implementing the CText Class

We have three functions to implement for the **CText** class:

▶ The constructor for a **CText** object.

▶ The virtual **Draw()** function to display it.

▶ The **MoveTo()** function to support moving a text object by dragging it with the mouse.

You can add these to the **Elements.cpp** file.

The CText Constructor

The constructor for a **CText** objects needs to initialize the class and base class data members:

```
CText::CText(CPoint Start, CPoint End, CString aString, COLORREF aColor)
{
    m_Pen = 1;                      // Pen width only for bound rectangle
    m_Color = aColor;               // Set the color for the text
    m_String = aString;             // Make a copy of the string
    m_StartPoint = Start;           // Start point for string
```

```
        m_EnclosingRect = CRect(Start, End);
        m_EnclosingRect.NormalizeRect();
}
```

This is all standard stuff, like we've seen before for the other elements.

Drawing a CText Object

Drawing text in a device context is different to drawing a geometric figure. The **Draw()** function for a **CText** object is as follows:

```
void CText::Draw(CDC* pDC, BOOL Select)
{
    COLORREF Color(m_Color);                // Initialize with element color

    if(Select)
        Color = SELECT_COLOR;               // Set selected color

    // Set the text color and output the text
    pDC->SetTextColor(Color);
    pDC->TextOut(m_StartPoint.x, m_StartPoint.y, m_String);
}
```

We don't need a pen to display text. We just need to specify the text color using the **SetTextColor()** function member of the **CDC** object, and then use the **TextOut()** member to output the text string. This will display the string using the default font.

Since the **TextOut()** function doesn't use a pen, it won't be affected by setting the drawing mode of the device context. This means that the ROP method that we use to move the elements will leave temporary trails behind when applied to text. We'll see how to fix this problem in the next chapter.

Moving a CText Object

The **Move()** function for a **CText** object is very simple:

```
void CText::Move(CSize& aSize)
{
    m_StartPoint += aSize;                  // Move the start point
    m_EnclosingRect+= aSize;                // Move the rectangle
}
```

All we need to do is alter the point defining the position of the string, and the data member defining the enclosing rectangle, by the distance specified in the **aSize** parameter.

Creating a Text Element

Once the element type has been set to **TEXT**, a text object should be created at the cursor position whenever you click the left mouse button and enter the text you want to display. We, therefore, need to open the dialog to enter text in the **OnLButtonDown()** handler. Add the following code to this handler in **CSketcherView**.

```
void CSketcherView::OnLButtonDown(UINT nFlags, CPoint point)
{
    CClientDC aDC(this);                // Create a device context
    OnPrepareDC(&aDC);                  // Get origin adjusted
    aDC.DPtoLP(&point);                 // convert point to Logical
    // In moving mode, so drop the element
    if(m_MoveMode)
    {
        m_MoveMode = FALSE;             // Kill move mode
        m_pSelected = 0;                // De-select element
        GetDocument()->UpdateAllViews(0);    // Redraw all the views
    }
    else
    {
        CSketcherDoc* pDoc = GetDocument();     // Get a document pointer
        if(pDoc->GetElementType() == TEXT)
        {
            CTextDialog aDlg;
            if(aDlg.DoModal() == IDOK)
            {
                // Exit OK so create a text element
                CSketcherDoc* pDoc = GetDocument();
                CSize TextExtent = aDC.GetTextExtent(aDlg.m_TextString);

                // Get bottom right of text rectangle - MM_LOENGLISH
                CPoint BottomRt(point.x+TextExtent.cx*m_Scale,
                                          point.y-TextExtent.cy*m_Scale);
                CText* pTextElement = new CText(point, BottomRt,
                                          aDlg.m_TextString, pDoc->GetElementColor());

                // Add the element to the document
                pDoc->AddElement(pTextElement);
                // Get all views updated
                pDoc->UpdateAllViews(0,0,pTextElement);
            }
            return;
        }

        m_FirstPoint = point;           // Record the cursor position
        SetCapture();                   // Capture subsequent mouse messages
    }
}
```

The code to be added is shaded. It creates a **CTextDialog** object and then opens the dialog using the **DoModal()** function call. The **m_TextString** member of **CTextDialog** will be automatically set to the string entered in the edit box, so we can just use this data member to pass the string entered back to the **CText** constructor if the OK button is used to close the dialog. The color and pen width are obtained from the document using the **GetElementColor()** and **GetPenWidth()** members that we have used previously. The position of the text is the **point** value holding the cursor position that is passed to the handler.

We also need to calculate the opposite corner of the rectangle that bounds the text. Because the size of the rectangle for the block of text depends on the font used in a device context, we use the **GetTextExtent()** function in the **CClientDC** object, **aDC**, to initialize the **CSize** object, **TextExtent**, with the width and height of the text string as it will be displayed. The width and height that are returned as a **CSize** object by the **GetTextExtent()** function are in logical coordinates.

Calculating the rectangle for the text in this way is a bit of a cheat, which could cause a problem once we start saving documents in a file, since it's conceivable that a document could be read back into an environment where the default font in a device context is larger that that in effect when the rectangle was calculated. This should not arise very often, so we won't worry about it here, but, as a hint - if you want to pursue it - you could use an object of the class **CFont** in the **CText** definition to define a specific font to be used. You could then use the characteristics of the font to calculate the enclosing rectangle for the text string.

You could also use the **CFont** to change the font size so that the text is also zoomed when the scale factor is increased. Note that the use of the scale factor when we create the text means that the bounding rectangle for the text zooms in and out appropriately. It's only the text itself that doesn't change in size when the scale is changed in our program. This means that the bounding rectangle is always appropriate for the size of the text at 1:1 scale, but will be too large for the other scales.

The **CText** object is created on the heap because the list in the document only maintains pointers to the elements. We add the new element to the document by calling the **AddElement()** member of **CSketcherDoc**, with the pointer to the new text element as an argument. Finally, **UpdateAllViews()** is called with the first argument 0, which specifies that all views are to be updated.

For the program to compile successfully, you need to add an **#include** statement for **TextDialog.h** to the **SketcherView.cpp** file. You should now be able to produce annotated sketches using multiple scaled and scrolled views such as that shown below:

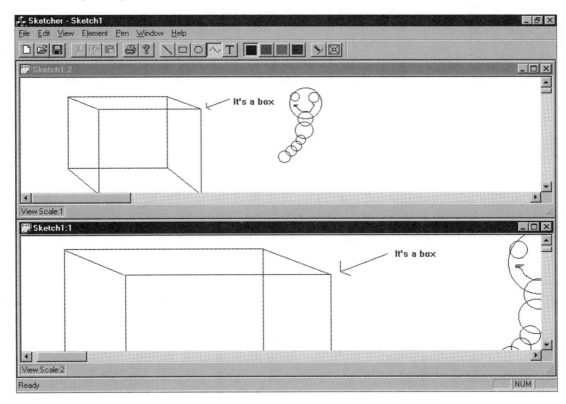

Summary

In this chapter, you have seen several different dialogs using a variety of controls. Although we haven't created dialogs involving several different controls, the mechanism for handling them is the same as we have seen, since each control can operate independently of the others.

The most important points that you have seen in this chapter are:

A dialog involves two components: a resource defining the dialog box and its controls, and a class that will be used to display and manage the dialog.

Information can be extracted from controls in a dialog using the DDX mechanism. The data can be validated using the DDV mechanism. To use DDX/DDV you only need to use ClassWizard to define variables in the dialog class associated with the controls.

A modal dialog retains the focus in the application until the dialog box is closed. As long as a modal dialog is displayed, all other windows in an application are inactive.

A modeless dialog allows the focus to switch from the dialog box to other windows in the application and back again. A modeless dialog can remain displayed as long as the application is executing if required.

Common Controls are a set of standard Windows 95 controls that are supported by MFC and the resource editing capabilities of Developer Studio.

Although controls are usually associated with a dialog, you can add controls to any window.

Storing and Printing Documents

With what we have accomplished so far in our Sketcher program, we can create a reasonably comprehensive document and create views at various scales, but the information is transient since we have no means of saving a document. In this chapter, we will remedy that by seeing how we can store a document on disk. We'll also see how we can output a document to a printer.

In this chapter, you will learn:

> What serialization is and how it works

> What you need to do to make objects of a class serializable

> The role of a **CArchive** object in serialization

> How to implement serialization in your own classes

> How to implement serialization in the Sketcher application

> How printing works with MFC

> What view class functions you can use to support printing

> What a **CPrintInfo** object contains and how it's used in the printing process

> How to implement multi-page printing in the Sketcher application

Understanding Serialization

Ordinarily, when you write data to a file and read it back, everything works in a straightforward way. As long as you know the file structure, reading it back isn't a problem. A document in an MFC-based program is not a simple entity, though, it's a class object that can be very complicated. It typically contains a variety of objects, each of which may contain other objects, perhaps descending to many levels of objects containing objects.

Writing a class object to a file represents something of a problem, as it isn't the same as a basic data item, such as an integer or a character string. Even if you write away all the data members of an object, it's no longer possible to get the original object back. Class objects contain function members as well as data members, and all the members, both data and functions, will have access specifiers. Therefore, to record objects in an external file, the information written to the file must contain complete specifications of the class structures involved. The read process must also be clever enough to synthesize the original objects completely from the data in the file. MFC supports a mechanism called **serialization** to help you to implement input and output to disk of your class objects with a minimum of time and trouble.

The basic idea behind serialization is that any class that is serializable must take care of storing and retrieving itself. This means that for your classes to be serializable - in the case of the Sketcher application this will include **CElement** and the shape classes we derived from it - they must be able to serialize themselves.

Serializing a Document

This all sounds like difficult stuff, but the basic capability for serializing your document was built into the application by AppWizard right at the outset. The handlers for File/Save, File/Save As..., and File/Open all assume that you want serialization implemented for your document and already contain the code to support this. Let's take a look at the parts of the definition and implementation of **CSketcherDoc** that relate to creating a document using serialization.

Serialization in the Document Class Definition

The code in the definition of **CSketcherDoc** that enables serialization of a document object is shown shaded in the following fragment:

```
class CSketcherDoc : public CDocument
{
    protected: // create from serialization only
        CSketcherDoc();
        DECLARE_DYNCREATE(CSketcherDoc)

    // Rest of the class as before...

    // Overrides
    // ClassWizard generated virtual function overrides
    //{{AFX_VIRTUAL(CSketcherDoc)
    public:
        virtual BOOL OnNewDocument();
        virtual void Serialize(CArchive& ar);
    //}}AFX_VIRTUAL

    // Rest of the class as before...

};
```

There are three items here relating to serializing a document object:

- The **DECLARE_DYNCREATE()** macro.
- The **Serialize()** member function.
- The default class constructor.

DECLARE_DYNCREATE() is a macro which enables objects of the **CSketcherDoc** class to be created dynamically by the framework during the serialization input process. It's matched by a complementary macro, **IMPLEMENT_DYNCREATE()**, in the class implementation. These macros only apply to classes derived from **CObject**, but they aren't the only pair of macros that can be used in this context, as we shall see shortly. For any class that you want to serialize, **CObject** must be a direct or indirect base, since it adds the functionality that enables serialization to work. This is why we took the trouble to derive our **CElement** class from **CObject**. Almost all MFC classes are derived from **Cobject** and, as such, are serializable.

The **Hierarchy Chart** in the **Class Library Reference** of Visual C++ **Books Online** shows those classes which aren't derived from **CObject**. Note that **CArchive** is in this list.

The class definition also includes a declaration for a virtual function **Serialize()** Every class that is serializable must include this function. It's called to perform both input and output serialization operations on the data members of the class. The object of type **CArchive** that's passed as an argument to this function determines whether the operation that is to occur is input or output. We'll look into this in more detail when we consider the implementation of serialization for the document class.

Note that the class also explicitly defines a default constructor. This is also essential for serialization to work, as the default constructor will be used by the framework to synthesize an object when reading from a disk file, which is then filled out with the data from the file to set the values of the data members of the object.

Serialization in the Document Class Implementation

There are two bits of the file containing the implementation of **CSketcherDoc** that relate to serialization. The first is the macro **IMPLEMENT_DYNCREATE()** that complements the **DECLARE_DYNCREATE()** macro:

```
// SketcherDoc.cpp : implementation of the CSketcherDoc class
//

#include "stdafx.h"
#include "Elements.h"
#include "Sketcher.h"

#include "SketcherDoc.h"
#include "PenDialog.h"

#ifdef _DEBUG
#define new DEBUG_NEW
#undef THIS_FILE
static char THIS_FILE[] = __FILE__;
#endif

/////////////////////////////////////////////////////////////////////////////
// CSketcherDoc

IMPLEMENT_DYNCREATE(CSketcherDoc, CDocument)

// Message maps and the rest of the file...
```

All this macro does is to define the base class for **CSketcherDoc** as **CDocument**. This is required for the proper dynamic creation of a **CSketcherDoc** object including members inherited from the base class.

The Serialize() Function

The class implementation also includes the definition of the **Serialize()** function:

```
void CSketcherDoc::Serialize(CArchive& ar)
{
   if (ar.IsStoring())
   {
      // TODO: add storing code here
   }
   else
   {
      // TODO: add loading code here
   }
}
```

This function serializes the data members of the class. The argument passed to the function is a reference to an object of the **CArchive** class, **ar**. The **IsStoring()** member of this class object returns **TRUE** if the operation is to store data members in a file, and **FALSE** if the operation is to read back data members from a previously stored document.

Since AppWizard can have no knowledge of what data your document contains, the process of writing and reading this information is up to you, as indicated by the comments. To understand how this is done, we need to look a little more closely at the **CArchive** class.

The CArchive Class

The **CArchive** class is the engine that drives the serialization mechanism. It provides an MFC-based equivalent of the stream operations in C++. An object of the MFC class **CArchive** provides a mechanism for streaming your objects out to a file, or recovering them again as an input stream, automatically reconstituting the objects of your class in the process.

A **CArchive** object has a **CFile** object associated with it which provides disk input/output capability for binary files and provides the connection to the physical file. Within the serialization process, the **CFile** object takes care of all the specifics of the file input and output operations, and the **CArchive** object deals with the logic of structuring the object data to be written or reconstructing the objects from the information read. You only need to worry about the details of the associated **CFile** object if you are constructing your own **CArchive** object. With our document in Sketcher, the framework has already taken care of it and passes the **CArchive** object, **ar**, that it constructs, to the **Serialize()** function in **CSketcherDoc**. We'll be able to use the same object in each of the **Serialize()** functions we need to add to the shape classes when we implement serialization for them.

CArchive overloads the extraction and insertion operators (**>>** and **<<**) for input and output operations respectively on objects of classes derived from **CObject**, plus a range of basic data types. These overloaded operators will work with the following types of objects:

Type	Definition
float	Standard single precision floating point.
double	Standard double precision floating point.
BYTE	8-bit unsigned integer.
int	16-bit signed integer
LONG	32-bit signed integer.
WORD	16-bit unsigned integer.
DWORD	32-bit unsigned integer.
CObject*	Pointer to **CObject**.
CString	A **CString** object defining a string.
SIZE and **CSize**	An object defining a size as a **cx,cy** pair.
POINT and **CPoint**	An object defining a point as an **x,y** pair.
RECT and **CRect**	An object defining a rectangle by its top left and bottom right corners.
CTime	A **CTime** object defines a time and a date.
CTimeSpan	A **CTimeSpan** object contains a time interval in seconds, usually the difference between two **CTime** objects.

For basic data types in your objects, you use the insertion and extraction operators to serialize the data. To read or write an object of a serializable class which you have derived from **CObject**, you can either call the **Serialize()** function for the object or use the extraction or insertion operator. Whichever way you use must be used consistently for both input and output, so you mustn't output an object using the insertion operator and then read it back using the **Serialize()** function, or vice versa.

Where you don't know the type of an object when you read it, as in the case of the pointers in the list of shapes in our document, for instance, you must only use the **Serialize()** function. This brings the virtual function mechanism into play, so the appropriate **Serialize()** function for the type of object pointed to is determined at run-time.

A **CArchive** object is constructed either for storing objects or for retrieving objects. The **CArchive** function **IsStoring()** will return **TRUE** if the object is for output, and **FALSE** if the object is for input. We saw this used in the **if** statement in the **Serialize()** member of the **CSketcherDoc** class.

There are many other member functions of the **CArchive** class which are concerned with the detailed mechanics of the serialization process, but you don't usually need to know about them to use serialization in your programs.

619

Functionality of CObject-based Classes

There are three levels of functionality available in your classes when they are derived from the MFC class **CObject**. The level you get in your class is determined by which of three different macros you use in the definition of your class:

Macro	Functionality
`DECLARE_DYNAMIC()`	Support for run-time class information.
`DECLARE_DYNCREATE()`	Support for run-time class information and dynamic object creation.
`DECLARE_SERIAL()`	Support for run-time class information, dynamic object creation and serialization of objects.

Each of these requires a complementary macro, named with the prefix **IMPLEMENT_** instead of **DECLARE_**, to be placed in the file containing the class implementation. As the table indicates, the macros provide progressively more functionality, so we'll concentrate on the third macro, **DECLARE_SERIAL()**, since it provides everything that the preceding macros do. This is the macro you should use to enable serialization in your own classes. It requires the macro **IMPLEMENT_SERIAL()** to be added to the file containing the class implementation

You may have noticed that the document class uses **DECLARE_DYNCREATE()** and not **DECLARE_SERIAL()**. The **DECLARE_DYNCREATE()** macro provides the capability for dynamic creation of the objects of the class in which it appears. The **DECLARE_SERIAL()** macro provides the capability for serialization of the class, plus the dynamic creation of objects of the class, so it incorporates the effects of **DECLARE_DYNCREATE()**. Your document class doesn't need serialization, since the framework only has to synthesize your document object and then restore the values of its data members. However, the data members of a document do need to be serializable, as this is the process used to store and retrieve them.

The Macros Adding Serialization to a Class

With the **DECLARE_SERIAL()** macro in the definition of your **CObject**-based class, you get access to the serialization support provided by **CObject**. This includes special **new** and **delete** operators that incorporate memory leak detection in debug mode. You don't need to do anything to use this, as it works automatically.

The macro requires the class name to be specified as an argument, so, for serialization of the **CElement** class, you would add the following line to the class definition:

```
DECLARE_SERIAL(CElement)
```

The macro **IMPLEMENT_SERIAL()**, which you need to place in the implementation file for your class, requires three arguments to be specified. The first argument is the name of your class, the second is the direct base class, and the third argument is an unsigned 32-bit integer identifying a schema number, or version number for your program. This schema number allows the serialization process to guard against problems that can arise if you write objects with one version of a program and read it with another where the classes may be different.

For example, we could add the following line to the implementation of the **CElement** class:

```
IMPLEMENT_SERIAL(CElement, CObject, 1)
```

If we subsequently modify the class definition, we would change the schema number to 2, say. If the program attempts to read data that was written with a different schema number from that in the currently active program, an exception will be thrown.

Where **CObject** is an indirect base of a class, as in the case of our **CLine** class, for example, each class in the hierarchy must have the serialization macros added for serialization to work in the top level class. For serialization in **CLine** to work, the macros must also be added to **CElement**.

How Serialization Works

The overall process of serializing a document is illustrated in a simplified form below:

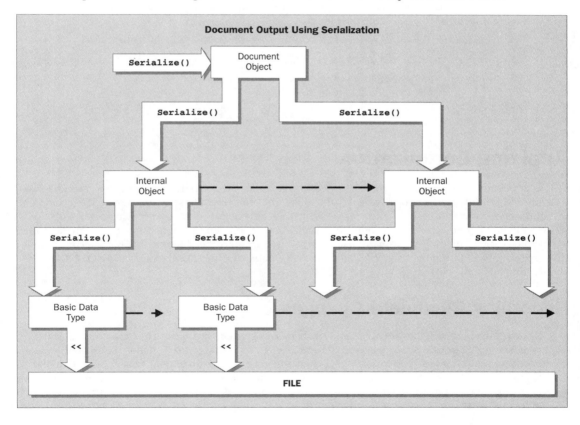

The **Serialize()** function in the document object needs to call the **Serialize()** function, or use an overloaded insertion operator for each of its data members. Where a member is a class object, the **Serialize()** function for that object will serialize each of its data members in turn, until ultimately basic data types are written to the file. Since most classes in MFC ultimately derive from **CObject**, they contain serialization support, so you can always serialize objects of MFC classes.

621

The data that you will deal with in the **Serialize()** member functions of your classes and the application document object will be just the data members in each case. The structure of the classes involved, and any other data necessary to reconstitute your original objects, is automatically taken care of by the **CArchive** object.

Where you derive multiple levels of classes from **CObject**, the **Serialize()** function in a class must call the **Serialize()** member of its direct base class to ensure that the direct base class data members are serialized. Note that serialization doesn't support multiple inheritance, so there can only be one base class for each class defined in a hierarchy.

How to Implement Serialization for a Class

From the previous discussion, we can summarize the actions that you need to take to add serialization to a class:

▶ Make sure that the class is derived directly or indirectly from **CObject**.

▶ Add the **DECLARE_SERIAL()** macro to the class definition and to the direct base class if the direct base is not **CObject**.

▶ Declare the function **Serialize()** as a member function of your class.

▶ Add the **IMPLEMENT_SERIAL()** macro to the file containing the class implementation.

▶ Implement the **Serialize()** function for your class.

Let's now see how we can implement serialization for documents in our Sketcher program.

Applying Serialization

To implement serialization in the Sketcher application, we need to complete the **Serialize()** function in **CSketcherDoc** to deal with all of the data members of that class. We need then to add serialization to each of the classes which specify objects that may be included in a document. Before we start on adding serialization to our application classes, let's make some small changes to the program to record when we change the document. This isn't absolutely necessary, but is highly desirable, since it will enable the program to guard against the document being closed without saving changes.

Recording Document Changes

There's already a mechanism for noting when a document changes. This uses an inherited member of **CSketcherDoc**, **SetModifiedFlag()**. By calling this function consistently whenever the document changes, you record in a data member of the document class object that the document has been altered. This will cause a prompt to be displayed automatically when you try to exit the application without saving the modified document. The argument to the function **SetModifiedFlag()** is a value of type **BOOL** which has a default value of **TRUE**. If you have occasion to specify that the document was unchanged, you can call this function with the argument **FALSE**, although circumstances where this is necessary are rare.

There are only three occasions when we alter a document object:

▶ When we call the **AddElement()** member of **CSketcherDoc** to add a new element.

▶ When we call the **DeleteElement()** member of **CSketcherDoc** to delete an element.

▶ When we move an element.

All three situations are very easy to deal with. All we need to do is to add a call to **SetModifiedFlag()** to each of the functions involved in these operations. The definition for **AddElement()** appears in the class definition. You can extend this to:

```
void AddElement(CElement* pElement)          // Add an element to the list
{
    m_ElementList.AddTail(pElement);  // Add the element to the list
    SetModifiedFlag();                     // Set the modified flag
}
```

You can get to the definition for **DeleteElement()** by clicking on its member name in the ClassView. You should add one line to it as follows:

```
void CSketcherDoc::DeleteElement(CElement* pElement)
{
    if(pElement)
    {   // If the  element pointer is valid
        SetModifiedFlag();                   // Set the modified flag

        // Find the pointer in the list and delete it
        POSITION aPosition=m_ElementList.Find(pElement);
        m_ElementList.RemoveAt(aPosition);
        delete pElement;                 // Delete the element from the heap
    }
}
```

Note that we must only set the flag if **pElement** is not **NULL**, so you can't just stick the function call anywhere.

Moving an element occurs in a view object in the **MoveElement()** member called by the handler for the **WM_MOUSEMOVE** message, but we only change the document when the left mouse button is pressed. If there's a right button click, the element is put back to its original position, so you only need to add the call to the **SetModifiedFlag()** function for the document to the **OnLButtonDown()** function as follows:

```
void CSketcherView::OnLButtonDown(UINT nFlags, CPoint point)
{
    CClientDC aDC(this);                       // Create a device context
    OnPrepareDC(&aDC);                         // Get origin adjusted
    aDC.DPtoLP(&point);                        // convert point to Logical
    // In moving mode, so drop the element
    if(m_MoveMode)
    {
        m_MoveMode = FALSE;                    // Kill move mode
        m_pSelected = 0;                       // De-select element
        GetDocument()->UpdateAllViews(0);      // Redraw all the views
        GetDocument()->SetModifiedFlag();      // Set the modified flag
    }
    // Rest of the function as before....
}
```

623

We just need to call the **GetDocument()** member inherited from **CView** to get access to a pointer to the document object, and then use this pointer to call the **SetModifiedFlag()** function. We now have all the places where we change the document covered.

If you build and run Sketcher, and modify a document or add elements to it, you'll now get a prompt to save the document when you exit the program. Of course, the File/Save menu option doesn't do anything yet except clear the modified flag. We need to implement serialization to get the document written away to disk, and that's the next step.

Serializing the Document

The first step is the implementation of the **Serialize()** function for the **CSketcherDoc** class. Within this function, we must add code to serialize the data members of **CSketcherDoc**. The data members that we have declared in the class are as follows:

```
class CSketcherDoc : public CDocument
{
protected: // create from serialization only
CSketcherDoc();
DECLARE_DYNCREATE(CSketcherDoc)
// Attributes
public:

protected:
    COLORREF m_Color;                                    // Current element color
    WORD m_Element;                                      // Current element type
    int m_PenWidth;                                      // Current pen width
    CSize m_DocSize;                                     // Document size
    CTypedPtrList<CObList, CElement*> m_ElementList;     // Element list

    // Rest of the class...
};
```

All we need to do is to insert the statements to store and retrieve these five data members in the **Serialize()** member of the class. We can do this with the following code:

```
void CSketcherDoc::Serialize(CArchive& ar)
{
    m_ElementList.Serialize(ar);      // Serialize the element list

    if (ar.IsStoring())
    {
        ar << m_Color                 // Store the current color
            << m_Element              // the current element type,
            << m_PenWidth             // and the current pen width
            << m_DocSize;             // and the current document size
    }
    else
    {
        ar >> m_Color                 // Retrieve the current color
            >> m_Element              // the current element type,
            >> m_PenWidth             // and the current pen width
            >> m_DocSize;             // and the current document size
    }
}
```

For four of the data members we just use the extraction and insertion operators overloaded by **CArchive**. This works for the data member **m_Color**, even though its type is **COLORREF**. This is because type **COLORREF** is the same as type **long**. We can't use the extraction and insertion operators for **m_ElementList** because its type isn't supported by the operators, but, as long as the **CTypedPtrList** class is defined from the collection class template using **CObList**, as we have done in the declaration of **m_ElementList**, the class will automatically support serialization. We can, therefore, just call the **Serialize()** function for the object.

We don't need to place calls to the **Serialize()** member of the object **m_ElementList** in the **if-else** statement because the kind of operation to be performed will be determined automatically by the **CArchive** argument **ar**. The single statement calling the **Serialize()** member of **m_ElementList** will take care of both input and output.

That's all we need for serializing the document class data members, but serializing the element list, **m_ElementList**, will cause the **Serialize()** functions for the element classes to be called to store and retrieve the elements themselves, so we need to implement serialization for these classes too.

Serializing the Element Classes

All the shape classes are serializable because we derived their base class from **CElement** which, in turn, is derived from **CObject**. The reason that we specified **CObject** as the base for **CElement** was solely to get support for serialization. We can now add serialization for each of the shape classes by adding the macros for serialization support to the class definitions and implementations and adding the code to the **Serialize()** function member of each class to serialize its data members. We can start with the base class, **CElement**, where you need to modify the class definition as follows:

```
class  CElement:public  CObject
{
  DECLARE_SERIAL(CElement)
    protected:
        COLORREF  m_Color;          // Color  of  an  element
        CRect  m_EnclosingRect;     // Rectangle  enclosing  an  element
        int  m_Pen;                 // Pen  width

    public:
        virtual  ~CElement(){}
// Virtual  destructor
        virtual  void  Draw(CDC*  pDC,  BOOL  Select=FALSE){}  // Virtual  draw  op
        virtual  void  Move(CSize&  aSize){}                   // Move  an  element
        CRect  GetBoundRect();      // Get  the  bounding  rectangle  for  an  element
    virtual void Serialize(CArchive& ar);          // Serialize function for CElement

protected:
    CElement(){}                    // Default  constructor
};
```

We have added the **DECLARE_SERIAL()** macro and a declaration for the **Serialize()** function as a virtual function.

We already had the default constructor defined as **protected** in the class. It doesn't matter what its access specification is, as long as it appears explicitly in the class definition. It can be **public**, **protected**, or **private**, and serialization will still work. If you forget to include it, though, you'll get an error message when the **IMPLEMENT_SERIAL()** macro is compiled.

You should add the **DECLARE_SERIAL()** macro to each of the classes **CLine**, **CRectangle**, **CCircle**, **CCurve** and **Ctext** with the relevant class name as the argument. You should also add a declaration for the **Serialize()** function as a **public** member of each class.

In the file **Elements.cpp**, you should add the following macro at the beginning of the code implementing **CElement**:

```
IMPLEMENT_SERIAL(CElement, CObject, VERSION_NUMBER)
```

You can define the constant **VERSION_NUMBER** in the **OurConstants.h** file by adding the lines:

```
// Program version number for use in serialization
   const UINT VERSION_NUMBER = 1;
```

You can then use the same constant when you add the macro for each of the other shape classes. For instance, for the **CLine** class you should add the line,

```
IMPLEMENT_SERIAL(CLine, CElement, VERSION_NUMBER)
```

and similarly for the other shapes classes. When you modify any of the classes relating to the document, all you need to do is change the definition of **VERSION_NUMBER** in the **OurConstants.h** file, and the new version number will apply in all your **Serialize()** functions. You can put all the **IMPLEMENT_SERIAL()** statements at the beginning of the file if you like. The complete set is:

```
IMPLEMENT_SERIAL(CElement, CObject, VERSION_NUMBER)
IMPLEMENT_SERIAL(CLine, CElement, VERSION_NUMBER)
IMPLEMENT_SERIAL(CRectangle, CElement, VERSION_NUMBER)
IMPLEMENT_SERIAL(CCircle, CElement, VERSION_NUMBER)
IMPLEMENT_SERIAL(CCurve, CElement, VERSION_NUMBER)
IMPLEMENT_SERIAL(CText, CElement, VERSION_NUMBER)
```

The Serialize() Functions for the Shape Classes

We need to implement the **Serialize()** member function for each of the shape classes. We can start with the **CElement** class:

```
void CElement::Serialize(CArchive& ar)
{
   CObject::Serialize(ar);              // Call the base class function

   if (ar.IsStoring())
   {
     ar << m_Color                      // Store the color,
        << m_EnclosingRect              // and the enclosing rectangle,
        << m_Pen;                       // and the pen width
```

```
        }
     else
     {
        ar >> m_Color               // Retrieve the color,
           >> m_EnclosingRect       // and the enclosing rectangle,
           >> m_Pen;                // and the pen width
     }
}
```

All of the data members defined in **CElement** are supported by the overloaded extraction and insertion operators, so everything is done using those operators. Note that we must call the **Serialize()** member for the **CObject** class to ensure that the inherited data members are serialized.

For the **CLine** class, you can code the function as:

```
void CLine::Serialize(CArchive& ar)
{
   CElement::Serialize(ar);         // Call the base class function

   if (ar.IsStoring())
   {
      ar << m_StartPoint            // Store the line start point,
         << m_EndPoint;             // and the end point
   }
   else
   {
      ar >> m_StartPoint            // Retrieve the line start point,
         >> m_EndPoint;             // and the end point
   }
}
```

Again, the data members are all supported by the extraction and insertion operators of the **CArchive** object **ar**. We call the **Serialize()** member of the base class **CElement** to serialize its data members, and this will call the **Serialize()** member of **CObject**. You can see how the serialization process cascades through the class hierarchy.

The **Serialize()** function member of the **CRectangle** class is very simple:

```
void CRectangle::Serialize(CArchive& ar)
{
   CElement::Serialize(ar);                 // Call the base class function
}
```

All it does is to call the direct base class function, since the class has no additional data members.

The **CCircle** class also doesn't have additional data members beyond those inherited from **CElement**, so its **Serialize()** function just calls the base class function:

```
void CCircle::Serialize(CArchive& ar)
{
   CElement::Serialize(ar);                 // Call the base class function
}
```

For the **CCurve** class, we have surprisingly little work to do. The **Serialize()** function is coded as follows:

```
void CCurve::Serialize(CArchive& ar)
{
   CElement::Serialize(ar);          // Call the base class function
   m_PointList.Serialize(ar);        // Serialize the list of points
}
```

After calling the base class **Serialize()** function, we just call the **Serialize()** function for the **CList** object, **m_PointList**. Objects of any of the **CList**, **CArray**, and **CMap** classes can be serialized in this way, since these classes are all derived from **CObject**.

The last class for which we need to add an implementation of **Serialize()** to **Elements.cpp**, is **CText**:

```
void CText::Serialize(CArchive& ar)
{
   CElement::Serialize(ar);          // Call the base class function

   if (ar.IsStoring())
   {
      ar << m_StartPoint            // Store the start point
         << m_String;               // and the text string
   }
   else
   {
      ar >> m_StartPoint            // Retrieve the start point
         >> m_String;               // and the text string
   }
}
```

After calling the base class function, we serialize the two data members using the insertion and extraction operators in **ar**. The class **CString**, although not derived from **CObject**, is still fully supported by **CArchive** with these overloaded operators.

Exercising Serialization

That's all we need for storing and retrieving documents in our program. The save and restore menu options in the file menu are now fully operational without adding any more code. If you build and run Sketcher after incorporating the changes we've discussed in this chapter, you'll be able to save and restore files and be automatically prompted to save a modified document when you try to close it or exit from the program, as shown here:

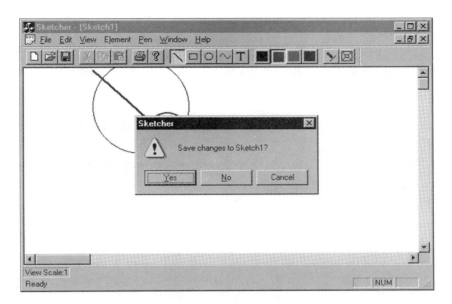

This works because
of the
SetModifiedFlag()
calls that we added
where we update the
document. If you
click on the Yes
button in the screen
above, you'll see the
File/Save As...
dialog as here:

This is the standard dialog for this menu item under Windows 95. It's all fully working,
supported by code supplied by the framework. The file name for the document has been
generated from that assigned when the document was first opened, and the file extension is
automatically defined as **.SKE**. In this particular instance, as you can see, there's already a file
with the same name, so selecting the Save button will generate a message box advising that we
are about to overwrite an existing file. Our application now has full support for file operations
on documents. Easy, wasn't it?

Moving Text

Now it's time to take a brief interlude to go back and fix a problem that we created in the last chapter. You'll remember that whenever you try to move a text element it leaves a trail behind it until the text is positioned on the document again. This is caused by our reliance on ROP drawing in the **MoveElement()** member of the view:

```
void CSketcherView::MoveElement(CClientDC& aDC, CPoint& point)
{
   CSize aSize = point - m_FirstPoint;
   m_FirstPoint = point;                // Set current point as 1st for next time

   // If there is an element selected, move it
   if(m_pSelected)
   {
      aDC.SetROP2(R2_NOTXORPEN);
      m_pSelected->Draw(&aDC,TRUE); // Draw over the element to erase it
      m_pSelected->Move(aSize);     // Now move the element
      m_pSelected->Draw(&aDC,TRUE); // Draw the moved element
   }
}
```

As we mentioned, setting the drawing mode of the DC to **R2_NOTXORPEN** won't remove the trail left by moving the text. We could get around this by using a method of invalidating the rectangles that are affected by the moving elements so that they redraw themselves. This, though, can cause some annoying flicker when the element is moving fast. A better solution would be to use the invalidation method only for the text elements and our original ROP method for all the other elements, but how are we to know which class the selected element belongs to? This is surprisingly simple. We can use an **if** statement as follows:

```
if (m_pSelected->IsKindOf(RUNTIME_CLASS(CText)))
{
   // Code here will only be executed if the selected element is of class CText
}
```

This uses the **RUNTIME_CLASS** macro to get a pointer to an object of type **CRuntimeClass**, then passes this pointer to the **IsKindOf()** member function of **m_pSelected**. This returns a non-zero result if **m_pSelected** is of class **Ctext** and returns zero otherwise. The only proviso is that the class we're checking for must be declared using **DECLARE_DYNCREATE** or **DECLARE_SERIAL** macros, which is why we left this fix until now.

The final code for **MoveElement()** will be as follows:

```
void CSketcherView::MoveElement(CClientDC& aDC, CPoint& point)
{
   CSize aSize = point - m_FirstPoint;
   m_FirstPoint = point;                // Set current point as 1st for next time

   // If there is an element selected, move it
   if(m_pSelected)
   {
      // If the element is text use this method...
      if (m_pSelected->IsKindOf(RUNTIME_CLASS(CText)))
      {
```

```
        CRect OldRect=m_pSelected->GetBoundRect();    // Get old bound rect
        m_pSelected->Move(aSize);                      // Move the element
        CRect NewRect=m_pSelected->GetBoundRect();    // Get new bound rect
        OldRect.UnionRect(&OldRect,&NewRect);         // Combine the bound rects
        aDC.LPtoDP(OldRect);                          // Convert to client coords
        OldRect.NormalizeRect();                      // Normalize combined area
        InvalidateRect(&OldRect);                     // Invalidate combined area
        UpdateWindow();                               // Redraw immediately
        m_pSelected->Draw(&aDC,TRUE);                 // Draw highlighted

        return;
    }
```

```
    // ...otherwise, use this method
    aDC.SetROP2(R2_NOTXORPEN);
    m_pSelected->Draw(&aDC,TRUE); // Draw over the element to erase it
    m_pSelected->Move(aSize);      // Now move the element
    m_pSelected->Draw(&aDC,TRUE); // Draw the moved element
  }
}
```

You can see that the code for invalidating the rectangles that we need to use for moving the text is much less elegant than the ROP code that we use for all the other elements. It works, though, as you'll be able to see for yourself if you make this modification and build and run the application.

Printing a Document

Now let's look at printing the document. We already have a basic printing capability implemented in the Sketcher program, courtesy of AppWizard and the framework. The File/ Print..., File/Print Setup..., and File/Print Preview menu items all work. The File/Print Preview will display a window showing the current Sketcher document on a page, as shown here:

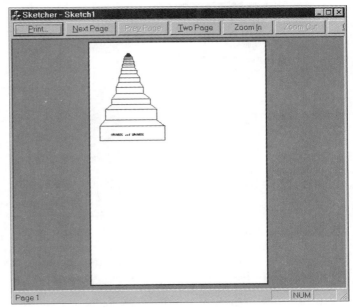

Whatever is in the current document is placed on a single sheet of paper at the current view scale. If the document's extent is beyond the boundary of the paper, it won't be printed. If you just select the Print... button, this page will be sent to your printer.

As a basic capability which you get for free, it's quite impressive, but it's not adequate for most purposes. A typical document in our program may well not fit on a page, so you would either want to scale the document to fit, or perhaps more conveniently, print the whole document over as many pages as necessary. You can add your own print processing code to extend the capability of the facilities provided by the framework, but to implement this you need to understand how printing has been implemented in MFC.

The Printing Process

Printing of a document is controlled by the current view. The process is inevitably a bit messy, since printing is inherently a messy business, and it potentially involves you in implementing your own versions of quite a number of inherited functions in your view class.

The logic of the process and the functions involved are shown in the diagram below:

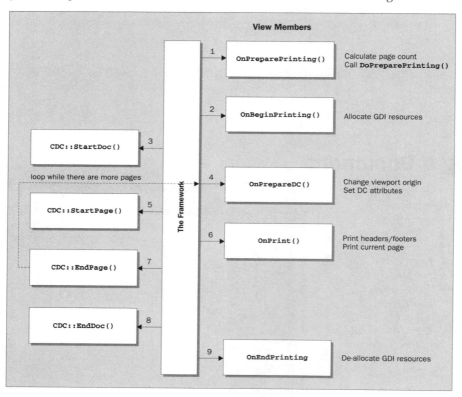

As you can see, the sequence of events is controlled by the framework and involves calling five inherited members of your view class that you may need to override. The **CDC** member functions shown on the left side of the diagram communicate with the printer device driver and are called automatically by the framework.

The typical role of each of the functions in the current view during a print operation is specified in the notes alongside them. The sequence in which they are called is indicated by the numbers on the arrows. In practice, you don't necessarily need to implement all of these functions, only those that you want to for your particular printing requirement. Typically, you'll want to at least implement your own versions of **OnPreparePrinting()**, **OnPrepareDC()** and **OnPrint()**.

You'll see an example of how these functions can be implemented in the context of the Sketcher program a little later in this chapter.

The output of data to a printer is done in the same way as outputting data to the display - through a device context. The GDI calls that you use to output text or graphics are device-independent, so they work as well for a printer as they do for a display. The difference is that the device that the **CDC** object applies to will be a printer instead of a display.

The **CDC** functions in the diagram of the process communicate with the device driver for the printer. If the document to be printed requires more than one printed page, the process loops back to call the **OnPrepareDC()** function for each successive new page, as determined by the **EndPage()** function.

All of the functions in your view class that are involved in the process are passed a pointer to an object of type **CPrintInfo** as an argument. This object provides a link between all the functions that manage the printing process, so let's take a look at the **CPrintInfo** class in more detail.

The CPrintInfo Class

A **CPrintInfo** object has a fundamental role in the printing process, since it stores information about the print job being executed and details of its status at any time. It also provides functions for accessing and manipulating this data. This object is the means by which information is passed from one view function to another during printing, and between the framework and your view functions.

An object of the **CPrintInfo** class is created whenever you select the File/Print... or File/ Print Preview menu options. After being used by each of the functions in the current view, it's automatically deleted when the print operation ends.

The data members of **CPrintInfo** are:

Member	Usage
m_pPD	A pointer to the **CPrintDialog** object which displays the print dialog box.
m_bDirect	Used by the framework and has the value **TRUE** if the print operation isn't to display the print dialog box, and **FALSE** otherwise.
m_bPreview	A **public** member of type **BOOL** which has the value **TRUE** if File/Print Preview was selected, and **FALSE** otherwise.
m_bContinuePrinting	A **public** member of type **BOOL**. If this is set to **TRUE**, the framework will continue the printing loop shown in the diagram. If it's set to **FALSE**, the printing loop will end. You only need to set this variable if you don't pass a page count for the print operation to the **CPrintInfo** object using the **SetMaxPage()** member function. In this case, you'll be responsible for signaling when you're finished by setting this to **FALSE**.

Table Continued on Following Page

Member	Usage
m_nCurPage	A **public** value of type **UINT** which stores the page number of the current page. Pages are usually numbered starting from 1.
m_nNumPreviewPages	A **public** value of type **UINT** which specifies the number of pages displayed in the print preview window. This can be 1 or 2.
m_lpUserData	This is of type **LPVOID** and stores a pointer to an object that you create. This is to allow you to create an object to store additional information about the printing operation and associate it with the **CPrintInfo** object.
m_rectDraw	A **public CRect** object which defines the usable area of the page in logical coordinates.
m_strPageDesc	A **CString** object containing a format string used by the framework to display page numbers during print preview.

When you're printing a document consisting of several pages, you need to figure out how many printed pages the document will occupy, and store this information in the **CPrintInfo** object to make it available to the framework. You can do this in your version of the **OnPreparePrinting()** member of the current view.

To set the number of the first page in the document, you need to call the function **SetMinPage()** in the **CPrintInfo** object which accepts the page number as an argument of type **UINT**. There's no return value. To set the number of the last page in the document, you call the function **SetMaxPage()** which also accepts the page number as an argument of type **UINT** and doesn't return a value. If you later need to retrieve these values, you can use the functions **GetMinPage()** and **GetMaxPage()** in the **CPrintInfo** object.

The page numbers that you supply will be stored in the **CPrintDialog** object pointed to by the **m_pPD** member of **CPrintInfo** and displayed in the dialog box which pops up when you select File/Print... from the menu. The user will then be able to specify the numbers of the first and last pages that are to be printed. You can retrieve these values by calling the **GetFromPage()** and **GetToPage()** members of the **CPrintInfo** object. In each case, the values returned are of type **UINT**. The dialog will automatically verify that the numbers of the first and last pages to be printed are within the range you supplied for the minimum and maximum page of the document.

We now know what functions in our view class we can implement to manage printing for ourselves, with the framework doing most of the work. We also know what information is available through the **CPrintInfo** object passed to the functions concerned with printing. We can get a much clearer understanding of the detailed mechanics of printing if we implement a basic multi-page print capability for Sketcher documents.

Implementing Multi-Page Printing

In the Sketcher program we use the **MM_LOENGLISH** mapping mode to set things up and then switch to **MM_ANISOTROPIC**. This means that our shapes and the view extent are measured in terms of hundredths of an inch. Of course, with the unit of size a fixed physical measure, objects should be printed at the same size as they appear in a view.

With the document size specified as 4000 by 4000 units in the document, we can create documents up to 40 inches square, which spreads over quite a few sheets of paper if we fill the whole area. It will require a little more effort to work out the number of pages necessary to print a sketch than with a typical text document because, in most instances, we'll need a two dimensional array of pages to print a complete sketch document.

To avoid overcomplicating the problem, let's assume that we're printing on something like a normal sheet of paper - either A4 size or 8 ½ by 11 inches, and in portrait orientation (which is the normal way up). With either paper size, we'll print the document in a central portion of the paper measuring 6 inches by 9 inches. With these assumptions, we don't need to worry about the paper size - we just need to chop the document into 600 by 900 unit chunks. For a document larger than one page, we'll divide up the document as illustrated in this example:

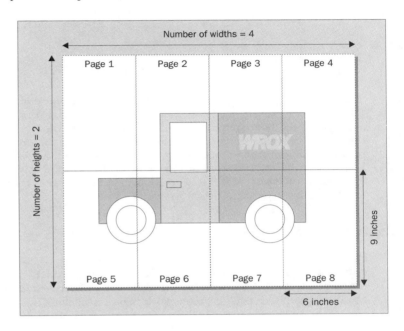

As you can see, we'll be numbering the pages row-wise, so, in this case, pages 1 to 4 are in the first row and pages 5 to 8 are in the second.

Getting the Overall Document Size

In order to figure out how many pages a particular document occupies, we are going to need to calculate the rectangle that encloses everything in the document. We can do this quite easily by adding a function, **GetDocExtent()** to the document class, **CSketcherDoc**. Add the following declaration to the **public** interface for **CSketcherDoc**:

```
CRect GetDocExtent();        // Get the bounding rectangle for the whole document
```

The implementation is no great problem. The code for it will be:

```
// Get the rectangle enclosing the entire document
CRect  CSketcherDoc::GetDocExtent()
{
    CRect DocExtent(0,0,1,1);     // Initial document extent
```

```
        CRect ElementBound(0,0,0,0); // Space for element bounding rectangle

        POSITION aPosition = m_ElementList.GetHeadPosition();

        while(aPosition)           // Loop through all the elements in the list
        {
            // Get the bounding rectangle for the element
            ElementBound=(m_ElementList.GetNext(aPosition))->GetBoundRect();

            // Make coordinates of document extent the outer limits
            DocExtent.UnionRect(DocExtent, ElementBound);
        }
        DocExtent.NormalizeRect();
        return DocExtent;
    }
```

You should add this function definition to the **SketcherDoc.cpp** file. The process loops through every element in the document, using the **aPosition** variable to step through the list and getting the bounding rectangle for each element. The **UnionRect()** member of the **CRect** class calculates the smallest rectangle that contains the two rectangles passed as arguments, and puts that value in the **CRect** object for which the function is called. Therefore, **DocExtent** will keep increasing in size until all the elements are contained within it. Note that we have to initialize **DocExtent** with **(0,0,1,1)** as the **UnionRect()** function doesn't work properly with rectangles that have zero height or width.

Storing Print Data

We'll need to store some data relating to the printing process that we will originate in the **OnPreparePrinting()** member of the view class so that we can use it later in other view functions involved. We'll store this data in our own class and store a pointer to it in the **CPrintInfo** object that the framework makes available. This is mainly to show you how this works but, in most cases, you'll find it easier just to store the data in your view object, mainly because it makes the notation for referencing the data much simpler.

We'll need to store the number of pages running the width of the document, **m_nWidths**, and the number of rows of pages down the length of the document, **m_nLengths**. We'll also store the top-left corner of the rectangle enclosing the document data as a **CPoint** object, **m_DocRefPoint**, because we'll use this when we need to work out the position of a page to be printed from its page number. We can also store the file name for the document in a **CString** object, **m_DocTitle**, so that we can add it as a title to each page. The definition of our class will be:

```
class CPrintData
{
    public:
        UINT m_nWidths;             // Number of pages for the width of the document
        UINT m_nLengths;            // Number of pages for the length of the document
        CPoint m_DocRefPoint;       // Top left corner of the  document contents
        CString m_DocTitle;         // The name of the document
};
```

You need to create a new file and add the class definition to it. Save the file as **PrintData.h**.

We don't need an implementation file for this class. The default constructor which is automatically generated will be quite adequate here. Since an object of this class is only going to be used transiently, we don't need to use **CObject** as a base, or to consider any other complication.

The printing process starts with a call to the view member **OnPreparePrinting()**, so let's see how we should implement that.

Preparing to Print

AppWizard added versions of **OnPreparePrinting()**, **OnBeginPrinting()**, and **OnEndPrinting()** to **CSketcherView** at the outset. The base code provided for **OnPreparePrinting()** calls **DoPreparePrinting()** in the **return** statement. This function will display the print dialog using information about the number of pages to be printed that is defined in the **CPrintInfo** object. Whenever possible, you should calculate the number of pages to be printed and store it in the **CPrintInfo** object before this call occurs. Of course, you may need information from the device context before you can do this, in which case it won't be possible to get the page count before you call **OnPreparePrinting()**. In this case, you can compute the number of pages in the **OnBeginPrinting()** member, which receives a pointer to the device context as an argument.

We're assuming that the page size is large enough to accommodate a 6 inch by 9 inch area to draw the document data, so we can calculate the number of pages in **OnPreparePrinting()**. The code for it will be as follows:

```
BOOL CSketcherView::OnPreparePrinting(CPrintInfo* pInfo)
{
    pInfo->m_lpUserData = new CPrintData;    // Create a print data object
    CSketcherDoc* pDoc = GetDocument();      // Get a document pointer

    // Get the whole document area
    CRect DocExtent = pDoc->GetDocExtent();

    // Save the reference point for the whole document
    ((CPrintData*)(pInfo->m_lpUserData))->m_DocRefPoint =
                            CPoint(DocExtent.left, DocExtent.bottom);
    // Get the name of the document file and save it
    ((CPrintData*)(pInfo->m_lpUserData))->m_DocTitle = pDoc->GetTitle();

    // Calculate how many printed page widths of 600 units are required
    // to accommodate the width of the document
    ((CPrintData*)(pInfo->m_lpUserData))->m_nWidths =
                        (UINT)ceil(((double)(DocExtent.Width()))/600.0);

    // Calculate how many printed page lengths of 900 units are required
    // to accommodate the document length
    ((CPrintData*)(pInfo->m_lpUserData))->m_nLengths =
                        (UINT)ceil(((double)(DocExtent.Height()))/900.0);

    // Set the first page number as 1 and
    // set the last page number as the total number of pages
    pInfo->SetMinPage(1);
    pInfo->SetMaxPage(((CPrintData*)(pInfo->m_lpUserData))->m_nWidths
                * ((CPrintData*)(pInfo->m_lpUserData))->m_nLengths);
```

```
        return DoPreparePrinting(pInfo);
    }
```

We first create a **CPrintData** object on the heap and then store its address in the pointer, **m_lpUserData**, in the **CPrintInfo** object passed to the function via the pointer **pInfo**. After getting a pointer to the document, we get the rectangle enclosing all of the elements in the document by calling the function **GetDocExtent()** that we added to the document class earlier in this chapter. We then store the corner of this rectangle in the **m_DocRefPoint** member of the **CPrintData** object and put the name of the file containing the document in **m_DocTitle**.

Referencing the **CPrintData** object through the pointer in the **CPrintInfo** object is rather cumbersome. We get to the pointer with the expression **pInfo->m_lpUserData**, but because the pointer is of type **void**, we must add a cast to type **CPrintData*** in order to get to the **m_DocRefPoint** member of the object. The full expression to access the reference point for the document is:

((CPrintData*)(pInfo->m_lpUserData))->m_DocRefPoint

We have to use this approach for all references to members of the **CPrintData** object, so any expression using them will be festooned with this notation. If we put the data in the view class, we would only need to use the name of the data member. Don't forget to add an **#include** directive for **PrintData.h** to the **SketcherView.cpp** file.

The next two lines of code calculate the number of pages across the width of the document and the number of pages required to cover the length. The number of pages to cover the width is computed by dividing the width of the document by the width of the print area of a page, which is 600 units or 6 inches, and rounding up to the next highest integer using the **ceil()** library function from **math.h**. An **#include** for this file needs to be added to **SketcherView.cpp**. For example, **ceil(2.1)** will return **3.0**, **ceil(2.9)** will also return **3.0**, and **ceil(-2.1)** will return **-2.0**. A similar calculation to that for the number of pages across the width of a document produces the number to cover the length. The product of these two values is the total number of pages to be printed and this is the value that we'll supply for the maximum page number.

Cleaning Up after Printing

Because we created the **CPrintData** object on the heap, we need to ensure that it's deleted when we are done with it. We do this by adding code to the **OnEndPrinting()** function:

```
void CSketcherView::OnEndPrinting(CDC* /*pDC*/, CPrintInfo* pInfo)
{
    // Delete our print data object
    delete (CPrintData*)(pInfo->m_lpUserData);
}
```

That's all we need to do for this function in the Sketcher program, but, in some cases, you'll need to do more. All your one time final clean up should be done here. Make sure that you remove the comment delimiters (**/* */**) from the second parameter name, otherwise your function won't compile.

We don't need to add anything to the **OnBeginPrinting()** function in the Sketcher program, but you would add code to allocate any GDI resources, such as pens, if they were required throughout the printing process. You would then delete these as part of the clean up process in **OnEndPrinting()**.

638

Preparing the Device Context

At the moment, our program calls **OnPrepareDC()** which sets up the mapping mode as **MM_ANISOTROPIC** to take account of the scaling factor. We need to make some additional changes so that the device context is properly prepared in the case of printing:

```
void  CSketcherView::OnPrepareDC(CDC*  pDC,  CPrintInfo*  pInfo)
{
   int Scale = m_Scale;                        // Store the scale locally
   if(pDC->IsPrinting())
      Scale = 1;                               // If we are printing, set scale to1

      CScrollView::OnPrepareDC(pDC,  pInfo);
      CSketcherDoc*  pDoc  =  GetDocument();
      pDC->SetMapMode(MM_ANISOTROPIC);         // Set  the  map  mode
      CSize  DocSize  =  pDoc->GetDocSize();   // Get  the  document  size

      // y extent  must  be  negative  because  we  want  MM_LOENGLISH
      DocSize.cy = -DocSize.cy;                // Change  sign  of  y
      pDC->SetWindowExt(DocSize);             // Now  set  the  window  extent

      // Get  the  number  of  pixels  per  inch  in  x  and  y
      int  xLogPixels  =  pDC->GetDeviceCaps(LOGPIXELSX);
      int  yLogPixels  =  pDC->GetDeviceCaps(LOGPIXELSY);

      // Calculate  the  viewport  extent  in  x  and  y
   long xExtent = (long)DocSize.cx*Scale*xLogPixels/100L;
   long yExtent = (long)DocSize.cy*Scale*yLogPixels/100L;

      pDC->SetViewportExt((int)xExtent,  (int)-yExtent);  // Set  viewport  extent
}
```

This function is called by the framework for output to the printer as well as to the screen. The only thing we need to worry about when we are printing is that a scale of 1 is used to set the mapping from logical coordinates to device coordinates. If you left everything as it was, the output would be at the current view scale, but you would need to take account of the scale when calculating how many pages you needed, and how you set the origin for each page.

We can determine whether we have a printer device context or not by calling the **IsPrinting()** member of the current **CDC** object. It returns **TRUE** if we are printing. All we need to do when we have a printer device context is to set the scale to 1. Of course, we need to change the statements lower down which use the scale value, so that they use the local variable **Scale**, rather than the **m_Scale** member of the view. The values returned by the calls to **GetDeviceCaps()** with the arguments **LOGPIXELSX** and **LOGPIXELSY**, return the number of logical points per inch in the x and y directions for your printer when we are printing, and the equivalent values for your display when we are drawing to the screen, so this automatically adapts the viewport extent to suit the device to which you are sending the output.

Printing the Document

We can write the data to the printer device context in the **OnPrint()** function. This is called once for each page to be printed. You will need to add this function to **CSketcherView**, using ClassWizard or the drop-down Messages list when viewing **SketcherView.cpp**.

We can obtain the page number of the current page from the **m_nCurPage** member of the **CPrintInfo** object and use this value to work out the coordinates of the position in the document that corresponds to the top-left corner of the current page. The way to do this is best understood using an example, so let's suppose that we're printing page seven of an eight-page document, as illustrated in the diagram below:

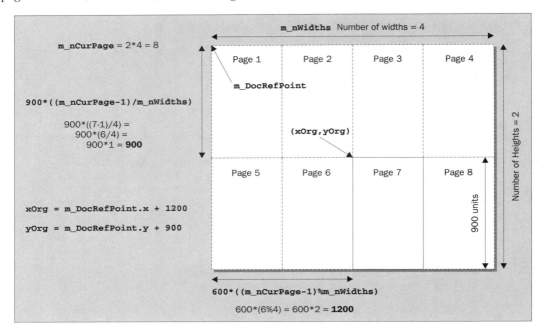

We can get an index to the horizontal position of the page by decrementing the page number by 1 and taking the remainder after dividing by the width of the printed area on the page, which is 600 units. Multiplying the result by 600 produces the x coordinate of the top-left corner of the page, relative to the top-left corner of the rectangle enclosing the elements in the document. Similarly, we can determine the index position of the document by dividing the current page number reduced by 1 by the length of a printed page, which is 900. By multiplying the remainder by 900 you get the relative y coordinate of the top-left corner of the page. We can express this in two statements as follows:

```
int xOrg = ((CPrintData*)(pInfo->m_lpUserData))->m_DocRefPoint.x +
              600*((pInfo->m_nCurPage - 1)%
                 (((CPrintData*)(pInfo->m_lpUserData))->m_nWidths));
int yOrg = ((CPrintData*)(pInfo->m_lpUserData))->m_DocRefPoint.y -
              900*((pInfo->m_nCurPage - 1)/
                 (((CPrintData*)(pInfo->m_lpUserData))->m_nWidths));
```

The statements look complicated because of the need to access the information stored in our **CPrintData** object through the pointer in the **CPrintInfo** object.

We want to print the file name for the document at the top of each page, and we want to be sure we don't print the document data over the file name. We also want to center the printed area on the page. We can do this by moving the origin of the coordinate system in the printer device context after we have printed the file name. This is illustrated in the diagram on the following page:

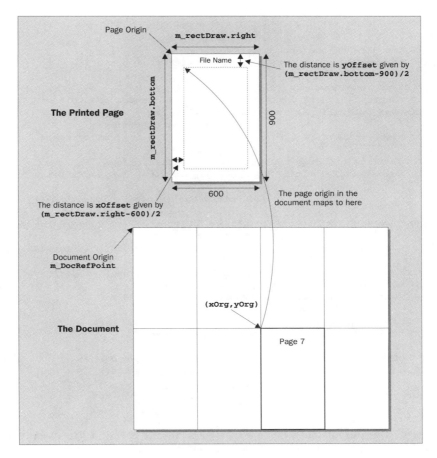

The diagram illustrates the correspondence between the printed page area in the device context and the page to be printed in the reference frame of the document data. Remember that these are in logical coordinates - the equivalent of **MM_LOENGLISH** in Sketcher - so y is increasingly negative from top to bottom. The page shows the expressions for the offsets from the page origin for the 600 by 900 area where we are going to print the page. We want to print the information from the document in the dashed area shown on the page, so we need to map the **xOrg,yOrg** point in the document to the position in the printed page shown, which is displaced from the page origin by the offset values **xOffset** and **yOffset**.

By default, the origin in the coordinate system that we use to define elements in the document is mapped to the origin of the device context, but we can change this. The **CDC** object provides a function **SetWindowOrg()** for this purpose. This enables you to define a point in the document's logical coordinate system that you want to correspond to the origin in the device context.

The point in the document that we want to map to the origin of the page has the coordinates **xOrg-xOffset,yOrg+yOffset**. This may not be easy to visualize, but remember that by setting the window origin, we're defining the point that maps to the viewport origin. If you think about it, you should see that the **xOrg,yOrg** point in the document is where we want it on the page.

The complete code for printing a page of the document will be:

```
// Print a page of the document
void CSketcherView::OnPrint(CDC* pDC, CPrintInfo* pInfo)
{
   // Output the document file name
   pDC->SetTextAlign(TA_CENTER);              // Center the following text
   pDC->TextOut(pInfo->m_rectDraw.right/2, -20,
                   ((CPrintData*)(pInfo->m_lpUserData))->m_DocTitle);
   pDC->SetTextAlign(TA_LEFT);                // Left justify text

   // Calculate the origin point for the current page
   int xOrg = ((CPrintData*)(pInfo->m_lpUserData))->m_DocRefPoint.x +
                600*((pInfo->m_nCurPage - 1)%
                          (((CPrintData*)(pInfo->m_lpUserData))->m_nWidths));

   int yOrg = ((CPrintData*)(pInfo->m_lpUserData))->m_DocRefPoint.y -
                900*((pInfo->m_nCurPage - 1)/
                          (((CPrintData*)(pInfo->m_lpUserData))->m_nWidths));

   // Calculate offsets to center drawing area on page as positive values
   int xOffset = (pInfo->m_rectDraw.right - 600)/2;
   int yOffset = -(pInfo->m_rectDraw.bottom + 900)/2;

   // Change window origin to correspond to current page
   pDC->SetWindowOrg(xOrg-xOffset, yOrg+yOffset);

   // Define a clip rectangle the size of the printed area
   pDC->IntersectClipRect(xOrg,yOrg,xOrg+600,yOrg-900);

   OnDraw(pDC);                               // Draw the whole document
}
```

The first step is to output the file name that we squirreled away in the **CPrintInfo** object. The **SetTextAlign()** function member of the **CDC** object allows you to define the alignment of subsequent text output in relation to the reference point you supply for the text string in the **TextOut()** function. The alignment is determined by the constant passed as an argument to the function. You have three possibilities for specifying the reference point for the text:

Constant	Alignment
TA_LEFT	The point is at the left of the bounding rectangle for the text, so the text is to the right of the point specified. This is default alignment.
TA_RIGHT	The point is at the right of the bounding rectangle for the text, so the text is to the left of the point specified.
TA_CENTER	The point is at the center of the bounding rectangle for the text.

We define the x coordinate of the file name on the page as half the page width, and the y coordinate as 20 units, which is 0.2 inches, from the top of the page. After outputting the name of the document file as centered text, we reset the text alignment to the default, **TA_LEFT**, for the text in the document.

The **SetTextAlign()** function also allows you to change the position of the text vertically by ORing a second flag with the justification flag. The second flag can be any of the following:

Constant	Alignment
TA_TOP	Aligns the top of the rectangle bounding the text with the point defining the position of the text. This is the default.
TA_BOTTOM	Aligns the top of the rectangle bounding the text with the point defining the position of the text.
TA_BASELINE	Aligns the baseline of the font used for the text with the point defining the position of the text.

The next action in **OnPrint()** uses the method that we've just discussed for mapping an area of the document to the current page. We get the document drawn on the page by calling the **OnDraw()** function that is used to display the document in the view. This potentially draws the entire document, but we can restrict what appears on the page by defining a **clip rectangle**. A clip rectangle encloses a rectangular area in the device context within which output appears. Outside the clip rectangle, output is suppressed. It's also possible to define irregularly shaped areas for clipping called regions.

The initial default clipping area defined in the print device context is the page boundary. We define a clip rectangle which corresponds to the 600 by 900 area centered in the page. This ensures that we will only draw in this area, and the file name will not be overwritten.

Getting a Printout of the Document

To get your first printed Sketcher document, you just need to build the project and execute the program once you have fixed any typos. If you try File/Print Preview, you should get something similar to the window shown here:

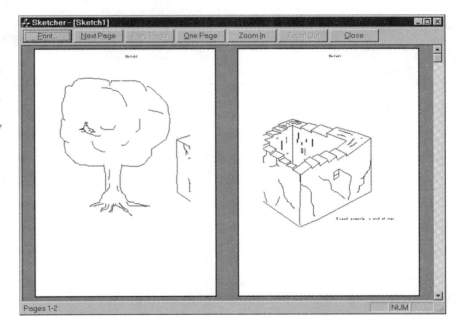

We get print preview functionality completely for free. The framework uses the code that you've supplied for the normal multi-page printing operation to produce page images in the print preview window. What you see in the print preview window should be exactly the same as appears on the printed page.

Summary

In this chapter, we've seen how to get a document stored on disk in a form that allows us to read it back and reconstruct its constituent objects using the serialization process supported by MFC. To implement serialization for classes defining document data, you must:

- Derive your class directly or indirectly from **CObject**.
- Specify the **DECLARE_SERIAL()** macro in your class implementation.
- Specify the **IMPLEMENT_SERIAL()** macro in your class definition.
- Implement a default constructor in your class.
- Declare the **Serialize()** function in your class.
- Implement the **Serialize()** function in your class to serialize all the data members.

The serialization process uses a **CArchive** object to perform the input and output. You use the **CArchive** object passed to the **Serialize()** function to serialize the data members of the class.

Implementing classes for serialization also has the side effect that it allows us access to run-time class information using the **RUNTIME_CLASS** macro and **IsKindOf()** function.

We have also seen how MFC supports output to a printer. To add to the basic printing capability provided by default, you can implement your own versions of the view class functions involved in printing a document. The principal roles for each of these function are:

Function	Role
OnPreparePrinting()	Determine the number of pages in the document and call the view member **DoPreparePrinting()**.
OnBeginPrinting()	Allocate the resources required in the printer device context which are needed throughout the printing process, and determine the number of pages in the document, where this is dependent on information from the device context.
OnPrepareDC()	Set attributes in the printer device context as necessary.
OnPrint()	Print the document.
OnEndPrinting()	Delete any GDI resources created in **OnBeginPrinting()** and do any other necessary clean up.

Information relating to the printing process is stored in an object of type **CPrintInfo** that's created by the framework. You can store additional information in the view, or in another object of your own. If you use your own class object, you can keep track of it by storing a pointer to it in the **CPrintInfo** object.

Writing Your Own DLLs

In this chapter, we will be investigating a different kind of library from the static libraries that contain standard C++ functions such as **sqrt()** or **rand()**. These libraries are called **dynamic link libraries**, or **DLLs**, and they provide a very powerful way of storing and managing standard library functions that is integral to the Windows environment. They also provide much more flexibility than static libraries.

A complete discussion of DLLs is outside the scope of a beginner's book, but they are important enough to justify including an introductory chapter on them. In this chapter, you will learn:

- What a DLL is and how it works
- When you should consider implementing a DLL
- What varieties of DLL are possible and what they are used for
- How you can extend MFC using a DLL
- How to define what is accessible in a DLL
- How to access the contents of a DLL in your programs

Understanding DLLs

Almost all programming languages support libraries of standard code modules for commonly used functions. In C++, we have been using lots of functions stored in standard libraries, such as the **ceil()** function that we used in the previous chapter which is declared in the **math.h** header file. The code for this function is stored in a library file with the extension **.lib**, and when the executable module for the Sketcher program was created, the linker retrieved the code for this standard function from the library file and integrated a copy of it into the **.exe** file for the Sketcher program.

If you write another program and use the same function, it too will have its own copy of the **ceil()** function. The **ceil()** function is **statically linked** to each application and is an integral part of each executable module, as illustrated on the following page.

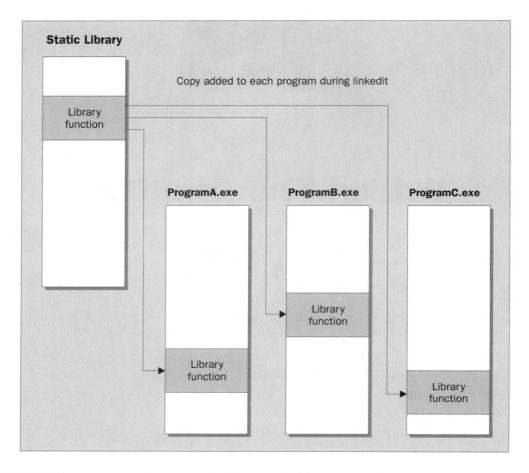

While this is a very convenient way of using standard functions with minimal effort on your part, it does have its disadvantages as a way of sharing common functions in the Windows environment. Since Windows can execute several programs simultaneously, a statically linked standard function in use by more than one concurrent program will be duplicated in memory for each program using it. This may not seem to matter very much for the **ceil()** function, but some functions, input and output, for instance, will invariably be common to most programs and are likely to occupy sizable chunks of memory. Having these statically linked would be extremely inefficient.

Another consideration is that a standard function from a static library may be linked into hundreds of programs in your system, so identical copies of the code for them will be occupying disk space in the **.exe** file for each program. For these reasons, an addition library facility is supported by Windows for standard functions, called a **Dynamic Link Library**, usually abbreviated to **DLL**. This allows one copy of a function to be shared among several concurrently executing programs and avoids the need to incorporate a copy of the code for a library function into a program that uses it.

How DLLs Work

A dynamic link library is a file containing a collection of modules that can be used by any number of different programs. The file usually has the extension **.dll**, but this isn't obligatory. When naming a DLL, you can assign any extension that you like, but this can affect how they are handled by Windows. Windows automatically loads dynamic link libraries that have the extension **.dll**. If they have some other extension, you will need to load them explicitly by adding code to do this to your program. Windows itself uses the extension **.exe** for some of its DLLs. You are likely to have heard of the extensions **.vbx** and **.ocx** which are applied to DLLs containing specific kinds of controls.

You might imagine that you have a choice about whether or not you use dynamic link libraries in your program, but you don't. The Win32 API is used by every Windows 95 program and the API is implemented in a set of DLLs. DLLs really are fundamental to Windows programming.

Connecting a function in a DLL to a program is achieved differently from the process used with a statically linked library, where the code is incorporated once and for all when the program is linked to generate the executable module. A function in a DLL is only connected to a program that uses it when the application is run, and this is done on each occasion the program is executed, as illustrated below:

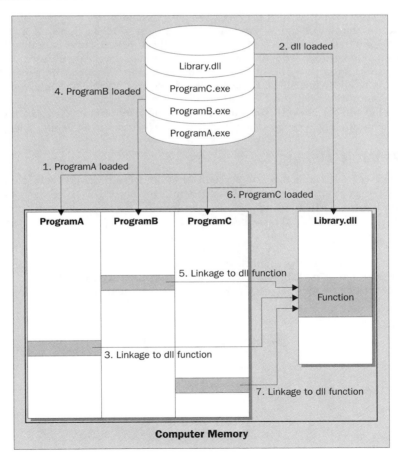

This illustrates what happens when three programs that use a function in a DLL are started successively, and then all execute concurrently. No code from the DLL is included in the executable module of any of the programs. When one of the programs is executed, the program is loaded into memory and if the DLL it uses isn't already present, it too is loaded separately. The appropriate links between the program and the DLL are then established. If, when a program is loaded, the DLL is already there, all that needs to be done is to link the program to the required function in the DLL.

Note that when your program calls a function in a DLL, Windows will automatically load the DLL into memory. Any program using the same DLL that is loaded subsequently into memory can also use any of the capabilities provided by the same copy of the DLL, since Windows recognizes that the DLL is already in memory and just establishes the links between the program and the DLL. Windows keeps track of how many programs are using each DLL that is resident in memory, so that as long as some program is still using a DLL, it will remain there. When a DLL is no longer used by any executing program, Windows will automatically delete it from memory.

MFC is provided in the form of a number of DLLs that your program can link to dynamically, as well as a library which your program can link to statically. By default, AppWizard generates programs that dynamically link to the DLL form of MFC.

Having a function stored in a DLL introduces the possibility of changing the function without affecting the programs that use it. As long as the interface to the function in the DLL remains the same, the programs can use a new version of the function quite happily, without the need for recompiling or re-linking them. This unfortunately also has a down side. It's very easy to end up using the wrong version of a DLL with a program. This can be a particular problem with applications which install DLLs in the Windows System folder. Some commercial applications arbitrarily write the DLLs associated with the program to this folder without regard to the possibility of a DLL with the same name being overwritten. This can interfere with other applications you already have installed and, in the worst case, can render them inoperable.

Run-time Dynamic Linking

The DLL that we'll create in this chapter will be automatically loaded into memory when execution of the program that uses it is loaded into memory. This is referred to as **load-time dynamic linking**, or **early binding**, because the links to the functions used are established as soon as the program and DLL have been loaded into memory. This kind of operation was illustrated in the previous diagram.

However, this isn't the only possibility. It's also possible to cause a DLL to be loaded after execution of a program has started. This is called **run-time dynamic linking,** or **late binding**. The sequence of operations that occurs with this is illustrated in the following diagram.

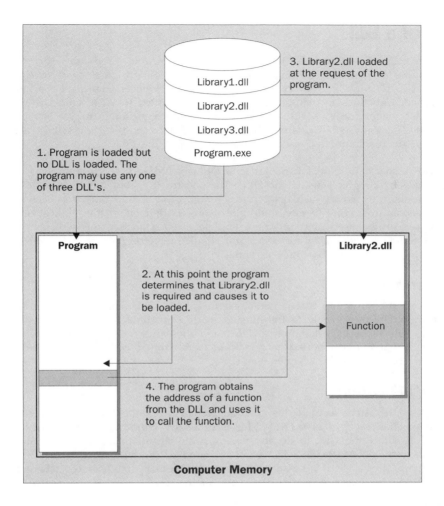

Run-time dynamic linking enables a program to defer linking of a DLL until it is certain that the functions in a DLL are required. This will allow you to write a program that can choose to load one or more of a number of DLLs based upon input to the program, so that only those functions that are necessary are actually loaded into memory. In some circumstances, this can drastically reduce the amount of memory required to run a program.

A program implemented to use run-time dynamic linking calls a function **LoadLibrary()** to load the DLL when it is required. The address of a function within the DLL can then be obtained using a function **GetProcAddress()**. When the program no longer has a need to use the DLL, it can detach itself from the DLL by calling the **FreeLibrary()** function. If no other program is using the DLL, it will be deleted from memory. We won't be going into further details of how this works in this book.

Contents of a DLL

A dynamic link library isn't limited to storing code for functions. You can also put resources into a DLL, including such things as bitmaps and fonts. The Solitaire game that comes with Windows uses a dynamic link library called **Cards.dll** which contains all the bitmap images of the cards and functions to manipulate them. If you wanted to write your own card game, you could conceivably use this DLL as a base and save yourself the trouble of creating all the bitmaps needed to represent the cards. Of course, in order to use it, you would need to know specifically which functions and resources are included in the DLL.

You can also define static global variables in a DLL, including C++ class objects, so that these can be accessed by programs using the DLL. The constructors for global static class objects will be called automatically when such objects are created. You should note that each program using a DLL will get its own copy of any static global objects defined in the DLL, even though they may not necessarily be used by a program. For global class objects, this will involve the overhead of calling a constructor for each. You should, therefore, avoid introducing such objects into a DLL unless they are absolutely essential.

The DLL Interface

You can't access just anything that is contained in a DLL. Only items specifically identified as **exported** from a DLL are visible to the outside world. Functions, classes, global static variables and resources can all be exported from a DLL, and those that are make up the **interface** to the DLL. Anything that is not exported cannot be accessed from the outside. We'll see how to export items from a DLL later in this chapter.

The DllMain() Function

Even though a DLL isn't executable as an independent program, it does contain a special variety of the main function called **DllMain()**. This is called by Windows when the DLL is first loaded into memory to allow the DLL to do any necessary initialization before its contents are used. Windows will also call **DllMain()** just before it removes the DLL from memory to enable the DLL to clean up after itself if necessary. There are also other circumstances where **DllMain()** is called, but these situations are outside the scope of this book.

Varieties of DLLs

There are three different kinds of DLL that you can build with Visual C++ using MFC: an MFC extension DLL, a regular DLL with MFC statically linked and a regular DLL with MFC dynamically linked.

MFC Extension DLL

You can use this kind of DLL to extend MFC by deriving additional classes from MFC for use in your programs. Accesses to classes in MFC by the DLL are resolved dynamically by linking to the shared version of MFC that is implemented in DLLs. If you create a DLL that exchanges pointers to MFC class objects with the program using the DLL, you need to create it as an extension DLL. Use of an extension DLL requires the shared version of MFC to be available in the environment where it is used. An MFC extension DLL can be used by the normal AppWizard generated application. It requires the option Use MFC In A Shared DLL to be selected under the General tab of the project settings, which you access through the Build/ Settings... menu option. This is the default selection with an AppWizard-generated program. An extension DLL can't be used by programs that are statically linked to MFC.

Regular DLL - Statically Linked to MFC

This is a DLL that uses MFC classes which are linked statically. Use of the DLL doesn't require MFC to be available in the environment in which it is used. This kind of DLL can be used by any Win32 program, regardless of whether it uses MFC or not.

Regular DLL - Dynamically Linked to MFC

This is a DLL that uses dynamically linked classes from MFC but doesn't add classes of its own. Use of the DLL requires MFC to be available in the environment where the DLL is used. This kind of DLL can be used by any Win32 program, regardless of whether it uses MFC itself or not.

You can use the AppWizard to build all three types of DLL that use MFC. You can also create a project for a DLL that doesn't involve MFC at all, by selecting the project type as Dynamic-Link Library.

Deciding What to Put in a DLL

How do you decide when you should use a DLL? In most cases, the use of a DLL provides a solution to a particular kind of programming problem, so, if you have the problem, a DLL can be the answer. The common denominator is often sharing code between a number of programs, but there are other instances where a DLL provides advantages. The kinds of circumstances where putting code or resources in a DLL provides a very convenient and efficient approach include the following:

> You have a set of functions or resources on which you want to standardize and which you will use in several different programs. The DLL is a particularly good solution for managing these, especially if some of the programs using your standard facilities are likely to be executing concurrently.

> You have a complex application which involves several programs and a lot of code, but which has sets of functions or resources that may be shared among several of the programs in the application. Using a DLL for common functionality or common resources enables you to manage and develop these with a great deal of independence from the program modules that use them and can simplify program maintenance.

> You have developed a set of standard application oriented classes derived from MFC which you anticipate using in several programs. By packaging the implementation of these classes in an extension DLL, you can make using them in several programs very straightforward, and in the process provide the possibility of being able to improve the internals of the classes without affecting the applications that use them.

> You have developed a brilliant set of functions which provide an easy to use but amazingly powerful tool kit for an application area which just about everybody wants to dabble in. You can readily package your functions in a regular DLL and distribute it in this form.

There are also other circumstances where you may choose to use DLLs, such as when you want to be able to dynamically load and unload libraries, or to select different modules at run time. You could use them to generally ease the development and updating of your applications.

The best way of understanding how to use a DLL is to create one and try it out. Let's do that now.

Writing DLLs

There are two aspects to writing a DLL that we will look at: how you write a DLL and how you define what is to be accessible in the DLL to programs that use it. As a practical example of writing a DLL, we'll create an extension DLL to add a set of application classes to the MFC. We will then extend this DLL by adding variables that will be available to programs using it.

Writing and Using an Extension DLL

We can create an extension DLL to contain the shape classes for the Sketcher application. While this will not bring any major advantages to the program, it will demonstrate how to write an extension DLL without needing to produce a lot of new code. The starting point is AppWizard, so create a new project workspace using the File/New... menu option and choose MFC AppWizard (dll) from the Type: list box, as shown below:

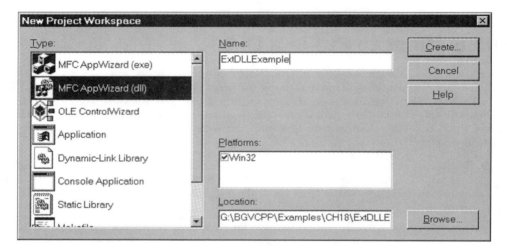

This selection identifies that we are creating an MFC-based DLL and will invoke the AppWizard. The option Dynamic-Link Library that you see a little lower down the list is for creating DLLs that don't involve MFC. You need to make sure that the Location: entry corresponds to the folder where you want the folder containing the code for the DLL to be placed. Once this is done, and you have entered a suitable name for the DLL as shown above, you can click on the Create... button to go to the next step.

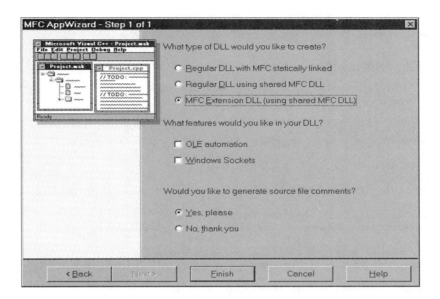

Here, you can see three radio buttons corresponding to the three types of MFC-based DLL that we discussed earlier. You should choose the third option, as shown above.

The two check boxes below the first group of three radio buttons allow you to include code to support **OLE automation** and **Windows Sockets** in the DLL. These are both advanced capabilities within a Windows program, so we don't need either of them here. OLE automation provides the potential for hosting objects created and managed by one application inside another, and we will be taking a tentative look into this before the end of the book. Windows Sockets provides classes and functionality to enable your program to communicate over a network, but we won't be getting into this as it is outside the scope of this book. The default choice to include comments is OK, so you can click on the Finish button and complete creation of the project.

Now that AppWizard has done its stuff, we can look into the code that has been generated on our behalf. If you look at the contents of the project using Windows Explorer, you'll see that AppWizard has generated a total of ten files in the project folder, including a **.txt** file which contains a description of the other files and one further resource file in the sub-folder **Res**. You can read what they are all for in the **.txt** file, but the following two are the ones of immediate interest in implementing our DLL:

Filename	Contents
ExtDLLExample.cpp	This contains the function **DllMain()** and is the primary source file for the DLL.
ExtDLLExample.def	The information in this file is used by Visual C++ during compilation. It contains the name of the DLL and you can also add to it the definitions of those items in the DLL that are to be accessible to a program using the DLL. We'll use an alternative and somewhat easier way of identifying such items in our example.

When your DLL is loaded, the first thing that happens is that **DllMain()** is executed, so perhaps we should take a look at that first.

Understanding DllMain()

If you take a look at the contents of **ExtDLLExample.cpp**, you will see that AppWizard has generated a version of **DllMain()** for us, as shown below:

```
extern "C" int APIENTRY
DllMain(HINSTANCE hInstance, DWORD dwReason, LPVOID lpReserved)
{
    if (dwReason == DLL_PROCESS_ATTACH)
    {
        TRACE0("EXTDLLEXAMPLE.DLL Initializing!\n");

        // Extension DLL one-time initialization
        AfxInitExtensionModule(ExtDLLExampleDLL, hInstance);

        // Insert this DLL into the resource chain
        new CDynLinkLibrary(ExtDLLExampleDLL);
    }
    else if (dwReason == DLL_PROCESS_DETACH)
    {
        TRACE0("EXTDLLEXAMPLE.DLL Terminating!\n");
    }
    return 1;    // ok
}
```

There are three arguments passed to **DllMain()**. The first argument, **hInstance**, is a handle which has been created by Windows to identify the DLL. Every task under Windows 95 has an instance handle which identifies it uniquely. The second argument, **dwReason**, indicates the reason why **DllMain()** is being called. You can see this argument being tested in the **if** statements in **DllMain()**. The first **if** tests for the value **DLL_PROCESS_ATTACH**, which indicates that a program is about to use the DLL, and the second **if** tests for the value **DLL_PROCESS_DETACH**, which indicates that a program is finished using the DLL. The third argument is a pointer that is reserved for use by Windows, so you can ignore it.

When the DLL is first used by a program, it is loaded into memory and the **DllMain()** function will be executed with the argument **dwReason** set to **DLL_PROCESS_ATTACH**. This will result in the function **AfxInitExtensionModule()** being called to initialize the DLL and an object of the class **CDynLinkLibrary** created on the heap. Windows uses objects of this class to manage extension DLLs. If you need to add initialization of your own, you can add it to the end of this block. Any clean-up you require for your DLL can be added to the block for the second **if** statement.

Adding Classes to the Extension DLL

We are going to use the DLL to contain the implementation of our shapes classes, so move the files **Elements.h** and **Elements.cpp** from the folder containing the source for Sketcher to the folder containing the DLL. Be sure that you move rather than copy the files. Since the DLL is going to supply the shape classes for Sketcher, we don't want to leave them in the source code for Sketcher.

You'll also need to remove **Elements.cpp** from the Sketcher project. To do this, simply change to the File View, highlight Elements.cpp by clicking on the file, then press *Del*. If you don't do this, Visual C++ will complain that it couldn't find the file when you try to compile the project.

The shape classes use the constants that we have defined in the file **OurConstants.h**, so copy this file from Sketcher to the folder containing the DLL. Note that the variable **VERSION_NUMBER** is used exclusively by the **IMPLEMENT_SERIAL()** macros in the shape classes, so you could delete it from the **OurConstants.h** file used in the Sketcher program.

We need to add **Elements.cpp** containing the implementation of our shape classes to the extension DLL project, so select the menu option Insert/Files into Project... and choose the file **Elements.cpp** from the list box in the dialog, as shown below:

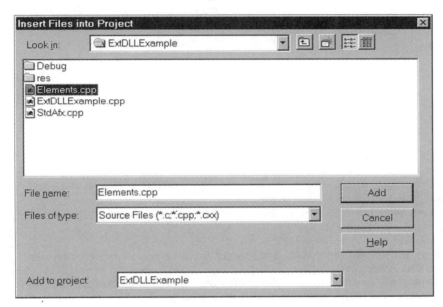

To make sure that the project includes the file containing the shape class definitions, select Build/Update All Dependencies... and choose both the debug and release versions of the project. This will add the files **Elements.h** and **OurConstants.h** to the dependencies for the project.

Exporting Classes from the Extension DLL

The names of the classes that are defined in the DLL and are to be accessible in programs that use it must be identified in some way so that the appropriate links can be established between a program and the DLL. As we saw earlier, one way of doing this is by adding information to the **.def** file for the DLL. This involves adding what are called **decorated names** to the DLL and associating the decorated name with a unique identifying numeric value called an **ordinal**. A decorated name for a object is a name that is generated by the compiler which adds an additional string to the name you gave to the object. This additional string provides information about the type of the object or, in the case of a function, for example, information about the types of the parameters to the function. Amongst other things, it ensures that everything has a unique identifier and enables the linker to distinguish overloaded functions from each other.

Obtaining decorated names and assigning ordinals to export items from a DLL is a lot of work, and isn't the best or the easiest approach with Windows 95. A much easier way to identify the classes that we want to export from the DLL is to modify the class definitions in **Elements.h** to include the keyword **AFX_EXT_CLASS** preceding each class name, as shown below for the **CLine** class:

```
// Class defining a line object
class AFX_EXT_CLASS CLine: public CElement
{
    DECLARE_SERIAL(CLine)
    public:
        // Function to display a line
        virtual void Draw(CDC* pDC, BOOL Select = FALSE);
        virtual void Move(CSize& aSize);       // Move an element
        // Constructor for a line object
        CLine(CPoint Start, CPoint End, COLORREF aColor, int PenWidth);
    virtual void Serialize(CArchive& ar);          // Serialize function for a line

    protected:
        CPoint m_StartPoint;       // Start point of line
        CPoint m_EndPoint;         // End point of line

        CLine(){}       // Default constructor - should not be used
};
```

The keyword **AFX_EXT_CLASS** indicates that the class is to be exported from the DLL. This has the effect of making the complete class available to any program using the DLL and automatically allows access to any of any of the data and functions in the public interface of the class. The collection of things in a DLL that are accessible by a program using it are referred to as the **interface** to the DLL. The process of making an object part of the interface to a DLL is referred to as **exporting** the object.

You need to add the keyword **AFX_EXT_CLASS** to all of the other shape classes, including the base class **CElement**. Why is it necessary to export **CElement** from the DLL? After all, programs will only create objects of the classes derived from **CElement**, and not objects of the class **CElement** itself. The reason is that we have declared public members of **CElement**, which form part of the interface to the derived shape classes and which are almost certainly going to be required by programs using the DLL. If we don't export the **CElement** class, functions such as **GetBoundRect()** will not be available.

The final modification needed is to add **#include <afxtempl.h>** to **StdAfx.h**, so that the definition of **CList** is available.

We have done everything necessary to add the shape classes to the DLL. All you need to do is compile and link the project to create the DLL.

Building a DLL

You build the DLL in exactly the same way as you build any other project - by using the Build/ Build menu option. The output produced is somewhat different, though. You can see the files that are produced in the **Debug** sub-folder of the project folder. The executable code for the DLL is contained in the file **ExtDLLExample.dll**. This file needs to be available to execute a program that uses the DLL. The file **ExtDLLExample.lib** is an import library file that contains the definitions of the items that are exported from the DLL, and it must be available to the linker when a program using the DLL is linked.

Using the Extension DLL in Sketcher

We now have no information in the Sketcher program on the shape classes because we moved the files containing the class definitions and implementations to the DLL project. However, the compiler will still need to know where the shapes classes are coming from in order to compile the code for the program. The Sketcher program needs to include a **.h** file defining the classes that are to be imported from the DLL. We can just copy the file **Elements.h** from the DLL project to the folder containing the Sketcher source. It would be a good idea to identify this file as specifying the imports from the DLL in the Sketcher source code. You could do this by changing its name to **DllImports.h**, in which case you will need to change the **#include** statements that are already in the Sketcher program for **Elements.h** to refer to the new file name (these occur in **SketcherDoc.h** and **SketcherView.h**).

When the Sketcher source has been recompiled, the linker will need to know where to find the DLL, in order to include information that will trigger loading of the DLL when the Sketcher program is executed, and to allow the links to the class implementations in the DLL to be established. We must, therefore, add the location of the DLL to project settings for the link operation. Select Build/Settings... and enter the name of the **.lib** file for the DLL, **ExtDLLExample.lib**, including the full path to it, in the Link tab of the Project Settings dialog, as shown below:

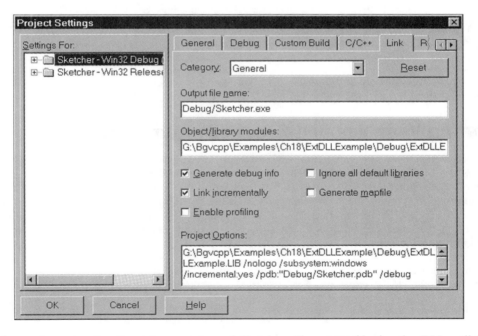

This shows the entry for the debug version of Sketcher. The **.lib** file for the DLL will be in the **Debug** folder within the DLL project folder, as you can see from the entry in the Object/library modules: entry in the dialog box shown. If you create a release version of Sketcher, you will also need the release version of the DLL available to the linker. You'll also need to enter the fully qualified name of the `.lib` file for the release DLL corresponding to the release version of Sketcher. The file to which the Link tab applies is selected in the Settings For: list box in the dialog box above.

You can now Build the Sketcher application once more. To enable Windows to load a DLL for a program, it's usual to place the DLL in your `\Windows\System` folder. Since you probably don't want to clutter up this folder unnecessarily, you can copy `ExtDllExample.dll` from the `Debug` folder of the DLL project to the `Debug` folder for Sketcher. Sketcher should execute exactly as before, except that now it will use the shape classes in the DLL we have created.

Files Required to Use a DLL

From what we have just seen in the context of using the DLL we created in the Sketcher program, to use a DLL in a program, three files must be available:

Extension	Contents
`.h`	Defines those items that are exported from a DLL and enables the compiler to deal properly with references to such items in the source code of a program using the DLL. The `.h` file needs to be added to the source code for the program using the DLL.
`.lib`	Defines the items exported by a DLL in a form which enables the linker to deal with references to exported items when linking a program that uses a DLL.
`.dll`	Contains the executable code for the DLL which is loaded by Windows when a program using the DLL is executed.

If you plan to distribute program code in the form of a DLL for use by other programmers, you need to distribute all three files in the package. For users, just the `.dll` is required.

Exporting Variables and Functions from a DLL

You have seen how you can export classes from an extension DLL using the `AFX_EXT_CLASS` keyword. You can also export objects of classes that are defined in a DLL, as well as ordinary variables and functions. These can be exported from any kind of DLL by using the attribute `dllexport` to identify them. By using `dllexport` to identify class objects, variables or functions that are to be exported from a DLL, you avoid getting involved in the complications of modifying the `.def` file and, as a consequence, you make defining the interface to the DLL a straightforward matter.

You must use the `dllexport` attribute in conjunction with the keyword `_declspec` when you identify an item to be exported. For example, the statement,

```
_declspec(dllexport) double aValue = 1.5;
```

defines the variable `aValue` of type `double` with an initial value of `1.5`, and identifies it as a variable that is to be available to programs using the DLL. To export a function from a DLL, you use the `dllexport` attribute in a similar manner. For example:

```
_declspec(dllexport) CString FindWinner(CString* Teams);
```

This statement exports the function **FindWinner()** from the DLL.

To avoid the slightly cumbersome notation for specifying the **dllexport** attribute, you can simplify it by using a preprocessor directive:

```
#define DllExport _declspec(dllexport)
```

With this definition, the two previous examples can be written alternatively as:

```
DllExport double aValue = 1.5;
DllExport CString FindWinner(CString* Teams);
```

This notation is much more economical, as well as being easier to read, so you may wish adopt this approach when coding your DLLs.

Obviously, only symbols which represent objects with global scope can be exported from a DLL. Variables and class objects that are local to a function in a DLL cease to exist when execution of a function is completed, in just the same way as in a function in a normal program. Attempting to export such symbols will result in a compile time error.

Importing Symbols into a Program

The **dllexport** attribute identifies the symbols in a DLL that form part of the interface. To use these in a program, they must be correspondingly identified as imported from the DLL. This is done by using the **dllimport** keyword in declarations for the symbols to be imported in a **.h** file. We can simplify the notation by using the same technique we applied to the **dllexport** attribute. We can define **DllImport** with the directive:

```
#define DllImport _declspec(dllimport)
```

We can now import the **aValue** variable and the **FindWinner()** function with the declarations:

```
DllImport double aValue;
DllImport CString FindWinner(CString* Teams);
```

These statements would appear in a **.h** file which would be included into the **.cpp** files in the program that referenced these symbols.

Implementing the Export of Symbols from a DLL

We could extend the extension DLL to make the symbols defining shape types and colors available in the interface to the DLL. We can then remove the definitions that we have in the Sketcher program and import the definitions of these symbols from the extension DLL.

We can first modify the source code for the DLL to add the symbols for shape element types and colors to the interface for the DLL. To export the element types and colors, they must be global variables. As global variables, it would be better if they appeared in a **.cpp** file, rather than a **.h** file, so move the definitions of these out of the **OurConstants.h** file to the beginning of **Elements.cpp** in the DLL source. You can then apply the **dllexport** attribute in their definitions in the **Elements.cpp** file, as follows:

```
// Definitions of constants and identification of
// symbols to be exported

#define DllExport __declspec(dllexport)

// Element type definitions
// Each type value must be unique
DllExport extern const WORD LINE = 101U;
DllExport extern const WORD RECTANGLE = 102U;
DllExport extern const WORD CIRCLE = 103U;
DllExport extern const WORD CURVE = 104U;
DllExport extern const WORD TEXT = 105U;
///////////////////////////////////

// Color values for drawing
DllExport extern const COLORREF BLACK = RGB(0,0,0);
DllExport extern const COLORREF RED = RGB(255,0,0);
DllExport extern const COLORREF GREEN = RGB(0,255,0);
DllExport extern const COLORREF BLUE = RGB(0,0,255);
DllExport extern const COLORREF SELECT_COLOR = RGB(255,0,180);
///////////////////////////////////
```

We first define the symbol **DllExport** to simplify the specification of the variables to be exported as we saw earlier. The symbol **VERSION_NUMBER** is only used in the DLL, so we don't need to export that. We then assign the attribute **dllexport** to each of the element types and colors.

You will notice that the **extern** specifier has also been added to the definitions of these variables. The reason for this is the effect of the **const** modifier. The **const** modifier indicates to the compiler that these values are constants and shouldn't be modified in the program, which was the effect that we wanted. However, by default, it also specifies the variables as having internal linkage, so they are local to the file in which they appear. We want to export these variable to another program so we have to add the modifier **extern** to override the default linkage specification due to the **const** modifier and ensure that they have external linkage. Symbols that are assigned external linkage are global and so can be exported. Of course, if the variables didn't have the **const** modifier applied to them, we wouldn't need to add **extern**, since they would be global automatically as long as they appeared at global scope.

The **OurConstants.h** file now only contains one definition:

```
// Definitions of constants

#ifndef OurConstants_h
#define OurConstants_h

// Define the program version number for use in serialization
UINT VERSION_NUMBER = 1;

#endif
```

You can now <u>B</u>uild the DLL once again, so it is ready to use in the Sketcher program. Don't forget to copy the latest version of the **.dll** file to the Sketcher **Debug** folder.

Using Exported Symbols

To make the symbols exported from the DLL available in the Sketcher program, you need to specify them as imported from the DLL. You can do this by adding the identification of the imported symbols to the file **DllImports.h** which contains the definitions for the imported classes. In this way, we will have one file specifying all the items imported from the DLL. The statements that appear in this file will be as follows:

```
// Variables defined in the shape DLL ExtDLLExample.dll
#ifndef DllImports_h
#define DllImports_h


#define DllImport    __declspec( dllimport )

    // Import element type declarations
    // Each type value must be unique
    DllImport extern const WORD LINE;
    DllImport extern const WORD RECTANGLE;
    DllImport extern const WORD CIRCLE;
    DllImport extern const WORD CURVE;
    DllImport extern const WORD TEXT;
    ////////////////////////////////////

    // Import color values for drawing
    DllImport extern const COLORREF BLACK;
    DllImport extern const COLORREF RED;
    DllImport extern const COLORREF GREEN;
    DllImport extern const COLORREF BLUE;
    DllImport extern const COLORREF SELECT_COLOR;
    ////////////////////////////////////

// Plus the definitions for the element classes...
#endif
```

This defines and uses the **DllImport** symbol to simplify these declarations, in the way that we saw earlier. You now need to make sure there is an **#include** statement for this file to the files that refer to these symbols, namely **SketcherView.cpp** and **SketcherDoc.cpp**.

This means that the **OurConstants.h** file in the Sketcher project is now empty and we can remove the file from the project, along with the **#include** of it in **Sketcher.h**.

That looks as though we have done everything necessary to use the new version of the DLL with Sketcher, but we haven't. If you try to recompile Sketcher, you will get error messages for the **switch** statement in the **CreateElement()** member of **CSketcherView**.

The values in the case statements must be constant, but, although we have given the element type variables the attribute **const**, the compiler has no access to these values because they are defined in the DLL, not in the Sketcher program. The compiler, therefore, can't determine what these constant case values are and flags an error. The simplest way round this problem is to replace the **switch** statement in the **CreateElement()** function by a series of **if** statements, as follows:

```
// Create an element of the current type
CElement* CSketcherView::CreateElement()
{
    // Get a pointer to the document for this view
    CSketcherDoc* pDoc = GetDocument();
    ASSERT_VALID(pDoc);                          // Verify the pointer is good

    // Now select the element using the type stored in the document
    WORD ElementType = pDoc->GetElementType();
    if(ElementType == RECTANGLE)
            return new CRectangle(m_FirstPoint, m_SecondPoint,
                            pDoc->GetElementColor(), pDoc->GetPenWidth());

    if(ElementType == CIRCLE)
            return new CCircle(m_FirstPoint, m_SecondPoint,
                            pDoc->GetElementColor(), pDoc->GetPenWidth());

    if(ElementType == CURVE)
            return new CCurve(m_FirstPoint, m_SecondPoint,
                            pDoc->GetElementColor(), pDoc->GetPenWidth());
    else            // Always default to a line
            return new CLine(m_FirstPoint, m_SecondPoint,
                            pDoc->GetElementColor(), pDoc->GetPenWidth());
}
```

We have added a local variable **ElementType** to store the current element type retrieved from the document. This is then tested against the element types imported from the DLL in the series of **if** statements. This does exactly the same job as the **switch** statement, but has no requirement for the element type constants to be explicitly known. If you now Build Sketcher with these changes added, it will execute using the DLL using the exported symbols as well as the exported shape classes.

Summary

In this chapter, you have learned the basics of how to construct and use a dynamic link library. The most important points we have looked at in this context are:

▶ Dynamic link libraries provide a means of linking to standard functions dynamically when a program executes, rather than incorporating them into the executable module for a program.

▶ An AppWizard-generated program by default links to a version of MFC stored in DLLs.

▶ A single copy of a DLL in memory can be used by several programs executing concurrently.

▶ An extension DLL is so called because it extends the set of classes in MFC. An extension DLL must be used if you want to export MFC-based classes or objects of MFC classes from a DLL. An extension DLL can also export ordinary functions and global variables.

▶ A **regular** DLL can be used if you only want to export ordinary functions or global variables that aren't instances of MFC classes.

▶ You can export classes from an **extension** DLL by using the keyword **AFX_EXT_CLASS** preceding the class name in the DLL.

▶ You can export ordinary functions and global variables from a DLL by assigning the **dllexport** attribute to them using the **_declspec** keyword.

▶ You can import the classes exported from an extension DLL by using including the **.H** file from the DLL that contains the class definitions using the **AFX_EXT_CLASS** keyword.

▶ You can import ordinary functions and global variables that are exported from a DLL by assigning the **dllimport** attribute to their declarations in your program by using the **_declspec** keyword.

Connecting to Data Sources

In this chapter, we will show you to how to interface to a database using Visual C++ and MFC. This is by no means a comprehensive discussion of the possibilities, since we'll only address retrieving data, but at least you'll take a few steps down this particular path.

In this chapter you will learn:

- What SQL is, and how it is used
- How to retrieve data using the SQL **SELECT** operation
- What a recordset object is, and how it links to a relational database table
- How a recordset object can retrieve information from a database
- How a record view can display information from a recordset
- How to create a database program using AppWizard
- How to add recordsets to your program
- How to handle multiple record views

Database Basics

This is not the place for a detailed dissertation on database technology, but we do need to make sure that we have a common understanding of database terminology. Databases come in a variety of flavors, but the majority these days are **relational databases**. It is relational databases that we will be talking about throughout this chapter.

In a database, your data is organized into one or more **tables**. You can think of a database table as being like a spreadsheet table, made up of rows and columns. Each row contains information about a single item and each column contains the information about the same characteristic from every item.

A **record** is equivalent to a row in the spreadsheet. Each record consists of elements of data that make up that record. These elements of data are known as **fields**. A field is a cell in the table identified by the column heading. The term *field* can also represent the whole column.

We can best see the structure of a table with a diagram:

Here you can see that this table is being used to store information on a line of products. Unsurprisingly then, the table is called Products. Each record in the table, represented by a record in the diagram, contains the data for one product. The description of a product is separated into fields in the table, each storing information about one aspect of a product: Product Name, Unit Price, etc.

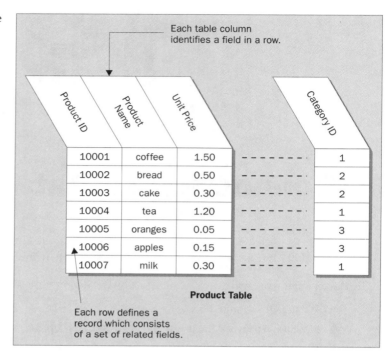

Each table column identifies a field in a row.

Product ID	Product Name	Unit Price		Category ID
10001	coffee	1.50	--------	1
10002	bread	0.50	--------	2
10003	cake	0.30	--------	2
10004	tea	1.20	--------	1
10005	oranges	0.05	--------	3
10006	apples	0.15	--------	3
10007	milk	0.30	--------	1

Product Table

Each row defines a record which consists of a set of related fields.

Although the fields in this table store only relatively simple information (character strings or numeric values), the type of data you decide to put in a particular field can be virtually anything you want. You could store times, dates, pictures or even binary objects in a database.

A table will usually have at least one field that can be used to identify each record uniquely and in the example above, the Product ID is a likely candidate for this. A field in a table that serves to identify each record within the table is called a **key**. A key which uniquely identifies each record in a table is referred to as a **primary key**. In some cases, a table may have no single field that uniquely identifies each record. In this circumstance, two or more key fields may be used. A key composed of two or more fields is called a **multi-value key**.

The relational aspect of a database, and the importance of keys, comes into play when you store related information in separate tables. You define relationships between the tables, using keys, and use the relationships to find associated information stored in your database. Note that the tables themselves don't know about relationships, just as the table doesn't understand the other bits of data stored in the table. It is the program that accesses the data which must use the information in the tables to pull together related data, whether that program is Access 95, SQL Server 6 or your own program written in Visual C++. These are collectively known as **relational database management systems** or **RDBMSs**.

A real, well-designed relational database will usually consist of a large number of tables. Each table usually has only several fields and many records. The reason for only having a few fields in each table is to increase query performance. Without going into the details of database optimization, have faith that it's much faster to query many tables with a few fields each than to query a single table with many fields.

We can extend the example shown in the previous diagram to illustrate a relational database with two tables: Products and Categories.

Product ID	Product Name	Unit Price	Category ID
10001	coffee	1.50	1
10002	bread	0.50	2
10003	cake	0.30	2
10004	tea	1.20	1
10005	oranges	0.05	3
10006	apples	0.15	3
10007	milk	0.30	1

Category ID	Category Name
1	Beverage
2	Baked goods
3	Fruit

The data in this field can only be used to obtain the category name from the category table.

As you can see from the diagram, the Category ID field is used to relate the information stored in the two tables. Category ID uniquely identifies a category record in the Categories table, so it is a primary key for that table. In the Products table, the Category ID field is used to relate a product record to a category, so the field is termed a **foreign key** for that table.

Relational databases can be created and manipulated in numerous ways. There are a large number of RDBMSs on the market that provide a wide range of facilities for creating and manipulating database information. Obviously, it's possible for you to add and delete records in a database table, and to update the fields in a record, although, typically, there are controls within the RDBMS to limit such activities, based on the authorization level of the user. As well as accessing information from a single table in a database, you can combine records from two or more tables into a new table, based on their relationships, and retrieve information from that. Combining tables in this way is called a **table join**. To program all these kinds of operations on a relational database, you can use a language known as SQL that is supported by most RDBMSs and programming languages.

A Little SQL

SQL stands for Structured Query Language. It's a relatively simple language, designed specifically for accessing and modifying information in relational databases. It was originally developed at IBM in a mainframe environment, but is now used throughout the computing world. SQL doesn't actually exist as a software package by itself. It's usually hosted by some other environment, whether that's an RDBMS or a programming language, such as COBOL, C or C++. The environment hosting SQL provides for mundane things such as regular I/O and talking to the operating system, and SQL is used to query the database.

MFC support for databases uses SQL to specify queries and other operations on database tables. These operations are provided by a set of specialized classes. You'll see how to use some of these in the example that we will write later in this chapter.

SQL has statements to retrieve, sort and update records from a table, to add and delete records and fields, to join tables and to compute totals, as well as a lot of other capabilities for creating and managing database tables. We won't be going into all the possible programming options available in SQL, but we'll discuss the details sufficiently to enable you to understand what's happening in the examples that we write, even though you may not have seen any SQL before.

When we use SQL in an MFC-based program, we won't need to write complete SQL statements for the most part because the framework takes care of assembling a complete statement and supplying it to the database engine you are using. Nevertheless, we'll look here at how typical SQL statements are written in their entirety, so that you get a feel for how the language statements are structured.

SQL statements are written with a terminating semicolon, just like C++, and keywords in the language are written in capital letters. Let's take a look at a few examples of SQL statements and see how they work.

Retrieving Data Using SQL

To retrieve data, you use the **SELECT** statement. It's quite surprising how much of what you want to do with a database is covered by the **SELECT** statement. The **SELECT** statement operates on one or more tables in your database. The result of executing a **SELECT** statement is always a **recordset**, which is a collection of data produced using the information from the tables you supply in the detail of the statement. The data in the recordset is organized in the form of a table, with named columns that are from the tables you specified in the **SELECT** statement, and rows or records that are selected, based on conditions specified in the **SELECT** statement. The recordset generated by a **SELECT** statement might have only one record, or might even be empty.

Perhaps the simplest retrieval operation on a database is to access all the records in a single table, so, given that our database includes a table called **Products**, we can obtain all the records in this table with the following SQL statement:

```
SELECT * FROM Products;
```

The * indicates that we want all the fields in the database. The parameter following the keyword **FROM** defines the table from which the fields are to be selected. We haven't constrained the records that are returned by the **SELECT** statement, so we'll get all of them. A little later we'll see how to constrain the records that are selected.

If you wanted all the records, but only needed to retrieve specific fields in each record, you could specify these by using the field names separated by commas in place of the asterisk in the previous example. An example of a statement that would do this is:

```
SELECT ProductID,UnitPrice FROM Products;
```

This statement selects all the records from the **Products** table, but only the **ProductID** and **UnitPrice** fields for each record. This will produce a table having just the two fields specified here.

The field names that we have used here don't contain spaces, but they could. Where a name contains spaces, standard SQL says that it has to be written between double quotes. If the fields had the names **Product ID** and **Unit Price**, we would write the **SELECT** statement as:

```
SELECT "Product ID","Unit Price" FROM Products;
```

Using double quotes with names, as we have done here, is a bit inconvenient in the C++ context, as we need to be able to pass SQL statements as strings. In C++, double quotes are already used as character string delimiters, so there would be confusion if we tried to enclose the names of database objects (tables or fields) in double quotes.

For this reason, when you reference database table or field names which include spaces in the Visual C++ environment, you should enclose them within square brackets rather than double quotes. Thus, you would write the field names from the example as **[Product ID]** and **[Unit Price]**. You will see this notation in action in the database program that we write later in this chapter.

Choosing Records

Unlike fields, records in a table do not have names. The only way to choose particular records is by applying some condition or restriction on the contents of one or more of the fields in a record, so that only records meeting the condition are selected. This is done by adding a **WHERE** clause to the **SELECT** statement. The parameter following the **WHERE** keyword defines the condition that is to be used to select records.

We could select the records in the **Products** table that have a particular value for the **Category ID** field, with the statement:

```
SELECT * FROM Products WHERE [Category ID] = 2;
```

This selects just those records where the **Category ID** field has the value **2**, so, from the table we illustrated earlier, we would get the records for coffee, tea and milk. Note that a single equals sign is used to specify a check for equality in SQL, not **==** as we normally use in C++.

You can use other comparison operators such as **<**, **>**, **<=**, and **>=** to specify the condition in a **WHERE** clause. You can also combine logical expressions with **AND** and **OR**. To place a further restriction on the records selected in the last example, we could write:

```
SELECT * FROM Products WHERE [Category ID] = 2 AND [Unit Price] > 0.5;
```

In this case, the resulting table would just contain two records, because milk would be out as it's too cheap. Only records with a **Category ID** of **2**, and a **Unit Price** value greater than **0.5** are selected by this statement.

Joining Tables Using SQL

You can also use the **SELECT** statement to join tables together, although it's a little more complicated than you might imagine. Suppose we have two tables: **Products** having three records and three fields, and **Orders** with three records and four fields. These are illustrated on the following page.

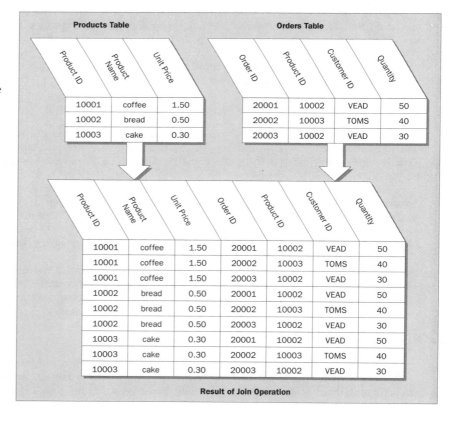

Products Table

Product ID	Product Name	Unit Price
10001	coffee	1.50
10002	bread	0.50
10003	cake	0.30

Orders Table

Order ID	Product ID	Customer ID	Quantity
20001	10002	VEAD	50
20002	10003	TOMS	40
20003	10002	VEAD	30

Here, we have a meager product set in the **Products** table, consisting of just coffee, bread and cake, and we have three orders as shown in the **Orders** table, but we haven't managed to sell any coffee.

We could join these tables together with the **SELECT** statement:

```
SELECT * FROM Products, Orders;
```

This statement creates a recordset using the records from both the tables specified. The recordset will have seven fields, three from the **Products** table and four from the **Orders** table, but how many records does it have? The answer is illustrated in the diagram here:

Products Table

Product ID	Product Name	Unit Price
10001	coffee	1.50
10002	bread	0.50
10003	cake	0.30

Orders Table

Order ID	Product ID	Customer ID	Quantity
20001	10002	VEAD	50
20002	10003	TOMS	40
20003	10002	VEAD	30

Product ID	Product Name	Unit Price	Order ID	Product ID	Customer ID	Quantity
10001	coffee	1.50	20001	10002	VEAD	50
10001	coffee	1.50	20002	10003	TOMS	40
10001	coffee	1.50	20003	10002	VEAD	30
10002	bread	0.50	20001	10002	VEAD	50
10002	bread	0.50	20002	10003	TOMS	40
10002	bread	0.50	20003	10002	VEAD	30
10003	cake	0.30	20001	10002	VEAD	50
10003	cake	0.30	20002	10003	TOMS	40
10003	cake	0.30	20003	10002	VEAD	30

Result of Join Operation

The recordset produced by the **SELECT** statement has nine records that are produced by combining each record from the **Products** table with every record from the **Orders** table, so all possible combinations are included. This may not be exactly what is required, or what you expected. Arbitrarily including all combinations of records from one table with another is of limited value. The meaning of a record containing details of the bread product and an order for cake is hard to fathom. You can also end up with an incredibly big table in a real situation. If you combine a table containing 100 products with one containing 500 orders and you do not constrain the join operation, the resulting table will contain 50,000 records.

To get a useful join, you usually need to add a **WHERE** clause to the **SELECT** statement. With the examples of tables we have been using, one condition that would make sense would be to only allow records where the **Product ID** from one table matched the same field in the other table. This would combine each record from the **Products** table with the records from the **Orders** table that related to that product. The statement to do this would be:

```
SELECT * FROM Products,Orders
                WHERE Products.[Product ID] = Orders.[Product ID];
```

Note how a specific field for a particular table is identified here. You add the table name as a prefix and separate it from the field name with a period. This qualification of the field name is essential where the same field name is used in both tables. Without the table name, there's no way to know which of the two fields you mean. With this **SELECT** statement and the same table contents we used previously, we'll get the recordset shown below:

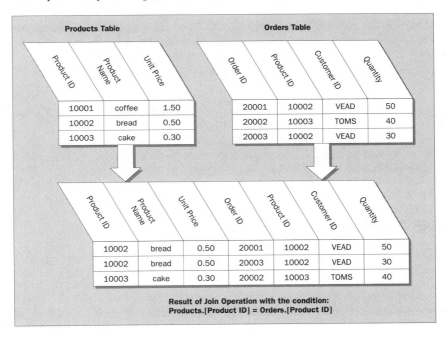

Result of Join Operation with the condition:
Products.[Product ID] = Orders.[Product ID]

Of course, this may still be unsatisfactory in that we have two fields containing the **Product ID** field, but you could easily remove this by specifying the field names you want, instead of the * in the **SELECT** statement.

Sorting Records

When you retrieve data from a database using the **SELECT** statement, you will often want the records sorted in a particular order. With the previous example, the tables shown are already ordered, but in practice this is not necessarily the case. You might want to see the output of the last example sorted in a different way, depending on the circumstances. At one time, it might be convenient to have the records ordered by **Customer ID**, and on another occasion perhaps ordered by **Quantity** within **Product ID**. The **ORDER BY** clause added to the **SELECT** statement will do this for you. For example, we could refine the last **SELECT** statement by adding an **ORDER BY** clause:

```
SELECT * FROM Products,Orders
                WHERE Products.[Product ID] = Orders.[Product ID]
                ORDER BY [Customer ID];
```

The result of this will be the same records that we obtained with the last example, but with the records arranged so that the **Customer ID** field is in ascending sequence.

If you wanted to sort on two fields, **Customer ID** and **Product ID** say, and you wanted the records arranged in descending sequence, you would write:

```
SELECT * FROM Products,Orders
                WHERE Products.[Product ID] = Orders.[Product ID]
                ORDER BY [Customer ID] DESC, Products.[Product ID] DESC;
```

We need to use the qualified name, **Products.[Product ID]**, in the **ORDER BY** clause to avoid ambiguity, as we do in the **WHERE** clause. The keyword **DESC** at the end of each field in the **ORDER BY** statement specifies descending sequence for the sort operation. There is a complementary keyword, **ASC**, for ascending sequence, although this is usually omitted because it is the default condition.

This is by no means all there is to SQL, or even all there is to the **SELECT** statement, but it's enough to get you through the database example that we will write.

 If you need to know more about SQL, there is an excellent book written by Joe Celko and published by Wrox Press entitled *Instant SQL Programming*.

Database Support in MFC

You're spoilt for choice when you use MFC for database application development, since two distinct approaches are supported, each of which uses its own set of MFC classes.

One approach is to use **Data Access Objects** (DAO). These objects provide an interface to the **Jet database engine**. The Jet database engine is a generalized piece of software that provides the ability to store data in, and retrieve data from, a range of database management systems. Jet is the engine used by Microsoft's Access DBMS. Whenever you manipulate a database in Access, you are actually getting Jet to do all the hard work. Jet is optimized for accessing Access (**.mdb**) database files directly, but will also enable you to attach to any database that supports the **Open DataBase Connectivity** interface, better known as **ODBC**. This allows you to manipulate databases in any format for which you have the appropriate ODBC driver. Databases that you can access using Jet, in addition to Microsoft Access, include Oracle, dBase 5, Btrieve 6.0, and FoxPro 2.6.

The other approach is ODBC specific, but since ODBC drivers are also available for **.mdb** files, both approaches cover essentially the same range of databases formats. How do you choose between them?

The first consideration is whether you are accessing your database in a client-server environment. If you are, you need to use ODBC. If you're not in a client-server situation, perhaps the most significant factor is whether you are going to use your program primarily with **.mdb** databases. If you are, the DAO-based approach will be more efficient than the ODBC approach. On the other hand, if you use the DAO approach with databases other than those in Microsoft Access format that do not use the Microsoft Jet engine to drive them, you'll be working through the ODBC interface included within the DAO implementation, and this will be less efficient than using the ODBC specific approach directly. The DAO-based classes also provide a more comprehensive range of capabilities than the ODBC classes, so you need to consider this aspect as well.

If you want to take a simplistic view, you could decide on the basis that if you intend to use Microsoft Access databases and you are not in a client-server situation, you should program using DAO, otherwise you use ODBC.

DAO versus ODBC

DAO uses objects for accessing and manipulating a database. There are objects representing tables, queries and the database itself. These objects insulate you from the detail of the specific database system implementation you are concerned with and provide you with a programming interface that is consistent with the object oriented approach to programming.

ODBC, on the other hand, is a system-independent interface to a database environment that requires an **ODBC driver** to be provided for each database system from which you want to manipulate data. ODBC defines a set of function calls for database operations that are system neutral. You can only use a database with ODBC if you have the DLL that contains the driver to work with that database application's file format. The purpose of the driver is to interface the standard set of system independent calls for database operations that will be used in your program to the specifics of a particular database implementation.

While the concept here is rather different from that of DAO, in Visual C++, the programming approach is very similar with both methodologies. MFC packages the ODBC interface in a set of classes that are structured in a very similar way to the classes that apply with DAO. The application of MFC classes for ODBC closely parallels the use of the equivalent DAO classes.

It would be useful now to take a broad view of the classes supporting DAO and ODBC in MFC. We won't go into detail at this point, but will use the programming example to understand the basic mechanics of how the ODBC classes can be used.

Classes Supporting DAO

The eight classes shown on the next page are used with the DAO approach:

675

Class	What it does
CDaoWorkspace	An object of this class manages a database session from start to finish. A **CDaoDatabase** object requires a **CDaoWorkspace** object to be available, and if you don't create one, the framework will supply one automatically when your **CDaoDatabase** object is created. A workspace object can contain several database objects.
CDaoDatabase	An object of this class implements a connection to a specific database. An object of this class will always be created when you access a database, but you don't necessarily have to create a database object explicitly. It can be created implicitly when you create a **CDaoRecordset** object.
CDaoRecordset	An object of a class derived from this class represents the result of an SQL **SELECT** operation, which is a set of records. The object makes available one record of the table produced by the **SELECT** at a time, and provides a range of functions to enable you to move backwards and forwards through the records available, and to search for records conforming to a set of search criteria.
CDaoRecordView	An object of a class derived from this class is used to display the current record from an associated recordset object. The record view object uses a child dialog to display data items from the DAO recordset object. There are automatic mechanisms for updating the controls in the dialog with current data from the DAO recordset object.
CDaoFieldExchange	This class supports the exchange of data between your database and a DAO recordset object. You can use objects of this class yourself, but AppWizard and ClassWizard will implement and maintain the use of these objects automatically.
CDaoQueryDef	An object of this class defines a query on your database that is usually stored in the database. These are typically standard queries that are used frequently. A **CDaoQueryDef** object can be used to create a **CDaoRecordset** object that represents a particular SELECT statement. An object of this class can also be used to execute SQL statements explicitly, by using its Execute() member function.
CDaoTableDef	An object of this class defines a table in your database. It can represent an existing table, or can be used to construct a new table.
CDaoException	An object of this class is constructed when an exception condition arises from a DAO database operation. All DAO errors cause exceptions and result in objects of this class being created. The CDaoException class members enable you to determine the cause of the exception.

The most essential classes that you'll use in DAO programming are a **CDaoDatabase** class that will represent your database, one or more classes derived from **CDaoRecordset** that will represent **SELECT** operations on your database, and one or more classes derived from **CDaoRecordView** that will display data made available by your **CDaoRecordset** based classes. As we shall see, an ODBC application involves a similar set of basic classes with the same sort of functionality. The **CDaoTableDef** and **CDaoQueryDef** classes provide capability that is not available within MFC support for ODBC.

Classes Supporting ODBC

MFC support for ODBC is implemented through five classes:

Class	What it does
CDatabase	An object of this class represents a connection to your database. This connection must exist before you can carry out any operations on the database. No workspace class is used with an ODBC database.
CRecordSet	An object of a class derived from this class represents the result of an SQL **SELECT** operation. This is the same concept that we saw with the **CDaoRecordset** class.
CRecordView	An object of a class derived from this class is used to display current information from an associated recordset object. This is the same concept that we saw with the **CDaoRecordView** class.
CFieldExchange	This class provides for the exchange of data between the database and a recordset object, in the same manner that we saw for DAO databases.
CDBException	Objects of this class represent exceptions that occur within ODBC database operations.

The ODBC classes look very much like a subset of the DAO classes and, in the sense that the interface they provide is similar to that of the equivalent DAO classes, they are. Of course, the underlying process for accessing the database is rather different.

We can best understand how database operations with MFC work by creating an example. We will use the ODBC approach, but apply it to accessing a Microsoft Access database. The database that we'll use is supplied on the Visual C++ CD. It has the merit of containing a considerable variety of tables that are populated by realistic numbers of records. This will give you a lot of scope for experimentation, as well as providing some feel for how well your code will work in practice. It's easy to be lulled into a false sense of security by running your program against a test database where the numbers of tables and records within a table is trivial. It can be quite a surprise to find out how long transactions can take in a real world context.

Creating a Database Application

For our example, we'll show how to use three related tables in the database contained in the **SampData.mdb** file. You'll find this file in the **\Msdev\Samples\Mfc\Database\Daoctl** folder on the Visual C++ CD. Copy this file to a suitable folder on your hard disk and make sure that the file is no longer set to read-only. (On Windows 95, you can alter this by right-clicking the file, selecting Properties from the pop-up menu and making sure that the Read-only attribute box is unchecked.) Since you'll always have the read-only version of the database on the CD to go back to if something goes wrong, you won't need to worry about messing it up, so feel free to experiment as we go along.

In the first step, we'll create a program to display records from the **Products** table in the database. We will then add code to allow us to examine all the orders for a given product using two other tables.

Finally, we'll access the **Customers** table to enable the customer details for an order to be displayed. Before we can start with the code, we need to identify the database to the operating system.

Registering an ODBC Database

Before you can use an ODBC database, it needs to be registered. You do this through the Control Panel that you access by selecting Settings from the Start menu. In the Control Panel, select the 32bit ODBC icon. To add the database that we're going to use, click on the Add button. You should then see a list of ODBC drivers that includes Microsoft Access Driver(*.mdb). This is automatically installed with the typical setup when you installed Windows. If you don't see this driver, you need to go back to Windows setup to install it. Select this driver and select OK and then enter Sample Data as the Data Source Name. We'll use this name to identify the database when we generate our application using AppWizard. You now need to click on the Select... button in the Database group and then select the **Sampdata.mdb** file in whichever directory it now sits. Finally, click on successive OK buttons and the final Close button, and you have registered the database.

We can now go ahead with our database application and, as ever, the starting point is AppWizard.

Using AppWizard to Generate an ODBC Program

Create a new project workspace in the usual way and give it a suitable name, such as DBSample. Choose the SDI interface for document support, since that will be sufficient for our needs. The document is somewhat incidental to operations in a database application, since most things are managed by recordset and record view objects. As you'll see, the main use of the document is to store recordset objects, so you won't need more than one document. Click on the Next > button to move to the next step.

In Step 2 you have a choice as to whether you include file support with the database view option. File support refers to serializing the document which is not normally necessary, since any database input and output that you need will be taken care of using the recordset objects in your application. Therefore, you should choose the option without file support, as shown here:

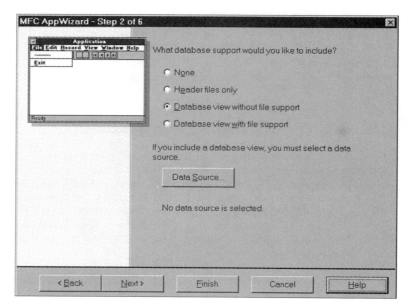

When you select either of the database options, the Data Source... button is activated. You now need to click on this button to specify the database that your application is going to use. This will display the dialog shown here:

ODBC is already selected as the database option and, if you expand the drop-down list, you should find Sample Data as one of the data sources available to you - that is if you have registered it correctly beforehand. In the dialog above, it has already been selected.

AppWizard will automatically equip your program with a recordset class and a record view class, and the dialog also shows a choice for the recordset your program will use. The grayed Table option only applies if you are using DAO. For ODBC, you have a choice between Snapshot and Dynaset for your initial recordset class. There is a significant difference between these options, so let's look at what they mean.

Snapshot versus Dynaset Recordsets

Your recordset object will provide you with the result of a **SELECT** operation on the database. In the case of a **snapshot** recordset, the query is executed once and the result is stored in memory. Your recordset object can then make available to you any of the records in the table that result from the query, so a snapshot is essentially static in nature. Any changes that might occur in the database due to other users updating the database will not be reflected in the data you have obtained with your snapshot recordset. If you need to see changes that may have been made, you'll need to re-run the **SELECT** statement.

There is another difference in snapshot recordsets that depends on whether you are using DAO or ODBC. A DAO snapshot can't be changed by your program - it is read-only. However, an ODBC snapshot can be either read-only or updatable. An updatable snapshot writes any modifications that you make to the table straight back to the underlying database, and your program can see the change. Other programs with a snapshot of the database will not, however, see the changes until they requery the database.

With the **dynaset** option, your recordset object will automatically refresh the current record from the database when you move from one record to another in the table generated by the query for the recordset. As a consequence, the record available in the recordset will reflect the up-to-date status of the database when you accessed the record, not when you first opened the recordset. The refresh only occurs when your recordset object accesses a record. If the data in the current record is modified by another user, this will not be apparent in your recordset object unless you move to another record and then return to the original record. A dynaset recordset uses an index to the database tables involved to dynamically generate the contents of each record.

Since we have no other users accessing the Sample Data database, you can choose the Snapshot option for our example. This will be adequate here because we'll only be implementing the retrieval of data from the database. If you want to try to add some update capability yourself, you should use the Dynaset option.

Choosing Tables

Once Snapshot has been chosen, you can click on the OK button to display the dialog which will determine the tables that the recordset class in your application will relate to. Here, you are effectively specifying the tables parameter for the **SELECT** statement that will be applied for the recordset. The dialog is shown here:

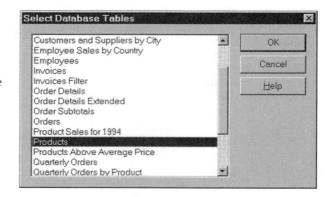

The dialog lists all the tables in the Sample Data database and, as you see, there are quite a few. You could select several tables to be associated with the recordset by holding down the *Shift* key as you click on entries in the list box, but here we only need one, so just select the Products table, as shown, and then click on the OK button.

You have now specified the operation for the recordset class that AppWizard will generate as:

```
SELECT * FROM Products;
```

The use of * for all fields is determined by the framework. It just uses the table names you choose here to form the SQL operation that will be applied for the recordset.

You can now move through the remaining steps for generating the project workspace without changing any of the options, until you get to the dialog displaying the class and file names to be used, which is Step 6, as shown here:

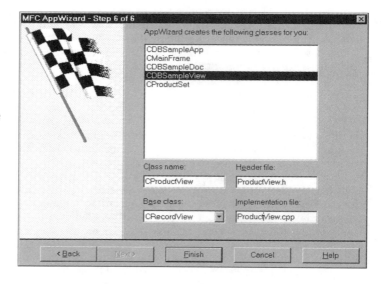

You should change the **CDBSampleSet** class name to **CProductSet** and the associated **.h** and **.cpp** file names to be consistent with the class name. Also change the **CDBSampleView** class in the same way, as shown above. Once that is done, you can click on Finish and generate the program.

Understanding the Program Structure

The basic structure of the program is as we have seen before, with an application class **CDBSampleApp**, a frame window class **CMainFrame**, a document class **CDBSampleDoc**, and a view class **CProductView**. A document template object is responsible for creating and relating the frame window, the document and the view objects. This is done in a standard manner in the **InitInstance()** member of the application object.

The document class is quite standard, except that AppWizard has added a data member, **m_productSet** which is an object of the **CProductSet** class. As a consequence, a recordset object will be automatically created when the document object is created in the **InitInstance()** function member of the application object. The significant departures from a non-database program arise in the detail of the **CRecordset** class, and in the **CRecordView** class, so let's take a look at those.

Understanding Recordsets

We can look at the definition of the **CProductSet** class that AppWizard has generated piecemeal and see how each piece works. The bits under discussion will be shown as shaded.

Recordset Creation

The first segment of the class definition that is of interest is:

```
class CProductSet : public CRecordset
{
  public:
    CProductSet(CDatabase* pDatabase = NULL);
      DECLARE_DYNAMIC(CProductSet)

    // Plus more of the class definition...

    // Overrides
    // ClassWizard generated virtual function overrides
    //{{AFX_VIRTUAL(CProductSet)
    public:
    virtual CString GetDefaultConnect();      // Default connection string
    virtual CString GetDefaultSQL();           // default SQL for Recordset
    virtual void DoFieldExchange(CFieldExchange* pFX);// RFX support
    //}}AFX_VIRTUAL

    // Plus some more standard stuff

};
```

The class has **CRecordset** as a base class and provides the functionality for retrieving data from the database. The constructor for the class accepts a pointer to a **CDatabase** object that is set to **NULL** as a default. The parameter to the constructor allows a **CProductSet** object to be created for a **CDatabase** object that already exists, which allows an existing connection to a database to be re-used. Opening a connection to a database is a lengthy business, so it's advantageous to re-use a database connection when you can.

If no pointer is passed to the constructor, as will be the case for the **m_productSet** member of the document class **CDBSampleDoc**, the framework will automatically create a **CDatabase** object for you and call the **GetDefaultConnect()** function member of **CProductSet** to define the connection. The implementation of this function provided by AppWizard is shown over the page.

```
CString CProductSet::GetDefaultConnect()
{
    return _T("ODBC;DSN=Sample Data");
}
```

This function is a pure virtual function in the base class, and so must always be implemented in a derived recordset class. The implementation provided by AppWizard will return the text string shown to the framework. This identifies our database by name and enables the framework to create a **CDatabase** object to provide the database connection automatically.

In practice, it's usually necessary to supply a user ID and a password before access to a database is permitted. You can add this information to the string returned by the **GetDefaultConnect()** function. Where this is necessary, you specify your user ID by adding **UID =** and your ID following the **DSN =** part of the string, and you specify the password by adding **PWD =** followed by your password. Each piece of the string is separated from the next by a semicolon. For example, if your user ID is Reuben and your password is Hype, you could specify these in the **return** statement in **GetDefaultConnect()** as:

```
return _T("ODBC;DSN=Sample Data ; UID=Reuben ; PWD=Hype");
```

You can also make the framework pop up a dialog for the user to select the database name from the list of registered database sources by writing the return as:

```
return _T("ODBC;");
```

Querying the Database

The **CProductSet** class includes a data member for each field in the **Products** table. AppWizard obtains the field names from the database and uses these to name the corresponding data members of the class. They appear in the block of code delimited by the **AFX_FIELD** comments in the following:

```
class CProductSet : public CRecordset
{
public:
    CProductSet(CDatabase* pDatabase = NULL);
    DECLARE_DYNAMIC(CProductSet)

// Field/Param Data
    //{{AFX_FIELD(CProductSet, CRecordset)
    long      m_ProductID;
    CString   m_ProductName;
    long      m_SupplierID;
    long      m_CategoryID;
    CString   m_QuantityPerUnit;
    CString   m_UnitPrice;
    int       m_UnitsInStock;
    int       m_UnitsOnOrder;
    int       m_ReorderLevel;
    BOOL      m_Discontinued;
    //}}AFX_FIELD

// Overrides
// ClassWizard generated virtual function overrides
    //{{AFX_VIRTUAL(CProductSet)
```

```
   public:
   virtual CString GetDefaultConnect();     // Default connection string
   virtual CString GetDefaultSQL();         // default SQL for Recordset
   virtual void DoFieldExchange(CFieldExchange* pFX);// RFX support
   //}}AFX_VIRTUAL

// Implementation
#ifdef _DEBUG
   virtual void AssertValid() const;
   virtual void Dump(CDumpContext& dc) const;
#endif
};
```

The type of each data member is set to correspond with the field type for the corresponding field in the **Products** table. You may not want all these fields in practice, but you shouldn't delete them willy-nilly in the class definition. As you will see shortly, they are referenced in other places, so always use ClassWizard to delete fields that you don't want. A further caveat is that you must not delete primary keys. If you do, the recordset won't work, so you need to be sure which fields are primary keys before chopping out what you don't want.

The SQL operation which applies to the recordset to populate these data members is specified in the **GetDefaultSQL()** function. The implementation that AppWizard has supplied for this is:

```
CString CProductSet::GetDefaultSQL()
{
    return _T("[Products]");
}
```

The string returned is obviously obtained from the table you selected during the creation of the project. The square brackets have been included to provide for the possibility of the table name containing blanks. If you had selected several tables in Step 2 of the project creation process, they would all be inserted here, separated by commas, with each table name enclosed within square brackets.

The **GetDefaultSQL()** function is called by the framework when it constructs the SQL statement to be applied for the recordset. The framework slots the string returned by this function into a skeleton SQL statement with the form:

```
SELECT * FROM < String returned by GetDefaultSQL()> ;
```

This looks very simplistic, and it is, but we can add **WHERE** and **ORDER BY** clauses to the operation, as you'll see later.

Data Transfer between the Database and the Recordset

The transfer of data from the database to the recordset, and vice versa, is accomplished by the **DoFieldExchange()** member of the **CProductSet** class. The implementation of this function provided by AppWizard is:

```
void CProductSet::DoFieldExchange(CFieldExchange* pFX)
{
    //{{AFX_FIELD_MAP(CProductSet)
    pFX->SetFieldType(CFieldExchange::outputColumn);
    RFX_Long(pFX, _T("[ProductID]"), m_ProductID);
    RFX_Text(pFX, _T("[ProductName]"), m_ProductName);
```

683

```
        RFX_Long(pFX, _T("[SupplierID]"), m_SupplierID);
        RFX_Long(pFX, _T("[CategoryID]"), m_CategoryID);
        RFX_Text(pFX, _T("[QuantityPerUnit]"), m_QuantityPerUnit);
        RFX_Text(pFX, _T("[UnitPrice]"), m_UnitPrice);
        RFX_Int(pFX, _T("[UnitsInStock]"), m_UnitsInStock);
        RFX_Int(pFX, _T("[UnitsOnOrder]"), m_UnitsOnOrder);
        RFX_Int(pFX, _T("[ReorderLevel]"), m_ReorderLevel);
        RFX_Bool(pFX, _T("[Discontinued]"), m_Discontinued);
    //}}AFX_FIELD_MAP
}
```

This function is called automatically by the framework to retrieve data from the database and to store data in the database. It works in a similar fashion to the **DoDataExchange()** function we have seen with dialog controls, in that the **pFX** parameter determines whether the operation is a read or a write. Each time it's called, it moves a single record to or from the recordset object.

The first function called is **SetFieldType()** which sets a mode for the **RFX_()** function calls that follow. In this case, the mode is specified as **outputColumn**, which indicates that data is to be exchanged between the database field and the corresponding argument specified in each of the following **RFX_()** function calls.

There are a whole range of **RFX_()** functions for various types of database field. The function call for a particular field will correspond with the data type applicable to that field. The first argument to an **RFX_()** function call is the **pFX** object which determines the direction of data movement. The second argument is the table field name and the third is the data member that is to store that field for the current record.

Understanding the Record View

The purpose of the view class is to display information from the recordset object in the application window, so we need to understand how this works. The bits of the class definition for the **CProductView** class produced by AppWizard that are of primary interest are shown shaded:

```
class CProductView : public CRecordView
{
    protected: // create from serialization only
        CProductView();
        DECLARE_DYNCREATE(CProductView)

    public:
        //{{AFX_DATA(CProductView)
        enum{ IDD = IDD_DBSAMPLE_FORM };
        CProductSet* m_pSet;
            // NOTE: the ClassWizard will add data members here
        //}}AFX_DATA

    // Attributes
    public:
        CDBSampleDoc* GetDocument();

    // Operations
    public:

    // Overrides
```

```
    // ClassWizard generated virtual function overrides
    //{{AFX_VIRTUAL(CProductView)
    public:
        virtual CRecordset* OnGetRecordset();
        virtual BOOL PreCreateWindow(CREATESTRUCT& cs);
    protected:
        virtual void DoDataExchange(CDataExchange* pDX);//DDX/DDV support
        virtual void OnInitialUpdate();//called 1st time after construct
        // plus printing functions...
    //}}AFX_VIRTUAL

    // plus implementation and generated message maps
    // that we have seen with standard view classes...
};
```

The view class for a recordset always needs to be derived because the class has to be customized to display the particular fields from the recordset that we want. The base class, **CRecordView**, includes all the functionality required to manage communications with the recordset. All we need to do is to use ClassWizard to tailor our record view class to suit our application. We'll get to that in a moment.

Note that the constructor is **protected**. This is because objects of this class are expected to be created from serialization, which is a default assumption for record view classes. When we add further record views to our application, we'll need to change the default access for their constructors to **public** because we'll be creating the views ourselves.

In the block bounded by the comments containing **AFX_DATA**, the enumeration adds the ID, **IDD_DBSAMPLE_FORM**, to the class. This is the ID for a blank dialog that AppWizard has included in the program. We'll need to add controls to this dialog to display the database fields from the **Products** table that we want displayed. The dialog ID is passed to the base class, **CRecordView**, in the initialization list of the constructor for our view class:

```
CProductView::CProductView():CRecordView(CProductView::IDD)
{
    //{{AFX_DATA_INIT(CProductView)
        // NOTE: the ClassWizard will add member initialization here
    m_pSet = NULL;
    //}}AFX_DATA_INIT
    // TODO: add construction code here
}
```

This links the view class to the dialog, which is necessary to enable the mechanism which transfers data between the recordset object and the view object to work.

There is also a pointer to a **CProductSet** object, **m_pSet**, in the **AFX_DATA** block of the class definition, which is initialized to **NULL** in the constructor. A more useful value for this pointer is set in the **OnInitialUpdate()** member of the class, which has been implemented as:

```
void CProductView::OnInitialUpdate()
{
    m_pSet = &GetDocument()->m_productSet;
    CRecordView::OnInitialUpdate();
}
```

This function is called when the record view object is created and sets **m_pSet** to the address of the **m_productSet** member of the document, thus tying the view to the product set object.

The transfer of data between the data members in the **CProductSet** object that correspond to fields in the **Products** table, and the controls in the dialog associated with the **CProductView** object, will be managed by the **DoDataExchange()** member of **CProductView**. The code in this function to do this is not in place yet, since we first need to add the controls to the dialog that are going to display the data and then use ClassWizard to link the controls to the recordset data members. Let's do that next.

Creating the View Dialog

The first step is to place the controls on the dialog, so go to ResourceView, expand the list of Dialog resources and double-click on **IDD_DBSAMPLE_FORM**. You can delete the static text object with the TODO message from the dialog. If you double-click on the dialog, you can view its properties, as shown here:

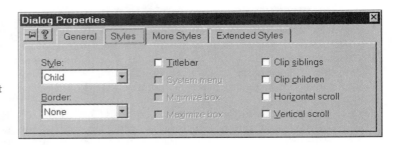

The Style: option has been set to Child because the dialog is going to be a child window and will fill the client area. The Border: style has also been set to None because if it fills the client area the dialog doesn't need a border.

We'll add a static text control to identify each field from the recordset that we want to display, plus an edit control to display it. The tab order of the text control should be such that each static text control immediately precedes the corresponding control displaying the data in sequence. This is because ClassWizard will determine the data member name to be associated with each control that is to display a field from the text in the static control immediately preceding it. The text you choose for the static control is, therefore, most important if this is to work.

You can add each static control, followed immediately by the corresponding edit control, to create the tab order that you want, or you can simply fix the tab order at the end using the Layout/Tab Order menu option.

You can enlarge the dialog by dragging its borders and then place controls on the dialog as shown on opposite page:

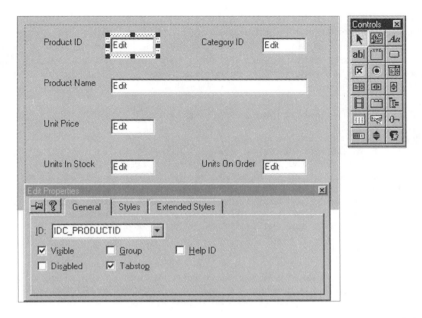

You can add the text to each static control by just typing it as soon as the control has been placed on the dialog. The Properties dialog box will open automatically. As you see, the text for each static control corresponds to the field name in the database. You need to make sure that all the edit controls have different IDs. It's helpful to use the field name as part of the control ID, as shown in the Properties dialog above. You need not worry about the IDs for the static controls, since they are not referenced in the program. After you have arranged the controls, you should check the tab order to make sure that each static control has a sequence number one less than its corresponding edit control.

You can add other fields to the dialog if you want. The one that is most important for the rest of our example is the **Product ID**, so you must include that. Save the dialog and then we can move on to that the last step, which is to link the controls to the variables in the recordset class.

Linking the Controls to the Recordset

Linking the controls to the data members of **CProductSet** is simplicity itself. Just double-click on the **Product ID** edit control while holding down the *Ctrl* key and you'll see the dialog box shown here:

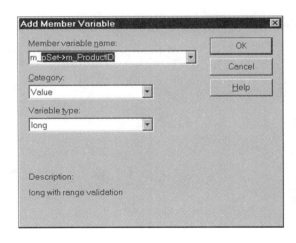

ClassWizard has filled in all the required values for you using the text from the preceding static control and the information from **CProductSet**. All you need to do is to verify that the variable name is correct - it should be if you put the right text in the static control - and click on OK. You then need to repeat this for the other edit controls on your dialog. This will enable ClassWizard to fill out the code for the **DoDataExchange()** function in the **CRecordView** class, which will now be implemented as:

```
void CProductView::DoDataExchange(CDataExchange* pDX)
{
    CRecordView::DoDataExchange(pDX);
    //{{AFX_DATA_MAP(CProductView)
    DDX_FieldText(pDX, IDC_PRODUCTID, m_pSet->m_ProductID, m_pSet);
    DDX_FieldText(pDX, IDC_CATEGORYID, m_pSet->m_CategoryID, m_pSet);
    DDX_FieldText(pDX, IDC_PRODUCTNAME, m_pSet->m_ProductName, m_pSet);
    DDX_FieldText(pDX, IDC_UNITPRICE, m_pSet->m_UnitPrice, m_pSet);
    DDX_FieldText(pDX, IDC_UNITSINSTOCK, m_pSet->m_UnitsInStock, m_pSet);
    DDX_FieldText(pDX, IDC_UNITSONORDER, m_pSet->m_UnitsOnOrder, m_pSet);
    //}}AFX_DATA_MAP
}
```

This function works in the same way you have seen previously with dialog controls. Each **DDX_()** function transfers data between the control and the corresponding data member of the **CProductSet** class which is accessed through the pointer **m_pSet**.

The complete mechanism for data transfer between the database and the dialog owned by the **CProductView** object is illustrated below:

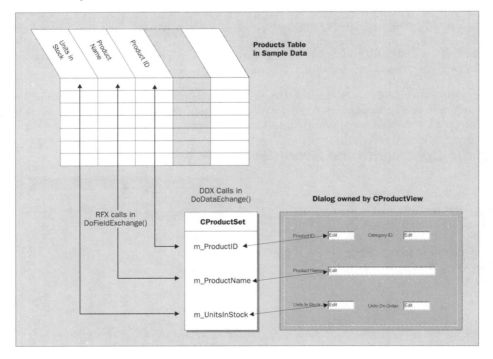

The recordset class and the record view class cooperate to enable data to be transferred between the database and the controls in the dialog. The **CProductSet** class handles transfers between the database and its data members and the **CProductView** deals with transfers between the data members of **CProductSet** and the controls in the dialog.

Exercising the Example

You can now run the example. Just build it in the normal way and then execute it. The application should display a window similar to that shown here:

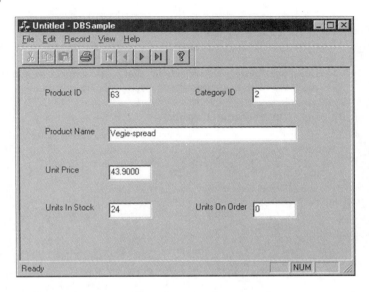

The **CRecordView** base class automatically implements toolbar buttons that step from one record in the recordset to the next or to the previous record. There are also toolbar buttons to move directly to the first or last record in the recordset. You'll notice that the products are in a somewhat arbitrary order. It would be nice to have them sorted in **Product ID** sequence, so let's see how we can do that.

Sorting a Recordset

As we saw earlier, the data is retrieved from the database by the recordset, using an SQL **SELECT** statement which is generated by the framework using the **GetDefaultSQL()** member. We can add an **ORDER BY** clause to the statement generated by setting a value in the **m_strSort** member of **CProductSet**, which is inherited from **CRecordSet**. This will cause the output table from the query to be sorted, based on the string stored in **m_strSort**. We only need to set the **m_strSort** member to a string that contains the field name that we want to sort on. The framework will provide the **ORDER BY** keywords. But where should we add the code to do this?

The transfer of data between the database and the recordset occurs when the **Open()** member of the recordset object is called. In our program, the **Open()** function member of the recordset object is called by the **OnInitialUpdate()** member of the base class to our view class, **CRecordView**. We can, therefore, put the code for setting the sort specification in the **OnInitialUpdate()** member of the **CProductView** class, as shown on the next page.

```
void CProductView::OnInitialUpdate()
{
    m_pSet = &GetDocument()->m_productSet;
    m_pSet->m_strSort = "[ProductID]";          // Set the sort fields
    CRecordView::OnInitialUpdate();
}
```

We just set **m_strSort** in the recordset to the name of the **ProductID** field. Square brackets
are useful, even when there are no blanks in a name, because they differentiate strings
containing these names from other strings, so you can immediately pick out the field names.
They are, of course, optional if there are no blanks in the field name.

If there was more than one field that you wanted to sort on here, you would just include each
of the field names in the string separated by commas.

Modifying the Window Caption

There is one other thing we could add to this function at this point. The caption for the
window would be better if it showed the name of the table being displayed. We can fix this by
adding code to set the title in the document object:

```
void CProductView::OnInitialUpdate()
{
    m_pSet = &GetDocument()->m_productSet;
    m_pSet->m_strSort = "[ProductID]";  // Set the sort fields

    // Set the document title to the table name
    if (m_pSet->IsOpen())                      // Verify the recordset is open
    {
        CString strTitle = _T("Table Name");   // Set basic title string
        CString strTable = m_pSet->GetTableName();
        if (!strTable.IsEmpty())               // Verify we have a table name
            strTitle += _T(":") + strTable; // and add to basic title
        GetDocument()->SetTitle(strTitle); // Set the document title
    }
    CRecordView::OnInitialUpdate();
}
```

After checking that the recordset is indeed open, we initialize a local **CString** object with a
basic title string. We then get the name of the table from the recordset object by calling its
GetTableName() member. In general, you should check that you do get a string returned from
the **GetTableName()** function. Various conditions can arise that will prevent a table name from
being set, for instance, if there is more than one table involved in the recordset. After appending
a colon followed by the table name we have retrieved to the basic title in **strTitle**, we set the
result as the document title by calling the document's **SetTitle()** member.

If you rebuild the application and run it again, it will work as before, but with a new window
caption and with the product IDs in ascending sequence.

Using a Second Recordset Object

Now that we can view all the products in the database, a reasonable extension of the program
would be to add the ability to view all the orders for any particular product. To do this, we'll
add another recordset class to handle orders information from the database and a complementary
view class to display some of the fields from the recordset.

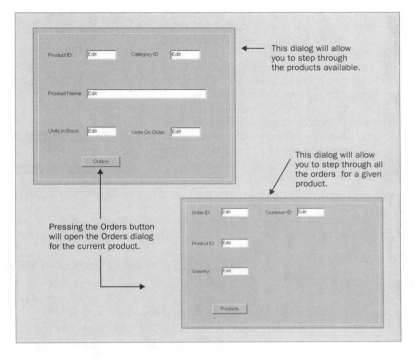

We'll also add a button to the **Products** dialog to enable you to switch to the **Orders** dialog when you want to view the orders for the current product. This will enable us to operate with the arrangement shown in the diagram:

This dialog will allow you to step through the products available.

This dialog will allow you to step through all the orders for a given product.

Pressing the Orders button will open the Orders dialog for the current product.

The Products dialog will be the starting position. You will be able to step backwards and forwards through all the available products. Clicking the Orders button will switch you to the dialog where you'll be able to view all the orders for the current product. You will be able to return to the Products dialog by clicking the Products button.

Adding a Recordset Class

We start by adding the recordset class using ClassWizard, so click on the ClassWizard toolbar button. Then click on the Add Class... button in the ClassWizard dialog and select New... from the pop-up. In the dialog, enter the name of the class as **COrderSet** and select the base class from the drop-down list box, as shown here:

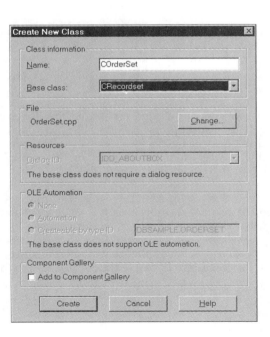

Make sure that the Add to Component Gallery check box is unchecked if you don't want it cluttered up with miscellaneous classes. If you now select the Create button, ClassWizard will take you to the dialog to select the database for the recordset class. Select Sample Data from the list box and leave the Recordset type as Snapshot, as before. Then click on the OK button to move to the table selection dialog shown here:

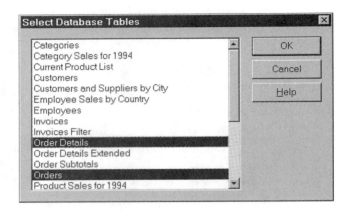

We'll select two tables to associate with the **COrderSet** class, so select the Orders and Order Details table names. You can then click the OK button to complete the process.

You can examine what has been created through ClassWizard. If you switch to the Member Variables tab, you'll see the dialog shown here:

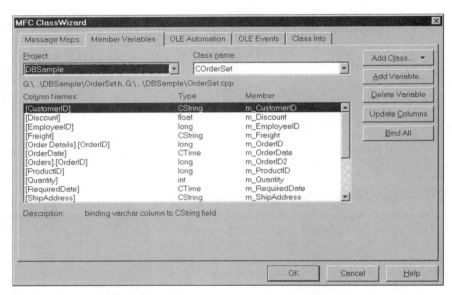

ClassWizard has created a data member for every field in each of the tables. Note that the OrderID field appears in both tables, so ClassWizard identifies these by prefixing the table name to the field names in each case. The data member for the OrderID field in the Orders table is differentiated from the member for the corresponding field in the Order Details table by adding a 2 to the name created from the field name.

If you don't want all these fields, you can delete any of them by selecting the appropriate record in the list and then clicking the Delete Variable button. You should, however, take care not to delete any variables that are primary keys. When you delete a data member for a table field, ClassWizard will take care of deleting the initialization for it in the class constructor and the **RFX_()** call for it in the **DoFieldExchange()** member function. The variables that we need are **m_OrderID**, **m_OrderID2**, **m_ProductID**, **m_Quantity** and **m_CustomerID**.

You can now close ClassWizard by clicking the OK button. To hook the new recordset to the document, you need to add a data member to the definition of the **CDBSampleDoc** class, so right-click the class name in ClassView and select Add Variable... from the pop-up. Specify the type as **COrderSet** and the variable name as **m_OrderSet**. You can leave it as a **public** member of the class. After clicking OK to finish adding the data member to the document, you need to make sure that the compiler understands that **COrderSet** is a class before it gets to compiling the **CBSampleDoc** class. The easiest way to ensure this is to add an **#include** statement for the definition of the **COrderSet** class to the top of **DBSampleDoc.h**:

```
#include "OrderSet.h"
class CDBSampleDoc : public Cdocument
{ // Rest of class definition }
```

Adding a Record View Class

Now, you need to create a dialog resource. You need to do this before you create the view class so that ClassWizard can automatically connect the dialog to the class for you.

Creating the Dialog Resource

Switch to ResourceView, right-click on the Dialog folder and select Insert Dialog from the pop-up. You can delete both of the default buttons from the dialog. Now change the name and styles for the dialog, so double-click on it to display the Properties box. Change the dialog ID to **IDD_ORDERS_FORM**. You also need to change the dialog style to Child and the border style to None. You do this on the Styles tab, as shown below:

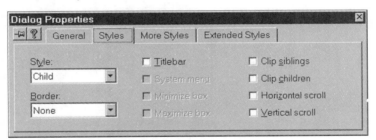

You're now ready to populate the dialog with controls for the fields that you want to display from the **Orders** and **Order Details** tables. If you switch to ClassView and extend the **COrderSet** part of the classes tree, you'll be able to see the names of the variables concerned while you are working on the dialog. Add controls to the dialog as shown here:

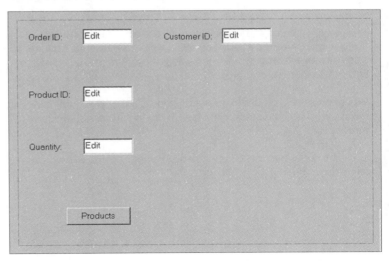

693

Here, we have four edit controls for the **OrderID**, **CustomerID**, **ProductID**, and **Quantity** fields from the tables associated with the **COrderSet** class, together with static controls to identify them. You can add a few more if you wish. Don't forget to modify the IDs for the edit controls so that they are representative of the purpose of the control. You can use the table field names as we did previously. You also need to check the tab order and verify that each static control immediately precedes the associated edit control in sequence. If they don't, just click on them in the sequence that you want.

The button control labeled Products will be used to return to the **Products** table view, so modify the ID for this button to **IDC_PRODUCTS**. When everything is arranged to your liking, save the dialog resource.

Creating the Record View Class

To create the view class for the recordset, right-click on the dialog and select ClassWizard... from the pop-up. You will then see a dialog offering you three options for identifying a class to associate with the dialog. If you elect to create a new class, you'll see the dialog for Create New Class:

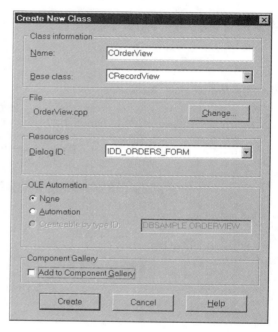

You need to enter the class name as **COrderView** and select the base class from the drop-down list box as **CRecordView**. You also need to select the ID for the dialog you have just created, **IDD_ORDERS_FORM**, from the Dialog ID: list box. As before, make sure that this class is not being added to the component gallery.

When you click on the Create button, ClassWizard will automatically choose **COrderSet** as the recordset class to be associated with the view class, so all you have to do is click the OK button.

You can see what the characteristics of the **COrderView** class are if you look at the Class Info tab shown on the opposite page:

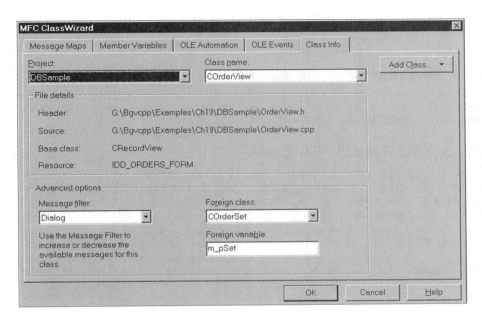

This tells you everything you need to know. The view class, which is derived from **CRecordView**, is hooked to the dialog resource you created with the ID, **IDD_ORDERS_FORM**, and has the **COrderSet** class associated with it. A data member **m_pSet** has also been added to hold the address of the associated **COrderSet** object.

Strangely, ClassWizard adds an unorthodox **#include** statement to the beginning of the **.h** file for **COrderView** which specifies a fully qualified name for the **OrderSet.h** file, even if the file is in the project directory. This can be a nuisance, particularly if you move the folder containing the project to somewhere else. It can also cause you to have multiple definitions of the **COrderSet** class in your program, about which the compiler will certainly complain by issuing an error message. I suggest that you simply alter the **#include** statement so that it contains only the name of the **OrderSet.h** file as shown below:

```
#include "OrderSet.h"
```

This is preferable to the fully qualified version, which probably looks like this:

```
#include "C:\MSDEV\Projects\DBSample\OrderSet.h"
```

Now would also be a good time to surround the **OrderSet.h** file with the standard preprocessor directives to prevent the redefinition of the class in case the file gets included more than once. So open that file and add the code that you see below to the very beginning and end of the file.

```
#ifndef CORDERSET_H
#define CORDERSET_H

class COrderSet : public CRecordset
{
    // rest of class definition
```

```
};
```

```
#endif
```

Linking the Dialog Controls to the Recordset

To link the controls to the recordset, you follow the same procedure as we did for the **CProductView** class. Go back to the dialog **IDD_ORDERS_FORM** and double-click each edit control while holding down the *Ctrl* key.

Customizing the Record View Class

As it stands, the SQL **SELECT** operation for a **COrderSet** object will produce a table which will contain all combinations of records from the two tables involved. This could be a lot of records, so we must add the equivalent of a **WHERE** clause to the query to restrict the records selected to those that make sense. There is another problem too. When we switch from the **Products** table display, we don't want to look at just any old orders. We want to see precisely those orders for the product ID we were looking at, which amounts to selecting only those orders that have the same product ID as that contained in the current **CProductSet** record. This is also effected through a **WHERE** clause. In the MFC context, the **WHERE** clause for a **SELECT** operation for a recordset is called a **filter**.

Adding a Filter to the Recordset

Adding a filter to the query is accomplished by assigning a string to the **m_strFilter** member of the recordset object. This member is inherited from the base class, **CRecordSet**. As with the **ORDER BY** clause, which we added by setting a value to the **m_strSort** member of the recordset, the place to implement this is in the **OnInitialUpdate()** member of the record view class, just before the base class function is called.

We want to set two conditions in the filter. One is to restrict the records generated in the recordset to those where the **OrderID** field in the **Orders** table is equal to the field with the same name in the **Order Details** table. We can write this condition as:

```
[Orders].[OrderID] = [Order  Details].[OrderID]
```

The other condition we want to apply is that, for the records meeting the first condition, we only want those with a **ProductID** field that is equal to the **ProductID** field in the current record in the recordset object displaying the **Products** table. This means that we need to have the **ProductID** field from the **COrderSet** object compared to a variable value. The variable in this operation is called a parameter and the condition in the filter is written in a special way:

```
ProductID  =  ?
```

The question mark represents a parameter value for the filter and the records that will be selected are those where the **ProductID** field equals the parameter value. The value that is to replace the question mark will be set in the **DoFieldExchange()** member of the recordset. We'll implement this in a moment, but first let's complete the specification of the filter.

We can define the string for the filter variable that incorporates both the conditions that we need with the statement:

```
// Set the filter as product ID field with equal order IDs
m_pSet->m_strFilter =
    "[ProductID] = ? AND [Orders].[OrderID] = [Order Details].OrderID";
```

We'll insert this into the **OnInitialUpdate()** member of the **COrderView** class, but first let's finish setting the parameter for the filter.

Defining the Filter Parameter

We need to add a data member to the **COrderSet** class that will store the current value of the **ProductID** field from the **CProductSet** object, and will also act as the parameter to substitute for the **?** in our filter for the **COrderSet** object. So right-click on the **COrderSet** class name in ClassView and select Add Variable from the pop-up. The variable type needs to be the same as that of the **m_ProductID** member of the **CProductSet** class, which is **long**, and you can specify the name as **m_ProductIDparam**. You can leave it as a **public** member. Now we need to initialize this data member in the constructor and set the parameter count, so add the code shown below:

```
COrderSet::COrderSet(CDatabase* pdb)
    : CRecordset(pdb)
{
    //{{AFX_FIELD_INIT(COrderSet)
    m_OrderID = 0;
    m_ProductID = 0;
    m_UnitPrice = _T("");
    m_Quantity = 0;
    m_Discount = 0.0f;
    m_OrderID2 = 0;
    m_CustomerID = _T("");
    m_EmployeeID = 0;
    m_ShipVia = 0;
    m_Freight = _T("");
    m_ShipName = _T("");
    m_ShipAddress = _T("");
    m_ShipCity = _T("");
    m_ShipRegion = _T("");
    m_ShipPostalCode = _T("");
    m_ShipCountry = _T("");
    m_nFields = 19;
    //}}AFX_FIELD_INIT

    m_ProductIDparam = 0L;      // Set initial parameter value
    m_nParams = 1;              // Set number of parameters

    m_nDefaultType = snapshot;
}
```

All of the unshaded code was supplied by ClassWizard to initialize the data members corresponding to the fields in the recordset and to specify the type as **snapshot**. Our code initializes the parameter to zero and sets the count of the number of parameters to **1**. The **m_nParams** variable is inherited from the base class, **CRecordSet**. Since there is a parameter count, evidently you can have more than one parameter in the filter for the recordset.

To identify the **m_ProductIDparam** variable in the class as a parameter to be substituted in the filter for the **COrderSet** object, we must also add some code to the **DoFieldExchange()** member of the class.

697

```
void COrderSet::DoFieldExchange(CFieldExchange* pFX)
{
    //{{AFX_FIELD_MAP(COrderSet)
    pFX->SetFieldType(CFieldExchange::outputColumn);
    RFX_Long(pFX, _T("[Order Details].[OrderID]"), m_OrderID);
    RFX_Long(pFX, _T("[ProductID]"), m_ProductID);
    RFX_Text(pFX, _T("[UnitPrice]"), m_UnitPrice);
    RFX_Int(pFX, _T("[Quantity]"), m_Quantity);
    RFX_Single(pFX, _T("[Discount]"), m_Discount);
    RFX_Long(pFX, _T("[Orders].[OrderID]"), m_OrderID2);
    RFX_Text(pFX, _T("[CustomerID]"), m_CustomerID);
    RFX_Long(pFX, _T("[EmployeeID]"), m_EmployeeID);
    RFX_Date(pFX, _T("[OrderDate]"), m_OrderDate);
    RFX_Date(pFX, _T("[RequiredDate]"), m_RequiredDate);
    RFX_Date(pFX, _T("[ShippedDate]"), m_ShippedDate);
    RFX_Long(pFX, _T("[ShipVia]"), m_ShipVia);
    RFX_Text(pFX, _T("[Freight]"), m_Freight);
    RFX_Text(pFX, _T("[ShipName]"), m_ShipName);
    RFX_Text(pFX, _T("[ShipAddress]"), m_ShipAddress);
    RFX_Text(pFX, _T("[ShipCity]"), m_ShipCity);
    RFX_Text(pFX, _T("[ShipRegion]"), m_ShipRegion);
    RFX_Text(pFX, _T("[ShipPostalCode]"), m_ShipPostalCode);
    RFX_Text(pFX, _T("[ShipCountry]"), m_ShipCountry);
    //}}AFX_FIELD_MAP

    // Set the field type as parameter
    pFX->SetFieldType(CFieldExchange::param);
    RFX_Long(pFX, "ProductIDParam", m_ProductIDparam);
}
```

The ClassWizard has provided code to transfer data between the database and the field variables it has added to the class. There is one **RFX_()** function call for each data member of the recordset.

Other than the comment, we only needed to add two lines to the code that ClassWizard has generated to specify **m_ProductIDparam** as a filter. The first line of code calls the **SetFieldType()** member of the **pFX** object. to set the mode for the following **RFX_()** calls to **param**. The effect of this is to cause the third argument in any succeeding **RFX_()** calls to be interpreted as a parameter that is to replace a **?** in the filter for the recordset. If you have more than one parameter, the parameters substitute for the question marks in the **m_strFilter** string in sequence from left to right, so it's important to ensure that the **RFX_()** calls are in the right order. With the mode set to **param**, the second argument in the **RFX_()** call is ignored, so you could put **NULL** here, or some other string if you want.

Initializing the Record View

We now need to add the code to the **OnInitialUpdate()** member of the **COrderView** class. As well as specifying the filter, we can also define a value for **m_strSort** to sort the records in **OrderID** sequence and add the code to change the window caption to match the tables we are dealing with:

```
void COrderView::OnInitialUpdate()
{
    BeginWaitCursor();        // This could take time so start the wait cursor
```

```
        CDBSampleDoc* pDoc = (CDBSampleDoc*)GetDocument();//Get the doc pointer
        m_pSet = &pDoc->m_OrderSet;                    // Get a pointer to the recordset

        // Use the DB that is open for products recordset
        m_pSet->m_pDatabase = pDoc->m_productSet.m_pDatabase;

        // Set the current product ID as parameter
        m_pSet->m_ProductIDparam = pDoc->m_productSet.m_ProductID;

        // Set the filter as product ID field
        m_pSet->m_strFilter =
            "[ProductID] = ? AND [Orders].[OrderID] = [Order Details].[OrderID]";
        GetRecordset();                                // Get the recordset

        // Now fix the caption
        if (m_pSet->IsOpen())
        {
            CString strTitle = "Table Name:";
            CString strTable = m_pSet->GetTableName();    //Get the table name

            //If the recordset uses 2 or more tables, the name will be empty
            if (!strTable.IsEmpty())
                strTitle += _T(":") + strTable;    // It is not so use the name
            else
                strTitle += _T("Orders - Multiple Tables");// Use generic name

            GetDocument()->SetTitle(strTitle);          // Set the document title
        }
    CRecordView::OnInitialUpdate();
    EndWaitCursor();
}
```

The version of the **COrderSet** class that has been implemented by ClassWizard does not override the **GetDocument()** member because it is not associated with the document class. As a result, we need to cast the pointer from the base class **GetDocument()** member to a pointer to a **CDBSampleDoc** object. Alternatively, you could add an override version of **GetDocument()** to **COrderSet** to do the cast.

Because we refer to the **CDBSampleDoc** class, you need to add three **#include** statements to the beginning of the **COrderView.cpp** file:

```
#include "ProductSet.h"
#include "OrderSet.h"
#include "DBSampleDoc.h"
```

The **BeginWaitCursor()** call added by ClassWizard at the start of the **OnInitialUpdate()** function displays the hourglass cursor while this function is executing. The reason for this is that, especially when multiple tables are involved, this function can take an appreciable time to execute. The processing of the query and the transfer of data to the recordset all takes place in here. The cursor is returned to normal by the **EndWaitCursor()** call.

The first thing that our code does is to set the **m_pDatabase** member of the **COrderSet** object to the same as that for the **CProductSet** object. If we don't do this, the framework will re-open the database when the orders recordset is opened. Since the database has already been opened for the products recordset, this would waste a lot of time.

699

Next, we set the value for the parameter variable to the current value in the **m_ProductID** member of the products recordset. This value will replace the question mark in the filter when the orders recordset is opened and so select the records we want. We then set the filter for the orders recordset to the string we saw earlier.

Next, the **GetRecordSet()** call supplied by ClassWizard is executed. This calls the **OnGetRecordSet()** member which creates a recordset object if there isn't one - in our case there is one because we added it to the document object - and then calls the **Open()** function for the recordset.

Finally, we have the code we saw earlier to define the caption for the window. The test for an empty table name is not strictly necessary, since we know that the table name will be empty because the recordset has two tables specified for it. You could just use the code to explicitly define the caption, but the code shown serves to demonstrate that the table name is indeed empty in this case.

Accessing Multiple Tables

Since we have implemented our program with the single document interface, we have one document and one view. The availability of just one view might appear to be a problem, but we can arrange for the frame window object in our application to create an instance of our **COrderView** class and switch the current window to that when the orders recordset is to be displayed.

We'll need to keep track of what the current window is which we can do by assigning a unique ID to each of the record view windows in our application. At the moment there are two: the product view and the order view. To do this, create a new file called **OurConstants.h** and add the following code to define the window IDs:

```
// Definition of our constants

#ifndef OURCONSTANTS_H
#define OUR_CONSTANTS_H

// Arbitrary constants to identify record views
const UINT PRODUCT_VIEW = 1U;
const UINT ORDER_VIEW = 2U;

///////////////////////////////////////////////////

#endif
```

We can now use one of these constants to identify each view and record the ID of the current view in the frame window object. To do this, add a **public** data member to the **CMainFrame** class of type **UINT** and give it the name **m_CurrentViewID**. Once you have done that, you can initialize it in the constructor for **CMainFrame**, by adding code as follows:

```
CMainFrame::CMainFrame()
{
    m_CurrentViewID = PRODUCT_VIEW;    // We always start with this view
}
```

Now add an **#include** statement for **OurConstants.h** to the beginning of **MainFrm.cpp** so that the definition of **PRODUCT_VIEW** is available here.

Switching Views

To enable the view switching mechanism, we are going to add a function member to the **CMainFrame** class, **SelectView()**, which will have a parameter defining a view ID. This function will switch from the current view to whatever view is specified by the ID passed as an argument.

Right-click on **CMainFrame** and select Add Function... from the pop-up. You can enter the return type as **void** and the Function Declaration: entry as **SelectView(UINT ViewID)**. The implementation of the function is as follows:

```
void CMainFrame::SelectView(UINT ViewID)
{
   CView* pOldActiveView = GetActiveView();      // Get current view

   // Get pointer to new view if it exists
   // if it doesn't the pointer will be null
   CView* pNewActiveView = (CView*)GetDlgItem(ViewID);

   // If this is 1st time around for the new view,
   // the new view won't exist, so we must create it
   if (pNewActiveView == NULL)
   {
      switch(ViewID)
      {
         case ORDER_VIEW:        // Create an Order view
            pNewActiveView = (CView*)new COrderView;
            break;
         default:
            AfxMessageBox("Invalid View ID");
            return;
      }

      // Switching the views
      // Obtain the current view context to apply to the new view
      CCreateContext context;
      context.m_pCurrentDoc = pOldActiveView->GetDocument();
      pNewActiveView->Create(NULL, NULL, 0L, CFrameWnd::rectDefault,
                                        this, ViewID, &context);

      pNewActiveView->OnInitialUpdate();
   }
   SetActiveView(pNewActiveView);                      // Activate the new view
   pOldActiveView->ShowWindow(SW_HIDE);                // Hide the old view
   pNewActiveView->ShowWindow(SW_SHOW);                // Show the new view
   pOldActiveView->SetDlgCtrlID(m_CurrentViewID);      // Set the old view ID
   pNewActiveView->SetDlgCtrlID(AFX_IDW_PANE_FIRST);
   m_CurrentViewID = ViewID;                           // Save the new view ID
   RecalcLayout();
}
```

The operation of the function falls into three distinct parts:

▶ Getting pointers to the current view and the new view.

▶ Creating the new view if it doesn't exist.

▶ Swapping to the new view in place of the current view.

701

The address of the current active view is supplied by the **GetActiveView()** member of the **CMainFrame** object. To get a pointer to the new view, we call the **GetDlgItem()** member of the frame window object. If a view with the ID specified in the argument to the function exists, it returns the address of the view, otherwise it returns **NULL** and we need to create the new view.

Since we will create a **COrderView** object on the heap here, we need access to the constructor for the class. The default access specification for the constructor **COrderView()** in the class definition is **protected**, so change it to **public** to make creating the view object legal, as in the following code:

```
class COrderView : public CRecordView
{
public:
   COrderView();            // we changed this to public

protected:
   DECLARE_DYNCREATE(COrderView)

   // rest of class definition
};
```

After creating a view object, we define a **CCreateContext** object, **context**. This object type ties together the document template, the document, the frame window and the view. Thus, before we create a window for a new view, we need to obtain the **CCreateContext** object for the current view setup. We then use it as an argument in the call to the **Create()** member of the view object which creates the window for the new view to establish a proper relationship with the document template, the document and the frame window. The argument **this** in the call to **Create()** specifies the current frame as the parent window, and the **ViewID** argument specifies the ID of the window. This ID enables the address of the window to be obtained with a subsequent call to the **GetDlgItem()** member of the parent window.

To make the new view the active view, we call the **SetActiveView()** member of **CMainFrame**. The new view will replace the current active view. To display the new view window, we call the **ShowWindow()** member of the view with the argument **SW_SHOW** . To remove the old view window, we call the same function with the argument **SW_HIDE**.

We restore the ID of the old active view to the ID value that we have defined for it from the **m_CurrentViewID** member of the **CMainFrame** class that we added earlier. We also set the ID of the new view to **AFX_IDW_PANE_FIRST** to identify it as the first window for the application. This is necessary because our application only has one view, so the first view is the only view. Lastly, we save our ID for the new window in the **m_CurrentViewID** member, so it's available the next time the current view is replaced.

You must add an **#include** statement for the **OrderView.h** file to beginning of the **MainFrm.cpp** file, so that the **COrderView** class definition is available here. Once you have saved **MainFrm.cpp**, we can move on to adding a button control to the products dialog to link to the order dialog, and adding handlers for this button and its partner on the orders dialog to call the **SelectView()** member of **CMainFrame**.

Enabling the Switching Operation

To do this, go back to ResourceView and open the **IDD_DBSAMPLE_FORM** dialog. You need to add a button control to the dialog as shown on the opposite page:

You can set the ID for the button to **IDC_ORDERS**, consistent with the naming for the other controls in the dialog.

After saving the resource, you can create a handler for the button by double-clicking it while holding down the *Ctrl* key. ClassWizard will add the function **OnOrders()** to the **COrderView** class and this handler will be called when the button is clicked. You only need to add one line of code to complete the handler:

```
void CProductView::OnOrders()
{
    ((CMainFrame*)GetParentFrame())->SelectView(ORDER_VIEW);
}
```

The **GetParentFrame()** member of the view object is inherited from **CWnd**, which is an indirect base class of **CMainFrame**. This function returns a pointer to the parent frame window and we use it to call the **SelectView()** function that we have just added to the **CMainFrame** class. The argument **ORDER_VIEW** will cause the frame window to switch to the orders dialog window. If this is the first time this has occurred, it will create the view object and the window. On the second and subsequent occasions that a switch to the orders view is selected, the existing orders view will be re-used.

You must add the following **#include** statements to the beginning of the **ProductView.cpp** file:

```
#include "OurConstants.h"
#include "MainFrm.h"
```

The next task is to add the handler for the button we previously placed on the **IDD_ORDERS_FORM** dialog. Double-click the button with the *Ctrl* key pressed, as before, and add the following code to the **OnProducts()** handler that is generated in the **COrderView** class.

```
void COrderView::OnProducts()
{
    ((CMainFrame*)GetParentFrame())->SelectView(PRODUCT_VIEW);
}
```

This works in the same way as the previous button control handler. Again, you must add **#include** statements for the **OurConstants.h** and **MainFrm.h** files to the beginning of the **.cpp** file, and then save it.

Handling View Activation

When we switch to a view that already exists, we need to ensure that the recordset is refreshed and that the dialog is re-initialized, so that the correct information is displayed. When an existing view is activated or deactivated, the framework calls the **OnActivateView()** member of the class. We need to override this function in each of our view classes. You should still have the **OrderView.cpp** file displayed, so you can add the function by extending the Messages list box and selecting OnActivateView. Click Yes when asked if you want to add a handler.

You can add the following code to complete the implementation of the function:

```
void COrderView::OnActivateView(BOOL bActivate, CView* pActivateView,
                                CView* pDeactiveView)
{
    if(bActivate)
    {
        // Get a pointer to the document
        CDBSampleDoc* pDoc = (CDBSampleDoc*)GetDocument();

        // Get a pointer to the frame window
        CMainFrame* pMFrame = (CMainFrame*)GetParentFrame();

        // If the last view was the product view, we must re-query
        // the recordset with the product ID from the product recordset
        if(pMFrame->m_CurrentViewID==PRODUCT_VIEW)
        {
            if(!m_pSet->IsOpen())    // Make sure the recordset is open
                return;
            // Set current product ID as parameter
            m_pSet->m_ProductIDparam = pDoc->m_productSet.m_ProductID;
            m_pSet->Requery();       // Get data from the DB

            // If we are past the EOF there are no records
            if(m_pSet->IsEOF())
                AfxMessageBox("No orders for the current product ID");
        }

        // Set the window caption
        CString strTitle = _T("Table Name:");
        CString strTable = m_pSet->GetTableName();
        if(!strTable.IsEmpty())
            strTitle += strTable;
        else
            strTitle += _T("Orders - Multiple Tables");
        pDoc->SetTitle(strTitle);
        CRecordView::OnInitialUpdate();           // Update values in dialog
    }
```

```
        CRecordView::OnActivateView(bActivate, pActivateView, pDeactiveView);
    }
```

We only execute our code if the view is being activated. If this is the case, the **bActivate** argument will be **TRUE**. After getting pointers to the document and the parent frame, we verify that the previous view was the product view, before re-querying the order set. This check is not necessary at present, since the previous view is always the product view but, when we add another view to our application, this will not always be true, so we might as well put the code in now.

To re-query the database, we set the parameter member of **COrderSet**, **m_ProductIDparam**, to the current value of the **m_ProductID** member of the product recordset. This will cause the orders for the current product to be selected. We don't need to set the **m_strFilter** member of the recordset here because that will have been set in the **OnInitialUpdate()** function when the **CRecordView** object was first created. The **IsEOF()** function member of the **COrderSet** object is inherited from **CRecordSet** and will return **TRUE** if the recordset is empty when it is re-queried.

You now need to add the **OnActivate()** function to the **CProductView** class and code it as follows:

```
    void CProductView::OnActivateView(BOOL bActivate, CView* pActivateView,
                                      CView* pDeactiveView)
    {
        if(bActivate)
        {
            // Update the window caption
            CString strTitle = _T("Table Name");
            CString strTable = m_pSet->GetTableName();
            strTitle += _T(":") + strTable;
            GetDocument()->SetTitle(strTitle);
        }

        CRecordView::OnActivateView(bActivate, pActivateView, pDeactiveView);
    }
```

In this case, all we need to do if the view has been activated is to update the window caption. Since the product view is the driving view for the rest of the application, we always want to return the view to its state before it was deactivated. If we do nothing apart from updating the window caption, the view will be displayed in its previous state.

Viewing Orders for a Product

You are now ready to try to build the executable module for the new version of the example. When you run the example, you should be able to see the orders for any product just by clicking the Orders button on the products dialog. A typical view of an order is shown on the following page.

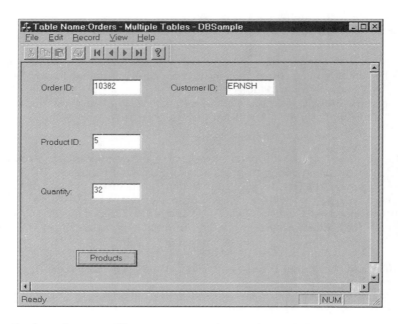

Clicking the Products button will return you to the products dialog, so you can browse further through the products. In this dialog, you can use the toolbar buttons to browse all the orders for the current product.

The Customer ID is a bit cryptic. We could add one more view to display the details of the customer's name and address. It won't be too difficult because we have built the mechanism to switch between views already.

Viewing Customer Details

The basic mechanism that we will add will work through another button control on the order dialog which will switch to a new dialog for customer data. As well as controls to display customer data, we'll add two buttons to the customer dialog, one to return to the order view, and the other to return to the product view. We'll need another view ID corresponding to the customer view, which we can add with the following line in the **OurConstants.h** file:

```
const UINT CUSTOMER_VIEW = 3U;
```

Let's now add the recordset for the customer details.

Adding the Customer Recordset

The process is exactly the same as we followed for the **COrderSet** class. You use the Add Class... button in ClassWizard to define the **CCustomerSet** class with **CRecordSet** specified as the base class. You select the database as Sample Data, as before, and select the Customers table for the recordset. The class should then be created with the data members shown on the opposite page:

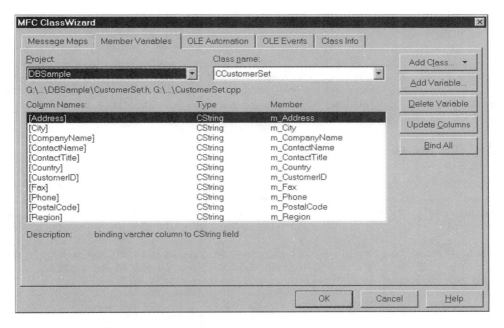

You can click on the OK button to store the class. At this point, you could add a **CCustomerSet** member to the document so that it will be created when the document object is created. Right-click on the **CDBSampleDoc** class name in ClassView and add a variable of type **CCustomerSet** with the name **m_CustomerSet**.

You will also need to add an **#include** statement for **CustomerSet.h** into **DBSampleDoc.h**. After saving all the files you have modified, you can move next to creating the customer dialog resource.

Creating the Customer Dialog Resource

This process is also exactly the same as you went through for the orders dialog. Change to ResourceView and create a new dialog resource with the ID **IDD_CUSTOMER_FORM**, not forgetting to set the style to Child and the border to None in the Properties box for the dialog. After deleting the default buttons, add controls to the dialog to correspond to the field names for the Customers table, as shown here:

707

The two buttons enable you to switch to either the Orders dialog, which will be how you got to here, or directly back to the Products dialog.

Specify the IDs for the controls, using the field names as a basis. You can get help with this by expanding the list of members of **CCustomerSet** in ClassView and keeping that visible while you work on the dialog. You can set the button IDs as **IDC_ORDERS** and **IDC_PRODUCTS**. Remember to check the tab order is as required and then save the dialog resource. Now we're ready to create the view class for the recordset.

Creating the Customer View Class

Right-click the dialog and select ClassWizard... from the pop-up. Create a new class based on **CRecordView** with the name **CCustomerView**, and select the **IDD_CUSTOMER_FORM** as the ID for the dialog to be associated with the class. ClassWizard should automatically choose **CCustomerSet** as the recordset for the view class. Complete the process and click on OK in ClassWizard. You can then associate the edit controls with variables in the recordset.

To tie the controls to the recordset data members, double-click on each edit control in turn with the *Ctrl* key held down. If the tab order for the controls is correct, all the variables should be selected automatically.

You can also process the button controls in the same way to add the **OnOrders()** and **OnProducts()** functions to the class. The code for these is very similar to the corresponding functions in the other views. The code you need to add to **OnOrders()** is:

```
void CCustomerView::OnOrders()
{
    ((CMainFrame*)GetParentFrame())->SelectView(ORDER_VIEW);
}
```

You can add a similar line of code to the **OnProducts()** function:

```
void CCustomerView::OnProducts()
{
    ((CMainFrame*)GetParentFrame())->SelectView(PRODUCT_VIEW);
}
```

We now need to add code to specify a filter for the customer recordset so that we only get the customer details displayed that correspond to the customer ID field from the current order in the **COrderSet** object.

Adding a Filter

We can define the filter in the **OnInitialUpdate()** member of **CCustomerView**. Since we only anticipate one record being returned corresponding to each customer ID, we don't need to worry about sorting. The code you need to add to this function is as follows:

```
void CCustomerView::OnInitialUpdate()
{
    BeginWaitCursor();

    CDBSampleDoc* pDoc = (CDBSampleDoc*)GetDocument();
    m_pSet = &pDoc->m_CustomerSet;  // Initialize the recordset pointer
```

```
    // Set the DB for the customer recordset
    m_pSet->m_pDatabase = pDoc->m_productSet.m_pDatabase;

    // Set the current customer ID as the filter parameter value
    m_pSet->m_CustomerIDparam = pDoc->m_OrderSet.m_CustomerID;
    m_pSet->m_strFilter ="CustomerID = ?";// Filter on CustomerID field

    GetRecordset();
    CRecordView::OnInitialUpdate();
    if (m_pSet->IsOpen())
    {
        CString strTitle = m_pSet->m_pDatabase->GetDatabaseName();
        CString strTable = m_pSet->GetTableName();
        if (!strTable.IsEmpty())
            strTitle += _T(":") + strTable;
        GetDocument()->SetTitle(strTitle);
    }
    EndWaitCursor();
}
```

After getting a pointer to the document, we store the address of the **CCustomerSet** object member of the document in the **m_pSet** member of the view. We know the database is already open so we can set the database pointer in the customer recordset to that stored in the **CProductSet** object.

The parameter for the filter will be defined in the **m_CustomerIDparam** member of **CCustomerSet**. We'll add this member to the class in a moment. It is set to the current value of the **m_CustomerID** member of the **COrderSet** object owned by the document. The filter is defined in such a way that the customer recordset will only contain the record with the same customer ID as that in the current order.

To handle activation of the customer view, you must add the **OnActivateView()** function by selecting it from the Messages drop-down list. You can implement it as follows:

```
void CCustomerView::OnActivateView(BOOL bActivate, CView* pActivateView,
                                                   CView* pDeactiveView)
{
    if(bActivate)
    {
        if(!m_pSet->IsOpen())
            return;
        CDBSampleDoc* pDoc = (CDBSampleDoc*)GetDocument();

        // Set current customer ID as parameter
        m_pSet->m_CustomerIDparam = pDoc->m_OrderSet.m_CustomerID;
        m_pSet->Requery();                 // Get data from the DB
        CRecordView::OnInitialUpdate();   // Redraw the dialog

        // Check for empty recordset
        if(m_pSet->IsEOF())
            AfxMessageBox("No customer details for the current customer ID");

        CString strTitle = _T("Table Name:");
        CString strTable = m_pSet->GetTableName();
        if (!strTable.IsEmpty())
            strTitle += strTable;
```

```
        else
            strTitle += _T("Multiple Tables");
        pDoc->SetTitle(strTitle);
    }

    CRecordView::OnActivateView(bActivate, pActivateView, pDeactiveView);
}
```

If this function is called because the view has been activated, **bActivate** will have the value
TRUE. In this case, we set the filter parameter from the order recordset and re-query the
database.

You will need to add the following **#include** statements to the beginning of the
CustomerView.cpp file:

```
#include "ProductSet.h"
#include "OrderSet.h"
#include "CustomerSet.h"
#include "DBSampleDoc.h"
#include "OurConstants.h"
#include "MainFrm.h"
```

The first three are required because of classes used in the definition of the document class.

At this point, you could save the current file and return to the definition of the
CCustomerView class. Delete any **#include** that has been added to the **.H** file. Add a
declaration for the **CCustomerSet** class just before the definition for the **CCustomerView** class.
You also need to change the constructor from **protected** access specification to **public** because
we need to be able to create a customer view object in the **SelectView()** member of
CMainFrame.

Implementing the Filter Parameter

Add a public variable of type **CString** to the **CCustomerSet** class to correspond with the type
of the **m_CustomerID** member of the recordset and give it the name **m_CustomerIDparam**. You
can initialize this in the constructor and set the parameter count as follows:

```
CCustomerSet::CCustomerSet(CDatabase* pdb): CRecordset(pdb)
{
    //{{AFX_FIELD_INIT(CCustomerSet)
    m_CustomerID = _T("");
    m_CompanyName = _T("");
    m_ContactName = _T("");
    m_ContactTitle = _T("");
    m_Address = _T("");
    m_City = _T("");
    m_Region = _T("");
    m_PostalCode = _T("");
    m_Country = _T("");
    m_Phone = _T("");
    m_Fax = _T("");
    m_nFields = 11;
    //}}AFX_FIELD_INIT
    m_CustomerIDparam = _T("");      // Initial customer ID parameter
    m_nParams = 1;                   // Number of parameters
```

710

```
        m_nDefaultType = snapshot;
    }
```

ClassWizard uses the comments containing **AFX_FIELD_INIT** as markers for updating the constructor when data members for table fields are added or deleted, so we add our initialization code outside that block. We set the parameter to an empty string and the parameter count in **m_nParams** to **1**.

To set up the parameter, you add statements to the **DoFieldExchange()** member, as before:

```
    void CCustomerSet::DoFieldExchange(CFieldExchange* pFX)
    {
        //{{AFX_FIELD_MAP(CCustomerSet)
        pFX->SetFieldType(CFieldExchange::outputColumn);
        RFX_Text(pFX, _T("[CustomerID]"), m_CustomerID);
        RFX_Text(pFX, _T("[CompanyName]"), m_CompanyName);
        RFX_Text(pFX, _T("[ContactName]"), m_ContactName);
        RFX_Text(pFX, _T("[ContactTitle]"), m_ContactTitle);
        RFX_Text(pFX, _T("[Address]"), m_Address);
        RFX_Text(pFX, _T("[City]"), m_City);
        RFX_Text(pFX, _T("[Region]"), m_Region);
        RFX_Text(pFX, _T("[PostalCode]"), m_PostalCode);
        RFX_Text(pFX, _T("[Country]"), m_Country);
        RFX_Text(pFX, _T("[Phone]"), m_Phone);
        RFX_Text(pFX, _T("[Fax]"), m_Fax);
        //}}AFX_FIELD_MAP
        pFX->SetFieldType(CFieldExchange::param);        // Set parameter mode
        RFX_Text(pFX, _T("CustomerIDParam"), m_CustomerIDparam);
    }
```

After setting the **param** mode by calling the **SetFieldType()** member of the **pFX** object, we call the **RFX_TEXT()** function to pass the parameter value for substitution in the filter. We use **RFX_TEXT()** because the parameter variable is of type **CString**. There are various **RFX_()** functions supporting a range of parameter types.

Once you have completed this modification, you can save the **CustomerSet.cpp** file.

Linking the Order Dialog to the Customer Dialog

To permit a switch to the customer dialog, we require a button control on the **IDD_ORDER_FORM** dialog, so open it in ResourceView and add an extra button, as shown here:

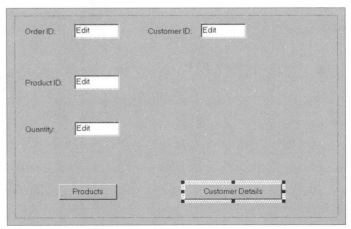

You can define the ID for the new button control as **IDC_CUSTOMER**. After you save the dialog, you can add a handler for the button by double-clicking on it while keeping the *Ctrl* key pressed. The handler only requires one line of code to be added to it, as follows:

```
void COrderView::OnCustomer()
{
    ((CMainFrame*)GetParentFrame())->SelectView(CUSTOMER_VIEW);
}
```

This obtains the address of the frame window and uses it to call the **SelectView()** member of **CMainFrame** to switch to a customer view. The final step to complete the program is to add the code to the **SelectView()** function that will deal with the **CUSTOMER_VIEW** value being passed to it. This requires just three additional lines of code, as follows:

```
void CMainFrame::SelectView(UINT ViewID)
{
    CView* pOldActiveView = GetActiveView();      // Get current view
    // Get pointer to new view if it exists
    // if it doesn't the pointer will be null
    CView* pNewActiveView = (CView*)GetDlgItem(ViewID);

    // If this is 1st time around for the new view,
    // the new view won't exist, so we must create it
    if (pNewActiveView == NULL)
    {
        switch(ViewID)
        {
            case ORDER_VIEW:        // Create an Order view
                pNewActiveView = (CView*)new COrderView;
                break;
            case CUSTOMER_VIEW:     // Create a customer view
                pNewActiveView = (CView*)new CCustomerView;
                break;
            default:
                AfxMessageBox("Invalid View ID");
                return;
        }

        CCreateContext context;
        context.m_pCurrentDoc = pOldActiveView->GetDocument();
        pNewActiveView->Create(NULL, NULL, 0L, CFrameWnd::rectDefault,
                                                this, ViewID, &context);
        pNewActiveView->OnInitialUpdate();
    }
    SetActiveView(pNewActiveView);                    // Activate the new view
    pNewActiveView->ShowWindow(SW_SHOW);              // Hide the old view
    pOldActiveView->ShowWindow(SW_HIDE);              // Show the new view
    pOldActiveView->SetDlgCtrlID(m_CurrentViewID);    // Set the old view ID
    pNewActiveView->SetDlgCtrlID(AFX_IDW_PANE_FIRST);
    m_CurrentViewID = ViewID;                         // Save the new view ID
    RecalcLayout();
}
```

The only change necessary is the addition of a **case** statement in the **switch** to create a **CCustomerView** object when one doesn't exist. Each view object will be re-used next time around, so they only get created once. The code to switch between views works with any number of views, so if you want this function to handle more views, you just need to add another **case** in the **switch** for each new view that you want.

Because we reference the **CCustomerView** class in the **SelectView()** function, you must add an **#include** statement for the **CustomerView.h** file to the block at the beginning of **CMainFrm.cpp**.

Exercising the Database Viewer

At this point, the program is complete. You can Build the application and execute it. As before, the main view of the database is the Products view. Clicking on Orders will, as before, take you to the Orders view. The second button on this form should now be active and clicking on it takes you to the details of the customer.

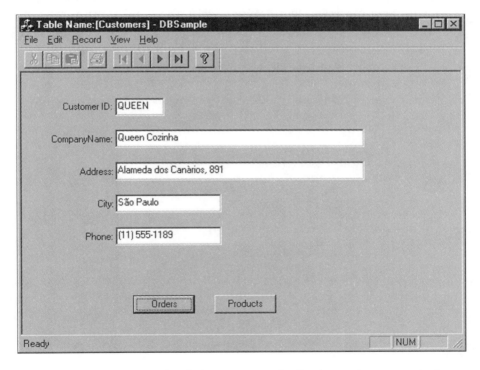

The two buttons take you back to the Orders view or the Products view respectively.

Summary

You should now be comfortable with the basics of how MFC links to your database. The fundamentals of the recordset and the record view are the same, whether you use the DAO or the ODBC classes. Although we have not covered adding records to tables or deleting them in our example, you should have little difficulty implementing this as the recordset already has the functions you need built-in.

The key points we have seen in this chapter are:

▶ MFC provides DAO and ODBC support for accessing databases.

▶ To use a database with ODBC the database must be registered.

▶ A connection to a database is represented by a **CDatabase** or a **CDaoDatabase** object.

▶ A recordset object represents an SQL **SELECT** statement applied to a defined set of tables. Where necessary, the framework will automatically create a database object representing a connection to a database, when a recordset object is created.

▶ A **WHERE** clause can be added for a recordset object through its **m_strFilter** data member.

▶ An **ORDER BY** clause can be defined for a recordset through its **m_strSort** data member.

▶ A record view object is used to display the contents of a recordset object.

Understanding OLE

OLE is a complex topic which many would argue is out of place in a beginner's programming book. However, because of the advantages it brings, more and more applications are making the most of OLE, so it's important to have a basic understanding of how it works.

There are whole books dedicated to OLE, so we'll only scratch the surface in this chapter. Fortunately, MFC hides most of the complexity and with the help you get from AppWizard you shouldn't find it difficult to implement some examples that use OLE. By the end of this chapter you will have learnt:

- What OLE is and how it can be used
- How the OLE mechanism works
- What OLE containers and OLE servers are
- How to write a simple OLE container using AppWizard
- How to write an OLE server using AppWizard

Object Linking and Embedding

Before we launch into writing code, we first need to get the ideas and terminology straight. **Object Linking and Embedding**, perhaps better known as **OLE**, is a mechanism which enables you to write a program, a text editor say, that will allow other applications to edit data within it that it can't handle itself, like graphics. OLE also allows an application that you write to handle data contained within other applications. This isn't the whole story, but it's what we'll concentrate on.

Once you allow your program to have these data objects in them, you can have any kind of object you like, and as many as you like. This is quite an amazing capability when you think about it. The program hosting these alien objects has no knowledge of what they are, but you can still edit and manipulate them as though they were handled by the same program. In fact, there is a different program involved for each variety of alien object you are working with.

An object from one program can appear in another in two different ways. An object from an external document can be **linked** to the document of another program, in which case the external object is not stored as part of the document for the current program, just a reference allowing it to be retrieved from wherever it is. An external document can also be **embedded** in the current document, in which case it is stored within the current document. A document that contains an embedded or a linked OLE object is called a **compound document**.

A linked object has the advantage that it can be modified independently from the compound document, so that when you open a document containing a linked object, the latest version of the object will automatically be incorporated. However, if you delete the file containing the linked object, or even move it to another folder, the compound document will not know about this and won't be able to find the linked object. With an embedded object, the object only exists in the context of the compound document and is, therefore, not independently accessible. The compound document with all its embedded OLE objects is a single file, so there's no possibility of the embedded objects getting lost. To the user, there appears to be no difference in the appearance of the compound document.

Containers and Servers

Clearly, to enable OLE to work, a program must contain special code supporting this sort of functionality. A program that can handle embedded objects is called an **OLE container** and a program that creates objects that can be embedded in an OLE container is referred to as an **OLE server**. OLE servers also come in two flavors. A **full server** can operate as an independent program, or can operate servicing an object embedded in a compound document. A **mini-server** can't operate in stand-alone mode. Its sole function is to support objects in a compound document.

It's possible that an application can be both an OLE server and an OLE container. The AppWizard can generate programs which have OLE container or OLE server functionality built in. All you have to do is to choose the appropriate options when creating an OLE project.

Compound Documents

When you work with an embedded object in a program, the code for the application that generated the embedded object can be automatically invoked to allow you to edit the object in the container application window. This is referred to as **in-place activation**. With an OLE server that supports in-place activation, you can edit an embedded object in an OLE container application just by double-clicking it. The menus and toolbars for the container application will then change to incorporate those required to use the server application to edit the object. More than that, if there are several different embedded objects, the menus and toolbars in the container will change to incorporate the menus and toolbars for whatever embedded object you are working with, all completely automatically.

With in-place activation, the appearance of the compound document comprising the natively supported object and the embedded object or objects is seamless, and generally hides the fact that several different programs may be involved in manipulating what you see in the application window.

If an OLE server doesn't support in-place activation, double-clicking the embedded object will open a separate window for the server application, allowing you to edit the embedded object. When you've finished editing the embedded object, you only need to close the server application window to resume work with the container application. Obviously, in-place activation is a much more attractive way of handling compound documents, as it appears to the user as a single application. Most containers also allow you to edit an embedded object in a server window, even when the server does support in-place activation. Double-clicking an object while holding down the *Ctrl* or the *Alt* key often initiates this mode of server operation.

A compound document is illustrated below:

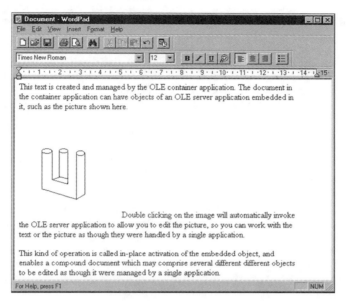

Activating an Embedded Object

Once an object has been embedded in a container, the server supporting it can be in two basic states. When the server has been activated in place for editing, the object is shown with a shaded border in the client area of the container. If you click once outside the object, the server will be deactivated and the shaded border will not be displayed. You can see both of these states in the following screen:

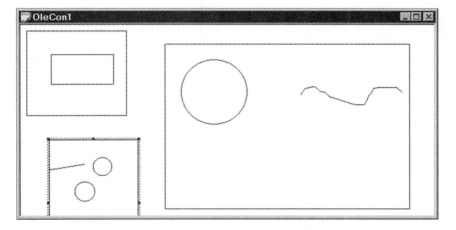

There are three embedded objects here. Only the object at the bottom left is fully in-place activated and only one object can be in this state at one time. The user interface is under the control of the server. The other two embedded objects are inactive. No communication between the container and server is necessary for the inactive objects. To change an inactive object to the fully in-place activated state, you just double-click on it. With the fully activated object, the server will advise the container each time the area occupied by the embedded object needs to be redrawn. This could be because the contents have changed or because a larger area is required.

If you click on an inactive object, the appearance of the object will be as an inactive object but with resize handles on the borders. In this situation, you can't edit the object, but you can resize the area it occupies by dragging the border. You can also move the object around in the client area. The container signals the server whenever the contents of the object needs to be redrawn because of changes to the size or position of the area occupied by the embedded object.

There is another state for a server supporting an embedded object when the object is opened in a completely separate window.

How Does OLE Work?

The communications between an OLE server application for an embedded object and the OLE container application are concerned primarily with the area occupied by the object, when it needs to be redrawn, and the resources the server needs to make available in the container for editing such as menus and toolbars. The container has no knowledge of what is to be displayed by the server. All it knows is that an area in its view is going to be used by the server and the server is going to sort out what needs to be displayed. Neither does the container know which menus or toolbars are required to use the server. All it does is provide space for them within its own menus and toolbars. It's a bit like the owner of a store, renting the premises out to someone. The person who uses the store does what he or she wants, within an agreed set of rules. The owner doesn't get involved in what goes on inside the store or what is displayed in the window. As long as the rent is paid and the rules are obeyed, everybody's happy.

As you have probably guessed, the communication between an OLE container and the servers supporting the embedded objects uses the Windows operating system as a go-between. Each OLE program uses a common OLE DLL which is part of Windows, and the functions in the DLL provide the means of passing information between them. Thus, the key to the operation of OLE is a **standard interface**. The standard interface that enables OLE to work is specified by the **Component Object Model**, or **COM**. This is essentially a definition of the appearance of an embedded object and how a container communicates with it. COM is a big topic. We won't be delving into the detail, but just looking close enough to understand the ideas involved.

The OLE Component Object Model

The component object model has sets of standard functions that are used for OLE communications, packaged in named groups called **interfaces**. This is analogous to a C++ class which defines an interface through its **public** function members. A complete discussion of COM is far beyond the scope of this book, and its operation is hidden in the framework that we get with an AppWizard- generated program, so you won't need to deal with the details. However, we'll look far enough into it to give you a feel for what's happening when we implement an OLE container and a server later in this chapter.

For an OLE object such as an OLE server, at least one interface (or group of functions) called **IUnknown** is always implemented. The **IUnknown** interface contains three standard functions:

Function	Usage
`QueryInterface()`	Tests whether a particular interface is supported by the object. If an interface that is queried is supported, a pointer to it is returned. The calling function can then access the functions in the queried interface through the pointer.
`AddRef()`	Increments a count of the number of clients using the interface. This count enables the object owning the interface to know when it is no longer required.
`Release()`	Decrements the count of the number of clients using the interface. When the count is zero, the object knows that it is no longer in use and can remove itself from memory.

You can do almost anything with these three functions. Since the `QueryInterface()` function allows you to ask about other interfaces, you can access any interface that an object supports, as long as you know about it. OLE defines a set of standard interfaces, each identified by an **interface ID**, or **IID**, which is passed as an argument in the `QueryInterface()` call. It's also possible to define your own custom interfaces which will also need to be identified by a unique IID. We won't need to look into the detail of these interface functions, as, for the most part, MFC takes care of using them.

IUnknown is by no means all there is to the component object model. There are several other interfaces involved, concerned with transferring data, managing memory and so on, but we can create a container and a server without knowing any more about COM, so let's press on.

The Registry

In order to use an OLE server, it must be identified in some way. When you run an OLE container, you wouldn't want to be just rummaging around your hard disk to see if any of the applications on your PC might support OLE, so how are OLE programs identified?

An **OLE object** can be a program, a document type, or, indeed, any kind of object that supports OLE. Each OLE object in your system is identified by a unique 128-bit numeric value, called a **class ID** or **CLSID**. These are also referred to as **globally unique Ids**, or **GUIDs**. Information about every OLE object in your system, including its CLSID, is stored on your hard disk in a database called the **system registry**.

You can look at the registry by executing the program **Regedit.exe**. A typical window is shown here:

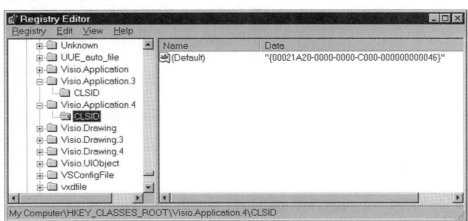

This shows the entry for the drawing package, Visio 4, and its class ID. You can see that there is also a key (it looks like a folder) for Visio.Drawing which represents a document type. Because it is also an OLE object, this also has its own CLSID. An OLE server can't be used until it has been entered in the system registry with all the information necessary to identify it.

MFC Classes Supporting OLE

MFC has a set of classes that represent OLE objects, as well as classes that represent documents that can contain OLE objects. The relationships between these classes are illustrated in the diagram below:

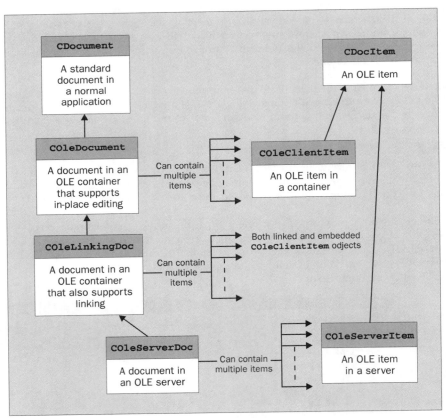

The arrows in the diagram point from a derived class towards a base class, so the **COleServerDoc** class, for example, inherits the functionality of its base class as well as its indirect base classes, which are **CDocument**, **COleDocument** and **COleLinkingDoc**.

OLE Object Classes

The two classes that are shown derived from the class **CDocItem**, **COleClientItem** and **COleServerItem** represent different perspectives on an OLE object corresponding to the point of view of a container and of a server, respectively, as shown in the diagram below:

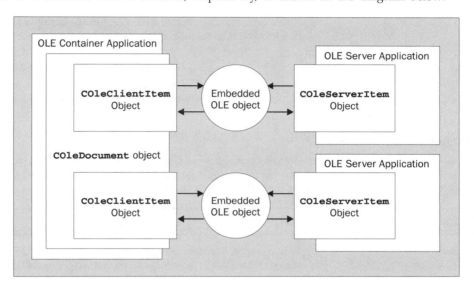

This shows two different OLE objects embedded in a container application. The class objects in the container corresponding to the embedded objects will both be included in the container document object. Each embedded object will have its own server application and each server will have a **COleServerItem** object corresponding to the object in the container for which it is responsible. This is a simplified representation here, since the OLE DLL is involved in the communications.

An Embedded Object in a Container

The class **COleClientItem** provides the interfaces required by a container to manage an embedded item. This involves a large number of functions which enable the object to be queried and manipulated, as well as functions which enable communications between the container and the server. The most important of these are the ones you will need to implement, which are as follows:

Function to implement	Usage
OnChange()	This function is called by the framework when a change to an embedded item is signaled by the item's server. The typical action is to invalidate the embedded object to get it redrawn in the container.
OnGetItemPosition()	This function is called by the framework to obtain the rectangle in the client area of the container where the OLE object is to be displayed.

Table Continued on Following Page

Function to implement	Usage
OnChangeItemPosition()	This function is called by the framework to indicate to the container that the extent of the embedded object has changed during editing.
Serialize()	If you add any members to the object in the container, you will need to serialize them in this function.

Drawing of an embedded object and any modifications made by the user are carried out by the server, but the object is displayed in an area in a window that is owned and managed by the container. Thus, the communications between the container and the server are fundamental to proper OLE operation.

An Embedded Object in a Server

An OLE object embedded in a container application is represented by an object of the class **COleServerItem** in the server. The interface supporting a server in **COleServerItem** also involves a large number of functions, but the most important of these are:

Function to implement	Usage
OnDraw()	This function is responsible for drawing the embedded object in the container when it isn't being edited, so it's essential to implement this function. When the object is in-place active, the object is drawn by the **OnDraw()** function in the server's view class. Drawing in the container has to be done by the server because the container has no knowledge of the internals of the embedded object. When the server runs stand-alone, of course the **OnDraw()** function in the view object is also responsible for drawing the object in the normal way.
Serialize()	This function is responsible for serializing the embedded object when required to do so by the container. This is usually implemented by calling the **Serialize()** function for the document object in the server.
OnGetExtent()	This function is called by the framework to get the actual extent of the embedded object. This is communicated to the container application.
NotifyChanged()	This function is called by the server application when it changes the embedded object. This signals the change to the framework which will call the **OnChange()** function in the corresponding **COleClientItem** object in the container.

OLE Document Classes

Specialized document classes are necessary for OLE applications because the documents must include the ability to deal with the added complexity of OLE objects. There are two document classes that are used in OLE container applications: **COleDocument** and **COleLinkingDoc**. **COleDocument** supports embedded objects that are edited in-place by a server. It represents the embedded objects as instances of a class derived from **COleClientItem**. The class **COleLinkingDoc** is derived from **COleDocument** and adds support for linked objects that are stored separately from the container document. The document class in a container application is typically derived from either **COleDocument** or **COleLinkingDoc** document. The container example that we'll implement later in this chapter will use the **COleDocument** class as a base.

A document in a server application is derived from the class **COleServerDoc**. When the server is supporting an embedded object, the OLE object is represented by a class derived from the **COleServerItem** class that we saw earlier. Of course, a server document will only include one instance of this class, which will represent the whole document when it is embedded in a container document. A document class for an OLE server must implement the member **OnGetEmbeddedItem()**, because this is a pure virtual function in the **COleServerDoc** class. If you don't implement it, your code won't compile. This function is called by the framework to get a pointer to the OLE object supported by the server and is used by the framework to call function members of the object.

Implementing an OLE Container

AppWizard makes it very easy to create an OLE container application, so let's try it out. Create a new project of type MFC AppWizard (exe). You could call it something meaningful, like OleContainer. Select the Create... button to create it, then click on the Next > button to accept the default MDI implementation and another Next > without electing for database support. The next part of the dialog is shown below:

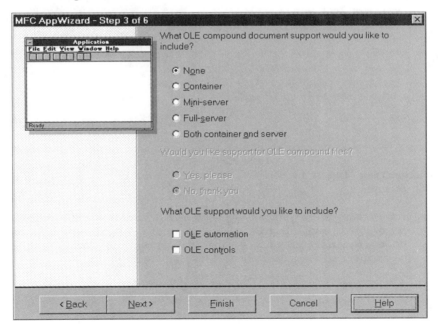

Select the Container radio button here to generate an OLE container. When you click on this, the option for compound files will be activated and selected automatically. The other options on this dialog are all the variations on a server that we referred to earlier. The Mini-server is just a server that can't be used independently of a container. The Full-server can operate as a stand-alone application or as a server to a container. We'll implement a full server a little later in this chapter. The third possibility, Both container and server, generates a program that can run stand-alone, can run as a server to a container and can itself act as a container for other embedded objects. This raises the possibility of an embedded object containing embedded objects.

The other two options, OLE automation and OLE controls provide additional levels of OLE functionality. OLE automation adds a programmable interface to your application so that other applications which have provision for doing so can make use of functions within your application. Selecting OLE controls adds the capability for your program to incorporate and use OLE controls. We'll be looking at creating an OLE control in the next chapter.

Click on Next > to go to Step 4 and select the Advanced... button. The dialog for this is shown here:

Enter the file extension con for container files. The entry in the File type ID: box, OleContainer.Document, will appear in the registry.

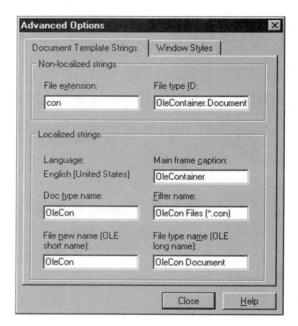

The only other change to make is on Step 6 when you get to the list of classes that AppWizard plans to generate. Select the class **COleContainerCntrItem**, and shorten it to **COleContainerItem**. This is just for our convenience. You can then proceed to the end and generate the program.

If you look at the classes in the program by selecting the ClassView tab, you'll see that we have the standard set of classes supporting the MFC document/view architecture. If you look at the definition of **COleContainerApp**, you'll see that it is perfectly standard. The differences really start to become apparent in the initialization of the application object.

Initializing a Container Application

The initialization is done in the **InitInstance()** member of the application class **COleContainerApp**. The code generated for it by AppWizard is as follows:

```
BOOL COleContainerApp::InitInstance()
{
    // Initialize OLE libraries
    if (!AfxOleInit())
    {
    AfxMessageBox(IDP_OLE_INIT_FAILED);
    return FALSE;
    }

    // Standard initialization
    // If you are not using these features and wish to reduce the size
    //  of your final executable, you should remove from the following
    //  the specific initialization routines you do not need.

#ifdef _AFXDLL
    Enable3dControls();         // Call this when using MFC in a shared DLL
#else
    Enable3dControlsStatic();// Call this when linking to MFC statically
#endif

    LoadStdProfileSettings();// Load standard INI file options

    // Register the application's document templates.  Document templates
    //  serve as the connection between documents, frame windows and views.

    CMultiDocTemplate* pDocTemplate;
    pDocTemplate = new CMultiDocTemplate(
                    IDR_OLECONTYPE,
                    RUNTIME_CLASS(COleContainerDoc),
                    RUNTIME_CLASS(CChildFrame), // custom MDI child frame
                    RUNTIME_CLASS(COleContainerView));
    pDocTemplate->SetContainerInfo(IDR_OLECONTYPE_CNTR_IP);
    AddDocTemplate(pDocTemplate);

    // The rest of the function definition is
    //  is as in a normal application that we have seen before...

}
```

We have used shading to highlight the differences between this code and that generated in a standard application. We'll just discuss these differences. The call to the global function **AfxOleInit()** initializes the system DLL that supports OLE operations. This establishes the links between the application and the DLL. If the initialization fails for some reason, perhaps because the version of the DLL required by the application isn't installed, a message will be displayed and the container will terminate.

The call to the member function **SetContainerInfo()** of the document template object transfers the ID of the menu to be used when an OLE object is embedded and in-place active. The container has three different menu resources that are shown in the following diagram.

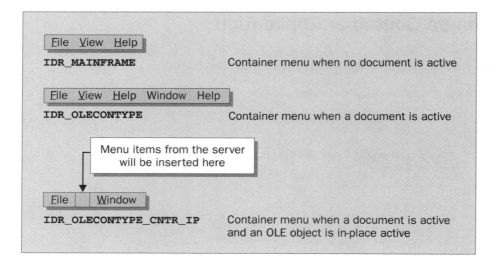

The menu corresponding to the ID passed to the **SetContainerInfo()** function has separator bars to identify where the menu items supplied by the server are to be inserted. The additional menu items are inserted automatically by the framework when the embedded object is active. We will look at the specific menu items that are inserted when we implement an OLE server, but it is essentially the set required to interact with the in-place object.

The COleContainerItem Class

Another differentiating feature of our container application is the class **COleContainerItem** which is derived from **COleClientItem**. As we have seen, an object of this class refers to an embedded OLE object which is supported by a server application. When you introduce an object into the container application, a **COleContainerItem** object is constructed and will only be destroyed when the container document is closed or the embedded item it corresponds to is deleted from the container. When a **COleContainerItem** is constructed, the constructor requires a pointer to the container's document object, so that the object being constructed is associated with the container document. The definition of the class provided by AppWizard is:

```
class COleContainerItem : public COleClientItem
{
    DECLARE_SERIAL(COleContainerItem)

    // Constructors
public:
    COleContainerItem(COleContainerDoc* pContainer = NULL);
    // Note: pContainer is allowed to be NULL to enable
    // IMPLEMENT_SERIALIZE.
    // IMPLEMENT_SERIALIZE requires the class have a constructor with
    //   zero arguments.  Normally, OLE items are constructed with a
    //   non-NULL document pointer.

    // Attributes
public:
    COleContainerDoc* GetDocument()
        { return (COleContainerDoc*)COleClientItem::GetDocument();}
```

```
        COleContainerView* GetActiveView()
            { return (COleContainerView*)COleClientItem::GetActiveView();}

    // ClassWizard generated virtual function overrides
    //{{AFX_VIRTUAL(COleContainerItem)
    public:
        virtual void OnChange(OLE_NOTIFICATION wNotification,
                                              DWORD dwParam);
        virtual void OnActivate();
    protected:
        virtual void OnGetItemPosition(CRect& rPosition);
        virtual void OnDeactivateUI(BOOL bUndoable);
        virtual BOOL OnChangeItemPosition(const CRect& rectPos);
    //}}AFX_VIRTUAL

    // Implementation
    public:
        ~COleContainerItem();
    #ifdef _DEBUG
        virtual void AssertValid() const;
        virtual void Dump(CDumpContext& dc) const;
    #endif
        virtual void Serialize(CArchive& ar);
};
```

As the note in the code indicates, the constructor will normally be called with a pointer to a container document as an argument. The default value of **NULL** for the parameter is only there because the serialization mechanism requires a default constructor.

One addition to the **COleContainerItem** class definition that we can make straight away is a data member to store the rectangle defining the position of the embedded object. Add the following declaration to the **public** section of the class definition:

```
    CRect m_Rect;       // Item position in the document object
```

You can do this by right-clicking the class name in ClassView and selecting Add Variable... from the pop-up. Now, each item can record where it is in the container document. You should also add initialization for the **m_Rect** member to the constructor:

```
COleContainerItem::COleContainerItem(COleContainerDoc* pContainer)
    : COleClientItem(pContainer)
{
    m_Rect.SetRect(10,10,100,100);       // Set initial item position
}
```

The statement initializes **m_Rect** by calling the **SetRect()** member of the **CRect** class. This sets an arbitrary position which will be overridden when an object is added to the container document. Note that the constructor explicitly calls the base class constructor in the initialization list for our constructor and passes the pointer to the document object to it.

We should also arrange to store and retrieve **m_Rect** by adding the following code to the implementation of the **Serialize()** function for the embedded object:

```
void COleContainerItem::Serialize(CArchive& ar)
{
```

```
        ASSERT_VALID(this);

        // Call base class first to read in COleClientItem data.
        // Since this sets up the m_pDocument pointer returned from
        //   COleContainerItem::GetDocument, it is a good idea to call
        //   the base class Serialize first.
        COleClientItem::Serialize(ar);

        // now store/retrieve data specific to COleContainerItem
        if (ar.IsStoring())
    {
        ar << m_Rect;
    }
    else
    {
        ar >> m_Rect;
    }
    }
```

The base class **Serialize()** function takes care of everything else, so we don't need to add anything further.

AppWizard has provided an implementation of **GetDocument()** which returns a pointer to the document object, and **GetActiveView()** which returns a pointer to the active view belonging to the document containing the embedded object. The next member function that we are interested in is **OnChange()**, which is called when an embedded object is fully open for editing and is modified in some way.

Reacting to OLE Object Modification

When the server modifies an embedded object, it calls a function to notify the framework that a change has occurred. The framework reacts by calling the **OnChange()** member of the object in the container application. The container owns the window in which the object is displayed, so it's up to the container to do something about the change.

The reason for calling the **OnChange()** function is indicated by the first argument passed, the two arguments being of type **OLE_NOTIFICATION** (nCode) and **DWORD** (dwParam). We need to deal with two possibilities: when **nCode** has the value **OLE_CHANGED**, which indicates that the object has been modified, and when **nCode** has the value **OLE_CHANGED_STATE**, which indicates the object has changed in some other way. You should add the code for this to the implementation of the **OnChange()** member, as follows:

```
    void COleContainerItem::OnChange(OLE_NOTIFICATION nCode, DWORD dwParam)
    {
        ASSERT_VALID(this);

        COleClientItem::OnChange(nCode, dwParam);

        // When an item is being edited (either in-place or fully open)
        //   it sends OnChange notifications for changes in the state of the
        //   item or visual appearance of its content.

    switch(nCode)
    {
        case OLE_CHANGED:               // Item appearance has been changed
```

```
                InvalidateItem();       // Invalidate the current item
                GetServerSize();        // Update to the size from the server
                break;
            case OLE_CHANGED_STATE:     // Item state has changed
                // Pass a hint to update all views in the document
                InvalidateItem();
                break;
        }
    }
```

Our code replaces the call to **UpdateAllViews()** in the default implementation. We will update selectively, depending on what is happening to the embedded object. Where the value of **nCode** indicates that there was a change to the content of the server, we need to get the object redrawn. We initiate this by calling the function **InvalidateItem()** which we'll add to the **COleContainerItem** class in a moment. We also need to deal with the possibility that the size of the object may be altered by the server, and we may want to record the area it occupies in the **m_Rect** member and resize it in the container document view. This will be done in the second function that we'll add to the **COleContainerItem** class, **GetServerSize()**.

The second value of **nCode** reflects a change in state such as occurs when an object is active but not being edited and the user double-clicks the object in the document view to edit it. In this case, we just need to get the object redrawn by calling the **InvalidateItem()** function. You'll need to add this function, so right-click the COleContainerItem class name in ClassView and select the Add Function... menu item from the pop-up. Specify the return type as **void** and enter the function name as **InvalidateItem()**. You can leave its access specification as **public**. Click on the OK button then add the following code to its implementation:

```
void COleContainerItem::InvalidateItem()
{
    // Pass a hint to update all views in the document
    GetDocument()->UpdateAllViews(0, HINT_UPDATE_ITEM, this);
}
```

This calls the **UpdateAllViews()** function member of the document object to get all the views redrawn. The second argument value, **HINT_UPDATE_ITEM**, indicates that there is a hint passed in the third argument which is the address of the current object. This will be used when the **OnUpdate()** function in the container document view is called as a consequence of the call to **UpdateAllViews()**. We'll be extending the implementation of the view a little later in this chapter.

We can define the value of the symbol **HINT_UPDATE_ITEM** within the definition file for the **COleContainerItem** class. Add it at the beginning of the **CntrItem.h** file with the directive:

```
#define HINT_UPDATE_ITEM 1    // Indicates a hint is present
```

When you have entered this definition, you can add the **GetServerSize()** function next. Just right-click the **COleContainerItem** class name again and select Add Function... from the pop-up. Enter the return type as **void** and the function name as **GetServerSize()**. You can implement the function as follows:

```
void COleContainerItem::GetServerSize()
{
    CSize aSize;                    // Create a size object
    if(GetCachedExtent(&aSize))    // Get the size of the current item
```

```
{
    // Size is specified by OLE in HIMETRIC units
    CClientDC aDC(0);            // Get a device context
    aDC.HIMETRICtoDP(&aSize);   // Convert size to device coordinates

    // Verify that size has changed and item is not in-place active
    if(aSize != m_Rect.Size() && !IsInPlaceActive())
    {
        InvalidateItem();           // Invalidate old item

        // Change the rectangle for the item to the new size
        m_Rect.right = m_Rect.left + aSize.cx;
        m_Rect.bottom = m_Rect.top + aSize.cy;

        InvalidateItem();           // Invalidate the item with the new size
    }
}
}
```

The size of the OLE object is stored in the **aSize** object by the **GetCachedExtent()** member function that is inherited from the base class, **COleClientItem**. If the object is blank, this function will return **FALSE** and we will do nothing.

Whenever size information about an OLE object is passed to or from the framework, it is always in **HIMETRIC** units to ensure that such information is handled uniformly. This provides a standard unit for specifying size information that has more precision than any of the other possible choices, such as **LOMETRIC**, **HIENGLISH** or **LOENGLISH**. This means that whenever you pass size information to the framework, you must convert it from whatever units you are using to **HIMETRIC**. Whenever you receive size information, you need to convert it to whatever units you require, if they are different from **HIMETRIC**. In the container, we need the rectangle to be in device units, which are pixels, so we get a **CClientDC** object which provides a conversion function from **HIMETRIC** to device coordinate units.

After converting **aSize** to pixels, we then check that the size is actually different from that recorded in **m_Rect** for the item and that the object is not still in-place active. We don't want to do anything if the size hasn't changed. If the item is in-place active and a change occurs, the framework will call **OnChangeItemPosition()**. We'll come to this shortly, so we don't need to handle that situation here.

The **Size()** member of the **CRect** class returns the size of the rectangle stored in **m_Rect**. The **IsInPlaceActive()** function inherited from **COleClientItem** returns **TRUE** if the object is current being edited, and **FALSE** otherwise. With a new size, we invalidate the object with its old extent, create a new extent, then invalidate the object with the new extent. We define the new extent corresponding to the new size by leaving the top left point of the rectangle in **m_Rect** in the same position and creating the bottom right point coordinates by adding the **cx** and **cy** components of **aSize** to the top left point coordinates.

Dealing with the Position of an Object in the Container

There are two members of the **COleContainerItem** class concerned with the position of the object in the view: **OnGetItemPosition()** and **OnChangeItemPosition()**.

As we noted earlier, the function **OnGetItemPosition()** is called by the framework when it needs to know where the object is to be displayed in the document view in the container. This occurs each time an item is in-place activated. A reference to a **CRect** object is passed as an argument in which you need to store the required information. You can do this quite simply by modifying the default implementation to correspond to the following:

```
void COleContainerItem::OnGetItemPosition(CRect& rPosition)
{
    ASSERT_VALID(this);

    rPosition = m_Rect;
}
```

We just set the **rPosition** variable that is passed as a parameter to the value we have in the **m_Rect** member of the object. This replaces the previous line of code . Since we update the rectangle in **m_Rect**, whenever we get a change signaled by the server, this will always be the current rectangle appropriate to the object.

The **OnChangeItemPosition()** member is called when you move the embedded object in the view, when you resize the borders of the object in the view or the server requests that the size of the object be altered. We, therefore, need to change the default implementation to the following:

```
BOOL COleContainerItem::OnChangeItemPosition(const CRect& rectPos)
{
    ASSERT_VALID(this);

    if (!COleClientItem::OnChangeItemPosition(rectPos))
        return FALSE;

    InvalidateItem();                 // Invalidate the item at the old position
    m_Rect = rectPos;                 // Set the item rectangle to the new position
    InvalidateItem();                 // Invalidate the item in the new position
    GetDocument()->SetModifiedFlag();    // Mark the document as changed

    return TRUE;
}
```

Since we are moving the object or altering its extent, we first invalidate it in its old position. We then set **m_Rect** for the object to the new extent passed in the parameter **rectPos** and then invalidate the object in its new position. Finally, we call the **SetModifiedFlag()** member of the document to indicate that the document in the container has been changed.

Managing Multiple Embedded Objects

The container program generated by AppWizard assumes that there is only one embedded object. To manage more than one, we must add functionality to the **COleContainerView** class to enable a user to switch from one embedded object to another. This means keeping track of a current active object, processing a single mouse click in a view to switch to the object at the cursor position and responding to a double mouse click by activating the object at the cursor position. The view class already contains a data member **m_pSelection** that is a pointer to an embedded item, so we can store the currently active item in this variable. AppWizard has already added statements to set this member to **NULL** in the constructor for the view class and in the **OnInitialUpdate()** member of the view, so we don't need to worry about initializing it.

Let's take a look at how we handle a single mouse click.

Selecting an Object

We need to add a handler for the **WM_LBUTTONDOWN** message to **COleContainerView**, so use ClassWizard to add this handler in the same manner that you have used with the Sketcher application and add code to the handler as follows:

```
void COleContainerView::OnLButtonDown(UINT nFlags, CPoint point)
{
    // Get address of item hit
    COleContainerItem* pHitItem = HitTestItems(point);
    SelectItem(pHitItem);                       // Now select the item

    if(pHitItem)      // As long as an item was selected
    {
        CRectTracker aTracker;                  // Create a tracker rectangle

        // Set the tracker rectangle to the item selected
        SetupTracker(pHitItem, &aTracker);
        UpdateWindow();                         // Get the window redrawn

        // Enable the rectangle to be resized
        // TRUE is returned from Track() if rectangle is changed
        if(aTracker.Track(this, point))
        {
            pHitItem->InvalidateItem();         // Invalidate the old item

            // Set the item rectangle to the new tracker rectangle
            pHitItem->m_Rect = aTracker.m_rect;
            // Invalidate the item with the new tracker rect
            pHitItem->InvalidateItem();
            GetDocument()->SetModifiedFlag();// Mark document as changed
        }
    }
    CView::OnLButtonDown(nFlags, point);
}
```

The handler uses several helper functions that we will add once we have discussed how this works. The first helper function, **HitTestItems()**, is used to initialize the pointer **pHitItem**. This function iterates over all the OLE objects in the container until it finds one that has the **point** object within its bounding rectangle. The **point** object is passed to the handler as an argument and contains the current cursor position, so the item containing it will be the item the user has clicked on. Its address is returned and stored in the local pointer **pHitItem**. If no item was hit, a null pointer will be returned from **HitTestItems()**.

If the user has clicked on an embedded item, we create an object of the class **CRectTracker**. An object of this class is a rectangle called a **tracker** that can be displayed in different ways to provide visual cues to different situations. A tracker can be set to display its border as solid, dotted or hatched. The interior of the tracker can be hatched and it can also have resize handles. You can use a **CRectTracker** object anywhere you need this kind of capability. The first thing we do with our tracker, **aTracker**, is to initialize it using the helper function **SetupTracker()**. This will set the tracker rectangle to be the same size as the rectangle stored in the embedded object pointed to by **pHitItem** and set its appearance according to the state of the object. Two examples of trackers appear in the following window.

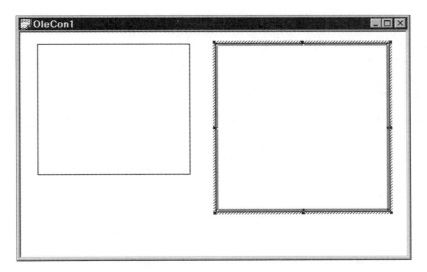

The one on the left represents an inactive object and the one on the right, with the hatched border and the resize handles, represents an active item.

The first thing we do with our tracker, **aTracker**, is to initialize it using the helper function **SetupTracker()**. This will set the tracker rectangle to be the same size as the rectangle stored in the embedded object pointed to by **pHitItem** and set its appearance according to the state of the object.

After initializing the tracker, we call the **UpdateWindow()** member function of **COleContainerView**. This is a function that is inherited indirectly from the **CWnd** class which causes the window to be redrawn immediately and will result in the tracker being displayed.

In the succeeding **if** statement, the **Track()** member of the tracker object is called. This is quite a sophisticated function that provides for the possibility that this **WM_LBUTTONDOWN** message was triggered by the user re-sizing the border of the embedded object. The arguments are a pointer to the current window and the current cursor position, **point**. The function captures the mouse and allows the user to resize the tracker rectangle by dragging its borders. As the border is dragged, the cursor is tracked and the border updated as long as the left mouse button is held down. The **track()** function stores the modified rectangle in the tracker object and returns **TRUE** if the tracker was re-sized, and **FALSE** otherwise.

If the tracker rectangle was changed, the current item with its old extent is invalidated to get the area it occupies redrawn. The **m_rect** member of the tracker object contains the new rectangle which is stored in the **m_Rect** member of the embedded object. Finally, the item with the new extent is invalidated to get it redrawn.

Finding the Object Selected

The helper function **HitTestItems()** searches through the embedded items in the document to find the one the user is clicking on. You can add this function to the class by right-clicking on COleContainerView in the ClassView. Specify its return type as **COleContainerItem***, and the name as **HitTestItems(CPoint aPoint)**. Select the OK button and enter its code as follows:

```
COleContainerItem* COleContainerView::HitTestItems(CPoint aPoint)
{
    COleContainerDoc* pDoc = GetDocument();
    COleContainerItem* pItem = 0;        // Place to store an item pointer

    // Get position of the first item
    POSITION aPosition = pDoc->GetStartPosition();

    while(aPosition)    // Iterate over items until one is hit
    {
        pItem = (COleContainerItem*)pDoc->GetNextItem(aPosition);
        if(pItem->m_Rect.PtInRect(aPoint))
            return pItem;      // Return pointer to item hit
    }
    return 0;                  // No item hit
}
```

After getting a pointer to the document object, we create a pointer, **pItem**, to store the address of the item hit. We get a position value for the first item in the document by calling the **GetStartPosition()** member of the document object. The value returned from this function is of type **POSITION** because pointers to the items stored in the document are maintained in a list. This is used in the same way as you have seen with the lists we used in the Sketcher application. We iterate through the list of embedded objects by calling the **GetNextItem()** member of the document object.

In the loop, the **m_Rect** member of each embedded object is tested using the **PtInRect()** member of **CRect** to see whether the **aPoint** object is inside the rectangle. As soon as an object is found where this is the case, the address of the embedded object is returned. If we reach the end of the list, **aPosition** will be zero and the **while** loop will end. In this case we haven't hit an item, so we return a null pointer value. This situation arises when the user clicks on a point in the view that is outside of all the embedded objects. This might be done to deactivate the current object, for instance, so that another object can be embedded in the document.

Setting an Object as Selected

When the user clicks on an item, we must deactivate any active item and activate the new item. This is carried out by the **SelectItem()** helper function that we used in the **OnLButtonDown()** handler. You can add this function by right-clicking on COleContainerView in ClassView and selecting Add Function... from the pop-up. You can specify the return type as **void** and enter the name as **SelectItem(COleContainerItem* pItem)**. You can then add the code for the function as follows:

```
void COleContainerView::SelectItem(COleContainerItem* pItem)
{
    if(m_pSelection != 0 && m_pSelection != pItem)
        m_pSelection->Close(); // De-activate current selected item

    if(m_pSelection != pItem)       // Only update view for a new selection
    {
        if(m_pSelection)            // Check there is an old selection
            // Update area for the old
            OnUpdate(0,HINT_UPDATE_ITEM, m_pSelection);

        m_pSelection = pItem;       // Set the current selection to the new item
        if(m_pSelection)            // Check there is a new selection
```

```
                 // Update area for the new
                 OnUpdate(0,HINT_UPDATE_ITEM, m_pSelection);
        }
   }
```

The first **if** statement deactivates the currently selected object which has its address stored in the **m_pSelection** member of the view, as long as there is a current selection that is different from the new item to be selected which has its address passed in the parameter **pItem**. Note that we won't deactivate the current item if it is the same as the new item.

The next **if** tests whether the address of the new item is different from that of the old. If they are the same, we have nothing further to do. Otherwise, we verify that the address of the current selected item is not zero before using it as the hint argument in the call to the **OnUpdate()** member of the view.

Finally, we store the address of the new embedded object in the **m_pSelection** member of the view. If it isn't zero, we use it as a hint in the call to the **OnUpdate()** function once more.

Setting the Tracker Style

The last helper function sets the style for the tracker which determines its appearance. You can add this function in the same way as the others by right-clicking on COleContainerView in ClassView. Set the return type as **void** and the name of the function as **SetupTracker(COleContainerItem* pItem, CRectTracker* pTracker)**. The code for the function is as follows:

```
void COleContainerView::SetupTracker(COleContainerItem* pItem,
                                                  CRectTracker* pTracker)
{
    pTracker->m_rect = pItem->m_Rect;

    if(pItem == m_pSelection)       // Check if the item is selected
        pTracker->m_nStyle |= CRectTracker::resizeInside;

    if(pItem->GetType() == OT_LINK)        // Test for linked item
        // Item is linked so dotted border
        pTracker->m_nStyle |= CRectTracker::dottedLine;
    else
        // Item is embedded so solid border
        pTracker->m_nStyle |= CRectTracker::solidLine;

    // If the item server window is open or activated in-place,
    // hatch over the item
    if(pItem->GetItemState() == COleClientItem::openState ||
                  pItem->GetItemState() == COleClientItem::activeUIState)
        pTracker->m_nStyle |= CRectTracker::hatchInside;
}
```

The **m_rect** member of the tracker object stores the rectangle representing the tracker in device coordinates. This is set up by storing the rectangle in the **m_Rect** member of the object, which has its address passed as the parameter **pItem**.

The style of the tracker object is stored in the member **m_nStyle**. This can consist of a number of different flags, so the style is set by ORing flags with **m_nStyle**. The symbols corresponding to possible values for the flags are defined in an enumeration within the definition of the **CRectTracker** class, so you must prefix them with **CRectTracker::**. The symbols defining valid flags are as follows.

Flag	Meaning
solidLine	Specifies the border of the rectangle as solid. This is used for an embedded object that is inactive.
dottedLine	Specifies the border of the rectangle as dotted. This is used to identify a linked object. We won't be dealing with linked objects.
hatchedBorder	Specifies the border of the rectangle as hatched. This identifies an embedded object as active, with the server menus displayed in the container.
resizeInside	Specifies that resize handles appear inside the border.
resizeOutside	Specifies that resize handles appear outside the border.
hatchInside	Specifies that the interior of the rectangle is to be hatched. This is used to identify an object that can't be edited in its present state.

The first **if** statement in the **SetupTracker()** function checks whether the object indicated by **pItem** is actually the current selection. If it is, the **resizeInside** style is set to allow the border to be resized. The next **if** checks whether the item is linked by calling the **GetType()** member of the object. If it is, the flag **dottedLine** is added, otherwise we assume that it is embedded and set the **solidLine** flag. The last **if** statement checks the state of the item by calling its **GetItemState()** member. The states that are tested for reflect conditions under which the item can't be edited, so the **hatchInside** style is set.

Setting the Cursor

Although we have implemented the capability to resize an object by dragging the tracker rectangle, the user has no indication of when this is possible. We really need to ensure that the cursor representation provides a cue for this by switching its appearance to a double arrow to indicate when a border can be dragged, or to a four-way arrow showing that the object can be moved in the view.

To do this, we must add a handler for the **WM_SETCURSOR** message. As long as the mouse hasn't been captured, this message is sent to the application whenever the cursor is moved. All we need to do is implement the handler to check where the cursor is in relation to the tracker for the currently selected object.

You can use ClassWizard to add the handler and then code it as follows:

```
BOOL COleContainerView::OnSetCursor(CWnd* pWnd, UINT nHitTest, UINT message)
{
    if(pWnd == this && m_pSelection)
    {
        CRectTracker aTracker;                  // Create a tracker rectangle
        SetupTracker(m_pSelection, &aTracker);  // Set the tracker style

        // Change the cursor if it is over the currently selected item
        // Check if the last hit was in the tracker rectangle
        if(aTracker.SetCursor(this, nHitTest))
```

```
            return TRUE;                        // and if so return TRUE
    }

        return CView::OnSetCursor(pWnd, nHitTest, message);
}
```

The first parameter passed to the handler is a pointer to the window that currently contains the cursor. The second parameter is a numeric value that identifies the area in the window where the cursor is. The third parameter, which we will ignore, is a mouse message number.

After verifying that the cursor is in the view window and that there is an object selected, we create a **CRectTracker** object and set its style to correspond to the state of the selected object. We then use the **SetCursor()** member of the tracker object, **aTracker**, which will take care of setting the cursor appropriately if it is over the tracker. If the cursor wasn't set, the **SetCursor()** function will return **0** and the message will be passed to the handler in the **CView** class to give it a chance to set the cursor.

Activating an Embedded Object

An object is activated by double-clicking it, so we need to add a handler for the **WM_LBUTTONDBLCLK** message to **COleContainerView**. You can use ClassWizard to do this and implement it with the following code:

```
void COleContainerView::OnLButtonDblClk(UINT nFlags, CPoint point)
{
    OnLButtonDown(nFlags, point);
    if(m_pSelection)
        m_pSelection->DoVerb((GetKeyState(VK_CONTROL)<0) ?
                                        OLEIVERB_OPEN:OLEIVERB_PRIMARY, this);
        CView::OnLButtonDblClk(nFlags, point);
}
```

Because the left button has been clicked, we first call the **OnLButtonDown()** handler. If **m_pSelection** is not zero, we use the pointer to call the **DoVerb()** member of the embedded item selected.

The word **verb** has been given a special meaning in the context of OLE. A **verb** specifies an action that an embedded object is to take, usually in response to some action by the user. The first argument to the **DoVerb()** function specifies a verb, which in our case is given by:

```
(GetKeyState(VK_CONTROL)<0) ? OLEIVERB_OPEN:OLEIVERB_PRIMARY
```

This is a conditional expression which will result in the verb **OLEIVERB_OPEN** if the function **GetKeyState()** returns a negative value, and the verb **OLEIVERB_PRIMARY** if it doesn't. The **GetKeyState()** function tests the status of keys, in this case the *Ctrl* key. If the *Ctrl* key is pressed, the function will return a negative value. If you double-click with the *Ctrl* key pressed, the verb **OLEIVERB_OPEN** will be selected, otherwise the other verb will be selected.

The verb **OLEIVERB_OPEN** opens the item for editing in a separate server window, although the object will remain embedded in the container. You will see that the object in the container window will be cross-hatched, because opening the server window modifies the style of the tracker for the object to do this. The verb **OLEIVERB_PRIMARY** activates the server and makes the item available for in-place editing in the container in the normal way. The second argument to **DoVerb()** identifies the current view in the container where the double-click occurred.

739

Drawing Multiple Embedded Objects

To draw objects in the container document, you must extend the **OnDraw()** handler in **COleContainerView**. The version provided by AppWizard assumes that there is only one object. We need it to iterate over all the objects in the document and draw each of them with an appropriate tracker. Change the code to the following:

```
void COleContainerView::OnDraw(CDC* pDC)
{
    COleContainerDoc* pDoc = GetDocument();
    ASSERT_VALID(pDoc);

    // Get the first item position
    POSITION aPosition = pDoc->GetStartPosition();

    while(aPosition)      // For each item in the list
    {
        // Get the pointer to the current item
        COleContainerItem* pItem =
                            (COleContainerItem*)pDoc->GetNextItem(aPosition);
        pItem->Draw(pDC, pItem->m_Rect);    // Now draw the item

        // Now create a suitable tracker for the item
        CRectTracker aTracker;              // Create a tracker rectangle
        SetupTracker(pItem, &aTracker);  // Set the style for current item
        aTracker.Draw(pDC);                // Draw the tracker rectangle
    }
}
```

This is very straightforward. We iterate through all the items embedded in the document in the **while** loop, using the **GetNextItem()** function member of the document object that you saw earlier.

For each item in the list, we call the **Draw()** function to get it to draw itself, passing the **m_Rect** member of the item as the second argument. We didn't implement a **Draw()** function for the **COleContainerItem** class. This function is inherited from the base class, **COleClientItem**. You will remember that we saw at the beginning of this chapter that the server, not the container, draws embedded objects. The object will be drawn by the **OnDraw()** member of the OLE object in the server. This drawing operation will generate the picture in an internal format called a **metafile**, which is a way of storing all the function calls you make to draw the image to produce a device- independent representation of the image. This can then be replayed in a specific device context. The **Draw()** function member of **COleItem** will access the metafile generated by the server and display it in the device context here.

After drawing an item, we create a tracker with a style based on the state of the current item and get it to draw itself by calling its **Draw()** member. Each time a tracker needs to be displayed for an item, we just generate a new one because it's only a visual aid to interaction. It doesn't need to be permanently saved with the item.

We have no local data in the container document. If the container application has its own document data, you would need to display that in the **OnDraw()** function as well.

Dealing with Object Insertion

AppWizard already provided the mechanism for handling the insertion of a new object into the container. This is in the implementation of the handler **OnInsertObject()** in the **COleContainerView** class. We can make two additions to improve it a little, though. We'll add code to update the rectangle for a new object to that corresponding to the size from the server, and replace the default code that redraws all the views in the container with code that only redraws the area occupied by the new object:

```
void COleContainerView::OnInsertObject()
{
    // Invoke the standard Insert Object dialog box to obtain information
    //  for new COleContainerItem object.
    COleInsertDialog dlg;
    if (dlg.DoModal() != IDOK)
        return;

    BeginWaitCursor();

    COleContainerItem* pItem = NULL;
    TRY
    {
        // Create new item connected to this document.
        COleContainerDoc* pDoc = GetDocument();
        ASSERT_VALID(pDoc);
        pItem = new COleContainerItem(pDoc);
        ASSERT_VALID(pItem);

        // Initialize the item from the dialog data.
        if (!dlg.CreateItem(pItem))
            AfxThrowMemoryException();  // any exception will do
        ASSERT_VALID(pItem);

        pItem->UpdateLink();             // Update the item display
        pItem->GetServerSize();          // Update the item size

        // If item created from class list (not from file) then launch
        //  the server to edit the item.
        if (dlg.GetSelectionType() == COleInsertDialog::createNewItem)
            pItem->DoVerb(OLEIVERB_SHOW, this);

        ASSERT_VALID(pItem);

        // As an arbitrary user interface design, this sets the selection
        //  to the last item inserted.

        // TODO: reimplement selection as appropriate for your application
        SelectItem(pItem);               // Select last inserted item
        pItem->InvalidateItem();         // then invalidate the item
    }
    CATCH(CException, e)
    {
        if (pItem != NULL)
        {
            ASSERT_VALID(pItem);
            pItem->Delete();
        }
```

```
        AfxMessageBox(IDP_FAILED_TO_CREATE);
    }
    END_CATCH

    EndWaitCursor();
}
```

In the **TRY** block, the default code creates a new **COleContainerItem** object associated with the document and stores its address in **pItem**. This is then initialized to the new embedded object through the **CreateItem()** member of the dialog object, **dlg**, which manages the selection of the type of object to be embedded. As long as everything works OK, the first two lines of code we have added are executed. The call to the **UpdateLink()** member of the new **COleContainerItem** object causes the contents of the embedded object to be drawn. We then call our **SetServerSize()** helper function to update the size to that required for the server.

The next **if** statement in the default code checks for a new embedded item being created, rather than one being loaded from a file. If it's a new item, it executes the **DoVerb()** member of the object to open it for editing. Our new code follows, which calls our **SelectItem()** function to select the new item and causes the area occupied by the new object to be redrawn. These lines replace the two default lines which set **m_pSelection** and call **UpdateAllViews()**.

Trying Out the OLE Container

The container is ready to run. You can build it in the normal way and, if you haven't made any typos, it should execute. You may well have applications installed on your system which are OLE servers, in which case you'll see a list of them when you select the Edit/Insert New Object... menu option:

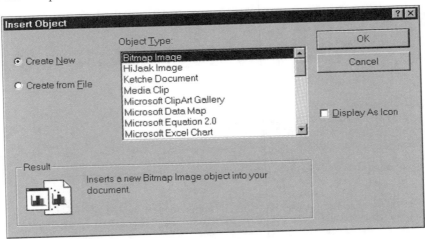

This shows some of the OLE servers that are around in my system. If you want to load a file, you should check the radio button Create from File on the left. Of course, you can add more than one embedded object, as shown in the following screenshot.

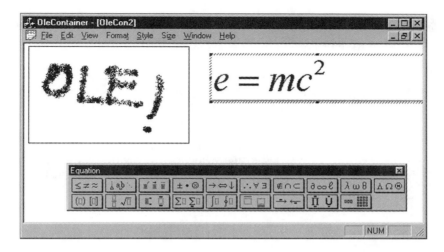

Here you can see an inactive bitmap on the left and an in-place active equation object on the right. The Equation toolbar shown here is supplied by the equation server application.

Implementing an OLE Server

It would be nice to have the Sketcher application working as a server. If we had chosen the options in AppWizard at the beginning, we would have the basics built in now, but that would have meant carrying a lot of excess baggage around in the early stages, which we really didn't want. However, we can quite quickly reconstruct a skeleton version of Sketcher to act as a full server. For this exercise, we'll just add the bare bones drawing capability that we had in the early versions of Sketcher, plus serialization of the document object. We'll go through the code that you need to add to the AppWizard-generated base program, but you should be able to steal a lot of it from versions of Sketcher that you have already. Of course, if you want to, you can add any of the other functionality that we implemented in earlier chapters, but here we'll just discuss the minimum we need to get an operational server going that we can exercise in our container.

The first step is to recreate the basic Sketcher application as an OLE server using AppWizard.

Generating a Server Application

Create a new project of type MFCAppWizard (exe) and call it Sketcher. Make sure that it's in a different folder from any of the other versions of Sketcher you may have around. The process is almost identical to what you did to generate the program in the first instance. It should be an MDI application - the only differences from the default options are in Step 3 and Step 4. In Step 3, make sure that you select the Full Server option as the type of application. In Step 4, select the Advanced button to bring up the Advanced Options dialog, then set the entries as you see in the following screenshot.

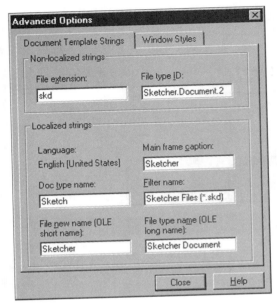

You can see that we have used a different File extension and File type ID for this version of the Sketcher application. Once this information has been filled in, you can click Close and then Finish to create the new project. You may find that you get the following message displayed, in which case, you should click No to ensure that a unique ID is used for your documents.

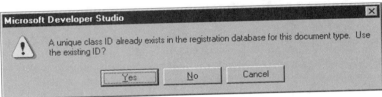

Adding Sketcher Application Functionality

The first step to recreating Sketcher is to copy the **Elements.h**, **Elements.cpp** and **OurConstants.h** files from an earlier version of Sketcher to the folder containing the current version. Make sure that it's a version containing serialization of the elements. The one you had at the end of Chapter 17 will do nicely. Then add the **Elements.cpp** file to the current project using the Insert/Files into Project... menu option.

We'll attempt to keep the code simple in this version of Sketcher, so we won't implement scrolling, text, different pen widths or the context menu. The only change that you'll need to make to the elements as we used them in Chapter 17 is to remove the **PenWidth** parameter from the constructors both in the class definitions and in the implementations. Set the **m_Pen** member to **1** in each element constructor. The easiest way to do this is to search for **,int PenWidth** in both the **Elements.h** and **Elements.cpp** files and replace this string with nothing using the Edit/Replace... menu item. Once that's done, go back to the **.cpp** file and replace all occurrences of **PenWidth** with **1**.

You can now follow what should be a well trodden path to add the basic drawing functionality to the project. You can do it in the following steps.

Document Data and Interface Functions

Add the **protected** data members to the **CSketcherDoc** class:

```
WORD m_Element;
COLORREF m_Color;
CSize m_DocSize;
```

To do this, you can right-click on the class name in ClassView or just copy the code from an earlier implementation. The third data item is a record of the document size which we'll use extensively when Sketcher is operating as an OLE server.

Next, you can add the **protected** data member for storing the list of elements:

```
CTypedPtrList<CObList, CElement*> m_ElementList;   // Element list
```

Note that you have to add this explicitly and that you must remember to add an **#include** for **afxtempl.h** to **StdAfx.h**. (Put it after the **#include** for **afxole.h**).

The first three data members must be initialized in the constructor for the document:

```
CSketcherDoc::CSketcherDoc()
{
   // Use OLE compound files
   EnableCompoundFile();

   // TODO: add one-time construction code here
   m_Element = LINE;            // Set initial element type
   m_Color = BLACK;             // Set initial drawing color
   m_DocSize = CSize(200,200);  // Set document size
}
```

Because we refer to the constants that we have defined for the element types and colors, you must add an **#include** directive for **OurConstants.h** to the beginning of **SketcherDoc.cpp**. We must also remember to clean up the **m_ElementList** object in the destructor for the document:

```
CSketcherDoc::~CSketcherDoc()
{
   // Get the position at the head of the list
   POSITION aPosition = m_ElementList.GetHeadPosition();

   // Now delete the element pointed to by each list entry
   while(aPosition)
      delete m_ElementList.GetNext(aPosition);

   m_ElementList.RemoveAll();    // Finally delete all pointers
}
```

You can copy the **public** interface functions for the document class directly from the Chapter 17 version of Sketcher. The ones that you need are:

```
WORD GetElementType()                    // Get the element type
          { return m_Element; }

COLORREF GetElementColor()               // Get the element color
```

```
                        { return m_Color; }

void AddElement(CElement* pElement)        // Add an element to the list
                { m_ElementList.AddTail((CObject*)pElement); }

POSITION GetListHeadPosition()             // return list head POSITION value
             { return m_ElementList.GetHeadPosition(); }

CElement* GetNext(POSITION& aPos)          // Return current element pointer
              { return m_ElementList.GetNext(aPos); }

CSize GetDocSize(){ return m_DocSize; }  // Return the current document size
```

Because we refer to the **CElement** class here, you should add an **#include** statement for
Elements.h to the **SketcherDoc.h** file.

You also need to implement the **Serialize()** member of the document:

```
void CSketcherDoc::Serialize(CArchive& ar)
{
    m_ElementList.Serialize(ar);         // Serialize the element list
    if (ar.IsStoring())
    {
        ar << m_Color                    // Store the current color
            << m_Element                 // the current element type,
            << m_DocSize;                // and the document size
    }
    else
    {
        ar >> m_Color                    // Retrieve the current color
            >> m_Element                 // the current element type,
            >> m_DocSize;                // and the document size
    }
}
```

The reason that you need serialization implemented for your server is that, when an embedded
object is deactivated, the framework uses it to save the document. When you reactivate the
object, it is restored using serialization. This is necessary because your server may be servicing
several embedded objects at one time.

Adding the Menus

Now you need to add the Element and Color menus that we had in earlier versions of Sketcher
(Chapter 13 and later). You should add them to the **IDR_SKETCHTYPE** menu, just as we did
before. You will see that this version of Sketcher contains a couple of menu resources in addition
to **IDR_SKETCHTYPE** and **IDR_MAINFRAME** which are for use when the program is operating as
a server, but ignore these for now. We'll get to them later. For each menu item, use the same
IDs and captions that we used before.

There is a shortcut you can use here to transfer your menus across from a previous version of
Sketcher. First, close all the open windows in Developer Studio, then open the **.rc** file for the
menu you want to copy. Double-click on the **IDR_SKETCHTYPE** menu resource for the newly
opened file to display the menu. Open **IDR_SKETCHTYPE** for the current project, then use the
Window/Tile Horizontally to view both menus simultaneously. You can copy the menu items that
you want by dragging them with the mouse while holding down the *Ctrl* key.

Now you should add the COMMAND and UPDATE_COMMAND_UI handlers for each menu item to the **CSketcherDoc** class, exactly as you did way back in Chapter 13. You can use ClassWizard to add these handlers, then copy the code for the command handlers (**OnColorBlack()**, etc.) and update handlers (**OnUpdateColorBlack()**, etc.) from an earlier version of Sketcher into the current one, or you can just enter the code - the functions are very simple. The typical command handler for an element is:

```
void CSketcherDoc::OnElementCircle()
{
   // TODO: Add your command handler code here
   m_Element = CIRCLE;          // Set element type as a line
}
```

A typical update command handler is:

```
void CSketcherDoc::OnUpdateElementLine(CCmdUI* pCmdUI)
{
   // TODO: Add your command update UI handler code here
   // Set Checked if the current element is a line
   pCmdUI->SetCheck(m_Element==LINE);
}
```

All the command and command update handlers are of a similar form.

Adding the Toolbar Buttons

You can also add the toolbar buttons for the menu items exactly as before. All you need are the buttons for the four element types and the four colors. You add these to the toolbar **IDR_MAINFRAME** and set the IDs to the same as those for the corresponding menu item.

If you like, you can also take a shortcut to this process. In the same way that you did for the menus, display the current project **IDR_MAINFRAME** toolbar and one containing the toolbar buttons you need - any version of Sketcher from the end of Chapter 13 onwards will be OK. You can then drag toolbar buttons from one toolbar to the other by holding down the *Ctrl* key. You only need the four buttons for colors and the four for element types.

Adding the View Application Functionality

The **protected** data items you need in the **CSketcherView** class definition are:

```
CPoint m_FirstPoint;       // First point recorded for an element
CPoint m_SecondPoint;      // Second point recorded for an element
CElement* m_pTempElement;  // Pointer to temporary element
```

Since the class definition uses the **CElement** class, we ought to add an **#include** statement for **Elements.h** to **SketcherView.h**.

The data members must be initialized in the constructor, so add the code to the constructor implementation to do this:

```
CSketcherView::CSketcherView()
{
   m_FirstPoint = CPoint(0,0);       // Set 1st recorded point to 0,0
   m_SecondPoint = CPoint(0,0);      // Set 2nd recorded point to 0,0
   m_pTempElement = 0;               // Set temporary element pointer to 0
}
```

The only message handling functions you need to add to the view class at this point are the handlers for **WM_LBUTTONDOWN**, **WM_LEFTBUTTONUP** and **WM_MOUSEMOVE**. Add these as before, by using ClassWizard or the Messages drop-down list box that is at the top of the window when you view the **SketcherView.cpp** file in the project.

You can use simple implementations of the handlers, similar to those from Chapter 15 without the context menu support but with the proper conversion from client coordinates to logical coordinates. The handler for **WM_LBUTTONDOWN** is:

```
void CSketcherView::OnLButtonDown(UINT nFlags, CPoint point)
{
   CClientDC aDC(this);               // Create a device context
   OnPrepareDC(&aDC);                 // Prepare the device context
   aDC.DPtoLP(&point);                // Convert point to Logical
   m_FirstPoint = point;              // Record the cursor position
   SetCapture();                      // Capture subsequent mouse messages
}
```

The implementation of the handler for **WM_LBUTTONUP** messages will be:

```
void CSketcherView::OnLButtonUp(UINT nFlags, CPoint point)
{
   CSketcherDoc* pDoc = GetDocument();      // Get the document pointer

   if(this == GetCapture())
      ReleaseCapture();                     // Stop capturing mouse messages

   // If there is an element, add it to the document
   if(m_pTempElement)
   {
      pDoc->AddElement(m_pTempElement);     // Add the element
      pDoc->SetModifiedFlag();              // Note the modification
      // Tell the other views about it
      pDoc->UpdateAllViews(0, 0, m_pTempElement);
      m_pTempElement = 0;                   // Reset the element pointer
   }
}
```

Finally, the code for the **WM_MOUSEMOVE** handler will be:

```
void CSketcherView::OnMouseMove(UINT nFlags, CPoint point)
{
   // TODO: Add your message handler code here and/or call default
   // Define a Device Context object for the view
   CClientDC aDC(this);
   OnPrepareDC(&aDC);                 // Prepare the device context
   aDC.SetROP2(R2_NOTXORPEN);         // Set the drawing mode

   if((nFlags & MK_LBUTTON) && (this == GetCapture()))
   {
      aDC.DPtoLP(&point);            // Convert point to logical
      m_SecondPoint = point;         // Save the current cursor position

      if(m_pTempElement)
      {
         // Redraw the old element so it disappears from the view
```

```
        m_pTempElement->Draw(&aDC);

        if(CURVE == GetDocument()->GetElementType())    // Is it a curve?
        {  // We are drawing a curve
           // so add a segment to the existing curve
           ((CCurve*)m_pTempElement)->AddSegment(m_SecondPoint);
           m_pTempElement->Draw(&aDC);                  // Now redraw it
           return;                                      // We are done
        }

        delete m_pTempElement;                          // Delete the old element
        m_pTempElement = 0;                             // Reset the pointer to 0
    }
    // Create a temporary element of the type and color that
    // is recorded in the document object, and draw it
    m_pTempElement = CreateElement();                   // Create a new element
    m_pTempElement->Draw(&aDC);                         // Draw the element
    }
}
```

All of this should be quite familiar to you now, so these additions shouldn't take very long.

We also need the **CreateElement()** function to create elements on the heap. Add a **protected** declaration for this function to the view class and implement it as:

```
CElement* CSketcherView::CreateElement()
{
    // Get a pointer to the document for this view
    CSketcherDoc* pDoc = GetDocument();
    ASSERT_VALID(pDoc);                       // Verify the pointer is good

    // Now select the element using the type stored in the document
    switch(pDoc->GetElementType())
    {
        case RECTANGLE:
            return new CRectangle(m_FirstPoint, m_SecondPoint,
                            pDoc->GetElementColor());
        case CIRCLE:
            return new CCircle(m_FirstPoint, m_SecondPoint,
                            pDoc->GetElementColor());
        case CURVE:
            return new CCurve(m_FirstPoint, m_SecondPoint,
                            pDoc->GetElementColor());
        case LINE:
            return new CLine(m_FirstPoint, m_SecondPoint,
                            pDoc->GetElementColor());

        default:                              // Something's gone wrong
            AfxMessageBox("Bad Element code", MB_OK);
            AfxAbort();
            return NULL;
    }
}
```

This is like the code you've seen in earlier chapters.

Drawing the Document

As you well know by now, we'll draw the document in the **OnDraw()** member of the view class. The implementation is:

```
void CSketcherView::OnDraw(CDC* pDC)
{
    CSketcherDoc* pDoc = GetDocument();
    ASSERT_VALID(pDoc);

    POSITION aPos = pDoc->GetListHeadPosition();
    CElement* pElement = 0;                    // Store for an element pointer
    while(aPos)                                // Loop while aPos is not null
    {
        pElement = pDoc->GetNext(aPos);        // Get the current element pointer
        // If the element is visible...
        if(pDC->RectVisible(pElement->GetBoundRect()))
            pElement->Draw(pDC);               // ...draw it
    }
}
```

This is identical code to that in earlier versions of Sketcher, so you can copy it from one of those if you like.

We must add the **OnUpdate()** function to respond to the **UpdateAllViews()** call that occurs when we add an element to the document, so add this handler to **CSketcherView** using ClassWizard or the drop-down Messages list. The implementation for it will be:

```
void CSketcherView::OnUpdate(CView* pSender, LPARAM lHint, CObject* pHint)
{
    // Invalidate the area corresponding to the element pointed to
    // if there is one, otherwise invalidate the whole client area
    if(pHint)
    {
        CClientDC aDC(this);                   // Create a device context
        OnPrepareDC(&aDC);                     // Prepare the device context

        // Get the enclosing rectangle and convert to client coordinates
        CRect aRect = ((CElement*)pHint)->GetBoundRect();
        aDC.LPtoDP(aRect);
        aRect.NormalizeRect();
        InvalidateRect(aRect);                 // Get the area redrawn
    }
    else
        InvalidateRect(0);
}
```

This is very similar to the code we've used in previous versions of Sketcher.

Finally, you need to add an **#include** statement for **OurConstants.h** to **SketcherView.cpp** after the **#include** for **Sketcher.h**.

Once you have added **OnDraw()**, **OnUpdate()**, the mouse handlers, the **CreateElement()** function and the **#include** statements, you should have a basic working version of Sketcher with the OLE server mechanism built in. You can build it and run it as a stand-alone application to check out all is well. Any omissions or errors should come out during the compilation. When it works stand-alone, you can try it out in the container.

Running Sketcher as a Server

Start the OleContainer application and select Insert New Object... from the Edit menu. The list of OLE servers available should include Sketcher Document, if that is how you identified the file type name in Step 4 of the AppWizard dialog to create the OLE version of Sketcher. If you select this, a Sketcher object will be loaded ready for editing, as shown in the next screen:

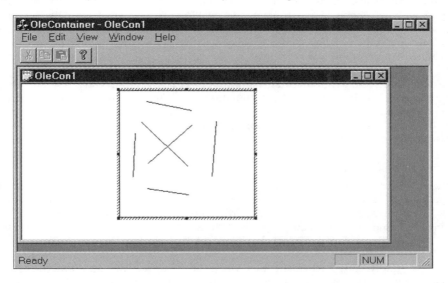

Unfortunately, we have no Sketcher menus or toolbars in the container, but at least you can draw black lines. However, there's another little problem. If you click outside the object to deactivate it, the contents of the object disappear. We clearly have a little more work to do on our server.

Server Resources

Let's go back to the Sketcher server and take a look at the menus. If you extend the Menu part of the resource tree, you'll see that there are two extra menu resources included in the server beyond the two menus that are used when Sketcher is running stand-alone. The contents of these are shown here.

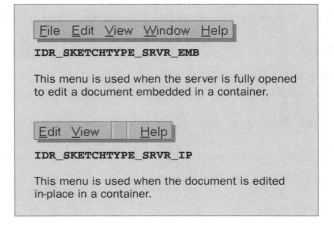

The menu corresponding to **IDR_SKETCHTYPE_SRVR_EMB** is used when you open the server to edit an object embedded in a container by double-clicking the object while holding down the *Ctrl* key. This will appear in a server window separate from the container, so this menu should contain all the items that appear in Sketcher when it's running stand-alone.

The **IDR_SKETCHTYPE_SRVR_IP** menu applies when you are editing an object in-place, which occurs when you just double-click on an object embedded in a container. The server menu will be merged with the menu in the container to enable you to interact with the server during editing, while still providing access to the essential container menus. The segments of the menus in the server and the container that are delineated by the separators will be merged in a predetermined sequence, as we shall see.

If you extend the Toolbar resources in the **Sketcher.rc** window, you'll see that there is also an extra toolbar with the ID **IDR_SKETCHTYPE_SRVR_IP**. This will replace the container's toolbar when you are editing an object in-place. We can copy the menu and toolbar resources that we need in the extra menus from the **IDR_SKETCHTYPE** menu and the **IDR_MAINFRAME** toolbar in the project.

Updating Menu Resources

The first step is to arrange to display the **IDR_SKETCHTYPE** and **IDR_SKETCHTYPE_SRVR_EMB** menus together. The easiest way to do this is to close all the windows in the project, then, with ResourceView displayed in the Project Window, extend the Menu resource tree in the **Sketcher.rc** window and double-click on **IDR_SKETCHTYPE** and **IDR_SKETCHTYPE_SRVR_EMB** to open both windows. Finally, select Tile Horizontally from the Window menu.

You can now simply copy each menu that you need in turn from **IDR_SKETCHTYPE** to **IDR_SKETCHTYPE_SRVR_EMB** by dragging it with *Ctrl* held down as we did before. You need to copy the Color and the Element menus. That completes the **IDR_SKETCHTYPE_SRVR_EMB** menu, so you can save it. All the links to the handlers for the menu items are already in place because they are the ones that are used normally.

After saving **IDR_SKETCHTYPE_SRVR_EMB**, you can close the window for this menu and open the menu **IDR_SKETCHTYPE_SRVR_IP**. Select Window/Tile Horizontally so that this menu and **IDR_SKETCHTYPE** are both visible. You can then copy the Element and Color menu items from **IDR_SKETCHTYPE** to **IDR_SKETCHTYPE_SRVR_IP**. The new menu should look like this:

The combined menu is now in a state where it will merge with the container menu to provide a composite menu in the container application for in-place editing of a Sketcher object.

How Container and Server Menus are Merged

If we assume the context of the container that we created earlier in this chapter, the menu for our server will be merged into the container's menu, as shown in the following diagram.

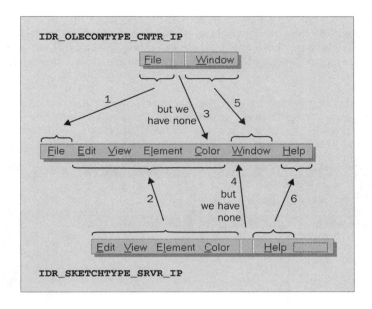

The diagram shows the composite menu in the center that is produced in the container by merging the menus from the container and the server. The numbers on the arrows indicate the sequence in which segments of the two menus are added to form the composite menu. There is actually more scope here than we are using, as we have no items between the separators in either the server or the container. The resulting menu has the File menu item and the Window menu item from the container, since a save operation will apply to the container document with its embedded objects and the window in which the object is displayed is owned by the container application. The application menu items and the Help menu item are contributed by the server.

Updating Toolbar Resources

You need to open both toolbars in the current project corresponding to the IDs **IDR_MAINFRAME** and **IDR_SKETCHTYPE_SRVR_IP** in the same way that you opened the menus previously. Then modify the toolbar with the ID **IDR_SKETCHTYPE_SRVR_IP** as shown in the diagram here.

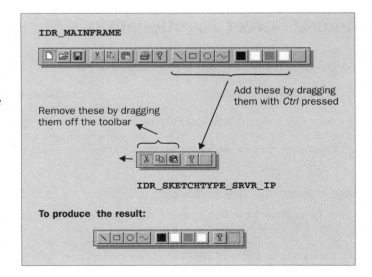

As we saw earlier, you can copy toolbar buttons using the same mechanism that you used for copying menu items. Just drag each button while holding down the *Ctrl* key. We need to remove the buttons indicated because these apply to server editing operations and, in the container context, the container operations will apply. We haven't implemented these functions in Sketcher anyway.

That completes updating the resources for the Sketcher project. Now would be a good time to save the resources if you haven't done so already. You can build Sketcher at this point to see how menu merging works out. If you run the container application and insert an object of the latest version of the Sketcher server, you should get something like the next screen:

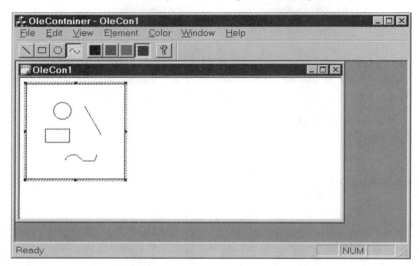

All the menus and toolbar buttons from Sketcher should work OK. You can draw any of the elements in any color. The only problem is that the picture just doesn't stay around when the object is deactivated, but we're getting there.

Adding Server Functionality

As we discussed early on in this chapter, a server object is an instance of the class **COleServerItem** in the server application. It is this object that is responsible for drawing the embedded item when it isn't active. In Sketcher, AppWizard has provided the class **CSketcherSrvrItem** which is derived from **COleServerItem**, so this class represents the embedded object in Sketcher. Whenever the embedded object is being edited, the drawing is being done by the **OnDraw()** function in **CSketcherView** and is being transferred to the container to be displayed. When the embedded object isn't active, the container is asking the **CSketcherSrvrItem** object to draw it, but we haven't provided the capability to do this. This is what we need to do now.

Implementing the Embedded Object

A **CSketcherSrvrItem** object has two essential jobs to do. It must draw the object when the object is embedded but not being edited in-place, and it must be able to supply the extent of the document when requested by the framework on behalf of the container. Drawing is done by the **OnDraw()** member of the **CSketcherSrvrItem** class and the document extent is supplied by the **OnGetExtent()** member.

Scaleable Mapping Modes

There are some complications arising from Sketcher being a server. We can no longer draw the document in the same way as before. You already know that there are two places in the Sketcher program where an embedded document will be drawn - in the **OnDraw()** function in the view object when it is being edited, and in the **OnDraw()** function of the **CSketcherSrvrItem** object when it isn't. Further complications arise because we'll be drawing the embedded document in a rectangle within a view of a container. This rectangle is inevitably small. After all, the whole point of embedding objects is that they should coexist with other objects. It may also be moved about and varied in size, so we need to use a flexible mapping mode.

There are two mapping modes that allow the mapping between logical coordinates and device coordinates to be altered: **MM_ISOTROPIC** and **MM_ANISOTROPIC**. We discussed these mapping modes back in Chapter 16, but it won't hurt to go over things again. The **MM_ISOTROPIC** mapping mode has the property that Windows will force the scaling factor to be the same for both the x and y axes, which has the advantage that your circles will always be circles, but you can't map a document to fit into a rectangle of a different shape. You will always leave part of the rectangle empty. **MM_ANISOTROPIC**, on the other hand, permits scaling of each axis independently, so that you can map an object to fit exactly into a rectangle of any shape, but, of course, shapes will deform in the process. Because it's the most flexible, we will use **MM_ANISOTROPIC** in our server version of Sketcher. This is necessary in the view class, as well as in the class representing the embedded object.

You'll remember that we saw the following equations which express device coordinates in terms of logical coordinates:

$$xDevice = (xLogical - xWindowOrg) * \frac{xViewPortExt}{xWindowExt} + xViewportOrg$$

$$yDevice = (yLogical - yWindowOrg) * \frac{yViewPortExt}{yWindowExt} + yViewportOrg$$

With a bit of algebraic juggling, you'll see that the conversion from device coordinates to logical coordinates will use the formulae:

$$xLogical = (xDevice - xViewportOrg) * \frac{xWindowExt}{xViewportExt} + xWindowOrg$$

$$yLogical = (yDevice - yViewportOrg) * \frac{yWindowExt}{yViewportExt} + yWindowOrg$$

With coordinate systems other than **MM_ISOTROPIC** and **MM_ANISOTROPIC**, the window extent and the viewport extent are fixed by the mapping mode, and you can't change them. Calling the functions **SetWindowExt()** or **SetViewportExt()** in the **CDC** object to change them will have no effect although you can still move the position of (0,0) in your logical reference frame around by calling **SetWindowOrg()** or **SetViewportOrg()**. With **MM_ISOTROPIC** and **MM_ANISOTROPIC**, you can mess everything around to your hearts content.

Updating the View

We need to adjust how the document is drawn by the view to take account of the implications of the server mode of operation. This means using a mapping mode that allows for flexibility in the way the conversion from logical to device coordinates occurs. In other words, we need to work with the **MM_ANISOTROPIC** mode. We can best do this by adding the **OnPrepareDC()** function to **CSketcherView** and setting up the mapping mode there, as we did in Chapter 16.

Changing the Mapping Mode

With the server version of Sketcher, we must define our logical units for drawing in the **MM_ANISOTROPIC** mapping mode so that Windows can determine the mapping to pixels. This is a bit more complicated than it seems at first sight, and requires a little more than we implemented in Chapter 16. You must take account of the scaling between the size at which you are drawing a document and the size of the document when it is displayed in the container.

The measure of this scaling between the server and the container is called a **zoom factor**. We'll use this zoom factor to provide true WYSIWYG drawing for embedded objects. If you don't adjust for the zoom factor, the size of a document object will vary, depending on whether it is being edited or not. The **GetZoomFactor()** member of **COleDocument** provides a value for the zoom factor that you can use to adjust the viewport extent in the device context to get the correct mapping.

We'll set up the mapping mode and the parameters that determine how our logical coordinates are converted in the **OnPrepareDC()** function member of **CSketcherView**. Of course, you'll need to add the function to the view class using ClassWizard. Its implementation will be as follows:

```
void CSketcherView::OnPrepareDC(CDC* pDC, CPrintInfo* pInfo)
{
    CView::OnPrepareDC(pDC, pInfo);
    CSketcherDoc* pDoc = GetDocument();
    pDC->SetMapMode(MM_ANISOTROPIC);
    CSize DocSize = pDoc->GetDocSize();

    // y extent must be negative because document assumes MM_LOENGLISH
    DocSize.cy = -DocSize.cy;   // Change sign of y
    pDC->SetWindowExt(DocSize); // Now set the window extent

    // Get the zoom factor for the server compared to the container
    // If the server isn't in place active, zoom factor will be 1 to 1
    CSize SizeNum, SizeDenom;                  // Places to store zoom factors
    pDoc->GetZoomFactor(&SizeNum, &SizeDenom);

    int xLogPixels = pDC->GetDeviceCaps(LOGPIXELSX);
    int yLogPixels = pDC->GetDeviceCaps(LOGPIXELSY);

    long xExtent = ((long)DocSize.cx*xLogPixels*SizeNum.cx)/
                                                (100*SizeDenom.cx);
    long yExtent = ((long)DocSize.cy*yLogPixels*SizeNum.cy)/
                                                (100*SizeDenom.cy);
    pDC->SetViewportExt((int)xExtent, (int)-yExtent);
}
```

Note that we add our code following the call to the base class function that was supplied in the default implementation. After setting the mapping mode to **MM_ANISOTROPIC**, we set the window extent to correspond to the size of the document, not forgetting that the y extent must be negative, because we are assuming **MM_LOENGLISH** compatibility with the origin at the top left corner of the client area. As we saw earlier, the conversion to device coordinates is determined by the ratio of the window extent to the viewport extent, so we need to set the viewport extent to be the number of pixels that are equivalent to the window extent we have specified, adjusted for the zoom factor.

As you have seen previously, the number of pixels in a logical inch is returned by the **GetDeviceCaps()** member of the **CDC** object. By using the argument **LOGPIXELSX**, we get the number of pixels in a logical inch on the x axis, and similarly for the y axis. A logical inch is a Windows invention which is an inch enlarged to make characters readable. For every 100 logical units, we want to set the viewport extent to a logical inch's worth of pixels, so the number of pixels for the viewport's x extent, before adjustment for the zoom factor, is:

$$\frac{DocSize.cx * xLogPixels}{100}$$

The zoom factor is returned as two **CSize** values - **SizeNum** and **SizeDenom** - corresponding to the numerator and denominator in the factor respectively. The ratio of the **cx** members of these apply to the x extent for the viewport and the ratio of the **cy** members apply to the y extent. Thus, the x extent, for example, is calculated by the expression:

$$\frac{DocSize.cx * xLogPixels * SizeNum.cx}{100 * SizeDenom.cx}$$

This is what we have in the code for the function above.

Drawing the Embedded Object

To draw the embedded object, we need to add code to the **OnDraw()** member of **CSketcherSrvrItem** as follows:

```
BOOL CSketcherSrvrItem::OnDraw(CDC* pDC, CSize& rSize)
{
    CSketcherDoc* pDoc = GetDocument();
    ASSERT_VALID(pDoc);

    // TODO: set mapping mode and extent
    //   (The extent is usually the same as the size returned from OnGetExtent)
    pDC->SetMapMode(MM_ANISOTROPIC);
    CSize DocSize = pDoc->GetDocSize();     // Get the current document size

    DocSize.cy = -DocSize.cy;               // Invert the y axis for MM_LOENGLISH
    pDC->SetWindowOrg(0,0);
    pDC->SetWindowExt(DocSize);

    // TODO: add drawing code here.  Optionally, fill in the HIMETRIC extent.
    //   All drawing takes place in the metafile device context (pDC).
    POSITION aPos = pDoc->GetListHeadPosition();
    CElement* pElement = 0;         // Store for an element pointer
    while(aPos)                     // Loop while aPos is not null
    {
        pElement = pDoc->GetNext(aPos);     // Get the current element pointer
        // If the element is visible...
        if(pDC->RectVisible(pElement->GetBoundRect()))
            pElement->Draw(pDC);            // ...draw it
    }

    return TRUE;
}
```

This is relatively straightforward. After setting the mapping mode, we retrieve the size of the document and use this to set the window extent. We make sure that the value for the y extent is negative. All our code in Sketcher assumes **MM_LOENGLISH** with the origin at the top left corner of the client area. We must, therefore, specify the *y* extent and set the origin here to be consistent with that assumption. Note that AppWizard already supplied the statement to set the mapping mode to **MM_ANISOTROPIC**. This is the standard approach to drawing an embedded server object.

After setting up the mapping mode and the window extent, we draw the document using the same code we used in the **OnDraw()** function in the view. Drawing here isn't directly to the screen. The GDI function calls that create the document image are stored in a metafile, which is a device-independent representation of the image. The viewport extent will be adjusted by the framework to map this metafile into the rectangle in the container view before the metafile is replayed to draw the document. This will result in the image being deformed if the rectangle enclosing the item in the container has been resized. If you want to prevent this, you need to include code here to do so. One possibility is to use **MM_ISOTROPIC** to force consistent scaling of the axes.

We haven't set the value of the second parameter, **rSize**, in the **OnDraw()** function. If you set this value it should be the size of the document in **MM_HIMETRIC** units. If you don't set it (we haven't here), the framework will call the **OnGetExtent()** function in the **COleServerItem** class object to get it from there. We'll implement that next.

Getting the Extent of an Embedded Object

The framework calls the **OnGetExtent()** member of the embedded object class in the server to get the size of the document that is to be displayed in the container. We need to implement this to return the size of the document object in Sketcher. The code to do this is as follows:

```
BOOL CSketcherSrvrItem::OnGetExtent(DVASPECT dwDrawAspect,
                                                   CSize& rSize)
{
    // Most applications, like this one, only handle drawing the content
    //   aspect of the item.  If you wish to support other aspects, such
    //   as DVASPECT_THUMBNAIL (by overriding OnDrawEx), then this
    //   implementation of OnGetExtent should be modified to handle the
    //   additional aspect(s).

    if (dwDrawAspect != DVASPECT_CONTENT)
        return COleServerItem::OnGetExtent(dwDrawAspect, rSize);

    // CSketcherSrvrItem::OnGetExtent is called to get the extent in
    //   HIMETRIC units of the entire item.  The default implementation
    //   here simply returns a hard-coded number of units.

    CSketcherDoc* pDoc = GetDocument();
    ASSERT_VALID(pDoc);

    // TODO: replace this arbitrary size
    rSize = pDoc->GetDocSize();   // Get the document size

    CClientDC aDC(0);             // Get device context for conversion
    aDC.SetMapMode(MM_ANISOTROPIC);  // Set map mode that is scaleable

    // Set window extent to 1 inch in each direction in MM_LOENGLISH
    aDC.SetWindowExt(100, -100);    // Set window extent with negative y

    // Set viewport extent to the number of pixels in 1 inch
```

```
        aDC.SetViewportExt(aDC.GetDeviceCaps(LOGPIXELSX),
                           aDC.GetDeviceCaps(LOGPIXELSY));

    aDC.LPtoHIMETRIC(&rSize);        // Convert document size to HIMETRIC
```

```
    return TRUE;
}
```

The comments explain what the framework expects from this function. Here, we take a simplistic approach and just retrieve the document size that is stored in the document. Ideally, the value returned should reflect the physical extent of the object to be drawn, not just the arbitrarily assigned extent for the document, but this will suffice to get our server working. The size must be returned in **HIMETRIC** units because this is the standard unit of measure set by the framework. Our document size is in **LOENGLISH** units, so we need to set up a mapping that will ensure that the logical unit in the device context is equivalent to this. We do this by setting the window extent to **100**, which is the equivalent of 1 inch in each direction in **LOENGLISH** units, and then setting the viewport extent to the number of logical pixels per inch in each direction.

The number of logical pixels per inch is obtained by calling the **GetDeviceCaps()** member of the **CClientDC** object with the arguments shown. You will remember we used this in Chapter 16 when we were implementing scaling, and in Chapter 17 to get the number of points per inch for the printer. By using suitable arguments, you can use this function to get at a vast range of parameters that apply to the device context. You can get the complete list of these through the <u>H</u>elp menu option. Finally, having set the scaling in the device context appropriately, we call the function **LPtoHIMETRIC()** to convert the document size to **HIMETRIC** units.

Add an **#include** directive for **Elements.h** to the beginning of the **SrvrItem.cpp** file because of the references to the **CElement** class in the **OnDraw()** member function.

Notifying the Framework of Changes

To communicate to the framework that we have altered the document, we need to call the function **NotifyChanged()** whenever we do so. This is a member of the document class that is inherited from the base class, **COleDocument**.

We need to call the **NotifyChanged()** function in the **WM_LBUTTONUP** handler in the view class:

```
    void CSketcherView::OnLButtonUp(UINT nFlags, CPoint point)
    {
        CSketcherDoc* pDoc = GetDocument();        // Get the document pointer

        if(this == GetCapture())
            ReleaseCapture();                      // Stop capturing mouse messages

        // If there is an element, add it to the document
        if(m_pTempElement)
        {
            pDoc->AddElement(m_pTempElement);      // Add the element
            pDoc->SetModifiedFlag();               // Note the modification
            // Tell the other views about it
            pDoc->UpdateAllViews(0, 0, m_pTempElement);
            m_pTempElement = 0;                    // Reset the element pointer
            pDoc->NotifyChanged();                 // Tell the container
        }
    }
```

759

There is just one place you need to add a call to **NotifyChanged()**, as highlighted above. This corresponds to when an element is being added to the document.

Executing the Server

Sketcher should now be ready to run as a server. You can try it out stand-alone first, to make sure nothing has been overlooked. To run as a server, Sketcher needs to be entered in the registry, but this will be done automatically for you when you build the application.

You can run Sketcher with the container we created at the beginning of this chapter. Run the container application and select Edit/Insert New Object... from the menu. Then choose Sketch Document from the list box in the dialog and click the OK button. You should then get an embedded Sketcher object, ready for editing.

You aren't limited to Sketcher. You can try embedding objects of other server applications. There are sure to be some on your system. Below, you can see an example of the container running with a Paintbrush object and a Sketcher object embedded:

Here, the Sketcher object is in-place active and currently being edited, as you can see from the hatched tracker border and the toolbar and menu items.

You may also like to try editing an embedded object in a server window. You'll remember that you do this by double-clicking the object while you hold down the *Ctrl* key.

Summary

In this chapter, we have taken a brief look into how to implement an OLE container and a server based on AppWizard-generated base code. The significant points that we have discussed in this chapter are:

▶ A program that can host OLE objects that are maintained and edited by an independent program is called an **OLE container**. An OLE container can typically accommodate multiple embedded objects of different types.

▶ OLE objects in a container can be **linked**, in which case they are stored separately from the container document, or **embedded**, in which case they are stored within the container document.

▶ A program that can support an object embedded in an OLE container application is called an **OLE server**. A server can also be a container.

▶ There are two kinds of server that you can create with AppWizard: a **mini-server** which can only operate in support of embedded objects, and a **full server** which can operate as a stand-alone application as well as a server.

▶ Embedded objects in a container are represented by instances of a class derived from the class **COleClientItem**. A server document that is embedded in a container is represented in the server application by an instance of a class derived from **COleServerItem**.

▶ Embedded objects are drawn in the container view by the server application. When an embedded object is being edited, it is drawn by the **OnDraw()** member of the document view object in the server, otherwise it is drawn by the **OnDraw()** member of the class derived from **COleServerItem**.

▶ An object is subjected to a scaling effect when it is displayed embedded in a container. Consequently, the server must use a mapping mode to allow the drawing operation to take account of the effect of this. This typically involves using **MM_ANISOTROPIC** as the mapping mode in the server.

OLE Controls

OLE controls are another powerful innovation which are becoming very important in the development of applications. This last chapter, therefore, ventures a few steps into the basic concepts of OLE controls and how they work. We'll create a simple OLE control example that you will be able to exercise using the test container provided with Visual C++.

By the end of this chapter, you will have learned:

- What OLE controls are
- What properties are and how they are used
- What ambient and stock properties are
- What methods in an OLE control are
- What events are and how they are used
- How to use Developer Studio to implement an OLE control
- How to add properties to a control
- How to add events to a control

What are OLE Controls?

Just like the Windows controls that we have seen in previous chapters, an OLE control is a facility for a programmer to use someone else's code. For instance, a Visual Basic programmer can use your C++ control in his code. An OLE control is often referred to as an **OCX**, because the extension for the executable module for an OLE control is usually **.ocx**.

OLE controls provide a way to implement component software. With the ever increasing complexity of applications, there is a growing requirement to be able to assemble applications from sets of components which, although written completely independently of one another, can be slotted together as required. An OLE server goes a little way along that path, in that an OLE container can execute any OLE server that is written to conform to the OLE standard.

The primary limitation of an OLE server is that it is anonymous as far as the container is concerned. The container has no knowledge of what the server does and has no mechanism for communicating with it. An OLE control is different. It can communicate with the container, so a degree of integration is possible between the container and the control.

First and foremost, an OLE control communicates with the program that is using it through a set of standard OLE interfaces, specific to OLE controls. The standard for OLE controls is an extension of the standard relating to an OLE compound document that we discussed in Chapter 20. An OLE control is easily reused in different application contexts, since a program that intends to use an OLE control uses the same interface, regardless of what the control does. A program that uses an OLE control is called an **OLE control container**, which implies that it supports the standard interfaces necessary to communicate with the OLE control. Obviously, an OLE control container is typically an application in its own right, which uses one or more OLE controls in its implementation. Because an OLE control uses the OLE interface, it is extremely portable, in that it can be used in any program designed to act as an OLE control container. An OLE control that you write using Visual C++ can be used in applications implemented in other programming languages, as long as they support the standard OLE control interface.

The major advantage of an OLE control over an OLE server is its potential for integrating with its container. There are three ways in which an OLE control and its container can interact. As well as being able to accommodate the transfer of data to and from an OLE container, an OLE control supports a programmable interface through which its container can alter the behavior of the control and the control can send messages to its container. The names for the mechanisms corresponding to these three capabilities are **properties**, **control methods** and **events**. Let's take a look at what each of these involve.

Properties

Properties are variables which specify things about an OLE control. Although they have names, properties are specifically identified by integer values called **DispID**s, which is an abbreviation for a **Dispatch ID**s. In the case of standard properties, which are properties defined within the OLE standard, the DispIDs are negative values.

There are three kinds of properties used in communications between an OLE control and its container:

- **Ambient properties**, which specify information about the environment provided by the container.

- **Control properties**, which are values determining aspects of the control and are set by the control.

- **Extended properties**, which are parameters that affect a control, such as the position where it is displayed, but which are set by the container.

Ambient Properties

Ambient properties are values that the container makes available to a control. A control cannot alter ambient properties, but it can use these values to provide better integration with the container. Through having access to such things as the screen background and foreground colors in use, the control can adjust its appearance to look consistent with that of the current container. More than that, a control may be displayed from various points in the code which goes to make up a container application, and the ambient properties may vary from place to place. The control can be programmed to automatically adapt to the conditions prevailing whenever it is displayed.

In order for ambient properties to be of any use, before you create a control you need to know which ambient properties are likely to be available. If you know what they are, you can incorporate code in your control to react to them. For this reason, the OLE controls specification defines a standard set of ambient properties. There are fifteen standard ambient properties in all, and they all have negative DispID values from -701 to -715 inclusive. We won't look at them all, but a few of the most common examples are as follows:

Name	Purpose	DispID
BackColor	Specifies the background color, in RGB values, used by the container.	-701
DisplayName	Specifies the name of the control for use in error messages.	-702
Font	Specifies the font used by the container.	-703
ForeColor	Specifies the foreground color, in RGB values, used by the container for the display of text and graphics.	-704
ScaleUnits	Specifies the name of the coordinate unit being used by container.	-707
TextAlign	Specifies how the container would like text displayed in a control to be aligned. A value of 0 indicates general alignment, which means text left justified and numbers right justified. A value of 1 is left justified. A value of 2 means text should be centered. A value of 3 means right justified, and 4 is full justification.	-708

These are the ones that you're likely to use most often, but you can get the complete set by looking up 'ambient properties' in Visual C++ help. You're not obliged to do anything about any of the ambient properties when you write an OLE control, but your control will look more professional if you react to those that are relevant.

Note that the names are not part of the OLE controls standard and, although you will find the same names are often used, you have no guarantee that they will always be used consistently. The DispIDs are the assured means of identifying the ambient properties. Visual C++ provides you with a set of symbols for these that, in the case of standard ambient properties, are all of the form **DISPID_AMBIENT_** followed by the property name in capitals. Thus, the symbol corresponding to the DispID for the background color ambient property is **DISPID_AMBIENT_BACKCOLOR**.

Control Properties

Control properties are variables which are set by, and give information about, the control. They can be any kind of attribute that is relevant to your control, but there is a standard set of these too, corresponding to control parameters that are also of interest to a container. The subset of standard control properties that are already included in the class **COleControl** are referred to as **stock properties**. There are nine stock properties, as shown on the following page.

Name	Purpose	DispID
BackColor	Specifies the background color for the control in RGB values.	-501
BackStyle	If this has the value **TRUE**, the control is opaque, otherwise it is transparent.	-502
BorderStyle	Determines whether a control is displayed with a border.	-504
Font	Defines the current font for the control.	-512
ForeColor	Specifies, in RGB values, the foreground color for the control that is used to display text and graphics.	-513
Enabled	When this has the value **TRUE**, it indicates that the control is enabled.	-514
hWnd	Specifies the handle of the control's main window.	-515
Text	Value for a text box, list box, or combo box in the control.	-517
Caption	Defines the caption for the control.	-518

The DispIDs for these properties can be specified by symbols consisting of the name for the property in capital letters with a prefix of **DISPID_**, so the symbol for the font property is **DISPID_FONT**.

It's possible to arrange that a container is automatically notified when a stock property is modified by a control. It's also possible to arrange that the control seeks permission from the container before a certain stock property is changed. You are under no obligation to implement support for any particular stock property in a control, although it makes sense to support some of the basic stock properties that relate to the appearance of a control. The usual approach in most cases is to synchronize them with the corresponding ambient property.

You will certainly be defining non-standard properties for your control. These are referred to as **custom properties**. Custom properties can be anything you need to provide a means of adapting the behavior of your control.

Extended Properties

Extended properties are properties that apply to a control, but are set by the container for the control. A control is able to access the extended properties defined by the container, but it is not usually necessary to do so. There are only five standard extended properties defined, with the names, **Name**, **Visible**, **Parent**, **Cancel** and **Default**. We won't dwell on these, as we won't be concerned with them in this book, but you should avoid giving your own properties names that are the same as these.

Property Pages

A **property page** is a dialog that is used to display an interface for modifying a group of properties so that the values assigned to the properties can be altered by the programmer.

With a complicated control, several property pages may be used, with a group of related properties being assigned to each page. A series of property pages like this is organized into a **property sheet**, which has the appearance of a tabbed dialog box. You have used such tabbed dialog boxes many times in Developer Studio, for example, when setting properties of controls during the creation of dialogs in the Sketcher program.

MFC includes the class **CPropertySheet** to define a property sheet, and the class **CPropertyPage** to defined individual tabbed pages within a property sheet. Each property page will use controls such as edit boxes, list boxes or radio buttons for the setting of individual property values. We'll see how to use controls on a property page to set values for properties in an OLE control when we come to implement an OLE control later in this chapter.

Control Methods

A control method is a function in a control that can be invoked to perform some action in response to an external request. Control methods are identified by DispIDs, just like properties. There are three standard methods defined:

Method Name	Purpose	DispID
Refresh()	Causes the control to be redrawn.	-550
DoClick()	Simulates a button being clicked with the left mouse button when the user presses the *Enter* or *Esc* keys.	-551
AboutBox()	Displays a modal About dialog box for the control.	-552

Of course, you can also add your own custom methods to a control that will execute when some specific action occurs. We'll be adding custom methods to an OLE control example later in this chapter.

Events

Events are signals that an OLE control sends to a container as a consequence of some action by the user on the control, or when some Windows message is received by the control. A control event can have parameters associated with it that provide additional information about the event. The container needs to implement functions to service these events in an appropriate way. The most common standard OLE control events are:

Event Name	Purpose	DispID
Click	Occurs when a mouse button is pressed and then released over a control.	-600
DblClick	Occurs when the control is double-clicked.	-601
KeyDown	Occurs when a key is pressed when the control has the focus.	-602
KeyPress	Occurs when a **WM_CHAR** message is received.	-603

Table Continued on Following Page

Event Name	Purpose	DispID
KeyUp	Occurs when a key is released when the control has the focus.	-604
MouseDown	Occurs when a mouse button is pressed while the cursor is over the control.	-605
MouseMove	Occurs when the cursor moves over the control.	-606
MouseUp	Occurs when a mouse button is released over the control.	-607
Error	Signals the container when some kind of error has occurred.	-608

All the standard events noted above are supported by the class **COleControl**.

The ability of an OLE control to communicate with a container through events, and the ability of a container to set properties which affect the operation of the control, is referred to as **OLE Automation**, although it is not limited to OLE controls. You can, for example, implement OLE automation in an OLE server to provide a programmable mechanism for a container to interact with the server.

The Interface to an OLE Control

In order to make the properties, events and methods of a control available to a container program, there needs to be an external description of what they are. Controls developed in Developer Studio make the external description available in a **type library** file, which has the extension **.tlb**. This file is produced from the definition of the interface elements expressed in the **Object Description Language**, or **ODL**, which is stored in a source file with the extension **.odl**.

You don't need to worry about the detail of the object description language, since this is all taken care of by ClassWizard when you add properties and other interface elements to your control. In the ODL file, you will find statements that associate the DispIDs for particular control properties with the variables in the code for your control which represent them. The same applies to the DispIDs for methods in your control that you make available to a container and the events that you implement. The appropriate entries will be added to the **.odl** file as you develop the source code for your control, and the type library file for your control will be generated automatically when you build the executable module.

Implementing an OLE Control

We can implement a model of a traffic signal as an OLE control. We'll expose properties for the period of time for which the stop or go light operates, and for the starting condition for the signal, to make it possible to change these externally.

The starting point for our example is a basic OLE control that we can create using ControlWizard in Developer Studio.

Creating a Basic OLE Control

Create a new project workspace with the Type: set to OLE ControlWizard, as shown below:

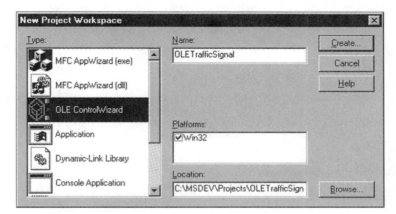

You can name the control as shown, or choose your own name for the project. Remember that the name you choose will eventually be entered in the registry, so you need to avoid conflicts. Before the code is generated, ControlWizard will check for conflicts with the existing registry entries and let you know if there is a potential problem.

You can go through the rest of the dialog to create the code for the control, accepting all the default options that are set.

Structure of the Program

If you look at ClassView for the program, you'll see that there are just three classes defined: the application class **COleTrafficSignalApp**, the control class **COleTrafficSignalCtrl** and the property page class **COleTrafficSignalPropPage**.

The Application Class

The application class **COleTrafficSignalApp** is very simple, containing just two members - the **InitInstance()** function in which you can include any initialization code you want to add, and the **ExitInstance()** function in which you can do any necessary clean-up when the control is terminated.

This external simplicity hides a good deal of internal sophistication. The base class for our application class is **COleControlModule** which is, in turn, derived from **CWinApp** which provides all of the functionality of any other Windows application. The default version of the **InitInstance()** function calls the version in **COleControlModule** which initializes the control.

The Control Class

The class **COleTrafficSignalCtrl** is derived from the MFC class **COleControl** and provides the interface to the control container. The definition provided by ControlWizard is shown on the next page.

```
class COleTrafficSignalCtrl : public COleControl
{
    DECLARE_DYNCREATE(COleTrafficSignalCtrl)

    // Constructor
    public:
        COleTrafficSignalCtrl();

    // Overrides

    // Drawing function
    virtual void OnDraw(CDC* pdc, const CRect& rcBounds, const CRect& rcInvalid);

    // Persistence
    virtual void DoPropExchange(CPropExchange* pPX);

    // Reset control state
    virtual void OnResetState();

    // Implementation
    protected:
        ~COleTrafficSignalCtrl();

    DECLARE_OLECREATE_EX(COleTrafficSignalCtrl)//Class factory and guid
    DECLARE_OLETYPELIB(COleTrafficSignalCtrl)  // GetTypeInfo
    DECLARE_PROPPAGEIDS(COleTrafficSignalCtrl) // Property page IDs
    DECLARE_OLECTLTYPE(COleTrafficSignalCtrl)  //Type name & misc status

    // Message maps
    //{{AFX_MSG(COleTrafficSignalCtrl)
        // NOTE - ClassWizard will add and remove member functions here.
        //    DO NOT EDIT what you see in these blocks of generated code !
    //}}AFX_MSG
    DECLARE_MESSAGE_MAP()

    // Dispatch maps
    //{{AFX_DISPATCH(COleTrafficSignalCtrl)
        // NOTE - ClassWizard will add and remove member functions here.
        //    DO NOT EDIT what you see in these blocks of generated code !
    //}}AFX_DISPATCH
    DECLARE_DISPATCH_MAP()

    afx_msg void AboutBox();

    // Event maps
    //{{AFX_EVENT(COleTrafficSignalCtrl)
        // NOTE - ClassWizard will add and remove member functions here.
        //    DO NOT EDIT what you see in these blocks of generated code !
    //}}AFX_EVENT
    DECLARE_EVENT_MAP()

    // Dispatch and event IDs
    public:
        enum {
    //{{AFX_DISP_ID(COleTrafficSignalCtrl)
        // NOTE: ClassWizard will add and remove enumeration elements here.
        //    DO NOT EDIT what you see in these blocks of generated code !
    //}}AFX_DISP_ID
```

```
      };
   };
```

You'll need to add application-specific data and function members to this class to customize the control to your requirements.

The **OnDraw()** function is called when a **WM_PAINT** message is sent to the control, so you add the drawing operations for your control to this function.

The **DoPropExchange()** member handles serialization of the properties for the control. ClassWizard will automatically extend this function for stock properties that you add, but, if your control requires custom properties, you must add code to serialize these yourself. It may not be immediately obvious why you would want to serialize the properties of a control, but think about what might be involved in setting up a complicated control that you are using in a program. There could be a significant number of properties that you need to set to achieve the behavior that you want and, without serialization, someone using your program would need to set every one, each time your application was executed. This could get tedious.

The **OnResetState()** member is called by the framework when the control properties need to be set to their default values. The default implementation of this member calls the **DoPropExchange()** function to do this. If your control needs special initialization, you can add it to the **OnResetState()** member.

You can ignore the group of four macros, starting with **DECLARE_OLECREATE_EX()**. These are included by ControlWizard to set up essential mechanisms required for the operation of an OLE control.

This class will eventually include the code to support the specifics of the interface to a container. You can see that there are three blocks at the end of the class, relating to **message maps**, **dispatch maps** and **event maps** definition, that are maintained by ClassWizard. The message maps are the same as the ones we have seen previously in an ordinary Windows program, providing Windows message handlers for the class. The dispatch maps referred to will specify the connection between internal and external names for properties and methods which are accessible by a container. The event maps will include the specification of the class function that is responsible for firing each event that the control can send to its container. Entries in all these maps are all handled automatically by ClassWizard, as and when you specify elements of the interface to a container that is supported by the control.

Implementation of the Control Class

The default implementation of the control class provided by ControlWizard in **OLETrafficSignalCtl.cpp** has the definitions for the maps we have just discussed, plus a lot of other stuff that is essential to the operation of the control. With the exception of the list of property pages, all of these are maintained by ClassWizard, so you can safely ignore their detailed contents. We'll just give the briefest indication of what they are, so that you get a basic understanding of what they do.

The maps are followed by the block that contains the list of property pages for the control. There is just one at present, but if you need to add more property pages to your control, for each page you must add an additional line which applies the **PROPPAGEID()** macro to the property page class name. You must also increase the count of the number of property pages to correspond to the total number of property pages that you have.

771

The next macro in the implementation of `COleTrafficSignalCtrl` is:

```
IMPLEMENT_OLECREATE_EX(COleTrafficSignalCtrl,
                       "OLETRAFFICSIGNAL.OleTrafficSignalCtrl.1",
                       0xf2e4bc3, 0x3ace, 0x11cf, 0xa3, 0xcb, 0x44,
                       0x45, 0x53, 0x54, 0, 0)
```

The purpose of this macro is to create a **class factory** for the control. A class factory is an object that has the ability to create OLE objects and, in this case, the objects it will be able to create are instances of our control. Instances of our control are identified by the CLSID which is specified here in the arguments to the macro. The class factory object implements another standard OLE interface, known as the `IClassFactory` interface, but you need not be concerned with the detailed mechanics of this - it's all handled by the framework.

The `IMPLEMENT_OLETYPELIB()` macro which follows creates a member of the control class that is used to retrieve information about the interface to a container that is supported by the control. The detail of this is also taken care of by the framework.

We then have definitions of two global constants, which are **struct**s that define unique identifiers for the interfaces to a container supported by our control. These identifiers are used to reference the interfaces. They are followed by a global constant which defines miscellaneous characteristics of the control's behavior, and a macro which implements these characteristics.

The definition of `UpdateRegistry()` overrides the base class implementation. The purpose of this member is to cause the control to be entered in the system registry. The control cannot be used until it has been registered.

The remainder of the class implementation contains simple default implementations of the class members, some of which we'll extend when we customize the control to behave as we want.

The Property Page Class

The class `COleTrafficSignalPropPage` implements the ability to set control properties through property pages. Each property page that is created for your control is managed by an instance of this class. The definition of this class provided by ControlWizard is:

```
class COleTrafficSignalPropPage : public COlePropertyPage
{
    DECLARE_DYNCREATE(COleTrafficSignalPropPage)
    DECLARE_OLECREATE_EX(COleTrafficSignalPropPage)

    // Constructor
public:
    COleTrafficSignalPropPage();

    // Dialog Data
    //{{AFX_DATA(COleTrafficSignalPropPage)
    enum { IDD = IDD_PROPPAGE_OLETRAFFICSIGNAL };
        // NOTE - ClassWizard will add data members here.
        //     DO NOT EDIT what you see in these blocks of generated code !
    //}}AFX_DATA

    // Implementation
protected:
    virtual void DoDataExchange(CDataExchange* pDX);// DDX/DDV support
```

```
    // Message maps
    protected:
      //{{AFX_MSG(COleTrafficSignalPropPage)
      // NOTE - ClassWizard will add and remove member functions here.
      //      DO NOT EDIT what you see in these blocks of generated code !
      //}}AFX_MSG
    DECLARE_MESSAGE_MAP()

};
```

The main activity supported by this class is the transfer of data that is set through a property page to update the variables that represent the properties in your OLE control implementation. The data is entered through controls, such as buttons and list boxes that you place on a property page, and the **DoDataExchange()** function handles the exchange of data between the controls, collecting the input and the variables in the control.

Implementation of the Property Page Class

If you look in the **OLETrafficSignalPpg.cpp** file for the property page class, you'll see that it contains code for defining a CLSID and an implementation of the **UpdateRegistry()** member function. This is because each property page is an OLE object in its own right and will have its own entry in the system registry.

The class constructor doesn't contain any code at present, but ClassWizard will add code to initialize any properties that we add to the property page. Similarly, the **DoDataExchange()** function will be extended by ClassWizard when we add variables to receive the values for properties from controls on the property page.

Defining a Traffic Signal Object

We can define the basic representation of a traffic signal in a class. The first thing we should consider is what we want the traffic signal to do. That will give us an idea of what function members we'll need to provide a satisfactory interface to the class.

A traffic signal object will represent the signal in a particular state. The change of state will be triggered externally to the class. We'll need the ability to set the initial state of the signal and step the signal from one state to another, keeping our traffic signal object very simple.

We can build in the ability for the signal to draw itself, but it would be useful if the size of the signal could adapt to the size of the control when it is displayed. If we decide that the signal will be the same height as the control, and will be positioned in the center of the control, we can pass sufficient information to a signal, so that it can draw itself to fit the control, with two functions in the class interface - one to set the position of the control, the other to set the height. We can calculate a value for the width based on the height.

With these considerations in mind, we can define the traffic signal class as follows:

```
class CTrafficSignal
{
  public:
    CTrafficSignal();                        // Constructor

    // Class interface
```

```
        void SetPosition(CPoint aPosition){m_Position = aPosition;}
        void SetHeight(int aHeight){m_Height = aHeight;}
        void Draw(CDC* pDC);                  // Draw the traffic signal
        void SetSignalState(int State){ m_SignalState = State;}
        int NextState();                      // Change to the next state

    private:
        CPoint m_Position;     // Bottom center of signal
        int m_Height;          // Height of signal
        int m_SignalState;     // State of signal

};
```

You can enter this code in a new header file, **TrafficSignal.h** and save it in the same folder as the source for the rest of the control, **OleTrafficSignal**. We have five functions defining the class interface to provide the capability we've just outlined, and three **private** data members for the position of the signal, the height of the signal and the state of the signal, which will determine which light is lit. The reference point for the position is arbitrarily the center point on the bottom edge of the signal.

The only functions that we haven't defined in the class definition are the **Draw()** function which will draw the signal using the **m_Position** and **m_Height** values, and the **NextState()** function which will change the signal to the next state in sequence by setting the value of **m_SignalState** appropriately. All we need to complete the class is to add the definitions for these.

Implementing the NextState() Function

Before we can implement the **NextState()** function, we need to define what we mean by a state. The signal has three different states - it can be at stop, at go, or it can be at get ready to stop. (British-style signals have an extra state, ready to go, between stop and go, but we won't implement that.) We can define these by a set of **const** variables that we can put in another file, so enter the following in a new source file and save it in the control project folder as **OurConstants.h**:

```
// Definition of constants

#ifndef OUR_CONSTANTS_H
#define OUR_CONSTANTS_H

const int STOP          = 101;
const int GO            = 103;
const int READY_TO_STOP = 104;

#endif
```

Now we can define the **NextState()** function using these constants. Add the following code in a new source file, save it in the control project folder as **TrafficSignal.cpp** and add it to the project:

```
#include "StdAfx.h"
#include "TrafficSignal.h"
#include "OurConstants.h"

// Change the signal state to the next in sequence
```

```
int CTrafficSignal::NextState()
{
   switch(m_SignalState)
   {
      case STOP:
         m_SignalState = GO;
         break;
      case GO:
         m_SignalState = READY_TO_STOP;
         break;
      case READY_TO_STOP:
         m_SignalState = STOP;
         break;
      default:
         m_SignalState = STOP;
         AfxMessageBox("Invalid signal state");
   }
   return m_SignalState;
}
```

This is very straightforward. The three cases in the switch correspond to the three possible states of the signal and each sets the **m_SignalState** variable to the next state in sequence. The action for the default case, which would only arise if an invalid state were set somewhere, is to arbitrarily set the signal state to **STOP** and to display a message.

Implementing the Draw() Function.

To draw the signal, we need a feel for how the width is set in relation to the height, and the positioning of the lights relative to the reference point, **m_Position**. The dimensions determining this are shown in the diagram here:

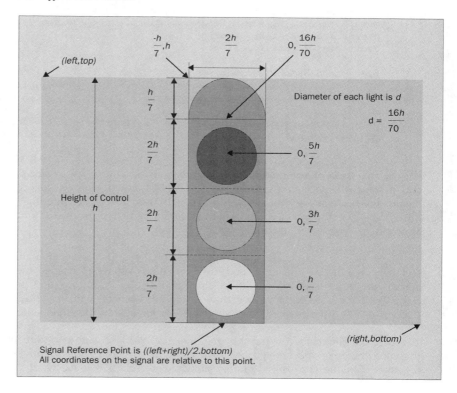

Signal Reference Point is *((left+right)/2,bottom)*
All coordinates on the signal are relative to this point.

The overall height of the signal is the same as that of the control. All the other dimensions for the signal have been defined in terms of the height to produce a consistently proportioned representation for it. All the coordinates for the centers of the lights and the top semicircular section are defined relative to the reference point for the signal which is set at the center of the base. The reference point is positioned at the midpoint on the bottom edge of the control.

There are several steps to drawing the complete signal, so let's build up the code for the **Draw()** function incrementally. Using the drawing above and the coordinates of the reference point for the signal stored in the data member **m_Position**, we can draw the basic outline of the signal with the following code, which you should add to the **TrafficSignal.cpp** file:

```
// Draw the signal
void CTrafficSignal::Draw(CDC* pDC)
{
    // Set the pen and brush to draw the signal
    CBrush* pOldBrush = (CBrush*)pDC->SelectStockObject(GRAY_BRUSH);
    CPen* pOldPen = (CPen*)pDC->SelectStockObject(BLACK_PEN);

    // Define the main body of the signal
    int Left = m_Position.x-m_Height/7;
    int Top = m_Position.y-(long)m_Height*6L/7L;
    int Right = m_Position.x+m_Height/7;
    int Bottom = m_Position.y;

    pDC->Rectangle(Left, Top, Right, Bottom);  // Draw the body

    // Define the semi-circular top of the signal
    CRect aRect(Left, Top-m_Height/7, Right, Top+m_Height/7);
    CPoint StartPt(Right, Top);
    CPoint EndPt(Left,Top);

    pDC->Chord(aRect, StartPt, EndPt);

    // Code to draw the lights goes here...

    pDC->SelectObject(pOldBrush);       // Get the old brush back
    pDC->SelectObject(pOldPen);         // Get the old pen back
}
```

We use the **SelectStockObject()** member of the **CDC** class to select a standard gray brush and a standard black pen into the device context, saving the old objects in each case, so we can restore them when we are done. The brush is used to fill the interior of any closed shapes we draw subsequently. We need to cast the pointer returned from **SelectStockObject()** to the appropriate type, as it returns a **void*** pointer.

The next step is to calculate the coordinates of the upper left and bottom right corners of the rectangle making up the main body of the signal. We won't change the mapping mode, so the default **MM_TEXT** will apply, with positive y from top to bottom, and positive x from left to right. With these coordinates, we draw a closed rectangle with the **Rectangle()** member of the **CDC** class. The interior of the rectangle will automatically be filled with the current brush color.

To draw the semicircle on the top of the signal, we calculate a **CRect** object corresponding to the coordinates of the top left and bottom right corners of the rectangle enclosing a full circle, together with the end points of the semicircular section that we want. The **Chord()** member of

CDC will draw a closed figure corresponding to the segment of the circle from **StartPt** to **EndPt** plus the chord, and fill the interior with the current brush color.

To draw the lights, we'll need to define the colors that we're going to use for them. We can add the definitions for the colors in the **OurConstants.h** file with the following code:

```
const COLORREF RED      = RGB(255,0,0);
const COLORREF ORANGE   = RGB(200,100,0);
const COLORREF GREEN    = RGB(0,255,0);
const COLORREF GRAY     = RGB(100,100,100);
```

The red, orange and green colors are the colors for the lights when they are on, and the gray color will be used for a light when it is off. If you don't like the way the colors come out, you can always mess around with the RGB values for them.

For each light, we'll need to create a brush to fill its interior depending on the state of the signal stored in **m_SignalState**. We can do this by adding code to the **Draw()** function, as follows:

```
// Draw the signal
void CTrafficSignal::Draw(CDC* pDC)
{
    // Code to draw the outline of the signal as before...

    // Create brushes for the lights
    CBrush StopBrush;           // A brush to fill the stop light
    CBrush ReadyBrush;          // A brush to fill the ready light
    CBrush GoBrush;             // A brush to fill the go light

    switch(m_SignalState)
    {
      case STOP:                              // Red only
         StopBrush.CreateSolidBrush(RED);
         ReadyBrush.CreateSolidBrush(GRAY);
         GoBrush.CreateSolidBrush(GRAY);
         break;
      case GO:                                // Green only
         StopBrush.CreateSolidBrush(GRAY);
         ReadyBrush.CreateSolidBrush(GRAY);
         GoBrush.CreateSolidBrush(GREEN);
         break;
      case READY_TO_STOP:                     // Orange only
         StopBrush.CreateSolidBrush(GRAY);
         ReadyBrush.CreateSolidBrush(ORANGE);
         GoBrush.CreateSolidBrush(GRAY);
         break;
      default:
         StopBrush.CreateSolidBrush(GRAY);
         ReadyBrush.CreateSolidBrush(GRAY);
         GoBrush.CreateSolidBrush(GRAY);
    }

    pDC->SelectObject(pOldBrush);       // Get the old brush back
    pDC->SelectObject(pOldPen);         // Get the old pen back
}
```

777

We create a **CBrush** object for each light which we will later use to fill the interior of the lights. We set the color for each **CBrush** object in the switch by calling the **CreateSolidBrush()** member of the object. The colors are determined by the state set in **m_SignalState**. If **m_SignalState** doesn't contain a valid state, all the lights will be out.

With the brush colors set, we're ready to draw the three lights. We can do this by adding the following code to the **Draw()** function:

```
// Draw the signal
void CTrafficSignal::Draw(CDC* pDC)
{
    // Code to draw the outline of the signal as before...

    // Code to create brushes for the three lights as before...

    // Define the rectangle bounding the stop light
    int Margin = (long)m_Height*18L/70L; // Ten percent of the width
    Left += Margin;                       // Left side of stop light
    Top += Margin;                        // Top of stop light
    Right -= Margin;                      // Right side of stop light
    int Step = (long)m_Height*2L/7L;      // Distance between lights
    Bottom = Top+Step-2*Margin;           // Bottom of stop light

    // Draw the stop light
    pDC->SelectObject(&StopBrush);
    pDC->Ellipse(Left, Top, Right, Bottom);

    // Set the position of the ready light
    Top += Step;
    Bottom += Step;

    // Draw the ready light
    pDC->SelectObject(&ReadyBrush);
    pDC->Ellipse(Left, Top, Right, Bottom);

    // Set the position of the go light
    Top += Step;
    Bottom += Step;

    // Draw the go light
    pDC->SelectObject(&GoBrush);
    pDC->Ellipse(Left, Top, Right, Bottom);

    pDC->SelectObject(pOldBrush);         // Get the old brush back
    pDC->SelectObject(pOldPen);           // Get the old pen back
}
```

To draw the lights, we'll be using the **Ellipse()** member of the class **CDC**. This requires an enclosing rectangle for the figure to be drawn, so we need to construct the coordinates of the top left and bottom right corners of the square enclosing each light. If we construct the square enclosing the red light, we can just displace this down by the appropriate amount to draw the orange light, and again by the same amount for the green light.

The diameter of each light is 20% less than the width of the signal, so we first calculate 10% of the width and store it in the local variable **Margin**. We'll use this value to decrease the size of the bounding rectangle for a light, all round. At this point, the coordinates stored in **Left** and

Top are the top left corner of the rectangle defining the main body of the signal. We can offset these by the value of **Margin** to get the top left corner of the square enclosing the red light. We can obtain the x coordinate of the bottom right corner of the square by subtracting the value of **Margin** from **Right**. To get the y coordinate, we increment **Top** by the value of **Step**, which we have set to the width of the signal, and subtract twice the value of **Margin**, that is 20% of the width. All we then have to do to draw the red light is to select the appropriate brush into the device context and use the **Ellipse()** function with the coordinates we have calculated.

Drawing the orange and red lights is simple. The orange is the same size as the red light, just displaced in the y direction by the width of the signal which we have stored in **Step**. The green light is displaced from the position of the orange light by a further distance **Step** in the y direction, .

Adding a Constructor

We need to add the implementation of the constructor to the file **TrafficSignal.cpp**. All this needs to do is to set some default values for the data members of the class:

```
// Constructor
CTrafficSignal::CTrafficSignal()
{
    m_Position = CPoint(0,0);    // Set arbitrary position
    m_Height = 1000;             // Set arbitrary height
    m_SignalState = STOP;        // Set initial state RED
}
```

All the data member values will eventually be set by the control, so the values given here are arbitrary.

Using a CTrafficSignal Object

To add a traffic signal object to the control, we need to add a **protected** member to the class **COleTrafficSignalCtrl**. You can do this either by right-clicking the class name in ClassView, and following the dialog after selecting Add Variable... from the pop-up, or by adding the following code directly to the class definition:

```
protected:
    CTrafficSignal* m_pSignal;       // Pointer to a traffic signal object
```

The merit of adding the code directly is that you can organize the class definition sensibly. Adding members using the dialog can put members of the class in rather bizarre places in the class definition.

Add a line just before the beginning of the **COleTrafficSignalCtrl** class definition to inform the compiler that **CTrafficSignal** is a class:

```
class CTrafficSignal;
```

We now need to create an object in the constructor, so amend the default constructor definition in the file **OleTrafficSignalCtl.cpp** by adding a line of code to it as overleaf.

```
COleTrafficSignalCtrl::COleTrafficSignalCtrl()
{
    InitializeIIDs(&IID_DOleTrafficSignal, &IID_DOleTrafficSignalEvents);

    m_pSignal = new CTrafficSignal;        // Create a signal
}
```

The first line of code in the constructor that was included by ControlWizard passes information to the base class about the interface to a container. This enables properties and events that we add to the control to be properly identified. Since we create a **CTrafficSignal** object on the heap, we should arrange to delete it in the class destructor, so modify the destructor as follows:

```
COleTrafficSignalCtrl::~COleTrafficSignalCtrl()
{
    delete m_pSignal;          // Delete the signal
}
```

If we now add some code to the draw function, we can try out the control to make sure that our traffic signal object displays as we expect it to. The default **OnDraw()** function in the control draws an ellipse, so you need to delete that code and add code to draw the traffic signal as follows:

```
void COleTrafficSignalCtrl::OnDraw(
            CDC* pdc, const CRect& rcBounds, const CRect& rcInvalid)
{
    // TODO: Replace the following code with your own drawing code.
    pdc->FillRect(rcBounds,
CBrush::FromHandle((HBRUSH)GetStockObject(WHITE_BRUSH)));

    // Set the height of the signal
    m_pSignal->SetHeight(abs(rcBounds.Height()));

    // The reference point for the signal is the middle of its base
    // so set the position of the signal at the midway point
    // along the bottom of the bound rectangle
    CPoint aPosition(((long)rcBounds.right+rcBounds.left)/2L, rcBounds.bottom);
    m_pSignal->SetPosition(aPosition);
    m_pSignal->Draw(pdc);                      // Draw the signal
}
```

The first statement in the default version fills the whole rectangle occupied by the control using a white brush. We'll be amending this later to use the background color defined by the ambient property, but for now you can leave it as it is.

The **rcBounds** parameter passed to the function defines the rectangle that the control occupies. We calculate the midpoint of the base of this rectangle and use this to set the position of the reference point in the traffic signal object. We then call the **Draw()** member of the object to get the traffic signal to draw itself.

Finally, we need to add **#include** statements to the beginning of the **OleTrafficSignalCtl.cpp** file for the **.h** files for the definition of the **CTrafficSignal** class and the constants we have defined:

```
#include "TrafficSignal.h"
#include "OurConstants.h"
```

Testing the Control

If you build the control, it should be ready to run. It won't do much, since we haven't built in any ability to interact with a container, or to sequence the traffic signal, but at least you can verify that it looks like a traffic signal and that it re-sizes itself satisfactorily.

Of course, you need a container to exercise the control and, conveniently, Developer Studio has one available in the Tools menu. Just select the OLE Control Test Container option. The control needs to be in the system registry before you can use it, but, if it is compiled and linked OK, it will have been registered automatically.

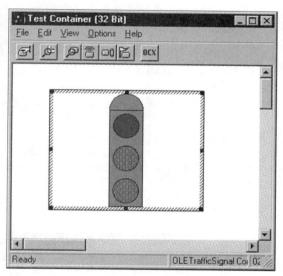

Once the test container is running, select Edit/Insert OLE Control... or click the first toolbar button on the left, to bring up a dialog displaying a list of OLE control objects that you can use. Select OLE TrafficSignal Control from the list to get our control to display in the container.

If you want to add another instance of our control, you can just click the toolbar button on the right, labeled OCX. You can resize the control and the signal should automatically alter its height and width.

The hatching around the control indicates that it is currently active. You can render it inactive by clicking anywhere outside it. A single-click in the control will reactivate it again.

Now that it works, we should think about extending the control to add some properties and to get the signal working.

Using Ambient Properties

We can see how we introduce stock properties into our control by using the **BackColor** property provided by a container. You use ClassWizard to add stock properties to the control. With the control project open, click on the ClassWizard toolbar button in Developer Studio, and select the OLE Automation tab. Make sure that **COleTrafficSignalCtrl** is shown in the Class name: list box and click on the Add Property... button. The resulting dialog is shown on the following page.

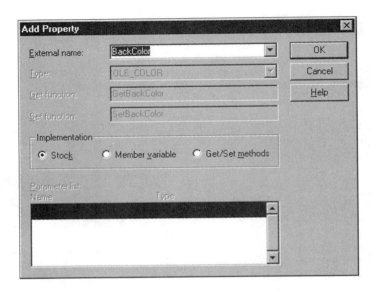

If you extend the Externaln name: list box, you'll see a list of stock properties. When you select BackColor, as shown in the dialog above, the other three list boxes will be set to appropriate values and grayed to indicate that you cannot change them. The Stock radio button is also selected automatically.

If you now select the OK button, you'll return to the ClassWizard dialog shown below:

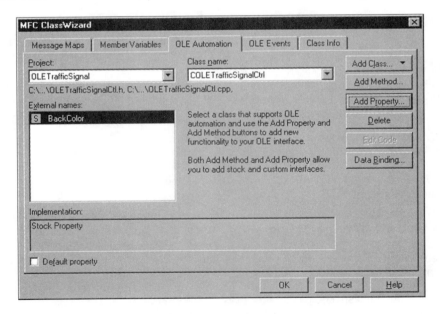

The list of External names: includes the name BackColor for the ambient property. The prefix S indicates that it is a stock property. Custom properties will be prefixed with C, as you'll see when we add some a little later. If you look in the implementation file for `COleTrafficSignalCtrl`, you'll see that the dispatch map has been modified by ClassWizard to the following:

```
BEGIN_DISPATCH_MAP(COleTrafficSignalCtrl, COleControl)
    //{{AFX_DISPATCH_MAP(COleTrafficSignalCtrl)
    DISP_STOCKPROP_BACKCOLOR()
    //}}AFX_DISPATCH_MAP
    DISP_FUNCTION_ID(COleTrafficSignalCtrl, "AboutBox", DISPID_ABOUTBOX,
                                AboutBox, VT_EMPTY, VTS_NONE)
END_DISPATCH_MAP()
```

This extra line of code ensures that the value for the ambient property BackColor, made available by a container, is accessible within our control as the equivalent stock property, but to make use of it we must add some code to the **OnDraw()** function:

```
void COleTrafficSignalCtrl::OnDraw(
        CDC* pdc, const CRect& rcBounds, const CRect& rcInvalid)
{
    // Set the background the same color as the container
    CBrush bgBrush(TranslateColor(GetBackColor()));

    pdc->FillRect(rcBounds, &bgBrush);   // Fill the background

    // Set the height of the signal
    m_pSignal->SetHeight(abs(rcBounds.Height()));

    // The reference point for the signal is the middle of its base
    // so set the position of the signal at the midway point
    // along the bottom of the bound rectangle
    CPoint aPosition(((long)rcBounds.right+rcBounds.left)/2L,rcBounds.bottom);
    m_pSignal->SetPosition(aPosition);
    m_pSignal->Draw(pdc);                           // Draw the signal
}
```

You should replace the default code that filled the background with the shaded lines of code above. The **GetBackColor()** function, which is inherited from `COleControl`, returns the color stored in the stock property in the control as type **OLE_COLOR**. The **OLE_COLOR** type defines a standard way of representing color values when they are transferred between OLE objects. The **OLE_COLOR** value is converted to a **COLORREF** value (RGB value) by the **TranslateColor()** function.

There are functions defined in the **COleControl** class for each of the stock properties that you may include in your control. Examples of these are **GetForeColor()** which returns the foreground color, and **GetScaleUnits()** which returns the type of units used in the container.

Note that the stock property in the control is set from the ambient property made available by the container when the control is first executed in the container. If the background color in the container later changes for some reason, the stock property in the container will not be updated. If you want to update a color directly from the current background color in the container, you can use the **AmbientBackColor()** function inherited from **COleControl**, instead of **GetBackColor()**.

You can easily see the differences between the effect of **GetBackColor()** and
AmbientBackColor() by trying two versions of the control in the test container. First, build a
version using **GetBackColor()**. Start the test container by selecting it from the Tools menu. You
can load the control by selecting Insert OLE Controls... menu from the Edit pop-up and selecting
the control from the list available in the dialog. There is also a toolbar button that you can use
corresponding to this menu item.

You can change the ambient background color by selecting Set Ambient Properties... from the
Edit menu, or by selecting the second toolbar button from the left. You can choose the property
that you want to set from the drop-down list box is the dialog, as shown:

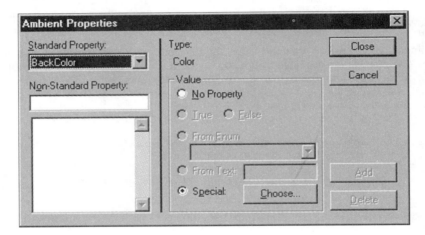

To select a color, click on the Choose... button in the dialog. Even though you change it, the
new background color will have no effect on the control. However, if you load another instance
of the control, it will use the new background color. Once you've added one instance of a
control, you can add another just by clicking on the toolbar button labeled OCX.

If you repeat the process with a version of the control that uses **AmbientBackColor()** instead
of **GetBackColor()**, you'll see that all of the controls can pick up a new **BackColor** value
when you change it in the test container. To see the difference between the two functions, you'll
need to get the original control to redraw, by moving it, for example.

Adding Custom Properties to the Control

There are actually four different flavors for the custom properties that you can define for an
OLE control. They reflect different ways in which the properties can operate:

> The simplest variety of custom property is of type **DISP_PROPERTY**. This is represented
> by a data member of the control class and is usually made available just for information.
> Because the property is freely accessible, this is referred to as **direct exposure** of the
> property.

> The **DISP_PROPERTY_NOTIFY** type of property is represented by a data member of the
> control class and has a function in the control class which is called if the property value
> is altered. This allows the control to adapt its operation to the new value for the control
> immediately. The notification function will typically cause the control to be redrawn.

▶ The **DISP_PROPERTY_EX** type of property is supported by functions accessible by a container to set the value of the property and to retrieve the current value of the property. These are usually referred to as **Get/Set** functions. This type of property is referred to as being **indirectly exposed**.

▶ The **DISP_PROPERTY_PARAM** type of property is similar to the **DISP_PROPERTY_EX** type in that is has **Get/Set** functions to manipulate it, but in addition can involve multiple parameter values stored in an array.

We'll try out custom properties by adding two to our control. One property that we might want to add is the duration of the stop or go period when the signal is running. A real signal might well operate so that the time that the signal was at red and green could vary, depending on traffic conditions. Another is the start-up conditions when the signal runs. Let's suppose that we'll allow it to start on either red or green. We can provide the option for the user to set this through a custom property.

Using ClassWizard to Add Custom Properties

First, we'll add the property to define which light is the start position when the signal runs. We can make this a logical value which will make the signal start on red if the property value is **TRUE**, and green otherwise.

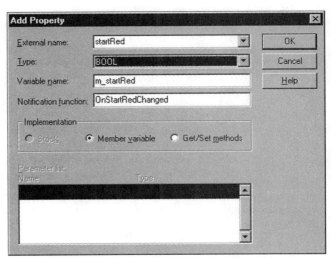

With the control project open, select the ClassWizard toolbar button and select the OLE Automation tab. Make sure the **COleTrafficSignalCtrl** class is shown in the Class name: list box and click on the Add Property... button. You can enter startRed as the external name and select **BOOL** from the Type: drop-down list box, as shown here:

The type for the member variable for a property must be one of those from the list. You can't use your own types here. ClassWizard has created a name for the class data member, representing the property, by prefixing the external name you supplied, with **m_**. It will also generate a notification function with the name shown, so here our property is of type **DISP_PROPERTY_NOTIFY**. The Member variable radio button has also been selected by default.

You can select the OK button to close this dialog and return to the OLE Automation tab. You'll see that the list of External names: includes startRed, which is shown with the prefix C because it is a custom property. We can now add the second custom property which will determine the time period for stop and go conditions for the signal, so select the Add Property... button once more.

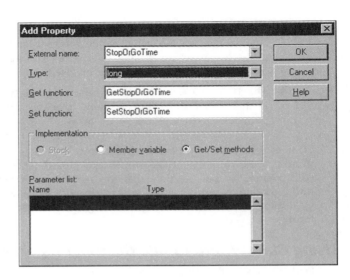

For this property, we'll make it of type **DISP_PROPERTY_EX**, just for the experience, so select the Get/Set methods radio button. You can enter the external name as StopOrGoTime, and select long from the Type: dropdown list box. The dialog will appear as shown here:

Here, we have a diminished set of types available and **long** is not the most convenient for a time interval, but it will have to do. Note that there are edit boxes showing the names that ClassWizard has assigned to the Get and Set functions. You can change these if you want, but they seem to be reasonable. You can select the OK button to return to the OLE Automation tab. We now have two custom properties listed, in addition to our stock property. The two functions that have been added to **COleTrafficSignalCtrl** are also noted, and we could go directly to them by selecting the Edit Code button, but we're not ready to do that yet. We have finished with ClassWizard for the moment, so click the OK button.

If you take a look at the dispatch map in the implementation of **COleTrafficSignalCtrl**, you'll see that the custom properties have been added and the types have been set based on the options we selected:

```
BEGIN_DISPATCH_MAP(COleTrafficSignalCtrl, COleControl)
 //{{AFX_DISPATCH_MAP(COleTrafficSignalCtrl)
 DISP_PROPERTY_NOTIFY(COleTrafficSignalCtrl, "StartRed", m_startRed,
                               OnStartRedChanged, VT_BOOL)
 DISP_PROPERTY_EX(COleTrafficSignalCtrl, "StopOrGoTime",
                               GetStopOrGoTime, SetStopOrGoTime, VT_I4)
 DISP_STOCKPROP_BACKCOLOR()
 //}}AFX_DISPATCH_MAP
 DISP_FUNCTION_ID(COleTrafficSignalCtrl, "AboutBox", DISPID_ABOUTBOX,
                               AboutBox, VT_EMPTY, VTS_NONE)
END_DISPATCH_MAP()
```

Initializing Custom Properties

We need initial values to be set for both our custom properties, but the **StopOrGoTime** property has no variable defined for it. This is because the Get/Set functions are the interface between the container and the property, and you must fill in the detail. You can add a data member to the **COleTrafficSignalCtrl** class definition directly by including the line:

```
long m_StopOrGoTime;   // Duration of stop period, or go period
```

You can put this in the **protected** section as there is no reason to make it **public**.

We can initialize this property and **m_startRed** by adding code to the **DoPropExchange()** member of the control class, which has the job of serializing properties.

```
void COleTrafficSignalCtrl::DoPropExchange(CPropExchange* pPX)
{
    ExchangeVersion(pPX, MAKELONG(_wVerMinor, _wVerMajor));
    COleControl::DoPropExchange(pPX);

    // TODO: Call PX_ functions for each persistent custom property.
    PX_Bool(pPX, _T("StartRed"), m_startRed, TRUE);
    PX_Long(pPX, _T("StopOrGoTime"), m_StopOrGoTime, 5000);
}
```

There is a global **PX_** function for each type of OLE property. They come in two versions. One version has three parameters and the other has an extra parameter. We're using the latter version here. The parameters to the function from left to right are:

▶ A pointer to a **CPropExchange** object which determines whether the function is storing or retrieving property values.

▶ The external name of the property. The **_T()** macro, which is used here, takes care of converting the text if the control is used in an environment using the Unicode character set. It must be used for all literal strings that are to be transferred across the OLE interface.

▶ A reference to the class data member that represents the property.

▶ A default value for the property which is used if the serialization process fails. The first time you use the control, the process will fail, of course, since the properties have not previously been saved.

The version of the **PX_** functions with three parameters omits the default value for the property. However, it's usually desirable to ensure that a value is set for all properties, so, if you use this, you would need to ensure that a value is set elsewhere. Of course, on the second and subsequent times your control is used, the properties will be initialized to the values that were last set.

We set **m_StartRed** to **TRUE** and **m_StopOrGoTime** to 5000 initially. Time intervals are measured in milliseconds, and we're setting the default red and green signal intervals to 5 seconds, so you need to be ready to floor the pedal.

Making the Signal Work

To get the signal running, we need three more data members in our **COleTrafficSignalCtrl** class. Add the following lines to the protected section of the class definition:

```
UINT m_ChangeTime;    // Duration of orange period, or red+orange period
BOOL m_SignalGo;      // TRUE indicates the signal is running
UINT m_Timer;         // Timer event ID
```

The first will define the duration of the transient state of the signal between red and green, the second is a flag which will be **TRUE** when the signal is running and **FALSE** when it is not, and the third is a variable identifying the timer we will use to control stepping the signal from one state to the next.

We can initialize these three members in the class constructor as follows:

```
COleTrafficSignalCtrl::COleTrafficSignalCtrl()
{
    InitializeIIDs(&IID_DOleTrafficSignal, &IID_DOleTrafficSignalEvents);

    m_pSignal = new CTrafficSignal;   // Create a signal
    m_SignalGo = FALSE;               // Signal not running initially
    m_ChangeTime = 1500U;             // Change over time in milliseconds
    m_Timer = 10;                     // Timer ID
}
```

Initially, the signal is not running since we have set **m_SignalGo** to **FALSE**. The change-over time is set to 1.5 seconds and the timer ID is set to an arbitrary integer value of 10.

Starting and Stopping the Signal

We need some external means of starting and stopping the signal and, for demonstration purposes, a convenient way to do this is using a mouse click. We can get it to operate like a flip-flop, so that clicking the control when the signal is not running will start it, and vice versa.

Add a handler for the **WM_LBUTTONDOWN** message to **COleTrafficSignalCtrl** using ClassWizard, and implement it as follows:

```
void COleTrafficSignalCtrl::OnLButtonDown(UINT nFlags, CPoint point)
{
    // If the signal is stopped, start it and
    // if the signal is running stop it
    m_SignalGo = !m_SignalGo;         // Invert signal go status
    if(m_SignalGo)
        StartSignal();
    else
        StopSignal();

    COleControl::OnLButtonDown(nFlags, point);
}
```

Since we want mouse clicks in the control to flip its operating state, the first action in the handler is to invert the value stored in **m_SignalGo**. If this value is now **TRUE**, we call a member function **StartSignal()** to start the signal, and if it is **FALSE**, we invoke the function **StopSignal()** to stop the signal.

Starting the Signal

You can add the **StartSignal()** member by right-clicking the COleTrafficSignalCtrl class name in ClassView and selecting Add Function... from the pop-up. Enter the return type as **void** and the name as **StartSignal()**. The code for this function will be:

```
void COleTrafficSignalCtrl::StartSignal()
{
    // Setup a timer with the required interval
    m_Timer = SetTimer(m_Timer, (UINT)m_StopOrGoTime, NULL);
```

```
    if(!m_Timer)
    {
       AfxMessageBox("No Timer!");
       exit(1);
    }
    InvalidateControl();    // Get the control redrawn
 }
```

We obtain a timer by calling the **SetTimer()** member of our class inherited from **CWnd**. The first argument is an ID for the timer which must be non-zero, and the second argument is the time interval we want, expressed in milliseconds as a **UINT** value. The third argument can be a pointer to a function that will be called when the time interval is up, but if it is **NULL**, as we have specified it here, a **WM_TIMER** message will be sent. We'll add a handler for this in a moment.

There are a limited number of timers available, so we need to make sure that we got one. If none are available, the **SetTimer()** function returns **FALSE**, in which case we display a message and end the program. If a timer is available, **SetTimer()** returns the ID of the timer. Once we have a timer, we get the control redrawn so that it always starts with the state determined by the **startRed** property. This will be set in the notification function for this property which we'll complete shortly.

Stopping the Signal

Add the **StopSignal()** function with a **void** return type and implement it as follows:

```
void COleTrafficSignalCtrl::StopSignal()
{
   KillTimer(m_Timer);          // Destroy the timer
   InvalidateControl();         // Redraw the control
}
```

The **KillTimer()** function kills the timer event specified by the ID passed as an argument and removes any **WM_TIMER** messages that have been queued for it. The function returns **TRUE** if it finds the specified event, and **FALSE** otherwise, so it copes with a non-existent timer event without any problem. We get the control redrawn to return it to its initial state.

Handling WM_TIMER Messages

Add a handler for the **WM_TIMER** message using ClassWizard. The process is exactly the same as for any other message handler. Add code to the handler as follows:

```
void COleTrafficSignalCtrl::OnTimer(UINT nIDEvent)
{
   UINT Interval = 0;    // Interval in milliseconds

   // Step to the next state and set the time interval
   // based on the new state
   switch(m_pSignal->NextState())
   {
      case STOP: case GO:
         Interval = (UINT)m_StopOrGoTime;           // Stop or Go interval
         break;
      default:
         Interval = m_ChangeTime;                    // Transient interval
```

```
    }

    InvalidateControl();                              // Redraw the signal

    KillTimer(m_Timer);                         // Make sure the old timer is dead
    m_Timer = SetTimer(m_Timer, Interval, NULL);    // Set a new timer event
    if(!m_Timer)
    {
        AfxMessageBox("No Timer!");
        exit(1);
    }
}
```

The signal is stepped to the next state by calling the **NextState()** member of the **CTrafficSignal** object. The new state is used to select the appropriate time interval for it. Having stored the time interval in the local variable **Interval**, we call **InvalidateControl()** to get the signal drawn in its new state and start a new timer period.

Implementing the Notify Function for the Control

The notify function will be called when the **startRed** property is modified externally, so we must add code to deal with this change, as follows:

```
void COleTrafficSignalCtrl::OnStartRedChanged()
{
    // Stop the signal if necessary
    if(m_SignalGo)
    {
        m_SignalGo = FALSE;     // Set signal not running
        StopSignal();           // Stop the signal
    }
    // Set the signal object to the appropriate state
    if(m_startRed)
        m_pSignal->SetSignalState(STOP);
    else
        m_pSignal->SetSignalState(GO);

    InvalidateControl();   // Get the control redrawn

    SetModifiedFlag();
}
```

Other than at initialization when the control is loaded, this is the only place the **startRed** property change is acted upon. We need to take account of the possibility that the signal is already running when the property is changed. We first check for this and stop the signal, since we're assuming that the user changed the starting condition because it will be restarted. To set the signal state, we use the **SetSignalState()** member of **CTrafficSignal** with a parameter determined by the value of the property. We then call **InvalidateControl()** to get the signal drawn in its latest state.

Implementing the Property Get/Set Functions

The **Get** function for the **StopOrGoTime** property is extremely simple since all we need to do is to return the current property value:

```
long COleTrafficSignalCtrl::GetStopOrGoTime()
{
    return m_StopOrGoTime;      // Return the current interval
}
```

The **Set** function requires a little more work:

```
void COleTrafficSignalCtrl::SetStopOrGoTime(long nNewValue)
{
    // Only alter the control if the value is different
    if(m_StopOrGoTime != nNewValue)
    {
        m_StopOrGoTime = nNewValue;       // Set the new stop or go time

        OnStartRedChanged();              // Set the initial state
    }
}
```

The value passed to the function is the new value for the property, but we don't want to do anything drastic unless it is different from the old value. If we have a new value, we store it in the **m_StopOrGoTime** member that we added for the purpose. We then set the signal state back to its initial starting state, according to the value of the property **startRed**, by calling **OnStartRedChanged()**.

Using the Property Page

Now let's move on to adding some controls to the property page that ControlWizard conveniently provided for us, to allow us to modify the values of the control's custom properties. To add controls to the property page, you need to be in ResourceView. Extend the Dialog part of the resource set, and double-click on IDD_PROPPAGE_OLETRAFFICSIGNAL to display the property page dialog. You can remove the static text control that has been added to the dialog by selecting it and pressing the *Delete* key.

We need to add two controls to the property page, corresponding to the **startRed** property which is Boolean and the **StopOrGoTime** property which is a **long** integer. The former we can handle with a check box control and, for the latter, we can use an edit box.

From the control palette, select a check box and place it at a suitable point on the property page. You can double-click it and enter the text as Start with Red Light. You may also like to check the Left text check box on the Styles tab. Next, you can add a static text control and place it on the property page. Double-click it to display its properties and change the text to Stop or Go Period:. Next, add an edit box to the property page and place it to the right of the static text box. Your property page should look something like that shown below:

We've finished laying out the property page, so you can save the resource. Now we need to connect the controls that we've added to the properties in our OLE control.

Connecting Controls to Properties

First, we'll connect the check box to the **startRed** property. Double-click on the check box control with the *Ctrl* key held down. You'll then see the Add Member Variable dialog box. You can complete the name for the variable to be added to the **COleTrafficSignalPropPage** class as **m_startRed** and the OLE property name as **startRed** in the bottom list box. The category and variable type boxes will already have been set as we are using a check box, so the dialog box will be as shown below:

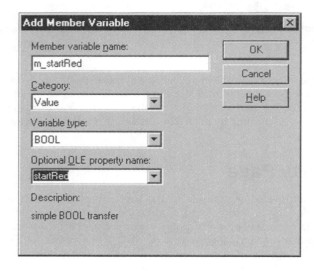

The drop-down list for OLE property names provides stock property names for when you are adding these to a property page. You can click on the OK button to complete the addition of the data member to the class.

Next, you should double-click the edit box while holding the *Ctrl* key down to add the data member to receive the value of the **StopOrGoTime** property from the control. Enter the information in the dialog box as shown here:

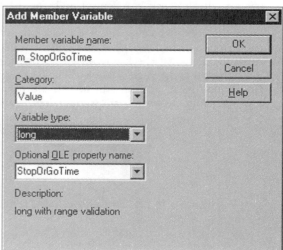

Here you must set the Variable type: to **long** to be consistent with what we have set previously for this value. Make sure the Category: entry is Value. As well as adding this data member, ClassWizard will make provision for range validation of the value entered, as indicated by the note at the bottom. You can click on the OK button to complete this operation and then save the property page.

In fact, ClassWizard has done rather more than just adding two data members to the **COleTrafficSignalPropPage** class. It has also included initialization for them in the class constructor:

```
COleTrafficSignalPropPage::COleTrafficSignalPropPage() :
                    COlePropertyPage(IDD, IDS_OLETRAFFICSIGNAL_PPG_CAPTION)
{
    //{{AFX_DATA_INIT(COleTrafficSignalPropPage)
    m_startRed = FALSE;
    m_StopOrGoTime = 0;
    //}}AFX_DATA_INIT
}
```

However, neither of these are good values for us, so set the initial value for **m_startRed** to **TRUE**, and the value for **m_StopOrGoTime** to **5000**.

The transfer of data between the controls and the variables we have added is accomplished using the **DDX** macros in the **DoPropExchange()** member of the property page class. These are exactly the same macros that we have seen used for controls in ordinary dialog boxes. ClassWizard has also added the code to do this, so the function implementation has already been created, as follows:

```
void COleTrafficSignalPropPage::DoDataExchange(CDataExchange* pDX)
{
    //{{AFX_DATA_MAP(COleTrafficSignalPropPage)
    DDP_Check(pDX, IDC_CHECK1, m_startRed, _T("startRed") );
    DDX_Check(pDX, IDC_CHECK1, m_startRed);
    DDP_Text(pDX, IDC_EDIT1, m_StopOrGoTime, _T("StopOrGoTime") );
    DDX_Text(pDX, IDC_EDIT1, m_StopOrGoTime);
    //}}AFX_DATA_MAP
    DDP_PostProcessing(pDX);
}
```

The **DDP** macros you see here are specific to OLE. These do the job of synchronizing the property values in the control with the values in the data members of the property page class, so all the updating of the property values has been taken care of.

The last thing you need to do is to set the range limits for the **m_StopOrGoTime** value. For this, you can add a **DDV** macro at the end of the block of **DDX** and **DDP** macros in the **DoDataExchange()** member, as follows:

```
void COleTrafficSignalPropPage::DoDataExchange(CDataExchange* pDX)
{
    //{{AFX_DATA_MAP(COleTrafficSignalPropPage)
    DDP_Check(pDX, IDC_CHECK1, m_startRed, _T("startRed") );
    DDX_Check(pDX, IDC_CHECK1, m_startRed);
    DDP_Text(pDX, IDC_EDIT1, m_StopOrGoTime, _T("StopOrGoTime") );
    DDX_Text(pDX, IDC_EDIT1, m_StopOrGoTime);
```

```
        DDV_MinMaxUInt(pDX, m_StopOrGoTime, 1000, 30000);
    //}}AFX_DATA_MAP
    DDP_PostProcessing(pDX);
}
```

You should add this line immediately after the last **DDX_TEXT()** macro. This will prevent values less than 1000 milliseconds or greater than 30000 milliseconds being accepted for the **StopOrGoTime** property. This is the same macro that is used for range checking values for controls in an ordinary dialog box.

Using the Control

You can now build the control once more, and exercise it using the test container. The window below shows three instances of the control running in the container, each having a different interval set for the **StopOrGoTime** property.

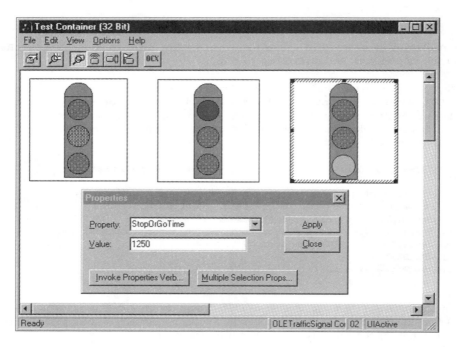

The Properties dialog box shown above is displayed when you select the View/Properties... menu option in the container, or the equivalent toolbar button. To display the property page for the control, you should click on the Invoke Properties Verb... button in the dialog box. Try setting the **StopOrGoTime** outside the permitted range. Whenever you set a property value, it only applies to the control that is currently active. An instance of the control which is running will continue to run when it is not active, so several can run simultaneously.

Adding Events to a Control

You will recall that events are used to tell a container that something has occurred in an OLE control. It might conceivably be useful for a container using our traffic signal control to know when the signal changed to red, and when it changed to green.

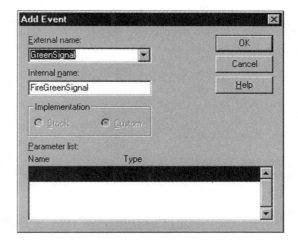

You can add events to the control using ClassWizard. Open ClassWizard and select the OLE Events tab. After making sure **COleTrafficSignalCtrl** is the class name selected, click on the Add Event... button. Enter the external name for the event as GreenSignal as shown here:

The drop-down list for the External name: list box contains names for standard events, but we don't need them here because we are creating a custom event. ClassWizard will fill in the internal name field. This will be the name of the function you call when you want to fire the event. Click the OK button to create the event, and repeat the process for an event with the external name RedSignal. The OLE Events tab will now show two custom events listed. Both events will have been entered in the event map in the **COleTrafficSignalCtrl** class definition, and the definition for the functions **FireGreenSignal()** and **FireRedSignal()** will also have been created. All we have to do is to use them.

The best place to fire these events is from the handler for the **WM_TIMER** message, because it is here that we progress the state of the signal object. Close ClassWizard by clicking the **OK** button and switch to the **OnTimer()** function implementation from ClassView. Add code to it as follows:

```
void COleTrafficSignalCtrl::OnTimer(UINT nIDEvent)
{
   UINT Interval = 0;   // Interval in milliseconds

   // Step to the next state and set the time interval
   // based on the new state
   switch(m_pSignal->NextState())
   {
      case GO:
         Interval = (UINT)m_StopOrGoTime;        // Stop or Go interval
         FireGreenSignal();                      // Signal the container
         break;
      case STOP:
         Interval = (UINT)m_StopOrGoTime;        // Stop or Go interval
         FireRedSignal();                        // Signal the container
```

795

```
        break;
    default:
        Interval = m_ChangeTime;                    // Transient interval
    }

    InvalidateControl();                            // Redraw the signal

    KillTimer(m_Timer);                    // Make sure the old timer is dead
    m_Timer = SetTimer(m_Timer, Interval, NULL);   // Set a new timer event
    if(!m_Timer)
    {
        AfxMessageBox("No Timer!");
        exit(1);
    }
}
```

Here, we've replaced the common handling of the stop and go states with two distinct cases to enable the appropriate event to be fired for each state. The rest of the handler remains as before.

With the events added, we can see how the control runs in the test container. You can view the event log by selecting the View/Event log... menu option in the container. The event log is shown below:

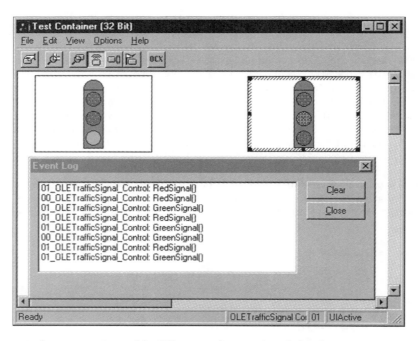

Here, two controls are running with different values assigned for the **StopOrGoTime** property. The individual instances of the control are indicated in the event log by the two digit prefix to the record of an event, the first instance of the control being numbered 00.

Of course, the control will also be usable from other OLE control container applications, including Visual Basic 4 or Visual C++ itself.

Summary

In this chapter, we have dug a little into the how and why of OLE controls. You should have a good idea of how an OLE control communicates with its container, and how the basic features of an OLE control can be implemented.

There is quite a lot more to learn about many of the topics we have covered, but if you have made it to here without too much trouble, you should have little difficulty progressing further into using Visual C++ and applying the more advanced capabilities of OLE. I hope that you've found as much pleasure in getting to here as I have. Enjoy your programming!

Keywords in Visual C++

Keywords are words used for special purposes. You must not use these words as names of objects in your program. The following is a list of C++ keywords:

asm	auto	bad_cast	bad_typeid
break	case	catch	char
class	const	const_cast	continue
default	delete	do	double
dynamic_cast	else	enum	except
extern	finally	float	for
friend	goto	if	inline
int	long	namespace	new
operator	private	protected	public
register	reinterpret_cast	return	short
signed	sizeof	static	static_cast
struct	switch	template	this
throw	try	type_info	typedef
typid	union	unsigned	using
virtual	void	volatile	while
xalloc			

The C++ language is still evolving. There are a number of C++ keywords not at present supported in Visual C++, but they may well be in the future. Other compilers support at least some of them at the moment. You should, therefore, also avoid using these for your own identifiers. Accidental use of some of them is quite possible, as you can see from the following list:

and	and_eq	bitand	bitor
bool	compl	false	mutable
not	not_eq	or	or_eq
true	typeidusing	wchar_t	xor
xor_eq			

You should also avoid using identifiers beginning with a double underscore as Visual C++ reserves a considerable number of keywords of this form.

The ASCII Table

The American Standard Code for Information Interchange or ASCII assigns values between 0 and 255 for upper and lower case letters, numeric digits, punctuation marks and other symbols. ASCII characters can be split into the following sections:

0 - 31	Control functions
32 - 127	Standard, implementation-independent characters
128 - 255	Special symbols, international character sets - generally, non-standard characters.

Since the latter 128 characters are implementation-dependent and have no fixed entry in the ASCII table, we shall only cover the first two groups in the following table:

ASCII Characters 0 - 31

Decimal	Hexadecimal	Character	Control
000	00	null	NUL
001	01	☺	SOH
002	02	•	STX
003	03	♥	ETX
004	04	♦	EOT
005	05	♣	ENQ
006	06	♠	ACK
007	07	•	BEL (Audible bell)
008	08		Backspace
009	09		HT
010	0A		LF (Line feed)
011	0B		VT (Vertical feed)
012	0C		FF (Form feed)
013	0D		CR (Carriage return)
014	0E		SO
015	0F	¤	SI
016	10		DLE
017	11		DC1

Decimal	Hexadecimal	Character	Control
018	12		DC2
019	13		DC3
020	14		DC4
021	15		NAK
022	16		SYN
023	17		ETB
024	18		CAN
025	19		EM
026	1A	→	SUB
027	1B	←	ESC (Escape)
028	1C	L	FS
029	1D		GS
030	1E		RS
031	1F		US

ASCII Characters 32 - 127

Decimal	Hexadecimal	Character	Decimal	Hexadecimal	Character
032	20	space	060	3C	<
033	21	!	061	3D	=
034	22	"	062	3E	>
035	23	#	063	3F	?
036	24	$	064	40	@
037	25	%	065	41	A
038	26	&	066	42	B
039	27	'	067	43	C
040	28	(	068	44	D
041	29	)	069	45	E
042	2A	*	070	46	F
043	2B	+	071	47	G
044	2C	,	072	48	H
045	2D	-	073	49	I
046	2E	.	074	4A	J
047	2F	/	075	4B	K
048	30	0	076	4C	L
049	31	1	077	4D	M
050	32	2	078	4E	N
051	33	3	079	4F	O
052	34	4	080	50	P
053	35	5	081	51	Q
054	36	6	082	52	R
055	37	7	083	53	S
056	38	8	085	55	U
057	39	9	086	56	V
058	3A	:	087	57	W
059	3B	;	088	58	X

Decimal	Hexadecimal	Character	Decimal	Hexadecimal	Character
089	59	Y	109	6D	m
090	5A	Z	110	6E	n
091	5B	[	111	6F	o
092	5C	\	112	70	p
093	5D	]	113	71	q
094	5E	^	114	72	r
095	5F	_	115	73	s
096	60	`	116	74	t
097	61	a	117	75	u
098	62	b	118	76	v
099	63	c	119	77	w
100	64	d	120	78	x
101	65	e	121	79	y
102	66	f	122	7A	z
103	67	g	123	7B	{
104	68	h	124	7C	|
105	69	i	125	7D	}
106	6A	j	126	7E	~
107	6B	k	127	7F	delete
108	6C	l			

Beginning
Visual C++
4

The Revolutionary Guide to MFC 4 with Visual C++

Written by one of Microsoft's leading MFC developers, this is the book for professionals who want to get under the cover of the Microsoft class library. It starts by putting the application architecture under the microscope, explaining the classes used in AppWizard generated code and examining their base classes. The use of threads is given special consideration, before the Document/View architecture is explained. Advanced user interface programming is also detailed. The book covers utility and exception classes, dealing with exception handling at both the MFC level and at the compiler level. It then describes how to write particular types of application: DLLs, console, database-enabled and OLE-enabled applications. The OLE coverage extends to writing OLE servers, containers, controls and control containers. The book also offers some great insights into writing applications specifically for Windows 95.

Author: Mike Blaszczak   ISBN: 1874416923
Price: $49.95 C$69.95 £46.99

The Revolutionary Guide to MS Office 95 Development

The book initially has primers for WordBasic and Visual Basic for Applications (VBA) and gives details of DDE and OLE technology which is the 'glue' which holds the Office 95 applications together. Stand-alone applications in Word, Excel and Access are developed to complete the readers understanding of these applications. The book then goes into detail of Client/Server design, before developing applications hosted in, again, Word, Excel and Access, that show how it is possible to combine functionality of the host application with the other applications in Office 95. Information on mail-enabling applications is also provided, using Exchange as well as the built-in mail capabilities. A detailed explanation of the workflow paradigm is given, before showing a complete office system built from the components so far discussed. The book finishes off with how to extend Word's capabilities by writing a WLL (using C) and finally considers what is required to make an application ready for distribution.

Author: Steve Wynkoop   ISBN: 1874416699
Price: $49.95 C$69.95 £46.99

The Revolutionary Guide to Visual Basic 4 Professional

This book focuses on the four key areas for developers using VB4: the Win32 API, Objects and OLE, Databases and the VB development cycle. Each of the areas receives in-depth coverage, and techniques are illustrated using rich and complex example projects that bring out the real issues involved in commercial VB development. It examines the Win32 API from a VB perspective and gives a complete run-down of developing multimedia apps. The OLE section includes a help file creator that uses the Word OLE object, and we OLE automate Netscape Navigator 2. The database section offers complete coverage of DAO, SQL and ODBC, finishing with a detailed analysis of client-server database systems. The final section shows how to design, code, optimize and distribute a complete application. The book has a CD including all source code and a hypertext version of the book.

Author: Larry Roof   ISBN: 1874416370
Price: $44.95 C$62.95 £49.99

Instant SQL Programming

This is the fastest guide for developers to the most common database management language. If you want to get the most out of your database design, you will need to master Structured Query Language. SQL is the standard database language supported by almost every database management system on the market. This book takes you into the concepts and implementation of this key language quickly and painlessly, covering the complete ANSI standard SQL '92 from basic database design through to some of the more complex topics such as NULLS and 3-valued logic. We take you through the theory step-by-step, as you put into practice what you learn at each stage, gradually building up an example database while mastering essential techniques.

WINNER OF A VBPJ READER'S CHOICE AWARD 96.

Author: Joe Celko   ISBN: 1874416508
Price: $29.95 C$41.95 £27.99

WIN FREE BOOKS

TELL US WHAT YOU THINK!

Complete and return the bounce back card and you will:

- Help us create the books you want.
- Receive an update on all Wrox titles.
- Enter the draw for 5 Wrox titles of your choice.

FILL THIS OUT to enter the draw for free Wrox titles

Name _____

Address _____

_____

_____

_____ Postcode/Zip _____

Occupation _____

How did you hear about this book?

- [ ] Book review (name) _____
- [ ] Advertisement (name) _____
- [ ] Recommendation
- [ ] Catalogue
- [ ] Other _____

Where did you buy this book?

- [ ] Bookstore (name) _____
- [ ] Computer Store (name) _____
- [ ] Mail Order
- [ ] Other _____

I would be interested in receiving information about Wrox Press titles by email in future. My email/Internet address is:

_____

What influenced you in the purchase of this book?

- [ ] Cover Design
- [ ] Contents
- [ ] Other (please specify) _____

How did you rate the overall contents of this book?

- [ ] Excellent
- [ ] Good
- [ ] Average
- [ ] Poor

What did you find most useful about this book? _____

What did you find least useful about this book? _____

Please add any additional comments. _____

What other subjects will you buy a computer book on soon? _____

What is the best computer book you have used this year? _____

Note: This information will only be used to keep you updated about new Wrox Press titles and will not be used for any other purpose passed to any other third party.

WROX

WROX PRESS INC.

Wrox writes books for you. Any suggestions, or
ideas about how you want information given in
your ideal book will be studied by our team.
Your comments are always valued at WROX.

Free phone in USA 800-USE-WROX
Fax (312) 465 4063

Compuserve 100063,2152.
UK Tel. (44121) 706 6826   Fax   (44121) 706 2967

―――― *Computer Book Publishers* ――――

NB. If you post the bounce back card below in the UK, please send it to:
Wrox Press Ltd. Unit 16, Sapcote Industrial Estate, 20 James Road, Birmingham, B11 2BA